THE BOOK is a commentary on the eighth century Kashmir Shaivism text *SpandaKārikā* – Verses on Divine pulsation. Modern physics agrees with the physical fact that the universe is a vibration of energy. Modern physics deals with phenomena, while this book is an outcome of research on the source of the phenomena. In the commentary on every verse, other texts such as *Shiv Sutras* and *Vijnāna Bhairava* and works of many Indian saints are quoted.

The main theme of the book is that one can remain aware of Supreme Consciousness in every moment of daily life. Thus sādhanā – spiritual quest – impacts every aspect of living. The experience transcends any religion, nationality, gender, family, upbringing or formal education.

This book is based on lectures given during 1980-81 in weekly satsangs, prayer meetings, of the meditation center which the authors ran from 1975 until 1982 under the guidance of their Guru Swami Muktanand.

This book is a testimonial that sadhana can be carried out under the guidance of a competent Guru while leading a householder life even in New York City.

The authors are professors of mathematics in two colleges of the City University of New York.

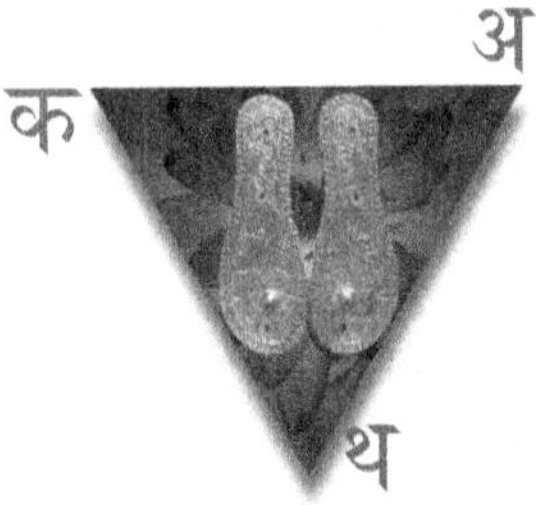

ON THE COVER, the Sandals, Triangle and Lotus describe the Gurupādukās, A-Ka-Tha triangle in the Sahasrār – thousand petal lotus. They exist in the cranium of every living being and can be seen in meditation by Guru's grace. This has been verified by thousands of yogis from ancient times to the present. Around the equilateral triangle are the first 48 letters of the Sanskṛt alphabet of 50 letters lined up counterclockwise: All 16 vowels starting with अ (A) on the horizontal upper side, 16 consonants starting with क (Ka) on the left side, the last 16 letters starting with थ (Tha) up to स (Sa) on the right side. The last two letters ह (Ha) and क्ष (Kṣa) are in the middle of the triangle representing Gurupādukās – Guru's sandals. The triangle represents Mātṛkā cakra, a detailed discussion of which is given in the Verse 45. Muktānand Bābā talked about this triangle in many of his talks.

References: Figure – *Saundarya-Laharī* by Sw.Viṣṇu Tīrtha, Page 144-145, verbal - *GuruGītā* verse 58.

SPANDAKARIKA

स्पंदकारिका

VERSES ON SPANDA
THE DIVINE PULSATION

A Commentary

by

UMESH AND CHITRA

NAGARKATTE

Edited by

AMBA CALDWELL

ACHARYA SHYAMSUNDAR JHA

Forewords by

MAHAMANDALESHWAR SWAMI NITYANAND SARASWATI

N.V. KAKATKAR

Shanti Mandir
51 Muktanand Marg, Walden, NY 12586
United States of America
http://www.shantimandir.com

Typesetting: Umesh Nagarkatte
Cover art: Michael Tobin, Goshen, NY, USA
Indexing: Amba Caldwell
Book design: Ron Carter
Publishing: Jude Berman

Printing:
10/2013

Publisher's Cataloging-in-Publication
Umesh and Chitra Nagarkatte
Spanda Kārikā: Verses on Spanda
Translation and Commentary – 1st ed.

Includes index.

ISBN 978-0-9886025-1-9

FOREWORD

Spanda Vijñāna

The eternal power that gives life to the manifest and non-manifest universe is called 'Śankara.' This is the state of oneness of Prakāśa and Vimarśa. This itself is the oneness of Śiva and Śakti. The differentiation between Śiva and Śakti is only documental. In reality they are inseparable just like the word and its meaning or the two sides of a coin. Śakti is called Vimarśa. This Vimarśa can be both in the 'Aham' and 'Idam' form. 'Aham' means Parāśiva and 'Idam' means Jagat (creation). Vimarśa itself is Spanda. This is the autonomy of Śiva. It is also known as Chetanā Śakti, Chiti Śakti and Samvit. Being conscious, Spanda Śakti eternally vibrates independently. At the very same time, it is both inwardly and outwardly faceted – inwardly in the form of 'Aham' and outwardly in the 'Idam' form. Even though perceived in the form of the universe, it is beyond the universe. Even though it is one, it is transmitted in various forms. The entire universe is the outward expansion of the Spanda Śakti of Śiva.

The simile of the ocean can be used to describe the Spanda Śakti. The ocean is sometimes full of waves and at other times, waveless. This Śakti is both full of waves and waveless at the very same time: this is its strangeness. Just like the magician takes out objects from his bag and presents them to the audience, the Spanda Śakti elaborates the universe hidden within itself and like the magician withdraws it again. This Śakti itself becomes both the Pramātā and Prameya. Even in these states of Pramātā and Prameya, it does not forget that its true state is beyond the universe. The Spanda Śakti can also be compared to the potter who creates many different kinds of pots from clay. The pots are preconceived in the mind of the potter. The only difference is that the potter has to utilize the Upādāna (material cause) from outside whereas the Spanda Śakti itself takes on the form of the Upādāna.

The following aphorism of the *Spanda Kārikā* outstandingly describes the absolute power of Spanda Śakti.

Na duḥkhaṁ na sukhaṁ yatra na grāhyo grāhako na ca
Na cāsti mūḍhabhāvo'pi tadasti paramārthatā
Spanda Kārikā 5

In that independent Spanda Tattva (Principle), there exists neither the state of sorrow nor joy. It is beyond the external measurements of Śabda (word), Sparśa (touch), Rūpa (form), Rasa (taste) and Gandha (smell). It also does not have the Mitapramātṛbhāva of the Jīva (individual being) who is limited in the body. Also, unlike the Jīva, the Spanda Tattva does not lack the ability to make any object the subject of its knowledge. This Tattva is always present in the eternal form.

This Spanda Śakti pervades each atom of the universe. It is because of which the inert sense organs function as conscious. Shaivism believes that the Jīvātmā (individual soul) can become Parameśwara by awakening his spiritual energy through Sādhanā. Two forms of Śiva have been described in Shaivism-Patipramātā and Paśupramātā. Patipramātā is Śiva because he is absolutely independent. He himself becomes Paśupramātā (Jīva) in the contracted autonomous state. He can once again grow to be Patipramātā by recognizing his true Self. The Spanda is so subtle that only those Siddhayogis who have received Śaktipāt from a Siddha Guru and are situated in the highest state through Sadhana, can experience it. In a way, this Tattva can be called indescribable.

My revered Gurudev Baba Muktananda Paramahamsa believed the *Spanda Śastra* to be completely scientific and would even discuss it with modern scientists.

I am very pleased to know that Chitra and Umesh Nagarkatte through great effort and Sādhanā have translated the *Spanda Kārikā*, an inexplicable scripture of Kashmir Shaivism, into English to present it to the modern scientists. They are worthy of appreciation.

It is my desire that the modern scientists study this scripture, integrate it into their practice and work for the welfare of the universe through the philosophy of the Supreme Principle.

Mahamandaleshwar Swami Nityananda Saraswati
Walden, New York
October 22, 2010

Photo: Suvarna at Foto Corner

Bhagawan Nityanand

Photo: Bill Carter

Swami Muktanand Paramhans (Muktanand Baba)

Photo: Vasudha Donnelly

Mahamandaleshwar Swami Nityanand Saraswati (Nityanand Baba)

ABOUT PRONUNCIATION AND DIACRITICAL MARKS

Diacritical marks in the text are used in transliteration of Devanagari verses. In the prose text diacritical marks are used only while introducing a Sanskrit or Hindi word and its pronunciation and a few more times.

The vowels are pronounced as follows:

a as in America	**ī** as in sweet	**ṛ** as in rim	**au** as in now
ā as in far	**e** as in they	**ṝ** as in reed	**u** as in push
i as in pin	**ai** as in aisle	**o** as in go	**ū** as in rule

The consonants are pronounced as follows:

Gutturals
(pronounced from throat)
- **k** as in kite
- **kh** as in Eckhart
- **g** as in give
- **gh** as in dig-hard
- **ṅ** as in sing

Palatals
(pronounced with middle of tongue against palate)
- **c** as in chair
- **ch** as in staunch-heart
- **j** as in joy
- **jh** as in hedge-hog
- **ñ** as in canyon

Cerebrals
(pronounced with tip of tongue against roof of mouth)
- **ṭ** as in print
- **ṭh** as in light-heart
- **ḍ** as in dog
- **ḍh** as in adhere
- **ṇ** as in don't

Dentals
(pronounced as cerebrals but with tongue against teeth)
- **t** as in with
- **th** as in thump
- **d** as in gather
- **dh** as in breathe-here
- **n** as in nut

Labials
(pronounced with the lips)
- **p** as in pine
- **ph** as in up-hill (*not* ***f***)
- **b** as in bird
- **bh** as in rub-hard
- **m** as in mother

Semivowels
- **y** as in yes
- **r** as in run
- **l** as in light
- **v** as in vine

Sibilants
- **ś** as in dish
- **ṣ** as in push
- **s** as in sun

Aspirate
- **h** as in home
- **ḷ** as in **rlu** (pronounced half r, l, u together with rolled tongue)
- **ḹ** pronounced like **ḷ** but with rolled tongue against the roof of mouth

Anusvāra
- **ṁ** a resonant nasal sound as in bon

Visarga
- **ḥ** as in half **huh**

FOREWORD

N. V. Kākatkar,
Former Editor of Sant Kṛpā (Marāṭhī monthly)
Shri

Pune
12-2-2009

(Translated from a hand-written Marathi letter – actual letter is scanned after this translation)

Dear Umesh and Chitra Nagarkatte,
Salutations with love and a special prayer.[1]

I read your commentary on *SpandaKārikā* with all my heart. It took me a little while to read. While reading, I was brimming with bliss. You have indeed done your sādhanā through the medium of writing. Your Guru directed you, and both of you after becoming completely one with the command, enjoyed the bliss of writing and distributed it to us with great ease. You are doubly blessed!

This writing, done with an attitude of a sādhaka – a seeker, unfolding the subject systematically, brings great bliss. Erudite scholars' writing falls short before a seeker's writing, from the point of view of experiencing bliss. Your experiences are uncommonly eloquent. In the commentary on the 51st verse, the nectar of the summary of *SpandaKarika* is extremely succinct and full of delight. This is the grace of the Guru!

That "you received guidance from me" is not true. I do not have that authority. Whatever I said in our personal meetings, your Guru told you through my mouth, making me a mere puppet! Asking you to bring in the references of *Shiva Sutras* and *Vijnana Bhairav* in your work is your Guru's command and not mine. The guidance of Revered late Lakshman Joo is also because of Him. You are affectionately indebted to Him!

---

[1] Translated from Original Marāṭhi – It is a Marāṭhi custom to start a letter with these words.

There is a verse in a book titled *Amanask Yog* by Revered Shri Gorakshanath:

ऊर्ध्वमुष्टिरधोदृष्टिरुर्ध्द्वभेदः अधः शिराः ।
धरायंत्रविधानेन जीवन्मुक्तो भविष्यति ॥

Ūrdhva-muṣṭi-radho-dṛṣṭi-rurddhva-bhedaḥ adhaḥ śirāḥ
Dharā-yantra-vidhānena jīvan-mukto bhaviṣyati.

Fist pointed upwards and sight downwards: the target upwards and the head bent downwards: practising this "Dharāyantra" posture a seeker attains liberation.

This verse reveals a mystery about how Arjuna pierced the fish eye[2] with the target on a pole and his head looking at its reflection at the time of Draupadi's "Husband Selection" celebration. The phrase "target above, look below" means "aim on the target outside, while looking outwards." Arjuna won the wager by means of this practice of "Dharāyantra" or "Śāṁbhavi Mudrā."[3] Śāṁbhavi Mudrā simultaneously keeps the aim inward while looking outward without "Nimeṣa and Unmeṣa."[4] In Śāṁbhavi Mudrā even while the eyes look outside, the mind is aimed within, then while looking outside there is neither Nimeṣa nor Unmeṣa. This is kept secret in all scriptures. This universe full of variety and duality is a reflection on the mirror of Self-Consciousness. With the ingenious assistance of the reflection, one will obtain the bliss of the highest liberation. This is the message of *SpandaKarika*. The individual being has forgotten his or her own Shiva nature. To remove this forgetfulness is the priceless undertaking of the philosophy of Spanda. So be it.

Note: It will be helpful to list the verses of *SpandaKarika* and their English meanings in an Appendix.[5]

---

[2] For his daughter's selection of her chosen husband, King Drupad built a machine which revolved a fish high on a pole above an oil tank. The contest was for prospective suitors to aim at the fish eye looking in the oil at its reflection and shoot an arrow to pierce the eye. *Mahābhārat*

[3] Śāṁbhavi Mudrā includes four types of mudras: 1. outer target, outward look 2. inner target, outward look 3. outward target, inward look 4. inward target, inward look

[4] See Verse 1 of the book, page 19.

[5] See Appendix.

Your writing is extremely simple and easy to understand, especially for us Indians. All references of Jnaneshwar Mauli are carefully chosen. He is the authority of this Science. He is a 'Chakreshwara.'[6]

In addition, all the quotes from the works of VasuGupta, BhattaKallata to Ramana Maharshi and Mata Amritanand Mayi are all appropriate and appealing to us. This is really great. It is indeed a festival of the Play of Consciousness! Lots of best wishes to you! Keep writing! You are doing an intense sadhana. That is the reason your Guru definitely is pleased. I pray that you always receive this incessant Love of the Guru.

Yours humbly,

N.V. Kākatkar

[6] Verse 51.

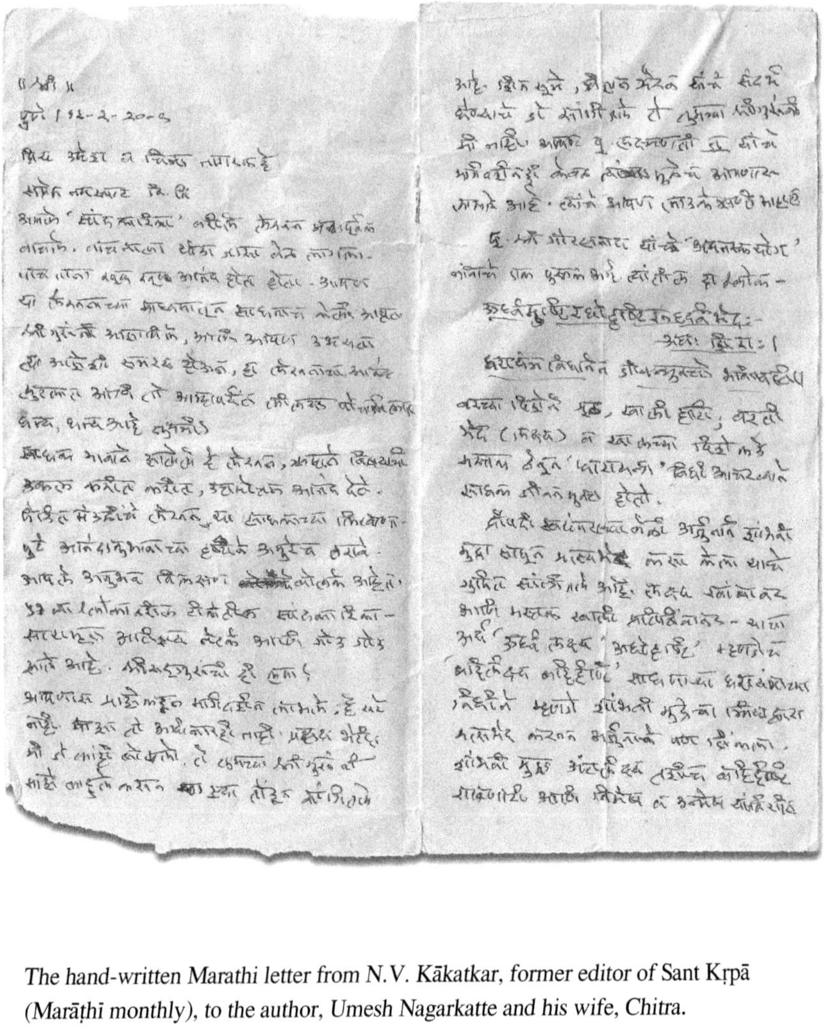

The hand-written Marathi letter from N.V. Kākatkar, former editor of Sant Kṛpā (Marāṭhī monthly), to the author, Umesh Nagarkatte and his wife, Chitra.

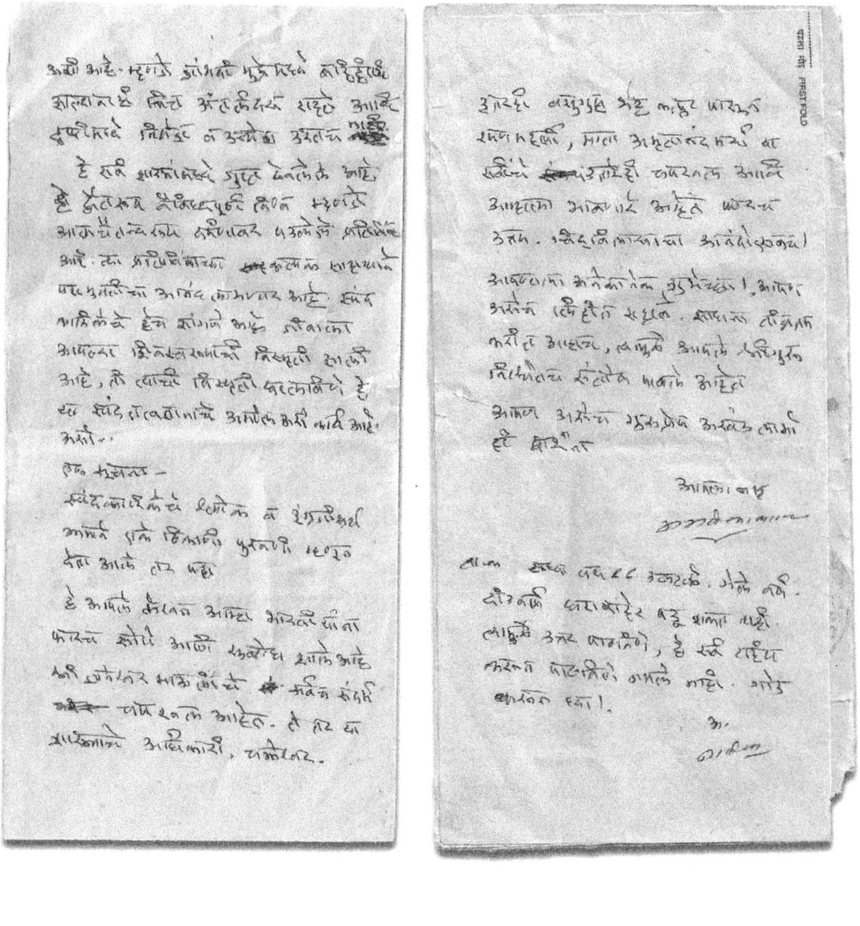

SPANDAKĀRIKĀ

PREFACE

श्री गुरुदेव

सर्वं स्वात्मस्वरूपं मुकुरनगरवत्स्वस्वरूपात्स्वतन्त्र-
स्वच्छस्वात्मस्वभित्तौ कलयति धरणीतः शिवान्तं सदा या ।
दृग्देवी मन्त्रवीर्ये सततसमुदिता शब्दराश्यात्मपूर्णा
हन्तानन्तस्फुरत्ता जयति जगति सा शांकरी स्पन्दशक्तिः ।।
सम्यक्सूत्रसमन्वयं परिगतिं तत्त्वे परस्मिन्परां
तीक्ष्णां युक्तिकथामुपायघटनां स्पष्टार्थसद्व्याकृतिम् ।
ज्ञातुं वाञ्छथ चेच्छिवोपनिषदं श्रीस्पन्दशास्त्रस्य तद्-
वृत्तावत्र धियं निधत्त सुधियः स्पन्दश्रियं प्राप्नुत ।।

मुक्तानंदाय गुरवे शिष्यसंसारहारिणे ।
भक्तकार्यैकदेहाय नमस्ते चित्सदात्मने ।।

ॐ नमः शिवाय गुरवे सच्चिदानन्दमूर्तये ।
निष्प्रपंचाय शान्ताय निरालम्बाय तेजसे ।।

Sarvaṁ svātma-svarūpaṁ mukura-nagaravat-svasvarūpāt-svatantra-
Svaccha-svātma-svabhittau kalayati dharaṇītaḥ śivāntaṁ sadā yā
Dṛgdevī mantra-vīrye satata-samuditā śabda-rāśyātma-pūrṇā-
hantānanta-sphurattā jayati jagati sā śāṁkarī spanda-śaktiḥ
Samyak-sūtra-samanvayaṁ parigatiṁ tattve parasmin-parāṁ
Tīkṣṇāṁ yukti-kathām-upāya-ghaṭanāṁ spaṣṭārtha-sadvyākṛtiṁ
Jñātuṁ vāñchatha cec-chivopaniṣadaṁ Śrīspanda-śāstrasya tad-
Vṛttāvatra dhiyaṁ nidhatta sudhiayaḥ spanda-śriyaṁ prāpnuta[7]
Muktānaṅdāya gurave śiṣya-saṁsāra-hāriṇe
Bhaktakāryaika-dehāya namaste cit-sadātmane
Oṁ namaḥ Śivāya gurave saccidānaṅda-mūrtaye

---

[7] Prayer of Kṣemarāja, a commentator of *Spandakārikā*, 11th Century

Niṣprapañcāya śāntāya nirālambāya tejase-

Just as a city reflected in a mirror
Everything is Her own Self
Out of her own free nature
On the clear canvas of her own Self,
She eternally creates the totality
From the earth up to Shiva.
She is goddess of knowledge.
She is always aware of the vitality of mantra,
She is the endless burst of perfect I-consciousness,
Whose essential nature encompasses the multitude of letters.
Hail to that Spanda Shakti[8] *of Shiva, which exults in the world.*
If you want to know the exact interconnection of all verses,
On the most excellent ascertainment of Reality,
With pointed precise statement of reasoning,
Right application of means
Exquisite exposition with clear meaning
Of the Shivopanishad, the Science of Divine Pulsation
Apply your mind to this work, O intelligent people, and attain the wealth of Spanda.
Salutations to Guru Muktananda,
You destroy disciples' worldliness
Your life was for the work of your devotees alone,
Your nature is Consciousness and Existence
Om! Salutations to Guru Lord Shiva,
You are an embodiment of Truth, Consciousness and Bliss
You transcend duality. You are peace itself
You are beyond all means. You are the Supreme illumination.

What is Spanda Kārikā? Why this book?

Spanda generally means vibration or pulsation. But in this work the word spanda is used in the sense of creative pulsation, the energy of the Highest Reality, that is the substratum of all phenomena, called Shiva, for short. According to the

[8] Energy of creative pulsation

science of the spanda the whole universe is a pulsation of energy, a view that accords with that of modern science. Astronomers say that the universe composed of dark energy, giving rise to the various celestial bodies in the universe, of which our solar system is only a tiny part. Modern science has theories of relativity and quantum mechanics to explain how the universe comes into existence, is maintained, and is destroyed.

Modern science says that the universe originated with the Big Bang - a great explosion. It was not a physical event. There was nothing else to cause it. Its existence is supported by overwhelming evidence. We have to understand that it was not like a giant firecracker that went "Kaboom." We must comprehend that before the Big Bang even space did not exist. Time did not exist. Einstein's theory of relativity forces us to think of the unified entity of SpaceTime rather than of space and time existing independently. All physical reality comes after the Big Bang.[9] (Weeks, 60)[10] The vibrations – in the form of radiation – set in motion at that time can be measured even now. These were first measured accidentally in 1965 by two Bell Lab scientists, Penzias and Wilson, and they received a Nobel Prize for their discovery in 1978.[11] (*Panda*, 27)

The Vedas say that the universe came into existence with the vibration of the Self, which is regarded as the sound vibration AUM. From Aum space came into existence. From space was generated air from air, fire: from fire, water and from water, earth. Everything on this earth is made from these five basic elements. If we chemically analyze the ingredients of air, fire, etc. further into elements of the modern Periodic Table this Vedic statement is consistent with science.

All physical phenomena occur as events. Science characterizes (as proven in the Copenhagen Theory of Niels Bohr)[12] a physical phenomenon as an 'event' composed of a 'triad' occurring in a field of energy, consisting of object, observation of the object, and the observer. Quantum mechanics recognizes that the subatomic particles, such as photons – packets of light, electrons, have waveform as well as corpuscular – or individual – form. Two subatomic particles could be in

[9] Weeks, J. - *The Shape of Space*, Page 269
[10] In this book we use the following reference style. It is not the APA style. (Weeks, 60) means the Author Weeks is listed as 60th in the detailed Bibliography.
[11] Panda, N. C. – *The Vibrating Universe*, Page 328
[12] Panda, N. C. – *The Vibrating Universe*, Page 228
[13] Overbye Dennis, *Quantum Theory Tugged, All of Physics Unraveled*

two places at once, everywhere, nowhere until someone measured it: light could be a wave or a particle.[13] (*Dennis*, 6) Obeying only the law of conservation of action, these particles arise from a field, appear for a while, disappear, or conceal their actual whereabouts. "According to the Copenhagen view, it was the act of observation that 'collapsed' the wave of function of some particle, freezing it into one particular state, a location or velocity."[14] But modern science does not turn its focus on the observer or the consciousness of the observer.

In fact, the study of science and the issue of the existence of the universe in particular, depend on existence or consciousness as well as on the waking state of the observer. If the observer did not exist or were not awake, then the event would not exist for the observer, since the observer and his/her capability or process of observation, two of the three components of the triad, would be missing. For instance, in a class where the teacher is explaining something, a student's mind wanders somewhere away and the student has no idea what the teacher is talking about. It is as if the student is not physically there. In this case the absence of capability or lack of process of observation negates even the physical presence of the observer.

The field of energy underlying all triads or 'events' is called Spanda. Spanda means conscious creative pulsation, the emphasis is on the creative pulsation being conscious or self-aware, independent of the states of waking, dream, or deep sleep. Its universal existence is proven by the individual's conscious self-aware existence.

Spanda, similar to physical forces like electricity and gravitation, is not visible, but its effects as waves are seen everywhere in the whole universe. A wave is a vibration, whether it is a waveform of an atom, a sound wave, a light wave, a heat wave, an electric current, a magnetic wave, or a wave in an ocean. From physical scientific view, whatever we perceive through our senses consists of vibrations. We hear a sound through our ears because of the vibrations of the eardrums. We perceive a touch through our skin by the vibrations of hair follicles. We see an object with our eyes when the light wave from the object passing through the eye's lens sets up vibrations on the retina. We taste with our tongue by the vibrations of the taste buds on the tongue. We smell a fragrance

---

[14] Overbye Dennis, *Quantum Theory Tugged, All of Physics Unraveled* - in the paragraph "*Quantum Wars.*"

with the nose due to vibration of the hairs in the nose. These five senses are the qualities of the five basic elements - space, air, fire, water, and earth, respectively and will be discussed in detail later in the text. All these five types of vibrational perception are carried to our brain as electrical impulses. We breathe due to the pumping of the heart, which is nothing but a vibration. The blood flows through our system due to the contraction and expansion of the blood vessels, which is a vibration. The nervous system according to neurologists consists of electrical impulses. For a radiologist the body consists of electro-magnetic vibrations. The involuntary actions in our body take place as vibrations – contractions and expansions. The heart pumps due to contraction and expansion. The organs of voluntary action perform due to the electrical impulses in our brain. Internally, when a thought arises in our mind it bubbles out like a bubble in an ocean. It slowly arises from the substratum, takes shape and stays for a while and subsides. There is a gap; some time elapses before the second thought arises. Sometimes the gap is large, sometimes it is small; and sometimes when the mind is agitated the gap is miniscule. When emotions like fear and exhilaration are experienced, they produce shivers in the body or the body hair stands on its end. These are vibrations. Thus, whether at the level of the universe or the individual, vibration pervades physical and mental existence. The vibration in an individual is a sign that the individual is conscious or alive. The non-relational universal vibration may appear to us as happening automatically without consciousness taking any part. But again this understanding of relational or non-relational vibration occurs in us due to consciousness. It is necessary to reemphasize that our own existence as consciousness is a proof for the existence of universal consciousness, but the universal consciousness itself transcends all individual existences or any universe.

Modern science is a search for Truth. Einstein says in his *Meaning of Relativity*, "We are accustomed to regard as real those sense perceptions which are common to different individuals, and which therefore are, in a measure, impersonal." (Einstein, 7) If we regard the sense perceptions as reality in science then science is limited to a conditional reality in a waking state only, and cannot be considered as absolute Truth that transcends all states. There is no objective experiment that can measure consciousness since it is consciousness that has to devise such experiments. Yet its effects can be measured as described earlier.

The same inquisitiveness, experimentation, openness, and logical thinking required in studying physical science (obviously in the waking state) is also necessary in studying spanda – the conscious pulsation. The experiences that the study of the conscious pulsation brings are real as per Einstein's definition since they also contain "sense perceptions that are common to different individuals and in a measure, impersonal." Many researchers, whom we call saints, separated by time and space and not in direct contact with one another, have reported the same sensory experiences. Also they have reported experiencing something common - that which is beyond sense perceptions.

The subject matter of the current text *Spanda Kārikās* (Verses on Spanda) is the study of general non-relational universal consciousness and special individual consciousness or awareness. The study leads one to experience that both are one and the same consciousness, whose essential nature is existence or truth and bliss, and whose manifestation is the entire universe regarded as consciousness' pulsation. This consciousness is also called Shiva, the Self, God, Brahman, Truth, and by other countless names. An intellectual can relate to a philosophy known as Kashmir Shaivism, the study of consciousness as "Prakāsh" – light of consciousness (or Shiva) and "Vimarsh" – self-awareness (or His energy – Shakti). Kashmir Shaivism is a philosophy that can be practiced; its statements can be experimented with and verified in the laboratory of everyday life without regard to time, place, age, caste, gender, creed, or nationality.

Our individual consciousness, also called our inner Self, creates three types of experiences for us: waking, dream and deep sleep. Physical experiences take place in our waking state through voluntary activities, using senses of perception and action. Mental experiences of thoughts and emotions take place in both the waking and dream states. Experiences such as breathing and digestion pertaining to the vital force (prāṇa) connected with involuntary bodily functions, metabolism, and the central nervous system, occur in the waking, dream and deep sleep states. Through this consciousness in the waking state we experience physical duality, such as subject and object, within and without, here and elsewhere. In our waking and dream states we experience mental duality such as unity and diversity, pain and pleasure, joy and sadness, happiness and sorrow, clarity and confusion, knowledge and ignorance. In our waking, dream and deep sleep states we experience the vital ('prāṇic') duality, such as hunger and satisfaction.

Because of our conditioning in duality we regard our consciousness to be separate from other fellow beings, possibly a part of some general non-relational Universal Consciousness. Without study and the guidance of a competent teacher or Guru, we cannot experience our changeless individual consciousness itself. This consciousness is the cause of our existence, which makes us individually feel 'I AM.' It is the substratum of all phenomena that we experience. But with study under the guidance of a Guru, we acquire a totally different quality of insight and get the experience of identity of our individual consciousness with the Universal Consciousness.

The rewards of this understanding abound. Following the Guru's teachings in our waking moments makes our search (sādhanā) full of vigor, meaning it creates in us a liking of our nature. We look forward to having that nice feeling about ourselves and everyone else continually. We do not like or we shun thinking about petty bothersome things regarding ourselves as well as others. We remain cheerful regardless of our circumstances. We become better human beings liked by all. We get the experience and understanding that the mind and the universe are one and the same conscious vibrating energy (spanda), the all encompassing "I AM" where there is no other. We experience a life filled with love, health, peace and harmony. In the ninth century there was a sage, Utpaladeva, who studied Kashmir Shaivism. He says that the greatness of this path called Shaivism is such that by following the path "pains become pleasure, poison becomes nectar and this world which otherwise binds becomes liberation."

दुःखान्यपि सुखायन्ते विषमप्यमृतायते ।
मोक्षायते च संसारो यत्र मार्गः स शाङ्करः ॥ (उत्पलस्तोत्र २०।१२)

Duḥkhānyapi sukhāyante viṣamapyamṛtāyate,
Mokṣāyate ca saṅsāro yatra mārga sa Śāṅkaraḥ.
(Utpalastotra 20|12)

In his work *Dāsabodh*, Samarth Ramdas, a saint who lived in the 17th century in a place called SajjanGaḍ about 200 miles south east from Mumbai, Maharashtra, India, says: (Samarth Ramdas, 29)

पाहावे आपणासी आपण । या नाव ज्ञान ॥ (दासबोध द.५,स. ६,ओ. १)

Pāhāve āpaṇāsi āpaṇa, yā nāva jñana.
(Dasabodh 5|6|1)

To discern oneself is called knowledge.

The Lord says to Arjuna in the *Bhagavad Gita*:

यत्रोपरमते चित्तं निरुद्धं योगसेवया ।
यत्र चैवात्मनात्मानं पश्यन्नात्मनि तुष्यति ॥
सुखमात्यन्तिकं यत्तद, बुद्धिग्राह्यमतीन्द्रियम् ।
वेत्ति यत्र न चैवायं स्थितश्चलति तत्त्वतः ॥ (गीता ६।२०-२१)

Yatroparamate cittaṁ niruddhaṁ yogasevayā
Yatra caivātmanātmānaṁ paśyannātmani tuṣyati
Sukhamātyaṅtikaṁ yattad buddhi-grāhyamatīndriyam
Vetti yatra na caivāyaṁ sthitaścalati tattvataḥ
(Gītā 6|20-21)

By the study of Yoga, direct the mind where it delights in itself by discerning your own Self. The happiness is limitless, which is beyond all senses but can be grasped by the intellect, and the mind does not move away from that happiness.

Spanda Kārikās is a text of Kashmir Shaivism. There are four main texts in Kashmir Shaivism: *Shiva Sutras, Spanda Kārikās, Vijñana Bhairava*, and *Pratyabhijñā Hridayam*. In the ninth century, Vasugupta received instruction in a dream that in Mahādev Mountain, he would find the esoteric *Shiva Sutras* engraved on the surface of a rock. With his revelation, experience and logical reasoning, he put the exposition on Spanda together in deep but lucid 51 sutras as *SpandaKarikas*.[15] Thus the exquisite greatness of the Self was revealed to Vasugupta and through his work humanity benefits.

Swami Muktananda Paramahansa (1908-1982), lovingly called Baba Muktananda, lived in Ganeshpuri, Maharashtra State, India. He was a great saint and teacher well-known throughout the world. He could instantly give a first-hand experience of the inner Self to an ardent visitor, by 'shaktipāt' or transference of energy, overcoming all blinding conditioning of the visitor. Through shaktipāt he would awaken the 'Kundalini' energy of the visitor. One aspect of the life-force remains dormant at the base of the spine in humans in a coiled form, called Kundalini in Yoga scriptures, until awakened by a competent teacher. Quite often the visitor's

[15] Sanskrit transliteration diacritical marks are used first to introduce the reader to the proper pronunciation and are not maintained afterwards.

readiness caused an automatic awakening of his or her kundalini in Baba's presence, or in Baba's āshrams and meditation centers around the world without Baba's physical presence. In his teachings and talks, Baba used Kashmir Shaivism along with Vedanta, other scriptures and other saints' works, but always emphasized one's own first-hand experience.

As has been said earlier in a different context, the first hand experiences of the Self have been chronicled for countless centuries throughout the works of various scientists or saints. They dedicated their lives to this study and regardless of the individual, upbringing, tradition, age and gender, the experiences turn out to be common. Of course, not every one gets exactly the same experiences in the same order. One's experiences can be compared with those chronicled and can be tested for authenticity like results of a reaction in a chemistry lab. Awakening of kundalini is like opening another dimension in human life. Even today people who have kundalini awakening under the guidance of various competent teachers – Gurus – have similar experiences of the Self, which shows that the power of kundalini is not limited to a particular teacher. But as in any other field, expert teachers who can awaken students' kundalini energy are not plentiful. Some well-known spiritual teachers who have not experienced kundalini awakening, out of ignorance, think 'Kundalini awakening' is imagination.

Chitra and Umesh Nagarkatte met Baba in August 1972 in Ganeshpuri during their summer vacation visit to India from the U.S.A. They had instant kundalini awakening with Baba's touch. But they did not attribute their experiences of spontaneous meditation to the kundalini awakening until 1974, since they never came across a saint of his stature, who could explain to them what was happening in them. In 1974 when Baba came to New York, they met Baba again and started attending his programs, he asked them to begin and run a meditation center for him under his direction. They ran the meditation center – Siddha Yoga Dham of Jersey City, New Jersey, USA, from 1975 to 1982. In this center several people had experiences of spontaneous kundalini awakening. From 1975 to 1982, being college teachers they could devote a lot of time, especially the summers, with him without leaving their jobs. In their visits with him, they cooked for him and sometimes cooked with him. Over the last three years, he gave them various assignments, through which he trained them in saints' teachings. In 1981 and 1982, they prepared weekly talks on *SpandaKarikas* for their meditation center programs. They would prepare one or two verses from the *SpandaKārikās* each time. Chitra had many dreams in which Baba appeared. A dream would precede a verse, but they would not know the meaning of the dream. But as they studied a particular verse, the meaning of the dream would be clear. Thus the talks were prepared with the first hand experience given by the Guru. To end each talk, they would find an appropriate song of a poet saint.

In summer 1981, among several of Baba's assignments to them, one assignment was to study poet saints' works, select songs on several subjects that he gave them, write them in notebooks and give these to Baba. The songs they chose to end a talk came from those notebooks. All these events have made *SpandaKarikas* a special text for Chitra and Umesh, through the medium of which the great Guru chose to give them the experience of the bliss of the Self. Hence they are making this attempt to share their experiences and subsequent great joy, with great humility knowing that their experiences are common to all who aspire under the direction of different Gurus and it is only the Guru's grace and not the aspirant's own effort that can bring such experiences and understanding. Words fall short in the description of the experience, but certainly words would dissolve in the mind of the reader and produce the required effect, just as sugar dissolves in the mouth of the taster and produces an experience of sweetness.

This book is based on the talks in their meditation center and what they learned over the years. It is a recollection of Baba's teaching of *SpandaKarikas* to them and such recollections of one's spiritual practices are necessary. Baba's rich tradition included Kashmir Shaivism, Vedanta, poet saints' works from all over India, especially Maharashtra, Sufi teaching stories and many more things. The original talks were based on Jaideva Singh's (Singh, 32) English translation of SpandaKarikas based on Kṣemarāja's (11th century) Commentary. For this text however the Hindi translation by Prof. Nīlkaṇṭha Guruṭū (Gurutu, 12) has been used as the basis. Prof. Guruṭū has written the commentary based on Bhaṭṭa Kallaṭa, who was a direct disciple of Vasugupta.

In short, this book is based on direct personal experiences and is a tribute to the Guru principle.

Acknowledgements

It was Nityanand Baba, Swami Muktananda's first successor, who showered his grace on Umesh, saying six years ago in Shanti Mandir Ashram, Pine Bush, New York, USA Ashram, "You have Baba's grace and Chitra's inspiration. You should write a commentary on the *SpandaKarikas.*" The commentary was finished in Nityanand Baba's beautiful Shanti Mandir Ashram, situated in mango groves in Magod, near Valsad, Gujarat, India on the auspicious day of Thursday, 5th June 2008, (Jyeṣṭha Śukla Dvitīyā, Sarvadhāri Samvatsara, Śālivāhana Śaka 1930 as per the Hindu calendar.) He also agreed to write a Foreword to the commentary.

Soon after the work of the present commentary started, Umesh and Chitra went to meet P.P. Sadyojāt Śankarāshram Swamiji in Chitrapur Math, Shirali, Karnatak, India their family math of Chitrapur Saraswat community. He was trained by revered Swami Ishwaranand Giri of Mount Abu and had recently been installed to continue the Chitrapur Guruparampara – lineage of Gurus. When Umesh told Sadyojat Shankarashram Swamiji about the *Spandakarika* project, Swamiji said, "Write it from an upāsak's (worshipper's or seeker's) point of view." This has what has taken place in the commentary.

Shri Nānā Kākatkar, the former editor of 'Sant Kripa' magazine, Pune, India whom Umesh and Chitra had gone to meet after writing commentary of a few verses, said, "In your commentary of every verse, you must bring in appropriate references from *Shiva Sutras* and *Vijnan Bhairava* also. Then it would be worthwhile." That has happened in most verses. Whenever they met him in his old simple Pune office, Shri Kakatkar always encouraged both Umesh and Chitra, saying they should keep writing. Review and reflection are good for seekers.

While writing, Baba Muktanand's favorite saints, Jnaneshwar, Eknath, Tukaram, Brahmanand, Purandardas, Ramana Maharshi, Lakshman Joo and so on all came to help out. Among them most quoted is Jnaneshwar, whose works *Cāngdev Pāsaṣṭi* (65 verses to Changadev), Jñāneśwari – a commentary on the *Bhagavad Gita, Haripāṭh* and *Amṛtānubhav* (*Nectar of Experience*) literature of the 12th century from Maharashtra fit in appropriately in *SpandaKarikas* of the 8th Century from distant Kashmir. Their help makes this work a rich tapestry of saints' writings in the tradition of Baba Muktanand.

Dr. Sarah (Amba) Caldwell, and Acharya Shyamsundar Jha, both disciples of Baba Muktanand and devotees of Swami Nityanand, promptly edited the manuscript for English and Sanskrit writing, transliteration respectively. Michael Tobin, Goshen, NY a devotee of Nityanand Baba designed the cover. The authors as well as the artist have seen the triangle on the cover in their meditation.

We thank Ron Carter for book design and Jude Berman for coordinating the publication of this book. Namdev Hayes rendered *Cāngdev Pāsaṣṭi* into English in 1982 which we had together prepared on the occasion of Baba's successors' installation ceremony.

We acknowledge the blessings and help of the people who made this work possible.

INTRODUCTION

The book *SpandaKarikas,** written by the sage Vasugupta and commented upon by Shri Bhaṭṭa Kallaṭa, a direct disciple of Vasugupta, as well as Kṣemarāj is a logical system. The subject matter of this book is the essential nature of Shiva, or the universal Self or Consciousness, as creative pulsation. The purpose for writing the book is to show that an individual can become aware of his or her consciousness as identical with Shiva and become liberated. Both liberation and bondage are relative ideas. Forgetfulness of one's own nature is regarded as bondage and its remembrance is liberation. All human suffering starts due to this forgetfulness. This is because feelings of limitation in knowledge and capability arise, and desires followed by anger, greed, infatuation or fear, pride and jealousy, collectively known as the six inner enemies, are born in the mind of the individual. Thus he or she acts under the sway of these feelings, troubling himself or herself and others. The remembrance of one's own nature brings about the liberation from the feeling of limitation and its consequences. This remembrance should be a constant awareness. It should become as natural as one's identification of oneself as a man or a woman. The goal of the book is to enable an individual to claim his or her already existing identification with Shiva. The book describes how to attain this identification.

The text is divided into three sections. The first section of twenty-five verses describes Shiva's creative pulsation, or Spanda, as the dynamic aspect, which is identical with the essential Self of each person. This part also teaches the means for experiencing the Spanda. The second section consisting of seven verses describes how the creative pulsation is identical with the whole universe, and teaches how to experience this aspect of the Spanda. Realization is not complete without experiencing both of these aspects of Spanda. The third section of eighteen verses describes mostly the supernormal powers attained by the realization of the Spanda. Some of these powers can easily serve as an exit from continuous experience of the Self and an entry into a cycle of misery and happiness. These verses so far form the fifty verses of the *Spanda Karika*. The fifty-first verse points to the good that accrues to people who take upon themselves the study of the Spanda principle and realize it. The last verse lauds the power of the Spanda state and simultaneously the power of the word of the Guru.

---

* referred to in this book in one of the four ways: *SpandaKarikas, Spanda Karikas, Spanda Karika, Spandakarika*

CONTENTS

PART I
NATURE OF SPANDA

PART II
SPONTANEOUS RISE OF KNOWLEDGE

PART III
POWERS OF SPANDA

PART I

स्वरूप-स्पंद - SVARŪPA SPANDA
NATURE OF SPANDA

VERSE 1
UNIVERSE A DIVINE THROB

यस्योन्मेषनिमेषाभ्यां जगतः प्रलयोदयौ ।
तं शक्तिचक्रविभवप्रभवं शंकरं स्तुमः ॥१॥

1. *Yasyonmeṣa-nimeṣābhyāṁ jagataḥ pralayodayau*
Taṁ śakti-cakra-vibhava-prabhavaṁ śaṁkararṁ stumaḥ.

भट्ट कल्लट – अनेन स्वस्वभावस्यैव शिवात्मकस्य संकल्पमात्रेण जगदुत्पत्तिसंहारयोः कारणत्वं, विज्ञानदेहात्मकस्य शक्तिचक्रैश्वर्यस्योत्पत्तिहेतुत्वं, नमस्कारद्वारेण प्रतिपाद्यते ॥१॥

Bhaṭṭa Kallaṭa: - 1. *Anena sva-svabhāvasyaiva Śivātmakasya saṅkalpamātreṇa jagadutpatti-saṁhārayoḥ kāraṇatvaṁ, vijñāna-dehātmakasya śakti-cakraiśvarya-syotpatti-hetutvaṁ, namaskāra-dvāreṇa pratipādyate.*

"*We praise that Śaṅkara, whose nature is the conglomeration of powers that evolve to cause the manifestation of the universe through their junction and disjunction. His expansion and contraction causes the universe to dissolve and arise."Another meaning will be given in the last part of the discussion.*

Bhaṭṭa Kallaṭa: "With this verse, Shiva's nature is recognized through salutations. The nature of Shiva, the Primal Cause, Whose mere will or pulsation of I-consciousness is the cause of the universe's creation and dissolution, is benevolent, being also the grace-bestowing power of establishing us in oneness. That Self-aware Pulsation is also recognized through salutations. While remaining general *non-different independent knowledge, It also has a potential of creating different energies flowing through myriads of specific forms."*

THE BOOK *SPANDAKARIKAS* consists of 52 verses. This is the first verse. It summarizes the subject matter of the book as experiencing the Self or Shiva. It describes the goal as well as the means of attaining the goal.

Jagat or The Universe

The Sanskrit word for the universe is "jagat" which means that which is constantly going, changing or moving. Science deals with the non-relational physical universe experienced in the waking state by the senses of perception: and it does not resort to concepts of creative agency or energy or consciousness to explain these manifestations. Of course, it is only because of our self-awareness in our waking state that we are able to decipher the sense perceptions of the universe around us. Kashmir Shaivism recognizes a conscious universe and emphasizes that the energy around is also conscious. Philosophy deals not only with the physical universe but also with all the states of an individual - embodied being: waking, dreaming, deep sleep and the fourth or super-conscious states. It is fascinating and yet to be expected that a philosophical system such as ancient Indian philosophy, that deals with Truth in all states, should be consistent with Truth discovered by modern discoveries of science perceptible in the waking state.

Among the ancient Indian philosophies, Kashmir Shaivism is available to anyone regardless of time, space, gender, caste, creed or nationality, and provides logical, scientific, and practical applications to every day life. The Kashmir Shaivite text under discussion, *SpandaKārikās*, composed about a thousand years ago, describes the universe through the workings of the throb of consciousness. In discussing this text, we will draw upon the insights of Kashmir Shaivism along with supporting statements from *Upanishads*, modern and ancient saints' literature, and personal experiences. The present authors were trained in this manner by their Guru. Whenever a comparison between statements of *Spanda Karika* and Science is under discussion, the authors' training in science and mathematics compel them to make sure that the philosophy discussed is truly universal, transcending all cultures, rigorously logical, and is consistent with scientific discoveries.

Our universe, which is constantly changing, consists of a general or impersonal set of names and forms, and a special or personal set of emotions and feelings.

The set of forms manifests from and shares its nature with the light of consciousness, called Prakāsh in Kashmir Shaivism; and the set of names associated with and uniquely identifying the set of forms, distinguishing each from all the rest, emerges from and shares the nature of Self-awareness, called Vimarsh in Kashmir Shaivism, meaning the energy of consciousness. Among the general aspect of the universe lie galaxies containing stars, planets and other celestial bodies; trees, mountains, rivers and oceans; various insentient objects and sentient beings; energies or forces of gravitation, magnetism, electricity; chemical and biological energy and atomic energy; vital life-force known as Prāṇa, and consciousness, which assures the existence of an embodied being and which, when it departs the being, causes the elements that comprise the body to wither away.

Einstein proved the basic identity of matter and energy. So even something that may appear insentient is also a manifestation of energy. Science has given an explanation of the origin and general working of the physical and biological universe. Physicists say that the universe began with the Big Bang - an explosion, which is a vibration. The vibrations set in motion at the time of the Big Bang can be measured even now as a background noise. This was conjectured by Princeton University scientists and discovered in 1965 by two Bell Lab scientists, Penzias and Wilson, for which they received a Nobel Prize in 1978. We have to understand that even space came out of the Big Bang.

The emergence of the universe from the Big Bang is consistent with the Vedic philosophy. In the *Māṇḍukya Upanishad* (*Nikhilanand*, 55) Kārikā Gauḍapādācarya says: "सर्वस्य प्रणवो ह्यादिर्मध्यमन्तस्तथैव च ।" "*Sarvasya praṇavo hyādirmadhyamantastathaiva ca*" [Mā.U. I, 27][16] "The sound Pranav - AUM is at the beginning, middle and the end."

This says that the universe began with the sound vibration AUM. Doesn't the sound OM itself sound like a 'humming' sound associated with a vibration of a string or a machine? Many saints over the ages also have trained and continue to train their disciples to hear the sound of OM in every vibration.

The *Bhagavad Gita* says, "ॐ इत्येकाक्षरं ब्रह्म ।" "*Om Ityekākṣaraṁ Brahma*" [BG 8, 13] "AUM is the one word signifying Brahman - the Self." In the Vedas the -

[16] References to all Upanishads and Bhagavad Gita are not in the Bibliography. All published versions are consistent with one another.

words Brahman and Atman are used interchangeably for the Self. How the universe manifests is also described in the Vedas.

The *Taittiriya Upanishad* (Swami Gambhiranand, 40) says,

> तस्माद्वा एतस्मादात्मन आकाशः संभूतः । आकाशाद्वायुः । वायोरग्निः । अग्नेरापः । अद्भ्यः पृथिवी ।
>
> *Tasmād-vā Etasmād-ātmana ākāśaḥ saṁbhūtaḥ, ākāśād-vāyuḥ, vāyor-agniḥ, agner-āpaḥ, adbhyaḥ pṛthivī. [T.U. II. i 1]*
>
> *"From the Self emerged space, from space air, from air fire, from fire water, from water earth." Space, air, fire, water and earth (solid matter) are the five elements from which everything in the physical world is made. If we look at the chemical and physical properties of the ingredients of five elements, we see that this Upanishadic statement is consistent with the modern science.*

According to modern physics, the universe will end in the Big Crunch. The Vedas also describe a similar end where the earth will merge into water, water into fire, fire into air, air into space and space into the Self, resulting in a void or black hole, except for the eternal Self, which just exists with or without creation.

As per the first part of Verse 1, it is the expansion and contraction of Shiva, the Self that creates and destroys the universe. Elsewhere, in *Pratyabhijñā - Hṛdayaṁ*, (Singh, 33) another text of Kashmir Shaivism there is an aphorism, "स्वेच्छया स्वभित्तौ विश्वं उन्मीलयति" [प्र. २] "*Svecchayā svabhittau viśvaṁ unmīlayati* / [PH, 2] "By Its own wish Consciousness reveals the universe on Its own canvas."

This general universe is a non-relational and common experience, corroborated by people in the waking state. Even then an individual's universe is limited to things, people, and life-experiences that surround him or her. The individual may not be concerned about the general universe. According to the science of Yoga, there are four bodies – स्थूल sthula gross or physical, सूक्ष्म sūkṣma subtle, कारण kāraṇa - causal and महाकारण mahākāraṇa - supracausal शरीर *śarīr* - body. The experience of the waking state takes place in the individual's gross or physical body. The word जगत् jagat – or universe used in this verse is not limited merely to a general or physical universe, but also includes a special inner personal universe. In our inner universes lie our ideating mind, discriminating intellect, and ego or "I-AM"-ness or self-awareness, our thoughts, memories, emotions and feelings. There are three states other than waking. Those are dream, deep sleep, and the fourth or super-conscious states, which an individual experiences the subtle, causal and supra-causal body, mutually exclusive, and are discussed in detail in later verses. They are considered briefly here.

In the dream state each individual has an experience of a reality that may or may not have some connection to the experiences of waking state. The dream experienced cannot always be corroborated by other people in the waking state. If I have a dream about some person whom I know, and if the person meets me later in the waking state, the person may not be able to confirm that I saw him or her in my dream. But there are exceptions to this. Some people have dreams about a person and the person meets and confirms appearing in the dream. We have had dreams of our Guru, which he had confirmed later. A person established in the Self may know about someone's dream and use it to give a lesson in reality. There are several examples of such instances.

There was such an incident in the life of a saint called Akkalkot Mahārāj, who lived in a place called Akkalkot in Mahārāshṭra, India. He remained unconcerned about the world and many would come to be in his presence. A scholar, Viṣṇubuvā Braḥmacārī, came to test his state and argue about some Vedantic phrase - *Brahma tadākāra vṛtti* - meaning "mind taking shape of Brahman or reality," in other words the state of mind where mind is merged in equality-consciousness. Akkalkot Maharaj ignored him for a few days. But when Viṣṇubuvā insisted, Akkalkot Maharaj asked him to come to him the next day. That night Viṣṇubuvā had a dream, in which scorpions were crawling all over his body. Viṣṇubuvā was petrified and woke up to find nothing around. The next day when he went to Akkalkot Maharaj to argue, Maharaj said, "Don't repeat the Vedantic phrases without experiencing them. When the scorpions were crawling all over your body where did your "*Brahma tadākār vṛtti*" go?" (Kelkar, 18) This illustrates that some people established in the state of Self can easily know about another's dreams and mental states in detail.

The dream state is experienced in the subtle body. For an external observer, the physical body of a dreamer appears to be undergoing various movements, brain waves may take a definite shape, and the dreamer may utter sounds while in the dream state. Sleep scientists call this REM (Rapid Eye Movements) state.

In the subtle body also lie the six chakras - nerve centers in the body through which the Kundalini energy (a subtle aspect of the life-force) flows. This aspect of energy remains dormant in the base of every animal's spine until it is awakened. When the energy is awakened, the experiences which people have of the chakras and the Kundalini energy itself can be corroborated, and have been chronicled from ancient times in the literature of Yoga and saints' lives. One of the important consequences of Kundalini awakening is spontaneous meditation, in which one experiences the core of one's being or innate nature, which is the fourth state in the supracausal body. Many scholars and lecturers of science and Vedanta who have not had Kundalini experiences describe it as mere imagination, but it is like the difference between the experience of driving a car and flying. It is a different dimension. A person who only drives a car has to imagine the experiences of one who flies. The experiences one gets of the awakened Kundalini, also called Ātmashakti – energy of the Self, are not ends in themselves, and not obtained by one's own volition, but are similar to those obtained by many other seekers whose Kundalini energy is also awakened. If they were merely imaginary as some scholars say, then how could it be that over the ages, regardless of erudition or culture, countless people have had similar experiences? Doesn't the test of empirical laboratory replicability used as the standard of Truth in sciences like chemistry or physics apply here? Here the lab is one's own body. Detailed discussions of Kundalini energy and the effects of its awakening are given in later paragraphs and later verses of the *SpandaKārikās*. For a person who has established himself in Consciousness (Shiva), even the waking state is as illusory as the dream state, because of the understanding that there is only one state of absolute Consciousness - Shiva.

In the deep sleep state no thought movement or experience occurs, though the individual being's metabolism continues. This state is absolutely essential for the rejuvenation of an individual's physical and mental faculties. This experience takes place in the causal body. The physical senses and mental activity are completely at rest. The physical body remains motionless. The seeds of objective experience that lie in potentiality in the deep sleep state, come back into full blossom as soon as the individual awakens. One's knowledge about oneself does not change in the deep sleep state.

The fourth state or Turiya in Sanskrit, can be experienced in meditation as a direct experience of the core of one's being, the pure substratum – Consciousness or the Self. This experience happens in the supracausal body. Even though the experience cannot be described in words, it can be apprehended as the content of the concept of a pure "I" devoid of attributes. Individual experience of the fourth state can also be corroborated by glimpses given in the words of saints' and yogic literature. The people who experience this state find that it exists within and transcends all the other three states. The bliss of experiencing this state surpasses any pleasure experienced by any senses. Human restlessness that plagues most people regardless of their worldly achievements comes to an end with the experience of this state. In this state people have had spontaneous experiences of deepest intuitive knowledge, both secular and scriptural.

If we focus only on the outer and inner diversity, we are sure to get confused. All our activities are consequences of our understanding. In order to get a correct understanding, we must look at the substratum. The first verse is about the substratum.

Consciousness as the Substratum

Logically, the substratum of all that lives as well as of the apparently insentient universe can only be one non-relational general conscious existence or Reality. Logical and scientific experimental analysis of creation points to one substratum to all creation. As discussed earlier, science has proven the existence of the Big Bang as the start of creation. It was not a physical event but a cosmic one, because neither time nor the five basic elements, which make up any physical event, existed. This is consistent with ancient Indian philosophy. Scientists have been trying and have succeeded to some extent at this time to develop a general unification theory of all physical energies or forces - such as atomic, magnetic, electrical, gravitational forces, which still needs to be verified.

According to the philosophy under discussion, what we call insentient and sentient are only relative in terms of exhibiting degrees of consciousness perceptible to the senses of an average human being. There can only be one creative force or energy, which is beyond all creation and pervading all creation. If there were two separate all-pervading or omnipresent substrata, one for the sentient and another for the insentient universe, this would require the existence of some omniscient and omnipotent creator equipped with all capabilities and awareness of the two substrata, directing the functioning of both the sentient and insentient; in which case, that awareness would become the substratum. No creation can take place without space, time and causation. The methodical intelligence with which the universe behaves naturally contradicts any assumption of the existence of a random non-conscious creative energy that is neither omniscient nor omnipotent. To claim the existence of such a non-conscious creative entity would still imply a conscious omnipresent observer prior to insentient creation! In Kashmir Shaivism, omniscience is described as *jñānashakti* - the power of knowledge, and omnipotence is described as *kriyāshakti* - power of action.

Even though it is eternally beyond name and form, we give the substratum the name 'Brahman' or Self, 'Shiva' or 'Shamkara' (or 'Shankara' using correct Sanskrit grammar).

Shankara and Five Functions

The word 'Shankara' means "That which bestows grace." Kashmir Shaivism recognizes Shankara as performing five acts or processes. They are 1. सृष्टि – *sṛṣṭi* creation, 2. स्थिति *sthiti* sustenance, 3. संहार *saṁhār* dissolution, 4. तिरोधान *Tirodhān* concealment, and 5. अनुग्रह *Anugraha* grace. The first four aspects are the same as postulates in the quantum field theory in modern physics. The grace aspect is not dealt with in science. According to quantum field theory, a particle arises out of the field of energy. It is sustained for a while. Then it dissolves. When it exists, it can be verified experimentally to exist as a particle. It can also remain in the waveform and conceal its exact location to an observer. It dissolves into the field. The objects in the universe, as well as the activities and experiences of the physical, mental and vital nature of an individual also follow these four processes. For example, our breathing consists of inhalation of air, a pause when the air is sustained inside for a while, and exhalation of the air. Then there is another pause, before the breathing process starts again. These four processes can be summarized as contraction and expansion.

The fifth aspect, called grace, is that process of consciousness by which the earlier four aspects are understood. Grace resides in the observer, distinct from the objective world that continually undergoes the first four processes. In the process of breathing, for instance, grace exhibits as: 1. understanding that breathing happens due to Prāṇa or the life-force; 2. the experience of stillness in the two pauses between the breaths; and 3. a subsequent blissful experience of the Self. Because of grace, Kundalini Shakti is awakened in an individual that leads to the understanding of the four other aspects of reality. In general, the grace aspect removes the confusion and subsequent affliction that arises out of regarding the first four processes of the world as four separate activities.

Salutation to Shankara

The phrase "We praise that Shankara" recognizes Shiva as the Reality of these five processes, that transcends the entire cosmos, yet is the warp and woof of the universe, creating everything including us. It not only creates living beings and substances, but also the non-living material world. Praise of Shankara means entrance into His being. The word "His" or "Her" does not refer to classification into male or female sexes. As per tradition, we call the principle of Reality "It," we refer to "Shiva" or "Shankara" as "He," and to Shakti, His energy, as "She." All the three terms are synonymous and used in the appropriate context. How can we bring about that entrance into Him? Since Shiva is all-pervasive, we are also made of and pervaded within and without by It. Shiva is the Self, our innate nature, or the core of our being. In other words, how can we experience our own nature or enter our supracausal body? The grace element brings this about.

A Guru who is established in the Self is regarded as embodying the grace-bestowing power of Shiva, and can give a seeker that experience without effort by a process called "Shaktipāt" or "transference of energy." By following the examples of the people, called saints, who have accomplished that entrance and established themselves in their true nature, we can also establish ourselves in Shiva, the Reality. Saint Jñaneśwar, a well-known great 12th century child saint from Mahārāshṭra, lived thousands of miles away from Kashmir, but knew the Shiva Sutras[17]. Jñāneśwar Mahārāj[18] says beautifully in his book *Amṛtānubhav – Nectar of Experiences:* (*Jnaneshwar*, 14)

अहो ऐक्याचे मुद्दल न ढळे । आणि साजिरेपणाचा लाभ मिळे ।
तरी स्वतरंगाचीं मुकुळें । तुरंबु कां पाणी ॥
म्हणोनि भूतेशु भवानी । वंदिलीं न करोनि सिनानीं ।
मी निघालों नमनीं । तें हें ऐसे ॥

[17] He mentions आणि ज्ञान बंधु ऐसें। शिवसूत्राचेनि मिसें। म्हणितले असे। सदाशिवें॥ (अमृतानुभव ३।१६) Āṇi jñāna bandhu aise, Śivasūtrāceni mise, mhaṇitale ase, Sadāśive. (Amṛtānubhav 3|16) In Shiva Sutras, Shiva states that knowledge is bondage for individuals. (Part 1, Aphorism 2)

[18] Great being - a common word in India to address a revered person.

दर्पणाचेनि त्यागें । प्रतिबिंब बिंबीं रिगे ।
कां बुडी दीजे तरंगें । वायूचा ठेला ॥
नातरी नीदजात खेवो । पावे आपुला ठावो ।
तैशी बुद्धित्यागें देवीदेवो । वंदिलीं मिया ॥
सांडुनि मीठपणाचा लोभु । मिठें सिंधुत्वाचा घेतला लाभु ।
तेवी अहं देऊनि मी शंभु । शांभवी जालों ॥
शिवशक्ति समावेशें । नमन केलें म्यां ऐसे ।
रंभागर्भ आकाशे । रिघाला जैसा ॥ (अमृतानुभव १।५९-६४)

Aho aikyāce muddala na ḍhaḷe, āṇi sājirepaṇācā lābha miḷe,
tarī svataraṅgāciṁ mukuḷeṅ, turaṁbu kā pāṇī.
Mhaṇoni Bhūteśu Bhavānī, vaṅdilīṅ na karoni sinānīṅ,
mī nighāloṅ namanī, teṅ heṅ aise.
Darpaṇāceni tyāgeṅ, pratibimba bimbī rige,
kāṅ buḍī dīje taraṅgeṅ, vāyūcā ṭhelā.
Nātarī nīdajāta khevo, pāve āpulā ṭhāvo.
taiśī buddhityāgeṅ devīdevo, vaṅdilīṅ miyā.
Sāṅḍūni mīṭhapaṇācā lobhu, miṭheṅ siṅdhutvācā ghetalā lābhu,
tevī ahaṁ deūni mī Śaṁbhu, śāṁbhavī jāloṅ.
Śivaśakti samāveśeṅ, namana keleṅ myāṅ aise,
raṁbhāgarbha ākāśe, righālā jaisā. (Amṛtānubhav 1|59-64)

Hey! without "losing the principal"
(without disturbing their oneness)
I have the opportunity of offering salutations
to Shiva and Shakti,
just as without disturbing oneness with water
the waves can be enjoyed.
I have offered my salutations,
without regarding Shiva and Shakti as separate,
in the following manner.
Just as when a mirror is taken away,
the reflection merges with the object,
or just as when the wind stands still,
the bubble merges with the water;
Or just as when sleep goes away with the dream,
the sleeping person wakes up,
I gave up my intellect and offered my salutations!

Just as salt gives up its desire for solidity and limitedness
to merge with the ocean,
I gave up my "I" to become one with the Self
and attained oneness with Shiva and Shakti.
Just as when the outer layers of a banana tree are peeled,
only space inside merges with the space outside,
Peeling of my identification with the four bodies,
I offered my salutations by merging with Shiva-Shakti.

Thus the saints and their writings teach us that by obliterating our identification with the outside we merge with Shiva. It is as simple as changing our attitude and the way we look at ourselves and at the world. The attitude of separateness is so ingrained in us that logical arguments, proofs, examples, our sense of time and space and our own practice following these examples are required to overcome our resistance and the logical objections that our intellect raises. They teach us those arguments and how to achieve that change in attitude.

Spanda as the creative energy

Shiva is never without His Shakti – the energy of pulsation, vibration or Spanda. Without this energy the universes cannot be generated. Shiva is the light of consciousness (Prakāsh) and Shakti is self-awareness - 'I AM' or Aham-Vimarsh. It is also called Chitishakti, Sāra, Samvit, or Urmi. Shiva and Shakti can never be without each other just as fire can never be without its power to burn. Just as an electric light or toaster are effects of the electricity at home and a proof of existence of the general principle of electricity in the universe, the fact that we are conscious and we have self-awareness is the proof that the substratum is consciousness (Prakash) and has self-awareness (Vimarsh).

The word Spanda arises from the Sanskrit root स्पद् - Spad, which means किञ्चित् चलनम्, *Kiṅcit calanam* 'a slight movement,' or the dynamic throb of "Aham-Vimarsh." Spanda is not itself the vibration, but it is the cause or energy of vibration. The Big Bang is a vibration. Astronomers talk about the dark energy that is everywhere, from which the new matter and antimatter emerges and into which it dissolves, while the universe keeps expanding. The people who have experienced Spanda say, "It is actually live breathing dark energy." In all activities we can experience this vibration. How does the Spanda work? The verse says, "Through "Unmesh-Nimesh" or simultaneous expansion and contraction, respectively. A detailed discussion of Unmesh-Nimesh follows. This process takes place simultaneously in the sense that expansion of one is contraction of another.

Several examples from everyday life can be given regarding experiences of Spanda. Spanda is not visible, but its effects as waves are seen everywhere in the whole universe. A wave is a vibration, whether it is a waveform of an atom, a sound wave, a light wave, a heat wave, an electric current, a magnetic wave or a wave in an ocean. According to science, whatever we perceive through our senses are vibrations. We hear a sound - a quality of space - through our ears, because of the vibrations of the eardrums. We perceive a touch, a quality of air - through our skin, because of the vibrations of the hair follicles. We see an object with our eyes, when the light wave - a quality of fire - from the object passing through the eyes' lenses sets up vibrations on the retina. Taste is a quality of water. We taste food with our tongue, because of the vibrations of the taste buds on the tongue. We smell fragrance - a quality of earth - with the nose, due to vibration of the hairs in the nose. All these five types of vibration of perception are carried to our brain as electrical impulses. The involuntary actions in our body take place as vibrations in the form of contractions and expansions. The heart pumps due to contraction and expansion. Blood flows by contraction and expansion of blood vessels. The organs of voluntary action perform due to the electrical impulses in our brain. We breathe due to the pumping of the heart, which is nothing but a vibration. The nervous system according to neurologists is comprised of electrical impulses. If we look at an MRI of a brain, we can see that it is all "wired" and functions with electrical impulses. For a radiologist, the body is an electro-magnet, again a form of vibration. The five sense organs of voluntary action also perform due to the electrical impulses from our brain. When we do any activity, it is due to Spanda.

Now let us look at our functioning as a human being. When a thought arises in our mind it bubbles out like a bubble in an ocean. It slowly arises from the substratum, takes shape and stays for a while and subsides. There is a gap; some time elapses before the second thought arises. Sometimes the gap is large, sometimes it is small; and sometimes when the mind is agitated the gap is miniscule. Emotions like fear and exhilaration produce shivers in the body or body hair stands on end. These are vibrations.

Thus, whether at the level of the universe or an individual, a vibration pervades physical and mental existence. The vibration in an individual is a sign that the individual is conscious or alive. The non-relational universal vibration may appear to us as happening automatically without consciousness taking any part. But again this understanding of relational or non-relational vibration occurs in us due to consciousness. It is necessary to reemphasize that our own existence as consciousness is a proof for the existence of universal consciousness, but the universal consciousness itself transcends all individual existences or any universe. Processes of expansion and contraction take place simultaneously. Expansion of light is contraction of darkness. Expansion of the waking state is contraction of the deep sleep or dream state. "When agitation of an individual mind subsides, his or her essential nature – the Self – appears as consciousness and bliss." [*Spanda Kārikā*, Verse 9] When agitation of the mind manifests, thoughts appear, the universe is experienced in terms of the senses, mind and ego; and the bliss of immortality or of the Self disappears. This fact will be discussed in the commentary on Verse 9. When the awareness of Shiva arises, awareness of the universe as a universe dissolves. When the universe is considered as an entity, awareness of Shiva drops away. This is also the reason physical scientists are not aware of Shiva as the substratum. When a movie is being projected on a screen, awareness of the screen goes away. An observer is not aware of his or her own consciousness within when the observer uses it to observe or perceive an object. In reality or from the point of view of Shiva nothing appears or disappears. Spanda is always arisen or emerged. It does neither emerge nor submerge, since there is nothing else except Itself. It is neither active nor inactive. Its dynamism, directed inward - Aham - "I AM" or outward – Idam – "That," is only of the nature of thought. The inward aspect transcends the creation of universes, being the form of knowledge as the light of Consciousness - Prakash. The outward aspect is the potency of creation of the universe – Vimarsh. But it is not actually separate creation; it is more like the potential for the variegated colors of peacock feathers that dwells in the fluids of a peacock egg. However, though the egg is destroyed when a chick is born, Vimarsh is not destroyed when the universe is born, since there is nothing else other than Itself.

There are two aspects of Spanda. One is general and the other is special. Vimarsh is the general aspect of Spanda. Because of Vimarsh, the potential manifestation of the outward universe of "That" rests in the inward "I AM," and the outward-oriented "That" idea of the universe arises in the inward "I AM"– self-awareness, while remaining indifferent. The outward "That" idea is also called Māyāśakti - – Power of illusion.

Vimarsh is total freedom, called "स्वातन्त्र्यशक्ति" "*Svātantryaśakti*" in Kashmir Shaivism. Without Vimarsh, Prakāsh can only be an inert light. Freedom is Its main power because there is nothing else besides It to oppose It. By Its freedom It dissolves a manifested object into Itself. It can keep an object in a submerged state. It can appear together with a manifested object - such as creating a living being and giving it self-consciousness. It can appear separate from a manifested object - such as creating different living beings. It can sport by hiding Itself, and manifesting at lightning speed, as succession or order where there is actually none, and as simultaneity. It creates every visible and invisible object, as well as empty sets or totally fictitious objects such as the child of a barren woman. While being eternal and all pervading, devoid of any limitations, It produces unlimited space, and other principles such as air, fire, water, and earth, as well as the limitations of location, time, name and form for created objects. It produces all seeming triads such as observer, observed, and observation and pervades them. It produces internal things such as mind, intellect, ego, feelings, and external things such as bodies and objects, and also transcends everything. It is important to keep in mind and to discern within ourselves this Vimarsh, which is beneath the emergence/submergence phenomena of the universe. We must reiterate that though from the point of an individual all this happens, from the point of view of the Self or Consciousness, nothing is actually happening apart from Itself, as there is nothing else except Itself.

As the general aspect of Spanda, Vimarsh appears in the Universal Self as चित् *Cit* – Consciousness, आनंद *Ānanda* – Bliss, and three powers – इच्छा *Icchā* - Will, ज्ञान *Jñāna* - Knowledge, and क्रिया *Kriyā* - Action. In the Universal Self, the innate Freedom is the mass of Bliss; the efflorescence of Bliss is Will power; Consciousness is Light; Vimarsh is the power of Knowledge; and the Power of Action is the ability to create individual forms, individual states and universes.

The special aspect of Spanda is the universe of myriad forms – sentient and insentient. It is clear that the entire universe is an expansion of the power of Freedom that belongs to the Self. It appears as individuals with प्राण *Prāṇa* - life-force, and अंतःकरण *Antaḥkaraṇa* – the inner psychic instrument consisting of mind, intellect, ego and the five subtle senses, as well as outer sense organs. While there are infinitely many forms, the power of Freedom always manifests mainly as three powers – Will, Knowledge and Action.

We conscious individuals, as special aspects of Spanda, have self-awareness, and through self-awareness we have the three powers – Will (Desire), Knowledge, and Action. Regarding our own selves, we feel we are free. We are free to turn or not to turn inward. We are free to perceive or not to perceive an object. We are free to make ourselves experience happiness or sorrow or transcend them. We are free to perform or not to perform a particular physical activity.

Suppose we desire a car. As a desire it is an object within, not separate from ourselves. Using the power of knowledge we discern how much money is required, the place where to get the car, and we know how to acquire the car. By the power of action we actually arrange for the money and contact the dealer and get the car. If a desire for a car happens to arise again we have the freedom of not acting on the desire. Many times when we desire something, we may not know how to acquire it. But the power of will is so strong that it knows how to bring the other required forces or factors together, and to attain the object. Time is a factor since we, the individuals, experience all events in time. Modern science has verified that there is a 'gene' in creatures that recognizes time.

In the universal Self a desire arises to create the myriad of forms. Through the power of Knowledge it is known how to create the individual forms each with its own characteristics. Through the power of Action the actual forms are created. In the universal Self, the Time element does not exist.

We have to understand that the power of will, knowledge and action in the Supreme Self and ourselves are all versions of "Idam" "That" or Māyāśakti - Power of illusion of Vimarsh – spanda shakti.

Unmesh-Nimesh

The words Unmesh-Nimesh in the first verse describe expansion and contraction, but also have deeper meanings.

Unmesh brings about the dissolution (Pralaya) and Nimesh brings about the arising (Udaya) of the universe. Jñāneṣwar (Jnaneshwar) Maharaj writes exactly the same thing as in Verse 1, in his work called *Cāngadev Pāsaṣtī* (65 verses on Reality written to Cāngadev) (*Jnaneshwari*, 15):

स्वस्ति श्री वटेशु । जो लपोनि जगदाभासु ।
दावी मग ग्रासु । प्रगटला करी ॥

Swasti Śrī Vaṭeśu, Jo laponi jagadābhāsu
Dāvī maga grāsu, pragaṭalā karī

Salutations to Shri Vatesha (Shiva)
Who, when hiding Himself,
makes the universe visible,
And when hiding the universe,
makes Himself appear.

Whatever exists is the inseparable pair of Unmesh-Nimesh, as used in the verse to connote Iccha Shakti (Will Power) of Vimarsh or Spanda. The word Iccha means Wish. The root verb is "इश्" - "*Ish*" meaning "to wish or will." Universal Consciousness, the substratum of everything that exists, is totally fulfilled. What kind of wish can Consciousness have? The Vedas declare that it is the wish: "एकोऽहं बहु स्याम्" – "*Eko 'haṁ Bahu Syām*" – "I am one. Let me be many." This wish or desire is the Idam - "That"- aspect of the original Spanda – the pulsation or stirring. The word Shakti originates from the root verb "शक्" "*Śak*" meaning "to be able." Universal Consciousness is capable of doing whatever It wishes since, as said earlier, there is nothing else to oppose It. This is total freedom or what is termed in Sanskrit as "स्वातन्त्र्य" – "*Swātantrya.*" The words Unmesh and Nimesh together describe this spiritual dynamism, total capability and total freedom. The word Unmesh describes the divine will of transcending (विश्वोत्तीर्णता - *Viśvottirṇatā*) the universe. The words "*Eko 'ham*" (I am one) signifies Unmesh. It is the doership aspect (अहम् - *Aham* or "I am") of the universe, in which the universe (इदम् - *Idam* - "That") is as yet submerged in oneness. The words "Bahu Syām" (Let me be many) signifies Nimesh. It is Consciousness' projection as the universe and varied forms of the universe. This projection must take place on the screen of Consciousness, and cannot take place anywhere else because there is nothing else. This projection is also called concealment (तिरोधान - *Tirodhān*) of the Self. This projection is due to Shiva's Māyāśakti, power of illusion.

The word Maya consists of two words: *Mā* and *yā*. *Mā* means 'No' and *Yā* means 'who.' Thus Maya means that which does not exist. *Mā* also means 'measurable' or limited and *Yā* means 'who.' Thus Maya is that which brings limitation. It is this Maya that manifests as the thirty-six principles from Shiva to earth. The thirty-six principles include the first five principles - Shiva, Shakti, Sadāshiva where will is predominant, Īśvara or Aiśvarya where knowledge is predominant, Śuddhavidyā where Kriya or activity is predominant. A detailed account of the thirty-six principles is given in a later verse.

Both Unmesh and Nimesh keep happening simultaneously. There is no time element or succession involved, since the concept of time applies to what is created, and exists only in the mind of the observer. Contemplation of Unmesh is grace, and that of Nimesh is bafflement, that results in going through the cycles of birth and death, pleasure and pain, and all such results of experiencing duality. It is the Divine Will that one individual is established in the Unmesh aspect and another individual is established in Nimesh aspect. It is also the Divine Will, which stirs in an individual to unravel the Nimesh and experience underlying Unmesh.

In an individual Unmesh is the self-awareness "I AM," while Nimesh is the conditional qualified "I am so and so." From Nimesh the individual's diverse world comes into being. It is comprised of sentient and insentient beings as external forms, and thoughts, memories, and emotions as internal forms. Whenever an individual creates something, a desire arises in the individual's mind followed by knowledge, which is followed by appropriate activity. We have discussed the powers of Will, Knowledge and Action earlier in explaining Vimarsh.

In an individual "Unmesh-Nimesh" describe a movement in awareness. Swami Ishwarananda Giri[19] (Swami Ishwaranand Giri, 41) describes this movement in a beautiful manner. He says, "The 'movement in awareness' manifests both action and cognition (knowledge)." Acharya Sureshwara, the most outstanding disciple of the Great Master Shankara, says: "When knowledge pulsates within as thought and will, the volitional force flows out of the body and is seen as action, initiating change." Therefore it is possible for man to cooperate with God, by lifting his own level of awareness during action, to be in tune with the Kāla or Kriyāśakti of the cosmic being. Every action springs from Will. Will is a mental force initiated in awareness. And that awareness is seemingly enclosed in your body, like a space in a room; whereas in truth, awareness (Chaitanya) is of such a nature that it cannot be divided. In pure self-awareness you can be one with the cosmic soul."

Shakti-chakra

The word Shakti-chakra or the conglomeration of powers consists mainly of the

[19] *Autumn Leaves*, P. 34

three shaktis or powers discussed earlier as will, knowledge and action. Shakti-chakra also includes the sounds or letters, which are manifestations of Vimarsh, the power of self-awareness (Spanda) that label or describe the objects of the universe. Words are formed of letters. In Sanskrit there is one letter for one sound. The Sanskrit alphabet consists of fifty letters divided in eight classes, starting with the letter अ (A) and ending with the letter क्ष (ksha). Each letter has a power instilled in it. These together are known as Mātṛkā - the unknown mother of the universe. The word *Mātṛ* means "mother" and *kā* means "who," thus signifying that all names of objects of the universe are generated by this mother–energy that most of us are unaware of. Each of the eight classes of letters in the Sanskrit alphabet is presided over by a deity or energy form. In addition, there are four energies called khechari, gochari, dikchari and bhuchari that preside over various internal and external functions, to wit: the sense of unlimitedness or limitedness, speech, the five senses of perception and action, and the five types of corresponding objects of the senses. Details about these energies appear in later verses. In short, every manifestation from Brahma to a blade of grass that becomes an object of perception is a conglomeration of infinitely many energies of the Self.

This Shakti-chakra is replete with vibhava – omnipotence, and has the capability of manifesting with total freedom - will. It can transcend the universe or become the warp and woof of this awesome universe. The origin or prabhava of the omnipotent Shakti-chakra is Shiva - Shankara. To that Shankara we offer our salutations. This is the meaning of the second line of the verse.

As said earlier, this salutation indicates entrance into Shiva. The means of this achievement is also given in the verse that follows.

There is an aphorism in *Shiva Sutras* –(*Singh*, 34) (*Swami Lakshman Joo*, 45)

शक्तिचक्रसंधाने विश्वसंहारः (शिवसूत्र १-४)

Śakticakra-sandhāne viśva-samhāraḥ (Shiva Sutras I-4)

By aligning oneself with or contemplating on the main energy – Vimarsh – underlying the conglomeration of energies, one's universe gets destroyed.

The destruction of the universe does not mean the objects of the universe actually get annihilated, but the sense of duality, of objects existing separately from the energy falls away. This contemplation of the main energy happens due to grace, the fifth process of Shankara. A guru is called the grace-bestowing power of Shiva – गुरुः पारमेश्वरी अनुग्राहिका शक्तिः - *Guruḥ pārameśwari anugrāhikā śaktiḥ*. A guru bestows grace on the seeker in one of the four ways – touch, look, thought, or word. A set of words is called a mantra. Grace awakens the kundalini shakti of the seeker and unravels the mystery behind the shakti-chakra. Grace removes the confusion and affliction that arises out of dealing with only the first four processes of the world as four separate activities. That is the reason we call that grace-bestowing power of the Universal Self Shamkara, wherein Sham means grace and kara means bestower.

In the light of our discussion, let us look at the first verse again.

यस्योन्मेषनिमेषाभ्यां जगतः प्रलयोदयौ ।
तं शक्तिचक्रविभवप्रभवं शंकरं स्तुमः ॥ १॥

1. *Yasyonmeṣa-nimeṣābhyāṁ, jagataḥ pralayodayau*
Taṁ śakti-cakra-vibhava-prabhavaṁ, Śaṁkaraṁ stumaḥ

The words Unmesh-Nimesh connote the freedom (or Iccha Shakti) of Spanda. The power of concealment inherent in Spanda is called Maya. Concealment hides the nature of reality. It shows duality or separateness where there is none. Because of Maya we experience the universe. It causes us to feel that there are two types of objects - insentient (jada) and sentient (chetan). Because of maya we make distinctions of high and low. Unmesh-Nimesh means the expansion and contraction of Spanda. When the awareness of Spanda expands, Shiva is experienced and the universe as universe made up of separate sentient and insentient objects dissolves, and when the awareness of Spanda contracts the universe as separate objects appears. The last part of the verse describes the means. Vibhava also means experience and Prabhava means manifestation of Shankara. By experiencing the conglomeration of Powers inherent in the universe through intensive and fixed awareness, the universe dissolves as a separate entity from Shiva, and we can find the manifestation of Shankara or that grace-bestowing power for ourselves.

BEFORE ENDING this discussion of the first verse we describe in the following an example of grace that took place in Chitra and Umesh's lives during the week preceding the series of talks on the *SpandaKarikas* given in their meditation center in New York.

It was the last week of December in the year 1980. Chitra and Umesh visited Miami Beach to spend time in the physical presence of their Guru. At the time the ashram was located in an old hotel right on the beach near the ocean. Chitra and Umesh spent all the time totally engrossed in doing guruseva (service to the guru), participating in the various chores around the ashram, and just being around Baba, their Guru. When it was time to return to New York, one morning Chitra and Umesh decided to visit a shopping mall located in downtown Miami.

Miami beach is a place well-known for its warm weather. Many retirees spend their 'sunshine' years in Miami or visit Miami to avoid the cold winters of their hometowns. After finishing shopping, Chitra and Umesh decided to have lunch in the restaurant of a department store. Sitting at a table next to them was an elderly couple, who had ordered plenty of very attractive-looking food. Just as they started to eat, the old man started coughing. The cough was very severe and would not stop. The old lady started stroking his back while repeating, "Take it easy, honey! Take it easy." But the old man's coughing continued. After finishing the lunch, Chitra and Umesh left to return to the Ashram. While riding the bus back to the ashram, Chitra and Umesh discussed with each other that people work so hard for many years and save money, so that they could retire and enjoy their retirement years in warm Florida. But when the time comes, many have no strength left in the body to enjoy life. That is life's irony. Why in vain do people struggle so much to achieve power and wealth? After all, every person's life ends with old age, sickness, and ultimately in death. Pondering over these ideas for quite some time made Chitra and Umesh sink into depression.

In this depressed mood they returned to the ashram, where they had their separate rooms and started packing their bags for the return trip. Soon the telephone rang in Umesh's room. It was Baba at the other end of the line. Umesh was thrilled to get this unexpected call. Baba said, "Oh, it's Umesh! Are you leaving today?" Umesh said, "Yes, Baba! We have to catch a plane to New York at 6 PM." Baba said, "Very Good! Meditate a lot. Run your meditation center with lot of love. Many people will come." In the few moments of the conversation Umesh felt so energized, encouraged and enthusiastic that the depression he felt a few minutes before had vanished. As he shared with Chitra the conversation Baba had with him, Chitra also felt elated.

After returning to New York, the whole week passed quickly. On Saturday the center had a satsang in a devotee's house in Jersey City, New Jersey. It was a bitter cold day in early January. During the satsang, Umesh spoke about the incident that happened in their visit to Miami Beach. He added, "Company of realized beings is essential. They have the power to wipe out depression from anyone's mind. Even though they might not have any particular personal interest or desire, they are enthusiastic about life; they do everything with great enthusiasm. They can make others enthusiastic as well."

The satsang was over and the host family was getting ready to distribute the prasad – blessed food. Chitra had an urge to leave everyone and be alone. She slipped away unnoticed from the group, went upstairs and sat in one of the bedrooms. In this room devotees' winter coats were piled up and little children were playing around. Chitra sat down on the floor resting her back against a wall. Her eyes closed. She started drifting into a different state. Gradually children's voices became inaudible. All objects began to disappear. When you are standing on a seashore, waves break on your feet and while returning to the ocean some sand below the feet slips away. Then it feels as if the whole earth is moving. This was the exact feeling. She felt she was going away from everybody. She did not have any inkling where she was.

She was aware only of a breathing presence. Like a giant dark balloon it was contracting and expanding. It was not at all an inanimate object. But in that pulsation there was not a single object. Some time passed in this state. She did not know how long. Slowly things were coming back. The next thing she realized was that once again she was becoming aware of some voices.

The first voice she heard was of Baba's. Baba was saying, "What you think about my being enthusiastic about life is actually this pulsation. Because of the Spanda (Divine Pulsation) you feel as if I am interested in different things, and I do them with enthusiasm. The reality is that there is nothing other than the Spanda. In doing anything, I am neither enthusiastic nor not enthusiastic." Chitra understood that when Baba laughs, jokes, does any activity, we feel how Baba is enthusiastic how interested he is. When we try to enjoy doing different things, we are the enjoyers. We are the doers. We are ready to label them good or bad. We feel Baba also behaves the same way. But here Baba was trying to tell Chitra, "Reality is never like that. There is only pulsation - Spanda. Everything is divine pulsation."

Baba was giving Chitra the experience of the teachings of the *SpandaKarikas* (Verses on Divine Pulsation). Chitra and Umesh had decided to study the *SpandaKarikas* regularly to prepare their talks in the weekly satsangs from the next time. And Baba was now giving her actual experience of the essence of the verses. After this experience she could not function as she did before. She did not feel like talking. She did not feel like walking. People were coming to her and asking something. But she could not respond. She was intoxicated. Finally Chitra and Umesh sat in the car to return home to New York City. Chitra shared her experience with Umesh. It was amazing that after doing sadhana for many years together the two had become 'one.' Both used to experience all the 'good feelings' together. Learning about Chitra's experience, Umesh also was exhilarated. In this floating state keeping the car in one lane was difficult. Umesh drove his car through the narrow lane of the Lincoln Tunnel with great difficulty. They did not know when they returned to New York City.

The next two days they were wondering, "If Baba was in this state all the time, how does he perform all his chores so efficiently? Here if we just have a glimpse of that state, we find it impossible to function. A strange intoxication takes over, and then we can't relate to the world. How can he do all the different things?" These questions obsessed them for two days. Here was meditation on one end, and there was work and only work on the other. "Meditation and work are not related to each other. Once we start meditating, then it is not possible to do any work. Once we start doing work, we cannot meditate. Why should this happen?" This question bothered Chitra all the time. Their two days' tasks were carried out automatically like a machine. Baba never lets go any questions unanswered. He has extraordinary ways of answering questions or of teaching. To answer Chitra's questions his method was to come into dreams. So Baba came into her dream after two days. In the dream she was sitting in a classroom with other familiar people in Baba's ashram. All people present had a notebook with them. They were busy studying. Chitra did not have anything in her hand or in her mind. Suddenly Baba entered the room and said, "Today I am going to test you. I want to examine how much you have absorbed of what I have taught you." She became quite nervous. She did not have a clue what Baba was going to ask.

As Chitra was a professor in a college, whenever a test was announced, it was her practice to assign the topics for the test. She said to her neighbor, "I have not studied anything. I don't know anything. What should I do?" But there was no time to do anything. Baba was staring at her. She had no idea what he was going to say. He said, "I am going to ask you the first question."

She was afraid to look at Baba. She stole a glance at him. Baba was looking at her with eyes full of compassion. In an instant her fear vanished. She was so calm that she felt she could do anything. Baba asked her, "Are the two, the mind and the Self, the same or different?"

Chitra thought for some time and said, "Baba, to function in the world it is necessary to distinguish between the two. But really speaking in the meditative state there is never a separate existence for the mind. Only the Self exists. Mind does not exist at all."

Chitra woke up as the dream was over. She had to go to the bathroom. She went to the bathroom. After she returned she went back to sleep. And a surprising thing was that her dream continued. Baba had a comment to make on her answer. Baba said, "As long as you have two answers for my one question, you have not understood anything that I have taught." She did not understand what Baba was saying. As she reflected on the dream the next day, it was clear that Baba was saying that because Chitra was differentiating between the meditative state and the mind while doing some chores.

Chitra had said that while doing some work it was necessary to differentiate between the mind and the Self. Whereas Baba was saying that even while working it is not necessary to differentiate between the two, because for him everything is meditation. There is nothing else. This was very clear to her. Because of that he could do all the work effortlessly. Baba had said that many times. But when it became her own experience, she had the correct understanding. After that she continued seeing duality as before. But her understanding was different. In spite of apparent duality she knew that in reality it was not so. Therefore she could do all her chores easily.

Even if she did not have fun while doing something, it did not matter; because fun is also imagination. Everything is imagination. It does not matter what work it is. It is going to change. Now there was no attachment regarding that work. Therefore every activity of her life became simple. She was at peace while doing work. Now there was absolutely no conflict while doing any work. Everything was simple. Only think of Baba. Even though she did not have her own strength, just by thinking about Baba, she could immediately experience his state. In a moment everything in her mind transformed. All problems are in the mind, and if the mind itself changes when and where can problems remain? In this manner, all her problems vanished.

Umesh's experience was similar. Once Baba in the past had said, "I have made both of you one." This experience was constant.

This experience of Guru's grace can be summed up by one verse of The *SpandaKarikas*:

प्रबुद्धः सर्वदा तिष्ठेज्ज्ञानेनालोक्य गोचरम् ।
एकत्रारोपयेत्सर्वं ततोऽन्येन न पीड्यते ।। (स्पंदकारिका - ४४)

Prabuddhaḥ sarvadā tiṣṭhej-jñānenālokya gocaram,
Ekatrā ropayet-sarvaṁ tato 'nyena na pīḍyate.
(Spaṅdakārikā - 44)

"*Observing all objective phenomena by the knowledge of external perception, one should deposit everything in one place, and see everything as identical with Spanda, which is our own essential Self. Thus, he is never troubled by another.*"

As the commentator of the *Karikas* says, in the waking, dream and deep sleep states and in the beginning, middle and end stages of these three states, the awakened ones regard their essential Self as the Spanda principle. They view all objective phenomena only as a manifestation of the Light of Consciousness and thus identical with It. Since there is nothing different from the Self, they have no trouble on any account.

The discussion of Verse 1 can be summarized by the following song.

ऐसा ज्ञान हमारा साधो । ऐसा ज्ञान हमारा रे ।। टेक ।।
जड़ चेतन दो वस्तु जगत में, चेतनमूल आधारा रे ।
चेतन से सब जग उपजत है, नहिं चेतन से न्यारा रे ।।
ईश्वर अंश जीव अविनाशी, नहिं कुच्छ भेद विकारा रे ।

सिंधु बिंदु सूरज दीपक में, एकहि वस्तु निहारा रे ।।
पशु पक्षी नर सब जीवन में, पूरण ब्रह्म अपारा रे ।
ऊँच नीच जग भेद मिटायो, सब समान निर्धारा रे ।।
त्यागग्रहण कुछ कर्तव्य नाहीं, संशय सकल निवारा रे ।
ब्रह्मानंद रूप सब भासे, यह संसारपसारा रे ।।

Ref. Aisā jñana hamārā sādho, aisā jñana hamārā re
Jaḍa cetana do vastu jagata meṅ, cetana mūla ādhārā re,
Cetana se saba jaga upajata hai, nahi cetana se nyārā re.
Īśvara aṅśa jīva avināśī, nahi kucha bheda vikārā re,
Siṅdhu biṅdu sūraja dīpaka me, Ekahi vastu nihārā re.
Paśu pakṣī nara saba jīvana me, pūraṇa Brahma apārā re,
Uṅca nīca jaga bheda miṭāyo, saba samāna nirdhārā re.
Tyāga-grahaṇa kucha kartavya nāhīṅ, saṅśaya sakala nivārā re,
Brahmānaṅda rūpa saba bhāse, yaha saṅsāra pasārā re.

(Refrain) This is what we know. Oh noble being!
This is what we know.
Insentient and sentient, these two objects in the world
are rooted in the substratum of consciousness.
From consciousness the whole world arises
from consciousness it is never separated.
The oneness of the Lord and Its part in every soul
imperishable, non-different, and unmodified;
The oneness of the ocean and its drop,
oneness of the sun and a flame, I identified.
In animals, birds, humankind and all that is animated
is the perfect Brahman perfused.
The world's differences of high and low have now evaporated,
and certainty that everything is the same is where I stand.
To renounce or accept I am not compelled
All doubt is now expelled.
"This expanse of the world" says Brahmānanda,
"is a form of the total bliss of Consciousness." - Brahmānanda.

VERSE 2
SUBSTRATUM AND ITS UNCONCEALABILITY

यत्र स्थितमिदं सर्वं कार्यं यस्माच्च निर्गतम् ।
तस्यानावृतरूपत्वान्न निरोधोऽस्ति कुत्रचित् ॥२॥

2. Yatra sthitam-idaṁ sarvaṁ kāryaṁ yasmācca nirgatam
Tasyānāvṛta-rūpatvān-na nirodho 'sti kutracit.

भट्टकल्लटः – कथं पुनः स्वस्वभावस्यैव संसारिणः शिवत्वेन निर्देशः – इति यद्युच्यते, तत् यत्र स्थितम् इदं जगत्, यस्मात् च उत्पन्नं तस्य संसार्यवस्था यामपि अनाच्छादित-स्वभावात् न क्वचित् निरोधः, अतः शिवत्वमुच्यते ॥ २ ॥

BhaṭṭaKallaṭa: 2. Kathaṁ punaḥ sva-svabhāvasyaiva saṁsāriṇaḥ Śivatvena nirdeśaḥ - iti yadyucyate, tat yatra sthitam idaṁ jagat, yasmāt ca utpannaṁ tasya saṁsāryavasthā yāmapi anācchādita-svabhāvāt na kvacit nirodhaḥ, ataḥ Śivatvam-ucyate.

Where this entire creation rests, and from where it has manifested, cannot be concealed by anything. Because of this nature It has absolutely no obstruction anywhere.

BhattaKallata: - The question arises, when by His own nature Shiva becomes bound in the cycle of worldliness, how can He still be called Shiva in that state? The answer is that this universe itself rests as one I-consciousness and is created from "That"-ness arising out of "I," yet there is nothing in the state of worldliness to hide its nature of existence as I-consciousness; hence there is no obstacle to Shiva's freedom.

SAGE VASUGUPTA shows that there is no difficulty to experience consciousness since It is everywhere and nothing can conceal It. It is out in the open for grasping. It is the substratum of everything and all creation starts from It. Just as a lump of sugar is sweet everywhere and it is not necessary to dissect it to taste the sweetness, everything in this universe is consciousness and to attain consciousness one need not make any effort of analyzing anything. A reporter came to Baba Muktanand, our Guru, and said, "You say that God is everywhere, can you show me that if there is God in that tree over there?" Baba said, "God has appeared as that tree." Baba always emphasized to see God in each other since God has appeared as each one of us!

Many people do not give credence to consciousness. In a philosophy class a student said to the professor, "Dr., I don't believe that consciousness exists everywhere." She said to the student, "Are you conscious?" The student said, "Yes I am!" The professor said, "This shows that there is consciousness. Once we know that there is consciousness, we have to be aware that we can experience it everywhere, which takes study and an effort on our part since we are trained to look at our sense perceptions as the only reality. Do you believe in the existence of gravity?" "Yes," the student said. The professor said, "Just as the existence of gravity can be judged by letting go an object in the hand and see it fall, existence of consciousness can be judged by Its effects as you and me and everything else in the universe. Consciousness gives rise to existence of everything else." There was another smart student in the class who said, "Professor! I may exist but I may not be conscious as in sleep. Gravity may exist, but it is not conscious." The professor said, "The word "I" that you uttered shows that you are conscious and awake. In sleep there is consciousness existing as life force. But in sleep you wouldn't experience the existence of the body and the world that you see in your waking state. The proof that consciousness exists in your body while you are asleep comes from the fact that after a sound sleep when you are awake, you say that you had a sound sleep. Who is it that keeps awake in you observing that you are sleeping soundly? No one outside is necessary to declare that you slept soundly. If consciousness did not exist in a body, the body would be dead, meaning it would cease to exist as a certain body, and perish. Thus your existence implies consciousness. What we call inanimate or not conscious is just the degree of movement of consciousness that is not perceived. At the atomic level there is nothing static, whatever propels the electron to move around the nucleus or whatever makes the subatomic particle appear or disappear and appear as a wave, is conscious energy. Gravity, electricity, magnetism, light, sound, mechanical and nuclear forces all originate from the universal energy of consciousness for proper functioning of the universe. Physical scientists may not call that universal energy conscious, because they would not know what to do with the consciousness aspect! Physical reality and scientific experiments are limited to the sense perceptions."

The words in the Verse 2, "यत्र स्थितमिदं सर्वम् " "Yatra sthitamidaṁ sarvam" mean "Where (in Him, Shiva or Consciousness) everything rests." The words existence and consciousness are synonymous. Existence of anything is consciousness, and consciousness means existence of anything. It is true from the above paragraph that existence of an object implies consciousness. One might argue that that does not mean consciousness implies existence of everything. The condition may be sufficient but not necessary. The quoted words of Verse 2 say that consciousness implies existence. In order to see whether something exists there has to be an observer. Somebody should actually perceive it. This means that whatever exists is known when the light of Consciousness shines upon it. Until that time it does not exist.

In quantum mechanics there is a 'thought experiment:' If a tree falls in a forest, will it make a noise? Its answer is: whether it makes a noise when falling depends upon whether there is somebody to hear it! When no one is there, there is no certainty of the actual event even happening! For any event to take place there has to be an observer to validate the event along with the observed and observation. If a fallen tree is seen later, the assertion that it must have made some noise is just a matter of inference, depending on the memory of some conscious individual regarding similar events. Without the memory or presence of an actual observer, there is no question of an entity's existence. Thus no existence implies no consciousness. Or as a contrapositive statement studied in Logic, consciousness implies existence. When we learn a new subject the light of our consciousness has to fall upon it. Once it is internalized or becomes a part of our memory, then we can say that we know the subject. When we perceive that something exists, it is the light of our consciousness that makes it so. When we are awake in the morning, awareness of our existence "I AM" comes first before our world dawns. In other words the world is the nature of "I AM" or "Aham Vimarsh." This vimarsh is the universal energy of consciousness. We will return later to this vimarsh aspect.

The next question then arises is: If the nature of Shiva is all consciousness and bliss, how is this material world formed? There must be a material cause for a material universe!" The answer to that question is as follows. There are two causes for anything to happen. One is the instrumental cause and the other is a material cause. For example, a potter is the instrumental cause and mud is the material cause of a pot to happen. The material cause transforms into the object. The object consists of the material cause. Whereas the instrumental cause does not transform, or become part of the object, just as a potter does not become the pot. Nothing happens to the potter. This material world cannot come forth from an insentient material cause. An insentient entity can never be an instrumental cause of creation. A lump of mud will remain a lump until a potter comes and mixes it with water and shapes it into a jar. There must be an instrumental cause to this universe, like a potter for the mud. The words of Verse 2 - कार्यं यस्माच्च निर्गतम् । *kāryaṁ yasmācca nirgatam* are "from where it has manifested." That is to say, all this has manifested from Consciousness. In other words, consciousness is the instrumental cause for all this manifestation.

There was a physicist who did not believe in consciousness as the cause of the material universe. His son started going to a Guru visiting from India and started repeating the mantra "Om Namah Shivaya." One day the scientist saw his son sitting quietly with his eyes closed muttering some words to himself, and felt kind of threatened, as if something had happened to his son. He said, "What were you muttering?" The son replied, "I am repeating the mantra honoring the Supreme Consciousness which is the cause of the universe, which is also within me."

The father said, "You must be out of your mind! You know that the universe came into being by the Big Bang or an explosion of energy. Fundamental particles were created - ν-(nu)mesons, π-(pi)mesons, etc. came into being, matter and antimatter came into being. I can describe to you in detail how the universe started. There is no such thing as supreme consciousness creating the universe. These gurus who have never learned modern theories come from India and preach something and brainwash the kids here. How can you be so gullible? We have brought you up as a rational person. You must question everything.

Don't accept what other people say, especially these so-called holy men. These people are always after money and sex while wearing an orange garb. They fool the gullible people. My son, don't ever be fooled by these people!"

The son who was an artist kept quiet for a few days. He secretly painted a beautiful picture. He kept the picture in his father's study. The father noticed the painting and asked the son who the artist was. The son replied, "Oh, it just happened by itself. Just like the pi-mesons, nu-mesons, atoms and molecules come together to form the universe, several paints from Pearl Paints and Artists Supplies Store came together and formed the picture. Just as you scientists have your beliefs or hypotheses about the universe, so also it is my hypothesis that the paints came together of their own and the picture happened. As for your remarks about the Gurus, many may be after money or sex, one who is going to them must watch, observe and question their behavior. You don't have to believe in them. The scientific hypotheses can be verified by experiments in the lab. Similarly, just like doing an experiment, the effects of going to a Guru, spending time in his/her presence, repeating a mantra and following his/her teaching for a while, can also be verified in the lab of life. If a so-called Guru has no effect on you, then it is not worth wasting your precious time. If the Guru transforms your life, after you have been in the Guru's presence and have practiced the Guru's teaching, so that you can experience consciousness within and experience its bliss, and you become peaceful, then naturally you trust the Guru. See whether your restlessness goes away. I have seen great achievers - scientists - who remain so restless to be creative, or get frustrated when they do not get anywhere, in spite of their past great accomplishments. Scientific research does not offer one peace, even if one does it in a solitary place or in a dedicated group. Research on consciousness through chanting or meditation done in a solitary place or in a dedicated group leads one to experience peace. Discoveries, whatever they are, are creations of the mind, and a mind at peace can become more creative than a restless mind. Moreover by meditating, one can find the answers to fundamental questions: Who am I? Why am I here? What is the meaning of this life? How can I bring out the best out of me? Who or what is the maker of this universe? In this manner Gurus go to the bottom of existence or truth." The point of the story is that consciousness is the instrumental cause of the universe and an individual's study of consciousness itself leads to peace of mind and creativity in the individual's life.

The next question that arises is, "Granted consciousness creates the universe. Is the material universe created by consciousness using any insentient material?" The answer is "If there was some material used to create the universe that material itself would require another material and this chain of prerequisites would continue ad infinitum. From modern scientists' point of view everything would go back to energy. Scientists are amazed to see the celestial bodies arising out of seemingly nothing in the space. Thus they believe there is energy everywhere out of which creation takes place." Just because the scientists do not know how to address the conscious aspect of energy, it does not mean that the energy from which material universe originates is insentient or is not conscious!

Another interesting example is a visit to Yellowstone National Park, Wyoming, USA. The park rangers keep emphasizing not to stray away from the stairs or path they have built, because the earth in the Park is such that it might break out as a geyser, or a boiling mud pot or some other geothermal activity.

Shaivism regards the conscious energy that exists everywhere as Shiva, and says that the universe exists in Shiva, in consciousness itself, in potential form, just as a banyan tree is contained in the seed, or just as mechanical energy is contained in potential form in the hand of a person because of the person's consciousness. Therefore it is valid to say the Lord Shiva materializes His essence in the form of the world. Still Shiva remains transcendent to the world, just as a potter does not get destroyed after creating pots. Lord Shiva can create countless universes by His will, just as a potter never runs of ideas after creating one pot. Therefore consciousness is not only the instrumental cause but also the material cause of the universe. This is the meaning of the words, "कार्यं यस्माच्च निर्गतम्" "*kāryaṁ yasmācca nirgatam*" "From where the creation is manifested." The Sanskrit word for transcending the world is विश्वोत्तीर्ण (*Viśvottīrṇa*) and that for becoming the warp and woof of the world is विश्वमय (*Viśvamaya*). Thus Lord Shiva is both Vishvottirna – transcendent and Vishvamaya - imminent.

Now a created thing cannot conceal or cover up the creator, just as a clay pot cannot conceal the nature of the potter who made the pot. Should a pot dissolve into mud or get destroyed, that has no reflection on the potter's existence. Therefore the nature of consciousness is to remain transcendent and eternal while also becoming the warp and woof of the universe. It cannot be hidden nor opposed by anything: any thought, word or form. The second part of Verse 2 says precisely this: "तस्यानावृतरूपत्वान्न निरोधोऽस्ति कुत्रचित्", "*Tasyānāvṛta-rūpatvān-na nirodho 'sti kutracit*" "That cannot be concealed by anything. Because of this nature It has absolutely no obstruction anywhere" indicates precisely this fact.

There is a deeper meaning to the universe. It is actually a different universe for each person. The set of objects existing in one's universe may not exist in another's universe. It has a three-fold nature, consisting of the subject (or a seer), object (or seen) and the process of perceiving (or seeing) the object. Vimarsh –

awareness - expresses Itself as I Am in the subject, and the object must exist internally within that mind or awareness to give reality to the object. The process of perceiving it is due to awareness. Thus the subject, object, and process of perception all consist of awareness. In Kashmir Shaivism, the Subject is "Aham" - "I," the object is "Idam" - this. Perception depends upon the faculty of the five senses or mind. Even if we see an object such as a book outside ourselves, it cannot exist for us until our own eyes, ears, hands, and sense of perception or awareness grasps the object. That is the reason a teacher has to remind her students to pay attention or bring awareness to the topic that is being taught in her class, since the mind has a tendency to occupy itself in useless wandering. The set of triads of subject, object and perception is what is called the universe. When the universe comes into being in awareness, it is maintained in awareness and it dissolves in awareness.

When an individual creates an object, first it is created or exists as a mental image or thought in the individual's mind. That is the seed form of the object. The individual's universe expands from those seeds. The object and its mental seed form are both "Idam" (that). All these seeds arise from the fundamental seed-thought "I AM," or initial functioning of the mind. The object may be inert, such as a pot, or alive, like a baby, a plant, or an organism in a lab. Along with the object come its accompanying name and qualities. Once the object is seen or the name is heard, an individual's awareness identifies it and distinguishes it from other objects in terms of its qualities. For example, the quality of a chalk is different from a pencil. A piece of chalk is brittle, while a pencil is not. We see chalk as chalk because the equation is not just chalk, but chalk equals the qualities of chalk plus the awareness of those qualities.

chalk = qualities of chalk + awareness (observer)
Similarly, pencil = qualities of pencil + awareness (observer)

So everything we perceive is actually the sum of the qualities of that thing plus our own awareness as observers. Another interesting example is when a couple is watching a movie, if the husband sleeps, only the wife would be able to say what the movie was about! The sleeping husband has no awareness to make sense of the movie. This is further elucidated in the book *In the Woods of God Realization - Collected Works of Swami Rama Tirth*. (*Swami Ram Tirth*, 57) Following Swami Rama Tirth's statements, if we close our eyes one fifth of the world is gone. If we close our ears one fifth more of the world is gone and so on.

Thus our five senses of perception make our world. Above all, if our awareness is not there to perceive, the whole world ceases to exit for us. Thus our world consists of sets of triads - observer, object and observation, and all the components of each triad are consciousness.

Even though everything is consciousness, we give different names to different forms or objects in order to identify them. The object is a manifestation of Vimarsh - ('I Am'ness). The manifold universe as it exists in thought form in Vimarsh is only oneness, like a city reflected in a mirror. It is unity in diversity. The manifested universe is diversity in unity.

In this manner there is no obstruction to consciousness in thought, word, or form, nor space, time and causation. Wherefrom did the world begin, when did the world begin, what is the cause of the world, are questions related to space, time and causation about the physical existence of the world. But one cannot answer them since, for example, should there be a place someone could go to see the world begin, that place would be included in the world. Time began after the Big Bang. But when the Big Bang happened cannot be answered. As per science there is no absolute time. Causation, as already discussed, in terms of material and instrumental cause is only consciousness. The world exists because we are there to observe it. It is the iccha-shakti, will power of the Vimarsh of Supreme consciousness that is behind the creation of the universe. It is the jñana-shakti or power of knowledge of Vimarsh that discerns the object and whatever is required to create the object. It is the kriya-shakti, power of action of the Vimarsh that manifests the object. Vimarsh's total freedom sometimes brings out the object in space, time, and causation and sometimes without requiring any space, time, or causation. For example, the Big Bang is a cosmic event. It is not a physical event. Consciousness through its Vimarsh aspect manifests as creation in 36 principles from Shiva to the earth. We will discuss the 36 principles at a proper place later. One of the 36 principles is Maya - or the power of concealment, and another is qualities, about which we discussed earlier. More details will be given in later verses. The existence of this universe-manifesting Vimarsh cannot be denied nor can it be hidden by any opposing power because there is nothing other. But because we are trained to look outside of ourselves rather than within, first-hand awareness or experience that consciousness exists everywhere requires consistent study and practice, and most importantly grace. It is within ourselves that we must first get the first-hand experience of the universal consciousness.

Even though the whole text of *SpandaKārikās* is a "how to" book, it is worthwhile to refer to some exercises from *Vijñana Bhairava*, another text from Kashmir Shaivisim, (*Singh*, 35) that we can start with. The closest experience to us is our breathing. The *Vijñana Bhairava* has several awareness of breathing exercises.

Dhāraṇā:

ऊर्ध्वे प्राणो ह्यधो जीवो विसर्गात्मा परोच्चरेत् ।
उत्पत्तिद्वितयस्थाने, भरणाद्भरिता स्थितिः ॥ (श्लोक २४, धारणा १)

Ūrdhve prāṇo hyadho jīvo visargātmā paroccaret
Utpatti-dvitayasthāne, bharaṇād-bharitā sthitiḥ.
(Verse 24, Dhāraṇā 1)

Watch the breath. From the time we are born till we die, we breathe. We normally breathe fifteen times a minute, 900 times an hour, 21,600 times during 24 hours. Our breath is the only constant thing in our life that we can observe physically. Breathing is closely connected to the mind. When we are excited, we breathe rapidly. When we are calm, we breathe slowly.

Fix your attention on breathing. Watch the breath coming in, filling the lungs. Watch the pause before it rises to go out. Watch the breath going out. After all the air has gone out through the nostrils, there is a momentary pause, watch that pause. Watch the breath coming in again.

Parā Devi or Highest Shakti is of the nature of visarga (:) two dots arranged vertically. The root (सृग्) सर्ज sṛg means to create. Visarga means letting go, projection, or creation. The creative principle involves two movements - outward and inward. These are exhalation (*prāṇa*) and inhalation (*apāna*) in living beings. The exhalation begins at the heart, which is a द्वादशान्त (*dvādaśānta*) or a distance of twelve fingers from the tip of the nose. The inhalation begins at a point outside the body, which is also a *dvādaśānta*. The upper dot in the visarga (:) represents the heart and the lower dot represents the outer dvādaśānta. At these points the Highest Shakti is in suspended animation. By the rhythm of inhalation and exhalation, Parā Devi carries on her play of life in microcosm or macrocosm. This movement is the ceaseless throb or स्पंदन (*spandana*). By steady fixation of the mind at the two places of dvādaśānta, one realizes the fullness of the Highest Shakti.

Another interpretation is that the breathing process is a continuous japa of Hamsah. Inhalation takes place with the sound Ha, and exhalation happens with the sound Sah. At the junction point in the center the nasal sound 'ṃ' is added. Sah represents Shiva (Consciousness), Ha represents Shakti (Vimarsh) and ṃ represents the individual (jiva). Many gurus give the Hamsah mantra to their disciples to repeat.

Now again, as in the previous exercise, focus on breathing. But this time try to lengthen the pauses between the exhalation and inhalation.

Dhāraṇā:

कुम्भिता रेचिता वापि पूरिता या यदा भवेत् ।
तदन्ते शान्तनामासौ शक्त्या शान्तः प्रकाशते ॥ (श्लोक २७, धारणा ४)

Kumbhitā recitā vāpi pūritā yā yadā bhavet.
Tadante śāntanā-māsau śaktyā śāntaḥ prakāśate
(Verse 27, Dhāraṇā 4)

The shakti is retained outside in the outer dvādaśānta in the form of exhalation and is retained inside in the form of inhalation. Then at the end of this practice, the duality between prāṇa and apāna ceases, the Shakti is tranquilized and Bhairava - the Self that transcends duality of name and form - shines forth.

These exercises can be performed at anytime when one is by oneself.

A yogi who is established in this awareness experiences the universe as his/her own body. The *Shiva Sutras*, Aphorisms on Shiva,[20] say, "दृश्यं शरीरम् (शिवसूत्र १।१४)" "*Dṛśyaṁ śarīram*" (Śivasutra 1|14) "Objects are seen as one's own body." *Kṣemarāja*, the commentator on the *Śivasutra* says, "Whatever is perceptible whether inwardly or outwardly, all that appears to the Yogi identical with himself and not something different from him. This is so because of his great accomplishment of identity with universal consciousness. His feeling is 'I am this,' just as the feeling of Sadāshiva (Consciousness as creator) regarding the entire universe is 'I am this.'" Kṣemarāja also interprets this sutra as "*Śarīram dṛśyam*" "The body is seen as an object." Unlike ordinary individuals who identify

[20] Jaidev Singh *Śiva Sūtra* P. 57

themselves with a male or female body, the yogi sees the body as a perceptible objective phenomenon like the color blue, whether that body is in the waking state, dwelling in the intellect or mind in the dream state, or as a void in the sleep state. More will be said about these states in the next verse of the *Spandakarika*.

The experience of this verse can be seen in many saints' writings and behavior or in the way they lived. *Jñāneśwar* Maharaj says in his letter - offering to Yogi *Cāngadev (Cāṅgadev pāsaṣṭī) Sixty-five Verses to Changadev* as follows: (*Jñāneṣwar Mahārāj*, 16)

बहु जंव जंव होये । तंव तंव कांहींच न होये ।
कांहीं नहोनि आहे । अवघाचि जो ॥
सोने सोनेपणा उणे । न येतांचि झाले लेणे ।
तेंवी न वेचितां जग होणे । अंगे जया ॥
कल्लोळकंचुक । न फेडितां उघडे उदक ।
तेंवी जगेसी सम्यक् । स्वरूप जो ॥
परमाणूंचिया मांदिया । पृथ्वीपणें न वचेचि वायां ।
तेंवी विश्वस्फूर्ति इयां । झांकवेना जो ॥
कळांचेनि पांघुरणे । चंद्रमा हरपों नेणे ।
कां वन्ही दीपपणे । आन नोहे ॥
म्हणोनि अविद्यानिमित्ते । दृश्य द्रष्टुत्व वर्ते ।
तें मी नेणें आइते । ऐसेंचि असे ॥
जेंवी नाममात्र लुगडे । येऱ्हवी सुतचि तें उघडें ।
कां माती मृद्भांडे । जयापरी ॥
तेंवी द्रष्टा दृश्य दशे । अतीत दृङ्मात्र जे असे ।
तेंचि द्रष्टादृश्यमिसे । केवळ होय ॥
अलंकार येणे नामे । असिजे निखिल हेमें ।
नाना अवयवसंभ्रमे । अवयविया जेंवी ॥
तेचि शिवोनि पृथ्वीवरी । भासती पदार्थांचिया परी ।
प्रकाशे तें एकसरी । संवित्ति हें ॥
(चांगदेव पासष्टी ३–१२)

Bahu jaṅva jaṅva hoye, taṅva taṅva kāṅhīṅca na hoye
kāṅhī nahoni āhe, avaghāci Jo.
Sone sonepaṇā uṇe, na yetāṅci jhāle leṇe
teṅvī na vecitāṅ jaga hoṇe, aṅge jayā.
Kalloḷa-kaṅcuka, na pheditā ughaḍe udaka
teṅvī jagesī samyak, svarupa jo.

Paramāṇuṅciyā māṅdiyā, pṛthvīpaṇeṅ na vaceci vāyāṅ
teṅvī viśva-sphurti iyā, jhākavenā jo.
Kaḷāceni pānghuraṇe, candramā harapoṅ neṇe
kā vanhī dīpapaṇe, āna nohe.
mhaṇoni avidyānimitte, dṛśya draṣṭrutva varte
teṅ mī neṇeṅ āite, aiseṅci ase.
Jeṅvī nāma-mātra lugaḍe, yerhavī sutaci teṅ ughaḍe
kāṅ mātī mṛdbhāṅḍe, jayāparī.
Teṅvī draṣṭā dṛśya daśe, atīta dṛṅmātra je ase
teṅci draṣṭā-dṛśyamise, kevaḷa hoya.
Alaṅkāra yeṇe nāme, asije nikhila hemeṅ
nānā avayava-saṅbhrame, avayaviyā jeṅvī.
Teci Śivoni pṛthvīvarī, bhāsatī padārthānciyā parī
prakāśe teṅ ekasarī, saṅvitti heṅ.
(Cāṅgadeva pāsaṣṭī 3-12)

Who, without becoming anything, Is everything,
And whose expansion results in nothing.
Who is not diminished,
When the many faceted world arises out of Him,
Just as gold remains gold, When it's made into an ornament,
Water is clearly water,
Even when it's covered with waves.
In the same way, it is He who is the world.
Just as the earth is not hidden by a pile of dirt,
He is not concealed, by the vibration of the universe,
As the moon has phases. yet remains the moon,
Or fire remains fire, though it takes the form of flames.
Solely because of ignorance, the Seer and the Seen exist.
Though not for me. that's how it is!
As what is called fabric, is made up of thread,
Or a clay pot is only clay,
In the same way, when there is a Seer and a Seen,
It is the Pure Awareness, beyond the two of them
That is experienced as both.
As what is called an ornament, is really gold,
Or a single body has several limbs,

So all things from Lord Shiva to earth
Are manifestations of Consciousness.

Oṁ Namaḥ Śivāya

VERSE 3

ONENESS OF NATURE OF SELF IN DIFFERENT STATES

जाग्रदादि-विभेदेऽपि तदभिन्ने प्रसर्पति ।
निवर्तते निजान्नैव स्वभावादुपलब्धृतः ॥३॥

3. Jāgradādi vibhede 'pi tadabhinne prasarpati
Nivartate nijānnaiva svabhāvād-upalabdhṛtaḥ

भट्ट कल्लटः – जाग्रदादिनापि भेदे प्रथमाने न तस्य स्वरूपम् आव्रियते, यस्माद् उपलब्धृत्वं त्रिष्वपि पदेषु साधारणम्, न तस्य स्वरूपान्यथाभावः, यथा विषस्याङ्कुरादिषु च पञ्चसु स्कन्धेषु ॥३॥

Bhaṭṭa Kallaṭa: - 3. Jāgradādināpi bhede prathamāne na tasya svarūpam āvriyate, yasmād upalabdhṛtvaṁ triṣvapi padeṣu sādhāraṇam, na tasya svarūpānyathābhāvaḥ, yathā viṣasyāṅkurādiṣu ca pañcasu skandheṣu.

The Spanda principle pervades waking, dream and deep sleep, even though they are different states, but never undergoes any change in such states. It remains as the sole knower of these states.

BhattaKallata: Even though an individual experiences mutual differences in waking and other states, the individual's nature itself cannot be hidden since the experiencer is common to all the three states, just as a plant of a poisonous seed has the same poison in all its five parts: root, branches, leaves, flowers and fruit.

IN THIS VERSE Vasugupta refers to the states experienced by every individual and shows that the true knower of these states is the Spanda principle. In the first verse he showed how the universe is created, maintained and destroyed by the opening and closing of Shiva's eyes or by the expansion and contraction of the Spanda principle. In the second verse he discussed that the substratum in which everything exists and from where everything manifests is Consciousness or Shiva and hence there is nothing - no word, thought or form, place, time or causation - that can hide Shiva. In this verse he shows that even if an individual experiences different states such as waking, there is something in every individual that is the real knower that remains unaffected.

If you ask a person who is just getting up how he or she slept, the person acknowledges, "I went to sleep. I had a dream and then had a sound sleep. But now I am wide awake." That "I," which did not change during all these states, is the unchanging Spanda principle. If the connecting common principle did not exist then the three states would be completely isolated and the person would not remember what happened in each state. The real experient or knower is the unchanging principle experienced in that continuum; it is not the individual who regards himself or herself as separate from that continuum. People regard themselves as unique individuals with a sense of doership, due to an illusion of individuality - or māyā. Removal of this illusion is essential to experience Shiva, and the way to do this will be discussed later in this exposition. In this and several verses following Vasugupta relates the Spanda principle to various common experiences that people have, to show that they can experience God within during those experiences.

The word तदभिन्ने *tadabhinne* in the verse is made of two words: तत् *tat* meaning "that" or "those" and अभिन्ने *abhinne* meaning "in non-difference." Hence the word तदभिन्ने *tadabhinne* can be interpreted two ways: 1. These states are not different from that Spanda principle or Shiva. Only Shiva makes the difference in his own nature by His own power of free will. 2. Even though the states of waking, etc. are mutually different, that Spanda principle of Consciousness - pervades the states as one observer.

The word प्रसर्पति *prasarpati* connotes spreading in all directions or pervading. The Spanda principle pervades all the different states - waking, dream, deep sleep, swoon, intoxication, dhyāna (meditation), dhāraṇā (centering - concentration), and samādhi (intense absorption) - experienced by an individual. The word prasarpati also implies that the Spanda principle appears so real in the waking, dream, and deep sleep states, that the person experiencing a particular state gets so absorbed in it that he or she identifies completely with that state and forgets that the true experient is one's own unchanging nature. The second part of the verse says that the Spanda principle never deviates from its nature as observer.

It is commonly understood that there are three main mutually exclusive states of consciousness - waking, dreaming and deep sleep. Hallucination, and intoxication fall in the category of the dream state and swoon in the sleep state. But in addition there are two more states - called *turya* - the fourth state, and *turyātīta* - the state beyond the fourth. These states intermingle in one another. The turya state acts as the background of all the three states. That is where the Spanda principle can be experienced first hand. It penetrates all the states simultaneously. In the Shiva Sutras Vasugupta says,

जाग्रत्स्वप्नसुषुप्त्यभेदे तुर्याभोगसंभवः । (शिवसूत्र १।७)

Jāgrat-svapna-suṣuptya-bhede turyā-bhoga-sambhavaḥ
(Śiva Sutras 1/7)

> *Even during the three different states of consciousness – waking, dreaming and profound sleep -- the rapturous experience of I-consciousness of the fourth state abides.*

The commentator Kṣemarāj quotes an experience of this turya state. "As the moon, pure as a flower, shines all round and delights the world in a moment by its delightful rays, even so, oh goddess (Pārvati), the great yogi, experient of the turya state, moves about in the world, delighting the entire variegated world from hell up to Shiva with the moonbeams of his knowledge - awareness." As one experiences the fourth state and gets established in it alone, not dwelling in any other, one experiences the state of total consciousness and bliss, the supreme state of the Self or the fifth state - Turyātīta. These two states are always full of knowledge, total awareness.

Saints who are experiencing God are permanently in turyātīta states. When we approach saints, and tell them about our worldly problems, how can they know our pain, anger, fear, anguish? They don't. Yet it's not that they cannot relate to you. Instead of coming down to your state, they will take you to that state where they reside, where there is no fear, afflictions, or inner enemies. In that state there is only rapture. Therefore, you feel lighter and happy after your meeting with saints.

The obstacle that prevents one from experiencing the turya state is that in the waking and dream states one totally identifies with the states or with the objects of those states. Many people came to our Guru, Muktananda Baba to describe to him the dream they had and to ask him the interpretation of that dream. Baba often said, "People are curious about their dream but no one thinks about the dreamer."

In the waking state all our five senses of cognition (touch, smell, taste, seeing and hearing), and action (speaking, locomotion, grasping, evacuation, and procreation) continually function. Along with the senses, the mind, intellect, ego sense "I," and the life-force also function. The objects one sees can be corroborated by other people who are also awake and seeing. The sense of time, place and causation seem to be logically relevant. The world is an objective world, called in Sanskrit विश्व - *Vishwa*. It is an effect of Sattva Guna - "pure" quality. *Shiva Sutra* I, 8 says, "ज्ञानं जाग्रत्" "*Jñānaṁ jāgrat*" "Knowledge obtained by direct contact with senses is called the waking state" Yoga scriptures say that one experiences the waking state in the "gross" body.

In the dream state only the mind, intellect, ego, and the life-force function. The outer senses come to stop. The objective world corroborated by others vanishes. Whatever objects are seen in the dream are all mental creations - even though most seem to be impressions left behind by the experiences of the waking state. The sense of time and logic seem irrelevant, and experiences cannot be corroborated by others as in the waking state. In Sanskrit, this world is called तैजस - *Taijas*.

Once Swami Ram Tirth was travelling by boat from Germany. He was lounging on the deck. A person nearby suddenly got up and ran up to him. He was frightened. He suddenly shouted and asked the Swami, "Where did the lion go?" Swami Ram Tirth asked him, "What lion?" The man said, "The one from my dream." Ram Tirth said, "How can I know the lion of your dreams? It does not exist for me."

Shiva Sutra I, 9 describes the dream state as "स्वप्नो विकल्पाः ।" "*Svapno vikalpāḥ*" "All knowledge obtained by the independent activity of the mind while one is not in direct contact with the external world on any plane is included in the category of the dream state." All dreams are thought constructs. This state is the expression of Rajoguna - the quality of activity. We experience the dream state in the subtle body.

Shiva Sutra I, 10 is about the deep sleep state: "अविवेको मायासौषुप्तम् ।" "*Aviveko māyā-sauṣuptam*" "Lack of awareness on any plane is the profound sleep of delusion."

While defining the deep sleep state the sutra invokes māyā - the power of delusion, which an individual needs to abolish in order to experience the Spanda Principle, our true nature, continually.

We experience the sleep state in the causal body. In Sanskrit the world experienced in the sleep state is called प्रज्ञा - *prajñā*. Even though there is no objective experience here and there is only void, the seeds of objective experiences are still present, and sprout when one wakes up. That is the reason for calling the sleep body causal. It is an expression of Tamoguna. Only the life force - prāṇa, and other vital functions are at work in the deep sleep state.

When we are in deep sleep, we are closest to the fourth state, but unaware of it. Regardless, we feel fresh after deep sleep, because the Self's rejuvenating freshness - its eternal nature - touches the deep sleep state with nothing else to distract, the mind and senses being absent. In the fourth state we experience the bliss of the Self. That fourth state is actually our foundational absolute consciousness - the Self. It is called the supracausal body. We can experience the fourth state by the grace of our Guru. This experience is what is described in the *Shiva Sutra* I, 7 quoted earlier. Becoming established in the fourth state one experiences the fifth - turyatita state. There will be more discussion about these states later since this experience is the most important goal of our life.

Swami Lakshman Joo (1907-1991), the well-known and most recent saint of the tradition of Kashmir Shaivism, has explained very succinctly the intricacies of the five states - waking, dream, deep sleep, turya, turyatita states -- discussed in the literature of Kashmir Shaivism. The following are quotes from the article The *Five States of the Individual Subjective Body*, in his book entitled *Kashmir Shaivism - The Secret Supreme. (Swami Lakshman Joo*, 47)

Jñānis (those with divine knowledge) experience the waking state as Shiva manifest in names, forms, space and time. They feel the Consciousness of Shiva everywhere, in whatever they are doing. Yogis call the ordinary waking state पिंडस्थ *Pinḍastha* "One with whatever you perceive." *Jñānis*' state is called सर्वतोभद्र *Sarvatobhadra* "Everywhere Divine" state.

Jñānis call the dream state व्याप्ति *Vyāpti* or the "pervasive" state. They pervade whatever they see in the dream - their body, car, road, the place they are going to. They exist in their own self. Jñānis call this state प्रचय *Pracaya* since they experience the entire universal existence as undifferentiated in the state of totality without any succession.

Ordinary deep sleep is तूष्णीभाव *Tūṣṇībhāva* "Absolute silence." People feel more peaceful after leaving sleep. Yogis feel that in the deep sleep is when they become attached to their own Self. Yogis call this state रूपस्थ *Rūpastha* "One (in touch) with nature." Jñānis call the state महाव्याप्ति *Mahāvyāpti* "Great pervasion" since there is absolutely no limitation of objectivity or impressions.

Ordinary people call turya the fourth state because they are unaware of it. Yogis call it रूपातीत *Rūpātīta* "established in one's self." They are beyond the "touch state." Yogis call the ordinary dream state पदस्थ *Padastha* "established in whatever you are." It is easier to experience the Turya state in the dream state than during the waking state since the deep sleep state is closer to the Self. Children exist primarily in the dream state. They have no external thoughts. If they receive Guru's grace they immediately experience samādhi.

The fifth state तुर्यातीत *Turyātīta* is the state of absoluteness of the Self. You not only find this state in samādhi, you also find this state in each and every activity of the world. In this state there is no practice of yoga. In practice there is a place to go to. But in this state there is nowhere to go, nothing to achieve. Yogis through their imagination and guesswork call this state सततोदितम् *Satatoditam* "that state which has no pause, no break." It is a continuous and unitary state. It is present in every individual in all states - samadhi, deep sleep, dream and waking. Jñānīs call this state महाप्रचय *Mahāpracaya* the unlimited and unexplainable supreme totality.

The first four states interplay and are not mutually exclusive as many think. The fifth state is absolute and does not mix with other four. Their interplay can be presented in a chart as follows:

The states are called:

जाग्रत् जाग्रत् *jāgrat jāgrat* waking waking	जाग्रत् स्वप्न, *jāgrat svapna* waking dream	जाग्रत् सुषुप्ति *jāgrat suṣupti* waking sleep	जाग्रत् तुर्या *jāgrat turyā* waking fourth
स्वप्न जाग्रत् *svapna jāgrat* dream waking	स्वप्न स्वप्न, *svapna svapna* dream dream	स्वप्न सुषुप्ति *svapna suṣupti* dream sleep	स्वप्न तुर्या *svapna turyā* dream fourth

सुषुप्ति जाग्रत् *suṣupti jāgrat* sleep waking	सुषुप्ति स्वप्न *suṣupti svapna* sleep dream	सुषुप्ति सुषुप्ति *suṣupti suṣupti* sleep sleep	सुषुप्ति तुर्या *suṣupti turyā* sleep fourth
तुर्या जाग्रत् *turyā jāgrat* fourth waking	तुर्या स्वप्न *turyā svapna* fourth dream	तुर्या सुषुप्ति *turyā suṣupti* fourth sleep	

There is no turya-turya (fourth-fourth) state since there is no higher experience than turya. The states are explained in the chart on pages 50A and 51A. Read the chart left to right.

In the *Vijñānabhairava*, a centering exercise gives a technique to transcend the differences felt in the waking, dream, and deep sleep states.

Dharana:

किंचिज्ज्ञातं द्वैतदायि बाह्यालोकस्तमः पुनः ।
विश्वादि, भैरवं रूपं ज्ञात्वानन्तप्रकाशभृत् ।।(श्लोक ८६, धारणा ६३)

Kiṅcijñātaṁ dvaitadayi bāhyālokastamaḥ punaḥ,
Viśvādi, Bhairavaṁ rūpaṁ jñātvā-nanta-prakāśabhṛt,
(Verse 86, Dhāraṇā 63)

"When the yogi knows the three states of consciousness, Viśwa - the world experienced in waking, producing duality; Taijas - the world experienced in dream, perception of the exterior; and Prajñā - the world experienced in deep sleep state with all darkness, as the form of Bhairava (Expression of Shiva), he is then filled with the splendor of infinite consciousness. In other words, when subject-object duality disappears i.e. in the turya state he/she is filled with the light of the Self."

There is another dhāraṇā which talks about the intermediate state between waking and sleep.

अनागतायां निद्रायां प्रणष्टे बाह्य गोचरे ।
सावस्था मनसा गम्या परा देवी प्रकाशते ।। (श्लोक ७५, धारणा ५२)

Anāgatāyāṁ nidrāyāṁ praṇaṣṭe bāhya gocare
Sāvasthā manasā gamyā parā devī prakāśate
(Verse 75, Dhāraṇā 52)

One should concentrate on that state when one is not yet asleep, and all external objects are not being perceived. In that state Supreme Goddess Spanda reveals herself. By concentrating on that intermediate state one can experience the Spanda principle.

Jñāneśwar Maharaj describes the continuum behind the different states. He says,

नाहीं तें चित्र दाविती । परि असे केवळ भिंती ।
प्रकाशे ते संवित्ति । जगदाकारे ।। १३।। चांगदेव पासष्टि

Nāhīṅ teṅ citra dāvitī, pari ase kevala bhintī
Prakāśe te saṁvittī, jagadākāre
(Cāṅgadeva Pāsaṣṭi, 13)

A picture is shown on a wall, but it is still a wall
Similarly, Samvitti (Spanda) remains, while shining as the world.

This constant first-hand experience is described by Jñāneśwar Maharaj in another abhang - (unchanging poem):

तुर्येमध्ये माझा अखंड रहिवास ।
निवृत्ति म्हणे अविनाश तूर्या करी ।।
स्थूळदेह निमतां सूक्ष्म उरतां ।
कारणीं हारपतां कैसे झाले ।।
ज्ञानदेव म्हणे महाकारणीं नांदे ।
निवृत्तिनें आनंदे दाखविले ते ।।

Turyemadhye mājhā akhaṇḍa rahivāsa
Nivṛtti mhaṇe avināśa turyā karī
Sthūḷadeha nimatā sūkṣma uratā
Kāraṇī hārapatā kaise jhāle
Jñanadeva mhaṇe mahākāraṇīṅ nānde
Nivṛttīne ānaṅde dākhavile te

In turya constantly I live
  Nivritti (My Guru) says, "Turya makes one immortal."
How the gross body vanished into the subtle.
  Then the subtle body into the causal,
Jñānadev says, "I rejoice in the supracausal body.
  Which Nivritti blissfully showed me."

In short, the Guru, who is experiencing the turyatita state, can easily explain the importance of the state to the disciple, and can gladly make the disciple experience it.

Once the bliss of the fourth state is tasted by the grace of the Guru, *Shiva Sutras* exhort us to consciously keep tasting it in all the other three states.

त्रिषु चतुर्थं तैलवद् आसेच्यम् । (शिवसूत्र ३। २०)

Triṣu caturthaṁ tailavad āsecyam
(Śiva Sūtra 3|20)

The fourth state should be poured like incessant flow of oil in the three states (of waking, dream, and deep sleep.)

This leads us to have all our moments of waking and dream full of bliss. When we awaken to this fourth state, i.e. when we become aware of this state throughout our day, the other three states and activities in those three states seem like a dream. This awakening requires a conscious effort of following the Guru's teachings on our part until it becomes a part of the behavioral system. That trust and teaching itself tears the veil of maya, the illusion of separate individuality, destroying the doership of the individual.

This is described by a poet saint *Krishnātmaj* as follows.

सद्गुरुनी अवचित मजला, निद्रेतुनी जागे केले ॥ ध्रु ॥
मी मी मम गृह सुत दारा, मी करितो देतो घेतो ।
ऐशापरी वरचे वरी मी, झोपेमधि बरळत होतो ।
परी आजी मजला कळलें, कीं सर्वही स्वप्नभ्रम ते ।
भ्रमशेजीं पडलो असतां
थापटिले गुरुनीं हातां ।

झडकरी मी उठूनि पहातां
सर्व ही तें शून्यचि झालें ॥ १॥
कवणाला मुख हे दावू, जाऊ मी आतां कोठे ।
मी कर्ता भोक्ता ऐसें, वदणे मज संकट मोठे ।
ठेपली घडी मरणाची
तैं विवाह वांछा कैसी ।
काय आतां चाड भोगाची
जैं मीपण खोटें ठरले ॥ २ ॥
ाटलो तयाच्या संगे, खंती ये त्या भ्रष्टांची ।
सद्गुरूनी दिधली मजला, पूर्व स्थिति ब्रह्मपणाची ।
देउनियां प्रायश्चित्ता,
मम मस्तकीं ठेवुनि हस्ता ।
घालुनिया मुखी पदतीर्था
आपुल्यापरी शुद्धचि केले ॥ ३ ॥
निःसंग निरंजन साक्षी, असुनी तू चिन्मय मूर्ती ।
प्रतिबिंब रूप म्यां जीवे, लोपिले तव निर्मळ कीर्ति ॥
दाविली व्यर्थ मूढत्वें, मी मी ही मिथ्या स्फूर्ती ।
या मिथ्यारोपा करितां
तुज शरण मी आलो आतां ।
बा तुझीच सर्व ही सत्ता
कृष्णात्मज ऐसे बोले ॥ ४ ॥

Ref.Sadgurunī avacita majalā, nidretunī jāge kele

1. Mī mī mama gṛha suta dārā, Mī karito deto gheto
Aiśāparī varace varī mī, jhopemadhi baraḷata hoto
Parī ājī majalā kaḷale, kī sarvahī svapnabhrama te
Bhramaśejī paḍalo asatāṅ
thāpaṭile Gurunīṅ hātāṅ
jhaḍakarī mī uṭhūni pahātāṅ
sarva hī teṅ śūnyaci jhāleṅ.

2. Beśuddhī je je kele, āṭhavunī maja lajjā vāṭe
Kavaṇālā mukha he dāvū, jāū mī ātā koṭhe
Mī kartā bhoktā aise,vadaṇe maja saṅkaṭa moṭhe
Ṭhepalī ghaḍī maraṇācī
taiṅ vivāha vāṅchā kaisī
kāya ātāṅ cāḍa bhogācī

jaiṅ mīpaṇa khoṭe ṭharale.

3. Saṅgatī pure maja ātāṅ, yā sthūlādika dehācī
Bāṭalo tayācyā saṅge, khaṅtī ye tyā bhraṣṭāṅcī
Sadgurunī didhalī majalā, pūrva sthiti Brahmapaṇācī
Devuniyā prāyaścittā,
mama mastakī ṭhevuni hastā
ghāluniyā mukhī pada-tīrthā
āpulyāparī śuddhaci kele.

4. Niḥsaṅga niraṅjana sākṣī, asunī Tū cinmaya mūrtī
Pratibiṁba rūpa myāṅ jīve, lopile tava nirmaḷa kīrtī
Dāvilī vyartha mūḍhatveṅ, mī mī hī mithyā sphūrti
Yā mithyāropā karitā
tuja śaraṇa mī ālo ātāṅ
bā tujhīca sarvahī sattā
Kṛṣṇātmaja aise bole.

Ref. Sadguru suddenly woke me up from sleep.

1. "I, I, my house, children, wife, I do, I give, I take."
I was repeatedly babbling while asleep,
But today I learned that it was all
but the delusion of a dream,
while in my sleep of delusion.
My Guru tapped on my arm
Waking up suddenly I saw
All of it had become a void.

2. In my swoon whatever I did,
I remember and feel ashamed.
Whom could I show my face, where could I go?
Now to say, "I am the doer, I am the enjoyer"
is so difficult,
When the time of death has arrived,
Where is the desire of marriage?
What is the longing for sense enjoyment?
When my "I"-ness itself was proven false.

	Waking	Dream
Waking	You lose consciousness of subjectivity. Unaware of inner nature, identify with objects. This state is called in Kashmir Shaivism अबुद्धावस्था Abuddhāvasthā unawareness.	You lose consciousness of objectivity. Live in the impressions of objectivity - "Day dreaming." Called बुद्धावस्था Buddhavasthā, some awareness.
Dream	You have impressions of the objective field; experience intermittently waves of impressions and waves of objectivity. You see a pencil and a knife in its place, but not aware of the change. Everything, normal or abnormal, seems normal and ordinary. Question "How is this so?" does not arise. Called गतागतम् Gatāgatam. "Come and go." Sometimes a pencil, sometimes not.	You completely travel in impressions, no relation to objectivity. You see a pencil, a book, drive a car, fly in the air, but everything seems perfectly alright. Called सुविक्षिप्तम् Suvikṣiptam 'absolutely dispersed consciousness.' You do this, you do that yet you do not know anything.
Sleep	Lose all impressions and thoughts, and remain in void. You later remember, "I experienced nothing." Called उदितम् Uditam full of rising. You are rising out of the world of impressions towards Shiva.	You have some impression of remaining in subjectivity. But it is not constant. Called विपुलम् Vipulam "Gets nourished." Impression that you are traveling in the subjectivity increases.
Fourth	Consciousness of turya is not vividly manifested; it is in the background. It is yet to be manifested. The state is called मनोन्मनम् Manonmanam "Beyond the span of the mind." It is complete thoughtlessness.	Consciousness of turya is more vividly manifested. Consciousness is stronger here. The state is called अनन्तम् Anantam "unlimited." It is the unlimitedness of the Self. There is no limitation of being here.

Sleep	Fourth
Experience no external objectivity, no internal subjectivity. Called प्रबुद्धावस्था Prabuddhāvasthā, with consciousness.	Move in the objective world while residing in Self Consciousness. Called सुप्रबुद्धावस्था Suprabuddhāvasthā, Absolutely full awareness.
You travel in the world of impressions and thoughts, also develop some awareness of subjectivity. If you see a pencil and then a knife you wonder why the pencil became knife. You realize that you are not awake and you must be dreaming. You question, argue and forget, and again travel in impressions. Called संगतम् Sangatam "touched by Consciousness"	You see an object, you become aware that you are not seeing the object but actually its impression and that you are dreaming and you are not awake. By the grace of your Guru, cast away the impressions and enter samādhi. You come back and forth from dream state to samādhi. Called सुसमाहितम् Susamāhitam "absolutely aware."
The impression that you are traveling in the subjectivity remains in the background throughout, without interruption. Called शान्तम् Shāntam "Peaceful." You are in absolutely peaceful state. No agitation.	You enter in samadhi, yet consciousness remains in the background. Here you experience the Bliss of the Self while remaining conscious. Called सुप्रसन्नम् Suprasannam. You are in absolute bliss but not aware of the bliss.
Consciousness is most vivid. It is the strongest. This state is called सर्वार्थम् Sarvārtham although you are unlimited, yet you find existing here all of the limitations of the universe.	There is no such state.

3. Enough of the company of the bodies - gross, subtle
I was ruined in their company,
I feel sorry for those fallen bodies
Sadguru gave me my original state of the Self
by giving me atonement putting his hand
on my head making me drink the water of
the holy feet (the elixir from the cranium)
He made me pure like himself.

4. "You are unattached, unblemished, a witness,
Consciousness-manifested
Your untainted glory made my individuality
that was only a reflection disappear
By senseless foolishness I was showing off my
throbbing false ego
To get rid of this false claim
I now surrender to You.
This is only Your kingdom."
Kṛṣṇātmaj says.

VERSE 4

SPANDA: WARP AND WOOF OF DIFFERENT EXPERIENCES

अहं सुखी च दुःखी च रक्तश्चेत्यादि-संविदः ।
सुखाद्यवस्थानुस्यूते वर्तन्तेऽन्यत्र ताः स्फुटम् ।।४।।

4. Ahaṁ sukhī ca duḥkhī ca raktaścetyādi-saṁvidaḥ
Sukhādyavasthānusyūte vartante 'nyatra tāḥ sphuṭam

भट्ट कल्लटः – स चानुस्यूत एव सर्वावस्थासु, यस्मात् य एव अहं सुखी स एव अहं दुःखी, रक्तो वा पश्चात् स्थित इति अनुस्यूतत्वेन; अन्यत्र अवस्थाव्यतिरिक्ते । यदागमः .....स स्वभावः परः स्मृतः । इति ।। ४।।

Bhaṭṭa Kallaṭa: - 4. Sa cānusyūta eva sarvāvasthāsu, yasmāt 'Ya eva ahaṁ sukhī sa eva ahaṁ duḥkhī, rakto vā paścāt sthita' iti anusyūtatvena; anyatra avasthāvyatirikte. Yad-Āgamaḥ '.....sa svabhāvaḥ paraḥ smṛtaḥ I' iti

It is evident that 'I am happy'; 'I am sad'; 'I am attached,' yet all such feelings exist in a different place, in which happiness and other states are strung together.

It is evident that this Spanda nature is interwoven through all states like a thread, because such experiences as "the one 'I' who was happy at first later became unhappy or attached" have a common thread of "I." The word 'anyatra' (different place) indicates that these experiences are different from that on which they are threaded. In Āgamas (revealed scriptures) it is said, "This nature is sublime and different from all things." What this emphasizes is that before you have the feelings of happiness or sadness the pure attributeless "I am" arises.

IN THIS VERSE Vasugupta shows to all humankind how to get out of the pairs of opposite emotions such as sorrow and happiness, love and hate. People identify themselves with these emotions and are swayed by them. Vasugupta says that those feelings are strung together on the Spanda principle like flowers on a string. By using the word स्फुटम् (Sphuṭam) "evident" or "open" he indicates that one needs to look beyond or underneath these feelings to see that which is actually revealed and not hidden by these feelings. He gives a technique of looking beyond or underneath the feelings in later verses – verses 41 and 44, but here he wishes to emphasize Spanda's open and foundational nature. If these various states were not connected, then the perceiver would be different in each case and ideas born out of their traces left behind in memory would be disconnected. In our sleep state we are not aware of anything. When we change from sleep to our waking and dream states first "I am" arises, then thoughts such as "I am so and so," and "I am a man or woman" come, and then we start to experience the pairs of opposites. Nisargadatta Maharaj, a modern saint, kept repeating the same message in his talks a few years before his death (*Nisargadatta Maharaj*, 26). He said, "Just as you are aware that you are a man or woman, become aware that you are consciousness, chaitanya. It is not necessary to do any other practices. Just become aware."

In America, people identify themselves with different things so routinely that the people from Asia find it very amusing. For example, somebody says in anger, "If you hit my car, you have hit me." This exemplifies what people do who do not know their own nature. In general, people identify themselves with so many external qualifications, becoming happy or sorry when changes occur. Working people identify themselves with their work and position. They become happy and celebrate when they get promoted. They become sad when they are not promoted, while they become jealous when another colleague, whom they consider less deserving, gets the promotion. They become happy when somebody praises them and get offended when they are insulted. People identify themselves with their children's accomplishments or failures. People love their children and spouse, but once the children or spouse start behaving contrary to their wishes, people start hating them. Thus they are under the sway of these opposites. This is all due to ignorance of the facts that Vasugupta has mentioned in this verse.

When a person is extremely sad due to losing a close relative, doctors prescribe a sedative to make the person sleep, so that the person gets some relief. This is because sorrow or happiness does not reach the causal body. These feelings reach only the gross body of the waking state and sometimes the subtle body of the dream state.

An individual, who knows his or her nature as the Self, can transcend the feelings of happiness or sorrow. We have a gurubhagini (sister devotee of our Guru) who lives in a town in New York State. Her husband passed away after a grave illness. On that day as all preparations for his cremation were being made, she kept losing her body consciousness because of deep meditation - samadhi. Her son and son-in-law thought she was extremely sad so she was passing out, and dialed 911, a phone number in America for emergency ambulance, etc. The paramedics came to check her pulse and to give a sedative or take her to a hospital. Hearing the commotion she came out of her samadhi, and asked what happened. A paramedic said, "You had passed out. So your son called and we came." "I am all right now," she said. Soon after the paramedics left the house she went back into meditation. Again the son dialed 911. Again a similar thing happened. This incident repeated several times. The last time the paramedic came who knew about meditation. He asked the people around whether the lady went into trance. When they said yes, he told the son that she went into meditation trance and they could not do anything about it, she was not in a shock, and if he called 911 again they would take her to a hospital and sedate her and she would not be able to come out of the hospital for a few days. In fact her trance helped her to overcome her feeling of pain. The point of this story is that by a regular practice of meditation, one can transcend the pairs of opposites, which trouble most people.

In the famous dialogue from *Bṛhadāraṇyaka Upaniṣad* Sage Yājñvalkya, imparting the teaching of supreme love of the inner Self to his wife Maitreyi, says,

न वा अरे पत्युः कामाय पतिः प्रियो भवति,
आत्मनस्तु कामाय पतिः प्रियो भवति ।
न वा अरे जायायै कामाय जाया प्रिया भवति,
आत्मनस्तु कामाय जाया प्रिया भवति ।
न वा अरे पुत्राणां कामाय पुत्राः प्रिया भवन्ति ।
आत्मनस्तु कामाय पुत्राः प्रिया भवन्ति
(बृहदारण्यक उप. २।४।५)

Na vā are patyuḥ kāmāya patiḥ priyo bhavati,
Ātmanastu kāmāya patiḥ priyo bhavati.
Na vā are jāyāyai kāmāya jāyā priyā bhavati,

Ātmanastu kāmāya jāyā priyā bhavati.
Na vā are putrāṇāṁ kāmāya putrāḥ priyā bhavanti,
Ātmanastu kāmāya putrāḥ priyā bhavanti.
(Bṛhadāraṇyaka Up. 2|4|5)

"Oh Maitreyi! A husband is loved not for the sake of the husband, but for the sake of the happiness of the Self. A wife also is loved not for the sake of the wife, but for the sake of the happiness of the Self. Children are loved not for the sake of the children, but for the sake of the happiness of the Self."

This conversation becomes clear in the light of this *Spanda Karika* verse. Love happens because of the "I" principle. "I" is also common to all other feelings. The foundation for such feelings is the Spanda principle or the Self which is beyond all of them, but which passes through them like a string through flowers in a garland.

The feelings of love, hatred, greed, infatuation, pride, and jealousy lie in the mind. However people first identify love or hate with their body and then identify with objects external to their bodies. If these emotions are not held in check, they can consume the individual's mind, body and health. To keep them in check once for all, we must understand their origin – the mind. An individual mind exists as mind as long as the veil of maya – illusion of individuality -- persists. Only the Guru can show how frail the veil is and remove it in no time by His or Her grace. The experience given by the Guru described at the end of the first verse shows that mind is nothing but vibration or spanda. When asked by a devotee the difference between the mind and the Self, Ramana Maharshi (*Sri Ramana Maharshi*, 37, page 91) said, "There is no difference. The mind turned inwards is the Self; turned outwards, it becomes the ego and all the world. The cotton made into various clothes, we call by various names. The gold made into various ornaments, we call by various names. But all the clothes are cotton and all the ornaments are gold. The One is real, the many are mere names and forms. But the mind does not exist apart from the Self, i.e., it has no independent existence. The Self exists without the mind, never the mind without the Self."

The word अनुस्यूत *anusyūta* in the verse means stringing together. All these feelings are strung together. The *Bhagavad Gita* uses similar wording.

मत्तः परतरं नान्यत्, किञ्चिदस्ति धनञ्जय !
मयि सर्वमिदं प्रोतं, सूत्रे मणिगणा इव ॥ (गीता ७।७)

Mattaḥ parataraṁ nānyat, kiñcidasti Dhananjaya.
Mayi sarvamidaṁ protaṁ, sūtre maṇigaṇā iva. (B.G. 7/7)

"Oh Dhananjaya, Arjuna! Whatever object is visible in the world is not different from me. This entire universe is woven on me alone - the warp and woof of all - like beads knotted on a string."

Swami Maheshwarananda[21] (*Swami Maheshwaranand Giri*, 49) in his Nectar of Discourses on the Seventh Chapter of the Gita says: "If you take the illustration to refer to Tulasi or Rudraksha beads threaded on a string, then the statement means that the universe is woven on God the way that special dissimilar wooden beads are woven on a string. This meaning is not consistent with the doctrine of Oneness. It implies that 'just as the thread occurs with the beads, but the beads are different from it, the Supreme Self occurs with the manifest and unmanifest universe, the universe is different from the Self and something other than the Self.' But this is inconsistent with the statements established in the scriptures .... The beads are knotted out of the same thread upon which they are strung, like beads knotted from silk in Panjab. An example such as this, like a chain with gold thread and gold beads, makes the illustration consistent with the doctrine of the one without a second." He reminds us that we have to realize that the chain or garland that is being referred to is a gold chain where even the beads are made of the same gold. Yet the gold is not delimited by becoming beads. Likewise, these emotions are made of the same Spanda principle, but the Spanda principle itself transcends all those emotions.

Vasugupta emphasizes this fact in the given verse by the word अन्यत्र *Anyatra*, meaning "another place." That can be clarified also as follows. According to Kashmir Shaivism it is the universal Self, which descends from its pure "I"ness – "Aham Vimarsh" without any attributes or Spanda principle, to become the individual self. This individual self has an ego, or sense of "I"ness with attributes, which is the 13th principle among the 36 principles of creation[22] and is a byproduct of the fifth principle māyā – the illusion of individuality. Mind is the byproduct of the individual ego and is the 15th principle. It is in the mind that emotions

[21] Swāmi Maheṣwarānanda *Nectar of Discourses* (Pravacan Sudhā) Verse 7

and other experiences reside. Thus even though everything is made of the Spanda principle, the principle Itself transcends all emotions and is not affected by it.

Rābia was a Sufi saint. Once she was sick and two Sufi saints 'Abd al-Wāhid' Amr and Sūfiyān Thawri went to see her. Sūfiyān said to Rābia, "If you would utter a prayer, God would relieve your suffering." She turned her face to him and said, "O Sūfiyān, do you know Who it is that wills this suffering for me, is it not God Who wills it?" He said, "Yes." She said, "When you know this, why do you bid me to ask for what is contrary to His will? It is not well to oppose one's Beloved." (Attar, 1) The point of the story is that by contemplating God constantly, one is not affected by the duality of this world.

Indian saints always emphasize that one should think of God incessantly to get out of this duality, which is the cause of sorrow and happiness. Saint Eknath says in his teaching to the common man as follows:

आवडीने भावे हरिनाम घेसी, तुझी चिंता त्यासी सर्व आहे ।
नको खेद करू कोणत्या गोष्टीचा, पति लक्ष्मीचा जाणतसे ॥
सकल जगाचा करितो सांभाळ, तुज मोकलील ऐसे नाही ॥
जैशी स्थिति आहे तैशापरी आहे, कौतुक तू पाहे संचिताचे ॥
एका जनार्दनी भोग प्रारब्धाचा, हरिकृपे त्याचा नाश झाला ॥

Āvaḍīne bhāve Harināma ghesī, tujhī cintā tyāsī sarva āhe.
Nako kheda karu koṇatyā goṣṭīcā, Pati Lakṣumīcā jāṇatase.
Sakala jagācā karito sāṁbhāḷa, tuja mokalīla aise nāhī.

---

[22] The 36 principles are as follows: four pure elements – Shiva (Self), Shakti (pure "I Am;" awarenss – Spanda), Sadāśiva (I ness-thisness together – I ness predominant), Īśvara (Thisness in I ness – Thisness predominant), Śuddha Vidyā (Pure knowledge – I and this separated – but with the knowledge they are the same as the Spanda); six coverings – māyā – illusion of individuality, kalā (creativity), vidyā (limitation in knowledge), rāga (limitation of attachment – limitation of incompleteness), kāla (limitation of time), niyati (limitation of place); five internal organs – antaḥkaraṇas – purusha (ego connected with subjectivity), prakṛti (nature), ahaṁkāra – (ego connected with objectivity), buddhi (intellect), manas (mind); five organs of cognition – jñānendriyas - śrotra (ears), cakṣu (eyes), tvak (skin - touching), rasanā (tongue), ghrāṇa (nose); five organs of action – karmendriyas - vāk (speech), pāṇi (hand), pāda (foot), pāyu (excretion), upastha (procreation); five subtle elements – tanmātras - śabda (sound), sparśa (touch), rūpa (form), rasa, (taste), gandha (smell); five gross elements - ākaśa (space), vāyu (air), agni (fire), jala (fluid - water), pṛthvi (earth - solid)

[23] Viṣṇu – Maintainer of the universe

Jaiśī sthiti āhe taiśāparī rāhe, kautuka tū pāhe saṅcitāce.
Ekā Janārdanī bhoga prārabdhācā, Harikṛpe tyācā nāśa jhālā.

Repeat Lord's name with love and feeling,
For all your worries He will be caring.
Do not worry whatsoever,
Lord of Goddess Lakshmi[23] knows forever.
The whole world He cares about
He is not going to leave you out.
Stay according to whatever situation,
Watch the play of destiny in admiration.
Janardan's Ekanath says, "Suffering due to past actions
With Lord Hari's grace went to annihilation."

This is sobering and urgent advice to people who are suffering. Ekanath brings out the principle of grace inherent in the Self. People can get out of their sorrow easily by remembering God, by contemplating That which is beyond the cycle of sorrow and happiness, by being a witness to the Divine play. The trouble is that people think of God only when they are in misery. When they are experiencing pleasure, happy events in their lives, they get attached to them and forget about God. But the only way not to be troubled by misery, is not to be overjoyed or attached to happiness either; but just to witness both misery and happiness while remaining aware of the reality - Spanda - beyond. Vasugupta, the author, supports by explaining that sorrow and happiness, love and hate are made of Spanda and strung together in Spanda which can be openly discerned in any condition.

In Verse 4, Vasugupta has refuted many ancient philosophers such as Bauddhas – followers of Buddhist philosophy; Mīmānsakas – logicians who propound sensory evidence, inference, deduction, – etc. as the means of checking reality; and Chārvāks – atheists who regard that there is no other consciousness except bodily consciousness and consciousness is born and dies with the body. This point is brought out here since many popular western philosophers subscribe to one of these ways of thinking of Reality. Vasugupta's refutation applies also to such philosophers.

The point of this verse is that when somebody says I am happy, I am sad, I am in love etc., even though they appear connected to the same "I." all these feelings are experienced within the ego, intellect, and mind. They do not come directly from the Spanda. It is the Spanda that empowers the ego and mind. To be free from the cycles of sorrow and happiness, love and hatred, we must contemplate our own nature - the Self – Existence, Consciousness and Bliss – Spanda.

The following song summarizes Verse 4. It also sets up a connection to the next verse. It is written from the view of the Self. The Self is saying (a poem of Hari Om Sharan):

मेरा सतचित- आनंद रूप, कोई कोई जाने रे ।।ध्रु ।।
द्वैत वचन का मैं हूँ दृष्टा, मनवाणी का मैं हूँ सृष्टा ।
ज्यूं माला में सूत कोई कोई जाने रे ।।१।।
तीन अवस्था से मैं हूँ न्यारा, तीन गुण है मेरा पसारा ।
मैं ही साक्षी भूप, कोई कोई जाने रे ।।२।।
चतुष्ट अंतःकरण मैं हूँ चतुष्ट साधन संपन्न मैं हूँ
मैं छाया मैं धूप, कोई कोई जाने रे ।।३।।
पंचकोश मेरे धरम नहीं है, पंच ग्यान और करम नहीं है ।
अनुभव सिर्फ अनूप, कोई कोई जाने रे ।।४।।

Ref. Merā sata-cita- ānaṁd rūpa, koyī koyī jāne re

1. *Dvaita vacana kā maiṁ hūṁ dṛṣṭa, manavāṇī kā maiṁ hūṁ sṛṣṭā*
   Jyūṁ mālā meṁ sūta koī koī jāne re.
2. *Tīna avasthā se maiṁ hūṁ nyārā, tīna guṇa hai merā pasārā*
   Maiṁ hūṁ sākṣī bhūpa, koī koī jāne re.
3. *Catuṣṭa aṁtaḥkaraṇa maiṁ hūṁ catuṣṭa sādhana saṁpanna maiṁ hūṁ*
   Maiṁ chāyā maiṁ dhūpa, koī koī jāne re.
4. *Paṅcakośa mere dharama nahīṁ hai,*
   paṅca gyāna aur karama nahīṁ hai
   Anubhava sirpha anūpa, koī koī jāne re.

My nature is Sat-Chit-Ananda – Existence, Consciousness and Bliss.
But only a few people know this.
Witness of the dual states[24] *am I. Source of mind and speech am I.*
Just as a string through a garland.

[24] love and hatred, happiness and sorrow

This, only a few people understand.
I am different from the three states.[25] *I am different from the three gunas*[26].
I am the witnessing King.
Few people have this understanding.
The fourfold inner instrument[27], *I am. The four types of sadhana*[28], *I am.*
Both the shade and the sun I am.
Only a few people know who I am.
The five sheaths[29] *are not my characteristics.*
The five senses of perception[30] *or action*[31] *are not my nature.*
I am only the indescribable experience.
Few people know my nature.

[25] waking, dream and deep sleep
[26] sattva (purity), rajas (activity), tamas (indolence)
[27] ego, mind, intellect and subconscious
[28] discrimination, dispassion, determination, desire to be "free." (These are the means of purification of the fourfold inner instrument.)
[29] food, prana (life force), mind, knowledge, Self-knowledge
[30] sound, touch, sight, taste, smell
[31] speaking, handling, locomotion, excreting, procreation.

VERSE 5

TRANSCENDENT SPANDA

न दुःखं न सुखं यत्र न ग्राह्यो ग्राहको न च ।
न चास्ति मूढभावोऽपि तदस्ति परमार्थतः ॥५॥

5. Na duḥkhaṁ na sukhaṁ yatra, na grāhyo grāhako na ca
Na cāsti mūḍhabhāvo 'pi tad-asti paramārthataḥ

भट्ट कल्लट – तस्य चायं स्वभावो यत् सुख-दुःख-ग्राह्यग्राहक-मूढतादिभावैरस्पृष्टः । स एव च परमार्थतोऽस्ति नित्यत्वात् । सुखादयः पुनः संकल्पोत्थाः क्षणभङ्गुरा आत्मस्वरूपबाह्याः शब्दादिविषयतुल्याः । न च, सुखादिस्वरूपो यदा नासौ तदा पाषाणप्रख्य एव ॥५॥

Bhaṭṭa Kallaṭa: - 5.Tasya cāyaṁ svabhāvo yat sukha-duḥkha-grāhya-grāhaka-mūḍhatādi-bhāvair-aspṛṣṭaḥa. Sa eva ca paramārthato 'sti nityatvāt. Sukhādayaḥ punaḥ saṅkalpotthāḥ kṣaṇa-bhaṅgurā ātma-svarūpa-bāhyāḥ śabdādi-viṣaya-tulyāḥ. Na ca, sukhādi-svarūpo yadā nāsau tadā pāṣāṇa-prakhya eva.

That is the Spanda principle in the highest sense, in which there is no sorrow, no happiness, no object, no subject, no insentience.

The nature of the Spanda Principle is such that it is not touched by happiness, sorrow, object, subject, or insentience, nor any other such feelings or states. That principle is the highest truth since it is eternal. Happiness and other feelings, being mental constructs, are momentary. They are external to the true nature of the Self. They can be categorized with objects like words. Yet it is also not correct to say that since Spanda does not have feelings such as happiness, It is insentient like a rock.

IN CONTRAST to the Verse 4, where Vasugupta shows that the feelings such that "I am happy," "I am afflicted," "I am in love" are connected by "I" like a string of a garland which is all manifestation of Spanda, in this verse he shows how Spanda transcends all these feelings. In Verse 3 he showed that the true experient of all experiences of all states is the Spanda principle, here he states that It transcends all of them. The emphasis of this Verse is on how subject-object relationships come into being out of Spanda, yet how Spanda is beyond these relationships.

When Spanda in its outward aspect takes the form of the subtle general life-force in order to generate the universe, it also becomes the *antaḥkaraṇa* (inner equipment) made of three guṇas (qualities) – *sattva* (light), *rajas* (restlessness) and *tamas* (darkness – indolence). The inner instruments are the five internal organs – *puruṣa* (ego connected with subjectivity), *prakṛti* (nature), *ahaṁkāra* – (ego connected with objectivity), *buddhi* (intellect), and *manas* (mind). The nature of the three qualities is happiness, sorrow and infatuation respectively. As such the feelings of happiness, sadness or attachment are not different from Spanda, from which they originate. Yet they reside not in the Spanda but rather in the ego and the mind.

When a visitor approached Ramana Maharshi[32] (*Sri Ramana Maharshi*, 37) and expressed his grief about losing his son, Ramana Maharshi was silent for a while, and then said, "Your worry is due to thinking. Anxiety is a creation of the mind. Your real nature is peace. The true remedy is to enquire into your nature. It is because you feel that your son does not exist, you feel grief. If you knew that he existed you would not feel grief. That means that the source of the grief is mental and not the actual reality. In deep sleep the thought of 'I' or 'child' or 'death' does not occur to you, and now you are the same person that existed in sleep. If you enquire in this way and find out your real nature you will know your son's real nature also. He always exists. It is only that you think he is lost. You create a son in mind, and think that he is lost. But in the Self he always exists." Similarly, all problems are in the mind. If we turn our minds inwards and experience our real nature our problems are dissolved. In *Shiva Sutras* it is said, सुखदुःखयोर्बहिर्मननम् (३,३३) "*Sukha-duḥkhayor-bahirmananam* I" (3:33) "Happiness

[32] *Ramana Maharshi Day by Day with Bhagavan* 31/5/46, p. 208.

and sorrow are in the outward-looking mind where subject and object relationship exists. When they are regarded as "Idam" - "This" separate from "Aham" – "I" there is no experience of the pangs of duality."

The words "grāhya - grāhaka" in the verse always go together, indicating that which is grasped or experienced, thus an object of experience for a certain subject or experient. For each object there must be a subject as well as the process of experiencing the object – thus creating a triad. Even in quantum mechanics importance is given to the triad. It is the observer or subject that gives validity to an event. It is the same Shakti that manifests herself as both internal and external objects. The internal objects are feelings such as pain, pleasure, and infatuation aroused by thinking and memories – saṁkalpa – vikalpa of the mind; and the subject is composed of the ego, intellect and mind. The external objects are the five types of sense objects perceived by the five senses of perception, which take shape only when connected with the inner instrument. Hence whether the object is internal or external the process of experience itself is the jñāna shakti – power of knowledge. Without the support of power of knowledge the triad of the Seen (the external or internal objects), Seer (the corresponding subjects) and Seeing cannot exist. Hence the triad and its components are of the form of power of knowledge.

There is a story written by Tolstoy. In a village there was a man who had an incurable and contagious disease. People built a hut for him outside the village. The man would sit outside his hut, and live on the scraps thrown to him by passersby. One day he died and people burned his body, his clothes and belongings. Fearing that the germs of his disease might have penetrated the ground the doctors ordered that the hut and the ground underneath be dug and burned as well. People started digging up. They found a large chest full of gems and gold ornaments. Here the man had died in ignorance of the treasure. As far as he was concerned the light of his consciousness had not fallen on the treasure.

The point of the story is that if a thing does not appear in the light of consciousness, it is as good as nonexistent. There is another point to this story. If we do not experience our real nature, which is the treasure of bliss and omniscience, we will also die as poor as that man hankering after bliss outside ourselves.

Jnaneshwar Maharaj brings out the concepts of Verse 5, beautifully in the letter to Changadev:

घडियेचेनि आकारें । प्रकाशिजे जेवीं अंबरें ।
तेंवी विश्वस्फूर्ति स्फुरें । स्फुर्तिचि हे ॥१५॥
न लिंपतां सुखदुःख । येणें आकारें क्षोभोनि नावेक ।
होय आपणिया सन्मुख । आपणचि जो ॥१६॥
तया नांव दृश्याचें होणे । संवित्ति द्रष्टुत्वा आणिजे तेणें ।
बिंबा बिंबत्व जालेपणें । प्रतिबिंबाचेनि ॥ १७ ॥
तेंवी आपणचि आपुला पोटीं । आपणया दृश्य दावित उठी ।
द्रष्टादृश्यदर्शन त्रिपुटी । मांडें तें हे ॥ १८ ॥
सुताचिये गुंजे । आंतबाहेर नाहीं दुजें ।
तेवी तिनपणेवीण जाणिजे । त्रिपुटी हे ॥ १९॥
नुसधें मुख जैसे । देखिजतसे दर्पणमिसें ।
वायांचि देखणे ऐसें । गमों लागे ॥ २०॥
तैसें न वचतां भेदा । संवित्ति गमे त्रिधा ।
हेंचि जाणे प्रसिद्धा । उपपत्ति इया ॥ २१॥
दृश्याचा जो उभारा । तेंचि द्रष्टुत्व होय संसारा ।
या दोहींमधला अंतरा । दृष्टि पंगु होय ॥२२ ॥
दृश्य जेधवां नाहीं । तेधवां दृष्टि घेऊनि असे काई ।
आणि दृश्येंविण कांहीं । द्रष्टुत्व असे ॥ २३॥
म्हणोनि दृश्याचे जालेपणें । दृष्टि द्रष्टुत्व असे ।
पुढती तें गेलिया जाणें । तैसेचि दोन्ही ॥२४ ॥
एवं एकचि झालीं ती होती । तिन्ही गेलिया एकचि व्यक्ति ।
तरी तिन्हीं भ्रांति । एकपण साच ॥२५ ॥
दर्पणाच्या आधि शेखीं । मुख असतांचि असे मुखीं ।
माजीं दर्पण अवलोकीं । आन कांहीं होये ? ॥२६॥
पुढें देखिजे तेणें बगे । देखतें ऐसे गमों लागे ।
परी दृष्टीतें वाउगें । झकवित असे ॥२७॥
म्हणोनि दृश्याचिये वेळे । दृश्य-द्रष्टुत्वा वेगळें ।
वस्तुमात्र निहाळे । आपणापाशीं ॥२८॥

15. *Ghaḍiyeceni ākāreṅ prakāśije jevīṅ aṁbareṅ*
    Teṅvī viśvasphūrti sphureṅ sphurtici he
16. *Na liṁpatāṅ sukha-duḥkha yeṇeṅ ākāreṅ kṣobhoni nāveka*
    Hoya āpaṇiyā sanmukha āpaṇaci jo
17. *Tayā nāṅva dṛśyāceṅ hoṇe Saṁvitti drṣṭutvā āṇije teṇeṅ*
    Bimbā biṁbatva jālepaṇeṅ pratibiṁbāceni
18. *Teṅvī āpaṇaci āpulā poṭīṅ āpaṇayā dṛśya dāvita uṭhī*
    Drṣṭā-dṛśya-darśana tripuṭī māṅḍeṅ teṅ he

19. *Sutāciye guṅje āṅta-bāhera nāhīṅ dujeṅ*
Tevī tinapaṇevīṇa jāṇije tripuṭī he
20. *Nusadheṅ mukha jaise dekhijatase darpaṇamiseṅ*
Vāyāṅci dekhaṇe aiseṅ gamoṅ lāge
21. *Taiseṅ na vacatāṅ bhedā saṁvitti game tridhā*
Heṅci jāṇe prasiddhā upapatti iyā
22. *Dṛśyācā jo ubhārā teṅci draṣṭutva hoya saṁsārā*
Yā dohīmājila aṅtarā dṛṣṭi paṅgu hoya
23. *Dṛśya jedhavāṅ nāhīṅ tedhavāṅ dṛṣṭi gheūni ase kāi*
Āṇi dṛśyeṅviṇa kāhīṅ dṛṣṭṛtva ase
24. *Mhaṇoni dṛśyāce jālepaṇeṅ dṛṣṭi dṛṣṭutva ase*
Puḍhatī teṅ geliyā jāṇeṅ taiseci donhī
25. *Evaṁ ekaci jhālīṅ tī hotī tinhī geliyā ekaci vyakti*
Tarī tinhnīṅ bhrāṅti ekapaṇa sāca
26. *Darpaṇācyā ādhi śekhīṅ mukha asatāṅciṁ ase mukhīṅ*
Mājīṅ darpaṇa avalokīṅ āna kāṅhīṅ hoye ?
27. *Puḍheṅ dekhije teṇeṅ bage dekhateṅ aise gamoṅ lāge*
Parī dṛṣṭīteṅ vāugeṅ jhakavita ase
28. *Mhaṇoni dṛśyāciye veḷe dṛśya-dṛṣṭutvā vegaḷeṅ*
Vastumātra nihāḷe āpaṇāpāśīṅ

A piece of cloth is cloth, even when it's folded.
In the same way, the Supreme Principle
Pulsates as the Universe.
And when, untouched by pain or pleasure,
He appears before Himself in different forms,
Consciousness becomes a Seer,
And what appears is called the Seen,
The way a face in a mirror
Becomes an object of perception.
He creates the Seen out of his own being
And shows it to Himself.
In this way, there appears the triad
Of the Seer, Seen and Seeing
But just as in a ball of string
There is nothing but string, inside and out,
Understand that this triad is not three.

A face, which is alone, sees itself in a mirror,
And as it looks, the act of seeing
Naturally occurs.
O Famous One, in the same way,
Consciousness, without being divided
Appears to become three.
Understanding this is the secret of everything!
When the Seen is created,
The Seer of the world comes into being.
In trying to perceive the distinction between them,
Seeing disappears.
How can there be Seeing, when there is no Seen?
And when there is no Seen,
How can there be a Seer?
When the Seen is created,
Then the Seer and Seeing are also created.
Should the Seen vanish, so will the other two.
In this way, one becomes three.
When the three disappear, only One remains.
The three were an illusion, oneness is real.
Before looking in a mirror, a face is a face.
After looking in a mirror
Does it become something else?
Though a face looking in a mirror, may appear to be a Seer,
Because it only sees itself,
Seeing is deceived.
Therefore when the Seen appears, know that it is That,
Beyond the Seer and the Seen
Which is looking at itself. (15-28)

The Seer, the Seen and Seeing – or the subject, the object and perception – are created by Maya, the power of delusion. If we realize that the object "Seen" has no separate existence from the Self, only the Self remains. If happiness and sorrow, or the triad of object, subject and perception of the object, do not exist, it does not mean insentience remains. As said by Jñāneṣwar, only the Self remains. Another saint, *Tukārām*, (Tukaram, 58) sings in one of his abhangas, "सांडिली त्रिपुटी, दीप उजळला घटी" - "*Sāṅḍilī tripuṭī, dīpa ujāḷalā ghaṭī*" "The triad dropped away, and Light pervaded the body." In short, one should never fear that if we lose our set of triads we would become inert or insentient, one would experience only the light of consciousness which is untouched by the cycles of pleasure and pain.

By one's own effort – disciplined thinking or outer rituals – it is difficult to transcend the mind and ego. When we go beyond the body identifications and mind, we experience the Self. Only a Sadguru can do that for us. This experience of the Self is readily wonderful. It is intoxicating. A song of a poet saint explains why this experience of Self is significant.

इक नशा है अजब, जो घटे ना बढे ।
जो कि छाया है ऐसा मिटे ना हटे ।।ध्रु.।।
जरा पहले था भ्रमका कुछ आवरण ।
अब पता चल गया क्या है जीवन मरण ।
ये बनते बिगडते रहे बुदबुदे ।
जो कि छाया है ऐसा मिटे ना हटे ।। १ ।।
सुखदुःख की मौजों का था जो असर ।
किश्ती मेरी कहीं डूबे ना था ये डर ।
अब तो तूफां के झोंके रूके या चले ।
जो कि छाया है ऐसा मिटे ना हटे ।।२।।
लोग पाने की खातिर भगे जा रहे ।
कुछ भी हासिल नही ठोकरे खा रहे ।
हम तो पहचान कर अपने दिल में जगे ।
जो कि छाया है ऐसा मिटे ना हटे ।। ३।।
ओ इन्सान कहलाने वाले सुन ।
जरा अपने मुर्शद के छू ले चरण ।
फिर तो कोऽहं और सोऽहं की गांठे खुले ।
जो कि छाया है ऐसा मिटे ना हटे ।।४।।

Ref. Ika naśā hai ajaba, jo ghaṭe nā baḍhe
jo ki chāyā hai aisā miṭe nā haṭe
1. Jarā pahale thā bhramakā kucha āvaraṇa
aba patā cala gayā, kya hai jīvana maraṇa
ye banate bigaḍate rahe buda-bude
jo ki chāyā hai aisā miṭe nā haṭe.
2. Sukha-duḥkha kī maujoṅ kā thā jo asara
kiśtī merī kahīṅ ḍūbe nā thā ye ḍara
aba to tūphāṅ ke jhoṅke ruke yā cale
jo ki chāyā hai aisā miṭe nā haṭe.

3. Loga pāne kī khātir bhage jā rahe
kucha bhī hāsila nahī ṭhokare khā rahe
hama to pahacāna kara apane dila meṅ jage
jo ki chāyā hai aisā miṭe nā haṭe.
4. O insāna kahalāne vāle suna
jarā apane Murśada ke chū le caraṇa
phira to ko 'haṁ aur so 'haṁ kī gāṅṭhe khule
jo ki chāyā hai aisā miṭe nā haṭe.

Ref. What strange intoxication, that does not diminish or swell.
It spreads over me so well, it does neither go away nor quell.

1. For some time there was a kind of delusion veil
But what life and death are, now I can tell.
These are the bubbles – that form and burst.
That intoxication spreads over me so well,
It does neither go away nor quell.

2. Cycles of happiness and sorrow used to have a spell.
A fear that my boat might sink would sometimes dwell.
But now may the waves of storms stop or swell.
That intoxication spreads over me so well, -
It does neither go away nor quell.

3. People ran in frenzy to attain the Bliss
But empty-handed they fell in an abyss.
Having found that out we became aware.
That intoxication spreads over me so well,
It does neither go away nor quell.

4. O the one who calls himself a human being, listen.
Just take refuge at your Guru's feet, hasten.
Then, the knots of 'Who am I?' and 'I am that' will unravel.
That intoxication spreads over me so well,
It does neither go away nor quell.

VERSES 6 AND 7

MANIFESTATION OF SPANDA

यतः करणवर्गोऽयं विमूढोऽमूढवत् स्वयम् ।
सहान्तरेण चक्रेण प्रवृत्ति-स्थिति-संहृतीः ॥६॥

6. *Yataḥ karaṇa-vargo 'yaṁ vimūḍho 'mūḍhavat svayam.*
   Sahāntareṇa cakreṇa pravṛtti-sthiti-saṁhṛtīḥ.

लभते, तत्प्रयत्नेन परीक्ष्यं तत्त्वमादरात् ।
यतः स्वतन्त्रता तस्य सर्वत्रेयमकृत्रिमा ॥७॥

7. *Labhate, tat-prayatnena parīkṣyaṁ tattvam-ādarāt.*
   Yataḥ svatantratā tasya sarvatreyam-akṛtrimā

भट्ट कल्लटः – यतः करणवर्गस्य अन्तश्चक्रसहितस्य विमूढस्याप्यमूढवत् उत्पत्तिस्थितिनिरोधाः, सोऽन्येषां चैतन्यापादने समर्थः कथं निःस्वभावः । तस्मात् तत् तत्त्वं यत्नेन परीक्षितव्यं योगिना । यथास्य करणादिषु चैतन्यदाने स्वातन्त्र्यम्, तथा परपुरादिष्वपि सम्भाव्यते; स्वातन्त्र्यस्य स्वस्वभावभूतस्य सर्वत्राकृत्रिमस्याभासात् यतो व्यक्तिः ॥६–७॥

Bhaṭṭa Kallaṭa: 6-7. *Yataḥ karaṇa-vargasya antaś-cakra-sahitasya vimūḍhasyāpyamūḍhavat utpatti-sthiti-nirodhāḥ, so 'nyeṣāṁ caitanyāpādane samarthaḥ kathaṁ niḥsvabhāvaḥ. Tasmāt tat tattvaṁ yatnena parīkṣitavyaṁ yoginā. Yathāsya karaṇādiṣu caitanyadāne svātantryam, tathā para-purādiṣvapi sambhāvyate svātantryasya sva-svabhāva-bhūtasya sarvatrākṛtrim asyābhāsāt yato vyaktiḥ.*

That Spanda principle, flowing as the group of inner causal divinities or Shaktis, *due to which all sense organs, though inert, acquire the ability of creation, sustenance, and dissolution, should be examined with great care and effort. By this examination Its innate independence pervading all can be experienced. (As such there is nothing inert per se but it is the degree of consciousness present in an object that makes it inert or insentient like a rock or sentient like a living creature.)*

Bhaṭṭa Kallaṭa: By contact with the power of this Spanda principle, the inner causal cycle of powers, such as Khechari (power of knowledge moving in the sky of consciousness), along with the inert sense organs, acquire the powers of creation, sustenance and dissolution. Then how can that principle itself be insentient, losing its own sentient nature? Therefore it is essential that the principle be examined tirelessly. Just as It is free to make consciousness flow through the inert limbs, animating them, It is also freely able to make another body and life-force sentient. The power of freedom of the universal "I AM" Aham-Vimarsh becomes the nature of every form, every thought. Hence by studying intuitively the inherent freedom of the universal I-consciousness, that freedom can be experienced effortlessly.

IN THE PREVIOUS VERSE the author, Vasugupta, showed that the Spanda principle transcends all feelings and subject-object relationships. In this verse, he shows that it is essential to examine with great honor the principle as the source empowering the presiding deities from which the inert sense organs – nose, ears, eyes, tongue, skin, larynx/tongue, hands, feet, organs of procreation and elimination – and the inner instruments – mind, intellect and ego – act as if they are sentient, performing their own cycles of creation, maintenance and dissolution. This independence of the Divine Power of Pulsation naturally pervades every atom of this universe including ourselves, and can be experienced by taking great interest and untiring efforts in examining this principle. The experience leads to human freedom, which is the fulfillment of life.

The word करणवर्ग - *Karaṇavarga* is the essential equipment without which creatures cannot function. In our functioning in the world we creatures as conscious beings experience a continuous interaction between the inner world of feelings - emotions or thoughts - and the outer world of names and forms. The outer world of names and forms causes emotions, thoughts and the sense of doership or ownership; and in turn, doership, thoughts and emotions cause or manipulate outer names and forms. The inner world consists of the three functions of thinking, deciding, and claiming or owning, conducted by mind, intellect and ego respectively as the instruments, and is based on the power of knowledge - ज्ञानशक्ति - *jñānaśakti*. The outer world consists of a set of senses of perception and senses of action. The five senses of perception - hearing, touching, seeing, tasting and smelling - functioning through ears, skin, eyes, tongue (taste buds of the tongue) and nose respectively are also based on the power of knowledge as products of ego. The five senses of action - speaking, touching/grasping, walking/moving, sexual gratification, and excreting, through the tongue and larynx, hands, feet, organ of sex and urination, and anus respectively - are also a product of ego, and are based on the power of action, क्रियाशक्ति - *kriyāśakti*. In this manner the thirteen instruments, three internal organs and ten external organs, perform thirteen functions. The organs form the *Karaṇavarga*, the set of essential equipment.

Though this equipment is inert, a particular type of flow of Spanda makes it appear sentient. For example, in deep sleep the equipment stays motionless, remaining inert, without the flow of Spanda, while in the waking state all equipment appears active. If the Spanda principle leaves the body then the body becomes inert and needs to buried or cremated. This easily shows that the body or the outer equipment is inert. Furthermore, the body is made of the five "inert" elements – space, air, fire, water, and earth. The inner equipment also is inert. A human mind and intellect depend very much upon food, consisting of the five elements, that is inert. For instance, when the sugar level goes down as in a diabetic patient, the patient's mind and intellect do not function properly. The patient gets agitated or sick. Because of chemical imbalance in the brain a person becomes depressed or insane. What about the ego? How is ego also inert? The ego is a mere reflection of the Spanda, like light in a mirror. The fact that ego, mind and intellect are inert, is stated in the *Bhagavad Gīta*.

भूमिरापोऽनलो वायुः, खं मनो बुद्धिरेव च ।
अहंकार इतीयं मे भिन्ना प्रकृतिरष्टधा ॥
अपरेयम् इतस्त्वन्यां प्रकृतिं विद्धि मे पराम् ।
जीवभूतां महाबाहो ! ययेदं धार्यते जगत् ॥ (गीता ७। ४–५)

Bhūmir-āpo 'nalo vāyuḥ, khaṁ mano buddhir-eva ca.
Ahaṅkāra itīyaṁ me bhinnā prakṛtir-aṣṭadhā.
Apareyam itas-tvanyāṁ prakṛtiṁ viddhi me parāṁ.
Jīvabhūtaṁ Mahabāho! yayedaṁ dhāryate jagat. (B.G. 7/4-5)

"Oh! Great Warrior Arjuna! My material, inert or gross nature is 'divided' *in eight ways: as earth, water, fire, air, and space and as mind, intellect, and ego. Know that my transcendental conscious nature which becomes the individual Self and which sustains this universe is different from the lower, subordinate, inert nature." Here the five elements earth, etc. are stated in their purest subtle form as "tanmātrās" or principles.*

Their combination, called पञ्चीकरण - *Pañcīkaraṇa* gives rise to the five gross elements. The ten sense organs - instruments of the outer equipment, again not in their physical but in their subtle functioning form, are products of the five principles. How the ten sense organs are created out of the five elements can be seen from the following table.

Principle	Organ (Sense) of Perception	Organ (Sense) of Action
Space	ears (hearing)	tongue/larynx (speech)
Air	skin (touch)	hands(touching, grasping)
Fire	eyes (seeing/"wandering")	legs (locomotion)
Water	tongue (tasting)	anus (excretion)
Earth	nose (smelling)	sex (procreation)

The relationship between the senses of perception and their corresponding principles is clear and well-known. But the relationship between the senses of action and these principles is not as well-known. The relation described in the table is based on Sage Vidyāraṇya's work titled *Pancadaśī*. He says,

रजोंऽशैः पञ्चभिस्तेषां क्रमात्कर्मेन्द्रियाणि तु ।
वाक्पाणिपादपायूपस्थाभिधानानि जज्ञिरे ॥ (१-२१)

Rajoṅ 'śaiḥ pañcabhis-teṣāṁ kramāt-karmeṅdriyāṇi tu
Vāk-pāṇi-pāda-pāyūpasthābhidhānāni jajñire (1-21)

From the Rajoguna aspect of the five elements, the organs of action in the respective order, called speech, hands, feet, anus, and genitals arose.

Based on the commentary on the work *Pancadaśī* written by Swami *Kāśikānanda*, (Swami *Kāśikānanda*, 42) we can see in reference to the above verse that from the rajoguna aspect of the elements the five organs of action are created. (From the sattvaguna aspect of the elements the five organs of perception are created.) Some might say even the eyelids keep fluttering so they could be classified as organs of action. But that is not correct. The organs of action include only those organs in which a voluntary function takes place. Eyelids flutter involuntarily, whereas the mind decides whether to function or not to function through the ten organs. There are certain activities which are allowed and some are prohibited for a seeker. For example, speaking to benefit someone or to communicate with others is allowed, but speech should not be used to hurt another being. Walking is allowed, but kicking is not. The awakening of Kundalini at Muladhar situated near the anus in front of a Guru is allowed but passing gas is not. Sex at the time of conception with one's spouse is allowed but sex with anyone else is not. Swami Kāśikānanda also says that it is easy to understand how space, hearing, and speech are related; but it is more difficult to relate other organs of action with the elements; though it is not impossible to speculate.

The five senses of perception and the three inner instruments are called the "city of eight" or "*puryaṣṭaka*" in Kashmir Shaivism.

In the verse of the *Bhagavad Gita* quoted above, the Lord says that the earth and other inert perceived objects are His material or subordinate, gross nature. One well-known meaning of "nature" is an "innate state." Two types of innate states seem to exist, one "as it is" and the other superimposed on it. Material nature, which is the product of māyā, is superimposed on the natural state, just as an individual's superimposed sorrow overlies the individual's natural state of bliss. The word "divided" refers to discernment of the Self as name and form, while "undivided" discernment transcends name and form, and sees the Self as Truth, Existence and Bliss.

Jnaneshwar Maharaj says regarding these verses in his *Jñāneshwari*, which is a commentary on the *Bhagavad Gita*:

तरी अवधारीं गा धनंजया । हे महदादिक माझी माया ।
जैसी प्रतिबिंब छाया । निजांगाची ॥
आणि इयेतें प्रकृति म्हणिजे । जे अष्टधा भिन्न जाणिजे ।
लोकत्रय निपजे । इयेस्तव ॥ (७। १५ – १६)

आणि या आठांची जे साम्यावस्था । ते माझी परम प्रकृति पार्था ।

तिये नाम व्यवस्था । जीवु ऐसा ॥
जे जडातें जीववी । चेतनेतें चेतवी ।
मनाकरवीं मानवी । शोक मोहो ॥
पैं बुद्धिचां अंगीं जाणणें । तें जियेचिये जवळिकेचें करणें ।
जिया अहंकाराचेनि विंदाणें । जगचि धरिजे ॥ (७। १९–२१)

Tarī avadhārīṅ gā Dhanañjayā, he mahadādika mājhī māyā
jaisī pratibiṁba chāyā, nijāṅgācī
Āṇi iyete prakṛti mhaṇije, je aṣṭhadhā bhinna jāṇije
lokatraya nipaje, iyestava (7 15-16)

Āṇi yā āṭhāñcī je sāmyāvasthā, te mājhī parama prakṛti Pārthā
tiye nāma vyavasthā, jīvu aisā
Je jaḍāteṅ jīvavī, cetaneteṅ cetavī
manākaravīṅ mānavī, śoka moho
Paiṅ buddhicāṅ aṅgīṅ jāṇaṇeṅ, teṅ jiyeciye javaḷikeceṅ karaṇeṅ
jiyā ahaṅkārāceni viṅdāṇeṅ, jagaci dharije (7 19-21)

"*Oh Arjuna! Then listen! These five primal elements, etc. are my maya, just as a body casts a shadow. It is called* प्रकृति *(Prakṛti) - the innate nature, and understand that it is made of eight different aspects and the "three worlds" are created due to the innate nature. And where these eight get merged with my innate nature, that is called 'jīva' a creature. ... The great nature makes the inert alive, a creature cognizant (of the manifestation), and makes the mind lament and become infatuated. Due to the proximity of this nature the intellect has power to discern, and it (this nature) gives credence to the universe by the dexterity of ego.*"

What Jnaneshwar Mahārāj says is the same as Kṣemarāja says in the text of Kashmir Shaivism, *Pratyabhijñāhṛdayam*,

स्वेच्छया स्वभित्तौ विश्वम् उन्मीलयति । (प्रत्यभिज्ञा. २)

Svecchayā svabhittau viśvam unmīlayati
(Pratyabhijñā. 2)

"*Chiti - the Universal Consciousness - unfolds the universe by Its own power of will projecting it on its own screen.*" And the will of

Consciousness is another name for Its Divine Pulsation - Spanda.

Jñāneśwar Mahārāj's commentary also brings out the gist of Verse 6, that the *Karaṇavarga*, the essential equipment for functioning for all creatures, is inert. What makes it function or appear sentient is Spanda. His use of the word "Jīva" is called Purusha in Kashmir Shaivism.

Verse 6 further states that the equipment functions by means of अंतरचक्र, - *Antar-cakra* - the group of inner powers or subtle causal divinities or the specific currents of the Spanda. This is a group of four types of powers: खेचरी - *Khecarī*, गोचरी - *Gocarī*, दिक्चरी - *Dikcarī*, भूचरी - *Bhūcarī*.

In the commentary of *Pratyabhijñāhṛdayam* aphorism 12, Kṣemarāja says:

> चितिशक्तिरेव भगवती विश्ववमनात् संसारवामाचारत्वाच्च वामेश्वर्याख्या सती, खेचरी – गोचरी – दिक्चरी – भूचरी –रूपैः अशेषैः प्रमातृ–अन्तःकरणबहिष्करण–भावस्वभावैः परिस्फुरन्ती, ...
>
> *Citiśaktireva Bhagavatī viśva-vamanāt saṁsāra-vāmācāratvācca Vāmeśvaryākhyā satī, Khecarī - Gocarī - Dikcarī - Bhūcarī -rūpaiḥ aśeṣaiḥ pramātṛ-antaḥ-karaṇa-bahiṣkaraṇa-bhāva-svabhāvaiḥ parisphu-rantī, ...*

The great consciousness-power, Spanda, is also called Vāmeśvarī since she

1. pours out (vama - means to pour out) or projects the universe (onto Herself)
2. behaves contrary (vāma - means contrary) to Her nature of all-pervasiveness, displaying the bound creatures passing through all lamentations, afflictions, cycle of birth and death
3. behaves contrary to the binding world for people who have received grace of the Guru.

The power of independence - Spanda - of Consciousness manifests in the form of the four types of powers खेचरी - *Khecarī*, गोचरी - *Gocarī*, दिक्चरी - *Dikcarī*, भूचरी - *Bhūcarī*. These powers infatuate Shiva who has manifested in the form of bound creatures. A seeker blessed by a Guru is helped by the same powers to experience innate independence. Thus the seeker becomes free.

Kṣemarāj states the 12th aphorism itself as follows:

तदपरिज्ञाने स्वशक्तिभिर्व्यामोहितता संसारित्वम् (प्रत्यभिज्ञा. १२)

Tada-parijñāne svaśaktibhir-vyāmohitatā saṁsāritvam
(Pratyabhijñā 12)

"Because of ignorance of one's being Universal consciousness itself, performing the five acts - creation, sustenance, dissolution, concealment and grace - a creature is deluded by its own powers and becomes bound by the world."

As the *Bhagavad Gita* and Jnaneshwar Mahārāj have said, the bound creature's ego holds the creature's universe together.

The bound creature only knows the first three acts: प्रवृत्ति-स्थिति-संहृति/ *Pravṛtti-Sthiti-Saṁhṛti* - creation, sustenance and dissolution, in whatever he or she does. In an individual's mind a thought arises, is maintained for a while, and dissolves as it makes room for the next thought. A person sees an object, keeps looking at it for a while and then turns his attention away. A hand grasps an object, holds it for a while and then releases it. These are various examples of creation, sustenance and dissolution. But the word used in the aphorism is not *utpatti* (creation) but *pravṛtti* which not only involves creation but also the intent that goes with creation and sets up a connection with the inner equipment. It indicates the independence of performing the voluntary action. Only when the inner equipment decides to do something can creation, sustenance and dissolution take place. Such is the power of the inner equipment. Thus along with creation, the equipment - with thirteen instruments - has the independence of performing or not performing a designated activity. This independence gives an individual the key to choose a life that sets him or her free. The three acts of creation, sustenance and dissolution are described in Verse 6. Kṣemarāja explains in the following commentary on the twelfth aphorism how the inner group of Shaktis - अंतश्चक्र - *Antaścakra* - the four set of Shaktis खेचरी - *Khecarī*, गोचरी - *Gocarī*, दिक्चरी - *Dikcarī*, भूचरी - *Bhūcarī* push bound creatures into further oblivion and at the same time help the seeker blessed by a Guru to experience independence and become Shiva while in the body. Further explanations are provided for a seeker's benefit.

- **Khecarī** This group of Shaktis move about in the infinite sky of knowledge. They actually move about in the sky of Consciousness. But when using the principle of Maya, Shiva gives up all-creativity, all-knowledge, all-power, timelessness, and omnipresence and becomes a limited creature taking on limited creativity, limited knowledge, attachment, time-bound in past, present and future, and limitation of place. These are known as five *Kañcukas* - *kalā, vidyā, rāga, kāla, niyati* respectively - in Kashmir Shaivism. Whereas a creature is usually bound by these five limitations, when blessed by a Guru, one breaks the five *kañcukas* and ascends to become Shiva and consequently has Shiva's unlimited qualities.

Gocari This group of Shaktis moves about in the four types of speech - परा, (*Parā*) subtlest, पश्यन्ती, (*Paśyantī*) subtler, मध्यमा (*Madhyamā*) subtle, वैखरी (*Vaikharī*) gross and inner instrument - mind, intellect, ego. For a bound creature it produces an endless chain of beneficial or harmful thoughts - "I will do this, then I will do that, I will go there..." or "If this doesn't work out ..., Why did I do that ..." and so on regarding planning and consequent lamentations. For a person blessed by a Guru this group of Shaktis gives a complete understanding of the seven items listed above, namely the four types of speech and mind, intellect and ego, and reveals the secret of the universe. For ages, countless saints all over India have extolled the value of importance of repetition of the name or mantra given by Guru. They have attained the goal of life by repeating just one name.

For example, Saint Tukārām says:

न कळे तें कळो येईल उगले । नामें या विठ्ठले एकाचिया ॥१॥
न दिसे तें दिसो येईल उगले । नामें या विठ्ठले एकाचिया ॥२॥
न बोलो तें बोलों येईल उगले । नामें या विठ्ठले एकाचिया ॥३॥
न भेटे तें भेटो येईल उगले । नामें या विठ्ठले एकाचिया ॥४॥
अलभ्य तो लाभ होईल अपार । नाम निरंतर म्हणतां वाचे ॥५॥
तुका म्हणे जीव आसक्त सर्वभावें । तरतील नांवें विठोबाच्या॥६॥

1. *Na kaḷe teṅ kaḷo yeīla ugale, nāmeṅ yā Viṭṭhale ekāciyā*
2. *Na dise teṅ diso yeīla ugale, nāmeṅ yā Viṭṭhale ekāciyā*
3. *Na bolo teṅ boloṅ yeīla ugale, nāmeṅ yā Viṭṭhale ekāciyā*
4. *Na bheṭe teṅ bheto yeīla ugale, nāmeṅ yā Viṭṭhale ekāciyā*
5. *Alabhya to lābha hoyīla apāra, nāma nirantara mhaṇatāṅ vāce*
6. *Tukā mhaṇe jīva āsakta sarvabhāveṅ, taratīla nāveṅ Viṭhobācyā*

What you don't understand will be understood by itself,
by just this one name of Vitthala.
What you don't see will be seen by itself,
by just this one name of Vitthala.
What you don't say will be said by itself,
by just this one name of Vitthala
What you don't meet will come to meet by itself,
by just this one name of Vitthala.
That which seems unattainable, will be attained to the fullest by itself,
by constant verbal repetition of the name.
Tukaram says, "The jiva bound in all kinds of ways,
will be redeemed by the one name of Vitthala."

(Viṭṭhala or Viṭhobā is a typical Maharashtrian name for the Lord of the Universe, Self.)

Dikcarī These shaktis work in the ten directions or senses - five senses of perception and five senses of action. For bound creatures these shaktis pull the attention to the world and away from the real treasure within, miring them in diversity and confusion. For a seeker blessed by a Guru the shaktis help turn attention within and dissolve the universe in Spanda. Only diligent examination or observation is adequate for this to occur. This will be explained later by a centering exercise.

Bhūcarī These shaktis function in the manifesting of the five basic principles - sound, touch, form, taste, smell - which for the bound creature make up the gross products or manifestations in the objective universe, while for the meditator they give the subtle inner divine experience of

1. various types of unstruck sound - *anāhata nāda*
2. touch - hair standing on end due to exhilaration or devotion
3. visions of inner chakras, saints, gods and goddesses, blue pearl
4. taste - of the sweet elixir - whose delicacy beats any delicious gross drink residing in the reservoir in front of head about which Saint Kabir talks in his work and
5. fragrances - a fragrance like Heenā.

In this manner the Spanda principle flowing through the inner group of shaktis makes the inert inner and outer equipment sentient, and makes it perform the three processes of creation, sustenance and dissolution just like Shiva. But in fact as the text *Pratyabhijñahṛdayam* says -

तथापि तद्वत्पञ्चकृत्यानि करोति ॥ (प्रत्यभिज्ञा.. १०)

Tathāpi Tadvat pañcakṛtyāni karoti. (Pratyabhijñāhṛdayam 10)

Even in the bound state the creature performs the five fold act of Shiva.

The fourth act of concealment and fifth of grace are hidden from the bound individual. What the bound creature does not know is the remaining two acts: तिरोधान - *Tirodhāna* concealment and अनुग्रह - *Anugraha* grace. This ignorance keeps the individual bound or belonging to the universe. The Seventh Verse gives a way of uncovering the secret and experiencing the innate Independence by directing our efforts into enquiring reverently into the Spanda Principle. In this inquiry we must transcend our "equipment" - ten senses or body, mind and intellect and ego. This can be done in a variety of methods. Depending on the mood, we can choose the method.

The three processes of creation, sustenance and dissolution have already been discussed earlier. The concealment and grace aspects can be discussed here. Let us take the examples of thought, seeing an object, and holding an object. When one thought dissolves and another thought arises, there is a gap. Actually, the gap describes a source of experiencing bliss. The longer the gap the greater is the experience of bliss. This will be discussed in the commentary on Verse 41. Giving importance or credence to a thought itself rather than to the gap between thoughts is concealment of essential bliss. Focusing instead upon the gap rather than the thoughts is grace. When a person sees an object, assigning solidity or reality to the object itself is concealment of the true nature of the object, while regarding the object as merely a triad of seer, seen and seeing exposes the reality of Vimarsh beneath, which is grace. When a hand grasps an object, giving solidity and claiming "I am holding the object," is an act of concealment, whereas becoming aware that the object has reality only so long as the mind is looking outward, is grace. There is nothing inherent in the three acts of creation, sustenance and dissolution to keep a person bound as long as doership or ownership of the individual is not involved. The key element in creation, as we have seen earlier, is the mind, transforming as the inner instrument. Here is a poem that teaches us to transform our outlook towards the world.

Once I met a man[33]

Once I met a man
His wife was buying corals
"Oh, these are so beautiful," she said
"Those won't look nice on me"
He turned to me and said,
"Oh, I don't see any difference.
All are Calcium Carbonate to me."
He knew the essence of it all
'Cause he was a chemical engineer.

Once I met a man
We were sitting on the edge of a lake
Water was calm, we saw our reflections
He pointed to them and said,
"It is easy to know
that these reflections we see
are not real.
If water was not there
We couldn't see them.
Now it is as easy to know
that these solid forms we see
are not real.
If mind was not there
We couldn't see them."
He knew the essence of it all
'Cause he was a Divine Engineer.

I bow to this man
He made this Life easy
As I understand

[33] The first man was the author's wife Chitra's great uncle, head of Associated Cement Companies in India, who visited them in the USA.
The second is author's Guru Baba Muktananda. The story is a narration of Chitra's dream of Baba in which he gave the teaching.

We don't need to look at
the phenomena
and get bewildered
Instead we could see
the Essence of it all
and just be surrendered. - *U.N.*

By grace of the Self, the act of concealment is known and the veil is removed to experience freedom.

Verse 7 describes the innate and spontaneous, effortless discovery of the Spanda Principle. Vasugupta says in his Shiva Sutras:

उद्यमो भैरवः ।
शक्तिचक्रसंधाने विश्वसंहारः । (शिवसूत्र १ – ५, ६)

Udyamo Bhairavaḥ.
Śakticakra-sandhāne viśva-saṁhāraḥ. (Shiva Sutra 1- 5, 6)

"An emergence of the 'I AM' awareness is Bhairava - Shiva. By union of the collective whole of shaktis through this intensive awareness the universe as something separate from consciousness disappears." In the commentary on the Sutras, Kṣemarāja says that this is the awareness which is also the power of independence – Svātantrya śakti. This innate independence is the warp and woof of the universe, including ourselves.

The effortless inquiry into this "I" is the means to experience our own independence as Shiva. Saints like Ramana Maharshi and Nisargadatta Maharaj always emphasized this inquiry. The first thought one gets after waking is "I AM." All other thoughts such as I am a man, I am a woman, are based on this I AM thought. Hence it is effortless to inquire into the first thought.

Inquiry includes examination. As one observes a particular activity performed by a sense organ one becomes conscious and the activity comes to stop and leads to the experience of Spanda. For example, when one watches the thought process it suddenly seems to slow down and stop. Thus the innate independence can be effortlessly experienced. A *dhāraṇā*, or a centering exercise given in the text *Vijñānabhairava* describes the following:

यत्र यत्राक्षमार्गेण चैतन्यं व्यज्यते विभोः ।
तस्य तन्मात्रधर्मित्वात् चिल्लयाद् भरितात्मता ॥ (श्लोक ११७, धारणा ९२)

Yatra yatrākṣa-mārgeṇa caitanyaṁ vyajyate Vibhoḥ.
Tasya tanmātra-dharmitvāt cillayād bharitātmatā.
(Verse 117, Dhāraṇā 92)

"On every occasion that the consciousness of the Omnipresent Reality is revealed through a sensory organ, in other words when a sense organ is functioning as a sentient object, one should contemplate upon the consciousness appearing through the sensory organ as the Universal Consciousness. Then one's mind will be dissolved in the Universal Consciousness and one will attain the State of Bhairava - Shiva."

The grace of saints transforms a person in a flash by giving the sincere seeker the experience of that Spanda. A repetition of the name given by a Guru or practicing inquiry into the "I AM" as shown by the Guru maintains only one thought in the mind and dissolves the endless chain of thoughts and the individual experiences freedom. The mind likes to form a habit of going to pleasurable objects. Once a Guru gives a seeker a taste of the inner bliss that transcends any external pleasure, the seeker's mind forms the habit of going inwards and experiencing the bliss and becomes free of worldly shackles. Thus a Guru established in consciousness is capable of establishing others in consciousness also. That is the purport of the sentence of BhattaKallata's commentary, "it is also freely able to make another body and life-force sentient."

It is for this reason that *Jñāneśwar Mahārāj* pays homage to Guru's grace. The following verses are the opening verses of the Chapter 12 of *Jñāneśwarī*. These verses are popular all over Maharashtra and it is a tradition to use them as the opening verses of a spiritual discourse among vārkaris – people who worship Lord Vithoba of Paṇḍharpur and do yearly pilgrimage. It is important to see that Jnaneshwar does not mention a specific Guru but rather the grace of the Guru, because Guru is a power of grace and is not a person. A person blessed by one Guru, experiences the same grace from all saints.

जय जय वो शुद्धे । उदारे प्रसिद्धे ।
अनवरत आनंदे । वर्षतिये ॥
विषयव्याळे मिठी । दिधलिया नुठी ताठी ।

ते तुझिये गुरुकृपादृष्टि । निर्वीष होय ॥
तरी कवणातें तापु पोळी । कैसेनि वो शोकु जाळी ।
जरी प्रसादरसकल्लोळी । पूरें येसी तू ॥
योगसुखाचे सोहळे । सेवका तुझेनि स्नेहाळे ।
सोऽहंसिद्धीचे लळे । लाविसी तू ॥
आधारशक्तिचिया अंकी । वाढविसी कौतुकी ।
हृदयाकाशपल्लकीं । परिये देसी निजे ॥
प्रत्यग्ज्योतीची वोवाळणी । करिसी मनपवनाची खेळणी ।
आत्मसुखाची बाळलेणी । लेवविसी ॥
सतराविये चे स्तन्य देसी । अनाहताचा हल्लरु गासी ।
समाधिबोधे निजविसी । बुझाऊनि ॥
म्हणोनि साधका तू माउली । पिके सारस्वत तुझिया पाउली ।
याकारणे मी साउली । न संडी तुझी ॥
अवो सद्गुरुचिये कृपादृष्टि । तुझें कारुण्य जयाते अधिष्ठी ।
तो सकळ विद्यांचिये सृष्टी । धात्रा होय ॥ (ज्ञानेश्वरी १२ । १-९)

Jaya jaya vo śuddhe, udāre prasiddhe
anavarata ānaṅde, varṣatiye
Viṣaya-vyāḷe miṭhī, didhaliyā nuṭhī tāṭhī
te tujhiye Gurukṛpādṛṣṭi, nirvīṣa hoya
Tarī kavaṇāteṅ tāpu poḷī, kaiseni vo śoku jāḷī
jarī prasāda-rasakalloḷī, pūreṅ yesī tū
Yogasukhāce sohaḷe, sevakā tujheni snehāḷe
So 'ham siddhice laḷe, lāvisī tū
Ādhāra-śaktīciyā aṅkīṅ, vāḍhavisī kautukī
hṛdyākāśapallakīṅ, pariye desī nije
Pratyag-jyotīcī vovāḷaṇī, karisī mana-pavanācī kheḷaṇī
ātmasukhācī bāḷaleṇī, levavisī
Satarāviyece[34] *stanya desī, anāhatācā hallaru gāsī*
samādhibodhe nijavisī, bujhāuni
Mhaṇoni sādhakā Tū māulī, pike sārasvata tujhiyā pāulī
yā kāraṇe mī sāulī, na saṅḍī tujhī

[35] Satarāvi means Seventeenth. Fifteen are the phases of the moon of worldly experiences - consisting of five tanmatras (sound, etc.), ten senses. The sixteenth phase is the individual self- which shines even in the dark phase of the moon. The seventeenth is the phase which has nothing to do with the objective, cognitive or subjective world. It is the phase where the nectar of God Consciousness flows. - *(Lakshman Joo, 46)*

Avo Sadguruciye kṛpādṛṣṭi, tujhe kāruṇya jayāte adhiṣṭhī
to sakaḷa vidyāñciye sṛṣṭī, dhātrā hoya
(Jñāneśvarī 12, 1-9)

Hail! Hail to Thee, Oh Purity! Generosity and Fulfilling!
You shower Bliss unceasing.
A person succumbs to poison
when the snake of worldliness entwines,
But the person is freed from poison
with just a look of Guru's grace.
In swelling waves of your cooling grace,
whom can the heat of misery raze
whom can grief set ablaze?
The bliss of Yoga celebrations,
Oh Source of Love! You've for those who serve you
The fulfillment feast of "I am That"
you treat them to.
From the lap of Ādhār Shakti[35]
you wake them up joyfully.
to the cradle of the sky of the heart,
take them to lie restfully.
The light of the Self You wave[36] *before them*
toys[37] *of the mind and prana You produce as a game.*
with ornaments of the Bliss of the Self You adore them.
You feed them the nectar of the Seventeenth[38]
lullabies of Anahata You sing
In the Samadhi of understanding
You leave them resting.
Therefore, You are the mother to seekers.
Knowledge ripens at your feet.
For this reason your shadow
I won't leave even a bit

Jai Gurudev!

---

[35] Kundalini situated at Muladhar Chakra
[36] Mothers, in India, worship their children as gods and goddesses and wave lights before them.
[37] controlling mind and prana is as easy as playing with a toy.
[38] Nectar in sahasrar

VERSE 8

TOUCH OF SPANDA WITH INDIVIDUAL

न हीच्छानोदनस्यायं प्रेरकत्वेन वर्तते ।
अपि त्वात्मबलस्पर्शात् पुरुषस्तत्समो भवेत् ॥८॥

8. Na hicchā-nodanasyāyaṁ prerakatvena vartate
Api tvātma-bala-sparśāt puruṣas-tatsamo bhavet.

भट्टकल्लटः – न च इच्छाप्रेषणेन करणानि प्रेषयति, अपि तु स्वस्वरूपे स्थित्वा केवलं यादृशी तस्येच्छा प्रवर्तते तथाविधमेव स बाह्यान्तरं कार्यमुत्पादयति, तेन न करणविषयमेव सामर्थ्यम्, किं तु तस्य सर्वत्र ॥८॥

Bhaṭṭa Kallaṭa: 8. Na ca icchā-preṣaṇena karaṇāni preṣayati, api tu svasvarūpe sthitvā kevalaṁ yādṛśī tasyecchā pravartate tathāvidhameva sa bāhyāntaraṁ kāryam-utpādayati, tena na karaṇa-viṣayam-eva sāmarthyaṁ, kiṁ tu tasya sarvatra.

Meaning of the verse, as per Kṣemarāj: It is not true that an individual behaves as the driving force of desires. It is due to the touch of Spanda - the power of the Self - that the individual becomes like That.

Another meaning: An individual does not live only as the driving force of the desires. But with just the touch of the power of the Self the individual will become like the Self.

(As continuation of the last verse-benefits of the inquiry:) Then (as a result of obtaining the innate independence of the Self), with just a touch of the Self an individual will become like the Self, then he no longer exists as the driving force of the desires.

(Continuation of the last verse:) Bhaṭṭa Kallaṭa says: Then an individual does not function according to the driving force of his or her desires; but abiding in one's nature, whatever Its wish is, following only that, he or she performs inner and outer activities. Then the individual's power is not limited to the objects of the essential equipment consisting of mind, intellect, and ego, and ten senses, but can work anywhere.

SEEKERS WANT to get in touch with their divinity. But whenever they close their eyes they find that their mind is spewing out thoughts after thoughts. They find they have so many desires, duties or obligations to attend to that they will never have time to find their mind at peace. These desires, problems, will, wishes, are called "इच्छा - *Icchā*" in the first part of the Verse. The restlessness they cause is like a driving force described by the word "नोदन - *nodana.*" The stimulation, direction, impelling is called "प्रेरकत्व - *prerakatva.*" "प्रेरकत्वेन - *prerakatvena*" means stimulated or driven by. People are stimulated to achieve the respective goals by their desires which act as a driving force. This is the story of existence of all humankind. In the first part of the verse, Vasugupta gives a hope to the seekers in this verse that an individual does not exist only as director of the driving force of desires. In the second part he assures us that with just a touch of the Spanda an individual can become free like Spanda.

In order to appreciate the importance and consequence of his statements, we need to consider the condition of people more fully. Seekers must know the answers to some essential questions: How do their desires arise? What is free will and can they exercise it? What is destiny and can they do anything about it? Does one have to live striving to attain desires? Can one live without having any desires? Does searching for Truth mean giving up all desires? Many philosophies and various saints have answered these questions.

How do desires arise? If a man is hungry he needs food. After he gets the food he is satisfied, and the desire for food is not there until all the food is digested. Such bodily needs are basic desires, which need to be fulfilled by every living creature. Then there are desires that arise in conjunction with the expression of one's innate talents. These talents can be regarded as products of the individual's destiny. There are some desires that arise by comparison with others, in a way arising out of jealousy. If somebody has a high-paying job then craving for a similar job is a worldly desire. To achieve all these desires people strive. These activities keep them busy. They identify themselves with their occupations.

Many people are bored soon after they retire from their occupations and die. Hardly any person feels fulfilled in his or her life.

The *Pratyabhijñā-hṛdayaṁ*, a text in Kashmir Shaivism, says:

चितिरेव चेतनपदादवरूढा चेत्यसंकोचिनी चित्तम् (प्रत्यभिज्ञाहृदयम् ५)

Citir-eva cetana-padād-avaruḍhā cetya-saṅkocinī cittam.
(Pratyabihijñāhṛdayam 5)

> *"Chiti - Universal Consciousness Itself descending from the stage of (unlimited) consciousness by contracting Itself becomes Chitta - a specific individual consciousness."*

This contraction limits total independence and omnipresence, omniscience and omnipotence, or *swātantrya, icchā, jñāna* and *kriyā śaktis* of Shiva, and an individual sentient form is created with an innate nature of limited *svātantrya* freedom, *icchā, jñāna* and *kriyā śaktis* – powers of desire, knowledge and action. In the creation of this world – plant life, viruses and bacteria, insects, fish, birds and mammals – Chiti (Self) expresses Itself as their respective natures. Thus a seed of a mango tree creates only a mango tree under suitable conditions and never a guava tree or coconut palm. A fish only exists in water and not outside. The intricacies and interdependence in nature are unfathomable. The plant life and creatures other than man behave in a very orderly fashion laid down by their respective natures. That nature is the *karaṇa varga* – mind, intellect, ego, and senses. Whereas the Self creates whatever It wishes and knows everything with total freedom, without limitations of space, time and causation, within Itself, since there is nothing besides It, creatures are limited by their body and create different things outside themselves in a certain time, space and causation. Yet basically there is no difference in the powers. Only the human being identifies himself or herself with the *karaṇa varga* - inner equipment, and tries to express the powers of independence, desire, knowledge and action, behaving as if independent of the universal I-consciousness. The purpose of inquiring into the power of the *karaṇa varga* is to come to touch the Self Itself. But people must inquire.

Most human desires start out of identification with the limited body. People are aware of their essential equipment - their senses and their mind, intellect and ego - but they are not aware of the power that drives the inner equipment. In the commentary on the Verses 26 and 27 in the Seventh Chapter of the *Bhagavad Gita*, Jñāneśwar Mahārāj describes beautifully how desires are born in individuals and the consequences an individual has to go through.

आतां थोडी ऐसी । गोठी सांगिजेल परियेसीं । जैं अहंकारतनूंसी । वाल्भ पडिलें ॥
तैं इच्छा हे कुमारी जाली । मग ते कामाचिया तारुण्या आली ।
तेथ द्वेषेंसी मांडिली । वराडिक ॥
तया दोघांस्तव जन्मला । ऐसा द्वंद्वमोह जाला । मग तो आजेन वाढविला । अहंकारे ॥
जो धृतीसि सदां प्रतिकूळु । नियमाही नागवे सळु । आशारसें दोंदिलु । जाला सांता ॥
असंतुष्टीचिया मदिरा । मत्त होवोनी धनुर्धरा । विषयांचां वोवरां । विकृतीसी असे ॥
तेणें भावशुद्धीचिया वाटे । विखुरले विकल्पाचे कांटे । मम चिरिले अव्हांटे । अप्रवृत्तीचे ॥
तेणें भूतें भांबावली । म्हणोनि संसाराचिया आडवामाजीं पडिली ।
मग महादुःखाचां घेतलीं । दांडेवरी ॥ (ज्ञानेश्वरी ७ । ६५–७१)

Ātāṅ thoḍī aisī, goṭhī sāṅgijela pariyesīṅ,
jaiṅ ahaṅkār-tanūṅsī, vālabha paḍileṅ.
Taiṅ icchā he kumārī jālī, maga te kāmāciyā tāruṇyā ālī,
tetha dveṣeṅsī māṅdilī, varāḍika.
Tayā doghāṅstava janmalā, aisā dvaṅdvamoha jālā,
maga to ājena vāḍahvilā, ahaṅkāre.
Jo dhṛtīsi sadāṅ pratikūḷu, niyamāhī nāgave saḷu,
āśāraseṅ doṅdilu, jālā sāṅtā.
Asaṅtuṣṭīciyā madirā, matta hovonī Dhanurdharā,
viṣayāṅcāṅ vovarāṅ, vikṛtīsī ase.
Teṇeṅ bhāva-śuddhīciyā vāṭe, vikhurale vikalpāce kāṅṭe,
mama cirile avhāṅṭe, apravṛttīce.
Teṇeṅ bhūteṅ bhāṁbāvalī, mhaṇoni saṅsārāciyā āḍavāmājiṅ padilī,
maga mahāduḥkhācāṅ ghetalī, dāṅḍevarī. (*Jñāneśvarī* 7/ 65-71)

Now I will tell you a little story; Listen. Ego and Body fell in love. From them was born a daughter, named Desire. She grew into a young maiden of passion. Desire wedded Jealousy.
From them was born a son, Infatuation-with-duality. The grandfather Ego nurtured him.
Infatuation-with-duality is always against pious Courage, and overstuffed with the juice of craving, he does not care for moral or society's rules.
O Arjuna! Drunk with the alcohol of dissatisfaction, he stays in the room of five senses with the wife named Temptation.

For the Inner Instrument, that Infatuation-with-duality spread thorns on the road of purity and opened the treacherous roads of forbidden acts. The people got confused by that and fell in the jungle of worldliness and were beaten by the huge rods of misery.

This is the tragedy of human life. That is the reason sages always emphasize the need to inquire into the Ego that falls in love with the body and starts the above-described tragedy.

Non-inquiry also leads most people to think only in terms of their capabilities. On the same lines as the first part of the current Verse, Ramana Maharshi says, "Man owes his movements to another Power, whereas he thinks that he does everything himself - just like a lame man bluffing that, were he helped to stand up, he would fight and chase away the enemy. ..."[39] They identify themselves as individuals separate from the universal I-Consciousness. They behave according to their memories and upbringing and work for the pursuit of happiness. They assume that in order to be happy they must fulfill their desires. Thus they behave as if they are the driving forces of their desires. Lord Krishna also says the same in the *Bhagavad Gita*:

प्रकृतेः क्रियमाणानि गुणैः कर्माणि सर्वशः ।
अहंकार-विमूढात्मा कर्ता ऽहमिति मन्यते ।। (भगवद् गीता ३।२७)

Prakṛteḥ kriyamāṇāni guṇaiḥ karmāṇi sarvaśaḥ,
Ahaṅkār-vimūḍhātmā kartā 'ham-iti manyate. (B.G. 3/27)

While all kinds of work are done by the modes of nature,
S/he who is ignorant of the Self thinks "I am the doer."

This doership has many consequences. After accomplishment of a certain task or desire the individual says, "I did this on my own. I am so happy I achieved my goal! I got what I wanted. ..." If the task is not accomplished, the same individual is disappointed, laments the actions taken, feels frustrated and becomes unhappy. Thus the individual goes through cycles of happiness and sorrow. Most people feel responsibility to work out their desires or obligations, and may

[35] *Talks with Sri Ramana Maharshi, Talk 210,* P. 184, Sri Ramanashramam, Tiruvannamalai, India, reprint 2000

sometimes feel helpless and limited. In both cases of success or failure they are stressed resulting in spoiling their health and premature aging. In success they are stressed to continue it and in failure they are stressed to get out of it. The poet king Bhartṛhari (600-700 A.D.) (*Bhartruhari*, 2) in his work titled *Vairāgyaśataka - Hundred Verses on Detachment* - says:

भोगा न भुक्ता वयमेव भुक्तास्तपो न तप्तं, वयमेव तप्ताः ।
कालो न यातो वयमेव यातास्तृष्णा न जीर्णा, वयमेव जीर्णाः ॥ (वैराग्य शतक ३४)

Bhogā na bhuktā vayameva bhuktās-tapo na taptaṁ, vayameva taptāḥ.
Kālo na yāto vayameva yātās-tṛṣṇā na jīrṇā, vayameva jīrṇāḥ.
(Vairāgya śataka 34)

"We did not enjoy the sense-pleasures, but the sense-pleasures enjoyed us. We have become victims to our sense objects. We did not experience any fire of purification, but we have surely been burnt by our activities in the world. We did not live to die, but we are dying to live trying to fulfill our desires; meaning that in living our life we have struggled so much that death is immanent for us. Our desires have not withered, but we have."

People become slaves to their senses. They do not know anything about their inner Self. That is the reason Kṣemarāj interprets the verse to let seekers know that it is the Spanda – the power of the Self, not they as individual entities, that acts through them as the driving force.

Because the ego is habituated to being extrovert, people feel that their happiness lies in obtaining some tangible things - such as money, good job, children, and so on. They make efforts to rearrange or manipulate various external situations to obtain the things they desire. Some offer prayers to various deities or visit temples on the advice of their friends or relatives so that their desires are fulfilled. Some might blame God who brings them suffering, while taking credit for good things happening in their life.

Because of worldly training, people may still give importance to their individuality. In working out their desires, people feel that they have free will and they are also bound by destiny. At any particular moment, they have freedom to take or not to take a specific action. Since they have no idea about the role of destiny and free will, people use their free will for striving after worldly gains while using the excuse of destiny for putting off the seeking the Self to a later date, not knowing whether they would be in a physical and mental condition needed to conduct an active search at that time. Some people also feel that they need to make effort for their successful life in the world, and turning within to touch the Self might be a waste of time. If a person turns to spirituality, the spouse may feel afraid that s/he would lose the good family life. For this reason, it is necessary to know what destiny and free will are.

One seeker asked of our Guru, Baba Muktananda, "Does man have free will or is everything destiny?" Baba answered, "Man does have free will; he can put forth his own self-effort. Whatever action you performed before becomes your destiny in the future. Therefore, in the *Bhagavad Gītā*[40] the Lord says to always put forth self-effort. Devotion to God comes from this free will.

Destiny cannot make your mind still. Destiny cannot make you meditate. Destiny cannot enter into you and make you become quiet. Therefore put forth self-effort. It is not good to depend on destiny all the time.

Always remember the Self. Always see your own Self. Look at others less. Always contemplate your own Self. There is nothing greater than you. ..."[41] (Swami Muktanand Paramhans, 53) This is where free will is to be used. It will be explained later how devotion for God comes from free will.

Destiny is that which brings our '*bhoga*' - our worldly pleasures and pains. Self-effort, free will is needed to attain '*yoga*' - union with the Self. Free will is that which gives us freedom to change our attitudes, our habits of turning outside to sense objects, and to touch the Self within.

When a question about free will and destiny was asked, Ramana Maharshi said,[42] "Whose will is it? 'It is mine,' you may say. You are beyond will and fate. Abide as that and you transcend them both. That is the meaning of conquering destiny by will. Fate can be conquered. Fate is the result of past actions. By association with the wise (satsang), the bad tendencies can be conquered. One's experiences are then viewed in their proper perspective.

---

[40] Several times - especially in Chapter 3

[41] *From the Finite to the Infinite*, Page 353.

[42] *Talks with Sri Ramana Maharshi*, Page 184

I exist now. I am the enjoyer. I enjoy the fruits of action. I was in the past and shall be in the future. Who is this 'I'? Finding this 'I' to be pure consciousness beyond action and enjoyment, freedom and happiness are gained. There is then no effort, for the Self is perfect and there remains nothing more to gain.

So long as there is individuality, one is the enjoyer and doer. But if it is lost, the divine Will prevails and guides the course of events. The individual is perceptible to others who cannot perceive divine force. Restrictions and discipline are for other individuals and not for the liberated.

Free will is implied in the scriptural injunctions to be good. It implies overcoming fate. It is done by wisdom. The fire of wisdom consumes all actions. Wisdom is acquired by association with the wise, or rather, their mental atmosphere."

This means that if we regard ourselves as individuals, we are subject to free will and destiny. But free will is actually the Independence of the Self, expressing as the present in our life with all Its power and knowledge.

A devotee asked Ramana Maharshi about the relation between free will and the overwhelming might of the Omnipotent (Self): "(a) Is the omniscience of God consistent with the ego's free will? (b) Is the omnipotence of God consistent with the ego's free will? (c) Are the natural laws consistent with God's free will?" Ramana Maharshi said:[43] "Yes. Free-will is the present appearing to a limited faculty of sight and will. The same ego sees its past activity as falling into a course of 'law' or rules - its own free-will being one of the links in that course of law.

The omnipotence and omniscience of God are then seen by the ego to have acted through the appearance of his own free-will. So he comes to the conclusion that the ego must go by appearances. Natural laws are manifestations of God's will and they have been laid down."

If we look at the present condition of our lives we see that we desired different things at different times and became restless by not attaining them. But destiny guided us in such a way as to find our niche in life that expresses all our talents and training. In other words there was always a divine intervention regardless of our desires. Then is there really a free will? As stated earlier by the people who

[43] *Talks with Sri Ramana Maharshi*, Page 31

were established in the Self, free will is the present moment, and it is our choice whether we direct our mind to the all powerful Self or to the limitations of ego, mind, intellect and body. So devotion for God can be practiced only in the present moment with free will. We always have a choice not to practice it.

In order to make the statement: "The individual does not exist as a stimulation of the driving force of the desires." which is the first part of the verse Vasugupta has prepared a background in terms of the previous verses.

In the verses discussed thus far, Vasugupta has shown us that Spanda, the universal I-consciousness of Shiva, creates the universe and creates experiences as an expression of its powers of desire, knowledge and action - *Icchā, jñāna* and *kriyā śaktis*. Because there is nothing opposing It, It is totally independent. It not only creates both sentient creatures and the insentient universe, but It also transcends the creation. It cannot be circumscribed by the phenomena of the universe. (Verse 1) We can experience the immanence and transcendence of the Self. (Verse 2) We experience three main states - waking, dreaming and deep sleep, and emotions of joy or sorrow, but actually there is something in us that is the real knower of these three states, that remains unaffected. (Verse 3) We become emotionally attached to our experiences, but it is Spanda that pervades all our experiences. (Verse 4) The Self is also beyond the triads of subject, object and perception, but It is never insentient. (Verse 5) Thus whatever states, feelings, or triads pertain to us as individual creatures, the Self creates these without modification in Itself, and it is for us to experience the Self through Its expressions. We can turn to It within as that which transcends our mind, intellect and ego. In the last two verses, Verses 6 and 7, Vasugupta talks about how we function. We function by means of our inert essential equipment, *karaṇavarga*, through which the light and power of the Self flows and makes these inert tools sentient. The inner equipment is the actual place where we experience the cycles of joy and sorrow, birth and death. Considering all these facts, we should contemplate with reverence the inner power of the Self, and experience Its independence or freedom. In the current verse Vasugupta gives us the details of the benefits of the inquiry into the Self.

There is another interpretation, which says that this verse elaborates the benefits of the inquiry described in the previous verse. Vasugupta says the result of Self-inquiry is that we are no more driven by the force of our desires, because with just a touch we would become like the omnipotent Self.

We see so many accomplished people in the world, who seem to have everything in terms of knowledge, societal position, fame and fortune, yet they are restless. There is a logical explanation to their state of mind in Vasugupta's current verse. Vasugupta's statement can be rewritten as a logically equivalent 'conditional' statement: If an individual does not behave as a driving force, then the individual is touched by the power of the Self and becomes like the Self. Consider the 'contrapositive'[44] of the verse: If an individual is not touched by the Self, or does not become like (does not identify with) the Self, s/he remains a driving force of her or his desires. Thus restlessness is common in man and continues till death, unless some time during the life he or she is touched by Spanda.

Seekers of Truth, as a consequence of contemplating the last verse and yet not knowing how to do Self-inquiry, might wonder where they stand between Universal I-Consciousness and Its power, working through their insentient, inert essential equipment to provide experiences of the sensory world and its pleasures. Universal grace descends upon those who sincerely question their existence. A Guru appears in their life, who by giving them the experience of peace and bliss of the inner Self, shows them that they are not different from the source of power within. When people experience directly that the happiness of the Self is far superior to whatever happiness they find from outer objects, they start Self-inquiry. They learn that the reason they feel happy when a desire gets fulfilled is that the mind gets quiet for a while soon after their desire is fulfilled; that it is the quiet mind that reflects the bliss of the Self. The Guru might even have powers because of abiding in the Self to fulfill the desire/s of the people taking refuge. The Guru shows people the difference between their wants and needs. Their wants are fulfillment of their desires, but their need is to be happy. Happiness is their innate nature independent of their desires. When they turn to the real power within and when their wants and needs are not in conflict their struggle is over; their happiness lies in the satisfaction of performing the actions caused by inner urges or inspiration, while abiding in the Self. Their will is not a separate driving force born out of ego's love for the body but is an expression of God's will. Their desires are the inner stirrings. The power of thought is such that it orients the person's capabilities, talents and other unknown factors of the universe necessary for the thought to come to fruition in such a way that success is automatic. That is also the purport of Bhaṭṭa Kallaṭa's commentary.

---

[44] A contrapositive is obtained by negating the first and second statements and reversing the order of If... then. For example, suppose p and q are statements. The contrapositive of "*If p then q*" is "*If not q then not p.*"

People get the experience of the Self by the grace of a Guru and want this experience to continue. But the seeds of desires – modifications of mind – called vṛttis in Sanskrit, are so strong that they keep drawing the individuals out. As soon as these seekers sit quietly for contemplation their minds become restless. They want to limit their desires. But the tendencies acquired keep making them work for desires.

Once Chitra, the author's wife and coauthor, had a dream. In the dream, she was standing close to the edge of a swimming pool. Nityananda Baba, one of the two successors of our Guru, Muktananda Baba, was resting on a lounge chair nearby on the deck. Chitra was standing facing Nityananda Baba with her back towards the pool. He looked at her and said, "People say that there is only one desire that needs to be fulfilled. But once that desire is fulfilled, one more desire follows it. And the cycle goes on. Since this is the situation, how can a person be free of desires?" Chitra felt that Nityananda Baba was describing precisely her predicament. She hesitated to answer the question. Suddenly she felt a jolt from inside, and she fell in the pool. She started to fight kicking and screaming, thinking that she was about to drown. She heard the words, "Relax! Relax!" These words were coming out from Nityananda Baba. The words were so soothing, that she started to relax.When she opened her eyes through shallow waters, she could see Nityananda Baba still sitting in the chair. As she relaxed completely she started floating in the water feeling very comfortable. At this time, Nityananda Baba got up, came to the edge of the pool, gave her a hand, pulled her out and said, "This is what you should do. You should take a plunge, a plunge into the Self." She understood that desires cannot be conquered by trying to fulfill them one by one. There is no end to this chain. Only by taking a plunge into the Self can one end the predicament.

In *Vijñānabhairava* there are several effective dhāraṇās to overcome desires and to experience the Self. One can use these dhāraṇās according to one's temperament.

झगितीच्छां समुत्पन्नामवलोक्य शमं नयेत् ।
यत एव समुद्भूता ततस्तत्रैव लीयते ॥ (श्लोक ९६, धारणा ७३)
इच्छायामथवा ज्ञाने जाते चित्तं निवेशयेत् ।
आत्मबुद्ध्यानन्यचेतास्ततत्सत्त्वार्थदर्शनम् ॥ (श्लोक ९८, धारणा ७५)
यत्र यत्राक्षमार्गेण चैतन्यं व्यज्यते विभोः ।
तस्य तन्मात्रधर्मित्वाच्चिल्लयाद्भरितात्मता ॥ (श्लोक ११७, धारणा ९२)

Zagitīcchāṁ samutpannām-avalokya śamaṁ nayet.
yata eva samudbhūtā tatas-tatraiva līyate.
(Verse 96, Dhāraṇā 73)
Icchāyām-athavā jñāne jāte cittaṁ niveśayet.
ātma-buddhyānanya-cetās-tat-sattvārtha-darśanam.
(Verse 98, Dhāraṇā 75)
Yatra yatrākṣa-mārgeṇa caitanyaṁ vyajyate Vibhoḥ.
tasya tanmātra-dharmitvāc-cillayād-bharitātmatā.
(Verse 117, Dhāraṇā 92)

Having observed a desire suddenly sprung up,
it should be calmed down.
Then it dissolves in the same place (Spanda)
from where it originated.
When a desire or knowledge arises,
one should focus on that desire or knowledge
With one-pointedness as the very Self.
Then one realizes the true Principle - Self.
Through whatever sense organ
the Omnipresent Reality's consciousness is revealed
Knowing that It is only the Reality Itself,
one's mind is filled with the Self.

In the second part of the verse Vasugupta discusses the advantages of touching the power of the Self or आत्मबलस्पर्श *Ātma-balasparśa*. He says the aspirant becomes like the Self. Bhaṭṭa Kallaṭa illustrates this point in his commentary. He emphasizes that the aspirant then performs all the inner and outer actions according to what the inner stirring, Spanda, directs. S/he is not limited to the sphere of influence of the inner equipment but is effective everywhere. The inner stirring is always there.

Question: Can one live without any desires or activities?
Answer: For a living being it is not possible to stay without performing any actions, says Lord Krishna in the *Bhagavad Gita*.

न हि कश्चित् क्षणमपि जातु तिष्ठत्यकर्मकृत् ।
कार्यते ह्यवशः कर्म सर्वः प्रकृतिजैर्गुणैः ॥ (भगवद् गीता ३।५)

Na hi kaścit kṣaṇam-api jātu tiṣṭhatyakarmakṛt.
Kāryate hyavaśaḥ karma sarvaḥ prakṛtijair-guṇaiḥ. (B.G. 3/5)

No one can remain even for a moment without doing work.
Everyone is made to act helplessly due to the qualities born of nature.

If we identify with the *karaṇavarga* - the inner equipment, we are led to actions limited to their sphere of influence as determined by sense objects, actions that create cycles of sorrow and happiness as discussed earlier. Instead, if we touch the power of Spanda, we are led to actions effective everywhere without limitations or hindrance as pointed by Bhaṭṭa Kallaṭa.

These actions are described in *Shiva Sutra* 1. 13:

इच्छाशक्तिरुमा कुमारी ।

Icchā śaktir-Umā kumārī

The will-power of the yogi who abides in the Self is the virgin Umā, the splendor of Śiva.

Its interpretation by Kṣemarāj brings out the full impact of the aphorism. The will-power of the Yogi is Umā - the splendor of Shiva - who, abandoning all attachment, brings about union with Shiva - the Self. This is the yoga of detached action and is also the message of the *Bhagavad Gītā*. The word *kumārī* ordinarily meaning a virgin can be interpreted as *ku* and *mārī*. *Ku* means the state of Māyā which brings out a sense of difference and *mārī* means who destroys. The word *kumārī* then means the one whose nature is to destroy a sense of difference. As a virgin she is never the object of enjoyment but she is the enjoyer. In abiding with the Self, the Yogi acquires Umā, the independent power of the Self intent on the play of manifesting the universe, regarding this universe is a play of consciousness. Thus the desire of the Yogi is superior to ordinary powers of knowledge and action. It is unimpeded everywhere.

In conclusion we can sing the following prayer for dissolving our limited individuality into the Self.

बना दो बुद्धिहीन भगवान
तर्क शक्ति सारी हीर लो, हरो ज्ञान विज्ञान ।
हरो सभ्यता शिक्षा संस्कृति, नये जगत की शान ॥
विद्या धन मद हरो हरो हे, हरे सभी अभिमान ।
नीति भीति से पिंड छुडा कर, करो सरलता दान ॥
नहीं चाहिये भोग योग कुच्छ, नहीं मान सम्मान ।
ग्राम्य गंवार बना दो तृणसम, दीन निपट निर्मान ॥
भर दो हृदय भक्तिश्रद्धा से, करो प्रेम का दान ।
प्रेम सिंधु निज मध्य डुबो कर, मिटाओ नाम निशान ॥

Banā do buddhi-hīna Bhagavān
Tarka śakti sārī hīra lo, haro jñāna vijñāna.
Haro sabhyatā śikṣā saṅskṛti, naye jagata kī śāna.
Vidyā dhana mada haro haro he, hare sabhī abhimāna.
Nīti bhīti se piṇḍa chuḍā kara, karo saralatā dāna.
Nahīṅ cāhiye bhoga yoga kucha, nahīṅ māna sammāna.
Grāmya gaṅvār banā do tṛṇasama, dīna nipaṭa nirmāna.
Bhara do hṛdaya bhakti-śraddhā se, karo prema kā dāna.
Prema siṅdhu nija madhya ḍubo kara, miṭāo nāma niśāna.

Refrain: O Lord, take away my differentiating intellect.
1. O, take away all the power of reasoning,
Take away knowledge - indirect and direct.
O, take away my civility, training, and culture,
This whole world's captivating effect.
2. Take away my learning, wealth and conceit.
Remove my ego in every respect.
Getting rid of my beliefs and fear,
Grant me simplicity that is direct.
3. I don't want any pain or pleasure, or union with god.
I want no acclaim or respect.
Make me rustic, unsophisticated, insignificant like grass,
humbly boundless in every aspect.
4. Fill this heart with devotion and conviction,
Grant me Love so perfect
Submerging me in the ocean of Your Love,
End this separate existence in effect.

VERSE 9

STOP AGITATING AND EXPERIENCE SPANDA

निजाशुद्ध्यासमर्थस्य कर्तव्येष्वभिलाषिणः ।
यदा क्षोभः प्रलीयेत तदा स्यात्परमम् पदम् ॥९॥

9. Nijāśuddhyā-asamarthasya kartavyeṣvabhilāṣiṇaḥ
Yadā kṣobhaḥ pralīyeta tadā syāt-paramaṁ padam.

भट्ट कल्लटः – स चास्य आत्मबलस्पर्शः सहजया अशुद्ध्या व्याप्तस्य कार्यमिच्छतोऽपि न भवति, किन्तु यदा क्षोभः अहमिति प्रत्ययभावरूपोऽस्य प्रलीयेत, तदास्य भवति परमे पदे प्रतिष्ठानम् ॥९॥

Bhaṭṭa Kallaṭa: - 9. Sa cāsya ātmabala-sparśaḥ sahajayā aśuddhyā vyāptasya kāryam-icchato 'pi na bhavati, kintu yadā kṣobhaḥ 'aham-iti' pratyaya-bhāva-rūpo 'sya pralīyeta, tadāsya bhavati parame pade pratiṣṭhānam.

Due to an individual's own impurity, the individual is incapacitated, unfulfilled, and is therefore desirous of worldly gains to attain fulfillment. When the individual's agitation disappears, the individual experiences the highest state.

An individual cannot touch the Spanda – the Power of Self, because the individual is pervaded with innate impurity, and also because the individual is involved in working towards fulfilling her/his desires. But when restlessness of the delusive belief 'I am the body,' dissolves, then the individual is established in the highest state.

IN THE EARLIER VERSES, it is said that an individual is a manifestation of the Self and the Self is the substratum of all thoughts and activities of the individual. Reading the last verse, one may then wonder why Vasugupta has mentioned the necessity of touching the Self. The reason for this is the fact that an individual assumes and experiences a separate position as compared to the Self and loses the contact with the Self. In this verse Vasugupta describes the various impurities, which make us think ourselves to be insignificant, separate or unworthy, and unfulfilled. These impurities come in the way of our touching the Self. He also says that no sooner do we clean up these impurities than we are in the highest state.

"What are these impurities, and how do they arise?" Analyzing this question leads to the methods of cleaning them up and establishes us in the state that Vasugupta has mentioned in the last part of the verse.

We human beings are reduced to the plight of regarding ourselves as limited in knowledge and capacity. However, the fact remains that we are manifestations of the omnipresent, omniscient and omnipotent Self. We are so wrapped up in carrying out our day-to-day duties that we don't find time or are not inclined to think about this fact. This negligence on our part makes us feel unfulfilled and crave for fulfillment in life. All our efforts seem to go towards achieving material fulfillment and basic sense pleasures. We could be fulfilled. Vasugupta says when क्षोभ *Kṣobha*, our agitation and stress caused by this running around, subsides, we are established in the Self. Our priorities are all mixed up. As seekers we know that we are consciousness. We agree with the first aphorism of *Shiva Sutras* "चैतन्यम् आत्मा" "*Caitanyaṁ Ātmā*" "Consciousness is the Self," but we do not do anything further with it. We do not enquire about why we feel separated, unfulfilled and bound. We just accept our limitations. We don't care for the full impact of the first aphorism. We do not know what it means to experience the Self in Its full splendor. That is because we are deluded by our limited knowledge. Actually, this forms the second aphorism of *Shiva Sutras*: "ज्ञानं बन्धः" "*Jñānaṁ bandhaḥ*" "Limited knowledge is bondage." We see our body and capability and have an innate feeling that we are limited. In addition, we see the world and many things we have to deal with in this world. We accept some and reject others. We look forward to the fruits of our actions. Some fruits turn out to be what we expect, which make us happy, and some disappoint us. We go through the swings of happiness and sorrow. We feel we are bound to the world. That takes away all our sense of freedom. The third aphorism says exactly that. "योनिवर्गः कलाशरीरम्" "*Yonivargaḥ kalāśarīram*" "The source of the world - Māyā and activities that are extensions of our body-mind complex - are also bondage." Studying these three aphorisms in detail is the answer to the question about the origin of the impurities. The impurities do not come from outside like a pile of dirt. These impurities are innate.

The word Chaitanya is derived from the Sanskrit verb "चित्", "*Chit*" which means to exist, to know, to understand, to observe, to perceive, to desire. Since there is nothing else to oppose It, the Self is free to know and do everything it desires. It does everything spontaneously, effortlessly. Thus the word chaitanya or consciousness implies total freedom to desire, know and act, transcending time, space, causation or effort. The Self is the mass of consciousness and bliss – चिदानन्द घनस्वात्मा - *cidānanda ghana-swātmā.* It performs the fivefold act - creation, sustenance, dissolution, concealment and grace. Its pulsation is the "Aham" - "I am" that expresses the existence of the Self, and is the root and potential of all creation. The Self with its independence contracts to "Idam" - "This" creating differences in the form of the universe and creatures. Only the total freedom is capable of doing all this. The rise of the desire to create differences and limit freedom is the foremost impurity. Out of this impurity arise the three impurities of limited existence, limited doership, limited desires and consequent experience of sorrow and happiness which are called *āṇava, kārma* and *māyīya malas* respectively.

It is the Self as a creature that, by deliberately training to external aspects, makes Itself forget Its unlimited nature. We look at our body and have the feeling that we are the body. This contraction leads to our first innate impurity of regarding ourselves as limited in body. The second aphorism "Limited knowledge is bondage" describes this innate impurity as "आणव मल" "*Āṇava mala,*" which is the impure feeling of "I am limited like an atom. I am insignificant." This limited knowledge or ignorance leads to two kinds of thoughts that reflect -

- "a loss of independence - contraction of our understanding that our nature is consciousness alone, that results in contraction of omniscience. That is one type of thought." स्वातन्त्र्यहानिर्बोधस्य - *Swātantrya-hānir-bodhasya,* बोधस्य चिन्मात्रस्य स्वातन्त्र्यहानिर्ज्ञातृत्वसंकोचः एकः प्रकारः- *Bodhasya cinmātrasya swātantrya-hānir-jñātṛtva-saṅkocaḥ ekaḥ prakāraḥ* - (Iṣwara Pratyabhijñā and Bhāskari commentary 3.2.4)
- "ignorance of independence – leading to a false pride of negating the omnipotence of that independence, regarding it as different from us. That is the second type of thought." स्वातन्त्र्यस्याप्यबोधता - *Swātantryasyāpyabodhatā,*

> स्वातन्त्र्यस्य कर्तृत्वस्य अबोधता बोधव्यतिरिक्ताभिमानः द्वितीयः प्रकारः - *Swātantryasya kartṛtvasya abodhatā bodha-vyatiriktābhimānaḥ dvitīyaḥ prakāraḥ* (Iṣwara Pratyabhijñā and Bhāskari commentary 3.2.4)

These are not two separate impurities, but two aspects of the ignorance of the independent nature. The first aspect leads to thinking the Self as non-Self and the second leads to identifying the body with the Self or the non-Self with Self, thus regarding the pieces of matter that comprise the body and mind as the Self. The first word "निजाशुद्ध्या" of the current verse describes this āṇava mala created by the Self's freewill to contract. Vasugupta says that an individual thus becomes incapacitated and imperfect.

There is a famous quotation of Shankaracharya: "ब्रह्म सत्यं जगन्मिथ्या जीवो ब्रह्मैव नापरः ।" "*Braḥma satyaṁ jaganmithyā jīvo Braḥmaiva nāparaḥ*" "The world as world is an illusion. And an individual is no other than the Self." There are some students of Kashmir Shaivism who disregard Shankaracharya's calling the world an illusion. There are some students of Vedanta who regard calling the world as play of consciousness, as in Kashmir Shaivism, equally absurd. But all the saints, such as our Guru Swami Muktanand, or Ramana Maharshi, who have gone beyond doctrines and are established in the state Vasugupta mentions, regard Vedanta and Kashmir Shaivism as equally important. They reconcile the various statements of Kashmir Shaivism and Vedanta. This can be seen in their works. For example, in many places in *Talks with Sri Ramana Maharshi*, Ramana Maharshi has pointed out the similarity of statements of both the doctrines. The following story illustrates a very important point.[45]

One day a sage was explaining Shankaracharya's verse cited above to his audience on the banks of the river Ganges. There was an intellectual who could not stand the sage's explanation. The intellectual started arguing with the sage. "How can this be? God as Universal Consciousness is unlimited. He has unlimited knowledge He is omniscient - He is a 'Sarvajna,' while an individual is limited in all respects. He has limited knowledge - He is an 'Alpajna'." The sage said, "Let go of these attributes - limited and unlimited - or Alpa and Sarva. What remains is only "Jna" or Knowledge. This way they are one." The intellectual still kept on arguing. The sage thought that this person needed a concrete example for

---

[45] Story from the *Nectar of Discourses on the Seventh Chapter of the Gita* - Swami Maheshwarananda.

understanding. He said, "I will explain to you another way. First bring me water of the Ganges in this *kamandalu* (water pot). I am very thirsty. Mind you I don't drink any other water. I only drink Ganges' water." So he gave his *kamandalu* – water pot - to the person. The person walked to the river, filled the *kamandalu* with water and brought it to the sage. The sage said, "Are you sure this water is Ganges' water?" The intellectual said, "Swamiji, you have seen me going to the Ganges and getting the water. Why do you ask?" The sage said, "On the banks of the Ganges, there are trees. In the river there are many boats. Many people are taking bath. But I don't see any trees, any boats in this water. The water is so little that let alone taking a bath, I can't even put my foot in it." The person said, "How is it that you don't understand that because of limitations of the pot you cannot see the trees, etc. There is no difference in the water." The sage said, "That's exactly what I have been trying to tell you. Just as purity, sweetness, and the cooling effect of the Ganges' water exists also in this limited pot, so purity, Existence, Consciousness, and Bliss are the nature of the Supreme Reality and also of every, seemingly limited, individual."

There is a similar dialogue between a devotee and Ramana Maharshi.[46] (*Sri Ramana Maharshi*, 38)

Devotee: 'Aham' (I) applies to the individual and also to Brahman. It is rather unfortunate.

Maharshi: It is *upādhi bheda* (differences in limiting adjuncts - attributes). The bodily limitations pertain to the aham of jīva (individual), whereas the universal limitations pertain to the 'aham' (I) of Brahman (Self). Take off the upādhi; the I is pure and single.

The pure "I am" is the Spanda and "this" is the bliss of the Self. If the "Idam" does not arise, there is no universe, there is no contraction of the Self, and there is no experience of limitation due to contraction. We cannot ask why it is necessary to have the second thought "Idam," but we can only observe that it invariably happens. "I am" is called the common Spanda and is different from the inert objects. Knowledge and action or Prakāśa (light) and Vimarśa ("I am" awareness) are not separate things but two aspects of the Spanda – the pulsating

[46] *Talks with Sri Ramana Maharshi* P.419 Sri Ramanashramam 2000

nature of the Self. Actually action is the manifestation of knowledge and knowledge is the precursor of action. Vimarśa is the external aspect of Prakāśa and Prakāśa is the internal aspect of Vimarśa. "This" is the dynamism of "I am." "I am" is the seed and "this" is Its extension. In the pulsating Shiva resides the universe and the universe is the efflorescence of Shiva. We also experience this every day. When we are asleep we are not aware of our existence. "I am" and the world are in the seed form in sleep. Yet as soon as we get up, the first thought is "Aham" - "I am" and then we become aware of "idam" - "this": the body and the world around. Yet it is still a thought.

Having the "this" thought is the impurity or dirt. This "dirty" feeling is due to the ignorance of our nature described earlier. As a result of this ignorance we feel we are imperfect and unfulfilled. We need to have something to make our life perfect. Because of *āṇava mala* our mind is ignorant of its perfect omniscient and omnipotent inherent nature, and our attention is directed to the world, actions, sense pleasures and sense objects. Our desires are born and we put in a lot of effort to fulfill those desires. This is also regarded as an impurity called "*Kārma mala.*" The effect of both *malas* is that while doing myriad activities we feel overwhelmed, incapacitated or stressed. Our desires, obligations and responsibilities seem endless. As a result another impurity called "*Māyiya Mala*" arises. It consists of cycles of happiness and sorrow, suffering and agitation. By the attainment of the desires we become happy for a few moments and by non-attainment we are sad. We also experience other emotions. We are angry - at ourselves if our actions fail, at somebody else if we think they are withholding our object, or at some thing or current situation. We are greedy, and we feel an insatiable appetite for sense-pleasures that is inherent in them. We are afraid or anxious that we may not get what we desire, or that we may lose what we have. We are attached to a person, to a career, or to an object. We are proud of our scholarship, our piety, our attainments, our possessions. We are jealous if somebody else has what we want or do not have. Since the chain of desires and actions continues, the cycle of happiness and sorrow continues. In addition, we may have bodily afflictions and health problems that arise out of no desire of our own. Some may be proud of their physique and beauty. Pertaining to the body other emotions such as anger, greed, fear, attachment, jealousy may also arise. These emotions also cause us happiness and sorrow. This is "*Māyiya mala.*" When we experience an emotion, we are overcome by it. In other words, our total being, actually our mind, seems pervaded by that emotion.

A poet saint, Sundardas says,

जो मन नारि कि ओर निहारत, तौ मन होतहि ताहिकु रूपा ।
जो मन काहुसूँ क्रोध करै पुनि, तौ मन है तबही तदरूपा ॥
जो मन मायहि माय रटै नित, तौ मन बूडत माय की कूपा ।
सुन्दर जो मन ब्रह्म विचारत, तौ मन होतहि ब्रह्मस्वरूपा ॥

Jo mana nāriki ora nihārata, tau mana hotahi tāhiku rūpā.
Jo mana kāhusūṅ krodha karai puni, tau mana hai tabahī tadarūpā.
Jo mana māyahi māya raṭai nita, tau mana būḍata māya kī kūpā.
Sundara jo mana Braḥma vicārata, tau mana hotahi Braḥma-svarūpā.

The mind that contemplates a woman, takes on the form of that woman.
The mind that harbors rage, instantly goes ablaze.
The mind that ruminates on (maya) delusion, sinks in the pit of delusion.
"The mind," Sundardas says, "that contemplates the Self, becomes the Self."

Since we want to get rid of our restlessness, we must study our strengths and weaknesses and get rid of our weaknesses. Our main strength is that we are not different from the Self. We must make our mind contemplate the Self. This happens if our mind tastes how profound the experience of the Self is. This can happen neither by reading, nor by self-effort, but only by the grace of the Guru - Self. Our weakness is that we have been baffled by maya. Out of the maya arise the three *malas* - impurities described earlier.

The word *māyā* - माया - is used in two ways. Maya is *māyā-śakti* – the power of maya; and maya is also *māyā-tattva* – the principle of maya. The desire to create the universe, to contract and create different creatures and things arises out of the Bliss (Ananda) of Spanda, the Shakti of Shiva. Out of Spanda thus arises the *Sadāśiva* principle - – the power of will (*icchā - śakti*) to affirm the "this" or objective aspect of Being. The "I am" aspect is still predominant in Sadashiva, and the objective or "this" aspect is still dormant. Both the subject and object are still pure consciousness, with consciousness appearing as an object to the subject. This universal experience can be expressed as "I am this." Out of Sadashiva arises the *Īśwara* principle –in which the power of knowledge – *jñāna śakti* - is predominant as the awareness, "This am I." The blossoming of the universe is yet more defined. Out of the Ishwara aspect arises the *Śuddha Vidyā* principle, in which the power of action – *kriyā śakti* - predominates. In the Shuddha Vidya stage, "I" and "This" are equally balanced, clearly distinguished, yet not separated from each other. The real nature of the Divine is still not veiled at this level. This is all the creation of Mayashakti. The powers of desire, knowledge, and action of the Self are its total fulfillment and require no effort on the part of the Self for their expression.

From there arises the *māyā tattva* or *māyā* principle, in which the veiling of the Self takes place. Omniscience and omnipotence are reduced to the limited knowledge of differences resulting in a limitation of power to act. This is accomplished by the five coverings of maya: omnipotence, the power of action - contracts to कला - *kalā* - limited creativity; the power of knowledge – *jñāna śakti* contracts to विद्या - *vidyā* - limited knowledge; the power of will - *icchā śakti* contracts to राग - *rāga* - desires and attachments; eternity – *nityatva* reduces to काल – *kāla* - limitation of time or succession; all pervasiveness – *vyāpakatva* reduces to नियति – *niyati* – limitations of space, cause and form. With these limitations in place, the Self contracts due to *mayashakti*, and individual souls appear. It is Shiva who forgets his own nature and becomes a jiva – an individual soul with limited powers. The individual is always aware of his or her smallness, imperfection. This impurity आणव मल - *āṇava mala* is the limitation of individuality. The power of knowledge becomes the intellect, mind, ego and the senses or the inner equipment – *karaṇa varga* of the individual soul. This limitation is मायीय मल - *māyīya mala* – impurity due to maya. It is the consciousness of differences. Then the limited power of action impels one to perform good and bad actions. Organs of action are formed. This impurity is कार्म मल – *kārma mala* – limitation of activity. Traces of actions arising from desires – called वासना – *vāsanā* become a propelling force for an individual thus going through the cycles of births and deaths. Thus the total freedom of the Self reduces to limited freedom or bondage.

This maya principle has many interpretations in Kashmir Shaivism.

- maya – comes from the Sanskrit root *mā* - to measure out, and *yā* who or which. Maya is that which is measurable thus the experience of Reality is limited, measurable.
- maya – comes from the Sanskrit root *mā* - to deny, and *yā* who or which. Maya is that which cannot be denied, meaning She is eternal. In the sense that she does not exempt anyone – sage or a rogue, rich or poor, learned or ignoramus - from her power of veiling. She puts her veil on every atom and molecule, so that the individual is diverted from the Self. Only from the Self's point of view is maya *mā* - no, and *yā* who; the one who does not exist.

- maya – comes from the fact that the universe remains in her womb. Maya is the mother of the universe - मात्यस्यां विश्वम् *mātyasyāṁ viṣvam* (*Tantrāloka Vivek* 9.152).(Mishra, 23)
- maya – is that which pervades the five senses – sound, touch, form, taste, and smell - सर्वत्र मातीति *sarvatra matiiti* – (Tantrāloka Vivek 9.152)
- maya – is that which the yogis regard worth rejecting and separate from themselves – मीयते हेयतया परिच्छिद्यते योगिभिः *mīyate heyatayā paricchidyate yogibhiḥ*. (*Tantrāloka Vivek* 9.152)
- maya – is that power through which the Self establishes the objective aspect, in which that which is non-different from Itself appears as different. – स्वात्माभिन्नमपि भावमण्डलं शिवो यया मिमीते भिदा व्यवस्थापयतीति *Svātmābhinnam-api bhāva-maṇḍalaṁ Śivo yayā mimīte bhidā vyavasthāpayatīti* (*Tantrāloka Vivek* 9.152)
- maya - is described as non-discrimination (ignorance) of the existence of the limiting principles ranging from contraction of creativity - kalā, etc. to earth कलादीनां तत्त्वानाम् अविवेको माया - *Kalādīnāṁ tattvānām aviveko māyā.* (*Śiva Sūtras* III - 3) The five principles discussed earlier and their consequences as individuals, senses, and the five subtle and gross principles upto earth conceal the individual's real nature.

Our agitation stops by cleansing ourselves of the three impurities - malas. Knowing that our malas or weaknesses arise due to the maya-principle, we must know how to overcome the maya-principle. Our strength is that we are not different from the Self, so we do not need do any further effort, we are established in the Self. In *Vijñānabhairava Bhairava* (Shiva) says to Devi (Parvati):

> माया विमोहिनी नाम कलायाः कलनं स्थितम् ।
> इत्यादिधर्मं तत्त्वानां कलयन्न (न्ना) पृथग्भवेत् ॥ (श्लोक ९५, धारणा ७२)

> *Māyā vimohinī nāma kalāyāḥ kalanaṁ sthitam.*
> *Ityādi-dharmaṁ tattvānāṁ kalayanna (nnā) pṛthagbhavet.*
> (Verse 95, – *Dhāraṇā* 72)

"Māyā is delusive, the function of kalā and four other coverings, and its function as previously discussed is limited activity. Considering the functions of the various principles (tattvas) in this way, one does not remain separate any longer. (A person becomes isolated from maya and is established in the Self.)"

This dharana – centering exercise – must be practiced by all seekers. Understanding of these functions and the conviction that maya is delusive is not easy to attain by one's own effort. We will go into more techniques in Verse 20. By knowing these functions of the principles, our restlessness due to the delusive knot or belief that 'I am the body,' dissolves, and as Bhatta Kallata says in his commentary, the individual is established in the highest state.

Swami Samartha Rāmdas (*Samarth Ramdas*, 29) says in his work *Dāsbodh*

देह तरी पांच भूतांचा । जीव तरी अंश ब्रह्मींचा । परमात्मा तरी अनन्याचा । ठाव पाहा ॥
उगेंचि पाहतां मीपण दिसे । शोध घेतां कांहींच नसे । तत्वें तत्व निरसे । पुढे निखळ आत्मा ॥
आत्मा आहे आत्मापणें । जीव आहे जीवपणें । माया आहे मायापणें । विस्तारली ॥
ऐसें अवघेंचि आहे । आणी आपणहि कोणीयेक आहे । हें सकळ शोधून पाहे । तोचि ज्ञानी ॥
(दासबोध ९।१०।२१-२४)

Deha tarī pāṅca bhūtāṅcā. Jīva tarī aṁśa Brahmīṅcā.
Parmātmā tarī ananyācā. Ṭhāva pāhā.
Ugeci pāhatāṅ mīpāṇa dise. Śodha ghetā kāṁhiṅcha nase.
Tatveṅ tatva nirase; puḍhe nikhaḷa Ātmā.
Ātmā āhe ātmāpaṇeṅ. Jīva āhe jīvapaṇeṅ.
Māyā āhe māyāpaṇeṅ; vistāralī.
Aiseṅ avagheṅci āhe. Āṇī āpaṇahi koṇīyeka āhe.
Heṅ sakaḷa śodhuna pāhe; toci jñānī.
(Dāsabodha 9/10/21-24)

The body is made of five elements, the individual self is essence of the Self. The Self transcends diversity. Discern the destination.
If you look casually, "I"ness appears. But if you investigate you find nothing there. If you probe one principle by another, everything unravels and Pure pristine nature, Self only remains.
Our own nature is the Self. The individual soul remains individualized. Maya has her mayic veil everywhere.
Thus everything seems to exist. And one feels, "I am also one of these things." But whoever investigates and discerns that what really exists is the real Knower.

In this verse, Vasugupta hints about a *Shivasutra* aphorism:

विद्यासमुत्थाने स्वाभाविकी खेचरी शिवावस्था ॥२-५॥

Vidyā-samuthāne svābhāvikī khecarī Śivāvasthā (II-5)

On the emergence of spontaneous supreme knowledge, occurs that state of movement in the vast unlimited expanse of consciousness which is Shiva's state – the Supreme state of Reality.

We conclude by saying that Guru's grace can effortlessly lift the veil of maya and thus remove the three impurities and calm all agitation.

There was a poet saint in the thirteenth century. He was a younger brother of Jñāneśwar Mahārāj. His name was Sopān. (*Sopan*, 34) His Guru was his brother, Nivṛtti Nāth. He says:

आम्हीं नेणो माया नेणों ते काया ।
ब्रह्म लवलाह्या आम्हांमाजी ॥१॥
मीं तूं गेलें ब्रह्मीं मन गेलें पूर्णीं ।
वासना ते जनीं ब्रह्म जाली ॥२॥
जिवशिव भाव आपणची देव ।
केला अनुभव गुरुमुखे ॥३॥
सोपान ब्रह्म वर्ततसे सम ।
प्रपंचाचा भ्रम नाही नाही ॥४॥

1. *Āmhī neṅo māyā neṇo te kāyā*
   Brahma lavalāhyā āmhāṅmājī
2. *Mī tū gele Brahmī mana gele pūrṇī*
   Vāsanā te janī Brahma jālī
3. *Jīva-Śiva bhāva āpaṇacī deva.*
   Kelā anubhava Gurumukhe.
4. *Sopāna Brahma vartatase sama*
   Prapapañcācā bhrama nāhī nāhī

We know neither the veiling power of the Self - maya,
nor the body - kaya.
Everything to us suddenly is only the Self.
You and I disappeared in the Self;

my mind went to completion.
All its traces of desire became the Self.
The Self took on the two roles of an individual soul
and Shiva.
I experienced that by the Guru's words.
To Sopana the Self exists equally forever.
Delusion of the world is nothing whatsoever

VERSE 10
EXPANSE OF KNOWING AND DOING

तदास्याकृत्रिमो धर्मो ज्ञत्वकर्तृत्वलक्षणः ।
यतस्तदीप्सितं सर्वं जानाति च करोति च ॥१०॥

10. Tadāsyākṛtrimo dharmo jñatva-kartṛtva-lakṣaṇaḥ
Yatas-tadīpsitaṁ sarvaṁ jānāti ca karoti ca.

भट्ट कल्लट : यतः तस्मिन् प्रलीनक्षोभात्मके काले अकृत्रिमः सहजो ज्ञत्वकर्तृत्वभावरूपो धर्मो यस्मात्, तस्मिन् एव प्राप्तयोगात्मके काले यद् यद् ज्ञातुम् इच्छति तत् तत् जानाति च करोति च, नान्यदा संसार्यवस्थायाम् ॥१०॥

Bhaṭṭa Kallaṭa: 10. Yataḥ tasmin pralīna-kṣobhātmake kāle akṛtrimaḥ sahajo jñatva-kartṛtva-bhāva-rūpo dharmo yasmāt, tasmin eva prāpta-yogātmake kāle yad yad jñātum icchati tat tat jānāti ca karoti ca, nānyadā saṁsāryavasthāyām.

Then the natural state of the individual, which has omniscience and omnipotence as its characteristics, flashes forth, due to which, the individual knows and does all that is desired with independence.

As perturbation dissolves, the individual's intuitive natural state which is of the form of 'knowing' and 'doing' manifests. The moment he has the touch of the power of the Self, whatever the individual wants to know, he/she independently knows and does. On the other hand, in the worldly plight this is never possible.

BHATTA KALLATA SAYS, "When agitation stops, limitation falls away and the natural state is experienced." The verse says that the natural state is omniscience and omnipotence. There is no compromise on anything that is desired and there is no sense of dependence. It is the experience of "being in charge" of our circumstances. It is "knowing" the essence of everything as the Self and it is "doing" from the state of oneness with Self.

It is a misconception among people that contact with our own being through meditation will spoil the fun they have. Usually a person feels, "If I get interested in spirituality, my spouse will leave me." Older people or friends who are still immersed in the world say to a married woman, "Don't let your husband do too much sadhana or think too much about God. He will leave you and your children, and become an ascetic, if he meditates." People are often scared that if they meditate and the thoughts dissolve, and the mind goes blank, then they might become weak like a vegetable and immune to their feelings, like a rock, and will be good for nothing. The commentary says that once agitation of the mind dissolves, the limited I-ness dissolves. It is never a vegetative state. When we lose the limited I-ness we experience the universal I-ness. That universal I-ness, Vimarsh, is all-powerful and all-knowing.

In order to stop the perturbation, it is not necessary to abandon the world. Moreover, it is impossible to abandon the world, because it is in the mind and its feelings and thoughts that our world resides. The world is not a hindrance. To see the world not as the world but as the Self is the natural state. Experiencing the Self requires giving up attachment to worldly objects, to stop giving them so much importance that they take over our life. When we experience the Self, perturbation stops. Perturbation is a pull by the senses towards sense objects in search of happiness. But when the Self is experienced once, it is ultimate happiness, and the mind is desirous of having that experience more and more, and the pull of senses is lessened to an equal extent. So to stop perturbation we have to experience the Self, and to experience the Self, we must stop the perturbation. This looks like an impossibility. This is where a Guru comes in. Whatever condition the disciple is in, if the disciple is earnest in coming out of the plight of limitation, and earnestly desires to experience the Self, the Guru takes the disciple within and makes the aspirant experience the Self, regardless of the pull of worldly tendencies. Then the real sadhana starts, to maintain the experience of the Self constantly, to be permanently established in the Self.

Swami Samarth Rāmdās describes the direction of sadhana in his *Dāsbodh*,

सागरामध्यें खसखस । तैसें परब्रह्मीं दृश्य । मतीसारिखा मतिप्रकाश । अंतरीं वाढे ॥
वृत्ति ऐसी वाढवावी । पसरून नाहींच करावी । पूर्णब्रह्मास पुरवावी । चहूंकडे ॥
वस्तु वृत्तीस कवळे । तेणें वृत्ति फाटोन वितुळे । निर्गुण आत्माच निवळे । जैसा तैसा ॥
(दासबोध ९।९।२९, ३५, ३७)

Sāgarāmadhyeṅ khasa-khasa, taiseṅ Parabrahmīṅ dṛśya.
Matīsārikhā matiprakāśa. Aṅtarīṅ vāḍhe.
Vṛtti aisī vāḍhavāvī. Pasaruna nāhica karāvī.
Pūrṇabrahmāsa puravāvi, cahuṅkaḍe.
Vastu vṛttīsa kavaḷe, teṇeṅ vṛtti, phāṭona vituḷe.
nirguṇa ātmāca nivaḷe, jaisā taisā. (Dāsbodh 9/9/29, 35, 37)

Like poppy seeds in an ocean, the seen universe, lies in the Supreme Self. The more an individual's intellect expands, the more it perceives the light of knowledge. ... One should develop the intellect and spread it to such an extent that it disappears and the perfect Self fills it everywhere. ... When Reality embraces our intellect, the mind breaks its bounds, and dissolves in the Supreme Self. Only the Self remains and experienced "as is."

That Being without any quality is like a calm waveless ocean. But it is not inert. It is both "knowing" - absolute knowledge, and "doing" - purposeful movement, the power of action harmonized with the power of desire. Our Being cannot be just existence without knowledge, because otherwise the knowledge of the world and of our own being would be impossible. If consciousness (knowledge) and Being were separate, knowledge would not exist.

The point is that when the agitation disappears, the universe of triads as separate entities disappears. But that does not mean powers of "knowing" and "doing" also disappear. All these powers are in equilibrium in a state of potentiality. Remaining in a static or dynamic state is up to the total independence of the Self. Regardless of the persistence of the so-called triads as the world, the Self is perceived as all three.

There is a story of a sixteenth-century poet saint named Dādu from Ahmedabad, India, who in his travels visited the Moghul king Akbar's royal court. King Akbar asked Dādu to illustrate with a practical example how a realized being sees the world. Dādu said, "A realized being sees the world in the same way you see water everywhere when you dive into a lake and open your eyes." (*Dadu*, 5)

Rāmakaṇṭha, a commentator on *Spandakrikas*, says, "वस्तुतः एकैव ईश्वरस्य स्वभावप्रत्यवमर्शरूपा शक्तिः, सा संवेदनरूपत्वाज् ज्ञानशब्देन उच्यते, तावन्मात्रसंरम्भरूपत्वात् क्रियाशब्देन च उद्घोष्यते ।" "*Vastutaḥ ekaiva Īśvarasya svabhāva-pratyavamarśa-rūpā śaktiḥ, sā saṁvedana-rūpatvāj jñānaśabdena ucyate, tāvan-mātra-saṁrambha-rūpatvāt kriyā-śabdena ca udghoṣyate.*"

Actually there is one Shakti of the divine, namely I-am awareness. The same Shakti in the form of perceiving or feeling, is known as jñāna-śakti or power of knowledge, in the form of its deliberate activity It is called kriyā-śakti or power of action.

When the three impurities - limitations of individuality, activity and attachment - discussed in the previous verse drop away, the perturbation stops. Then the individual does not remain as individual or ego, but becomes the Self, acquiring the qualities of bliss and light. He becomes a manifestation of knowledge and creativity. When desire is not there, there is no perturbation.

In *Vijnānabhairava* Verses 97-98, Dhāraṇās - 74 -75, the author says,

यदा ममेच्छा नोत्पन्ना ज्ञानं वा, कस्तदास्मि वै ।
तत्त्वतोऽहं तथाभूतस्तल्लीनस्तन्मना भवेत् ।।९७।।
इच्छायामथवा ज्ञाने जाते चित्तं निवेदयेत् ।
आत्मबुद्ध्यानन्यचेतास्ततस्तत्त्वार्थदर्शनम् ।।९८।।

Yadā mamecchā notpannā jñānaṁ vā, kas-tadāsmi vai.
Tattvato 'haṁ tathābhūtas-tallīnas-tanmanā bhavet. (97)
Icchāyām-athavā jñāne jāte chittam nivedayet.
Ātma-buddhyā-nanya-cetās-tatas-tattvārtha-darśanam. (98)

"When desire or knowledge (or activity) has not arisen in me, then what am I in that condition? In principle, I am that Reality itself – consciousness, bliss. Thus, he will be absorbed in that Reality and will become identified with It.
When a desire or knowledge (or activity) appears, the aspirant should, with the mind withdrawn from all objects (of desire, knowledge and

> *activity) fix his mind on it (desire, knowledge, activity) as the very Self, then he will have the realization of the essential Reality."*

This shows how the Self is experienced when there is no perturbation, and explains how to center the mind when perturbation begins, to get rid of the perturbation, thus continuing the experience of the Self.

It is Spanda that can simultaneously appear as the universe full of triads – seen, seer and seeing - in its external manifestation, while inwardly remaining as the power of desire, knowledge and activity. Those who have experienced It say It is a breathing presence in which no objects exist, just as in the verse earlier quoted Jñāneṣwar says, "If the mirror is removed, seer, seen and seeing go away, but does the face go away?" This Spanda is called common pulsation - पतिप्रमातृ भाव - *Patipramātṛ bhāva*, or the creator state. While manifesting as the universe and creatures, the Spanda is called special pulsation – पशुप्रमातृ भाव - *paśupramātṛ bhāva* - the creature state. The Self cannot be a remote onlooker, who just watches the phenomena, but It is the warp and woof of the universe, the knower and doer of the universe. In the two states the Self does not undergo any change in Its powers of knowledge and action. In the creature state It necessarily takes on a limited form bound by space, time and causation, and feelings of 'mine'-ness towards the forms, which creates perturbation. That is not the 'onlooker' or 'inactive' state.

Creatures of the world forget their nature as pulsation and run after the mirage of insatiable desires, accepting what they like and rejecting what they don't, caught up in the agitation of dualities and falling prey to a constant struggle of emotions. But when blessed by the Guru, the creature experiences the Self as the innate nature and body, and the creature's feeling of attachments, etc. are seen as Its manifestation, and the Universe as its own span.

This results in the constant experience of the independence of the powers of knowledge and action. The creature no longer remains fettered to limitations, and becomes master of the natural knowledge and action.

In this verse Vasugupta tells us that in order to experience our all-powerful Self we do not need to exert any extra efforts. We just need to quell our perturbations. For that we have to experience our Self once. The grace of a Guru is essential to break our mold and experience that Self. In the second part of the verse Vasugupta describes the benefits of getting established in the Self: One knows what one desires and one does whatever is necessary without any restrictions because omniscience and omnipotence is experienced.

Pratyabhijñāhṛdayam aphorism 15 says, "बललाभे विश्वम् आत्मसात् करोति" "*Balalābhe viṣvam ātmasāt karoti*" "In acquiring the inherent power of the Self, the aspirant assimilates the universe within him/herself." In the commentary on this aphorism Kshemaraj says, "When we gain the power of the Self, we accept our own emergent nature, we make the universe from the earth to Sadashiva our own, then the universe appears as identical with our Self." Thus nothing remains to be desired which we don't have and nothing remains to be done which we cannot do. In other words, all limitations regarding knowing and doing fall away. What is there to know if all knowledge is at hand, and what is there to do if one does not need anything? In the *Chāngadev Pāsaṣṭi*, Jñāneṣwar says exactly the same thing to Chāngadev.

जें जाणणेचि कीं ठाईं । नेणणें कीर नाहीं ।
परि जाणणें म्हणोनियांही । जाणणें कैंचें ।।३२।।
यालागीं मौनेंचि बोलिजे । कांहीं नहोनि सर्व होई ।
नव्हतां लाहिजे । कांहींच नाहीं ।।३३।।

Jeṅ jāṇaṇeci kī ṭhāīṅ, neṇaṇeṅ kīra nāhī.
Pari jāṇaṇeṅ mhaṇoniyāṅhī, jāṇaṇeṅ kaince (32)
Yālāgīṅ mouneṅci bolije, kāhī nahoni sarva hoī.
Navhatāṅ lāhije, kāhīṅca nāhī (33)

In that One who is Knowledge, there is no trace of ignorance.
So even if that One wanted to, what would there be to know?
That is why to speak of It, you must speak in silence.
Without becoming anything, It is everything,
So without your doing or becoming, it is attained.

If there is a desire to know or do at this stage of experience, it is divine will without causing any agitation or restlessness in the mind in the individual.

In conclusion, it is the Guru who breaks the perpetuating perturbation and gives the taste of the Self and makes an individual totally fulfilled, full of the power of knowing and doing. Thus a disciple always feels gratitude towards his or her Guru and sings with saint Jñāneṣwar as follows:

श्रीगुरुसारिखा असतां पाठिराखा । इतरांचा लेखा कोण करी ॥
राजयाची कांता काय भीक मागे । मनाचिया जोगे सिद्धि पावे ॥
कल्पतरुतळवटी जो कोणी बैसला । काय वाणी त्याला सांगिजो जी ॥
ज्ञानदेव म्हणे तरलो तरलो । साच उद्धरलो गुरुकृपे ॥

ŚrīGurusārikhā asatāṅ pāṭhirākhā, itarāṅcā lekhā koṇa karī.
Rājayācī kāntā kāya bhīka māge, manāciyā joge siddhi pāve.
Kalpataru-taḷavaṭī jo koṇī baisalā, kāya vāṇī tyālā sāṅgi jo jī.
Jñānadeva mhaṇe taralo taralo, sāca uddharalo Gurukṛpe.

When Shri Guru is behind you as a protector,
Who cares for anyone else?
Does a queen beg in need?
Whatever is in her mind, she gets indeed.
If a person sits under a wish-fulfilling tree,
Does he lack anything? Tell me.
Jnanadev says: I am redeemed, I am redeemed.
Truly I was uplifted by Guru's grace.

VERSE 11
SUBSIDENCE OF WORLDLINESS

तमधिष्ठातृभावेन स्वभावमवलोकयन् ।
स्मयमान इवास्ते यस्तस्येयं कुसृतिः कुतः ॥११॥

11. Tamadhiṣṭhātṛ-bhāvena svabhāvam-avalokayan
Smayamāna ivāste yas-tasyeyaṁ kusṛtiḥ kutaḥ.

भट्ट कल्लट : तदेवम्, यतः सर्वानुस्यूतः सर्वसामर्थ्ययुक्तश्च आत्मस्वभावः, तस्मात् तम् अधिष्ठातृभावेन सर्वव्यापकत्वेन स्वभावं पश्यन् , विस्मयाविष्ट इव यस्तिष्ठति, तस्य कुत्सिता सृतिः सरणं न भवति ॥११॥

Bhaṭṭa Kallaṭa: 11. Tadevam, yataḥ sarvānusyūtaḥ sarva-sāmarthya-yuktaśca ātma-svabhāvaḥ, tasmāt tam adhiṣṭhātṛ-bhāvena sarva-vyāpakatvena svabhāvaṁ paśyan, vismayāviṣṭa iva yastiṣṭhati, tasya kutsitā sṛtiḥ saraṇaṁ na bhavati.

How can the wretched cycle of birth and death exist for an aspirant who observes with amazement one's own nature, that is Spanda, that presides over all activities of life, and that pervades the entire universe?

The foregoing discussion has clearly established that one's own nature is the general principle of Spanda that is endowed with every power and pervades everything in the universe. Thus whoever experiences it as the presiding power present everywhere remains amazed and transcends the awful cycle of birth and death.

THE EXPERIENCE of the Spanda is so magnificent that any earthly experience pales before it. Once it is firmly in hand, pervading one's being, one doesn't want to let it go. In the last part of the verse the word "आस्ते" "āste" - 'adorns' -

describes this state. The experience adorns or beautifies everything. It is the mundane desires and outward-going tendencies of the mind that give rise to the cycle of births and deaths. With a proper understanding, the 'mind,' if such a thing can really be said to exist separately within an individual, no longer considers itself to be limited. Hence where is the possibility for desire?

All saints describe this sublime experience in many beautiful ways. Saint Jñāneśwar says:

हेचि आत्मप्रभा नीच नवी । तेचि करूनि ठाणदिवी ।
जो इंद्रियांते चोरूनि जेवी । तयासीच फावे ॥ ज्ञानेश्वरी ६-२३॥

Heci ātmaprabhā nīca navī, teci karūni ṭhāṇadivī.
Jo indriyānte corūni jevī, tayāsīca phāve. (Jñāneśvarī 6-23)

This light of the Self is ever new and ever bright.
The one who makes It his sole guiding light,
who enjoys It stealing away from the senses, attains It.

Ramana Maharshi describes this Spanda or 'Sphuran' (vibration) in answering a question from a devotee.[47] He says, "Sphuran is a foretaste of Realization. It is pure. The subject and object proceed from it. If the man mistakes himself for the subject, objects must necessarily appear different from him. They are periodically withdrawn and projected, creating [both] the world and the subject's enjoyment of the same. If, on the other hand, the man feels himself to be the screen on which the subject and object are projected there can be no confusion, and he can remain watching their appearance and disappearance without any perturbation to the Self." (*Sri Ramana Maharshi*, 38, P. 70) On another occasion he says, "The fact that the man considers himself limited, there arises the trouble. The idea is wrong. He can see it for himself. In sleep, there was no world, no ego (no limited self), and no trouble. Something wakes up from that happy state, and says, 'I.' To that ego the world appears. Being a speck in the world he wants more and gets into trouble.

How happy he was before the rising of the ego! Only the rise of the ego is the cause of the present trouble. Let him trace the ego to its source and he will reach that undifferentiated happy state which is sleepless sleep. The Self remains ever

---

47 *Talks with Sri Ramana Maharshi*, P.70-72

the same, here and now. There is nothing more to be gained. Because the limitations have wrongly been assumed there is need to transcend them. It is like the ten ignorant fools who forded a stream and on reaching the other shore counted themselves to be nine only. They grew anxious and grieved over the loss of the unknown tenth man. A wayfarer, on ascertaining the cause of their grief, counted them all and found them to be ten. But each one of them had counted the others leaving himself out. The wayfarer gave each in succession a blow telling them to count the blows. They counted ten and were satisfied. The moral is that the tenth man was not got anew. He was there all along, but ignorance caused grief to all of them." (*Sri Ramana Maharshi*, 38)

With Guru's grace a seeker can get an experience of Spanda in meditation. After the meditation is over the seeker may not be able to relate to the world he or she sees, or to the duties he or she must carry out, even though they happen without deliberate exertion on the seeker's part. If the seeker continues to wonder about the feeling of duality then the Guru dispels the doubt about the duality and convinces the seeker that it is the 'ego' or mind due to which the differences are felt. In reality there is no such difference. The mind and the Self - Spanda principle are the same. The case in point is the experience described at the end of the first verse on pages 20-24, since it is consistent with the word "स्मयमान" "*Smayamāna*," meaning constantly wondering with amazement, used at the beginning of the second part of the present verse. With the understanding Baba gave, in a moment everything in Chitra's, coauthor's, mind transformed. All problems are in the mind, and if the mind itself changes when and where can problems remain? In this manner, all her problems vanished.

A devotee asked Ramana Maharshi,[48] "Without the mind concentrating on it the work cannot be performed satisfactorily. How is the mind to be spiritually disposed and the work kept going as well?" Ramana Maharshi said, "The mind is the only a projection from the Self, appearing in the waking state. In deep sleep, you do not say whose son you are and so on. As soon as you wake up you say you are so and so, and recognize the world and so on. The world is only lokah, lokayate iti lokah (what is perceived is the world.) That which is seen is lokah or the world. Which is the eye that sees it? That is the ego, which rises and sinks periodically. But you exist always. Therefore that which lies beyond the ego is consciousness – the Self.

---

[48] *Talks with Sri Ramana Maharshi*, P. 81

In deep sleep mind is merged and not destroyed. That which merges reappears. It may happen in meditation also. But the mind which is destroyed cannot reappear. The yogi's aim must be to destroy it and not to sink in *laya*. In the peace of *dhyana*, *laya* ensues but it is not enough. It must be supplemented by other practices for destroying the mind. Its destruction is the non-recognition of it as being apart from the Self. Even now the mind is not. Recognize it. How can you do it if not in everyday activities. They go on automatically. Know that the mind promoting them is not real but a phantom proceeding from the Self. That is how the mind is destroyed."

Kṣemarāj, (*Singh*, 32) the commentator on *SpandaKarikas*, gives supplementary practices that destroy the mind as a separated entity. He says, "A yogi who closely observes his own (inmost) nature which is the Spanda principle experienced by means of the reasoning (already) mentioned, apprehends It as the 'I' that is the presiding principle of knowledge and activity, pervading the normal consciousness even after meditation has ceased." With this knowledge beyond knowledge, if a yogi has to carry out any entrusted earthly responsibilities or activities, he or she carries them out effortlessly.

The word "स्मयमान" "*Smayamāna*" used in the beginning of the second part of the verse, meaning constantly wondering with amazement at the experience of Spanda, is also mentioned in *Shiva Sutras* and *Vijnana Bhairava*. *Shiva Sutras* say, "विस्मयो योगभूमिकाः ॥१२॥" "*12. Vismayo Yogabhūmikāḥ*" – The stages of Yoga cause a fascinating wonder. In the commentary Kṣemarāj says, "As a person is filled with wonder at seeing something fantastic, likewise yogis abiding in the discernment of the Self, experience such extraordinary ever-new miracles at the dawning of the mass of consciousness which is their own Self, that remembering these often find It expanding throughout the entire complex of senses, mind, intellect, and ego. The constant wonderful experience blossoms into the bliss of the Self. They never tire of the taste of that uninterrupted bliss; they want it again and again." The same idea is expressed in Kulayukti, "When seekers realize the Self by themselves, then the Self experiences a pleasant surprise within itself."

As Ramana Maharshi has said in the earlier quotation, loka is the world, that which is perceived by senses. Shiva Sutras say, "लोकानंदः समाधिसुखम् ॥१८॥" "*18. Lokānandaḥ samādhi sukham*" "The delight felt in abiding as the knower in respect to both the subject and object in the world, is the delight of samādhi." As per Kṣemarāj , the commentator on Shiva Sutras, though this distinction of subject and object is evident in the world, the yogi experiences a unique delight of I-consciousness, which results from his continuous awareness of knowership. *Vijñāna Bhairava* Verses 106 and 65 – Dharana 42 describe this experience as follows:

ग्राह्यग्राहक- संवित्तिः सामान्या सर्वदेहिनाम् ।
योगिनां तु विशेषोऽस्ति संबन्धे सावधानता ॥१०६॥
सर्वं जगत्स्वदेहं वा स्वानन्दभरितं स्मरेत् ।
युगपत्स्वामृतेनैव परानन्दमयो भवेत् ॥६५॥

Grāhya-grāhaka-saṁvittiḥ sāmānyā sarva-dehinām,
Yoginām tu viśeṣo 'sti saṁbandhe sāvadhānatā (106)
Sarvaṁ jagat-svadehaṁ vā svānaṅda-bharitaṁ smaret,
Yugapat-svāmṛtenaiva parānanda-mayo bhavet (65)

Consciousness appearing as the subject and object is common to all embodied ones (individuals). Yogis are special in this respect that they are aware of this connection. (106)
"This entire universe and my body are full of the joy of the Self." This immortal nectar-like bliss at once makes a person one with the Supreme bliss. (65)

This experience is the recognition of and firm conviction regarding one's own nature. If that is attained, where is worldliness? The reason for experiencing worldliness and for going through the cycle of birth and death is described in the *Pratyabhijñāhṛdayam*:

तदपरिज्ञाने स्वशक्तिभिर्व्यामोहितता संसारित्वम् ॥१२॥

Tadaparijñāne svaśaktibhir-vyāmohitatā saṁsāritvam (12)

Because of ignorance of the fivefold act of the Spanda, one gets deluded by one's own powers and worldliness is experienced.
The consequence of worldliness is the cycle of birth and death.

In the commentary on this aphorism Kṣemarāj quotes a verse from *Īśwara-pratyabhijñā* which connects the earlier discussion.

सर्वो ममायं विभवं इत्येवं परिजानतः ।
विश्वात्मनो विकल्पानां प्रसरेऽपि महेशता ॥४, १, १२॥

Sarvo mamāyaṁ vibhavaṁ etyevaṁ parijānataḥ.
Viśvātmano vikalpānāṁ prasare 'pi Maheśatā (4, 1, 12)

The one who knows that "all this glory is mine," who realizes that the entire cosmos is his Self, possesses Lordship even when differentiating thoughts are present.

The aspirant does not experience Spanda by remaining separate from Spanda; it is impossible to do that. That is why the famous 17th century saint Tukaram Maharaj says,

देव माझा मी देवाचा । हीच माझी सत्य वाचा ॥
देहीं देवाचे देऊळ । आंत बाहेर निर्मळ ॥
देव पहाया मी गेलों । तेथें देवचि होउनि ठेलो ।
तुका म्हणे धन्य जहालो। आज विठ्ठला भेटलो ॥

Deva mājhā mī Devācā, hīca mājhī satya-vācā.
Dehīṅ Devāce Deūḷa, āṅta bāhera nirmaḷa.
Deva pahāyā mī gelo, tetheṅ devachi houni ṭhelo,
Tukā mhaṇe dhanya jahalo, āja Viṭṭhalā bheṭalo

God is mine and I am God's. This I truly claim.
In this body is the temple of God, pure inside and out.
I went to see God, there I myself became God.
Tuka says, "I am blessed. Today I met Viṭṭhala."

The consequence of this experience is described just as in the last part of the current verse, in another song of Tukaram :

आतां बरे झाले । माझे माथांचे निघाले ॥
चुकली हे मरमर । भार माथांचे डोंगर ॥
जाला झाडापाडा । तुका म्हणे गेली पीडा ॥

Ātāṅ bare jhāle, mājhe māthāṅce nighāle.
Cukalī he marmar, bhāra māthāṅce ḍoṅgara.
Jālā jhāḍā-pāḍā, Tukā mhaṇe gelī pīḍā.

Now, it is really good. The burden from my head has gone.
My repeated birth and death have escaped me.
The weight of many mountains has lifted from my head.
I have cleaned up everything.
Tuka says, "Oh, I am so glad to get rid of the pain."

Whereas ordinary people are overwhelmed and bewildered by the variety of worldly phenomena of knowledge and activity, the experiencer of Spanda is amazed by the experience and sees it as the presiding principle of all knowledge and activity. When people have lots of things to take care of, many times they get stressed out just listing the tasks mentally. However if instead of thinking about the things to be done, if people would simply perform actions without any sense of doership, and without regard to whether they could attend to all of them, they would not suffer stress. For an experiencer of Spanda the daily chores do not cause any stress. He or she has a "be there, and watch the work being done" attitude toward any chore. By "being there" it means remaining completely focused. He or she knows that it is Spanda that presides and that is the sole doer. As one watches an enormous amount of things getting done brilliantly, an amazement about the workings of Spanda arises.

The *Pratyabhijñāhṛdayam* has an aphorism that describes the constant experience of Spanda.

समाधि-संस्कारवति व्युत्थाने भूयो भूयश्चिदैक्यामर्शान्नित्योदितसमाधिलाभः ॥१९॥

Samādhi-saṁskāravati vyutthāne bhūyo bhūyaś-Cidaikyā - marśān – nityodita - samādhi - lābhaḥ (19)

After returning again and again to normal consciousness following the after-effects of samadhi, conviction regarding the oneness of Chiti - the Self - causes experience of the continuous, permanent samadhi state.

The word samadhi needs explanation. Samadhi is popularly known as a trance. Samadhi made of the word 'sama' or equalizing, or equilibrium and the word 'dhi' or intellect, is a state where intellect is in equilibrium, like a calm lake without ripples, where there is no triad of subject, object, and observation present except for the all-pervading breathing presence. There are two kinds of samadhi states. One is "निमीलन" "*nimīlan*" - of being one with the Self without perceiving the world, and the other is "उन्मीलन" "*unmīlan*" of being one with the Self while perceiving the world as non-different from oneself. In the latter state all objects of sense - of sound, touch, sight, smell and taste - are nothing but Spanda. This is an intoxicating state wherein the yogi reels with joy. Love for the entire universe oozes out through every pore of the body, and the mind returns to the meditation on one's identity with Chiti - the Self. Kṣemarāj's commentary on this aphorism is worth noting. First he quotes *Krama-Sutras*:

> क्रममुद्रया अन्तःस्वरूपया बहिर्मुखः समाविष्टो भवति साधकः । तत्रादौ बाह्यात् आन्तः प्रवेशः, आभ्यन्तरात् बाह्यस्वरूपे प्रवेशः आवेशवशात् जायते – इति सबाह्यान्तरोऽयं मुद्राक्रमः
>
> "*Kramamudrayā antaḥsvarūpayā bahirmukhaḥ samāviṣto bhavati sādhakaḥ, Tatrādau bāhyāt āntaḥ praveśaḥ, ābhyantarāt bāhya-svarūpe praveśaḥ āveśa-vaśāt jāyate - iti sabāhyāntaro ' yaṁ mudrā-kramaḥ.*"
>
> *By utilizing krama-mudrā the aspirant remains assimilated with the inner nature or Self while gazing outward. Because of the great force -* आवेश *āveśa - of the experience of the Self, the aspirant is drawn from the external world to the inner nature, and returns from the internal to the external marked with a stamp of the Self. Thus the internal and the external is "mudrā-kramaḥ."*

Krama means the successive cycle of consciousness as creation, maintenance and re-absorption, the world process. Mudrā means a stamp and "mudrayati" - seals up. Mudrā also can be interpreted as "mudam rāti" - that which gives joy. A third meaning of "Mudrā" is "mum drāvayati" - that which dissolves bondage. Thus krama-mudra means assimilating into oneself the process of world succession - creation, maintenance and re-absorption. With krama-mudrā the aspirant thus constantly experiences the innate nature of Spanda - Its simultaneous internal full 'Aham' (I am) and external 'Idam' (this) aspects - and is filled with joy. The following song of saint Jñānagiri brings out the full import of the verse as a conclusion:

हरी अंतरी ज्यासी पटला । हा भव तयाचा मिटला ।।ध्रु.।।
श्री गुरुचरणीं भाव जयाचा । तोचि भवांतुनी सुटला ।।१।।
ज्ञान–अज्ञान कर्म विवंचुनी । संशय ज्याचा फिटला ।।२।।
संतसमागमीं निजबोधाचा । शिक्का मोर्तब उठला ।।३।।

सोऽहंपणाचा जाणिव तंतु । समभावानें तुटला ॥४॥
ज्ञानगिरी हरी गोकुलवासी । अनंतस्वरूपीं नटला ॥५॥

Ref. Harī antarī jyāsi paṭalā, hā bhava tayācā miṭalā
1. Śrī Guru-caraṇiṅ bhāva jayācā, toci bhavāṅtunī suṭalā
2. Jñāna-ajñāna karma vivancunī, saṅśaya jyācā phiṭalā
3. Saṅta-samāgamiṅ nijabodhācā, śikkā mortaba uṭhalā
4. So 'haṅ-paṇācā jāṇiva taṅtu, sama-bhāvāneṅ tuṭalā
5. Jñānagirī Harī Gokula-vāsī, anaṅta-svarupiṅ naṭalā

Whoever has got conviction of Hari within,
    his cycle of births and deaths ends.
Whoever has all feeling set on the Guru's feet,
    is alone redeemed from worldliness.
Leaving behind knowledge-ignorance and actions,
    his doubts have disappeared.
In the company of saints the seal of the Self
    marked the world process.
Equanimity broke individuality,
    the conscious thread of So'ham.
Jñānagiri discerned the Lord residing in Gokul (Lord Krishna)
    adorned as countless forms.

VERSE 12

REFUTATION OF ABSOLUTE VOID AND NON-EXISTENCE OF THE SELF

नाभावो भाव्यतामेति न च तत्रास्त्यमूढता ।
यतोऽभियोगसंस्पर्शात्तदासीदिति निश्चयः ॥१२॥

12. Nābhāvo bhāvyatām-eti na ca tatrāstyamūḍhatā
Yato 'bhiyogasaṁsparśāt-tadāsīd-iti niścayaḥ

भट्ट कल्लटः न तु अभावो भावनीयो, यथा अन्यैर्योगिभिः उपदिश्यते, अभावं भावयेत्तावद्यावत्तन्मयतां व्रजेत् इति । न चैतत् युक्तम्, यस्मात् नाभावे भावना युज्यते मूढावस्थैव सा यस्मात् उत्तरकालम् अभियोगसंस्पर्शात् अभिलापसंयोगात् - सा शून्यावस्था अतीता मम इति स्मर्यते, न च आत्मस्वभाव एषः, यस्मात् न त्वेवं चिद्रूपत्वं मूढावस्थावत् स्मर्यते, तस्य सर्वकालमनुभवितृत्वेनानुभवो नित्योदितत्वात् ॥१२॥

Bhaṭṭa Kallaṭa: 12. Na tu abhāvo bhāvanīyo, yathā anyair-yogibhiḥ upadiśyate, abhāvaṁ bhāvayet-tāvad-yāvat-tanmayatāṁ vrajet iti. Na caitat yuktam, yasmāt nābhāve bhāvanā yujyate mūḍhāvasthaiva sā yasmāt uttarakālam abhiyoga-saṁsparśāt abhilāpa-saṁyogāt - "sā śūnyāvasthā atītā mama" iti smaryate, na ca ātma-svabhāva eṣaḥ, yasmāt na tvevaṁ cidrūpatvaṁ mūḍhāvasthāvat smaryate, tasya sarva-kālam-anubhavitṛtvena-anubhavo nityoditatvāt.

Void cannot be contemplated. Similarly, insentience cannot exist, since the recollection or inference regarding insentience indicates the existence of something. The Principle of Spanda must be present in order to recall or infer something.

BhattaKallata: Some yogis preach, "The void should be contemplated until the individual self merges in the void." But, the 'void' is an inert condition and hence cannot be a subject of contemplation. In fact, this instruction is impractical, since 'void' being an inert condition cannot logically be said to be the subject of contemplation. After samadhi if a yogi tries to describe contemplation of void, he or she can only say, "There was nothing," since it is merely an experience of the void. However that is not the nature of the Self, since consciousness being continually luminous cannot be remembered as void. Since the Self is the eternal luminous substratum, Its experience is of the omnipresent knower as the independent power of knowledge and (creative) action.

IN THIS VERSE, Vasugupta counters the theory of people who say that the ultimate goal of meditation is the Void, where there is no seer, seen or seeing; no subject, object, or the process of perception.

Some consider that nonexistence gave rise to existence. They even quote the statement of *Chāndogya Upaniṣad*, "असदेवेदमग्रमासीत्" (३।१९।१) "*Asad-evedam-agram-āsīt*" (III, 19, 1) - "In the beginning all this was indeed unmanifest (nonexistent)." But the same text emphasizes in Chapter 6, "By what means of proof can existence come out of nonexistence?" (VI, 2, 1) So those who emphasize Void or nonexistence as the origin and end of all creation and as the ultimate reality cannot substantiate their statement. It is worth noting that similar to the Vedantic proponents of Void, some modern scientists also propose that the universe was created out of nothing. Quantum Theory gives prominence to the observer in the fourth principle of concealment – that leads to light as a particle or a wave. However, since science cannot address anything happening beyond the domain of senses, further inference by some scientists that creation or universe came out of the void is not correct. Hence discussion of the Void in this verse is important.

No one can logically prove the existence of reality as Void. In fact, the words, "existence" and "void" are self-contradictory. In order to experience the Void there must be an observer – experiencer or some existence. The main point is that the Void is an experience and no experience can be the ultimate reality.

People would come to our Guru, Muktanand Baba, and explain a dream they had and ask the significance of that dream. Muktanand Baba used to say, "But nobody asks who the dreamer is." In other words the Self as the observer is beyond any experience, however lofty the experience is. The Void is a lofty experience. The Self cannot be Void.

Some regard the Self as 'void' but 'conscious.' How is this possible? Void or nonexistence of any object cannot be conscious, because consciousness implies existence. Void cannot exist by itself, because whoever shows that there is void, must be present thereby proving the existence of the Self as the observer. People who meditate say the 'void' exists because they experience it in meditation. If the void is experienced, it must be insentient, just like the void we experience in deep sleep. But then that void whether experienced in meditation or sleep cannot be the Self, and recollection of it is memory. The Self cannot be the object of memory and memory cannot be the Self. Hence the Self cannot be a 'void.' The Self is the observer of the void. So void is not the Self.

Besides, for the seekers of Truth there is a danger in regarding the Self as the 'void.' For then the Self is identified with the state of deep sleep, whereas the Self illumines all three states of waking, dream and deep sleep. Why meditate on an insentient thing like 'void' when our habitual meditation on external insentient objects of the senses or the world as well as on insentient thoughts and emotions about imagined objects has caused us so much suffering?

If the void exists, know that there is a substratum of the Self on which the experience of the void is projected. If there is a non-ripple state of mind, we should not mistake that Void for the Self. When there is no triad of seen, seer and seeing, it is possible to mistake this quiescence for the Void. But it is only the non-qualified Self that exists. As Jñāneṣwar Mahārāj says in his letter to Cāngadev which is known as *Cāngadev Pāsaṣṭi* (*Jnaneshwar*, 15) as seen in Verse 5 page 66:

नुसधें मुख जैसें । देखिजतसें दर्पणमिसें ॥
वायाचि देखणे ऐसें । गमों लागे ॥२०॥
तैसें न वचतां भेदा । संवित्ति गमे त्रिधा ।
हेंचि जाणे प्रसिद्धा । उपपत्ति इया ॥२१॥
दृश्याचा जो उभारा । तेंचि द्रष्ट्रत्व होय संसारा ।
या दोहींमाजिला अंतरा। दृष्टि पंगु होय ॥२२॥

20. *Nusadheṅ mukha jaiseṅ, dekhijataseṅ darpaṇamiseṅ .*
    Vāyāci dekhaṇe aiseṅ, gamoṅ lāge.
21. *Taiseṅ na vacatāṅ bhedā, saṁvitti game tridhā,*
    Heṅci jāṇe Prasiddhā, upapatti iyā.
22. *Dṛśyācā jo ubhārā, teṅci draṣṭṛtva hoya saṁsārā,*
    Yā dohṅimājilā aṅtarā, dṛṣṭi paṅgu hoya.

20. *A face which is alone, sees itself in a mirror,*
And as it looks, the act of seeing, naturally occurs.
21. *O Famous One, in the same way,*
Consciousness, without being divided
Appears to become three.
Understanding this is the secret of everything!
22. *When the Seen is created,*
The Seer of the world comes into being.
In trying to perceive the distinction between them,
Seeing disappears.

In short, when there is no triad perceived or conceived, it does not mean that there is void, it is the Self which is the substratum of everything that exists, which is all-knowing and capable of all action.

In void one cannot experience limitations of space, time, or matter. There is no such limitation in the Self either. Yet that does not mean the Self is void. A void is nothing, whereas the Self is everything. Since some modern scientists believe in the void and not the Self as the all-pervading substratum, some discussion of limitless Self is in order. In the Vedas the Self is 'दिक्कालवस्तुभेदातीत' '*dikkālavastubhedātīta*' i.e. beyond divisions of space, time and matter. That the Self is beyond divisions of space, time and matter can be seen as follows. Limitation of space comes in terms of a physically limited object, such as a person. If a person is inside a house, he cannot be outside the house. The limitless Self like space is all-pervasive. But the Self cannot be the space since before the 'big bang' space was not there. Space was created out of the first explosion. Space can be perceived by consciousness or Self. A person in deep sleep cannot conceive space. Also when the universe is dissolving, earth merges into water, water into fire, fire into wind, wind into space and space is sucked into the big bang or the black hole. To accomplish all this some 'doer' must exist beyond all of them. That 'doer' is the Self. As per Einstein's *Theory of Relativity*, space and time are always together. The Self cannot be time. Because time is relative and the idea of 'time' can only be conceived because of the Self or consciousness. So the Self transcends time. Self manifests as energy which in turn manifests as matter. That the Self or consciousness manifests as energy can be seen from one's own example of energy required performing physical or mental actions. That energy manifests as matter is again proved by relativity. Hence the Self cannot be matter or bound by matter. Also matter can only be perceived by the light of consciousness. Hence the Self is beyond divisions of space, time and matter. That is the reason why the saints sing the glories of the Self as follows:

शून्य स्थावर जंगम व्यापुनि राहिला अकळ ।
बाप रखुमादेवीवरु विठ्ठल सकळ ॥

Śūnya sthāvar jaṅgama vyāpuni rāhiḷā akaḷa,
Bāpa Rakhumādevīvaru Viṭṭhala sakaḷa.

Jñāneṣwar Maharaj says, "Viṭṭhala, the Self, has pervaded everything, void, sentient and insentient still remain unfathomable."

देशकाळवस्तुभेद मावळला । आत्मा निरवाळला विश्वाकार ॥

Deśa-kāḷa-vastu-bheda māvaḷalā, Ātmā niravāḷalā viṣvākāra

Tukārām Maharaj says, "The Self was experienced as the universe. The differences of space, time and matter dissolved."

Some yogis believe experiencing Laya (Void) is attaining the Self. In *Shiva Sutras* the aphorism 3.31 "स्थितिलयौ ।" "*Sthitilayau*" meaning "This universe is the expansion of the yogi's energy in objective impressions and the void or dissolution of those impressions" describes the state of a yogi established in the Self. It is the Kriyāshakti (creative power) of the Spanda, not different from the yogi, that not only expands as the appearance of the objective universe (creation), but also as the impressions of the objective world left behind in the mind (sthiti) and in the void where these impressions are absorbed. In the commentary Swami Lakshman Joo (*Swami Lakshman Joo*, 43) says, "If God consciousness were not existing throughout, then how would you be able to travel from one state to the next, from the dreaming state to the state of deep sleep, and from deep sleep state to the waking state? Between each (any two) of these states, there is a gap, a point where one state has ceased to exist and the next state has yet to begin. How could you travel through the gap if God consciousness did not exist in that gap?" It is because of this continuity of consciousness that one feels one is unchanged through childhood, youth and old age, and in all states of waking, dream and deep sleep. However this constant movement is not establishment in the Self. Hence, the yogis' belief that Laya (Void) is attaining the Self is not correct. To be established in the Self, which is our nature, it is necessary by practice to remove the different triads that fill our waking and dreaming moments from the mind. There are twelve *dhāraṇās* – centering exercises – in *Vijñānabhairava* concerning the Void. They consist of:

1. meditating on the five voids (tanmatras – sources of senses which have no concrete appearance, hence voids) in the heart (Dhāraṇā 9);
2. mindfulness on any void (empty space), on a wall, or on some excellent person established in the Self (10);
3. perfect repetition of pranav (Aum, Hūm or Hrīm) and contemplation over the void at the end of the protracted phase of it, which contains the most eminent energy (16);
4. moving from gross utterance to subtle vibration and mental reflection upon letters such as Aum, H, and R, which have a connecting vowel at the end (19);
5. contemplating within one's body, Void (spatial vacuity) in all directions simultaneously without any thought-construct (20);
6. contemplating the void above, at the base, in the heart (22);
7. contemplating the body as void even for a while (23);
8. concentrating intensely on the idea that this universe is totally void, thereby absorbing in the Absolute Void – the Self (35);
9. considering one of the limiting principles, such as maya, as delusion that brings about identity of the Self with the not-self such as void, intellect and the body (72);
10. void is that which is free of all attributes, all principles, and all residual traces of pains. The Ultimate Reality which cannot be reduced to an object, which is the void, and which also penetrates even non-existence should be contemplated (102);
11. fixing the mind on the external space which is eternal, without support, void, omnipresent, devoid of limitation (103);
12. regarding the universe as a magical spectacle, hence essentially void. How can there be knowledge of activity in the unchangeable Self? All external objects are dependent on knowledge; therefore this world is void (109).

These dharanas should be practiced by a seeker only one or two at a time according to the disposition of the seeker.

In the Sanskrit commentary on this verse, Bhaṭṭa Kallaṭa said, "Some yogis preach, 'The void should be contemplated until the individual self merges in the void.' But, the 'void' is an inert condition hence cannot be a subject of contemplation." The discussion until now shows it is essential to experience the void as a means to recognize the Self, on the substratum of which the void appears, but at the same time to recognize that the void itself is not the Self.

It is fascinating to see how the saints quoted above have the same experience as discussed in these dhāraṇās. Tukārām Mahārāj says in one of his abhangs (unperishable songs), "सांडिली त्रिपुटी दीप उजळला घटी ।" "*Sāṅḍilī tripuṭī dīpa ujaḷalā ghaṭī.*" "The triads dropped away, only the light (of consciousness) arose in the body."

Jñāneṣwar Mahārāj's abhang summarizes very well this discussion of Void and the Self.

शून्याशून्याधार शून्यशेजे हरि । शून्यामाजीं घरीं बिंबलासे ॥१॥
आधीं आप पाहीं शून्याशून्य देही । मग उमजोनि ठायीं घेईजे सुखे ॥२॥
शून्य तें काई शून्याशून्य पुशिलें । हृदयस्था जालें कोण्या गुणें ॥३॥
बाप रखुमादेविवर विठ्ठल अवघा । शून्याशून्य वेग ज्ञानघन ॥४॥

1. *Śūnyā-śūnyā -dhāra śūnyaśeje Hari,*
   śūnyāmājī gharī bimbalāse.
2. *Ādhīṅ āpa pāhīṅ śūnyā-śūnya dehī,*
   maga umajoni ṭhayīṅ gheīje sūkhe.
3. *Śūnya teṅ kāī śūnyāśūnya puśileṅ,*
   hṛdayasthā jāleṅ koṇyā gūṇeṅ.
4. *Bāpa Rakumādevi-vara Viṭṭhala avaghā,*
   śūnyāśūnya vega jñānaghana.

1. *The substratum of Void and non-void is the Lord who is beside the Void and whose abode appears as the Void.*
   [In this sense, he warns us not to mistake the dwelling for the indweller.]
2. *First investigate what is in your void and non-void – or subtle and gross - bodies. Then you will experience the bliss that indwells.*
3. *Investigate what is Void in the void and non-void, then you will know how the Lord is seated in the heart.*

The verses 2 and 3 are related to the *Shiva Sutras* aphorism 3-16 "आसनस्थः सुखम् हृदे निमज्जति ।" "*āsanasthaḥ sukhaṁ hṛde nimajjati.*" "Seated in that real posture, he effortlessly dives in the ocean of nectar." In the commentary on this Sutra, Kṣemarāj says, "This diving means he/she lets the impressions of the physical body, of the breath, of the eight subtle constituents (five subtle senses and the mind, intellect and ego) sink into that ocean and he/she becomes one with that nectar. This state, which is the real nature of Shiva is not revealed; this state is the revealer. This state is subjective and not objective."

4. *Jñāneṣwar says, "It is the father Viṭṭhala, Lord of Rakhumai, who is mass of knowledge and everything that is void and non-void."*

VERSE 13
DIFFERENCE OF THE VOID AND THE SELF

अतस्तत्कृत्रिमं ज्ञेयं सौषुप्तपदवत्सदा ।
न त्वेवं स्मर्यमाणत्वं तत्तत्वं प्रतिपद्यते ॥१३॥

*13. Atastat-kṛtrimaṁ jñeyaṁ souṣupta-padavat sadā,
Na tvevaṁ smaryamāṇatvaṁ tattavaṁ pratipadyate*

भट्ट कल्लटः – अभावभावनालब्धभूमिकस्यापि कृत्रिमा अनित्या सा अवस्था, यथा, सौषुप्ते पदे, यस्मात् चिद्रूपत्वं तु आत्मनः स्वरूपं नित्यसन्निहितं तदेव गुरूपदेशेन नित्यमेवानुशीलनीयम् ॥१३॥

Bhaṭṭa Kallaṭa: 13 - Abhāva-bhāvanā-labdha-bhūmikasyāpi kṛtrimā anityā sā avasthā, yathā, souṣupte pade, yasmāt cidrūpatvaṁ tu ātmanaḥ svarūpaṁ nitya-sannihitaṁ tadeva gurūpadeśena nityam-evānuśīlanīyam.

Hence that void, like sleep, should always be regarded as artificial. Mere nonexistence or void cannot be contemplated. Spanda Itself cannot be proposed as an object of recollection.

Bhaṭṭa Kallaṭa: The state experienced by contemplation on the Void is only artificial and temporary, because the nature of the Self is eternity. That eternity should always be pursued according to the Guru's instructions.

IN THIS VERSE, Vasugupta describes the state experienced by contemplating the Void as temporary, comparing it emphatically with deep sleep. Even though both the previous verse and current verse are about the Void, the difference between the two verses is that the previous one showed that Void is not Spanda, and this one says that the experience of Void is akin to deep sleep, while that of Spanda is awareness. The experience of deep sleep is void–in it there are no triads of seer, seen and seeing, and also no awareness; while the experience of Samadhi also is void of the triads of seer, seen and seeing, yet is characterized by full awareness. Muktananda Baba always said that in the state of Samadhi there are no visions or experiences of any kind, but only a kind of subtle living vibration remains.

Shiva Sutra (I, 10) describes deep sleep thus: "अविवेको मायासौषुप्तम्" "*Aviveko Māyāsauṣuptam*" "Lack of awareness is delusive deep sleep." Maya or ignorance of the Self is delusion. In ordinary deep sleep there is no awareness of any kind. There are no triads of "seer, seen, and seeing" as in the waking or dream states. At the same time there is no awareness of the Self either. The state of sleep is inert. In sleep the person's consciousness is entirely removed from the physical body, intellect, and prana or breath, and remains concentrated as the experiencer of the eight subtle constituents – the five senses, mind, intellect, and ego. Impressions of activities and personality remain in a seed form. The experience is temporary. After waking from deep sleep, one feels physically and mentally refreshed and one says, "I slept soundly, I was not aware of anything," but one is no wiser. This state is artificial since it is a state or an object in the memory. After waking from Samadhi, one is not only refreshed but is also wiser. The wisdom one obtains is never clouded by delusion and is permanent. Jñāneṣwar says in one of his abhangs, "परतोनि अज्ञान न ये घरा ।" "*Paratoni ajñāna na ye gharā* ।" "Ignorance will never be back to this place." Tukārām says, "सांडिली त्रिपुटी दीप उजळला घटी ।" "*Sāṇḍilī tripuṭī dīpa ujaḷalā ghaṭī*" "The triad (of seen, seer, and seeing) dropped away, a light emerged in the body." This state is natural, since it is not an object of memory but it is always continually arising or experienced. This is the difference between ordinary sleep and Samadhi.

Gurutu in his Hindi commentary of *Spanda Kārikās* makes an interesting comment on this verse about yoga teachers who advise their students to contemplate "I am not" or self-denial as the goal of meditation. Self-denial is like denying one's own existence. He says it is like a person who is sitting in his room and when called by someone outside says, "I am not here." The person's reply itself gives himself away.

Jñāneṣwar in his letter to Cāngadev discusses the consequences of losing the triad and experiencing pure consciousness.

पुढे देखिजे तेणे बगे । देखतें ऐसे गमो लागे ।
परी दृष्टिते वाउगे । झकवित असे ।।२७।।
म्हणोनि दृश्याचिये वेळे । दृश्य द्रष्ट्त्वावेगळे ।
वस्तुमात्र निहाळे । आपणापाशी ।।२८।।
वाद्यजातेविण ध्वनी । काष्टजातेविण वन्ही ।
तैसे विशेष ग्रासुनी । स्वयेंचि असे ।।२९।।
जे म्हणता नये काही । जाणो नये कैसेही ।
असतचि असे पाही । असणे जया ।।३०।।
आपुलिया बुबुळा । दृष्टि असोनि अखम डोळा ।
तैसा आत्मज्ञानी दुबळा । ज्ञानरूप जो ।।३१।।

27. *Puḍhe dekhije teṇe bage, dekhateṅ aise gamon lāge,*
Parī dṛṣṭite vāuge, jhakavita ase.
28. *Mhaṇoni dṛśyāciye veḷe, dṛśya draṣṭṛtvā-vegaḷe,*
Vastumātra nihāḷe, āpaṇāpāśī.
29. *Vādya-jāteviṇa dhvanī, kāṣṭa-jāteviṇa vanhī,*
Taise viśeṣa grāsunī, svayeṅci ase.
30. *Je mhaṇatā naye kāhī, jāṇo naye kaisehī,*
Asataci ase pāhī, asaṇe jayā.
31. *Āpuliyā bubuḷā, dṛṣṭi asoni akhama ḍoḷā,*
Taisā ātmajñānī dubaḷā, jñānarūpa jo.

27. *Though a face looking in a mirror*
May appear to be a Seer,
Because it only sees itself,
Seeing is deceived.
28. *Therefore, when the Seen appears,*
Know that it is That
Beyond the Seer and the Seen
Which is looking at itself.
29. *Sound exists without an instrument;*
Fire exists without wood;
And It, having devoured all forms,
Exists by Itself.
30. *Nothing can be said about It.*
It cannot be known in any way.

It is that which exists eternally
As Existence Itself.
31. Even if an eye can see
It cannot see itself.
In the same way, the One who is
Knowledge cannot know Himself.

Seekers need to experience the Self by removing all triads from their mind, which can be done by visualization as given in *Vijñānabhairava*. Two dhāraṇās, 95 and 97, follow:

क्वचिद्वस्तुनि विन्यस्य शनैर्दृष्टिं निवर्तयेत् ।
तज्ज्ञानं चित्तसहितं देवि शून्यालयो भवेत् ॥ (श्लोक १२०, धारणा ९५)
वस्त्वन्तरे वेद्यमाने सर्ववस्तुषु शून्यता ।
तामेव मनसा ध्यात्वा विचितोऽपि प्रशाम्यति ॥ (श्लोक १२२, धारणा ९७)

Kvacid-vastuni vinyasya śanair-dṛṣṭiṁ nivartayet,
Taj-jñānaṁ citta-sahitaṁ devi śūnyālayo bhavet.
(Verse120, Dhāraṇā 95)
Vastvantare vedyamāne sarva-vastuṣu śūnyatā,
Tāmeva manasā dhyātvā vicito 'pi praśamyati.
(Verse122, Dhāraṇā 97)

120. O Goddess, if one, after casting the gaze on some object, withdraws it and slowly eliminates the knowledge of that object along with the thought and impression of it, one abides in the void.

122. When one perceives a particular object, vacuity is established regarding all other objects. If one contemplates this vacuity with a mind freed of all thought, then even though the particular object still be known or perceived, the aspirant has full tranquility.

As one can see, these two exercises complement each other. In the first the object is transformed into void. In the second only one object and nothing else remains. Whether it is void or just one object, both contemplations lead to the experience of the Self.

As Bhaṭṭa Kallaṭa says, the Guru's guidance is essential in order to understand the significance of the Void and the Self, and not to confuse the two. Here also Jñāneṣwar has an abhanga that summarizes this.

शून्याचे जे बीज योगियांचे गुज । स्वानंदाचे निजब्रह्म रया ॥१॥
त्रिगुण त्रिविध तो सच्चिदानंद । शब्दाचा अनुवाद नसे जेथे ॥२॥
ज्ञानदेव म्हणे सद्गुरु जाणती । इतरांची वृत्ति चालेचीना ॥३॥

1. *Śūnyāce je bīja yogiyāṅce guja, svānaṅdāce nijabrahma rayā.*
2. *Triguṇa trividha to saccidānaṅda, śabdācā anuvāda nase jethe.*
3. *Jñānadeva mhaṇe sadguru jāṇatī, itarāṅcī vṛtti cālecīnā.*

1. *Oh my friend! The seed of the Void is the secret of Yogis.*
   It is our own blissful Self.
2. *Triguna (three qualities), triad, Sat-chit-ananda,*
   These words cannot describe It.
3. *Jñānadev says, "Sadguru knows this Brahman,*
   Others' intellect cannot fathom It."

VERSES 14, 15 AND 16
DOERSHIP, SAMADHI AND SELF

अवस्थायुगलं चात्र कार्यकर्तृत्वशब्दितम् ।
कार्यता क्षयिणी तत्र कर्तृत्वं पुनरक्षयम् ॥१४॥

14. Avasthā-yugalaṁ cātra kārya-kartṛtva-śabditam,
Kāryatā kṣayiṇī tatra kartṛtvaṁ punar-akṣayam.

भट्ट कल्लटः –अवस्थायुगलम्, अवस्थाद्वयमेव कार्यकर्तृत्वसंज्ञं भोग्यभोक्तृभेदभिन्नम्, तत्र यो भोग्यरूपो भेदः स उत्पद्यते नश्यति च, भोक्तृभेदस्तु चिद्रूपः पुनर्न जायते न कदाचिद् विनश्यति तेन नित्यः ॥१४॥

Bhaṭṭa Kallaṭa: 14. Avasthāyugalam, avasthādvayameva kārya-kartṛtva-saṁjñaṁ bhogya-bhoktṛ-bheda-bhinnam, tatra yo bhogya-rūpo bhedaḥ sa utpadyate naśyati ca, bhoktṛ-bhedastu cidrūpaḥ punar-na jāyate na kadācid vinaśyati tena nityaḥ.

कार्योन्मुखः प्रयत्नो यः केवलं सोऽत्र लुप्यते ।
तस्मिँल्लुप्ते विलुप्तोऽस्मीत्यबुधः प्रतिपद्यते ॥१५॥

15. Kāryonmukhaḥ prayatno yaḥ kevalaṁ so 'tra lupyate,
Tasmiṁllupte vilupto 'smītyabudhaḥ pratipadyate.

भट्ट कल्लट :– कार्यसंपादनसामर्थ्यं बाह्यकरणव्यापाररूपं केवलं विलुप्यते, स्थगितेन्द्रियस्य तस्मिन् विलुप्ते सामर्थ्ये स्वभावो मे विलुप्त इति अबुधो जानाति, न तु भावस्य विनाशोऽस्ति ॥१५॥

Bhaṭṭa Kallaṭa: 15. Kārya-saṁpādana-sāmarthyaṁ bāhya-karaṇa-yāpāra-rūpaṁ kevalaṁ vilupyate, sthagitendriyasya tasmin vilupte sāmarthye 'svabhāvo me vilupta' – iti abudho jānāti, na tu bhāvasya vināśo 'sti.

न तु योऽन्तर्मुखो भावः सर्वज्ञत्वगुणास्पदम्
तस्य लोपः कदाचित् स्यादन्यस्यानुपलम्भनात् ॥१६ ॥

16. Na tu yo 'ntarmukho bhāvaḥ sarvajñatva-guṇāspadam,
Tasya lopaḥ kadācit syād-anyasyānupalambhanāt.

भट्ट कल्लटः – न तु यः अन्तर्मुखः अन्तश्चक्रारूढस्वभावः सर्वज्ञत्वादिगुणाश्रयः तस्य विनाशः कदाचित्, तस्मात् द्वितीयस्यान्यस्याभावात् तत्स्वरूपमेव व्योमवत् चिद्रूपतया सर्वत्र अनुभवति इति॥१६॥

Bhaṭṭa Kallaṭa: – 16. Na tu yaḥ antarmukhaḥ antaś-cakrārūḍha-svabhāvaḥ sarvajñatvādi-guṇāśrayaḥ tasya vināśaḥ kadācit, tasmāt dvitīyasyānyasyābhāvāt tat-svarūpam-eva vyomavat cidrūpatayā sarvatra anubhavati iti.

14. Our own nature – consciousness (Self) and awareness (Pulsation) – has two states called deed and doer. The deed is temporary and the doer is eternal.
15. When the effort directed towards any deed vanishes, only a fool thinks that he has ceased to exist.
16. But that inner nature, which has qualities of omniscience, etc., never disappears, as there is no other conscious power that experiences all states.

Bhaṭṭa Kallaṭa: – 14. Our own nature – consciousness and awareness – has two states. These two states are called deed and doer. The difference between the two is that one is experience and the other experiencer. The state called experience emerges and dissolves, while the state called experiencer is of the nature of consciousness, hence the experiencer neither emerges nor dissolves. Therefore, the state of experiencer is eternal.
15. The ability to accomplish various activities stops; outer sense organs of sensing 'sound, touch, sight, taste, and smell,' stop functioning. But upon inactivity of the organs, it is only a fool who thinks, "I cease to exist." The Being never perishes.
16. Our own nature is the inner cycle of consciousness constantly pulsating. It is the abode of omniscience, omnipotence, and omnipresence. It is imperishable. Therefore there being no power of desire, knowledge, action other than the inner nature, It is clear and all pervasive as the sky, and It is conscious, experiencing all states.

THESE THREE VERSES describe the special and general nature of Spanda. The description is essential for us to live a fulfilled life. We give importance to things happening around us, done by us, or done to us. They affect our emotions making us depressed or elated. We think a lot about incidents that take place. We take the responsibility, credit, and blame for our actions as the doers or actors. But Verse 14 says our nature – Consciousness and "I am" awareness - has two states, namely the action or deed and the doer. The deed or activity (kārya, in Sanskrit) is not something that can be attributed to a person, and doership (kartṛtva) also is not personal.

There are two states of Spanda, Divine Pulsation. One is general and the other special. In the general state of 'doer', there are no objects, attributes, or forms. Only It remains as absolute Consciousness. In this state all forms remain potential as Vimarsha - "I am"- awareness. Whereas in the special, dynamic, state It takes on different forms, while concealing Its real nature. It performs actions, creating out of Itself animate objects such as body, life force, senses of perception and action, and inert objects such as rocks, jar, cloth, etc. Thus both the deed or activity and the specific non-physical or physical products are manifestations of Spanda. The word 'deed' involves both the action and the end result or product. This is the special state. The general state is the 'doer' in the present verse. And both states – deed and doer - are impersonal.

Acharya Abhinavagupta says, "निरावरणमाभाति भात्यावृतनिजात्मकः । (तंत्रालोकः १.९३) "*Nirāvaraṇam-ābhāti bhātyāvṛta-nijātmakaḥ*" (*Tantrālokaḥ* 1.93) "(By Its free will), without any covering It shines, and with coverings It appears as individual forms." That principle exists simultaneously in both the states of 'doer' and 'deed.' While the deeds are effects – temporary and perishable, doership is eternal and the root cause.

Even though it is the universal "I am" awareness (Spanda) that contains the two states of deed and doer, it is we, individual human beings, who identify ourselves with a particular deed and take on personal doership, thereby getting stuck and attached, resulting in a mental state of elation or depression. The first lesson Verse 14 gives us is that there is nothing to be elated or depressed about in our actions or any need to take responsibility for the actions. This does not advocate irresponsibility, as being irresponsible is merely taking responsibility for inaction. Rather, the correct attitude is to let an activity happen, with awareness of abiding in Spanda.

The second part of the Verse 14 gives us the second lesson that any deed – action and product – is temporary, whereas the state of the doer is eternal. Hence products - names and forms – dissolve after some time. By claiming some as ours, we enjoy or suffer. We differentiate between these names and forms, liking some and disliking others. This forms a triad of object, subject, and perception in each case. But instead of regarding ourselves as subjects, if our attitude is that 'It is the eternal Spanda that is the doer in each case,' we transcend the cycle of joy and sorrow. No action will be regrettable to anyone.

Everyone who has experienced Samadhi, experiences the general aspect of Spanda. Those who are established in this fourth state, the substratum of the three states of waking, dream and deep sleep, emphasize that they experience the divine pulsation devoid of the triads of seer, seen, and seeing. This divine pulsation never undergoes any changes even in the presence of the triads. Saint Kabir, who was established in the fourth state says:

दरियाव की लहर दरियाव है जी ।
दरिया और लहर में भिन्न कोयम् ॥
उठे तो नीर है बैठे तो नीर है ।
कहो जो दूसरा किस तरह होयम् ॥
उसी का फेर के नाम लहर धरा ।
लहर के कहो क्या नीर खोयम् ॥
जक्त ही फेर जब जक्त परब्रह्म में ।
ज्ञान कर देख माल गोयम् ॥

Dariyāva kī lahara dariyāva hai jī,
Dariyā aur lahara meṅ bhinna koyam.
Uṭhe to nīra hai baiṭhe to nīra hai,
Kaho jo dūsarā kisa taraha hoyam.
Usī kā phera ke nāma lahara dharā,
Lahara ke kaho kyā nīra khoyam.
Jakta hī phera jaba jakta Parabraḥma meṅ,
Jñāna kara dekha māla goyam.

The waves of an ocean are also ocean.
What is the difference between a wave and the ocean?
If the wave arises, it is water, if it subsides still it is water.
So tell me is there any difference?
If you change the name of water and call it a wave,
Will the water disappear?

See this with understanding: Universe after universe moves in the Supreme Self, like beads on a chain.

Vijñānabhairava describes a centering practice based on the same simile in Dhāraṇā 86.

जलस्येवोर्मयो वह्नेर्ज्वालाभङ्ग्यः प्रभा रवेः ।
ममैव भैरवस्यैता विश्वभङ्ग्यो विभेदिता
(श्लोक ११०, धारणा ८६)

Jalasyevormayo vahner-jvālā-bhangyaḥ prabhā raveḥ,
Mamaiva bhairavasyaitā viśva-bhangyo vibheditā.
(Verse 110, Dhāraṇā 86)

110. Just as waves arise from water, flames from fire, rays from the sun, similarly the universe manifests as waves from Me, Bhairava, supreme I-consciousness.

The practice of identifying ourselves with Spanda rather than with the limitations of the gross, subtle, or causal bodies leads us to the experience described by sages, the experience described in *Shiva Sutra* 14: "दृश्यं शरीरम् ।" "*Dṛśyaṁ śarīram* ।" "This universe is my own body" or "This body is an object." Just as the world seen from a keyhole does not give us any idea about its vastness, the universe seen from the attitude of limitations of the body and mind is also limited and leads to wrong identifications. The universe is vast yet not really separate from us. Separation occurs if we regard ourselves as limited, our individual 'I am' different from the universal 'I am.'

As objects, the body and the universe are perishable. Even though the substratum never undergoes any modification, the universe changes every moment. The mind goes from one object to another. As the objects differ, perception differs, and the triad changes. For example, if you look at a jar, you will see only a jar and not something else, such as a cloth. The universe keeps changing. Actually, every moment our eyes look at a different triad. At the very moment our eyes look, a different triad takes birth, and the next moment it dissolves. It is like a movie, every few seconds we see different frames but our eyes deceive us – by optical illusion the movie appears to be continuous. In order to avoid being deluded by the sense objects or countless 'seens,' it is necessary to understand the temporary nature of the triads, and to perceive the eternal nature of the Divine Pulsation as the seer underlying both seen and seeing.

Jñāneṣwar in his letter to Cāngdev describes how the Self is experienced at the occasion of a prospective meeting of two people – Cāngdev and himself. The terms 'deed' and 'doer' of the Verse 14 are described using several examples in these verses. The discussion is also a lesson for seekers to practice experiencing the indescribable Self at every instant. The knowledge is especially essential to practice the teaching "परस्पर-देवो भव ।" "*Paraspara-Devo bhava*" "See God in each other." This teaching is an antidote to conflicts that arise in transactions between people.

Cāngdev was a yogi with supernormal powers living for 1400 years and proud of his accomplishments. He was disturbed to hear reports about the greatness of Jñāneṣwar and his two brothers and one sister, who were only children. He was coming with his multitude of disciples, riding a tiger and carrying a whip made from a snake, to check them out. He did not know how to address them, whether to bless them or offer salutations to them. He sent them a message with a disciple, which turned out to be a blank paper. Muktābāi, Jñāneṣwar's sister, remarked: "1400 years of austerities and he's still blank!" The letter is Jñāneṣwar's loving reply.

Some verses of this letter have been quoted in the discussion on earlier Verses of *SpandaKarikas*. This is a continuation of the letter from the Verse 13 of SpandaKarikas. The letter first describes the unity of 'seen' and 'seer' and affirms the connection of all triads in the Divine Pulsation (Verses 34-37). It then describes how a conversation – speaking and listening – happens when the Self is recognized as the doer (Verses 38-40). Mutual love and thinking about the person one is about to meet are then shown to transcend the two people involved (Verses 41-43). The word "कर्तृत्व "– doership – is brought out in different aspects, but later the nature of the Self is shown to be beyond both doing and not doing any actual activity, devoid of triads (Verses 45-48). This connects to Verse 15 of *SpandaKarikas*. The Self is then shown to be the perfect Union (Verses 49-52). This Union is the Bliss of the Self, and the enjoyer and enjoyed cannot be separate from that bliss (Verses 53-55). The last five verses describe the Self as a treasure of Knowledge, beyond the knower and the known, and advice that using the means outlined in the earlier verses in practice, one can be established in the Self and Its Bliss. This connects with Verse 16 of *SpandaKarikas*. Understanding that everything is the blissful Self is the essence of all philosophy and the experience of all 'realized' beings. Hardly any single piece of literature brings out the message in such detail as this letter of Jñāneṣwar. (*Jnaneshwar*, 15)

नाना बोधाचिये सोयरिके । साचपण जेणें एके ।
नाना कल्लोळमाळिके । पाणि जेंवि ।।३४।।
जे देखिजतेविण। एकलें देखतेपण ।
हे असो आपणीया आपण । आपणचि जे ।।३५।।
जें कोणाचे नव्हतेनि असणें । जें कोणाचे नव्हतां दिसणें ।
कोणाचें नव्हतां भोगणें । केवळ जो ।।३६।।
तया पुत्र तूं वटेश्वराचा । रवा जैसा कापुराचा ।
चांगया मज तुज आपणयाचा । बोल एके ।।३७।।
ज्ञानदेव म्हणे । तुज माझा बोल ऐकणें ।
ते तळहाता तळीं मिठी देणे । जयापरि ।।३८।।
बोलोचि बोल ऐकिजे । स्वादेंचि स्वाद चाखिजे ।
कां उजिवडे देखिजे । उजिडां जेंवि ।।३९।।
सोनियां वरकल सोनें जैसा । कां मुख मुखा हो आरिसा ।
मज तुज संवाद तैसा । चक्रपाणि ।।४०।।
गोडिये आपली गोडी । घेतां काय न माये तोंडी ।
आम्हां परस्परें आवडी । तो पाडू असे ।।४१।।
सखया तुझेनि उद्देशें । भेटावया जीव उल्हासे ।
कीं सिद्धभेटी विसकुसे । ऐशिया बिहे ।।४२।।
घेवों पाहे तुझे दर्शन । तंव रूपा येवों पाहे मन ।
तेथे दर्शना होय अवजतन । ऐसे गमों लागे ।।४३।।
कांहीं करी बोले कल्पी । कां न करी न बोले न कल्पी ।
ये दोन्ही तुझ्या स्वरूपीं । न घेति उमसू ।।४४।।
चांगया तुझेनि नांवें । करणें न करणें न व्हावें ।
हें काय म्हणों परि न धरवे । मीपण हे ।।४५।।
लवण पाणियाचा थावो । माजि रिघोनि गेलें पाहो ।
तंव तेंचि नाहीं मा काय घेवो । माप जळा ! ।।४६।।
तैसें तुज आत्मयातें पाही । देखो गेलिया मीचि नाहीं ।
तेथें तूं कैचा काई । कल्पावया जोगा ।।४७।।
जो जागोनि नीद देखे । तो देखणेपणा जेंवि मुके ।
तेंवि तूंतें देखोनि मी ठाके । कांहीं नहोनि ।।४८।।
आंधाराचे ठाई । सूर्यप्रकाश तंव नाहीं ।
परी मी आहें हें कांहीं । न वचेचि जेंवि ।।४९।।
तेंवि तूंतें मी गिवसी । तेथें तूंपण मीपणेंसी ।
उखते पडे ग्रासीं । भेटीची उरे ।।५०।।

डोळ्याचे भूमिके । डोळा चित्र होय कौतुकें ।
आणि तेणेंचि तो देखे । न डंडळितां ॥५१॥
तैसी उपजतां गोष्टी । न फुटतां दृष्टि ।
मीतूंवीण भेटी । माझी तुझी ॥५२॥
आतां मी तूं या उपाधी । ग्रासूनि भेटी नुसधी ।
ते भोगिली अनुवादीं । घोळघोळू ॥५३॥
रूजतियाचेनि मिसें । रूचितें जेविजे जैसें ।
कां दर्पणव्याजें दिसे । देखतें जेंवि ॥५४॥
तैसी अप्रमेयें प्रमेये भरलीं । मौनाची अक्षरें भलीं ।
रचोनि गोष्टी केली । मेळियाची ॥५५॥
इयेनें करूनि व्याज । तूं आपणयातें बुझ।
दीप दीपपणें पाहे निज । आपुलें जैसें ॥५६॥
तैसी केलिया गोठी । तया उघडिजे दृष्टी ।
आपणिया आपण भेटी । आपणामाजी ॥५७॥
जालिया प्रळयीं एकार्णव । अपार पाणियाची धांव ।
गिळी आपुला उगव । तैसें करी ॥५८॥
ज्ञानदेव म्हणे नामरूपें । विण तुझें साच आहे आपणपें ।
तें स्वानंदजीवनपे । सुखिया होईं ॥५९॥
चांगया पुढत पुढती । घरा आलिया ज्ञानसंपत्ति ।
वेद्यवेदयत्वही अतीतीं । पदीं बैसें ॥६०॥

34. *Nānā bodhāciye soyarike, sācapaṇa jeṇeṅ eke,*
Nānā kalloḷa-māḷike, pāṇi jeṅvi.
35. *Je dekhijateviṇa, ekaleṅ dekhatepaṇa,*
Heṅ aso āpaṇīyā āpaṇa, āpaṇaci je
36. *Jeṅ koṇāce navhateni asaṇeṅ,*
jeṅ koṇāce navhatāṅ disaṇeṅ,
Koṇāceṅ navhatāṅ bhogaṇeṅ, kevaḷa jo.
37. *Tayā putra tūṅ Vaṭeśvarācā, ravā jaisā kāpurācā,*
Cāṅgayā maja tuja āpaṇayācā, bola eke.
38. *Jñānadeva mhaṇe, tuja mājhā bola aikaṇeṅ,*
Te taḷahātā taḷiṅ miṭhi deṇe, jayāpari.
39. *Boloci bola aikije, svādeṅci svād cākhije,*
Kāṅ ujivaḍe dekhije, ujiḍāṅ jeṅvi.
40. *Soniyāṅ varakala soneṅ jaisā,*
kāṅ mukha mukhā hoya ārisā,
Maja tuja saṁvāda taisā, Cakrapāṇi.
41. *Goḍiye āpalī goḍī, ghetāṅ kāya na māye toṅḍī,*

Āmhāṅ parspareṅ āvaḍī, to pāḍū ase.
42. *Sakhayā tuzeni uddeśeṅ, Bheṭāvayā jīva ulhāse,*
Kīṅ siddha-bheṭī visakuse, aiśiyā bihe.
43. *Ghevoṅ pāhe tujhe darśana,*
taṅva rūpā yevoṅ pāhe mana,
Tethe darśanā hoya avajatana, aise gamoṅ lāge.
44. *Kāṅhīṅ karī bole kalpī, kāṅ na karī na bole na kalpī,*
Ye donhī tujhyā svarūpīṅ, na gheti umasu.
45. *Cāṅgayā tujheni nāṅveṅ,*
karaṇeṅ na karaṇeṅ na vhāveṅ,
Heṅ kāya mhaṇoṅ pari na dharave, mīpaṇa he
46. *Lavaṇa pāṇiyācā thāvo, māji righoni geleṅ pāhoṅ,*
Taṅva teṅci nāhīṅ mā kāya ghevo, māpa jaḷā !
47. *Taiseṅ tuja ātmayāteṅ pāhī,*
dekho geliyā mīci nāhīṅ,
Tetheṅ tūṅ kaiṅcā kāī, kalpāvayā jogā.
48. *Jo jāgoni nīda dekhe, to dekhaṇepaṇā jeṅvi muke,*
Teṅvi tūṅteṅ dekhoni mī ṭhāke, kāṅhīṅ nahoni.
49. *Āṅdhārace ṭhāī, sūryaprakāśa taṅva nāhīṅ,*
Parī mī āheṅ heṅ kāṅhī, na vaceci jeṅvi.
50. *Teṅvi tūṅteṅ mī givasī, tetheṅ tūṅpaṇa mīpaṇeṅsī,*
Ukhate paḍe grāsīṅ, bheṭici ure.
51. *Doḷyāce bhumike, ḍoḷā citra hoya kautuke,*
Āṇi teṇeṅci to dekhe, na ḍaṅḍaḷitā.
52. *Taisī upajatāṅ goṣṭī, na phuṭatāṅ dṛṣṭi,*
Mī tūṅviṇa bheṭī, mājhī tujhī.
53. *Ātāṅ mī tūṅ yā upādhī, grāsūni bheṭi nusadhī,*
Te bhogilī anuvādīṅ, ghoḷa-ghoḷū.
54. *Rujatiyāceni miseṅ, ruciteṅ jevije jaiseṅ,*
Kāṅ darpaṇa-vyājeṅ dise, dekhateṅ jeṅvi.
55. *Taisī aprameyeṅ prameyeṅ bharalīṅ,*
mounācī akṣareṅ bhalīṅ,
Raconi goṣṭī kelī, meḷiyāci.
56. *Iyeneṅ karuni vyāja, tūṅ āpaṇayāteṅ bujha,*
Dīpa dīpapaṇeṅ pāhe nija, Āpuleṅ jaiseṅ.
57. *Taisi keliyā goṭhī, tayā ughaḍije dṛṣṭī,*
Āpaṇiyā āpaṇa bheṭī, āpaṇāmājī.
58. *Jāliyā praḷayīṅ ekārṇava, apāra pāṇiyācī dhāṅva,*

Giḷī āpulā ugava, taiseṅ karī.
59. Jñānadeva mhaṇe nāma-rupeṅ,
viṇa tujheṅ sāca āhe āpaṇapeṅ,
Teṅ svānaṅda-jīvanape, sukhiyā hoī.
60. Cāṅgayā puḍhata puḍhatī,
gharā āliyā jñānasaṁpatti,
Vedya-vedayatvahī atitīṅ, padīṅ baiseṅ.

34. *Just as in a series of waves, there is only water,*
Connecting all experiences, there is only one Truth.
35. *Though invisible, it is the only Seer.*
It is everything to Itself.
36. *It exists without support;*
It sees without there being anything to see;
It enjoys without enjoying anything; It is everything to Itself.
37. *You are the Son of That Vateshwara, (Shiva),*
As grains of camphor are to camphor.
Cāngayā, listen to what I have to say
About my relationship to you!
38. *Jñānadev says: When you listen to my words,*
It is like a hand clasping itself,
39. *Like speech hearing speech, taste tasting taste,*
Light seeing light.
40. *It's like gold testing gold, or a face becoming its own mirror.*
O Cakrapāṇī, this is how our conversation is!
41. *When sweetness tastes its own sweetness*
Won't its mouth hold it all? Our mutual love is like that.
42. *O Dear Friend, my heart is thrilled,*
At the prospect of meeting you.
But I am afraid that our meeting, will disturb perfect Union.
43. *As I yearn to see you,*
My mind begins to take on your true nature,
And then it seems as though, no meeting can occur.
44. *Doing, speaking or thinking,*
Or not doing, not speaking or not thinking –
None of these takes place in your true nature.
45. *In your true nature, Chāngayā,*
Doing or not doing does not occur.

What can I say? I can't even hold onto my "I."

46. *If salt, trying to fathom the water's depth,*
Enters the water and dissolves, who is left to fathom it?
47. *In the same way, when I try to see you,*
My "I" disappears. Then who is left even to think of you?
48. *Just as a person cannot see sleep when awake,*
In the same way, when I try to see you,
there is no "I" to do it.
49. *Just as in a dark place, devoid of sunlight,*
One's sense of "I Am" remains,
50. *In the same way, as I seek you*
And your "You" and my "I" are completely destroyed,
Only Union remains.
51. *On the screen of the eye, images are formed;*
The eye sees them, without being affected.
52. *Similarly,*
When we converse,
The knowledge of our Oneness is not disturbed
And Union takes place without a "You" and "Me."
53. *And, so having destroyed, these titles, "You" and "Me,"*
That Union described, is enjoyed again and again!
54. *Just as because of the taster, taste tastes itself,*
Or because of a mirror, a seer sees himself,
55. *In the same way, with letters of silence*
Beautifully explaining the inexplicable,
Union has been spoken of.
56. *Using these means, know your Self,*
Just as a flame, knows it is light.
57. *Because of what's been said,*
Open your eyes
And meet your Self within yourself.
58. *Do what countless rivers do, at the final deluge:*
Engulfing their own headwaters
And becoming the sea.
59. *Jñānadev says:*
Your true nature is without name and form.
Experience your own bliss. Be happy!
60. *Cāngayā, I repeat: Attaining the treasure of knowledge,*

Establish yourself in that state
Beyond the Knower and Known.

Jñāneṣwar in his letter acknowledges his Guru, Nivṛtti, for this loving gift of a delicious treat: the experience of the Self. He says the meeting of Cāngdev and Jñāneṣwar is like two clean mirrors facing each other, wherein all sense of difference vanishes. He further blesses the seekers who use these verses as a mirror to discern their own Self, asserting that they will obtain the bliss of the Self -- that which is but cannot be described, which is apparent but cannot be seen, which exists but cannot be "known." He says, "This is about the Sleep beyond sleep, the Waking beyond waking."

COMING BACK to Verse 14, we see that its second part describes the temporary nature of objects. Yet people are busy experiencing these objects. When no action is taking place, people feel their existence is coming to an end. In the society we see people always wanting to do some activity. They get bored if there is nothing to be done. They do not know how to pass their available time fruitfully. Many thrive on the recognition and honors they receive from society for their activities or position. When recognition and honors stop, many people get restless. Many people die soon after they retire from their career, having spent most of the waking moments in the adult life in pursuing that career. Many fall into dementia or get Alzheimer's disease, partly because their brain is no longer engaged in any activity. Therefore nowadays brain exercises are prescribed to seniors to keep their brain active. For some seniors, worry is the constant companion. But a seeker is never found to be bored, never needs any brain exercises, nor does s/he worry. The seeker is using the mind investigating not the "object" but the "subject." The subject is eternal, ever new, ever fresh, and full of delight.

This is where Verse 15 comes in with further explanation. When an effort directed towards any object vanishes, only a fool thinks that he/she has ceased to exist." When the effort of making mental triads vanishes, it is the Universal "I am" that remains. As seen earlier in the discussion of the Verses 12 and 13, when there is an experience of the Void, It is the Self resident in the Void that is experienced. In that "I am"-ness, there is a power of experiencing, discerning, and understanding. But the Self cannot be described by any words. It cannot be a triad. So if all doership also vanishes into nothingness along with triads, who is there to experience that Void? It is the Self that makes one experience even the Void as the absence of everything.

Jñāneṣwar Maharaj gives an example of a stallion in another work, Amritanubhava. A stallion sleeps in a standing position. And when he is awake, he remains standing. Similarly, whether there are triads or not, It is the Self that exists without modifications. In another place Jñāneṣwar describes an example of a man sleeping in a forest, where there is nobody else. Who wakes the man up? It is he himself. He is the subject and the object without undergoing any changes except the roles. Likewise, whether the work of the inner instrument – the mind and the senses – ceases or continues, the Self remains unchanged. It remains as consciousness and awareness. In samadhi, there is no distraction towards the absolute 'seer' as in the presence of triads.

A seeker asked a similar question to Ramana Maharshi (*Sri Ramana Maharshi*, 38) in February 1935. This also shows the similarity of the experiences various realized beings have from time immemorial:

D: How is that Self to be known or realized?

M: Transcend the present plane of relativity. A separate being (Self) appears to know something apart from itself (non-self). That is, the subject is aware of the object. The seer is '*drik*'; the seen is '*drishya*.'
There must be unity underlying these two, which arises as 'ego.' This ego is the nature of chit (intelligence); *achit* (insentient object) is only negation of chit. Therefore the underlying essence is akin to the subject and not the object. Seeking the *drik*, until all *drishya* disappears, the *drik* will become subtler and subtler until the absolute drik alone survives. This process is called *drishya vilaya* (the disappearance of the objective world).

D: Why should the objects *drishya* be eliminated? Cannot the Truth be realized even keeping the object as it is?

M: No. Elimination of *drishya* means elimination of separate identities of the subject and object. The object is unreal (temporary). All *drishya* (including ego) is the object. Eliminating the unreal, the Reality survives. When a rope is mistaken for a snake, it is enough to remove the erroneous perception of the snake for the truth to be revealed. With out such elimination the (experience of) Truth will not dawn.

D: When and how is the disappearance of the objective world (drishya vilaya) to be effected?

M: It is complete when the relative subject, namely the mind, is eliminated. The mind is the creator of the subject and the object and is the cause of the dualistic idea. Therefore it is the cause of the wrong notion of limited

> self and the misery consequent on such erroneous idea. If the inquiry into the ultimate cause of manifestation of mind itself is pushed on, mind will be found to be only the manifestation of the Real, which is otherwise called Atman or Brahman.

In another place, in the same book, Ramana Maharshi says that one should regard oneself as the screen where the subject and object are projected, rather than identifying oneself as the subject.

Tukārām Mahārāj describes in one of his abhangs the result of meditating on the Lord: "चित्तचैतन्या पडतां मिठी । दिसे हरिरूप अवघी सृष्टि ।।" "*Citta-Caitanyā paḍatāṅ miṭhī, dise Harirūpa avaghī sṛiṣṭi.*" "When the mind embraces consciousness, the whole universe looks like the Self."

From the above we can see that when the Self is experienced no triads remain in the observer's awareness, whether there is an external activity – like a meeting or discerning an object, or an internal activity – such as meditating on the Self. In the case of physical or mental inactivity – as in sleep or swoon, it is the Self which remains as doer with no object.

It is worth noting that just as in modern science, scientists thrive and get excited by the replication of an experiment in a lab, so also in the Science of Self, seekers replicate what has been discovered by sages before and arrive at the same exciting conclusions. Experiencing the Blissful Self continuously has effects on whatever we do in day-to-day life.

The sixteenth verse describes the inner nature as having the qualities of omniscience, etc., and explains that it can never disappear, even if no object is perceived. It can also be interpreted as in the beginning, "That omniscient inner nature can never disappear, as there is no other conscious power which experiences all states."

As discussed by Bhaṭṭa Kallaṭa in the commentary on Verse 16, the Self has three main powers: Icchāśakti, Jñānaśakti and Kriyāśakti – powers of will, knowledge, and activity. When activity ceases, It remains merely as the power of knowledge. The use of this awareness is extremely useful for all of us in daily activities. Whatever desire arises in our mind, we have the knowledge of how to carry out activities to fulfill the desire, and the power to do the activities appropriately. We can see examples of this statement in people, who are established in the Self, from the past as well as present. Instead of struggling through a life of individuality not being aware of the Self, a life that results in suffering, inadequacies, compromises and disharmony, we must opt for a life established in the Self that is fulfilled, harmonious, and blissful. This is the message of Verse 16.

By bringing the lessons into our practice we are able to sing the following concluding song by Hari Om Sharan:

मुझे मेरी मस्ती कहाँ लेके आयी ।
जहाँ मेरे अपने सिवा कुच्छ नहीं है ॥१॥
  लगा अब पता मुझ को हस्ती का मेरी ।
  बिना मेरे थारा जहाँ कुच्छ नहीं है ॥ ध्रु. ॥
सभी में सभी से परे मैं ही मैं हूँ ।
सिवा मेरे अपने कहाँ कुच्छ नहीं है ॥२॥
  न दुःख है, न सुख है नहीं शोक कुच्छ भी ।
  अजब है यह मस्ती पिया कुच्छ नहीं है ॥३॥
यह सागर ये लहरें,ये झाग और बुदबुद ।
ये कल्पित हैं जल के सिवा कुच्छ नहीं है ॥४॥
  अरे मैं हूँ आनंद, यह आनंद है मेरा ।
  है मस्ती ही मस्ती यहाँ कुच्छ नहीं है ॥५॥
ये परदा दुई का हटा के जो देखा ।
सभी एक मैं हूँ जुदा कुच्छ नहीं है ॥६॥

1. *Mujhe merī mastī kahāṅ leke āyī,*
   Jahāṅ mere apane sivā kucha nahīṅ hai.
Ref. *Lagā aba patā mujha ko hastī kā merī,*
   Binā mere thārā jahāṅ kucha nahīṅ hai.
2. *Sabhī meṅ sabhī se pare maiṅ hī main hūṅ,*
   Sivā mere apane kahāṅ kucha nahīṅ hai.
3. *Na duḥkha hai, na sukha hai nahīṅ śoka kucha bhī,*
   Ajaba hai yah mastī, piyā kucha nahīṅ hai.
4. *Ye sāgar ye lahareṅ, ye jhāga aur buda-buda,*
   Ye kalpita hai jala ke, sivā kucha nahīṅ hai.
5. *Are maiṅ hūṅ ānaṅd, yah ānaṅd hai merā,*
   Hai mastī hī mastī, yahāṅ kucha nahīṅ hai.
6. *Ye paradā duī kā, haṭā ke jo dekhā,*
   Sabhī eka maiṅ hūṅ, judā kucha nahīṅ hai.

My ecstasy has brought me to that state
Where there is nothing else besides my own Self.
Now I understand my existence
There is nothing else in my existence.
I am in all, I am beyond all,
There is nothing else except my Self.
There is no sorrow, no pleasure, nor any remorse.
This intoxication is strange, for I didn't drink anything.
The ocean, these waves, this stream, and the froth.
This is all imagination. It is nothing but water.
Oh, I am Bliss, This is my bliss.
This is all intoxication,
There is nothing else but intoxication.
I lifted this veil of duality
And saw that everything is I, and there is nothing else.

VERSE 17
EXPERIENCES OF THE ENLIGHTENED AND OTHERS

तस्योपलब्धिः सततं त्रिपदाव्यभिचारिणी ।
नित्यं स्यात् सुप्रबुद्धस्य, तदाद्यन्तेऽपरस्य तु ॥१७॥

17. *Tasyopalabdhiḥ satataṁ tripadā - vyabhicāriṇī,*
Nityaṁ syāt suprabuddhasya, tadādyante 'parasya tu.

भट्ट कल्लटः – तस्य चिद्रूपस्य सर्वगतस्य स्वभावस्य उपलब्धिः त्रिषु जाग्रदादिषु पदेषु नित्यं सुप्रबुद्धस्य भवति, तदाद्यन्ते अपरस्य प्रबुद्धस्य स्वप्नसुषुप्तादौ, जाग्रत्तुर्यौ त्वागममात्रगम्यौ ॥१७॥

Bhaṭṭa Kallaṭa: 17. Tasya cidrūpasya sarva-gatasya svabhāvasya upalabdhiḥi triṣu jāgradādiṣu padeṣu nityaṁ suprabuddhasya bhavati, tadādyante aparasya prabuddhasya svapna-suṣuptādau, jāgrat-turyo tvāgama-mātra-gamyau.

That Spanda in Its pure state is incessantly available. The fully enlightened yogi always experiences It in all the three states of waking, dreaming and deep sleep. But It is available to others who are not enlightened only at the beginning and the end of these states.

BhattaKallata: The enlightened yogi experiences his or her nature as all-pervasive consciousness uninterruptedly in all the three states of waking, dreaming and deep sleep, but the one who is a seeker (partially awakened yogi) experiences It only at the beginning and end of the states of dream and deep sleep, and can attain It in the waking and the fourth state only with Guru's grace.

SPANDA – DIVINE PULSATION is always present; and hence It is present in all the three conscious states – waking, dreaming and deep sleep - of human beings. Does everyone experience It? No. The verse says that only *suprabuddhas*, the enlightened yogis, are always aware of It, and for others It is available only at the end of one state and the beginning of the other state. Among 'others' are included *prabuddhas*, the partially enlightened or seekers; buddhas, the unenlightened; and *abuddhas*, those who are in the process of total destruction, and are not even aware of any bliss at all. *Prabuddhas* are aware of that experience, may have had a glimpse of the experience, and are yet to be established in the experience. *Buddhas* are those who want the experience but still feel that they can get it from their senses and who do not have even a glimpse of their own Spanda nature. They are not interested in finding out. *Abuddhas* do not experience any emotions at all. They do not distinguish between sentient and insentient.[49]

Enlightened beings experience that their consciousness is not separate from the universal consciousness. Even when they may look at and appreciate the names and forms of the world in their waking or dream states, they experience Spanda that pervades these states. It is like a goldsmith who recognizes the gold with which an ornament has been made while appreciating the artwork of the ornament. The universal phenomena do not confuse them. They do not have conflicts with the world. They know the same Spanda as the universe and also the maker of the universe.

In the following discussion, we will see how to discern enlightened beings so that by following their examples and teachings, we can strive to experience Spanda at will, as they do. The benefit is enormous. As the saints say, to experience It is the greatest joy, bliss surpassing any sense pleasure, it is the end of all suffering, and it is freely available to us right where we are. The main experience is described in the *Spandakārikās* Verses 18 and 19. All saints' works point to the experience, which is beyond all senses and which cannot be described in words. The saints' words bring one to the shore of the ocean of bliss and stop there; and with Guru's and saints' grace one then takes a plunge into that ocean of bliss.

In the *Bhagavad Gītā* the state of enlightened yogis is described in several places. The thirteenth chapter describes the universe, the maker of the universe, and the

---

[49] This classification of humans is given in the texts Mālinīvijaya (1/42-47) and Svacchanda Tantra (11/91-130).

characteristics of Knowledge observed in those who are enlightened. This study is also important in order to understand why some people experience Spanda and some do not. *Jñāneṣwar* has explained all the topics very lucidly in his great commentary on the *Bhagavad Gītā* called *Jñāneṣwarī*. The following has been adapted from the summary given by the recent saint *S.V. Dānḍekar* in his Marathi translation of *Jñāneṣwarī*.

First the Lord describes the individual body and the phenomenal universe perceived as *kṣetra*, meaning the field. The field consists of thirty-six components. They are: 1-5. five elements – earth, water, fire, wind, and space; 6. ego (limited I-am awareness); 7. intellect (understanding); 8. the unmanifested or *jīva* meaning individual nature; 9-13. five senses of perception – nose, tongue (to taste), eyes, skin, ears; and 14-18. five senses of action – anus, genitals, hands, feet, tongue (organ of speech), 19. mind; 20-24. the five objects of perception – smell, taste, sight, touch, and hearing; 25-29. the five objects of action (activities); 30-31. desire and hatred; 32-33. pleasure and pain; 34. consciousness; 35. *sanghāt* meaning that which brings the five elements, which are enemies[50] of each other, together; and 36. organism or group of the above thirty-five principles regarded as one thirty-sixth component.[51]

Following this, Knowledge as observed in the behavior of enlightened people is described as eighteen-fold: 1. humility (absence of pride), 2. integrity (absence of deceit), 3. non-violence, 4. patience - compassion, 5. uprightness - straightforwardness, 6. service to the Guru, 7. mental and physical purity, 8. steadfastness – ability to keep mind steady in the presence of disturbing circumstances, 9. self-control – keeping the mind away from the sense objects and focused on the Self, 10. detachment – nonattachment to sense enjoyments, 11. self-effacement – doing everything nicely but having no pride, 12. reflection on birth, death, old age, pain, and suffering, 13. non-attachment to spouse, children, house, and so on, 14. equal mindedness – neither happy nor sad regardless of such events, 15. one-pointed devotion – conviction that there is nothing more beautiful than the Self, 16. introverted – liking for solitude and disliking crowds, 17. insight that only the Supreme Self is knowledge and everything else is non-knowledge, 18. attainment

[50] Enemies – e.g. water destroys (submerges) earth, fire absorbs water, wind absorbs fire, space absorbs wind.

[51] Thirty-six components – Many of these components are different from the thirty-six fundamental principles of Kashmir Shaivism. But a connection of some of these components will be established with malas in Kashmir Shaivism in the later paragraphs.

of the Self – whose mind is so pure that the words 'he has knowledge' is a misnomer but 'he is knowledge' is a fact. Qualities opposite to the above belong to the unenlightened. There is a detailed description of the qualities of the unenlightened in *Jñāneṣwarī*. The goal of knowledge is to attain the Self, which is everywhere densely packed, and which has become everything. More detail about the goal is given in the *SpandaKārikā* Verse 18. The knower of the field is the Self and is called *Kṣetrajña*. Then there is a discussion of the Self and the universe as per the *Sānkhyaśāstra* (doctrine of Sage Kapila). *Kṣetra* is called *Prakṛti* or nature and *Kṣetrajña* is called *Puruṣa* or witnessing consciousness. Even though nature is not separated from consciousness they are regarded as twins and beginningless. The intellect, sense organs, and qualities are generated from nature. Different qualities give rise to different types of deeds from which pain and pleasure, birth and death are produced. It appears that *Puruṣa* has to experience the pain and pleasure, birth and death; but actually *Puruṣa* is beyond all these experiences.

As another summary of the thirteenth chapter of the *Bhagavad Gītā* Abhinava Gupta, the venerable teacher of Kashmir Shaivism, says:

पुमान्प्रकृतिरित्येव भेदः संमूढचेतसाम् ।
परिपूर्णास्तु मन्यन्ते निर्मलात्ममयं जगत् ॥

Pumān-prakṛtir-ityeva bhedaḥ saṁmūḍha-cetasām,
Paripūrṇāstu manyante nirmalātma-mayaṁ jagat.

> *The differentiated perception of Puruṣa and Prakṛti is the field of the ignorant. The fulfilled ones – enlightened - accept (experience) this universe as a pure reflection of the Self.* (Sw. Lakshman Joo, 46)

In these two summaries the qualities of the enlightened and unenlightened are given. In the philosophy of Kashmir Shaivism, the main reason for not experiencing Spanda always is the three malas or limitations: *āṇava*, *kārma*, and *māyīya* malas, which were discussed in detail in Verse 9. As one can see, they are inherent in an individual. We have discussed earlier the thirty-six components of the individual and universe. The component *jīva*, individual consciousness, brings about the '*āṇava*' - limitation to omniscience of Spanda. Components ego and its supporting components – intellect, mind, and ten senses bring about the *kārma* - limitation to omnipotence of Spanda. Components desire and hatred, pleasure and pain bring about the *māyīya* - limitations to omnipresence of Spanda – maya. The three kinds of sufferings – worldly (*ādhibhautik*), emotional (*ādhyatmik*), and natural or destined (*ādhidaivik*) are the result of these limitations. Because of these limitations one regards one's consciousness as separate from Spanda and becomes deluded.

There is a Sufi story that illustrates the delusion. One night Nasruddin was walking by a well. He had an impulse to look into it. He saw the moon's reflection on the water. He thought that the moon had fallen in the water, and that he had to save it, otherwise the new-moon night, when he was to break his month-long fast of Ramadan, would never come. He took a rope and tied a knot and tried to lasso the moon. It so happened that the noose caught a rock in the well. So Nasruddin felt the rope very heavy. He yanked it; the rope got loose and Nasruddin fell flat on his back on the ground. He saw the moon in the sky, and said, "Glad to be of service to you! Just as well I came along, isn't it?"[52] (Shah, 30)

We are like Nasruddin. We see the reflection of the Self in our mind, body and senses. We regard them as what we are. Like Nasruddin we are worried about things that may never happen, and make efforts to prevent them. In that process if our mind has a moment of rest we think that the happiness due to peace is because of our efforts, like Nasrudddin who tried to pull out the moon and after falling on his back, saw the real moon and credited his own efforts. Only a sane person knows that the moon never left its place and did not fall in the well, and there is only a reflection on the surface of water. Likewise an enlightened sage (called *Suprabuddha* in this verse) such as Abhinava Gupta knows that our bliss never leaves us, and that the bliss we experience in sense objects is only the bliss of Spanda. It is not because of objects that we experience bliss.

For the partially awakened or the seeker, the experience of the Self comes between the two states – waking and dream, dream and deep sleep, deep sleep and waking. Consciously a seeker can experience it effortlessly between waking and dream or deep sleep and waking. This is because the mind is thoughtless at such times. In that stillness our Self shines. But in order to experience it between the dream and sleep states, as well as during all states, Guru's grace is necessary.

Our activities in the waking state have a tremendous effect on the dream state.

[52] See Nasruddin – Idries Shah, Page 42.

Here is an experience the author had. Since this experience deals with computers those who are unfamiliar with computers can skip the story. He was downloading some printer drivers from a website on the internet for a long time. Before going to bed according to his habit of reading saints' works, he read some parts of the book, *Talks with Sri Ramana Maharshi* aloud so that his wife also could listen. Nonetheless, that night in his dream, he was downloading the drivers, and started saying aloud to his wife "I have downloaded it, downloaded it." His wife got up and tried to wake him up and he again said in his dream aloud, "I have just downloaded it." This was very scary to his wife. She told her husband she was going to call emergency 911 number, so that the doctors can check if something had gone wrong with his mind. This shook her husband up and completely woke him up. He felt bad that even in his dream he should be downloading instead of dreaming something spiritual. He prayed to his Guru and remembered the sloka from *Shiva Sutras*, त्रिषु चतुर्थं तैलवत् आसेच्यम् । (सूत्र ३।२०) "*Triṣu caturthaṁ tailavat āsechyam*" (Sūtra 3/20), "In all the three states, the Fourth state – turiya – should be poured like oil." And again he slept. Later he had a dream of his Guru and lineage in which his Guru was pleased and said, "Everything is alright. Don't be afraid." This dream was a lesson to the author – "We should do our activities, but should not get obsessed by them. Keep remembering the Supreme Self constantly in the waking state."

There will be more explanation of the conscious effort in the waking state later in Verse 21,

अतः सततमुद्युक्तः स्पन्दतत्त्वविविक्तये ।
जाग्रदेव निजं भावं न चिरेणाधिगच्छति ॥

Ataḥ satatam-udyuktaḥ spanda-tattva-viviktaye,
Jāgradeva nijaṁ bhāvaṁ na cireṇādhigacchati.

Therefore one should be always vigilant to discern the Spanda principle.
Such a person attains his own state in the waking condition quickly.

Being vigilant due to kundalini awakening also will be discussed later in Verse 25:

तदा तस्मिन् महाव्योम्नि प्रलीनशशिभास्करे ।
सौषुप्तपदवन्मूढः प्रबुद्धः स्यादनावृतः॥

Tadā tasmin mahāvyomni pralīna-śaśi-bhāskare,
Sauṣupta-padavan-mūḍhaḥ prabuddhaḥ syād-anāvṛtaḥ.

There the unenlightened yogi by considering that state a kind of deep sleep remains stupefied, while the one who is not covered with infatuation is established in 'the space where the sun and moon get merged' and abides as fully enlightened.

In *Vijñānabhairava* there is a centering technique, *Dhāraṇā 72*, about experiencing the Spanda consciously between the waking and deep sleep states about which the given verse talks.

अनागतायां निद्रायां प्रणष्टे बाह्य-गोचरे ।
सावस्था मनसा गम्या परा देवी प्रकाशते (श्लोक ७६, धारणा ७२)

Anāgatāyāṁ nidrāyāṁ praṇaṣṭe bāhya-gocare,
Sāvasthā manasā gamyā parā devī prakāśate.
(Verse 76, Dhāraṇā 72)

"When sleep has not yet fully appeared i.e. when one is about to fall asleep, and all the external objects (though present) have faded out of sight, then the state between sleep and waking is the one on which one should concentrate. In that state, the Supreme Goddess shines." This state is the turiya or fourth state, which is the substratum of all states. By focusing on this thoughtless state one can experience one's nature. That nature is beyond all thought constructs. That is the reason that state is called Parā Devi.

The rapture experienced by the fully enlightened is an incentive for the partially awakened, as discussed in *Shiva Sutra* 11, त्रितयभोक्ता वीरेशः। "*TritayaBhoktā Vīreśaḥ* " "The one who enjoys oneness in the three states becomes the master of all senses."

This can happen by Guru's grace. Eknath Maharaj says in his Abhang,

गुरुकृपांजन पायो मेरे भाई, राम बिना कच्छु जानत नाहीं ।
अंतर राम बाहर राम, जहाँ देखूँ तहाँ राम ही राम ।
जागत राम सोवत राम सपने में देखूँ तो राजा ही राम ।
एका जनार्दनी भाव ही नीका, ज्यों देखूँ सो रामसरीखा ।।

Guru-kṛpāñjana pāyo mere bhāī, Rāma binā kachu jānata nāhī.
Aṅtar Rāma bāhara Rāma, jahāṅ dekhūṅ tahāṅ Rāma hī Rāma.
Jāgata Rāma sovata Rāma, sapane meṅ dekhūṅ to Rājā hī Rāma.
Ekā Janārdanī bhāva hī nīkā, jyoṅ dekhūṅ so Rāma-sarīkhā.

I received the collyrium of Guru's Grace.
I do not know anything except Ram.
Inside I see Ram, outside I see Ram.
Wherever I see I see Ram.
When awake I see Ram,
in my dreams I see just King Ram.
Janardan's (that is the name of his Guru) Eka says,
"The conviction is very important, whatever I see is like Ram."

What is Guru's grace? Ramana Maharshi describes Guru's grace as follows.

Someone asks him, "What is Guru's grace? How does it work?"
Maharshi says: "Guru is the Self."
Devotee: "How does it lead to realization?"
Maharshi: "Ishwaro Gururatmeti - God is the same as Guru and Self. A person begins with dissatisfaction. Not content with the world he seeks satisfaction of desires by prayers to God; his mind is purified; he longs to know God more than to satisfy his carnal desires. Then God's grace begins to manifest. God takes the form of a Guru and appears to the devotee; teaches him the Truth; purifies the mind by his teachings and contact; the mind is able to turn inward; with meditation it is purified yet further; and eventually remains still without the least ripple. That stillness is the Self. The Guru is both exterior and interior. From the exterior he gives push to the mind to turn inward; from the interior he pulls the mind towards the Self and helps the mind to achieve quietness. That is Grace. Hence there is no difference between God, Guru and Self."

The Guru transforms the disciple's mind. Since all dualities that are felt, all problems that are experienced, and all hindrances to experiencing one's nature constantly reside in mind, when the mind itself is destroyed or transformed, the dualities, problems and hindrances also vanish. This is not possible without Guru's grace, since one's Self-awareness is veiled by the mind and the three malas. Guru's grace has to remove this veil.

In conclusion the detailed work of Guru's grace can be summarized in the following song of Hari Om Sharan.

सतगुरु ऐसी लगन लगाई ॥
अचल भयो मन चंचल मेरो ।
इंद्रियदमन कराई ॥
ऐसो बाण हृदयबिच मारो । देहबुद्धि बिसराई ॥
अंतर बाहर सकल चराचर ।
एक ही रूप दिखाई ॥ ऐसी लगन लगाई सतगुरु
जनम मरण के बीज मिटे जब । अंतर ज्योत जगाई ।
मनवाणी का अविषय है सो ।
वस्तु अलख लखाई ॥ ऐसी लगन लगाई सतगुरु
जीव और शिव का भेद मिटायो । सोऽहं नाद सुनायी ।
सदा एकरस विभु प्रकाशक ।
सौलज रूप बतायी ॥ ऐसी लगन लगाई सतगुरु
प्रगट्यो नित्यानंद हृदय में । पाही में मृत्यु समाई ॥
नित्यमुक्त साक्षी अविनाशी ।
तत्त्वम पद समझाई ॥ ऐसी लगन लगाई सतगुरु
बलिहारी ऐसो सतगुरु की । जिन मेरी बंध छुडाई ॥
हरिरेव जगत जगदेव हरी सब ।
झूम झूम बन गाई ॥ ऐसी लगन लगाई सतगुरु

Sataguru aisī lagana lagāī.
Acala bhayo mana caṅcala mero,
Indriya-damana karāī.
Aiso bāṇa hṛdaya-bica māro, dehabuddhi bisarāī.
aṅtara bāhara sakala carācara,
Ekahī rūpa dikhāī. Aisī lagana lagāī Sataguru...
Janama maraṇa ke bīja miṭe jaba, aṅtar jyota jagāī,
mana-vāṇī kā aviṣaya hai so,
Vastu alakha lakhāī. Aisī lagana lagāī Sataguru...
Jiva aur Śiva kā bheda miṭāyo, So 'haṁ nāda sunāyī,
Sadā ekarasa vibhu Prakāśaka,
Saulaja rūpa batāyī. Aisī lagana lagāī Sataguru...
Pragaṭyo Nityānaṅda hṛdaya meṅ, Pāhī meṅ mṛtyu samāī,
Nityamukta sākṣī avināśī,
Tattvama pada samajhāī. Aisī lagana lagāī Sataguru...

Balihārī aiso Sataguru kī, jina merī bandha chuḍāī,
Harireva jagata jagadeva Harī saba,
Jhūma jhūma bana gāī. Aisī lagana lagāī Sataguru.

Sadguru created such a longing in me.
My restless mind came to a stop.
My senses were subdued.
He released such an arrow in my heart,
that my identification with the body dropped away.
Inside and out, everywhere in the sentient and insentient,
He showed me only one Form.
All seeds of birth and death were destroyed,
when He kindled the inner flame.
Only That, which cannot be the subject of mind and speech
Started shining in all Its splendor.
He removed the difference between Jiva and Shiva –
that is the individual and the Self.
He made me listen to the nada – inner music of So 'ham.
He made me experience That which is all-pervading bright light,
which is eternal and nectarian.
Nityananda – meaning everpresent bliss – manifested in my heart.
Death vanished in oblivion,
I became free, I became witness, I became immortal.
He made me understand the meaning of "Thou art That."
I take refuge in such a Sadguru,
who freed me from my bondage.
I swayed, I danced, I sang that –
The Lord has become the universe
and the whole universe has become the Lord.

VERSE 18

UNDIFFERENTIATION OF SELF IN DIFFERENT STATES

ज्ञानज्ञेयस्वरूपिण्या शक्त्या परमया युतः ।
पदद्वये विभुर्भाति तदन्यत्र तु चिन्मयः ॥१८॥

18. Jñāna-jñeya-svarūpiṇyā śaktyā paramayā yutaḥ,
Padadvaye vibhur-bhāti tadanyatra tu cinmayaḥ.

भट्ट कल्लटः – ज्ञानज्ञेयभेदेन द्विरूपे जाग्रत्स्वप्नात्मके पदद्वये संवेदनम्, सुषुप्ततुर्यात्मके पदद्वये पुनश्चिद्रूपत्वेन केवलम् अनुभवः, न तु द्वितीयमन्यत्वेन उपलभ्यते ॥१८॥

Bhaṭṭa Kallaṭa: 18. Jñāna-jñeya-bhedena dvirūpe jāgrat-svapnātmake padadvaye saṁvedanaṁ, suṣupta-turyātmake padadvaye punaś-cidrūpatvena kevalam anubhavaḥ, na tu dvitīyam-anyatvena upalabhyate.

To the enlightened one, Spanda appears with all Its power in the form of the goal of knowledge and as knowledge itself in the waking and dream states respectively, and only as consciousness in the other state/s.

Bhaṭṭa Kallaṭa: Spanda is experienced in two ways: as objects of knowledge in the waking state, and as knowledge alone in the dream state.Its experience in deep sleep and turiya states is only as consciousness and not in any other way.

THE THIRD VERSE discussed the three states of waking, dream and deep sleep from a general point of view, stating that Spanda pervades all the three states in spite of the differences between them. But here these states are discussed from the point of view of the knower of Spanda. In the last Verse, the knower of Spanda was described as the one who experiences It in all three states. This verse explains how the knower experiences It.

To the knower, objects of the world appear as manifestations of consciousness in full power in both the waking and dream states--in the waking state as objects inseparable from consciousness, and in the dream state as mental knowledge of the objects. In the sleep state there are no objects and no mind, thus the goal of knowledge does not exist. Whatever exists in this state is consciousness alone. Since the fourth state is pure consciousness, which is the substratum of all the states, Kṣemarāj says in his commentary on *Spandakarika* that the word 'other' in this verse does not include the fourth state.

Swami Lakshman Joo instructed his students to associate the word *jñeya* – object or goal of knowledge -- with the waking state, and the word *jñāna* with the dream state. In the waking state there is the 'I-thought' from which the physical body consciousness arises and the waking world blossoms. In the dream state there is also the "I-thought" from which the subtle body consciousness arises and the dream world comes into being. In general, we regard that in a perception of an object in waking or dream states, there is a triad – subject or knower, *jñātā*, object of knowledge, *jñeya*, and knowledge, *jñāna*. We distinguish between the three. But why do Swami Lakshman Joo and this *Spandakarika* verse talk about only the object of knowledge and knowledge? The reason is that this verse is about the experience of the enlightened, the Knower of Spanda. The individual mind creates the triad – starting with "I am" itself as the subject. But in the case of the enlightened, the individual doership, I, is absent, and only knowledge and the object of knowledge remain.

Ramana Maharshi also says the same thing:[53] "What is this 'I-thought' (the ego)? Is it the subject or the object in the scheme of things?" Inasmuch as it witnesses all other objects in the waking and dream states, or at any rate we think that it does so, it must be considered to be the subject. On realizing the Pure Self, however, it will be an object only."

He also gives a technique for obviating the individual mind or 'I.' He says,

---

53 *Talks with Sri Ramana Maharshi*, Sri Ramanashram, Tiruvannamalai, 2000, Page 301.

"Whose is this 'I-thought' (the ego)? This investigation forms the *vichār*. (contemplation). 'I-thought' ('*Aham*') and 'this'-thought ('*Idam*') are both emanations from the same light. They are related to *rajoguṇa* and *tamoguṇa* respectively. [Incidentally, the next verse, Verse 19, speaks about these gunas in almost the same way. – Commentators.] In order to have the Reflected Light (pure sattva), free from *rajas* and *tamas* it must shine forth as 'I-I' [what *Spandakarikas* call as 'Aham' Vimarsh - Commentator], unbroken by 'this'- thought. This pure state momentarily intervenes between sleep and waking. If prolonged it is cosmic consciousness, or even *Iśvara*. This is the only passage to the Realization of the Self-shining Supreme Being."

In *Spandakarikas* this state between the waking and dreaming is called unmesh. In the last verse, Verse 17, we have discussed this intervening state in detail.

The waking state is defined in *Tantrāloka* as follows:

यदधिष्ठेयमेवेह नाधिष्ठातृ कदाचन ।
संवेदनगतं वेद्यं तज्जागृत्समुदाहृतम् ॥१०.२३१॥
तथा हि भासते यत्तन्नीलमन्तः प्रवेदने ।
संकल्परूपे बाह्यस्य तदधिष्ठातृ बोधकम् ॥
यत्तु बाह्यतया नीलं चकास्त्यस्य न विद्यते ।
कथञ्चिदप्यधिष्ठातृभावस्तज्जाग्रदुच्यते ॥ १०.२३४-३५॥

Yad-adhiṣṭheyameveha nādhiṣṭhātṛ kadācana,
Saṁvedana-gataṁ vedyaṁ tajjāgṛt-samudāhṛtam. (10.231)
Tathā hi bhāsate yattan-nīla-mantaḥ-pravedane,
Saṅkalpa-rūpe bāhyasya tad-adhiṣṭhātṛ bodhakam.
Yattu bāhyatayā nīlaṁ cakāstyasya na vidyate,
Kathañci-dapya-dhiṣṭhātṛ-bhāvastaj-jāgrad-ucyate.(10.234-235)

Where there can only be a sense of dependence (of being governed or controlled) and never a sense of presider (governer, controller), whatever is sensed is the known – the object or goal of knowledge; this is called waking state. The external objects grasped by senses such as jar, cloth, etc create sankalpa or thoughts, images in the mind, and only then are they experienced. The presider or doer is within the internal organ – mind – and does not exist externally. The external objects have to form mental impressions allowed by the mind, otherwise the existence of the objects does not take place.

Since a knower of the Spanda has no doership as an 'individual' and the goal of knowledge or object as only the manifestation of Spanda as vimarsh, the waking state for the knower is *jñeya* - the goal of knowledge only.

The dream state is described in *Tantrāloka* as follows:

मानभूमिरियं मुख्या स्वप्नो ह्यामर्शनात्मकः ।।१०.२५६।।
यत्त्वधिष्ठानकरणभावमध्यास्य वर्तते ।
वेद्यं सत्पूर्वकथितं भूततत्त्वाभिधामयम् ।।
तत्स्वप्नो मुख्यतो ज्ञेयं तच्च वैकल्पिके पथि ।।१०.२४७–४८।।

Mānabhūmir-iyaṁ mukhyā svapno hyāmarśanātmakaḥ (10.256)
Yattvadhiṣṭhāna-karaṇa-bhāvamadhyāsya vartate,
Vedyaṁ satpūrva-kathitaṁ bhūta-tattvābhidhāmayam,
Tatsvapno mukhyato jñeyaṁ tacca vaikalpike pathi. (10.247-48)

In the main dream state only vikalpa *or impressions of the objects already seen in the waking state exist. This is again only perception, never a perceiver. (Moreover, there is no questioning 'why,' it is just perception of the objects.) In the dream state both the subject and object are mental or in the form of* jñāna *-knowledge only.*

Since the dream state only reflects what is seen in the waking state and the knower sees 'this' – or the goal of knowledge - as a manifestation of Spanda as 'Aham' Vimarsh, what is seen in the dream state is also Spanda, but only as knowledge.

The sleep state has been described in *Tantrāloka* as follows:

यत्त्वधिष्ठातृभूतादेः पूर्वोक्तस्य वपुर्ध्रुवम् ।
बीजं विश्वस्य तत्तूष्णींभूतं सौषुप्तमुच्यते ।।
अनुभूतौ विकल्पे च योऽसौ द्रष्टा स एव हि ।
न भावग्रहणं तेन सुष्ठु सुप्तत्वमुच्यते ।।१०.२५७–५९।।
मुख्या मातृदशा सेयं सुषुप्ताख्या निगद्यते ।।१०.२६०।।

Yattva-dhiṣṭhātṛ-bhūtādeḥ pūrvoktasya vapur-dhruvam,
Bījaṁ viśvasya tattūṣṇīm-bhūtaṁ sauṣuptam-ucyate.
Anubhūtau vikalpe ca yo 'sau draṣṭā sa eva hi,
Na bhāva-grahaṇaṁ tena suṣṭhu suptatvam-ucyate. (10.257-59)
Mukhyā mātṛ-daśā seyaṁ suṣuptākhyā nigadyate (10.260)

The state wherein the above-quoted steadfast presiding power residing in waking creatures' bodies, making internal impressions of the objects of the external world, becomes dormant as the seed form, is called the sleep state. The state wherein the experiencing power of impressions, the subject of waking and dream states, ceases to perform its function, is called the sleep state. It is called the "main mother state" of the known and knowledge because all the activity ceases in this state yet is ready to be born again, creating the duality of "I" and "this."

The fourth state is described in *Tantrāloka* as follows.

पूर्णतागमनौन्मुख्यमौदासीन्यात्परिच्युतिः ॥
तत्तुर्यमुच्यते शक्तिसमावेशो ह्यसौ मतः ॥१०.२६५॥

Pūrṇatā-gamanaunmukhyam-audāsīnyāt-paircyautiḥ.
Tatturyamucyate śakti-samāveśo hyasau mataḥ.
(10.265)

That nature of "pramā" (knowledge) higher than "pramātā" (individual limited knower) greeting the arrival of fulfillment and obliteration of depression is Turya state. It is regarded as merging with Shakti.

In this verse the last three words of the first part are 'शक्त्या परमया युतः' '*Shaktyā paramayā yutaḥ*' which means endowed with Its supreme power. This is visible in the enlightened being's functioning in the world. The enlightened experiences all the power of Spanda. This naturally results in dexterity in all activities in the waking state. In the dream state there is total awareness of knowledge. The three qualities of *sattva*, *rajas* and *tamas* do not affect the enlightened. More about this experience is given in the next verse, Verse 19.

Swami Lakshman Joo, (*Sw. Lakshman Joo*, 47) has described the waking-fourth (*jagrat-turiya*), dream-fourth (*svapna-turiya*) and sleep-fourth (*sushupta-turya*) state of the knower of Spanda, which explains the meaning of 'endowed with Its supreme power.' The entire matrix of intermingling states was discussed in Verse 3. Here only the part pertaining to the knower of Spanda has been revisited:

waking – fourth: Move in the objective world while residing in Self Consciousness. It is called सुप्रबुद्धावस्था *Suprabuddhāvasthā* - the state of absolutely full awareness.

dream-fourth: You see an object, you become aware that you are not seeing the object but actually its impression and that you are dreaming and you are not awake. By the grace of your Guru, cast away the impressions and enter samādhi. You come back and forth from dream state to samādhi.The state is called सुसमाहितम् *Susamāhitaṁ* - "absolutely aware."

sleep-fourth: You enter in samādhi, yet consciousness remains in the background. Here you experience the Bliss of the Self while remaining unconscious. The state is called सुप्रसन्नम् *Suprasannaṁ* - in absolute bliss but not aware of the bliss.

Shiva Sutra 11 also makes the same point.

त्रितयभोक्ता वीरेशः ॥११॥

11. Tritayabhoktā vīreśaḥ.

The one who enjoys the rapture of oneness of the three states of waking, dream and sleep is the master of senses. This leads directly to the Verse 17 where we discussed that the knower always experiences Spanda in all the three states.

When the dualistic thoughts go away, oneness of the Spanda is experienced, with an inherent rapture sometimes called the bliss of the bliss –'आनंदी आनंद – '*Ānaṁdī ānaṁd*' by saints. This bliss transcends what the senses receive as *jñeya* - objects of knowledge - in the waking and *jñāna* in the dream states, thus making the knower the master of the senses. The saints describe their experience in the following manner. Jñāneśwar says, "A chrysanthemum has hundreds of petals, but they are not different from the flower. There might be hundreds of clay jars but the clay is just one. There are many fibers in a cloth but the cotton is just one. There are many words, but the power of speech is the same." Likewise there are multitude of names and forms in this universe, but they are only Spanda. Tukaram, the poet saint from Maharashtra says, "तुका म्हणे जे जे भेटे । ते ते वाटे मी ऐसा ।।" "*Tukā mhaṇe je je bheṭe, te te vāṭe mī aisā.*" "Whatever I come across, I feel I am that." He says elsewhere "चित्तचैतन्या पडे मिठी । विष्णुरूप झाली अवघी सृष्टि ।।" "*Citta-caitanyā paḍe miṭhī, Viṣṇurūpa jhālī avaghī sṛṣṭi.*" "When the mind embraced consciousness, the whole creation became Vishnu's form." Kabir, a Hindi poet saint says, "Oh my mind, now you can wander anywhere, because you will see God wherever you go."

A seeker can make an effort to attain this knower's state only in the waking state, since only in this state he or she can make a conscious effort to enhance the understanding. The text *Vijñānabhairav* has many centering techniques for this effort. Here are two of them.

Dhāraṇā: सर्वं देहं चिन्मयं हि जगद्वा परिभावयेत् ।
युगपन्निर्विकल्पेन मनसा परमोदयः ।।४०।।
(श्लोक ६३, धारणा ४०)

Sarvaṁ dehaṁ cinmayaṁ hi jagad-vā paribhāvayet,
Yugapannirvikalpena manasā paramodayaḥ.
(Verse 63, Dhāraṇā 40)

Even as you are sitting or walking, contemplate that the whole body and all its surroundings are both replaced by vibrating consciousness and that there are no other forms, just a living presence. When you contemplate with one-pointed and unwavering mind that your body and the entire universe are both of the nature of consciousness, you experience Supreme Awakening, meaning you experience the entire universe enveloped in and pervaded by Divine Light. The contemplation should be done spontaneously and without hesitation, with unwavering mind not subject to doubts.

Dhāraṇā: सर्वं जगत्स्वदेहं वा स्वानन्दभरितं स्मरेत् ।
युगपद्स्वामृतेनैव परानन्दमयो भवेत् ।।
(श्लोक ६५, धारणा ४२)

Sarvaṁ jagat-svadehaṁ vā svānand-bharitaṁ smaret,
Yugapad-svāmṛtenaiva parānandamayo bhavet.
(Verse 65, Dhāraṇā 42)

Contemplate in one sweep the entire universe and your body in its totality filled with the bliss of the Self. Through your own ambrosia-like bliss, you will become identified with supreme bliss.

To summarize the discussion how the knower sees the goal of knowledge and knowledge we hear Tukaram saying:

आणिक दुसरे मज नाही आतां ।
नेमिले या चित्तापासूनियां ।।१।।
पांडुरंग ध्यानी पांडुरंग मनी ।
जागृती स्वपनी पांडुरंग ।।२।।
पडिले वळण इंद्रियां सकळा ।
भाव तो निराळा नाही दूजा ।।३।।
तुका म्हणे नेत्री केली ओळखण ।
तटस्थ तें ध्यान विटेवरी ।।४।।

1. *Āṇika dusare maja nāhī ātāṅ*
   Nemile yā cittāpāsūniyāṅ.
2. *Pāṅḍuraṅga dhyānī Pāṅḍuraṅga manī,*
   Jāgṛtī svapanī Pāṅḍuraṅga.
3. *Paḍile vaḷaṇa iṅdriyāṅ sakaḷā,*
   Bhāva to nirāḷā nāhī dūjā.
4. *Tukā mhaṇe netrī kelī oḷakhaṇa,*
   Taṭastha teṅ dhyāna viṭevarī.

1. *Nothing more is there for me to do now.*
   From the time this mind got focused how!
2. *Pāṇḍurang is in meditation, in my mind Pāṇḍurang.*
   In waking and dream Pāṇḍurang.
3. *It has become a habit to senses all.*
   There is no other disposition at all.
4. *Tukaram says, "My eyes adore with appreciation*
   that Form standing aloof on the brick, in meditation."

VERSE 19

THE ENLIGHTENED AND SPECIAL SPANDA

गुणादिस्पन्दनिःष्यन्दाः सामान्यस्पन्दसंश्रयात्
लब्धात्मलाभाः सततं स्युर्ज्ञस्यापरिपन्थिनः ॥१९॥

*19. Guṇādi-spanda-niḥṣyandāḥ sāmānya-spanda-saṁśrayāt,
Labdhātma-lābhāḥ satataṁ syur-jñasyā-pari-panthinaḥ.*

भट्ट कल्लटः – गुणस्पन्दस्य सत्त्वरजस्तमोरूपस्य ये निःष्यन्दाः प्रवाहाः,ते सामान्यस्पन्दमाश्रित्य प्रसृता अपि सततं ज्ञस्य विदितवेद्यस्य योगिनः स्युर्भवेयुः,भवन्त्यपरिपन्थिनः अनाच्छादकाः स्वभावस्य ॥१९॥

Bhaṭṭa Kallaṭa: – 19. Guṇa-spandasya sattva-rajas-tamo-rūpasya ye niḥṣyandāḥ pravāhāḥ, te sāmānya-spandam-āśritya prasṛtā api satataṁ jñasya vidita-vedyasya yoginaḥ syurbhaveyuḥ, bhavantyapari-panthinaḥ anācchādakāḥ svabhāvasya.

Different guṇas which are special emanations of Spanda acquire their individual power from and are always dependent upon the general Spanda. They can never be the enemies of the Knower of the Spanda.

Bhaṭṭa Kallaṭa: Sattva guṇa, Rajo guṇa, Tamo guṇa are the particular qualified streams emanating from the general Spanda. They are always flowing but can never antagonize the knower yogi, who has attained what is to be known, by covering the essential nature of consciousness.

IN THE PREVIOUS VERSE we have seen *how* the knower experiences Spanda in all the three states of waking, dream and deep sleep. This verse answers the question *why* is it that the knowers of the Spanda experience It all the time, while the next verse answers *why* don't we, people in general, become aware of It.

This verse explains that the three coverings or guṇas – Sattva, Rajas and Tamas – emanate from the general Spanda. The knowers of the Spanda being one with the Spanda have transcended these guṇas, so even though they may be aware of them they cannot be bound by them. This is similar to how a person who has flown in an airplane in daylight sees that before the plane takes off the sky may be cloudy, but once the plane has established its assigned height she can see the clouds far below, while for her the sun is shining ever so brightly.

In the 14th chapter of the *Bhagavad Gita* Lord Krishna tells Arjuna about the guṇas and about the person who transcends them. In *Jñāneśwari* there is a beautiful explanation which is summarized in the following.

We forget that our nature is knowledge – consciousness. This ignorance also called *māyā* gives rise to the individual (*kṣetrajña* or "knower of the field") and what is known as *Prakṛti* – nature (*kṣetra*). This forgetfulness creates the three guṇas – Sattva, Rajas and Tamas. In the individual, intellect, mind, and ego are created from the three guṇas. Out of ego the five elements – earth, water, fire, air and space - become visible, as also the corresponding objects and senses of perception and action. The guṇas reside simultaneously in a person, just as fire takes form as wood. They become the gross and subtle bodies of a person. One quality dominates others at different times. Accordingly a person has different tendencies and moods. It is the guṇas which make one identify oneself with the body. Then one sees the universe and its objects which are also products of the three guṇas. Each guṇa binds a person to the world. Sattva guṇa binds a person with fetters of happiness and knowledge. A person thinks he or she is great because of scholarship, knowledge of the external world, material possessions and honors received from the society. *Rajoguṇa* is derived from '*Raja*' Sanskrit root meaning 'to enjoy.' It binds a person in the enjoyment of sense objects and hankering after them. It creates desires, and makes a person restless for activity. *Tamoguṇa* is the dark cloud of the night of infatuation and ignorance. Because of *Tamoguṇa* a person becomes lethargic, gets into dangerous situations without thinking. All guṇas create the cycle of birth and death. By predominance of *Sattva* guṇa a person is born in a learned family, that of *Rajoguṇa* a person is born in an active and ritualistic family, and that of *Tamoguṇa* a person is born as an animal, bird, worm or tree. But a person who knows Spanda goes beyond the guṇas and is not affected by them and is freed from the cycle of birth and death.

When Arjuna asks about the signs of the person who has transcended the guṇas, how he behaves, how he conquers the guṇas, Jñāneśwar says, "ShriKrishna says to Arjuna that his method of asking questions is unusual. 'What actions does the person who has transcended guṇas perform, how he conquers guṇas?' is a self-contradictory question like asking 'How is this truth false?' The one who is beyond the three guṇas is never caught by the guṇas and if such a one is caught among the guṇas, that one is never entangled by them. So ShriKrishna modifies the question as, 'When a person is caught among the guṇas how can one know whether the person is entangled by them or not?' Even though different guṇas become dominant at different times in his body, the person who has transcended the guṇas does not identify with them. When *Sattva guṇa* dominates, the person does not regard him/herself as happy. When *Rajoguṇa* dominates the person is not attached to karmas; and when *Tamoguṇa* dominates, the person does not become infatuated. The person who has transcended guṇas does not identify with the body. Lord Krishna says, 'न द्वेष्टि संप्रवृत्तानि न निवृत्तानि न कांक्षते । *Na dveṣṭi saṁprvṛttāni na nivṛttāni na kāṅkṣate.*' "Such a person does not hate when guṇas arise nor does he long for them when they cease. He never puts himself in opposition with the guṇas."

Muktanand Baba, our Guru, used to quote the second part of verse 23 from the 14th chapter of the *Bhagavad Gita*, saying, " गुणा वर्तन्त इत्येव योऽवतिष्ठति नेङ्गते ।" "*Guṇā vartanta ityeva yo 'vatiṣṭhati neṅgate* " "The knower thinks, 'Guṇas are working according to their nature, but they have nothing to do with me,' remains steadfast and is not swayed by them." Jñāneśwar says in his commentary on the verse, "It is like the sky which cannot be shaken by a wind, or the sun which cannot be swallowed by darkness."

In one evening program Muktanand Baba said, "Guṇas and malas are 'same, same'." Exploring this point connects Jñāneśwar's exposition and the fourteenth chapter of the *Gita* discussed earlier with this verse. In *Shiva Sutras*, there are two aphorisms (sutras)

अ)ज्ञानं बन्धः । (शिवसूत्र ३.२)
(A) Jñānaṁ Bandhaḥ. (Shiva Sutras 1 . 2, 3.2)

योनिवर्गः कलाशरीरम् ॥ (शिवसूत्र १.३)
Yonivargaḥ Kalāśarīram. (Shiva Sutras 1. 3)

Aphorism 2 can be interpreted in two ways, with or without the prefix A. When interpreted with the prefix it means ignorance of the Self is bondage. When interpreted without the prefix A, it means 'differentiated knowledge is bondage.' This aphorism also appears in the third section *Āṇavopāya* of *Shiva Sutras* as the second aphorism, where knowledge from an individual's point of view, i.e. differentiated knowledge, is discussed. Differentiated knowledge regards the individual consciousness and Supreme consciousness as different. This is called *Āṇava mala*. This ignorance of oneness that arises due to contraction of Vimarsha – general spanda – leads to identification with body, forgetting the pulsation of pure "I-I" and identifying with individual ego which is the cause of the universe (*Yonivarga*). That is *Māyīya mala* in which one takes on individual doership which is the embodiment of actions (*Kalā śarīra*), thus giving rise to *Kārma mala*. Thus out of *Āṇava mala* arise *māyiya* and *kārma malas*. *Āṇava mala* is the contraction of the general spanda through māyā tattva taking on the five kanchukas – limitations, namely, *kalā* (limitation of power of action), *rāga* (limitation of free will - attachment), *vidyā* (limitation of knowledge), *kāla* (limitation of omnipresence – experiencing time), *niyati* (limitation to objects) brings out the individual self (*puruṣa*) and limited nature (*prakṛti*) with which the three guṇas coexist. In this manner, existence of malas implies the existence of guṇas. While if one is bound by the three guṇas one exhibits the three malas or limitations described above. In this manner existence of guṇas imply existence of malas. Muktanand Baba's statement that guṇas and malas are the same is thus true. The guṇas are individualized experiences of malas which act like causes.

As the verse asserts, the knower of Spanda transcends the three guṇas not by denying or fighting and defeating them; rather the knower always stays in the blissful state by discerning the general Spanda through them. In *Vijñāna Bhairava* there are several *dhāraṇās* (techniques) to achieve this state.

समः शत्रौ च मित्रे च समो मानावमानयोः ।
ब्रह्मणः परिपूर्णत्वादिति ज्ञात्वा सुखी भवेत् ॥ श्लोक १२५, धारणा १००॥

Samaḥ śatrau ca mitre ca samo mānāva-mānayoḥ,
Brahmaṇaḥ paripūrṇa-tvāditi jñātvā sukhī bhavet.
(Verse125, Dhāraṇā 100)

When the seeker has the same attitude towards enemy and friend, towards honor and insult, with the understanding that Brahman is all-pervasive, the seeker becomes happy.

न द्वेषं भावयेत्क्वापि न रागं भावयेत्क्वचित् ।
रागद्वेषविनिर्मुक्तो मध्ये ब्रह्म प्रसर्पति ॥ श्लोक १२६. धारणा १०१॥

Na dveṣaṁ bhāvayet-kvāpi na rāgaṁ bhāvayet-kvacit,
Rāga-dveṣa-vinir-mukto madhye Brahma prasarpati.
(Verse 126, Dhāraṇā 101)

The seeker should neither maintain hatred nor attachment for anyone, including oneself, or any thing. Freed of both attachment and aversion there arises in his/her heart the awareness of Brahman.

The first part of the two verses lists practices one needs to practice in all waking hours while dealing with the world. At first it might be difficult due to old habits of deprecating others or oneself. But after a while this equal vision becomes a habit. Its effect is described in the second part of each verse. These effects happen when the individual ego vanishes. These practices become effortless when the Guru's blessing is received.

One great being, Kashi Vishweshwar Baba, wrote in his reply to one of his disciples who complained of worldly conflicts, "मी ह्या जगांत परमेश्वराशिवाय आणखी कांहींच पाहिलेले नाहीं." "I have not seen anything else except the Lord in this world." The summary of the verse is contained in that sentence. So even when the guṇas are at play the knower experiences only the general Spanda – or "I-I" or "Aham Vimarsh."

The discussion can be summarized in Jñāneṣwar's words. He says in his work, *Haripāṭh*, that it is better to leave alone the discussion of the guṇas or attributes and connect to that Self which is beyond, both with and without attributes.

त्रिगुण असार निर्गुण हें सार । सारासार विचार हरिपाठ ॥ १॥
सगुण निर्गुण गुणाचें अगुण । हरिवीण मन व्यर्थ जाय ॥२॥
अव्यक्त निराकार नाही त्या आकार । जेथोनि चराचर हरिसी भजे ॥३॥
ज्ञानदेवा ध्यानीं रामकृष्ण मनीं । अनंत जन्मोनी पुण्य होय ॥४॥

Triguṇa asāra nirguṇa he sāra, sārāsāra vicāra Haripāṭha.
Saguṇa nirguṇa guṇāceṅ aguṇa, Harivīṇa mana vyartha jāya.
Avyakta nirākāra nāhī tyā ākāra, jethoni carācara Harisī bhaje.
Jñānadevā dhyānīṅ Rāma-Kṛṣṇa manīṅ, anaṅta janmonī puṇya hoya.

What is composed of the three guṇas is unreal, and what is without guṇas is the real. Repeating 'Hari' is discriminating between the real and unreal.
Mind thinking about form and formless is wasted, without thinking of Hari who is beyond both.
Worship Hari, who is without manifestation or form and has no shape, but from where the sentient and insentient universe arises.
Jñānadev's mind meditates on Rāma Kṛṣṇa, that is the result of merits of countless lifetimes.

VERSE 20

THE UNENLIGHTENED AND SPECIAL SPANDA

अप्रबुद्धधियस्त्वेते स्वस्थितिस्थगनोद्यताः ।
पातयन्ति दुरुत्तारे घोरे संसारवर्त्मनि ॥२०॥

20. Aprabuddha-dhiya-stvete svasthiti-sthaganodyatāḥ,
Pātayanti duruttāre ghore saṁsāra-vartmani.

भट्टकल्लटः – स्वल्पप्रबोधांस्तु स्वस्थितेः चिद्रूपायाः स्थगनं कृत्वा, ते गुणाः पातयन्ति दुरुत्तारे अस्मिन् विषमे संसारवर्त्मनि, यतस्तदात्मकमेव नित्यमात्मानं पश्यन्ति, न तु शुद्धबुद्धस्वरूपतया ॥२०॥

Bhaṭṭa Kallaṭa: 20. Svalpa-prabodhāṅstu svasthiteḥ cidrūpāyāḥ sthaganaṁ kṛtvā, te guṇāḥ pātayanti duruttāre asmin viṣame saṁsāra-vartmani, yatas-tadātmakam-eva nityam-ātmānaṁ paśyanti, na tu śuddha-buddha-svarūpatayā.

The guṇas and other special currents of the general Spanda are always active in covering the natural state of those who are ignorant of the Spanda. They push them down further in the fearsome path of worldliness so hard to go across.

Bhaṭṭa Kallaṭa: The guṇas cover the nature of Supreme Consciousness of those who have limited knowledge. They push them down in this dangerous path of worldliness which is hard to go across, so that they see their individual self only in terms of the guṇas, not as their own pure omniscient nature.

THIS VERSE answers the question why an individual with limited understanding does not experience the Self all the time just as the knower of Spanda does.

The three guṇas and the special currents of sound, touch, form, taste and smell arising from the Spanda cover the natural state of an individual. They push the individual down by making the understanding limited. First of all limited understanding makes us look outside and enquire only about the outside world but never go within. Whatever we perceive by our senses, we regard as true. Thus our life consists entirely of our world, our body, and our emotions. Most of us don't even have a clue that there is anything beyond. Thus utmost importance is given to the happenings in the physical world and our mind. We spend our attention, time and effort in amassing different sense objects around us. We are subject to ups and downs, and go through the cycles of happiness and sorrow. We regard it as 'normal' to worry about different things happening and some other things not happening in our lives. We have desire, anger, craving, pride, infatuation or fear, and jealousy, and we regard them as normal. We are afraid of dying. Finally we go through the cycles of birth and death, but we do not believe that there is such a cycle. We forget that this is all temporary. But no sense object can give us true happiness.

A story[54] illustrates how the objects of sense pleasures which one regards as true can stop being pleasurable and can become source of despair in a moment. A very prosperous businessman, who lived in an affluent city, returned from his office by his fancy automobile to his mansion. His chauffeur tapped on the horn to let the people at home know that the master of the house had arrived. After parking the car, the chauffeur and his servants rushed out and with great respect helped him out of his car. When he saw his beautiful expensive car, his luxurious decorated mansion, and inside it his beautiful beloved wife, elegantly dressed and adorned with jewelry, and his dear and tender children, adorably dressed in latest fashion for youngsters, he was greatly pleased. He was certain that he was indeed getting joy from his wife, children and wealth. Soon it was dinner-time. The chef appeared and announced that the dinner was ready. With the couple's permission, he served an array of hot tasty delicacies on platters on the huge dining table. The family began their meal. Again the businessman was certain that the spicy basmati rice, puranpolis and patra[55] were giving him sheer pleasure. As they ate, their conversation was full of laughter, frolic and fun.

---

[54] Original story is in *Pravachan Sudha - Nectar of Discourses* by Swami Maheshwaranand Giri, English Translation by Umesh Nagarkatte.

[55] Indian delicacies

Suddenly the phone rang. Still at the table, the businessman lifted the receiver near him. As he listened to the news he seemed benumbed, as if struck with lightening. His face became pale, as if he had just drunk castor oil. He had just learned that the price of his biotech firm's stock had suddenly plummeted, and as a consequence he had lost billions of dollars. Now the delicious dinner, which had been so delectable earlier, suddenly lost all its juice and became as appetizing as mud. He had lost his appetite. Saying he had a stomachache, he got up from the table, and went over and slumped in his comfortable office chair. Now all the laughter, fun and frolic was over, and his mind wandered restlessly. His mansion was still there, and so were his wife, his children, their beautiful clothes, and their diamond and pearl ornaments. All the objects of the five senses: sound, touch, form, taste, and smell were around. Now, though, nothing was pleasing him. He was full of consternation, and worried, "What is going to happen now? What can I tell my shareholders and employees? Will I lose the office building or my mansion? Will I lose the beautiful things I have in life?" His mind, which never before remembered God even by mistake, was now quietly muttering, "My Lord! Be merciful to the poor! Now saving my dignity is in Your hands."

Now it was late at night. The wealthy man lay in his bed with velvet sheets. But the soft velvet did not comfort him; it pierced his skin like thorns. He was praying to the Goddess of sleep to bless him. The Goddess of Sleep is an ambassador to God's abode. She only takes one there, when one abandons all worries, turns away from the world's cares, thinks noble thoughts, spreads hands and feet, and closes one's eyes.

This anecdote illustrates that there is definitely no happiness in external sense objects. If there were, wouldn't his mansion, his beautiful family, and his tasty banquet have given him as much happiness in distress as they did before? If it is in the nature of objects to produce happiness, why does happiness disappear when the mind becomes restless? Only in peace of mind is there happiness - never in outer things. Only when the mind-waves are directed to one point and become quiet, does the bliss of the Self get reflected in the mind-waves, and through them, in outer objects. When the mind-waves get scattered, they do not reflect the bliss of the Self; consequently when one views the world through these distressing mind-waves, one experiences only sorrow, not happiness, in outer objects.

Therefore it is necessary to examine the gunas and the other currents with the correct perspective. In essence this verse is related to Kashmir Shaivism's thirty-one lower principles arising out of maya and its coverings, which pervade us inside and out. We forget to turn inside and experience the general Spanda - Self, the root of both our being and the universe, pulsating in us as 'I-I' without any attributes, even when It makes the mind and senses function within us.

In *Shiva Sutras*, sage Vasugupta says:

कलादीनां तत्त्वानामविवेको माया ॥ शिवसूत्र ३.३॥

Kalādīnāṁ tattvānām-aviveko māyā (Śiva sūtra 3.3)

> *Without discrimination regarding the thirty-one principles starting with Kalā people live in the energy of illusion - māyā.*

If we do not discriminate the lower thirty-one principles, we are entangled by maya. We must contemplate about how maya and the other lower thirty-one impure principles bind us. Then we can turn away from them and contemplate the first five pure principles to free us. To recall all the thirty-six principles expounded in Kashmir Shaivism, we study the following table to see which principles we should contemplate. (*Kashmir Shaivism – The Secret Supreme –* Swami Lakshman Joo.)

The thirty-one principles arise from the Māyā shakti – energy of illusion by which we are limited and we experience the duality and suffer from the gunas that are produced out of Nature – Prakṛti, the consequences of worldliness – happiness, sadness, delusion, and the cycle of birth and death.

Five Pure Elements	Six Coverings
Self - **Śiva**	Illusion of Individuality - Māyā
"I"ness – **Śakti** (Spanda)	Limitation of creativity - Kalā
"This"ness predominent in "I"ness - Iśwara (Icchā)	Limitation of knowledge - Vidyā
"I"ness in "This"ness - Sadāśiva (Jñāna)	Limitation of attachment - Rāga
Pure Knowledge "I"-"this" separate - Śuddha Vidyā (kriyā)	Limitation of time - Kāla
	Limitation of place – Niyati

Five Internal Organs	Five Organs of Cognition	Five Organs of Action	Five Subtle Senses
Ego connected with subjectivity- Puruṣa	Ears – Śrotra	Tongue/larynx – Speech – Vāk	Sound – Śabda
Nature - Prakṛti	Skin – Tvak	Hands – Pāṇi	Touch – Sparśa
Ego connected with objectivity- Ahaṁkār	Eyes – Cakṣu	Feet – Pada	Form – Rūpa
Intellect - Buddhi	Tongue – Rasanā	Procreation – Upastha	Taste – Rasa
Mind - Mānas	Nose – Grhāṇa	Excretion – Pāyu	Smell – Gandha

Five Gross Elements
Space – Ākāsh
Air – Vāyu
Fire – Agni
Water – Jala
Earth – Pṛthvi

Maya is a power of concealment or contraction of Svatantrya – freedom of the Spanda. It is accompanied with its five kañcukas, coverings or limitations: 1. Kalā: means limitation in arts. Unbounded creativity of the Spanda is reduced in us as limited creativity. We have only a few artistic talents. We can functionn only in a limited number of fields. 2. Vidyā: means differentiated knowledge. Our knowledge is limited to knowledge of duality. 3. Rāga: means attachment. We become aware that we are not full. We are attached to people, sense objects, position, house, clothes, body. We are dissatisfied and crave for more sense pleasures. This creates in us pride of possessing a beautiful object. We are proud of our accomplishments. We are jealous if some one else gets the object we desire instead of us. We are angry if someone criticizes us, or takes our possessions. We are fearful whether we will lose something we have. We are fearful of terrorists. We are infatuated by someone's charms. Thus the six inner enemies always play havoc in us. 4. Kāla: means limitation of time. We become aware of the past, present and future. We become aware of our age: I am old, I am young. I am twenty years old. I am sixty five years old. We also become aware of death. 5. Niyati: We line up our daily chores in a sequence of actions. We form rules of behavior. We are subject to destiny or fruits of our past actions. We become aware that we reside in such and such a place, and that we do not reside everywhere.

Maya makes individual beings take birth and have specific personality and nature. Because of Maya's coverings we are confined to experience above limitations. Our nature consists of the three gunas: sattva, rajas and tamas. The puryaṣṭaka – consisting of three antaḥkaraṇ - inner instruments: mind, intellect, and ego; and five subtle senses, five organs of perception, five of action, and five gross elements, make up our world of duality and the knowledge of differentiation. The five columns of five principles in the above table are actually shown to be embodiments in the respective order of the five subtle senses of sound, touch, form, taste and smell, which are also described as the five currents in the beginning. Thus for example, mind, nose, anus, and the earth are all manifestations of smell. So in the beginning of the third chapter of *Tantrālok*, the author Abhinav Gupta describes the world as a reflection of theses five subtle senses.

Thus we are too enmeshed to think of God, even if we have come across the first five principles.Our priorities are reversed. We think first of worldly attainment and then only of the attainment of God, or we do not even think of God. We struggle night and day to carry out our daily chores. So Saint Jñāneśwar says in his *Haripāṭh*, 4th abhang, the third verse,

सायास करिसी प्रपंच दिननिशीं । हरिसी न भजसी कवण्या गुणे

Sāyāsa karisī prapañca dina-niśīṁ, Harīsī na bhajasī kavaṇyā guṇe.

"*You struggle in the world, day and night, why don't you think of the Lord?" Logically, this also means that if we think of the Lord, we do not need to struggle day in and day out. The worldly life becomes divine in itself. Of course, the world does not go away.*

In *Vijnanabhairav*, there is a centering technique, dharana regarding this:

इन्द्रियद्वारकं सर्वं सुखदुःखादिसङ्गमम् ॥ श्लोक १३६, धारणा १११ ॥

Indriya-dvārakaṁ sarvaṁ sukha-duḥkhādi-saṅgamam.
(Verse 136, Dhāraṇā 111)

All contact with pleasure and pain is through the senses. Knowing this we should detach ourselves from the senses, and withdrawing within we should abide in our essential Self, which is pure and omniscient.

This technique shows that we have to rise above our senses, mind, intellect and ego. The simplest way to do this is to be in the constant company of saints.

When we come in the company of saints their grace acting on us pierces through the impure thirty-one principles, we get undifferentiated knowledge, and we experience the five pure principles. We become aware of "I, I" even though we are aware of 'this' i.e. all world as mere expression of the "I, I" – common spanda. The experience is so blissful that we have 'daring courage' in bouncing between 'this' and 'I.' Vatulnath, a siddha who practiced Kashmir Shaivism around the twelfth century, writes in the first sutra – aphorism of his *Vātulnāth Sutras.* (*Swami Lakṣman Joo*, 48)

महासाहसवृत्त्या स्वरूपलाभः ॥१॥

Mahāsāhasavṛttyā Svarūpa-lābhaḥ. (1)

By daring courage our real nature is exposed.

While dealing with the world it is not possible to experience just the subjective "I, I"; we must also deal with the world as an expression of 'I.' At first, we have to make an effort – daring courage - to rise above the cognitive world and experience the Self as "I Am." Then without losing the awareness of the 'I AM' experience we must come down to the cognitive world. In the text there are several aphorisms that show us how this happens. "One gets entry in the great fullness states simultaneously by bursting open the boards of both subjectivity and objectivity." (Sutra 3) "By tasting the power of Divine will, knowledge and action (third, fourth and fifth principles) the unfettered state unfolds within." (Sutra 8) "By giving rise to the twelve-fold flow of energy consisting of five senses of perception, fives senses of action, mind and intellect, we must make an effort to make these experiences transformed into ullās - upward flows of shaktis, then only we experience the Swātantrya Śakti – Power of freedom of the Self." (Sutra 10).

There was a saint, Gondavalekar Maharaj (1845-1913) (*Gondavalekar Maharaj*, 9) who was a householder and contemporary of other famous saints Akkalkot Maharaj, Shirdi Sai Baba, Gajanan Maharaj in Maharashtra, India. Like all saints he said, "It is not necessary to leave the world to do effort to experience God. Both can be done simultaneously. Because there is worldly life, it is important to understand the spiritual life. When we use discrimination in prapanca, worldly life, paramārtha – spiritual life or experiencing the highest truth is not far. Both are two sides of a coin. When we lift a coin, we lift both its sides. Similarly, when we look at the world the underlying truth is also there. But we have to be aware of It. Since we have so much attraction for the one side, the saints have to show its shortcomings and emphasize the other side. But when the attachment, and ego about the world is reduced and the Lord is remembered, that is experiencing the second side."

He further says that just as we need love in the world, we need love and faith in searching for the Lord. In worldly life however much effort we put in, that much payoff is not guaranteed, but in spiritual life the more effort we put in, the more the payoff. If the Lord is behind us in the world, that world itself makes life spiritual. "I am the doer" is the first step in worldly life; while "the Lord is the doer" is the first step in spiritual life. To be with sense pleasures away from the Lord is called worldly life, whereas remaining in the sense objects while in the company of the Lord is spiritual life. To perform actions with ego is the worldly life while performing them without ego is living a spiritual life.

Living a spiritual life breaks the world's hold on us. That is why Saint Jñāneśwar says in his *Haripāṭh*, in the same 4th abhang quoted earlier, as the last line:

ज्ञानदेव म्हणे हरिजप करणें । तुटेल धरणे प्रपंचाचे

Jñānadeva mhaṇe Harijapa karaṇeṅ tuṭela dharaṇe prapañcāce

> *Jñānadev says, doing Hari japa breaks the world's hold on you. Then you lose all sorrow and gain all joy.*

In conclusion, we must rise above gunas and the thirty-one impure principles. Jñāneśwar mahārāj shares a secret of his heart with all of us in the following 'Abhang'

योग तो कठीण साधिता साधेना ।
जेणें गा चिद्घना न पाविजे ।।१।।
याचि लागी आतां सांगणे हे तुज ।
माझे निजगुज अंतरींचे ।।२।।
इंद्रिये कोंडावी आवरावे मन ।
सहज ब्रह्मज्ञान लाधलाशी ।।३।।

जेथे जेथे मन धांवोनिया जाय ।
तेथे गुरुचे पाय बसवावे ।।४।।
ज्ञानदेव म्हणे होई तूं निर्गुण ।
कळेल तुज खूण पूर्ण तेव्हां.

1. *Yoga to kaṭhiṇa sādhitā sādhenā*
Jeṇeṅ gā cidghanā na pāvije.
2. *Yāci lāgī ātāṅ sāṅgaṇe he tuja*
Mājhe nijaguja aṅtarīṅce.
3. *Iṅdriye koṅḍavī āvarāve mana*
Sahaja Brahma-jñāna lādhalāśī.
4. *Jethe jethe mana dhāṅvoniyā jāya*
Tethe Guruce pāya basavāve.
5. *Jñānadeva mhaṇe hoi tū nirguṇa*
Kaḷel tuja khuṇa purṇa tevhāṅ.

Becoming one with the Self is difficult even if you try.
That is why awareness of Pure Consciousness is unattainable,
For this reason, I am now revealing
The secret of my heart.
Lock your senses inward, and control your mind
You will naturally obtain the knowledge of the Self.
Wherever your mind runs away
Place the feet of the True Guru there.
Jñānadev says: go beyond the three gunas.
Only then you know the complete sign of the Self.

VERSE 21

NECESSITY OF INCESSANT EFFORT

अतः सततमुद्युक्तः स्पन्दतत्त्वविविक्तये ।
जाग्रदेव निजं भावं न चिरेणाधिगच्छति ॥२१॥

21. Ataḥ satatam-udyuktaḥ spanda-tattva-viviktaye.
Jāgrad-eva nijaṁ bhāvaṁ na cireṇādhi-gacchati.

भट्टकल्लटः – अतः सततं सर्वकालं यः करोत्युद्योगं स्पन्दतत्त्वस्य स्वरूपाभिव्यक्त्यर्थं,
स जाग्रदवस्थायामेव निजमात्मीयं तुर्यभोगाख्यं स्वभावम् अचिरेणैव कालेन प्राप्नोति ॥२१॥

21.Bhaṭṭa Kallaṭa – Ataḥ satataṁ sarva-kālaṁ yaḥ karotyudyogaṁ spanda-tattvasya svarūpābhivyaktyarthaṁ, sa jāgrad-avasthāyām-eva nijam-ātmīyaṁ turya-bhogākhyaṁ svabhāvam acireṇaiva kālena prāpnoti.

Therefore, the one who incessantly strives for discerning the Spanda principle attains one's own nature in the waking state itself without any delay.

Bhaṭṭa Kallaṭa: - Therefore, whoever struggles at all times to experience the nature of the Spanda principle, that person gets to experience his/her own nature, which is the Spanda principle and is called the fourth state, in the waking state itself without any delay.

THIS IS A CONTINUATION of the discussion started in the Verse 20. The effort to come out of the effect of the gunas, or fetters of the sensory world, must be maintained vigilantly by focusing on Spanda underlying the familiar experiences.

Saint Tukaram Maharaj says:

क्षणक्षणा हाचि करावा विचार । तरावया पार भवसिंधु ॥१॥
नाशिवंत देह जाणार सकळ । आयुष्य खातो काळ सावधान ॥२॥
संतसमागमीं धरावी आवडी । करावी तांतडी परमार्थी ॥३॥
तुका म्हणे इहलोकींच्या वेव्हारे । नये डोळे धुरें भरूनि राहे ॥४॥

1. *Kṣaṇa-kṣaṇā hāci karāvā vicār, tarāvayā pāra bhavasiṅdhu.*
2. *Nāśivaṅta deha jāṇāra sakaḷa, āyuṣya khāto kāḷa sāvadhāna.*
3. *Saṅta-samāgamīṅ dharāvī āvaḍī, karāvī tāṅtaḍī parmārthī.*
4. *Tukā mhaṇe iha-lokīṅcyā vevhāre, naye ḍoḷe dhureṅ bharūni rahoṅ.*

Moment-by-moment you should think
of going across the ocean of worldliness
The mortal body will all vanish,
as Death is swallowing life. Be vigilant.
Develop love for the company of saints.
Make haste in spirituality.
Tukaram says, "Never let your eyes be blinded
with the smoke of the transactions of this world."

If we are not constant in our efforts it is just a waste of time. Constancy or earnestness of effort builds the intensity to achieve the constant experience of Spanda. Earnestness is devotion. Without a mind full of devotion, the experience is not possible. If we want to do something which requires physical strength and we don't have the strength, how can we do it? Suppose we want to go somewhere by car and we do not have gas in the car. Then our thought of going somewhere just remains a thought. We don't go anywhere. Similarly, spiritual practice without feeling does not attain anything. That intensity is one-pointedness. When we study we must study with intensity, without the mind wandering, without the mind thinking about anything else. The intense emotion is the driving force in whatever we want to accomplish. That intense emotion can be termed as pure love.

The pure love underlying the constant effort toward experiencing Spanda is the driving force in transforming ourselves to transcend the effect of gunas. That is an experience and cannot be described in words. The sage Narada says, "अनिर्वचनीयं प्रेमस्वरूपं । मूकास्वादनवत् ।" *Anirvacanīyam Prema-svarūpam.*

Mūkāswādanvat. (*Narada Bhakti Sutra* 11) "The nature of Love is indescribable, like a mute tasting something delicious but unable to describe it." The twelfth chapter of Jnaneshwari, a commentary on the *Bhagavad Gita* originally written in Marathi by Jnaneshwar Maharaj, is all about divine love. It describes in detail how a devotee carries out daily transactions, and as a consequence how knowledge arises effortlessly from within the devotee, how the Lord comes to embrace the devotee.

Many people limit their spiritual practices - sādhanā - to their time spent in meditation or reading scriptures or saints' literature. They do not realize the goal of spiritual practices if they don't know that sādhanā truly means practicing the teaching in all waking moments. Sadhana actually starts when the reading or meditating is over. How we behave with ourselves, how we behave with others, how we carry out our daily activities are all sadhana. If in our waking moments there is any discrepancy between our behavior in transactions with the world and the teachings of sages read in our daily spiritual reading, then our "experiencing spanda" or liberation remains only a fantasy.

From the point of view of experiencing Spanda, we start with a prayer in the morning as we get up: "Lord, through all my transactions, please express Yourself. May none of my activities be under the influence of the six inner enemies."

At my mind often, I must peek,
For it alone makes me strong or weak.
What is it thinking? Inferiority or superiority?
Good of me and everyone? What is its priority?
I Pray, "Oh my mind, think only good thought.
To be depressed or arrogant, you ought not."
My thinking machine forms its habit
It's up to my intelligence what I feed it.

By conscious practice of the feeling that everything is a manifestation of Spanda, while carrying out our day-to-day transactions that feeling turns into bliss when we relate to people, and when we carry out our daily chores with our total concentration. Good thoughts breed more good thoughts, and bad thoughts breed bad thoughts.

At the end of the day we must survey whether we did anything during the day out of fear, jealousy, pride, arrogance, anger or desire. If so, then we should forgive ourselves, offer our work to the Lord, and decide that the next day we are not going to do that anymore. Then we should sleep without any guilt feelings. A similar advice was given by the Bengali saint Ānandmayi Ma to a government officer who asked her how to perform desireless actions.

Devotion with love transforms the seeker, and his/her transformation can be seen from his/her behavior and actions in the waking state.

We may not be aware that the physical universe is all a vibration. When we hear sound, physics and physiology tell us that sound is a vibration, and as the sound vibrations carried through the air fall on our eardrums, the eardrums vibrate and the attached nerves carry on the vibrations as electric signals to the receptors in our brain where our inner instrument – our mind and intellect - identify the sound. The other four sensory perceptions – form, touch, taste and smell – are likewise vibrations. Similarly, all our actions – speech, grasping, locomotion, excretion and procreation – are commands, electric signals from the brain, controlled by the inner instrument; and as such are all vibrations. Observed scientifically or clinically, our perceptions and actions are vibrations or manifestations of Spanda. The other body systems, such as breathing, circulation, digestion and the nervous system, work in us automatically and are observed as vibrations. The emotional reactions after perception of objects produced in us and the responses or actions produced by us, are also vibrations, as is the subject of discussion in the next verse. Our thoughts are manifestations of Spanda. There is only one thought at a given time. It rises, stays and subsides as a wave in the mind and there is a gap between two thoughts. Thus if we are keen on experiencing Spanda, we can be aware of it at every moment of our waking state. Of course, by Spanda we do not mean the actual vibration but the conscious power behind, that produces the vibration. In general, without focusing on specific details, we can constantly maintain an attitude that everything in our life is a manifestation of Spanda.

Native Americans emphasize being always attentive and listening to nature around us. A native American chief named Beautiful Painted Arrow writes in his book *Being and Vibration*[56]

---

[56] *Being and Vibration* – Joseph Rael, Council Oak, Tulsa, Oklahoma 1993, page 67

> Listening is understanding the mystery of vibration because listening has to do with the inner vibration of the descending intelligence of the moment. Meditators become silent so that they can go to true vibration, which becomes the audible workings of vibration, of which ideas are made ... Inner listeners, or people who are continually listening to life as it is unfolding, are true humans because they are picking up vibrational messages before the messages become crystallized energy or perceptual forms that can then be articulated by the brain. Sensitivity, then, is paramount in developing the ability to be a good listener. In that process, the voice of guidance is found. This is the place where inspiration hides. At this level of vibration, one receives direct knowing. Decisions which are made are right decisions for that moment because the energy that is being tapped is the voice of the intuitive silent vibration. I have found that any physical task, no matter how mundane, that allows me to apply effort, keeps me intimately connected to the source of the creative insight.

It is much easier to learn to maintain that constant connection in the company of saints. Our sincere efforts, which are miniscule compared to the goal of attaining the Self or Spanda, bring us into the company of saints. Grace of such saints is unconditional, like rain showers that fall equally on a cultivated field as well as on a rock. Saints are knowers of Spanda and experience Spanda all the time, as discussed in Verse 18. They embody pure Spanda. Spanda can be worshipped by worshipping the saints. An individual seeker is too conditioned and is powerless himself or herself to control the mind from going towards the sensory objects and turning within. The author and his wife can corroborate their own experience with the testimony given by many over the ages that in spite of different malas or impurities being present, a special saint, the Guru, pierces through them and gives the seeker instantly an experience of the Self, even though that experience may not be permanent. Our Guru, Swami Muktanand Paramhansa, caused a meditation revolution during 1970-1982 around the world by giving the experience of the Self through shaktipat, transference of divine shakti to awaken kundalini shakti of thousands of people, whether they had undergone any conscious preparation or not. That experience of the Self is far more blissful than any concept of happiness of the seeker. The nature of the mind is such that it hankers after what it likes. Hence the seeker's mind now strives to have the blissful experience constantly. A complete transformation takes place in the seeker. The three malas – āṇava, kārma, māyīya - leave the seeker as the mind becomes pure in the quest of the Self. The mind that was restless and full of thought waves becomes calm, introverted, focused on the Self and makes an effort to get established there. It is not just some abstract Spanda which the mind has to contemplate, but it is the Spanda embodied as the Guru, that the mind has to contemplate. This contemplation is effortless because of Guru's love.

Poet Sundardas says: (*Sundardas*, 39)

सुंदर जो मन श्रीगुरु विचारत, तौ मन होतहि गुरुस्वरूपा ॥

Suṅdara jo mana Śriguru vicārata, tau mana hotahi Guru-svarupā

O Sundar, the mind that thinks only of the Guru,
itself becomes the Guru.

When the mind loves the Guru, thinks only of the Guru, it becomes the Guru himself/herself. It takes on the state of the Guru.

A saint, Kashi Vishwanath Baba[57] writes to his disciples: "In the contemplation of and communion with the Self natural blissful knowledge is born, feelings of benevolence blossom and life becomes blessed. Until the mind blossoms fully like a fragrant flower, protect your environment and nurture its tendencies with discrimination. A flower's existence and beauty are in its fragrance. Feeling is the fragrance of remembrance of the Self. As we contemplate more and more the Lord with love and His unconditional loving grace on us, our feeling, spirituality and righteousness also increase more and more, become active and cover various aspects of our actions in day-to-day life. Only then peace, bliss and knowledge arise; peace fills the mind and luster of knowledge radiates. Instead of thinking that we love the Lord, remember the Lord's love for us; then happiness and active feeling of service will joyfully course through the mind and Life will be fulfilled."

The second aphorism from the Second Awakening – Shāktopāya - of the *Shiva Sutras* describes the result of this attitude as: प्रयत्नः साधकः । *Prayatnaḥ Sādhakaḥ* "Incessant effort brings about the attainment of God consciousness." The Sanskrit

[57] *Sadguru Prasad* compilation of letters to devotees by Kashi Vishwanath Maharaj in Marathi.

word Prayatna – means effort and sādhaka – means that which attains. A brief discourse[58] on the Sutra by Swami Muktanand Paramhansa follows:

> This is an indication regarding what happens to a seeker who constantly strives to contemplate the Self. That spiritual practice which brings about unification of the Self and the seeker, makes them one, is called 'Prayatna' - effort. Just as an arrow accurately aimed and released from a bow hits the bulls' eye, likewise such a practice takes the seeker to the goal of being firmly established in the seeker's own Self. That practice is not a manual effort of repeating a certain seed mantra by tongue, lips or teeth in a specific manner for a certain period. It is that oneness of the principle being meditated upon by the meditating seeker.
>
> आत्मनो भैरवं रूपं भावयेद्यस्तु पूरुषः ।
> तस्य मन्त्राः प्रसिद्ध्यन्ति नित्ययुक्तस्य सुन्दरि ॥ (स्वच्छन्दतन्त्र)
>
> *Ātmano Bhairavaṁ rūpaṁ bhāvayed-yastu pūruṣaḥ*
> *Tasya mantrāḥ prasiddhyanti nitya-yuktasya Sundari*
> *(Svacchanda-tantra)*
>
> *"That being who has a feeling that his own nature is Bhairava (Self), in whose mind constant oneness of the great mantra arises, who is always connected (nitya-yukta), attains the goal of the mantra."* With the seeker's effort that mantra comes alive, becomes a conscious mantra. It is also called an awakening of the mantra. That mantra becomes alive when by Guru's grace the goal of the mantra – Kundalini (more about Kundalini in *Spanda Karika* verses 23-25) becomes active. That seeker who sets the goal of the mantra as Consciousness which manifests as the inner light and inner activity and identifies his prāṇa and apāna with the letters of the mantra and regards oneness of the mantra, the repeater of the mantra, and the Self always in his meditation, in his functioning in the world, and in the actions of his all sense organs is regarded as 'always connected.' Identifying prana and apana with the letters of the mantra means the Guru-given great mantra is repeated in unison with the outgoing and incoming breath. This effort is called sādhaka – achiever of the goal.

[58] गुरुदेव आश्रमपत्रिका *Gurudev Ashram Patrika* – Ashram Newsletter (Hindi) – July 1976, Volume 5 #7.

> Shiva, the supreme non-dual Master, is the Self of all. He is the instrument functioning in all bodies. By making the world conglomerate of 25 elements[59] He Himself has become the food, water and life situations. He himself has manifested as knowledge, devotion and yoga. That is why Shiva is called the supreme non-dual Master. The practice of feeling that I am Shiva with great devotion is the effort one must make.

The second part of Verse 21 says that by such an effort, which can only be made in the waking state, the seeker is quickly established in the Spanda. How quickly? Another aphorism in *Shiva Sutras* answers: उद्यमो भैरवः । (१.५) *Udyamo Bhairavaḥ (1.5)* "That effort – flashing forth of active awareness that instantaneously shines as the Universal Consciousness – is Bhairava." This active effort which can only be made in the waking state carries the seeker in a flash, in one flight, to the state of Bhairava. The effort is called Bhairava because it dissolves all different energies into Svātantrya – Divine freedom. The universe is then filled with Svatantrya and differentiation of perception ends. It transcends all confining feelings of nationality, education, duality, and makes one a universal being and one practices universal brotherhood in its greatest sense.

Tukārām Mahārāj extols the grace of the saints and admires how quickly they transform a seeker who takes refuge in them. He says:

आपणासारिखे करिती तात्काळ, नाही काळवेळ तयालागी ।

Āpaṇāsārikhe kariti tātkāḷa nāhī kāḷaveḷa tayālāgi

They make us like themselves instantaneously, It doesn't require any time or duration for this.

The text *Vijnana Bhairava* offers several centering techniques – dharanas – which when practiced can take the seeker away from the senses and sense objects and bestow the experience of Bhairava - Self.

क्रमद्वादशकं सम्यग् द्वादशाक्षरभेदितम् ।
स्थूलसूक्ष्मपरस्थित्या मुक्त्वा मुक्त्वान्ततः शिवः ॥ (श्लोक ३०, धारणा ७)

[59] Five inner organs – purusha, prakriti, mind, intellect, ego, Five senses of perception – seeing, etc, Five senses of action – locomotion, etc, Five pure senses – form, etc., and Five gross elements – light, etc. as in the table given in the Verse 20.

शिखिपक्षैश्चित्ररूपैर्मण्डलैः शून्यपञ्चकम् ।
ध्यायतोऽनुत्तरे शून्ये प्रवेशो हृदये भवेत् ॥ (श्लोक ३२, धारणा ९)
ईदृशेन क्रमेणैव यत्र कुत्रापि चिन्तना ।
शून्ये कुड्ये परे पात्रे स्वयं लीना वरप्रदा ॥ (श्लोक ३३, धारणा १०)
स्वदेहे जगतो वापि सूक्ष्मसूक्ष्मतराणि च ।
तत्त्वानि यानि निलयं ध्यात्वान्ते व्यज्यते परा ॥ (श्लोक ५४, धारणा ३१)

Krama-dvādaśakaṁ samyag dvādaśākṣara-bheditam
Sthūla-sūkṣma-para-sthityā muktvā muktvāntataḥ Śivaḥ
(Verse 30, Dhāraṇā 7)
Śikhi-pakṣaiś-citra-rūpair-maṇḍalaiḥ śūnya-pañcakam
Dhyāyato 'nuttare śūnye praveśo hṛdaye bhavet
(Verse 32, Dhāraṇā 9)
Īdṛśena krameṇaiva yatra kutrāpi cintanā
Śūnye kuḍye pare pātre svayaṁ līnā vara-pradā
(Verse 33, Dhāraṇā 10)
Svadehe jagato vāpi sūkṣma-sūkṣma-tarāṇi ca
Tattvāni yāni nilayaṁ dhyātvānte vyajyate parā
(Verse 54, Dhāraṇā 31)

These dharanas are explained in the following.

Dharana 7: There are two significant words in the first part which are explained as follows:

Succession of twelve centers of energy - kramadvādaśakaṁ is as follows:
Four lower centers signifying differences (bheda):

1. Janmāgra - head of the generative organ;
2. Mūla - spinal center below genitals, midway between genitals and anus;
3. Kanda – bulbous muscle at the root of the generative organ, above mula, formed by nerve fibers;
4. Nābhi – navel;

Five subtler centers of difference in non-difference (bhedābheda):

5. Hṛd – heart;
6. Kaṇṭha – the cavity at the base of the throat;
7. Tālu - palate;
8. Bhrūmadhya – centre between the eye-brows;
9. Lalāṭa – forehead;

Three centers signifying non-difference (abheda):

10. Brahmarandhra – The apex of the cranium;
11. Śakti – pure energy transcending the body;
12. Vyāpini – the all pervasive light of consciousness which appears when Kuṇḍalini finishes its journey.

Twelve letters – dvādaśākṣaraṁ are the twelve Sanskrit vowels
अ, आ, इ, ई, उ, ऊ, ए, ऐ, ओ, औ, अं, अः - a, ā, i, ī, u, ū, e, ai, o, au, aṁ, aḥ

(The four vowels ऋ, ॠ, ऌ, ॡ - ṛ, ṝ, ḷ, ḹ are regarded eunuch vowels and are left out)

The meaning of the dharana is: The succession of twelve centers is to be meditated upon with the sequence of the twelve letters in reverse order in each of the gross, subtle and supreme phases, leaving one phase after another until the meditator becomes one with Shiva.

Dharana 9: The seeker should meditate in his/her heart on the five voids – subtle sources of the five subtle senses which are like five circles – one above, one below, one in the middle, one on each side - on a peacock feather. Then the seeker will be absorbed in Absolute void which transcends senses and the mind; although from the point of view of Reality this state is most full. The word mandala used in the verse also means subtle senses that carry the essence of the five physical objects of sense.

Dharana 10: The seeker whose mind is one-pointed on the twelve centers in a succession, or void, or a blank wall, or twelve centers in some excellent person, that mind is absorbed by itself in the Self and that state is benefaction (of the highest spiritual experience.)

Dharana 31: If the seeker thinks of fusion of gross into subtle and then into subtler constitutive principles in the body and the world then the supreme Goddess – Parādevi is revealed.

The five gross principles in the universe are earth, water, fire, air and space. They exist in the body as bones and flesh, dermis, and refuse; body fluids, fat; light in the eyes, digestive fire, fire that keeps the body warm; five vital airs – prāṇas;[60] the space within, which prevents the organs functioning in place without collapsing into each other. There are also five corresponding organs of action and perception. In this meditation all of these get successively absorbed into their sources: five pure subtle senses – smell, taste, form, touch, sound. These five dissolve into the ego, ego into intellect, intellect into mind, mind into nature and the objective individual awareness that responds to the nature. The individual is blinded by the six coverings of maya discussed in Verse 20. By Guru's grace when that veil of maya is lifted one realizes the reality of one's own nature. One is in Shuddha Vidya or Pure knowledge. But this realization is flickering. The experience is "I am Shiva, this universe is in duality. This universe is real, I am Shiva."[61] This dissolves into the more subtle principle of Iśvara – "This universe is my own expansion. It is not an illusion, it is my expansion." This dissolves into the still more subtle principle of Sadāśiva where the experience is "I am this universe. Oh myself, I am this universe." This dissolves into subtler inseparable two principles: Vimarsha (Shakti, Spanda) and Shiva (Self): The impression is "I, the pure I, the universal I." It is not "This universe is my expansion or I am the whole universe." It is just pure "I, I, universal I."

In the 10th dharana, concentration on *pare pātre* – on some excellent person -- is mentioned, which is explained in *Pātanjala Yogasutra* (I, 37) : "वीतरागविषयं वा चित्तम् । *Vitarāga-viṣayaṁ vā cittam*" "Meditate on the person/s whose mind is devoid of thoughts of sense objects." If one meditates on the state of the Guru or saints who experience the Spanda all the time, one's mind is absorbed by itself in the Supreme and gets the highest spiritual experience. This interpretation is not traditionally given, but the saints have emphasized it as a very effective practice from their own experiences. As a result of our conscious effort and the grace of the Guru the process is effortless, juicy, and quick in experiencing the Self.

That is the reason the saint Kabir sings:

हमारे गुरु मिले ब्रह्मज्ञानी । पाई अमर निशानी ।।टेक।।
काग पलट गुरु हंसा कीन्हे, दीन्ही नाम निशानी,
हंसा पहुँचे सुखसागर पर, मुक्ति भरे जहाँ पानी ।।१।।
जलविच कुंभ, कुंभविच जल है, बाहर भीतर पानी ।

---

[60] vital airs – Life energy ('mind-body' connection) five names for five functions: Prāṇa exhaling – perception, works with sensory nerves of the respiratory system, Apāna inhaling – works with excretory system, Vyāna pervading through body - digestion, Udāna rising – cause of thinking, works with muscular system keeps a person stand erect on his legs, the soul is conducted through body at death, Samāna circulating, balancing nutrients throughout body, in meditation – 'purifying the centers such as the center between eyebrows'-Baba Muktanand

[61] *Kashmir Shaivism* by Swami Lakshmana Joo in Thirty Six elements, Sri SatGuru Publications, Delhi, 1991, page 9

विकस्यो कुंभ-जल, जलहि समाना,ये गति विरले ने जानी ।।२।।
है अथाह थाह संतन में, दरिया लहर समानी ।
धीवर जाल डाल काह करि है, (जब) मीन पिघल भये पानी ।।३।।
अनुभव का ज्ञान, उजलता की वाणी, सो है अकथ कहानी ।
कहै कबीर गूँगे की सैना, जिन जानी उन मानी ।।४।।

Ref. Hamāre Guru mile braḥmajñānī, pāyī amar niśānī.
1. Kāga palaṭa Guru hansā kīnhe, dīnhī nāma niśānī,
Hansā pahunce sukhasāgar par, mukti bhare jahān pānī.
2. Jala-vica kumbha, kumbhavica jala hai, bāhar bhītar pānī.
Vikasyo kumbha-jala, jalahi samānā, ye gati virale ne jānī.
3. Hai athāh thāh santana men, dariyā lahar samānī
Dhīvar jāla ḍala kāha kari hai, (jaba) mīna pighala bhaye pānī.
4. Anubhava kā jñāna, ujalatā kī vāṇī, so hai akatha kahānī.
Kahai Kabīr gūnge kī sainā, jina jānī una mānī.

We met a Guru who is established in the Self,
From him we received an immortal sign.
He transformed a crow into a swan
when he gave the Name and the Sign of Self.
The swan reached the ocean of bliss,
where liberation is serving by drawing water.
A jug is immersed in water, water is in the jug, inside and out.
When the water inside the jug expands
to the water outside, all water is the same.
This state only a rare one knows.
Saints' depth is fathomless,
For them the sea and a wave are the same.
What can a fisherman do by throwing his net,
if fish melt and become water.
Knowledge of experience, speech of the enlightened is
like a story untold,
Says Kabir, this is a troop of mutes.
Whoever knows understands

VERSE 22
EXPERIENCING SPANDA IN WAKING STATE

अतिक्रुद्धः प्रहृष्टो वा किं करोमीति वा मृशन् ।
धावन् वा यत्पदं गच्छेत्तत्र स्पन्दः प्रतिष्ठितः ॥२२।

22. *Atikruddhaḥ prahṛṣṭo vā kiṁ karomīti vā mṛśan*
Dhāvan vā yatpadaṁ gacchet-tatra Spaṅdaḥ pratiṣṭhitaḥ.

भट्टकल्लटः – तस्य च स्पन्दतत्त्वस्य अतिक्रुद्धे प्रहृष्टे धावमाने च किं करोमि, इत्येवं चिन्ताविष्टे यदा शक्तिप्रत्यस्तमयः, तदा स्पन्द तत्त्वस्य स्फुट एवोदयो गुरूपदेशात् अधिगन्तव्यः ॥२२॥

Bhaṭṭa Kallaṭa: – 22 - Tasya ca spanda-tattvasya atikruddhe prahṛṣṭe dhāvamāne ca kiṁ karomi, ityevaṁ cintāviṣṭe yadā śakti-pratyastamayaḥ, tadā Spanda tattvasya sphuṭa evodayo Gurū-padeśāt adhigantavyaḥ.

At the height of anger, or in extreme joy, or in a quandary as to 'what am I to do?,' or in a desperate situation such as running for one's life, whatever state is reached, there Spanda is established.

Bhaṭṭa Kallaṭa: When one is extremely angry, or extremely joyful, or running away in desperation and extremely worried as to 'what should I do now?', at such moments the energy of Spanda seems to be stalled in that emotion, and the principle of Spanda is revealed. This has to be attained with the guidance of a Guru.

THERE ARE EVENTS during one's waking state when suddenly the mind becomes so one-pointed on one emotion that it reaches a climax that is reflected in the entire physical system by momentarily bringing to halt all other functions of the body. This state is called by BhattaKallata शक्तिप्रत्यस्तमयः "Śaktipratystamayaḥ" "setting (blocking) of all powers." Normally people are totally caught up in the emotion and look outside to the senses, an event, or a person to blame or credit. They say, "That person made me so mad that my blood started boiling." "That person made me so happy." "I am stumped, I don't know what to do." "I had an anxiety attack." "I am terrified." If it is anger, depression, jealousy, they react and do something drastic and harmful. Even while experiencing extreme joy in events such as winning a lottery or suddenly meeting a long lost friend, people cry and hair stands on end. It has also been clinically shown that a mental shock, or stress due to these emotions does cause rapid aging, overnight graying of hair, thus affecting the physical body. But this verse says that one need not get caught up in the flow of the extreme emotion, it is actually the momentary experience of pure Spanda that manifests as that emotion. The only thing needed to transcend the emotion at the moment is to turn inward and experience the pure Spanda independent of the source of that emotion.

There are events in every day life which throw a person in situations which trigger emotions and reflex actions which are automatic. But a person who is always aware that there is nothing other than Shiva (consciousness) and Shakti (its power), that is also called Spanda, is at even keel in any circumstances. In the *Bhagavad Gita* Lord Krishna tells Arjuna in the second chapter:

यदा संहरते चायं कूर्मोऽङ्गानीव सर्वशः।
इन्द्रियाणीन्द्रियार्थेभ्यस्तस्य प्रज्ञा प्रतिष्ठिता ।।५८।।

58. Yadā saṁharate cāyaṁ kūrmo 'ṅgānīva sarvaśaḥ,
Indriyāṇīndriyārthebhyas-tasya prajñā pratiṣṭhitā.

Just as a tortoise draws in all its limbs, he withdraws all his senses from their objects, then understand that his mind has become steadfast in the Self.

A few verses after the above verse, Lord Krishna tells Arjuna the genesis of desire, anger and infatuation-delusion, and the benefits that occur when such detrimental reactions do not happen:

ध्यायतो विषयान्पुंसः संगस्तेषूपजायते ।

संगात् संजायते कामः कामात् क्रोधोऽभिजायते ॥६२॥
क्रोधाद् भवति संमोहः संमोहात् स्मृतिविभ्रमः ।
स्मृतिभ्रंशात् बुद्धिनाशो बुद्धिनाशात् प्रणश्यति ॥६३॥
रागद्वेषवियुक्तैस्तु विषयानिन्द्रियैश्चरन् ।
आत्मवश्यैर्विधेयात्मा प्रसादमधिगच्छति ॥६४॥

62. *Dhyāyato viṣayān puṁsaḥ saṅgas-teṣūpajāyate,*
saṅgāt saṁjāyate kāmaḥ kāmāt krodho ' bhijāyate.
63. *Krodhād bhavati sammohaḥ sammohāt smṛti-vibhramaḥ,*
smṛti-bhraṁśāt buddhināśo buddhināśāt praṇaśyati.
64. *Rāga-dveṣa-viyuktaistu viṣayān-indriyaiś-caran.*
Ātmavaśyair-vidheyātmā prasādam-adhigacchati.

The person thinking about sense objects develops an attachment to them. From the attachment arises desire, and from desire arises anger. (62) From anger arises infatuation-delusion. From infatuation-delusion memory is corrupted. From the corruption of memory intellect is destroyed. When intellect is destroyed, the person is destroyed. (63) But the person who is devoid of attachment and jealousy, has the senses under control even when they are going through the sense pleasures or reactions, and one who has the mind under control attains contentment. (64)

Saint Jñāneśwar comments in his *Jñāneśwari* that just as the sun touches the world by his rays but is never contaminated, the person who is unattached and immersed in the bliss of the Self is never affected by sense objects. That person's mind is steadfast.

If one's mind is not steadfast it does not matter whether one is a renunciant, highly respected by society for learning or accomplishments, or one has done years of sadhana, these inner enemies are ready to pounce. All discrimination goes out the window, all consequences are forgotten, and the whole mind is saturated with one emotion such as anger or lust and a person runs away with the emotion.

The present verse of *Spanda Karika* suggests a remedy to a situation where one is likely to run away with a single emotion. The only thing to do is to momentarily turn inward and experience the common source of that emotion, Spanda, which stands revealed swallowing up that particular emotion.

Vijñān Bhairav describes several centering techniques (dharanas) to experience Spanda in the midst of extreme emotions or even some mundane situations which we regard as insignificant.

कामक्रोधलोभमोहमदमात्सर्यगोचरे ।
बुद्धिं निस्तिमितां कृत्वा तत्तत्त्वमवशिष्यते ॥ श्लोक १०१, धारणा ७८॥
शक्तिसङ्गमसंक्षुब्ध-शक्त्यावेशावसानिकम् ।
यत्सुखं ब्रह्मतत्त्वस्य तत्सुखं स्वाक्यमुच्यते ॥ श्लोक ६९, धारणा ४६॥
लेहनामन्थनाकोटैः स्त्रीसुखस्य भरात्स्मृतेः ।
शक्त्यभावेऽपि देवेशि भवेदानन्दसंप्लवः ॥ श्लोक ७०, धारणा ४७॥
आनन्दे महति प्राप्ते दृष्टे वा बान्धवे चिरात् ।
आनन्दमुद्गतं ध्यात्वा तल्लयस्तन्मना भवेत् ॥ श्लोक ७१, धारणा ४८ ॥
जग्धिपानकृतोल्लास-रसानन्दविजृम्भणात् ।
भावयेद्भरितावस्थां महानन्दस्ततो भवेत् ॥ श्लोक ७२, धारणा ४९ ।
क्षुताद्यन्ते भये शोके गह्वरे वा रणाद्द्रुते ।
कुतूहले क्षुधाद्यन्ते ब्रह्मसत्तामयी दशा ॥ श्लोक ११८, धारणा ९२॥

Kāma-krodha-lobha-moha-mada-mātsarya-gocare
Buddhiṁ nistimitāṁ kṛtvā tat-tatvam-avaśiṣyate.
(Verse 101, Dhāraṇā 78)
Śakti - saṅgama - saṅkṣubdha - śaktyāveśāvasānikam
Yatsukhaṁ Brahma-tattvasya tatsukhaṁ svākyamucyate.
(Verse 69, Dhāraṇā 46)
Lehanā-manthanā koṭaiḥ strī-sukhasya bharāt-smṛteḥ
Śaktyabhāve 'pi Deveśi bhaved-ānanda-saṁplavaḥ.
(Verse 70, Dāraṇā 47)
Ānande mahati prāpte dṛṣṭe vā bāndhave cirāt
Ānandam-udgataṁ dhyātvā tallayas-tanmanā bhavet.
(Verse 71, Dhāraṇā 48)
Jagdhi - pāna - kṛtollāsa - rasānanda - vijṛmbhaṇāt
Bhāvayed-bharitāvasthāṁ mahānanda-stato bhavet.
(Verse 72, Dhāraṇā 49)
Kṣutādyante bhaye śoke gahvare vā raṇād-drute
Kutūhale kṣudhādyante Brahma-sattāmayī daśā.
(Verse 118, Dhāraṇā 93)

When one of the six inner enemies – desire or lust, anger, greed, infatuation, pride, and jealousy - arises, suppressing other emotions, one

> *should use discrimination, withdraw from the emotion and direct the intellect inward, then the Spanda principle only remains. The emotion dissolves and only Spanda is revealed. (78) When one is united with woman (Shakti) and one is absolutely embracing, the joy that ensues at orgasm, is the joy of Brahman. It is the joy of one's own Self. If one doesn't know this, it is only the union of two beasts. (46) O Goddess, the fact that even in the absence of woman (Shakti), by making an effort in recalling the intensity of the joy of sexual union in the form of licking, tasting the nectar of lips, prolonged kissing, embracing, pressing, making amorous marks with nails or teeth, or churning, joy surges and one gets lost in the joy, shows that the joy does not depend on a person or act, but the joy is within. That joy is to be remembered as the joy of the Self, without any person or act. (47) When great joy arises in the company of the beloved or lover, or after seeing a relative after a long time, one should meditate on that joy itself then the mind merges in the Spanda and becomes full of Spanda. (48) When one starving starts eating (the word jagdhi also means eating meat) or one extremely thirsty starts drinking (pāna also means drinking liquor), every bite or every sip starts producing greater and greater delight, increasing strength and suppleness in the physical body; juices start flowing through the dried up veins; one starts feeling full, touching one's hands, feet, stomach in great satisfaction, that delight is the great bliss of Spanda. (49) At the beginning and end of sneeze, in terror, in sorrow, in deep sigh, or in flight from the battlefield, or in keen curiosity, or at the beginning or end of hunger, one's state is that of Brahman. (93)*

Sneeze, hunger, relieving and other bodily functions which every person normally performs daily seem insignificant events to experience Spanda. But when one closely examines these functions, there is sometimes urgency at the commencement and only one thought of performing the bodily action remains and feeling of satisfaction or a sigh of relief at the end. The last centering technique is to make one aware of the experience of Spanda at such times.

In fact, any daily activity performed with just one thought regarding the activity gives satisfaction and fulfillment. In other words, this state can be termed as being in the now. This 'being in the now' generates joy which is an experience of Spanda, even though one may not call it Spanda.

That is the reason in *Shiva Sutras* Lord Shiva says:

त्रिपदाद्यनुप्राणनम् ॥३, ३८॥

Tripadādyanuprāṇanam (III, 38).

Emerging from the state of Turya, insert the absolute bliss of that state into the waking, dreaming and deep sleep states, they will become one with that of state of turya

There is another aphorism in *Shiva Sutras*:

त्रिषु चतुर्थं तैलवदासेच्यम् ॥३, २०॥

Triṣu caturthaṁ tailavad-āsecyam (III, 20)

The fourth state, turya, should be poured like a continuous flow of oil to pervade all the three waking, dream and deep sleep states.

For most people the experience of Spanda, or the turya state, is at the beginning or end of the waking, dreaming and deep sleep states as described in the *SpandaKarika* Verse 17. The aphorism III, 20 describes an effort to be put forth to cause the turya state to pervade the experience in all three states. In the aphorism III, 38 it gives more details as how to perform that effort; namely by inserting the experience of Spanda into every act of waking as described above.

Regardless of the desirable or undesirable nature of the sensory experiences described above, one point common to all of them is that they are momentary, and one gets bored, sick or disgusted if they are prolonged. There are records of kings who with hundreds of wives finally got bored and committed suicide. Food is pleasurable only up to certain extent, after which one cannot stand the sight of food. The reason the Verse is given is to understand that every event is filled with the bliss of Spanda and not to let the mind run away with that emotion. This awareness of Spanda is an experience that is not momentary, but is a continuous surge of bliss. The wise seeker should stay at the Source and experience the bliss of Spanda and then through that bliss carry out the transactions of the day-to-day world. If it so happens that some of the above events arise then the experience of Spanda will remain transcending the event. This can happen only by the grace of the Guru.

The last statement of Bhatta Kallata in his commentary is very meaningful to the author and his wife. They used to run a meditation center for their Guru, Baba Muktanand, in Jersey City, New Jersey, USA from 1975-1982. In 1981 they started to prepare talks for weekly satsangs on *SpandaKarikas* with Jaidev Singh's English commentary with translation of Kshemaraj's Sanskrit commentary. From time to time, Baba used to come into Chitra's dreams and give some teaching. Here is Chitra's account on the above Verse.

> Once for no apparent reason, I started feeling terribly depressed. I was sure of one thing that this depression was not of the normal kind because the feeling was very intense. I felt I did not belong to this world. That night I saw Baba in a vision. I would hear the sound of Om Namah Shivaya at a distance. I told Baba that I was feeling very depressed. He asked me whether I could hear Om Namah Shivaya at that particular time. All of a sudden I became aware of the sound which I was already hearing at a distance. Now the whole atmosphere was pulsating with Om Namah Shivaya. At the moment there was no Baba, no Chitra, nothing else. There was only the vibration of Om Namah Shivaya. I did not understand the meaning of this vision, until a few days later, when we came across the Verse 22.
>
> "When a person is extremely angry, extremely joyful or is extremely depressed or is dumbfounded wondering what to do or is running for life, in that state the Spanda principle, i.e. the Bliss of the Self pulsates steadily."
>
> It is very simple to experience God when one is elated. But Baba demonstrated in my state of depression that the Spanda, which he called the sound of Om Namah Shivaya can be experienced at the other extreme, namely depression. What I understood was that whenever I feel emotional, whether it is anger, happiness, or depression, I just have to focus on the source of that emotion from where the emotion arises. Baba directs me to this source, and the emotion itself completely dissolves in the vibration of Om Namah Shivaya.

The poet saint Dadu Dayal's various couplets (*Dadu*, 5) summarize the lesson of this verse as follows:

दादू देखु दयाल की, गुरू दिखाई बाट,
ताला कूंची लाई करि, खोलै सबै कपाट ॥
दादू सद्गुरु अंजन बाहिकर, नैन पटल सब खोले,
बहरे कानों सुनने लगे, गूँगे मुख से बोले ॥
सद्गुरु दाता जीव का, श्रवण शीश कर नैन,
तन मन सौंज संवारि सब, मुख रसना अरु बैन ॥
सद्गुरु कीया फेरिकर, मन का औरे रूप,
दादू पंचों पलट कर, कैसे भये अनूप ॥
दादू सद्गुरु मारे शब्द से, निरख निरख निज ठौर,
राम अकेला रह गया, चित्त न आवे और ॥

Dadū dekhu Dayāl kī, Gurū dikhāī bāṭ,
Tālā kūṅcī lāī kari, kholai sabai kapāṭ.
Dadū sadguru aṅjana bāhikar, naina paṭala saba khole,
Bahare kānoṅ sunane lage, gūṅge mukha se bole
Sadguru dātā jīva kā, śravaṇa śīśa kara naina,
Tana mana souṅja saṅvāri saba, mukha rasanā aru baina
Sadguru kīyā pherikar, mana kā aure rūpa,
Dādū paṅcoṅ palaṭa kar, kaise bhaye anūpa
Dādū Sadguru māre śabda se, nirakha nirakha nija ṭhaur,
Rām'a akelā raha gayā, citta na āve aur.

Dadu Dayal sees the path shown by the Guru,
Who opened the locks of all cabinets of binding karmas
with the key of knowledge.
Sadguru opened all the veils on Dadu's eyes
by anointing collyrium,
Deaf started hearing and mute started speaking.
Sadguru is the bestower of the knowledge of the Self.
He cleanses ears, head, eyes, mouth, tongue, and speech,
all the equipment of the body and mind.
Sadguru transformed the outgoing tendency
of mind into something else.
See, how Dadu's five senses of perception have
become indescribable.
Turning away from the sense objects
they are enjoying the Self.

Sadguru searching constantly killed all enemies
such as desire and anger one by one
by the arrows of his Word (mantra and teaching).
Only Lord Rama remained alone,
nothing else now comes in mind.

Sadgurunath Maharaj ki Jaya.

VERSES 23, 24 AND 25

ONE-POINTEDNESS OF MIND – THE MOON AND THE SUN (KUNDALINI AWAKENING AND HER WORK)

यामवस्थां समालम्ब्य यदयं मम वक्ष्यति ।
तदवश्यं करिष्येऽहमिति संकल्प्य तिष्ठति ।।२३।।
तामाश्रित्योर्ध्वमार्गेण सोमसूर्यावुभावपि ।
सौषुम्नेऽध्वन्यस्तमितो हित्वा ब्रह्माण्डगोचरम् ।।२४।।
तदा तस्मिन् महाव्योम्नि प्रलीनशशिभास्करे ।
सौषुप्तपदवन्मूढः प्रबुद्धः स्यादनावृतः ।।२५।।

23. *Yāmavasthāṁ samālambya yadayaṁ mama vakṣyati*
Tadavaśyaṁ kariṣye 'hamiti saṅkalpya tiṣṭati.
24. *Tāmāśrityordhvamārgeṇa soma-sūryā-vubhāvapi*
Sauṣumne 'dhvanyastamito hitvā brahmāṇḍa-gocaram
25. *Tadā tasmin mahāvyomni pralīna-śaśi-bhāskare*
Sauṣupta-padavan-mūḍhaḥ prabuddhaḥ syādanāvṛtaḥ

भट्ट कल्लटः – यां स्पन्दस्वरूपरूपामवस्थामवलम्ब्य यत्किंचित् अयं मम वक्ष्यति, तत् अवश्यं करिष्यामि इत्यध्यवसायेन स्पन्दतत्त्वमधिष्ठाय यो वर्तते,
तस्य, तामवस्थामाश्रित्य पुरुषस्य, सोमसूर्यौ द्वावपि सौषुम्ने अध्वनि मध्यनाड्यभिधाने, अस्तमयं कुरुतः, ब्रह्माण्डगोचरं शरीरमार्गं परित्यज्य योगिनः,
तस्मिन् महाव्योम्नि प्रत्यस्तमित–शशिभास्करे यस्य स्वस्वभावाभिव्यक्तिः न, सम्यक् वृत्ता, स स्वप्नादिना मुह्यमानोऽप्रबुद्धो निरुद्धः स्यात्, प्रबुद्धः पुनरनावृत एव भवति ।।२३, २४, २५।।

Bhaṭṭa Kallaṭa: 23. Yāṁ spanda-svarūpa-rūpām-avasthām-avalambya "Yatkiṅcit ayaṁ mama vakṣyati, tat avaśyaṁ kariṣyāmi" ityadhyavasāyena Spanda-tattvam-adhiṣṭhāya yo vartate.

24. Tasya, tām-avasthām-āśritya puruṣasya, soma-sūryau dvāvapi sauṣumne adhvani Madhya-nāḍyabhidhāne, astamayaṁ kurutaḥ, brahmāṇḍa-gocaraṁ śarīra-mārgaṁ parityajya yoginaḥ.

25. Tasmin mahāvyomni pratyastamita-śaśi-bhāskare yasya sva-svabhāvābhivyaktiḥ na samyak vṛttā, sa svapnādinā muhya-māno 'prabuddho niruddhaḥ syāt, prabud-dhaḥ punar-anāvṛta eva bhavati.

23. This verse is interpreted in two ways: the Seeker's interpretaion and the Knower's interpretation.

Seeker's interpretation: When his mind has nothing else except the only firm resolve, "Whatever this Master of mine will order me to do (easy or difficult to attain), that I will certainly carry out."

Knower's interpretaion: When he remains with no other thought except the resolve, "In whatever way this energy of Spanda makes me experience awareness of my nature I will stay in it."

24. Then in that state both the moon and the sun or Apāna and Prāṇa or mind and Prāṇa, travel fast by the higher path in the Sushumna and abandoning the limitations of body-consciousness merge with the space of Universal consciousness. (Both interpretations of sun and moon happen in devotee's life. See discussion.)

25. Then in that sublime space, where the moon and the sun have dissolved, one ignorant remains in a state of deep sleep while the knower-yogi's experience of the Self is not covered by anything.

Bhatt Kallata: 23. Taking refuge in one's own state of the nature of Spanda with the resolve that 'However it wants to move (direct) me to merge in the Turya state, I will certainly follow the directions'; the seeker remains established in the Spanda principle.

24. Based on that seeker-yogi's state, both his moon and sun abandon the path of the body, meaning abandoning the outward-going tendency to run out to the universe of five elements, and set in the central nerve called Sushumna.

25. Then in the great sky of the fourth state of universal consciousness, the sun and moon having set, the unaware yogi remains in dream or deep sleep; but the fully awakened yogi's own consciousness shines without any covering.

VERSE 23

The human mind forms habits of doing something over and over, and always hankers after more and more blissful experience. According to the first interpretation of Verse 23, it is the consequence of Verse 22, where the beginning seeker is told to experience the Spanda that is at the root of the intense emotion. Whenever such emotion arises, it normally drowns the common individual not exposed to spirituality or who is not aware of the omnipotence of Spanda, and as a result the individual sometimes suffers dire consequences. That experience of the general nature of Spanda makes the seeker in Verse 23 take refuge in Spanda to have that transcendental experience. The second interpretation is that when the mind tastes the most blissful experience of Spanda by the grace of Guru, it finds that compared to the bliss of Spanda all sensory experiences are insipid. It is convinced that there is nothing better. Hence it is enthusiastic to maintain that experience. Thus in Verse 23, the seeker who is not established in Spanda wants to surrender to Spanda and the accomplished seeker established in Spanda surrenders to Spanda and remains in it, just as a river becomes the ocean when it meets the ocean.

Just as there are two interpretations of Verse 23 according to the state of the yogi, so also in the *Bhagavad Gita* there are two different occurrences when Arjuna tells Lord Krishna that he is taking refuge in Him in two different ways. In the second chapter, when Arjuna is in the beginning seeker state, Lord Krishna tells Arjuna that there is a higher state than the state of infatuation he is currently in, where there is neither sorrow nor happiness. The second instance is after Arjuna experiences the glorious Self in the eighteenth chapter.

In the second chapter, Arjuna says:

कार्पण्यदोषोपहतस्वभावः,पृच्छामि त्वां धर्मसम्मूढचेताः ।
यच्छ्रेयः स्यान्निश्चितं ब्रूहि तन्मे, शिष्यस्तेऽहं शाधि मां त्वां प्रपन्नम् ॥
(भगवद्गीता २।७)

Kārpaṇya-doṣopahata-svabhāvaḥ,
pṛcchāmi tvāṁ dharma-sammūḍha-cetāḥ,

Yacchreyaḥ syān-niśchitaṁ brūhi tanme,
śiṣyaste 'haṁ śādhi māṁ tvāṁ prapannam.
(B.G. 2/7)

"Having lost my intellect in the fault of ignorance, deluded regarding what is right and what is wrong, I am asking You. Tell me what is truly beneficial to me. I am your disciple. Direct me who has surrendered to You." Arjuna, who cannot decide clearly because of attachment to the world, takes refuge in Krishna so as to overcome darkness.

At the end of the eighteenth chapter, having experienced the glorious Self by the grace of his Guru Lord Krishna, Arjuna says:

नष्टो मोहः स्मृतिर्लब्धा त्वत्प्रसादान्मयाच्युत ।
स्थितोऽस्मि गतसन्देहः करिष्ये वचनं तव ॥
(भगवद्गीता १८।७३)

Naṣṭo mohaḥ smṛtir-labdhā tvat-prasādān-mayācyuta
Sthito 'smi gata-saṅdehaḥ kariṣye vacanaṁ tava.
(B.G.18/73)

"O Lord! By Your grace my infatuation is all destroyed, I remember my own nature. I am free of doubt. I will carry out Your command."

The following discussion of the statements of Arjuna, who moves from the seeker to the Knower's state, is based on Jnaneshwar's commentary on this verse. After merging with the Lord, Arjuna is free of his identification as Arjuna. By the Lord's grace, the knowledge of the Self is attained, and ignorance, the root of infatuation, is abolished. In duality one always wonders whether this or that needs to be done. But once the surrender to the Self is made the individual has no choices. It is only the Self working. In other words, when one desires to do the Lord's will, all other desires vanish. There is no other sight throughout the duality of the world except that of the Lord everywhere. The Lord is Arjuna's Guru. To get the Guru's love Arjuna needs to go beyond even the understanding of non-duality, which helps attain oneness. The Lord graciously shares His state with Arjuna. Likewise, by surrendering to the Guru who is a manifestation of the Consciousness-Awareness, a seeker surrenders to Spanda.

There is a story of Swami Ram Tirth (*Swami Ram Tirth*, 57, Vol. II, p. 312). There was a beautiful organ in a church. The organ was so fine that no one except the organist was allowed near the organ. Once a poorly dressed stranger came in and wanted to play the organ, but he was not allowed near it. After the service was over and the organist had left the organ, this man stealthily crept up to the organ. The minute he laid his hands upon it, the organ recognized its master, and such music poured forth that even though the congregation was about to leave the church, they were spell-bound, enraptured, and could not leave the church. This wielder of wonderful harmony was the master musician, the inventor of the organ himself.

We do not give the Self, God, Love, a chance to do for us; we think we need to care for this body and mind, and so only common-place notes come forth from us. Let the Master play upon the organ of our body-mind, and the minute Love's hands touch the chords, music will pour forth – music that we have never dreamt of before – wonderful light and harmony will begin to flow, divine melodies will begin to burst out, and celestial rhapsodies will emanate.

Just as the involuntary actions of a creature such as the growth of the body, growth of hair, and digestion of food, happen perfectly without our effort, even so the voluntary actions need to happen pefectly by letting the Lord do them, by letting the individual 'I' merge in the universal 'I'!

For the beginning seeker who comes in contact with his or her Guru, by the blessing of Spanda, good things start happening in life due to Guru's grace, even though the seeker may not give credit to grace or may not even realize it. Long pending worldly goals are attained effortlessly. Relationships with relatives, colleagues, friends and strangers get better. Any inferiority or superiority complex one has felt for a life time is overcome. There is clarity in thinking. One becomes confident in attaining any task at hand. Meditation starts happening spontaneously. Life becomes simpler. The Guru's unconditional compassionate elevating love is experienced, unlike any love experienced anytime in life. Because of this love, regardless of external situations in the world, the seeker thinks about the Guru incessantly. This is the way the seeker experiences the Verse 23 in practice. The seeker's condition is much like that of Arjuna in the verse quoted from the second chapter. Knowledge of scriptures manifests spontaneously in a seeker's life, as it did in Arjuna's, soon after Arjuna says to Krishna, "I am Your disciple" in Chapter 3 of the *Bhagavad Gita*. Thus learning and practicing yogas of desireless action, meditation, and so on enrich a seeker's life.

In the present author's life the meaning of the *Bhagavad Gita* was revealed spontaneously through Guru's grace. A few years after meeting Baba,[62] he learned the importance of the twelfth chapter when he was taking a shower. As the shower started the meaning of the whole *Gita* flashed before him. To put it into words would take some time! In the first chapter Arjuna is infatuated with the world and says he is not going to fight, because in doing so he would kill his relatives and teachers. So in the second chapter Krishna tells him the importance of doing one's assigned duty without looking at the fruit of his actions. Arjuna's duty according to his situation in life, as Krishna makes clear, is to fight with all his might. The Lord guarantees Arjuna the ultimate reward for his desireless action, better than any mundane outcome, and that reward is equal vision under all circumstances. Arjuna accepts Lord Krishna as his Guru in the second chapter as described earlier.

In the third chapter, Lord Krishna introduces Arjuna to Karma Yoga, the yoga of desireless action. From the fourth chapter onwards Krishna introduces Arjuna to different types of sadhanas – spiritual practices – so that Arjuna can perform his actions more effectively.

In the fourth chapter, Krishna introduces Arjuna to the yoga of renunciation of actions. The fifth chapter begins with Arjuna's confusion, because he does not know whether he should perform the actions or renounce actions. So Krishna explains that the real meaning of renouncing actions is to transcend the triad of "doer, deed, and doing." In the sixth chapter Krishna teaches him how to meditate so that Arjuna can focus one-pointedly on the Self. In the seventh chapter, the Lord talks about Maya and the Self and about having direct and indirect knowledge of the Self. The eighth chapter explains seven technical terms, such as adhiyajna and adhibhuta that enable one to focus on the Self with body, mind and speech. In the ninth chapter on Raja Yoga, Krishna elaborates on the direct and indirect knowledge presented in the seventh chapter. He speaks about having one-pointed devotion with the feeling and knowledge that the all-pervasive Self is the essence of all knowledge. In the ninth chapter Krishna also talks about 'नवविधा भक्ति (*Navavidhā bhakti*) – nine ways of practicing devotion. In the tenth chapter the Lord describes how He himself has manifested as the different forms of the universe; the important point is to pay attention to the Self, the seed of all manifestation.

[62] Baba – Swami Muktananda, authors' Guru.

Thus preparing Arjuna for a direct experience through various yogas until the end of the tenth chapter.

In the eleventh chapter the Lord gives Arjuna Shaktipat – transference of Energy to awaken Arjuna's dormant Kundalini energy by hugging him. Arjuna then gets a direct experience of the Universal form of the Lord. Only after this experience does the Lord talk about the Yoga of Devotion, in the twelfth chapter. *A person develops true devotion only after having the direct experience of the divine.* This is the importance of the twelfth chapter. This devotion is necessary to remain established in the bliss of the Self, once one has the direct experience. Through devotion, one becomes friendly to all beings, and sees the Lord everywhere, and has the knowledge of the world and Self.

The discussion about knowledge that arises from devotion continues in the thirteenth chapter with the idea of the field – or the perceptible and non-perceptible universe and the knower of the field. The gunas – sattva, rajas and tamas – are discussed in the fourteenth chapter; with the explanation that the knower of the Self goes beyond the three gunas.

The fifteenth chapter explains the illusory nature of the world as an effect of the gunas, and presents the importance of being established in the bliss of the Self as the essential condition to go beyond the cycle of birth and death.

In the sixteenth chapter Krishna says that when knowledge arises in a person, divine qualities are reflected in the person's worldly behavior. These divine qualities are explained. A knower of the Self wonders why people suffer so much in the grip of demonic qualities. For seekers also, in order to get established in the Self, practicing the divine qualities and avoiding demonic qualities is essential.

In the seventeenth chapter Krishna explains how one's actions should be performed in a righteous manner. It is not enough to have faith in the all-pervasiveness of the Lord; it is necessary to dedicate body, mind and speech in the service of the Lord.

In the eighteenth chapter Krishna clarifies that all doership must go from any action so that it does not bind us. This chapter is the crest jewel of the *Gita*, since all yogas are summarized here. The individual ego must leave. His ego thus being dissolved, nothing remains for Arjuna but to say to the Lord, "I shall do thy bidding," and thus remain established in the bliss of experiencing the Lord.

In the study of *SpandaKarikas* also when all the previous verses come into one's experience at different times, one experiences Verse 23 in life. This experience of Spanda transforms the seeker.

While in the state described by Verse 23, the transformation that takes place is described in the following verse.

VERSE 24

The experience which Arjuna received in the eleventh chapter of the *Bhagavad Gita* due to Krishna's grace is explained in Verse 24 by describing the transformation itself, rather than the consequences experienced by the seeker (Arjuna). Due to the spiritual practice of various yogas, and the effects of the delightful experience of Spanda, the sun and moon – meaning the prana and mind, respectively, of a seeker leave their tendency of flowing outward. Prana and Apana are also known as the sun and moon, and these become stabilized. The mind then longs for saints' or Guru's company, turns inward to experience Love, just as a bee seeks and gets absorbed in drinking the nectar of a flower.

Jnaneshwar in his commentary on the sixth chapter of the *Bhagavad Gita* describes in detail the experience of Verse 24 when the prana and apana as well as prana and mind merge and rise up the central nerve – Sushumna – and become one with the Self. We paraphrase Jnaneshwar.

As a result of the respectful contemplation of the Guru, the entire being is filled with auspicious feelings and the hardness of the ego melts away. The senses forget their sense objects, and the mind becomes steady within the heart. In that state when one starts meditating automatically three bandhas or locks – 'Mūla bandh' (or vajrasana posture), 'Jālandhar bandh' and 'Uddiyān bandh' take place. Baba always insisted that these locks should happen spontaneously; then the seeker does not suffer any harm.

The mind loses its fickleness. Thus the body and mind are quiet. The force of Apāna that got contracted in the Mula bandh starts going upward and starts knocking at the 'Manipur Chakra' near the navel. It removes all impurities collected from childhood from stomach, it sucks up cough and bile. It stirs all the seven constituents of the body: *majjā* marrow, *asthi* bones, *meda* fat, *pala* flesh, *rakta* blood, *charma* dermis (inner layers of skin), and *tvak* epidermis (outer skin with hair), opens up nerves. It dissolves all earthly matter into watery matter of the body. Diseases appear during the cleansing action and disappear soon. The seeker should remain calm in such situations.

On the other side, the heat of vajrasana awakens dormant serpentlike Kundalini energy curled up in three and a half coils with mouth pointed below. As she awakens she grips the body and appears mounted upon the mound below the navel. She turns her mouth upward, eats up all the air filled in the cavity below the heart. She spreads her fire up and down, she takes a bite of the fleshy tissue of the heart, sips the blood from the palms and soles, and drinks the vitality of the nails and skin making the skin cling to the bones, penetrates and cleanses the joints, hollow of the bones, and muscles; due to her thirst she drinks up the seven bodily costituents and dries the entire body. Prana, or the air that is exhaled is pulled inward, and apana is compressed upward. In the merging of prana and apana the only barriers are the petals of the six chakras. After consuming the two primordial elements – earth and water, she lies quietly near the 'Sushumna' – the central nerve. The poison which she lets out from her mouth is the nectar by which vitality is restored. The fire that rises from the poison begins to cool down both internal and external body. The limbs regain the strength which they had lost. The 'ida' (moon) left and 'pingala' (sun) right nerves merge loosening their three knots – Braḥma, Viṣṇu, and Rudra granthis. Kundalini along with the intellect and power of smell enter Sushumna. Slowly the cranial reservoir tilts downwards on one side and the moon-nectar pours into the mouth of the Kundalini. This nectar fills the passages, circulates, the body and the life-force gets dissolved where it originates.

As a result, the body becomes radiant. Old age vanishes, the knot of youth is loosened, and the lost bloom of childhood reappears. Grasping prāṇa by the hand, Kundalini ascends the stairway of space in Sushumna and enters the heart, awakens the heart-center, 'anāhat chakra' and because of the intellect clinging to Kundalini, celestial sound (nada) is faintly heard. In the container of Parā vāṇi, all forms of sound of madhyamā reside as Auṁ. But since the mind does not exist at this place, that cannot be imagined. So long as the air exists the sound arises in the space and vibrates like thunder by which the door of the crown center – sahasrār - is spontaneously burst open. The space in the cranium is like the inside of a lotus. Shiva, Consciousness, resides in this space. Kundalini merges her brilliance and intellect with the life-force – Prana. Until this point the water principle has swallowed the earth principle, and fire (light) has swallowed the water principle. Prana (Air) has swallowed the fire principle. Now prana merges into the space of the cranium – Mūrdhni-ākāsh. Kundalini is now called "Mārut" –

wind – but retains her distinction from Shiva. Stepping over the region of 'pashyanti vani' (between the throat and the heart) riding the soundwave of Aum, she transcends the 'Jalandhar bandh' (the lock formed by the pressing of chin on the ribcage) and comes to a point just above the palate - called 'Kākī mukha' where nine sense organs originate. She breaks that barrier, and merges in the Brahma-randhra – center of the lotus at the top of cranium, with Shiva. Thus the veil of all five elements is overcome and difference between Shakti and Shiva disappears. The space of cranium (Mūrdhni-ākāsh) merges into the space of consciousness (Cidākāsh). This cannot be imagined or explained in words, but can be experienced. This is because 'Vaikhari' which forms the words to describe is far away from the Self, even in the "Ājñā Cakra" the 'ṁ' – nasal sound – component of Aum – cannot penetrate. It is at the Ajna chakra that prana enters the space of cranium. This can be understood only by direct experience.

At that state there is nothing more to be known. Even a semblance of a thought cannot enter there. It is the Supreme Principle transcending the mind. It is the pure Turya state. It is the end of form. It is the destination of liberation. Beginning and end are dissolved in that state, it is omnipresence. It is the root of the universe. It is bliss alone. It is consciousness – Shiva.

In *Shiva Sutras* there are two related sutras - aphorisms:

नाडीसंहार-भूतजय-भूतकैवल्य-भूतपृथक्त्वानि । (३-५)

Nāḍīsaṇhāra-bhūtajaya-bhūtakaivalya-bhūtapṛthaktvāni. (3-5)

Dissolution of prana in the nerves into the central nerve - Sushumna, control over the elements, withdrawal of the mind from elements and separation from grip of the elements are to be brought out by the Yogi by one-pointed attention.

भूतसंधान-भूतपृथक्त्व - विश्वसंघट्टाः (१-२०)

Bhūta-sandhāna-bhūta-pṛthaktva-viśva-saṁghaṭṭāḥ. (1-20)

By the greatness of this achievement of the energy of will, the yogi can focus his awareness and heal the sick and suffering, separate elements from his body and be free from the limitations of space-time.

The earlier discussion from Jnaneshwari describes in detail how the control over the elements happens, how the five principles - earth, water, fire, air, space comprising the seeker's body merge successively one into another and the space also vanishes in universal space of consciousness. For a beginning seeker there is an effort involved as indicated in the first quoted *Shiva Sutra*, whereas there is no such effort for an accomplished yogi as in the second aphorism. Jnaneshwari, in the verses following the quoted verses, also describes how the siddhis – occult powers – come to serve the accomplished Yogi.

In *Vijnana Bhairava* there are several centering techniques that aid to attain the state described in Verse 24 which a seeker can practice:

आमूलात्किरणाभासां सूक्ष्मात् सूक्ष्मतरात्मिकाम् ।
चिन्तयेत्तां द्विषट्कान्ते शाम्यन्तीं भैरवोदयः ॥
(श्लोकः २८, धारणा ५)

Āmūlāt-kiraṇābhāsāṁ sūkṣmāt sūkṣma-tarātmikām
Cintayet-tāṁ dviṣaṭkānte śāmyantīṁ Bhairavodayaḥ.
(Verse 28, Dhāraṇā 5)

Meditate on the Shakti arising from the mūlādhār chakra, scintillating like rays of the sun, and getting subtler and subtler till at last she dissolves in Dvādaśānta – a distance of twelve fingers from the middle of the eyebrows (i.e. top of cranium). Thus does Bhairava become manifest.

This is known as chit-kundalini or akrama-kundalini where Kundalini, without passing successively through the chakras, goes directly to Brahmarandhra.

उद्गच्छन्तीं तडिद्रूपां प्रतिचक्रं क्रमात्क्रमम् ।
ऊर्ध्वं मुष्टित्रयं यावत् तावदन्ते महोदयः ॥
(श्लोकः २९, धारणा ६)

Udgacchantīṁ taḍid-rūpāṁ prati-cakraṁ kramāt-kramam
Ūrdhvaṁ muṣṭi-trayaṁ yāvat tāvadante mahodayaḥ.
(Verse 30, Dhāraṇā 6)

Meditate on that very lightning-like śakti (Kundalini) moving upwards successively from one chakra – center of energy – to another, up to

Brahmarandhra located three fists (twelve fingers) from the middle of the eye brows.

This is known as prana-kundalini. The process has been described earlier.

कपालान्तर्मनो न्यस्य तिष्ठन्मीलितलोचनः ।
क्रमेण मनसो दार्ढ्यात् लक्षयेल्लक्ष्यमुत्तमम् ॥
(श्लोकः ३४, धारणा १०)

Kapālāntar-mano nyasya tiṣṭhan-mīlita-locanaḥ
Krameṇa manaso dārḍhyāt lakṣayel-lakṣyam-uttamam.
(Verse 34, Dhāraṇā 10)

Fixing one's attention on the interior everpresent light of the cranium and seated with eyes closed and firm mind, one gradually discerns that which is eminently discernible.

Ka - also means shakti –Vimarsh and pāla – means Shiva. Thus the technique also means: Having fixed one's mind on the union of Shiva and Shakti, and seated with eyes closed, gradually with firm mind, one discerns what is most eminently discernible.

मध्यनाडी – मध्यसंस्था बिससूत्राभरूपया ।
ध्यातान्तर्व्योमया देव्या तया देवः प्रकाशते ॥
(श्लोकः ३५, धारणा १२)

Madhyanāḍī-madhya-saṁsthā bisa-sūtrābha-rūpayā
Dhyātāntar-vyomayā devyā tayā devaḥ prakāśate.
(Verse 35, Dhāraṇā 12)

The medial nerve – Sushumna - is in the center. It is as slender as the stem of a lotus. If one meditates on the inner vacuity of this nerve, it helps in revealing the Divine.

The same idea is expressed in the Verse 25 of *Spandakarika*.

Constant repetition of the mantra given by the Guru has tremendous power to awaken the Kundalini. The power of mantra is explained in the next *Spanda Karika* verses: 26-27.

Before discussing Verse 25 some experiences of Kundalini that happen in the lives of thousands of devotees of Baba are described in order to show that the truth of Verse 24 can be verified anywhere in the world and that the tradition is still alive. Devotees of other Gurus also have logged in various places similar experiences showing that the Science of Spanda like physical sciences can be tested in a laboratory - the inner laboratory of the seeker.

When the author and his wife met Baba, their Kundalinis were awakened spantaneously and effortlessly. Meditation started happening to them regularly, without their making any effort at meditation. When they ran a meditation center under Baba's directions for about seven years from 1975 to 1982, many people attending satsangs in the center had experiences of Kundalini awakening while chanting, meditating, or performing arati. Thousands around the world who came in contact with Baba corroborated this testimony of people in the center with their own experience. Sometimes there is an intense pain at the base of the spine when Kundalini awakens, and it can start even when one is in a shopping center and is not sitting in meditation. The only thing one can do at such times is to sit at a quiet place until the pain subsides which takes a few minutes. The interior gray colored covering of Sushumna is seen while chanting or meditation. Some feel electricity coursing through the body. Exhilaration supersedes any sensual experience in intensity and duration. Sexual experience seems insipid and momentary. Some have physical yogic kriyas in which the bandhas – locks – take place spontaneously. Some experience other physical kriyas such as hatha yoga postures, classical dancing, or cleansing kriyas, some utter animal sounds aloud during meditation. Visions of saints and deities appear in devotees' meditations. Some have visions of their past lives and connection with their Guru and relatives. Chakras are seen in meditation, especially the 'Manipur Chakra' with its ten crimson petals. The petals of the heart chakra, where the mind resides, are felt churning gently. At the center of the eye-brows, 'Ajna chakra' is seen with its two white petals – first the two petals appear connected and then the two petals separated. *Gurugita* describes a place in the Sahasrar, where the Guru has to be meditated upon: namely, the inverted triangle with sides – अ क थ - a k th - the triangle with fifty letters of Sanskrit alphabet – one side starting with vowels अ'a' 17 letters, another side starting with consonant क 'k' 17 letters and the third side with consonant थ 'th' and 16 letters, with 'padukas' – in the middle. The triangle, the letters and padukas appear in devotees' meditation.

This happens repeatedly. Cranial nectar is tasted which beats the taste of any earthly nectar. The blue pearl – signifying the supracausal body – mahākāraṇ sharir starts showing up in meditation or while reading spiritual work. A universal vision similar to what Arjuna received in the eleventh chapter is also seen. Knowledge of scriptures arises spontaneously. For example, if one goes through Upanishads, one feels that its statements agree with one's experience.

On the whole, a seeker's life becomes simple, joyful, profound and fulfilling when Kundalini awakens by Guru's grace. The following describes a common experience of seekers.

"You have read about It,
You have heard about It.
But you won't believe It,
Until you have seen It.
That Awesome Light
When starts shining
Will bring you Joy
And stop your whining."
So saying He tapped
Gently on the child's head.
And a light of thousand suns
Shimmered through his head.
In that light the child kept jumping in his place
Unable to bear the light never yet seen
The light steadied and said, "Never forget.
The Light is what you've always been."

In that light the body reduced to an atom
And vanished saying,
"The life you live now on
is for the world's wellbeing."
He went away, sat aloof and quiet,
As the child was absorbed, in his lesson required.

VERSE 25

In spite of the sublime experience of the Self, where the moon and the sun have dissolved, the ignorant yogi remains in a state of deep slumber following this experience, while the knower yogi's experience of Self is not obscured by anything. It all depends upon the seeker's earnestness, love for his or her Guru, and understanding. It requires self-effort on the part of the beginning seeker to keep awake and not to slight the immeasurable gift received. For the knower yogi the experience of Self is constant with no effort involved.

Baba always said just seeing the chakras, even sahasrar or having visions is not enough. One must keep meditating and practicing devotion, until meditation happens in all waking hours (of course, continuing in other hours as well). The visions or any dramatic experiences have a beginning and an end. What matters is the constant experience of the Self. The sleep which the Verse 25 talks about even after the experiences of Kundalini awakening refers to the fact that a seeker may not understand their importance and may not respect the Guru or the experiences. A seeker might get so wrapped up in organizational efforts or a position given by the Guru that he or she might loose sight of the goal of life, which is to be established in the constant bliss of the Self. A seeker may be so tempted by the importance given by others that he or she might lose sight of the cause. Baba used to say, "One must be important, but one should never feel so." Another seeker may be baffled by the circus that sometimes goes on around the Guru and lose focus. Direct contact with the Guru and practicing the Guru's directions in all waking hours is extremely important. Baba was gracious enough always to have direct contact with the author and his wife, helping them to stay focused. Even after our Guru's physical demise, just as he did while in the physical body, the Guru keeps directing us through dreams and meditations, such as in writing this commentary. In spite of having the experience of the Self with one Guru's guidance, one might go to a different Guru due to slight discouragement or after the Guru's physical demise before the spiritual quest bears fruit, and waste one's time in learning new techniques or verbiage. After the spiritual quest is over, of course, one does not feel any difference anywhere. Before the spiritual quest is over, attending satsang with the correct attitude does help. There are always distractions of relatives and friends to dissuade a seeker from putting in self-effort. Thus there are lots of exits one can take from the highway to the destination, landing oneself right in the experience of the deep slumber described in Verse 25.

A seeker with understanding does not rest until the veil of the five elements goes away and the oneness of Spanda is discerned fully revealed all twenty four hours of the day in all states and activities.

In conclusion of the discussion of the Verses 23, 24, 25 and the first part of *Spanda Karika* known as Swarup Spanda – nature of Spanda -- we offer Adi Shankaracharya's composition, salutations to the Guru's sandals, which give experience of Spanda and redeem the seeker.

गुरुपादुकापंचकम्
ॐ नमो गुरुभ्यो गुरुपादुकाभ्यो
नमः परेभ्यः परपादुकाभ्यः ।
आचार्य-सिद्धेश्वर-पादुकाभ्यो
नमो नमः श्रीगुरुपादुकाभ्यः ॥१॥

ऐंकार-ह्रींकार-रहस्य-युक्त
श्रींकार-गूढार्थ-महाविभूत्या ।
ॐकारमर्मप्रतिपादिनीभ्याम्
नमो नमः श्रीगुरुपादुकाभ्याम् ॥२॥

होत्राग्नि-हौत्राग्नि-हविष्य-होतृ
होमादि-सर्वाकृति-भासमानम् ।
यद्ब्रह्म-तद्बोध-वितारिणीभ्याम्
नमो नमः श्रीगुरुपादुकाभ्याम् ॥३॥

कामादि-सर्पव्रज-गारुडाभ्याम्
विवेक-वैराग्य-निधीप्रदाभ्याम् ।
बोधप्रदाभ्याम् द्रुतमोक्षदाभ्याम्
नमो नमः श्रीगुरुपादुकाभ्याम् ॥४॥

अनंत-संसार-समुद्रतार
नौकायिताभ्यां-स्थिरभक्तिदाभ्याम् ।
जाड्याब्धि-संशोषण-वाडवाभ्याम्
नमो नमः श्रीगुरुपादुकाभ्याम् ॥५॥
ॐ शान्तिः शान्तिः शान्तिः ॥

Gurupādukā-pañcakam
1. *Oṁ namo Gurubhyo Guru-pādukābhyo*
Namaḥ parebhyaḥ para-pādukābhyaḥ,
Ācārya - siddheśvara - pādukābhyo
Namo namaḥ Śrīguru-pādukābhyaḥ.

2. *Aiṁkāra-hrīṅkāra-rahasya-yukta-*
Śrīṅkāra-gūḍhārtha-mahāvibhūtyā,
Oṁkāra - marma - pratipādinībhyāṁ
Namo namaḥ Śrīguru-pādukābhyām.

3. *Hotrāgni-hautrāgni-haviśya-hotṛ-*
Homādi- sarvākṛti - bhāsamānam
Yad-brahma-tad-bodha-vitāriṇībhyāṁ
Namo namaḥ Śrīguru-pādukābhyām.

4. *Kāmādi-sarpa-vraja-gāruḍābhyāṁ*
Viveka-vairāgya-nidhī-pradābhyām
Bodha-pradābhyāṁ druta-mokṣadābhyāṁ
Namo namaḥ Śrīguru - pādukābhyām.

5. *Ananta - saṁsāra - samudratāra-*
Naukāyitābhyāṁ-sthira-bhakti-dābhyām
Jāḍyābdhi-saṁśoṣaṇa-vāḍavābhyāṁ
Namo namaḥ Śrīguru-pādukābhyām

Oṁ Śāntiḥ Śāntiḥ Śāntiḥ ।

1. *Salutations to Gurus, to the Guru's sandals,*
Salutations to Gurus' Gurus, and to their sandals
To sandals of Teachers, of masters of Siddhas,
Repeated salutations to the holy sandals of Gurus.

2. *The sandals reveal the secrets of 'aiṁkār'[63] 'hrīṅkār '[64]*
They reveal the secret meaning of 'Śrīṁkār'[65]
With that power they reveal the essence of Aum
Repeated salutations to the auspicious sandals of Guru.

---

[63] ऐं aiṁ – is a bījākṣar – seed mantra to be meditated at Muladhar chakra signifies the fire principle also 'vāgbīja' seed of speech

[64] ह्रीं hṛīṁ – is a seed mantra to be meditated at the Anahat chakra in the heart signfies the maya principle crossing which one enters the temple of Guru.

[65] श्रीं śrīṁ – is a seed mantra to be meditated at the Sahasrar signifies the glory and magnificence of Guru at the thousand petal lotus (based on the Guru pujan – explanation by Sw. Ishwaranand Giri, Mt. Abu)

3. *In the fires of 'Hotra' and 'Hautra,' the oblation to be offered,*
And the person offering in the fire ritual and the intention,
The One manifesting is Brahman, whose direct experience
the sandals give.
Repeated salutations to such great sandals of Guru.

4. *The herders who round up the flock of snakes of desire, etc.*
The bestowers of the treasure of discrimination and detachment
The imparters of knowledge and swift givers of liberation
Repeated salutations to such powerful sandals of Guru.

5. *For taking across the infinite ocean of worldliness*
They navigate the boat and they bestow firm devotion
They are the fire drying up the ocean of dullwittedness (ignorance)
Repeated salutations to these redeeming sandals of Guru.

इति श्री कल्लटाचार्यविरचितायां स्पन्दकारिकावृत्तौ स्वरूपस्पन्दः नाम प्रथमो निष्यन्दः ॥१॥

1. *Iti ŚrīKallaṭācārya-viracitāyāṁ Spanda-kārikā-vṛttau*
"Svarūpa-spandaḥ" nāma prathamo niṣyandaḥ.

This concludes the first part called 'Svarūpaspanda' – 'The nature of Spanda,' of the commentary on SpandaKārikā written by Shri Kallaṭācārya.

Sadgurunāth Mahārāj ki Jai.

SUMMARY OF SPANDAKARIKAS VERSES 1-25

Verse 1 describes the general Spanda or dynamism of Shiva, His expansion and contraction causes the universe to contract and expand the universe, and by taking refuge in that Prakāsh - Vimarsh nature (consciousness - awareness nature) is the most beneficial way of offering salutations to Shiva. In Verse 2 we are told that the entire work, creation rests on the Spanda, Vimarsh – awareness nature of Shiva. Verse 3 teaches us that the states of waking, dream and deep sleep appear so different from one another, but Spanda remains as the unchanging experiencer of these states. Verse 4 indicates the Spanda Principle as the thread on which experiences of sorrow, happiness, etc. are strung and appear continuous. Actually, it is like a necklace of a cotton string where the beads are also made of cotton. Verse 5 says that from the highest point of view in Spanda there is neither sorrow nor happiness, neither perception nor the perceptor; at the same time there is no inertness like a rock. Verses 6 and 7 introduce the seeker freedom of the Spanda, power of Will or Iccha Shakti being one of the three aspects, the other two being Jnana – knowledge and Kriya – action, through which Spanda acts; they exhort the seeker to examine with respect, the principle because of which the senses and the inner instrument become alive and carry out their respective functions. In verse 8, we learn that an individual is not only an instrument to carry out the Will, but with the touch of the strength of the Self experiences the Freedom of will. In verse 9 the cause of agitation is given as the existence of three malas arising out of maya principle with the emphasis on ending the agitation to experience the highest state. Verse 10 explains that when agitation stops it is the spanda that remains uncovered, just as when the waves subside, the still blue ocean shimmers. The creation cannot cover or hinder Spanda in any way. Verse 11 extols the yogi who is in the state of amazement by his or her Spanda nature's pervasion everywhere in the atoms of the universe and asks - how will such a yogi go into the cycle of birth and death?

There never is complete Void, the absence of anything. The experience of the yogis who emphasize meditation on the Void is denounced in Verses 12 and 13. In verses 14, 15, 16 we learn that there are two special states of Spanda of doer or the subject and deed or the object of which the deed is temporary while the doer is imperishable. In the meditation on the Void if the objects disappear then the objectivity, of course, vanishes, but that does not mean the doer or consciousness also disappears. Only the triad goes away. The foundation of all the triads, the

Spanda Principle, does not. Verse 17 shows that the fully enlightened yogi has an incessant experience of Spanda in all the three states of waking, dreaming and deep sleep states, while the partially awakened has the experience only in the states as one state is subsiding and the other rising. In verse 18 we see how Spanda appears as knowledge and objects of knowledge in the waking and dream states and only as consciousness in the deep sleep and turya states. While, in verse 19 the author emphasizes that gunas cannot cover the general Spanda for those who have experienced their own Spanda nature, since gunas are only special manifestations of Spanda. Verse 20 shows how the three gunas in the nature cover the experience of Spanda principle for those people who are not vigilant.

Thus the verses 12-20 describe the Spanda principle as the substratum of everything including the void and experience of subjective and objective universe as special manifestations of Spanda.

Verse 21 guarantees that if the seeker is alert to discern the Spanda principle, the seeker attains It without delay. Verse 22 shows how experience of Spanda is possible in daily life when the mind is filled with one emotion and nothing else, by drawing in the mind and directing it to the source of that emotion. The discussion showed that the verse implied that when the mind is 'in the now' state contemplating only the chore at hand it is possible to experience Spanda by just becoming aware of the source. The only common requirement in all acts is that the mind be filled by only one thought one hundred percent. This easily happens in the extreme emotional state.

Thus the text *SpandaKarika* starts with verse 1 making the point of taking refuge, and in subsequent verses shows Spanda as the substratum and manifestation as the nature of the universe and each individual, while the verses 23-25 show how to take refuge in Spanda and as a result what transformation happens in the individual.

PART II

सहजविद्योदयः । - SAHAJA VIDYODAYAḤ SPONTANEOUS RISE OF KNOWLEDGE

In the previous part the author, Vasugupta, shows by various examples and arguments that every particle of the universe is pervaded by the Spanda – Divine pulsation. It is possible to experience it by purifying the mind and consistently practicing the various techniques laid down by the Guru. Then one transcends the restricted individual I-nature and experiences the all pervasive total I-Am – Aham Vimarsha - nature.

In the next part Vasugupta describes the consequence of experiencing the 'I-Am' nature, which is experience of the Matravīrya (the essence of the mantra).

In the next two verses Vasugupta describes the nature of the 'chaitanya' (conscious) or 'sabīja' (seeded) mantras given by Siddha Gurus who have realized their power. These are not just a collection of letters found in a book, but have the power of transforming a seeker from bondage to liberation.

VERSES 26 AND 27

MANTRA AND MANTRA VĪRYA

तदाक्रम्य बलं मन्त्राः सर्वज्ञबलशालिनः ।
प्रवर्तन्ते ऽधिकाराय करणानीव देहिनाम् ।।२६।।
तत्रैव संप्रलीयन्ते शान्तरूपा निरञ्जनाः ।
सहाराधकचित्तेन तेनैते शिवधर्मिणः ।।२७।।

26. *Tad-ākramya balaṁ mantrāḥ sarvajña-bala-śālinaḥ,*
Pravartante 'dhikārāya karaṇānīva dehinām

27. Tatraiva sampralīyante śānta-rūpā nirañjanāḥ,
Sahārādhaka-cittena tenaite Śiva-dharmiṇaḥ.

भट्ट कल्लट – तत् बलं निरावरणचिद्रूपमधिष्ठाय,मन्त्राः सर्वज्ञत्वादिना बलेन श्लाघायुक्ताः प्रवर्तन्ते अनुग्रहादौ स्वाधिकारे। करणानि यथा देहिनाम्, नान्येन आकारादिविशेषेण ।।२६।।
तत्रैव स्वस्वभावव्योम्नि निवृत्ताधिकाराः प्रलीयन्ते, शान्तरूपाः, मायाकालुष्यरहिताः, सह साधकचित्तेन; अनेन कारणेन शिवसंयोजनास्वभावेन, इति शिवात्मका उच्यन्ते ।।२७।।

Bhaṭṭa Kallaṭa: – 26. Tat balaṁ nirāvaraṇa-cidrūpam-adhiṣṭhāya, mantrāḥ sarvajñatvādinā balena ślāghāyuktāḥ pravartante anugrahādau svādhikāre. Karaṇāni yathā dehinām, Nānyena ākārādi-viśeṣeṇa.
27. Tatraiva sva-svabhāva-vyomni nivṛttādhikārāḥ pralīyante, śāntarūpāḥ, māyā-kāluṣya-rahitāḥ, saha sādhakacittena; anena kāraṇena Śiva-saṁyojanā-svabhāvena, iti Śivātmakā ucyante.

Mantras, having arisen from the Supreme I-Consciousness, Spanda, have the power of omniscience, etc. They carry out their assigned functions just as the senses of individual beings function as assigned by the individuals' decisions. Their nature is peace – pure consciousness, and pristine – free of any taints of Maya, and after their work of lifting an aspirant's conditioned mind to its nature of Consciousness is done, they dissolve into consciousness along with the aspirants' minds. Thus, all - the mantra, the repeater of the mantra, and consciousness - are one.

Bhaṭṭa Kallaṭa: *Having been endowed with the power of unmasked consciousness as their substratum, all mantras with powers such as omniscience (listed later in discussion) become venerable. Just as the senses of individuals perform their actions in their intended manner, mantras with their authority of bestowing grace, etc. perform their actions. Without being endowed with the power of the Self, mantras with their specific shape of letters and sounds (as given in a book) alone cannot perform any function.*

The mantras endowed with power, having discharged their duty become tranquil; free of the turbidity of maya, they dissolve in the space of their own nature of general Spanda along with the mind of the seeker. For this reason, because of their nature of making an individual soul one with Shiva, they are said to be of the nature of Shiva or Shiva Himself.

JUST AS THE ENTIRE CREATION arises from 'I AM' awareness - general Spanda - mantras also arise from the 'I AM' awareness. Mantras acquire powers from the 'I AM' awareness. The powers are called 'Māheshwar bala' (powers of Shiva). They fall into six types: सर्वज्ञता - sarvajñatā - omniscience, तृप्ति - tṛpti – contentment, अनादिबोध - anādibodha - knowledge of the eternal, अप्रतिहत-स्वातन्त्र्य - apratihata svātantrya – unimpeded independence, शक्ति का निर्बाध प्रसार - śakti kā nirbādh prasār – unhindered expansion of energy, विश्वरूप में विकसित अनन्त शक्तियों का ऐश्वर्य - viśvarūpa me vikasit anant śaktiyon kā aiśvarya – greatness of infinitely many energies manifesting in the universal form. (*Gurutu*, 11, p. 113). A person when her/his 'mind has become the mantra' is an embodiment of these powers.

In *Shiva Sutras* there is a sutra – an aphorism:

चित्तम् मन्त्रः ।।२,१।।

Chittaṁ mantraḥ (2.1)

The mind is the mantra and the mantra is the mind.

Swami Muktanand[66] Paramhans [1976] says, "This aphorism is of great importance, for a seeker it is the goal to be attained. Based on the understanding or not understanding this aphorism, a seeker can become free or bound. In this aphorism Supreme Shiv is explaining the secret of the mantra. He says that the seeker who worships the mantra as his/her mind itself becomes the mantra. That with which we contemplate the Supreme Principle, think about the mantra, absorb the mantra, understand the essence of the mantra, and the goal of mantra, for which we search within, that mind is called mantra. Never regard the mind as ordinary. By the power of the mind we obtain Lord's blessing."

The only way the mantra bears fruit is when the seeker repeats it regarding the deity of the mantra, the mantra, and the seeker him/herself as one and the same. If one considers there to be any difference between the mantra deity, mantra, and the repeater of the mantra, the mantra does not bear fruit. Saint Rama Vallabh Das says, "हरि होउनि हरिगुण गावे, तेणे आपण उद्धरावे ।" "Hari ho-uni Hariguṇa gāve, teṇe āpaṇa uddharāve." 'By becoming Hari, praise Hari's qualities, by which we will uplift ourselves.'

---

[66] *Gurudev Ashram Patrika* – Ashram Newsletter – Yr. 5, issue 8, August 1976.

Swami Muktanand used to say, "For a seeker, mantra japa is a spiritual practice. But for a realized being mantra is God –मन्त्रः महेश्वरः । *Mantraḥ Maheśvaraḥ*'." This is also said in the second part of Verse 27.

The mantra to be repeated should be 'Sabīja' – a seeded or conscious mantra. It must arise from 'I AM' awareness. A mantra has two aspects. One is a form -- the word, which can be written or uttered, and the other is formless - the power inherent in the mantra which can be experienced individually. The formless is the essence and cannot be obtained from books. BhattaKallata says mantras with form or shape alone cannot perform any function. One might look into books for a mantra, but unless a saint who has realized the power in a mantra has directed a person to do so, the mantra in the book has a form but no power. The formless aspect, the power, of which the mantra becomes an embodiment, comes from Spanda, specifically from the saints who are established in Spanda – the perfect "I AM." A saint's mantra forms a conduit for the power of Spanda.

Mantras from Siddha Gurus wield power. The mantra may not necessarily be the same one that has been used by the Guru or saint in his/her spiritual practice. Gurudev Rānaḍe (1886-1957) used to initiate a would-be disciple with 'sabīja nām' (seeded name) mantra. Even now at his samadhi shrine in Nimbāḷ, District Bijāpur, Karnāṭak State, India, a person can initiate himself/herself by choosing a name and offering it to his Samadhi. Mr. Pāṭhak, one of his disciples who runs a Rānaḍe meditation center in Bikāner, Rājasthān State, India, more than a thousand miles away from Nimbāḷ, asked one of the aspirants, (*Śekhāvat*, 31, p. 6) on March 24, 1980, to take a 'name' of the aspirant's choice, offering it to His Guru – Gurudev Rānaḍe, whose picture was in the meditation room. He took the name Shri Ram which Mr. Pāṭhak repeated aloud three times followed by repetition of the aspirant. Mr. Pāṭhak explained to him, "In the shell of the word, conscious energy has been filled and inserted inside you. This name is a means to attain God, from where the conscious energy has descended into the name, and that conscious energy will take you to the same place." In his spiritual diary the aspirant describes his experiences of the workings of the mantra of his choice which became a conscious mantra. Thus the diary stands as a recent testimony of the power of a conscious mantra.

Several autobiographical accounts of saints repeatedly confirm the validity of these two verses. They also confirm that only in the company of saints can such experiences happen.

BhattaKallata says that a mantra or Divine Name becomes venerable, because it has a unique function of bestowing grace and becoming a wish-fulfilling tree, making the seeker contented. Saints have described the power of repeating a Divine Name (mantra) given by the Guru, as well as the power of the company of saints. Mantra with its nature of Spanda - divine pulsation, helps an individual in worldly attainments also, since the whole world is Spanda's manifestation. There is nothing in the world that cannot be attained by the repetition of the conscious name and the company of saints.

Jñāneśwar Mahārāj (1274-1296) in his work titled *Haripāṭh* – "Study of the Divine Name (Hari)" which is a collection of 28 abhangs (Jnaneshwar, 16) ('indestructible poems'), gives another testimony and explanation of the two verses under discussion, with examples from nature. He describes the powerful effect of saints' company on the seeker when the mantra repetition comes to fruition and how it liberates the seeker. Regarding realizing the power of the name occurring in *Spandakarika* Verse 26 he says:

ज्ञानदेवा पाठ हरि हा वैकुंठ । भरला घनदाट हरि दिसे ॥ [हरिपाठ २]

Jñānadevā pāṭha Hari hā vaikuṇṭha, bharalā ghana-dāṭa Hari dise.
[Haripāṭh 2]

For Jñānadev, chanting Hari (the Lord) is heaven itself. You see the world densely pervaded by Hari.

भावेविण देव न कळे निःसंदेह । गुरुविणे अनुभव कैसा कळे ॥
ज्ञानदेव सांगे दृष्टांताची मात । साधुचे संगतीं तरणोपाय ॥ [५]

Bhāveviṇa deva na kaḷe nis-saṅdeha, Guruviṇe anubhava kaisā kaḷe.
Jñānadeva sāṅge dṛṣṭāṅtācī māta sādhuce saṅgatīṅ taraṇopāya. [5]

Without devotion, it is certain that you will not understand God. How will you get the experience without the Guru? Jñānadev describes what he has seen, remaining in the company of the saints is the means to go across the ocean of worldliness.

एक नाम हरि द्वैतनाम दुरी । अद्वैतकुसरी विरळा जाणे ॥१॥
समबुद्धि घेतां समान श्रीहरि । शमदमा वरी हरि झाला ॥२॥

सर्वांघटीं राम देहादेही एक । सूर्यप्रकाशक सहस्ररश्मी ॥३॥
ज्ञानदेवा चित्तीं हरिपाठ नेमा । मागिलिया जन्मा मुक्त झालों ॥४॥ [१५]

Eka nāma Hari dvaita-nāma durī, advaita-kusarī viraḷā jāṇe.
Sama-buddhi ghetāṅ samāna Śrihari, śama-damā varī Hari jhālā.
Sarvāṅ-ghaṭiṅ Rāma dehādehī eka, sūrya-prakāśaka sahasra-raśmī.
Jñānadevā cittī Hari-pāṭha nemā, māgiliyā janmā mukta jhāloṅ. [15]

With the name of Hari alone, any trace of duality disappears. Rarely does anyone know the secret of non-duality.
With the intellect full of equality the Lord is experienced equally everywhere. Transcending tranquility and self-restraint, one becomes Hari.
One Rāma exists in all different forms, just as the same sun is in thousands of rays.
Jñānadev says, "My mind is set to Haripāṭh (repetition of Hari), I became free from future births."

Many seekers feel they are not worthy or pure enough, they have committed too many mistakes/sins, or they are confused by the dualities of the world, and this feeling itself needs to be dispelled also by mantra repetition. Jñāneśwar Maharaj addresses such seekers' feelings:

ज्ञानदेव म्हणे हरिजप करणें । तुटेल धरणे प्रपंचाचे ॥ [४]

Jñānadeva mhaṇe Harijapa karaṇeṅ tuṭela dharaṇe prapaṅcāce. [4]

Jnanadev says, "Doing Hari japa (repetition) breaks down the world's hold on you."

ज्ञानदेव म्हणे सगुण हें ध्यान । नामपाठ मौन प्रपंचाचे ॥ [९]

Jñānadeva mhaṇe saguṇa heṅ dhyāna,
Nāmapāṭha mouna prapaṅcāce [9]

Repeating the name is meditation on the form of the Lord, which silences the world.

हरि उच्चारणीं अनंत पापराशी । जातील लयासी क्षणमात्रे ॥१॥
तृण अग्निमेळे समरस झाले । तैसे नामें केलें जपतां हरि ॥२॥
हरि उच्चारण मंत्र पैं अगाध । पळे भूतबाधा भेणें तेथें ॥३॥
ज्ञानदेव म्हणे हरि माझा समर्थ । न करवे अर्थ उपनिषदां ॥४॥ [११]

Harī uccāraṇīṅ anaṅta pāparāśī, jātīla layāsī kṣaṇamātre.
Tṛṇa agni meḷe samarasa jhāle, taise nāmeṅ keleṅ japatāṅ Hari.
Hari uccāraṇa maṅtra paiṅ agādha, paḷe bhūtabādhā bheṇeṅ tetheṅ.
Jñānadeva mhaṇe Hari mājhā samartha, na karave artha upaniṣadāṅ.
[11]

As you utter the name of Hari,
infinite piles of sins are destroyed in a moment.
When grass touches fire, it burns to ashes,
so do sins burn down when touched by Hari's name.
Therefore the power of Hari mantra is unfathomable.
Affliction of the five elements runs away in fear.
Jñānadev says my Hari is all-powerful.
Even the Upaniṣads cannot describe His power.

Regarding the effects of the Divine Name on the seeker and people close to the seeker, he says:

हरिपाठ कीर्ति मुखे जरि गाय, पवित्रचि होय देह त्याचा ॥१॥
तपाचें सामर्थ्यें तपिन्नला अमूप । चिरंजीव कल्प वैकुंठी नांदे ॥२॥
मातृ पितृ भ्राता सगोत्र अपार । चतुर्भुज नर होउनि ठेले ॥३॥
ज्ञान गूढगम्य ज्ञानदेवा लाधलें । निवृत्तिनें दिधलें माझे हातीं ॥४॥ [१७]

Haripāṭha kīrti mukheṅ jarī gāya, pavitraci hoya deha tyācā.
Tapāceṅ sāmarthye tapinnalā amūpa, ciraṅjīva kalpa vaikuṇṭhī nānde.
Mātṛu pitṛu bhrātā sagotra apāra, caturbhuja nara houni ṭhele.
Jñāna gūḍha-gamya Jñānadevā lādhaleṅ,
Nivṛttine didhale mājhe hātīṅ.[17]

The person who sings the glory of Hari's name, his body itself is purified. By the power of austerity of Hari's name when the body and mind get immersed, he becomes immortal and enjoys millions of years in Viṣṇu's abode.

His mother, father, brother and all relatives become one with Lord Viṣṇu, (receive liberation).
Jñānadev received this secret knowledge, Nivṛtti (Guru) bestowed it in my hands.

हरिपाठीं गेले ते निवांतचि ठेले । भ्रमर गुंतले सुमनकळिके ॥
ज्ञानदेवा मंत्र हरिनामाचे शस्त्र । यमें कुळगोत्र वर्जियेलें ॥ [२०]

Haripāṭhīṅ gele te nivāṅtaci ṭhele, bhramara guṅtale sumana-kaḷike.
Jñānadevā mantra Hari-nāmāce śastra, Yameṅ kuḷagotra varjīyeleṅ.
[20]

Those who go on repeating Hari remain at peace. They are like the bees absorbed in enjoying honey in the flower-buds.
For Jñānadev, the mantra of Hari's name is a weapon that makes the Lord of death stay away from one's family and lineage.

नित्यनेम नामीं ते प्राणी दुर्लभ । लक्ष्मीवल्लभ तयांजवळी ॥१॥
नारायण हरि नारायण हरि । भुक्ति मुक्ति चारी घरीं त्यांच्या ॥२॥
हरिविणें जन्म नरकचि पैं जाणा । यमाचा पाहुणा प्राणि होय ॥३॥
ज्ञानदेव पुसे निवृत्तिसी चाड । गगनाहुनि वाड नाम आहे ॥४॥ [२२]

Nitya-nema nāmīṅ te prāṇī durlabha, Lakṣmī-vallabha tayāṅjavaḷī.
Nārāyaṇa Hari Nārāyaṇa Hari, bhukti mukti cārī gharīṅ tyāṅcyā.
Hariviṇeṅ janma narakaci paiṅ jāṇā, Yamācā pāhuṇā prāṇi hoya.
Jñānadeva puse Nivṛttisī cāḍa, gaganāhuni vāḍa Nāma āhe.
[22]

Those beings are rare who repeat the Name incessantly.
The Lord of Lakṣmi is close to them.
Bhukti (material fulfillment) and four-fold Mukti[67] (liberation) reside in the homes of those who repeat Nārāyaṇa Hari Nārāyaṇa Hari.
Know that without Hari life is hell itself.
That individual is the guest of the Lord of death.

---

[66] Four-fold mukti – *Samīpatā* – closeness with the Lord, *Sāyujyatā* - oneness with the Lord, *Salokyatā* - dwelling in the same place with the Lord, *Sarūpatā* - being of the same nature as the Lord.

When Jñānadev asked Nivṛtti (his Guru), he said, "The Name is wider than the sky."

Considering that out of primal sound Oṁ or the Universal 'I AM' - Aham, the space (sky) arose as the first element, this statement of Nivṛtti is so true!

नामापरते तत्त्व नाही रे अन्यथा । वायां आणिक पंथा जाशील झणी ॥
ज्ञानदेवा मौन जपमाळ अंतरी । धरोनि श्रीहरी जपे सदा ॥ [२६]

Nāmā-parate tattva nāhī re anyathā, vāyāṅ āṇika panthā jāśila jhaṇī.
Jñānadevā mouna japamāḷa antarī, dharūnī Śhrīharī jape sadā. [26]

There is no principle other than the Name.
Don't waste your time by going on different paths.
For Jnānadev, it is the Lord who repeats the name
holding the silent japa-mala within.

In the last verse he means that with one's own breath that goes on incessantly, it is the Lord who repeats the name silently. It also means that after the Divine Name is repeated audibly, it descends to subtle levels of 'madhyamā,' 'pashyanti' and 'parā' and the Divine Name goes on continuously. More on this in later part of the discussion.

असावें एकाग्र स्वस्थचित्त मन । उल्हासेंकरूनी स्मरण दीवीं ॥
अंतकाळीं तैसा संकटाचे वेळीं । हरि तया सांभाळी अंतर्बाह्य ॥
संतसज्जनानी घेतली प्रचीति । आळशी मंदमति केवीं तरे ॥
श्रीगुरु निवृत्ति वचन प्रेमळ । तोषला तात्काळ ज्ञानदेव ॥ [२८]

Asāveṅ ekāgra svastha-citta mana, ullhāseṅ karūnī smaraṇa Dīviṅ.
Anta-kāḷiṅ taisā saṅkaṭāce veḷīṅ, Hari tayā sāṁbhāḷī antarbāhya.
Santa-sajjanānī ghetalī pracīti, āḷaśī mandamati kevīṅ tare.
Śrī Guru Nivṛtti vacana premaḷa, toṣalā tātkāḷa Jñānadeva. [28]

The mind should be at peace and one-pointed,
and should remember the Lord cheerfully.
At the time of death as well as calamity,
Hari protects that person within and without.
The saints and good people have verified this for themselves.

How can a lazy dull-witted person go across?
By Shri Guru Nivritti's loving words,
Jñānadev is instantly delighted.

Many educated people do not give credence to Gurus' grace but emphasize individual effort alone. One such person came to Baba Muktanand and said, "Why should the mantra be given by a Guru? If we choose it by ourselves and repeat say, '1, 2, 3,' or 'table, table' will it not have the same effect?" Baba said, "There are centers in the body. When I give the mantra 'Om Namah Shivaya,' I know its effect on the different centers. But I don't know which centers will be affected by repeating '1, 2, 3,' or 'table, table, …'!"

The second part of Spanda Verse 26 says mantras perform their intended functions just as the senses of individual creatures function according to those individual's decisions. In terms of the mantra it is the 'sankalpa' – decision – of the saint who gives the mantra to the seeker. The *Gurugita* (Swami Narasimha Saraswatī, 55) which emphasizes that Guru's grace is a wish-fulfilling tree says in Verse 76.

मंत्रमूलं गुरोर्वाक्यं मोक्षमूलं गुरोः कृपा ।

Mantramūlaṁ Gurorvākyaṁ mokṣamūlaṁ Guroḥ kṛpā.

For a disciple Guru's words are a mantra, and Guru's grace is the root of liberation.

The saints give a mantra to an aspirant to fulfill his worldly aspirations to obtain a spouse, a child, to obtain success in an endeavor, to cure some disease, to end any conflicts, to attain wealth or some goods. The aspirant attains these worldly objects by repeating the given mantra. Baba Muktanand used to say, "When you do not want any of these things, and you repeat the mantra, the Lord Himself stands before you!"

Thus the mantras act like different senses of a creature performing their assigned functions, assigned in the case of mantras by a totally free Sadguru. One might ask, "When the senses and mantras all arise from the same Spanda principle, how come the senses do not have the omniscience and omnipotence of the mantras?" The reason is that their functions are opposite of each other. The function of the senses is to make the universe perceptible by making one aware of differences, while the function of the mantras is to create unity awareness. In other words, senses cause the problems of individuals who are not blessed by a Guru, perceiving this duality in the universe, the ocean of worldliness, while the mantra becomes the boat to take one across the ocean of worldliness, thus resolving the problems of individuality. The word mantra means that which redeems the person who repeats it. "मननात् त्रायते इति मन्त्रः ॥" "*Mananāt trāyate iti mantraḥ.*"

Saint Tukaram says, "मुखीं नाम हातीं मोक्ष । ऐसी बहुतांची साक्ष ॥" "*Mukhī nāma hātīṅ mokṣa, aisī bahutānci sākṣa*"- "Have the (divine) name on your lips and receive liberation in your hand. Many witnesses say what I am saying."

It is not surprising to read about the power of a mantra as described in Verse 26, since words have so much power. There is a story of Ramakrishna Paramahansa, a famous 19th century saint of Bengal, India. Once he was talking about the importance of chanting the name. A young man, who was a lawyer by profession, did not believe in what Ramakrishna was saying. He became annoyed and impatient and could not sit quietly in his place. He got up and said, "This is nonsense. A divine name is a bunch of words. What can mere words achieve?" Ramakrishna shouted, "You stupid fool! Shut up and sit down." The lawyer's blood was boiling. His face was red. He said, "You are called a great saint, and you are insulting me. I am a lawyer." Ramakrishna smiled and said, "I was just showing you the effect of a word on a person's mind and body. If the swear words have such an impact upon you, imagine what effect the blissful divine name will have!"

The power of Mantra is called mantra-vīrya – essence of the mantra – in *Shiva Sutras* (translation by Swami Lakshmanjoo):

महाह्रदानुसंधानान्मन्त्रवीर्यानुभवः १,२२॥

Mahā-hradānusandhānān-mantra-vīryānubhavaḥ (1, 22)

By the attentive continuity of meditation on the great ocean of Supreme Consciousness, the power of Supreme I is attained.

Out of the I-Am awareness or Spanda, different currents of senses - sound, touch, light, taste and smell - are formed, and the phenomenal universe arises. That is why the Supreme Consciousness is called the great ocean.

The poet saint Kabir says:

सत्तनाम है सबते न्यारा । निर्गुन सर्गुन शब्द पसारा ॥
निर्गुन बीज सर्गुन फल-फूला । साखा ज्ञान नाम है मूला ॥
मूल गहेतें सब सुख पावै । डाल-पात में मूल गंवावै ॥
सांई मिलानी सुख दिलानी । निर्गुन-सर्गुन भेद मिटानी ॥

Satta-nāma hai sabate nyārā, nirguna sarguna śabda pasārā.
Nirguna bīja sarguna phala-phulā, sākhā jñāna nāma hai mūlā.
Mūla gaheteṅ saba sukha pāvai, ḍāla-pāta meṅ mūla gaṅvāvai.
Sāīṅ milānī sukha dilanī, nirguna - sarguna bheda miṭanī.

The true nature of mantra is different from objects and experiences.
The form and the formless – saguna and nirguna –
are two aspects of the mantra.
The seed is nirguna; but the flowers and fruit are saguna.
The name is the root and knowledge (of the world) the branches.
One who goes to the root obtains complete happiness.
One who gets entangled in the branches and
leaves loses (forgets) the root.
Kabir says, "I will obtain the happiness of the Self by removing
the differences between Saguna and Nirguna,
by going to the Sadguru (and taking the mantra from him)."

As Kabir says, when an aspirant turns his/her mind from the external phenomena to the divine name "I AM" under the direction of the Sadguru, the essence of the Mantra is experienced. Human beings are enveloped by words/sounds which generate from the universal "I AM" – Spanda Shakti. This cycle of words is called 'Mātṛkā chakra.' It is the creative energy of Spanda in the fifty/fifty one sounds/letters of the Sanskrit alphabet 'A' to 'Kṣa.'[68] How these letters are generated from the letter अ**A** signifying Anuttara (beginning), Shiva, is a subject of one of the later *SpandaKarika* verses which deals with the cycle of words and

---

[68] अ आ इ ई उ ऊ ए ऐ ऋ ॠ ऌ ॡ ओ औ अं अः, क ख ग घ ङ, च छ ज झ ञ, ट ठ ड ढ ण, त थ द ध न, प फ ब भ म, य र ल व श ष स ह ळ क्ष - a ā i ī u ū ṛ ṝ ḷ ḹ e ai o au aṁ aḥ, *ka kha ga gha ṅga, ca cha ja jha yṅa, ṭa ṭha ḍa ḍha ṇa, ta tha d dha na, pa pha ba bha ma, ya ra la va śa ṣa sa ha ḷa kṣa* 51 letters, some omit ḷa and put the count at 50. The letter ḷa resides in the sahasrār, as per ShriVidya while other letters

how a creature gets entangled in it. Here it suffices to say that the words are speech forms of the world. Any object in the world identified by a human being has a name. Hence names and forms make up the universe. If we give importance to the names and forms of the world, and not to the root 'I AM' from which letters arise, as Kabir says in the above song, we are lost. It is true that mantra is also sound or letters. But as Ramakrishna Paramahansa used to say, "To remove one thorn from your foot, you use another thorn and afterwords you throw both away." Mantra is regarded as a word-form of the Lord. That is the reason Baba Muktanand emphasized it to be "Mantraḥ Maheśvaraḥ" "Mantra is the Great Lord."

Verse 27 explains the nature of the mantra as taintless, peaceful, one with the nature of Shiva. Mantra are of the nature of Supreme I which is peaceful and free of any taint of maya. It describes that once the mantras have performed their duty of bestowing grace in all the different ways described earlier, then have no outward function to perform. They remain as peace and taintless, free of maya, but they also uplift the seeker to merge with Supreme Consciousness along with themselves. Jnaneshawar Maharaja also in his *Haripath* makes this clear with similes:

साधुबोध झाला तो नुरोनिया ठेला । ठायींच मुराला अनुभव ॥१॥
कापुराची वाती उजळली ज्योती । ठायींच समाप्ती झाली जैशी ॥२॥
मोक्ष रेखे आला भाग्यें विनटला । साधूंचा अंकिला हरिभक्त ॥३॥
ज्ञानदेवा गोडी संगती सज्जनीं । हरि दिसे जनींवनीं आत्मतत्त्वीं ॥ ४॥

Sādhubodha jhālā to nuroniyā ṭhelā, ṭhāyīṅca murālā anubhava.
Kāpurāci vātī ujaḷalī jyotī, ṭhāyīṅca samāpti jhālī jaiśī.
Mokṣa rekhe ālā bhāgyeṅ vinaṭalā, sādhūṅcā ankilā Hari-bhakta.
Jñānadevā goḍī saṅgatī sajjanīṅ, Hari dise janīṅ-vanīṅ ātma-tattvīṅ.

Whoever attains the understanding of the saints, loses his separateness, which dissolves in the experience of the Self, just as the lighted camphor shines and ends then and there, leaving no trace.
One flourishes in fortune in the territory of liberation, when he becomes God's devotee in the company of saints.

---

reside in different six centers in the body. The importance of 50/51 letters is that any pure - basic sound correspond to only one letter whereas in English alphabet there are 26 letters so one needs to use 2 letters for a sound.

Jñānadev experiences the nectar name in the company of saints, and sees Hari in people, the forest and Self.

ज्ञानदेवा पाठ नारायण नाम । पाविजे उत्तम निजस्थान ॥ [१४]

Jñānadevā pāṭha Nārayaṇa nāma, pāvije uttama nijasthāna. [14]

Jñānadev says, "Repeating the name 'Nārāyaṇa,' attain the supreme Destination (Self.)"

All sounds and letters exist in a state of potentiality in the 'Parā vāṇī' – meaning 'supreme speech' or that which transcends, which is another name for common spanda or Vimarsha. Parā vāṇī resides in the region below the navel in the body of a human being. At this stage vibration is only potential and is not felt. It then manifests as 'paśyanti' – the level of speech 'that observes.' Residing between the navel and heart, it is the subtle level of speech, only a vibration, where objects are not different from each other. One observes a kind of oneness, just as the earth is observed like a blue ball from a space ship. Speech or sound is not decipherable as separate words at this point, but rather is like music from a stringed instrument, or during the 'riaz' or music practice of a vocalist where only one or more prolonged sounds are vocalized but not actual words. Speech then manifests as 'madhyamā' – the intermediate stage, in thought form, residing between the heart and throat as unpronounced words. Here there is no separation between the word and its meaning or the indicated objects. An example where the speech and objects are not distinguishable is the sound produced by the leather surface of a drum when tapped by fingers or drumsticks.[69] Music consists of speech at 'pashyanti' and 'madhyama,' which is closer to the original parā – tranquil or blissful level; hence people find it sweet and are absorbed in it.

The gross level of speech consists of 'words,' when the object and its name are separated. This speech resides in the body or 'vikhara' in Sanskrit, hence it is called 'Vaikhari,' pronounced by lips and tongue. A person familiar only with gross speech does not have a clue about the power inherent in the letters of the alphabet. Only a Guru can reveal the power of the mantra to the seeker. Mantra repetition properly done connects one to the great ocean of consciousness. It submerges consciousness to madhyama and pashyanti, makes one transcend the

[69] See writings of Swami Lakshman Joo on the four levels of speech, and *Tantrāloka* Chapter 3.

names and forms of the world, and takes one to the root from which the mantra has originated. That is why Jnaneshwar Maharaj says, "For Jnanadev, it is the Lord who repeats the silent japa-mala of mantra within."

In his commentary on the *Shiva Sutra* 1.22, (महाह्रदानुसंधानात् मंत्रवीर्यानुभवः। *Mahāhradānusandhānāt mantra-vīryānubhavaḥ*' "By the attentive continuity of meditation on the great ocean of Supreme Consciousness, the power of Supreme I is attained,") Kshemaraj says, "Mātṛkā Chakra is the successive creative means of the universe of I-consciousness, while Mālinī[70] is the successive destructive (dissolving) means of the universe of I-consciousness. The successive creative means is represented by Aham while the successive destructive means is represented by Ma-ha-a. A yogi experiences the state of I-consciousness in both these ways. The mantra has its origin and its being in the Supreme Consciousness.[71]

In *Vijnana Bhairava*, there are several centering exercises – dhāraṇās – based on sound and music and which can be used by the seeker to become one with Spanda.

अनाहते पात्रकर्णेऽभग्नशब्दे सरिद्द्रुते । शब्दब्रह्मणि निष्णातः परं ब्रह्माधिगच्छति ॥
श्लोक ३८, धारणा १५
प्रणवादिसमुच्चारात् प्लुतान्ते शून्यभावनात् । शून्यया परया शक्त्या शून्यतामेति भैरवि ।
श्लोक ३९, धारणा १६
यस्य कस्यापि वर्णस्य पूर्वान्तावनुभावयेत् । शून्यया शून्यभूतोऽसौ शून्याकारः पुमान्भवेत्
श्लोक ४०, धारणा १७
तन्त्र्यादिवाद्यशब्देषु दीर्घेषु क्रमसंस्थितेः । अनन्यचेताः प्रत्यन्ते परव्योमवपुर्भवेत् ॥
श्लोक ४१, धारणा १८
गीतादिविषयास्वादा-समसौख्यैकतात्मनः । योगिनस्तन्मयत्वेन मनोरूढेस्तदात्मता ॥
श्लोक ७३, धारणा ५०

Anāhate pātrakarṇe 'bhagna śabde sarid-dṛute,
Śabda-Brahmaṇi niṣṇātaḥ paraṁ Brahmādhigacchati.
Verse 38, Dhāraṇā 15

Praṇavādi-samuccārāt plutānte śūnyabhāvanāt,

[70] The letters of Mālinī are the same as those of Mātṛkā but in a different order: न ऋ ॠ ऌ ॡ थ च ध ई ण उ ऊ ब क ख ग घ ङ इ अ व भ य ड ढ ठ झ ञ ज र ट प छ ल आ स अः ह ष क्ष म श अं त ए ऐ ओ औ द फ - *na ṛ ṝ ḷ ḹ tha ca dha ī ṇa u ū ba ka kha ga gha ṅga i a va bha ya ḍa ḍha ṭha jha yṅa ja ra ṭa pa cha la ā sa aḥ ha ṣa kṣa ma śa aṁ ta e ai o au da pha.*

[71] See page 70 *Shiva Sutras Revealed* by Swami Lakshman Joo.

Śūnyayā parayā śaktyā śūnyatāmeti Bhairavi
(Verse 39, Dhāraṇā 16)

Yasya kasyāpi varṇasya pūrvāntāvanubhāvayet.
Śūnyayā śūnya-bhūto 'sou śūnyākāraḥ pumān bhavet.
(Verse 40, Dhāraṇā 17)

Tantryādi-vādya-śabdeṣu dīrgheṣu krama-saṅsthiteḥ,
Ananya-cetāḥ pratyante para-vyoma-vapur-bhavet
(Verse 41, Dhāraṇā 18)

Gītādi - viṣayāsvādā - samasoukhaikatātmanaḥ,
Yoginas - tanmayatvena mano-rūḍhes-tadātmatā.
(Verse 73, Dhāraṇā 50)

When one is steeped in Nāda, the Self in the form of spontaneous sound vibration, produced without any impact, continually going on in all creatures (and also in the universe as discovered by scientists), which is heard by those who have been made fit by the blessing of a Guru, and which rushes like a river, one attains to the Self. (15)

O Bhairavi, after a drawn-out utterance of Praṇava (Auṁ, Hūm or Hrīm) and contemplating the silence that follows, the seeker attains to the Void by the energy of the void, the power of parā itself. (16)

Whatever sound or letter is uttered, the void existing before the utterance and prevailing after it should be contemplated. Then that individual by the power of the Void - parā - will become one with the nature and form of the Void. (17)

If one listens with undivided attention to the sound of a stringed instrument or other musical instruments produced in a prolonged succession, attending to the resonance and reverberation thus produced, one experiences the body merged with the space of Consciousness. (18)

When a yogi's mind becomes one with the joy of a melody or other object, by becoming one with the joy (transcending the melody or object in question), the Yogi experiences oneness with the blissful Self. (50)

This dissolution of the world for the seeker and oneness with the Self is described in the aphorism from the Shiva Sutras 2.1 : "चित्तम् मन्त्रः ।, *Cittaṁ Mantraḥ* - Mind is mantra and Mantra is Mind." That mind is called mantra when it arises as the Praṇava mantra and as the Prāsāda mantra. Pranava mantra flows in two directions, one arising from the subjective Supreme God consciousness and moving outward to objective God consciousness as "अहम्" "*Aham*" - "I AM," the potential to create the universe; and then returning from objective to subjective God consciousness as "महअ" "Ma-ha-a." The letter A – stands for shiva, ha – for shakti and m – for the individual; thus aham represents Supreme consciousness descending to individual consciousness through shakti, and mahaa represents individual consciousness through shakti ascending to Shiva. The Prasada mantra is "सौः" "*Sauḥ*," representing the thirty-six principles of the Universe, which flow out from the "I AM" awareness to the objective universe. This is the realization of the perfect "I Am"-ness. This is the experience Jnaneshwar describes when he says, "Hari is seen in the people, forest and the Self." or "The world is seen densely pervaded by Hari."

That is the reason *Spandakarika* Verse 27 says along with the mind of the seeker the mantra dissolves in and becomes one with the Supreme Consciousness.

The importance of the Sadguru in transforming an individual into the Self using the mantra is given by Saint Kabir.

सतगुरु हो महाराज, मोपे साईं रंग डारा ।
सब्द की चोट लगी मेरे मन में, बेध गया तन सारा ।
औषध-मूल कछू नहीं लागै, का करै वैद बिचारा ।
सुर-नर मुनिजन पीर-औलिया, कोई न पावे पारा ।
साहब कबीर सर्व रंग - रंगिया, सब रंग से रंग न्यारा ।

Sataguru ho Mahārāja, mope sāīṅ ranga ḍārā
Sabda kī coṭa lagī mere mana meṅ, bedha gayā tana sārā
Auṣadha-mula kachu nahīṅ lāge, kā karai vaida bicāra
Sura-nara muni-jana pīra-auliyā, koyī na pāve pārā
Sāhaba Kabīr sarva ranga -rangiyā, saba ranga se ranga nyāra

My Sadguru Maharaj dyed me in the color of Consciousness.
His words - the mantra – pierced my mind,
and the whole body was transformed into pure consciousness.

My state cannot be cured by any medicine, roots or herbs.
The poor doctor is totally helpless!
Without mantra gods, men, sages, or renunciants
  cannot cross the ocean of worldliness.
Kabir says, "My Lord, the Guru, has showed me all colors.
And this color of consciousness is totally different
  from any other color."

VERSES 28, 29 AND 30
OBJECTS OF PERCEPTION AND ALLPERVASIVENESS OF THE SELF

यस्मात् सर्वमयो जीवः सर्वभावसमुद्भवात् ।
तत्संवेदनरूपेण तादात्म्यप्रतिपत्तितः ॥२८।
तेन शब्दार्थचिन्तासु न सावस्था न यः शिवः ।
भोक्तैव भोग्य-भावेन सदा सर्वत्र संस्थितः ॥२९॥
इति वा यस्य संवित्तिः क्रीडात्वेनाखिलं जगत् ।
स पश्यन् सततं युक्तो जीवन्मुक्तो न संशयः ॥३०॥

28. *Yasmāt sarvamayo jīvaḥ sarva-bhāva-samudbhvāt*
Tat-saṁvedana- rūpeṇa tādātmya-pratipattitaḥ.
29. *Tena śabdārtha-cintāsu na sāvasthā na yaḥ Śivaḥ*
Bhoktaiva bhogya-bhāvena sadā sarvatra saṁsthitaḥ.
30. *Iti vā yasya saṁvīttiḥ krīḍātvenākhilaṁ jagat*
Sa paśyan satataṁ yukto jīvan-mukto na saṅśayaḥ.

भट्टकल्लटः – सर्वात्मक एवायमात्मासर्वानुभावोत्पत्तिद्वारेण अनुभूयमानस्यैव संवेदनात् बाह्यार्थमनुभूयमानमेव शरीरत्वेन गृह्णाति,न तु शिरःपाण्यादिलक्षितम् एकमेवास्य शरीरम् ॥२८॥
तेन तथाविधेन सर्वात्मकेन स्वभावेन, शब्दार्थयोः चिन्तासु न सा अवस्था या शिवस्वभावं न व्यञ्जयति, अतो भोक्तैव हि भोग्यभावेन सर्वत्रावस्थितो, न त्वन्यत् भोग्यमस्ति ॥२९॥
एवं स्वभावं यस्य चित्तं, यथा – मन्मयमेव जगत् सर्वम् इति, स सर्वं क्रीडात्वेन पश्यन् नित्ययुक्तत्वात् जीवन्नेव ईश्वरवत् मुक्तो, न त्वस्य शरीरादि बन्धकत्वेन वर्तते ॥३०॥

BhaṭṭaKallaṭa – *28. Sarvātmaka evāyam-ātmā sarvānubhāvotpatti-dvāreṇa anubhūyamānasyaiva saṁvedanāt bāhyārthamanubhūyamānameva śarīratvena gṛhṇāti, na tu*

śiraḥ-pāṇyādi-lakṣitam ekam-evāsya śarīram.
29. Tena tathāvidhena sarvātmakena svabhāvena, śabdārthayoḥ cintāsu na sā avasthā yā Śiva-svabhāvaṁ na vyanjayati, ato bhoktaiva hi bhogya-bhāvena sarvatrāvasthito, na tvanyat bhogyam-asti.
30. Evaṁ svabhāvaṁ yasya cittaṁ, yathā - "Manmayam-eva jagat sarvaṁ iti," sa sarvaṁ krīḍātvena paśyan nityayuktatvāt jīvanneva Īśvaravat mukto, na tvasya śarīrādi bandhakatvena vartate.

Meaning of each verse followed by BhattaKallata's commentary:

28. A person is all-pervasive because he becomes one with the internal and external objects and participates in their process of creation (creation, sustenance, dissolution, concealment and grace).

Indeed, every being is all-pervasive; by creating every sense object one experiences it through one's own consciousness alone. Any external object, when experienced, is regarded as a part of one's own body. Thus the body is not limited to what is indicated by the head, hands, and so on.

29. Therefore, among a word, the meaning or the object it stands for, and a thought, there is no state which is not the Self. It alone exists always everywhere as the experiencer as well as the experience.

Therefore because of all-pervasiveness of the individual there is no state among word, its indicated object, and thought which is different from the nature of Shiva. Hence it is the experiencer alone that exists everywhere as an experienced object, and no object to be experienced exists by itself without the experiencer.

30. The one who is aware of one's universal nature of consciousness-awareness regards the entire world as one's own play, and watching it, the one remains always merged with the Self and is liberated while alive. There is no doubt about this.

The one who has this nature as the mindset, as if 'this entire universe is my own Self,' sees everything as a play and being always one with the Self, that person is the master of the universe while still alive, and is not bound by current restrictions of the physical body.

THE UNIVERSE APPEARS from Supreme consciousness. With our

consciousness and awareness, which is also a manifestation of that Supreme consciousness, we make distinctions between words, objects and thoughts. We distinguish between objects as sentient and insentient. If we want to experience consciousness everywhere, we must start from ourselves. Let us take a close look at ourselves. We regard ourselves to be a physical body limited to our head, hands and other limbs, limited to a fixed spot at any given moment. But when we consider our mind we don't experience those limitations. We can think of anything. We can think of the sun, galaxies, countries, people and various objects. We can think of the past. We can imagine which does not even exist in the universe as an object. Our mind can travel fast – faster than light. Actually, this habit of globe-trotting is a nuisance when we need our mind to concentrate on the task at hand! So our mind is not limited to a fixed place and fixed time. Thus as our mind indicates, we are not limited. We can stand apart from our mind and can observe its functioning with amazement. This shows that we are greater than mind or wider than the reach of mind. Of course, if we investigate further, we transcend the mind, or we find that there is no mind! As we wake up from our sleep, the first thing we notice is that we become aware of our 'I' and then awareness of our body and our universe starts. Thus our 'I' is the origin of our mind. The whole problem is that we regard this 'I' as different from the Universal 'I' - Consciousness.

Our true nature is described by the verses 28 and 29 in a beautiful manner. Every individual is identical with the entire universe because all entities arise from him; by his perception of the entities he experiences his identity with them. Therefore, whether it is a word, object or thought, there is no state, which is not consciousness – Self. An experiencer himself resides always everywhere in the form of the experience. But the experiencer should not identify himself with any experience.

The saints say the world exists because you exist. If you did not exist, the world would not exist for you. This means the world exists because of our existence – our consciousness and awareness.

For instance, let us consider a painting of a natural scene. That painting would not exist for us if we were not conscious of it. When we look at the painting our mind takes on that form. When our mind looks at the house, stream, grass and trees in the painting, it takes the form of different objects. While looking at the house if the mind did not take the form of the house, then the house will not be perceived by us at all. In short, our mind becomes the object. When we look away from the painting and look at another object, the painting created and sustained in mind for a while is now dissolved and the mind takes the form of the new object. When we do not perceive an object, though its existence is guaranteed by others, it is the power of concealment that is acting for us! We find concealed electrical wiring in modern houses. Thus when we turn the switch on somewhere, the light goes on somewhere else with no directly visible connection. But we know there is a connection behind the wall. We have nowadays a wireless communications. For which, even wiring is not necessary. Thus the connections are available but they are all invisible. Similarly the act of concealment, the fourth process of Shiva, is experienced by us in the form of our separate 'I' feeling hiding from us 'the connected wiring' – universal consciousness. When the 'concealed wiring' or 'wireless connections' is observed, we can sing like Saint Jnaneshwar 'भरला घनदाट हरि दिसे । *Bharalā ghanadāṭa Hari dise* – The Lord is discerned densely packed everywhere.' Understanding this connection is grace. That grace comes to us in the form of saints and their teachings. In these two verses, Vasugupta, the author of *SpandaKarikas*, has indicated that we reside everywhere in the form of the experienced objects and that is why, whether it is a word, the meaning of the word, or the object the word stands for, or a thought, the beginning, middle or the end of any state cannot be devoid of consciousness. Hence we are that consciousness.

Thus similar to the five processes of the Supreme Consciousness, our individual consciousness performs the same five functions of creation, sustenance, dissolution, concealment and grace. In *Pratyabhijñā Hṛdayam*, a text of Kashmir Shaivism, (Singh, 33) there are two aphorisms, "चितिरेव चेतनपदादवरूढा चेत्यसंकोचिनी चित्तम् ॥५॥ तथापि तद्वत्पंचकृत्यानि करोति ॥१०॥" "*Citireva cetana-padādavarūḍhā cetya-saṅkocinī cittam. Tathāpi tadvat pañcakṛtyāni karoti.*" (5, 10) "It is Chiti which contracts from her Supreme Consciousness state to become the individual mind. Still, the individual performs the five-fold processes like Chiti." The five-fold processes are not the underlying reality; rather the substratum Chiti – Consciousness is reality.

Hence we should never regard any change, or even the world in itself as real; only the Self is real. We should consider ourselves as the compact mass of Supreme consciousness. The text *Pratyabhijñā Hṛdayam* says, "तदपरिज्ञाने स्वशक्तिभिर्व्यामोहितता संसारित्वम् ॥१२॥ तत्परिज्ञाने चित्तमेव अन्तर्मुखीभावेन चेतनपदाध्यारोहात् चितिः॥१३॥" "*Tad-aparijñāne svśaktibhir-vyāmohitatā saṁsāritvam. Tatparijñāne cittameva antarmukhī-bhāvena cetana-padādhyārohāt Citiḥ.*" (12, 13) "Not knowing our true nature and the five fold process we experience limited power, the duality-ridden universe, and then we suffer the cycles of pleasure and pain, birth and death. While knowing these, the mindset itself turning inwards rises to and becomes the state of Consciousness – Chiti." Thus the mind does not exist as an entity.

Verse 29 says that even when the three states – word, object or thought, are present we have to become aware of the substratum – Supreme consciousness, Shiva.

An important consequence of this teaching is that we should never regard ourselves as limited and imperfect, whether it is our body or mind. All the resources of the universe for our functioning are available to us.

Once a lion cub got away from his pack and found himself with a group of donkey foals. The foals accepted him as one of their own. The owner of the donkeys also accepted the lion cub along with his donkeys. The lion cub played with donkeys, ate with them and stayed with them. There was nothing to complain about. He brayed like the donkeys. One day the donkeys and the cub were passing through a forest. A lion was watching this interesting sight from a distance. The lion came out. The donkeys saw him. Frightened by the lion, the donkeys started running helter-skelter. As the lion cub saw his friends taking off he also decided to do the same. Suddenly the big lion pounced upon him and said, "You are not one of them. You are great. You are the king of the jungle. If you don't believe me, let us take a look at our faces in a nearby lake." The cub followed the lion. He looked at the reflection of their faces in the lake. The older lion further said to the cub, "Don't bray like those helpless donkeys. Roar like me! You are not helpless. You are all powerful. You are the king of the jungle!" Instantly, the lion cub became the lion again.

We are like that lion cub. We have kept company with thoughts of limitation, thoughts of helplessness, and thoughts of misery. Our nature is all power, all knowledge and all bliss. Only the grace of the Guru, his word, his teachings, can make our habits change and reveal our true nature.

As we were preparing these verses for presentation at weekly satsang, the author's wife, Chitra, had a dream where she was with Muktanand Baba. Baba was sitting at a desk; Chitra was sitting on the floor near his feet. She heard some people shouting curse words directed at Baba. Baba was very quiet. Chitra shouted back saying, "You don't know, how great a saint he really is. You should come and stay with him, follow his teachings and then you would know!" Baba turned to Chitra and said, "People say many things. But if you think highly of yourself, nothing will touch you. Never put yourself down." As Baba was talking to Chitra, the voices subsided.

In the Thirteenth Chapter of the *Bhagwad Gita* the Lord talks about the same ideas. The following verses are similar to the verses 28 and 29.

यावत्संजायते किंचित् सत्त्वं स्थावरजंगमम् ।
क्षेत्रक्षेत्रज्ञसंयोगात् तद् विद्धि भरतर्षभ ।।(भगवद् गीता १३।२६)

Yāvat saṁjāyate kiṁcit sattvaṁ sthāvara-jaṅgamam
Kṣetra-kṣetrajña-saṁyogāt tad viddhi Bharatarṣabha. (B.G. 13/26)

O Arjuna, whatever object, sentient or insentient, arises,
know that it emanates from the union of consciousness and matter.

Jnaneshwar Maharaj comments: When the wind blows over the water, waves are formed. When the Spring arrives, the trees have new buds. Similarly, know that an individual being is formed from matter and consciousness.

The next verse says:

समं सर्वेषु भूतेषु तिष्ठन्तं परमेश्वरम् ।
विनश्यत्स्वविनश्यन्तं यः पश्यति स पश्यति।।(भगवद् गीता १३।२७)

Samaṁ sarveṣu bhūteṣu tiṣṭhantaṁ Parameśvaram
Vinaśyatsvavinaśyantaṁ yaḥ paśyati sa paśyati (B.G. 13/27)

Whoever sees Supreme Consciousness abiding equally in all perishable things, as the only imperishable substance, he is the seer.

Jnaneshwar Maharaj comments, "Cloth may not look like yarn; but it is made of yarn. We see many different things; their names are different; their characteristics are different. But the principle in each of them is the same. It is like pumpkins growing on a vine, which may be of different sizes and shapes but their nature is the same. Or like sparks of a charcoal may be different but they produce the same heat." Just as the electricity is the same in all electric appliances.

The *Gita* further says:

यदा भूतपृथग्भावमेकस्थम् अनुपश्यति ।
तत एव च विस्तारं ब्रह्म संपद्यते तदा ॥ (भगवद् गीता १३।३०)

Yadā bhūta-pṛthag-bhāvam - ekasthaṁ anupaśyati.
Tata eva ca vistāraṁ Brahma saṁpadyate tadā. (B.G. 13/30)

Whenever he perceives the diversified existence of beings as rooted in the Supreme consciousness, and as the manifestation of That Consciousness, that very moment he attains the true knowledge – the knowledge of the Self.

Our basic instinct is that we want to be happy. We want to be in bliss. We want to experience love. We want to excel in everything we do. We do not want stress in our lives. We want to be creative. We are tired of competing, hating, and worrying. When we live life and experience the universe in proper perspective, we are in bliss. That is the reason we are here. The understanding of the two verses 28 and 29 is the key to happiness and total fulfillment.

The consequence is total delight and total satisfaction, when the Universe is seen to be a play of consciousness. That is why the Verse 30 following the above two verses says, "He who continually perceives this universe as a sport of the Universal Consciousness is immersed in the bliss of Shiva and is truly free in his body. There is no doubt about this."

Vasugupta says the same thing in his *Shiva Sutras*,"शुद्धतत्त्वानुसंधानाद्वाऽपशुशक्तिः ॥१-१६॥ *Śuddha-tattvānusaṅdhānādvā 'paśu-śaktiḥ* (1-16)" "Or by aiming at the Pure Principle one possesses Shiva's unlimited energy." The Pure Principle here is Shiva. We compromise this experience by aiming to obtain mundane objects that give only temporary satisfaction. This leads to the cycle of happiness and sadness. Any achievement in this world is very limited in comparison to the unlimited power of Shiva. Thus aiming at Shiva and attaining it once for all is the only true attainment.

Vijñānabhairava comes to our help by providing a centering technique:

सर्वं जगत्स्वदेहं वा स्वानन्दभरितं स्मरेत् ।

युगपत्स्वामृतेनैव परानन्दमयो भवेत् ॥ (श्लोक ६५, धारणा ४२)

Sarvaṁ jagat-svadehaṁ vā svānand-bharitaṁ smaret.
Yugapat-svāmṛtenaiva parānanda-mayo bhavet.
(*Verse 65, Dhāraṇā 42*)

The seeker should contemplate simultaneously this entire universe and his own body in totality full of bliss. Through this immortal nectarlike bliss, the seeker will become immersed in the Supreme bliss.

Baba Muktananda has described clearly in his spiritual autobiography *Play of Consciousness – Chitshakti Vilas*, (Swami Muktanand Paramhans, 52, p. 175-182) – how this liberation leads to bliss, total satisfaction and universal love. He sets us his own example, so we do not have to imagine such lofty ideas. What good are the ideas if they cannot be translated into practice? In this book Baba says:

The world which we live in is the play of that self-effulgent, all knowing energy of consciousness. The one who has this outlook is neither bound nor liberated. There are no means, nor an end. There are no contractions for him, since his eye of knowledge has opened by Guru's blessing. For him, the curtain of differentiation that creates duality is torn. If one does not have the grace of the Guru, then that playful conscious Shakti does not reside in one's eyes and does not reveal the true nature of the universe. When with Guru's grace that Shakti penetrates the seeker, She pervades his entire body and purifies his entire being, makes him like Herself, sits in his eyes, heart and mind. Then this universe appears to the seeker a play of the energy of Consciousness. This world is nothing else. The nature of Consciousness is total freedom and total knowledge. Consciousness creates, sustains and dissolves everything. It is the root of everything. That is why it is the means for everyone's happiness. It is beyond place, time and form, but manifests as place, time and form. Even though It manifests in the universe, It is all pervading, always full, complete, and ever-light. So it is undivided and one perfect.

Its expansive tendency creates this universe out of Itself, still It transcends the universe and remains total light and knowledge, and extremely pure. In the human being, that expanding tendency creates the four bodies – physical, subtle, causal and supracausal, five sheaths, four states, the inner instrument of mind, intellect, subconscious and ego. It combines the five elements and 36 principles to create the human body of 72000 nerves, seven vital fluids, five senses of perception and five of action and their respective sense objects; five pranas and their functions, from head to toe. It takes on innumerable forms. It creates happiness, sorrow, fear, pain and childhood, youth and old age out of Itself. It still remains untouched and pure. It transcends the waking state, where we see the common universe, and the good and bad actions performed. It is beyond the dream state and the happenings in the dreams. It is distant from the deep sleep and the void of the deep sleep. It is different from the turiya state perceived in the supracausal body. It appears as the universe and still stays as the witness to the universe.

As a result of Guru's grace if we remain in the sahasrar even for a moment, then we do not see anything else besides our Self, know nothing else besides our Self. It is an intoxication. We enjoy the bliss of the Self. We experience our perfection – there is only awareness of aham -"I AM." That awareness is Brahman, Kundalini and Consciousness. When that aham takes on the form of idam - this and appears as the world, It goes from the Turiya – fourth – state to deep sleep to dream and from dream to waking from head to toe, and becomes the entire world.

The two essential principles of Consciousness appears as the subject and object. What we call 'This' is the object principle, and the principle which distinguishes 'this' in terms of this world, this pot, this cloth is "I AM" – Aham Vimarsha – the subject principle. As man is not different from his four states, Consciousness is not different from the universe. 'You', 'I,' 'this' are just the manifestations of Chiti. Just as drops, foam, waves, and bubbles are not different from the ocean, the names, forms and qualities are not different from Consciousness. Coolness of water is not different from water, likewise this universe – play of consciousness cannot be different from us. The cloth is not separate from the yarn, out of which the cloth is made, similarly the universe is consciousness.

Thus the saints want us to live a happy, fulfilled life. Regarding life as a play, they want us to live our life dancing and never crawling. We have to practice the teachings of the saints and by investigating the culprit, the differentiating 'I,'merge with the Universal 'I.' With their grace, which is the fifth or grace-bestowing power of the universal consciousness, we can live life as described by Verse 30.

This can be summarized in the words of Dharmadas as follows:

खुदी का जब उठा परदा, अजब ही माज़रा देखा ।
जिसे बंदा मैं जाना था, उसे फिर खुद खुदा देखा ।।टेक ।।
यही कसरत की सूरत जो, नज़र आने लगी वहदत ।
अव्वल फ़ानी जो जाना था, उसी को फिर बक़ा देखा ।।१।।
मैं जिस को ढूँढता फिरता था, जा कर जा बजा प्यारे ।
खुली जब आँख रूहानी, उसी को जा बजा देखा ।।२।।
हुआ जब कतर-ए-पानी, हकीकत आब से वाकीफ़ ।
तो कुल फ़ानी को फिर उस ने, यहीं घर में छुपा देखा ।।३।।
नज़र आती है हर इक शै, किताबे मानवी मुझ को ।
जहाँ देखा वही देखा, न उस बिन कुछ जुदा देखा ।।४।।
बुजज़ उस के न कुछ देखा, जो देखा भी वो ना देखा ।
जो देखा आप ही देखा, न न्यारा ना मिला देखा ।।५।।
रहा हवाब खुद जब तक, न समझा आप को दरिया ।
हुआ जब बहर की सूरत, जब उस ने खुद गँवा देखा ।।६।।
सिवा इस के न था, न होगा, न है, यह बात सत समझो ।
किताबें और ग्रंथों का, यही ही मुद्दा देखा ।।७।।
न देखा यार को जिस ने , न उस ने और कुछ देखा ।
तमाशा कुल, उसे दीखा, है जिस ने दिलरुबा देखा ।।८।।
नज़ारा यार होता है, दिलादिल की सफाई से ।
उसी में रुख नज़र आया, जो आईना, सफ़ा देखा ।।९।।
रहो खामोश, मत कर, अब ये बातें तू धरमदासा ।
बता किस को, है देखा तू,और हो के उस को क्या देखा ।।१०।।

Ref: Khudī kā jaba uṭhā paradā, ajaba hī mājarā dekhā
Jise baṅdā maiṅ jānā thā, use phir khud Khuda dekhā.

1. *Yahī kasarata kī sūrata jo, najar āne lagī vahadata*
   Avval phānī jo jānā thā, usī ko phir bakā dekhā
2. *Maiṅ jisa ko ḍhūṇḍhatā phirtā thā, jā kara jā bajā pyāre*
   Khulī jaba āṅkha rūhānī, usī ko jā bajā dekhā.
3. *Huā jaba katar-e-pānī, hakīkata āba se vākifa*
   To kula fānī ko phir usa ne, yahīṅ ghar meṅ chupā dekhā.
4. *Najar ātī hai har ikaśai, kitābe mānavī mujha ko*
   Jahāṅ dekhā vahī dekhā, na usa bina kucha judā dekhā.

5. Bujaja usa ke na kucha dekhā, jo dekhā bhī vo nā dekhā
Jo dekhā āpa hī dekhā, na nyārā nā milā dekhā.
6. Rahā havāba khud jaba tak, na samajhā āpa ko dariyā
Huā jaba bahar kī sūrata, jaba usa ne khud gaṅvā dekhā
7. Sivā isa ke na thā, na hogā, na hai, yaha bāta sata samajho
Kitāboṅ aura granthoṅ kā, yahī hī muddā dekhā.
8. Na dekhā yāra ko jisa ne, na usa ne aur kuch dekhā
Tamāśā kula, use dīkhā, hai jisa ne dilarubā dekhā
9. Najārā yāra hotā hai, dilā-dila kī safāī se
Usī meṅ rukha nazar āyā, jo āīnā, safā dekhā
10. Raho khāmośa, mata kara, aba ye bāteṅ tū Dharamadāsā
Batā kisa ko, hai dekhā tū, āur ho ke usa ko kyā dekhā

When the veil of ego was lifted
I saw a wonderful sight
Myself, whom I thought to be an ordinary bound soul
Was God Himself.

I perceived Oneness in the expanded form of Consciousness
At first I used to think of myself as mortal
Now, once again, my self turned out to be immortal.

I used to wander searching for God in different places
When the eye of knowledge opened
I saw him everywhere.

Just as a drop of water is truly water itself
I found perfection hidden within this mortal frame.
I see everything exactly the same way
As the scriptures say
Wherever I see, I see only God
And nothing different from God

Except God I see nothing else
Whatever I used to see, I don't see it anymore.
Whatever I see is myself.
And I see nothing new.

As long as a bubble of water remained a bubble,
It did not know that it was the ocean
When the bubble lost itself, it became the ocean.

Understand this to be the truth
There was nothing, there is nothing,
and there will be nothing other than this.
All scriptures and books make the same point.

The one who has not seen the Friend, God,
has seen nothing.
The one who has seen his beloved, the Lord,
sees everything as a play.

One can see the Friend's face,
By purifying the heart.
Only in a clean mirror,
Can one see oneself.

Oh Dharmadas, please be quiet
and do not talk about these things.
After all tell me, Whom did you see?
And becoming Him what did you see?

The point is that there is nothing other than one's own Self. So there is nothing new to talk about.

Of course, this condition of remaining silent comes only when Guru lifts the curtain of one's ego.

VERSES 31 AND 32
DEITY OF MANTRA AND MIND

अयमेवोदयस्तस्य ध्येयस्य ध्यायिचेतसि ।
तदात्मतासमापत्तिरिच्छतः साधकस्य या ॥३१॥
इयमेवामृतप्राप्तिरयमेवात्मनो ग्रहः ।
इयं निर्वाणदीक्षा च शिवसद्भावदायिनी ॥३२॥

31. Ayam-evodayas-tasya dhyeyasya dhyāyi-cetasi
Tadātmatā-samāpattir-icchataḥ sādhakasya yā.
32. Iyam-evāmṛta-prāptir-ayam-evātmano grahaḥ
Iyaṁ nirvāṇa-dīkṣā ca Śiva-sadbhāva-dāyinī

भट्टकल्लटः- तत्संवेदनद्वारेण यः तदात्मग्रहो मन्त्रन्यासात्मकः स एवोदयः तस्य ध्येयस्य मन्त्रात्मनः साधकचेतसि, तादात्म्यं तत्स्वभावत्वप्राप्तिः मन्त्रदेवतया सह साधकस्य मन्त्रोच्चारणेच्छया संपादिता ॥३१॥ इयमेव सा मिथ्याज्ञानशून्यस्य साधकस्य निरावरणस्वस्वरूपसंवित्तिः अमृतत्वप्राप्तिः न तु रसास्वादरूपस्य धातुसारस्य स्थूलस्यास्वादनम् अमृतप्राप्तिरुक्ता, यैव मन्त्रोच्चारणमात्रेणैव मन्त्रस्वरूपावस्थितिप्राप्तिः सैवात्मनो ग्रहणमित्युक्ता । यस्मात् आत्मनो ग्रहणं कुर्याद्दीक्षाकाले गुरुर्धिया इति । न पुनर्लोष्टादिवत् हस्तेन तस्यामूर्तस्य ग्रहणं भवति, अत एव चेयमेव सा निर्वाणदीक्षा शिवसद्भावदायिनी, परमशिवस्वरूपाभिव्यञ्जिका ॥३२॥

BhaṭṭaKallaṭa –31. Tat-saṁvedana-dvāreṇa yaḥ tadātma-graho mantra-nyāsātmakaḥ sa evodayaḥ tasya dhyeyasya mantrātmanaḥ sādhaka-cetasi, tādātmyaṁ tat-svabhāvatva-prāptiḥ mantra-devatayā saha sādhakasya mantroccāraṇecchayā saṁpāditā.
32. Iyam-eva sā mithyā-jñāna-śūnyasya sādhakasya nirāvaraṇa-sva-svarūpa-saṁvittiḥ amṛtatva-prāptiḥ na tu ras-āsvāda-rūpasya dhātu-sārasya sthūlasyāsvādanam amṛta-

prāptir-uktā, yaiva mantroccāraṇa-mātreṇaiva mantra-svarūpāvasthiti-prāptiḥ saivātmano grahaṇamityuktā. Yasmāt "ātmano grahaṇaṁ kuryād-dīkṣā-kāle gurur-dhiyā" iti. Na punar-loṣṭādivat hastena tasyāmūrtasya grahaṇaṁ bhavati, ata eva ceyam-eva sā nirvāṇa-dīkṣā Śiva-sadbhāva-dāyinī, parama-Śiva-svarūpābhivyañjikā.

Meaning of each verse followed by BhattaKallata's commentary:

31. The goal of meditation is attained in the meditating seeker's mind when the seeker experiences oneness with the Deity merely upon willing to see that Deity. That perception of oneness with the Deity of the mantra is the realization of the Deity itself in the seeker's mind. Oneness with the Deity and attainment of the Deity's state is accomplished by the seeker's mere will to repeat the mantra.

32. This is the acquisition of nectar of immortality. It is the attainment of the Self. This is an initiation into liberation, and it is that which bestows the nature of Shiva on the seeker.

This perception is verily the awareness of one's own nature without any covering. This is the attainment of the nectar of immortality for a seeker devoid of any pretense of knowledge; whereas tasting of some gross concocted nectars or consuming of some gross mineral essence supplements does not bestow immortality. When a person acquires the state of the nature of the mantra merely by pronouncing the mantra, that state is called attainment of the Self. From this it is said, "At the time of initiation, Guru's intellect should take hold of the disciple's Self." It is not possible to grasp the formless Self in hand like a lump of clay or any other gross object. Therefore the "initiation bestowing liberation" is that which bestows on the disciple the experience of the auspicious state of Shiva manifesting as the disciple's nature of the Supreme Self.

THE FIRST VERSE describes the ultimate state of assimilation of the mantra in the system within the disciple. It shows effortlessness and spontaneity in experiencing oneness with the Deity of the mantra. At first the seeker repeats the mantra by lips – Vaikhari (audible) level of speech. By constant repetition with feeling, the mantra descends to the throat – Madhyama (subtle) level of speech, then to the heart - Pashyanti speech and finally the mantra is at the navel – Parā level of speech, where it is one with the individual's entire system. At that stage just remembrance or thought of the mantra makes the Deity appear, perceive Its presence within. This is the stage where even without uttering the mantra -'calling the Deity to appear,' the Deity appears. The verse celebrates the ultimate attainment of the spiritual practice of repeating mantra. All saints continually celebrate this state. Hence in the following discussion, different aspects of these two verses are brought out mainly through the words of different saints.

Jnaneshwar Maharaj says in an abhang (imperishable poem),

गोपाळा रे तुझे ध्यान लागो मना । अणु न विसंबे हरि जगत्रय जीवना ॥
सोनियाचा दिवस आजि अमृतें पाहिला । नाम आठवितां रूपीं प्रगट पैं झाला ॥
तनु मनु शरण तुझ्या विनटलों पायीं । बाप रखुमादेवीवरा वांचोनि आनु नेणें कांहीं ॥

Gopāḷā re tujhe dhyāna lāgo manā,
aṇu na visaṁbe Harī jagatraya jīvanā.
Soniyācā divasu āji amṛteṅ pāhilā,
nāma āṭhavītāṅ rūpīṅ pragaṭa paiṅ jhālā.
Tanu manu śaraṇa tujhyā vinaṭaloṅ pāyīṅ,
Bāpa Rakhumā-devīvarā vāṅconi ānu neṇe kāṅhī.

O Gopal (Master of senses!) Let Your meditation remain in my mind,
I can't forget You even for a moment, O Lord!
The Life of the three worlds!
Today is a golden day! I see You with immortal eyes,
At remembrance of Your name alone, You appeared in Your form.
Surrendering my body and mind I take refuge at your feet,
I don't know anything else except the Father, Lord of Rukmini.

The name – mantra – is so powerful that its remembrance alone, even before uttering aloud by the lips, suffices to give the experience of oneness with the Lord which is described in the second line of the abhang. For that to happen, the seeker has to have desperation of seeing Him, incessant remembrance of Him as given in the first line. That urge bestows on the seeker the immortal vision of Oneness. As described in the third line, the body and mind get surrendered to Him, since there is nothing else in this world to draw the senses out. Jnaneshwar Maharaj says in other abhangs, "I see the Lord densely packed. The Lord is imprinted on my mind, because of which in all directions I experience the Self. The Lord appears in people, forest and the Self." For this he gives credit to his Guru, Nivritti in another abhang, saying "Nivritti placed this secret knowledge in my hand." This is the same as in the second verse, Verse 32, under discussion.

In the work titled, *Amritanubhav – Nectar of experiences* Jnaneshwar Maharaj says,

द्वैतदशेचें आंगण । अद्वैत वोळगे आपण ॥
भेदु तंव तंव दुण । अभेदासी ॥ (९, २८)

Dvaita-daśece āṅgaṇa, advaita volage āpaṇa
Bhedu tava tava duṇa, abhedāsī. (9, 28)

In the courtyard of multiplicity, expresses Itself Unity.
The more we break It into duality, the more is the experience of non-duality.

When we meditate on the Self, we experience the Self. In Kashmir Shaivisim, that is known as '*ātma-vyāpti*' – recognizing the inner Self as Shiva. However that is not all there is to realization. When we open our eyes, we see a myriad of names and forms. To a knower of the Self each object, name or form, is a manifestation of his own Self. Thus the experience of the Self is multiplied by the number of objects he comes in touch with. The knower retains the experience of unity in the midst of apparent diversity. Paraphrasing Jnaneshwar Maharaj's further elaboration, "this experience is like that of a chrysanthemum flower, which is one in spite of its thousands of petals. As the camphor presents its white color to the eyes, its fragrance to the nose and its softness to the fingers that touch the camphor, the pulsation of Shiva appears to the knower in the multitude of names and forms. All differences vanish for him, as the parts of sugarcane are lost in the sugarcane juice." No trace of duality is found in him. This attitude of the knower of Shiva is called '*Śiva-vyāpti*' – recognizing the universe as Shiva.

This is the rise of natural knowledge or 'pure knowledge' - *śuddha vidyā*. It transcends the Maya principle. Because of Maya and its five kanchukas, the immeasurable infinite nature appears measurable and finite in perception. The first part of *SpandaKarikas* – verses 1 through 25 -- describes the individual self as Shiva, the supreme consciousness - *ātmavyāpti*. We learn that the various states we experience – waking, dream, deep sleep and turiya, various qualities as sattva, rajas and tamas, various thoughts and emotions, and the space between two thoughts -- all such phenomena are vibrations of Spanda. In short the first part *SpandaKarikas* describes to us how to experience the Supreme consciousness within ourselves. In the second part, verses 26-32, the *SpandaKarikas* tells us about the rise of pure knowledge - seeing everything as Shiva. We have seen the mantra as a form of 'Vimarsh' or Spanda in verses 26-27, and mantra's power is to uplift from finiteness – Maya to infiniteness - Spanda. In verses 28-29-30 we saw that the word, the object which is the manifestation of the word, and thought itself are all Shiva; and the effect on the seeker who starts regarding the universe as the play of the seeker's own Self. Verses 31-32 discuss the result of these practices - pure knowledge arising within - and extol the Guru's initiation that makes this pure knowledge arise.

The rise of natural knowledge – śuddha vidyā is also the subject of the *Shiva Sutra* 2.5.

विद्यासमुत्थाने स्वाभाविके खेचरी शिवावस्था ॥

Vidyā-samutthāne svābhāvike khecarī śivāvasthā.

> *The pure knowledge of God-consciousness effortlessly arises, and this state of Shiva is realized as one with the state of khechari (roaming in the space of Supreme knowledge).*

When the natural pure knowledge arises, one realizes that one is Shiva. Here, the word khechari is not the yogic posture called 'khechari mudra,' but it is the awareness that in every individual the whole universe exists. Saint Kabir gives a simile: "Everyone agrees that a drop of ocean is contained in an ocean, but very few are aware that in a drop the whole ocean is contained."

The next aphorism, *Shiva Sutra* 2.6 says: गुरुरुपायः । (शिवसूत्र २.६) Gururupāyaḥ. Guru is the means. It is the Guru that bestows on the disciple the experience of the reality of Supreme consciousness. The grace of the Guru has great energy that causes the understanding as explained in Verse 32 under discussion here. Thus the two sutras – aphorisms - go together and the two verses of *SpandaKarikas* go together and convey the same point.

In *VijnanaBhairava* there is a centering technique –

सर्वत्र भैरवो भावः सामान्येष्वपि गोचरः ।
न च तद्व्यतिरेकेण परोऽस्तीत्यद्वया गतिः ॥ (श्लोक १२४, धारणा ९९)

Sarvatra Bhairavo Bhāvaḥ sāmānyeṣvapi gocaraḥ

Na ca tad-vyatirekeṇa paro 'stītyadvayā gatiḥ.
(Verse 124, Dhāraṇā 99)

The reality of Bhairava is apparent everywhere – even among common folk. One who is convinced that, "There is nothing other than He" attains the non-dual condition.

Even a common individual knows the individual 'I,' but when one knows with conviction that this 'I-consciousness' throbbing in each person is the eternal 'I' of Bhairava, and knows Bhairava to be existing everywhere as manifestation, then that one is identified with Bhairava and enjoys oneness with Him.

Saints say throughout their works that to attain the state described in Verse 31, individual effort is necessary in addition to Guru's grace. That individual effort is the practice of repeating the name of the Deity – mantra – by being one with the deity. It is the easiest way to attain the Self. Swami Muktanand Paramhansa, the author's Guru, emphasized that the attitude is very important in spiritual practices. 'शिवो भूत्वा शिवं यजेत्' *'Śivo bhūtvā Śivaṁ yajet'* - Shiva should be worshipped by becoming Shiva. 'पृथक् मन्त्रः पृथक् मन्त्री न सिध्यति कदाचन' *'Pṛthak mantraḥ pṛthak mantrī na sidhyati kadācana'* – If the mantra and repeater of the mantra are separate the mantra does not reach fruition.

RamaVallabh Das (*RamāVallabh Dās*, 28) says:

हरि होउनि हरिगुण गावे । तेणे आपण उद्धरावे ॥
स्वयें हरि झाला नाहीं । तोंवरी हरिभक्ति कैंचि पाही ॥
नये स्वयें हरिपण ज्यासी । हरिभक्ति कैंचि त्यासी ॥
रमावल्लभदास हरि । आपली कथा आपण करी ॥

Hari ho-uni Hari-guṇa gāve, teṇe āpaṇa uddharāve.
Svayeṅ Hari jhālā nāhīṅ tovarī, Hari-bhakti kaiṅci pāhī.
Naye svayeṅ Hari-paṇa jyāsī, Hari-bhakti kaiṅci tyāsī.
Ramā-Vallabha-dāsa Hari, āpalī kathā āpaṇa karī.

By becoming Hari, sing Hari's praises,
by which you can uplift yourself.
As long as you yourself have not become Hari,
where is the devotion to Hari?

If Hari's nature has not manifested
within an individual, what kind of Haribhakti
- devotion to Hari – is it for that individual?
Rama-Vallabh-das, the poet, is Hari, and
Hari does his own kirtana (discourse).

Kabir says in one of his poems, "हमारा जप करे राम । हम बैठे आराम ॥ - *Hamārā japa kare Rāma, hama baiṭhe ārām.*" - "The Lord is doing our japa, and we are relaxing" Until this happens, we should not relax in our spiritual practices. Jnaneshwar says, "ज्ञानदेवा मौन जपमाळ अंतरी । धरोनि श्रीहरी जपे सदा ॥ - *Jñānadevā mouna japamāḷa antarī, dharonī Śhrīharī jape sadā.*" - "For Jnānadev, it is the Lord who repeats the name holding the silent japa-mala within." By that he means that the breath that goes on incessantly is the japamala (string of beads) Lord holds and repeats the name silently. Our meditation has borne fruit only when we start experiencing the state described in Verse 31.

In the *Gurugita* we see,

ज्ञेयं सर्वस्वरूपं च ज्ञानं च मन उच्यते ॥
ज्ञानं ज्ञेयसमं कुर्यात् नाऽन्यः पंथा द्वितीयकः ॥ (गुरुगीता १००)

Jñeyaṁ sarva-svarūpaṁ ca, jñānaṁ ca mana uccyate
Jñānaṁ jñeya-samaṁ kuryāt, n'ānyaḥ panthā dvitīyakaḥ.
(Gurugītā 100)

It is said that the goal is the nature of all, the Supreme Self and the knowledge is the mind.
That goal and the knowledge have to merge into one. There is no other path than this.

In other words, mind must merge into oneness with the Supremes Self. This is true devotion. It is focusing the mind one-pointedly on the Self. The saint Dadu, the poet saint who lived in the fifteenth century in Ahmedabad and Rajasthan area of India, says, "as the mother takes care of her child every moment, as a trapeze artist while performing acrobatics has her attention focused on the rope, as the larva meditates on the bee, as the fish die without water, the true devotee should be one-pointed on the Deity." (*Dādu*, 5) Such devotion leads to the attainment of the goal.

Once oneness with the mantra Deity is constant, just remembrance of the mantra makes one aware of the Deity of the mantra. This is the essence of verse 31. The consequence of experiencing the Deity is experiencing Its nature - bliss. The Deity is experienced with exhilaration, like electricity passing through the body, just as extreme joy is experienced, but many times stronger and lasting longer than earthly pleasures. Sometimes there is tranquil awareness like a calm lake without any ripples.

The verse 32 of *SpandaKarikas* says the realization of the Self is ambrosia. It liberates one from death. As BhattaKallata puts it, people might try lotions on their body to remain young, or may take elixirs to prevent death. But the lotions and elixirs are powerless. Jnaneshwar says that the ambrosia comes on its own to the seeker. What the Gods tasted after churning the ocean of milk with the mountain Meru is nothing compared with the ambrosia of the Self.

This ambrosia is available to those who have received Guru's grace. Verse 32 is about Guru's grace. Dadu says, "The bliss of the Self is available freely in all directions. But how can the ignorant individual taste it without Guru's grace?" "Without Guru how can one get to know the Experience?" says Jnaneshwar.

That grace is possible only with Guru's initiation called Shaktipat diksha. By touch, look, word or thought – mukti-sankalpa, desire for freeing the disciple, Guru awakens the kundalini of the disciple. He does not even have to be in the physical vicinity. Of course, in His physical presence there is a lot of fun. This is the greatest expression of love of the Guru for humanity. Once the kundalini is awakened, seeker's earnestness and own effort to follow Guru's teaching definitely leads the spiritual practice to fruition.

In the United States, the last weekend of November is celebrated as Thanksgiving Day holiday. On Thanksgiving Day weekend in 1974 a retreat was held in Washington, D.C. with Baba, Swami Muktananda. At that time the author and his wife had not yet accepted Baba as their Guru nor did they realize the importance of a personal Guru, but because he had showered so much love on them in September-October when he was visiting New York City during their visits to his temporary school house ashram, they were participating with hundreds of other seekers in the retreat. In the morning meditation session, Baba circulated among the men giving each of them initiation. The author's eyes were closed. As Baba touched the author's head, and bopped the head with peacock feathers, which was his style of giving shaktipat, Baba stood beside him for a while. During that time, he heard a voice saying within, "With his help realization is as easy as drinking tea." In the afternoon meditation session, he went to the women's side giving shaktipat. When Baba stood near author's wife, Chitra, she felt "With his help realization is as natural as breathing." Experiences from a Guru, such as these and many more, make the sadhana – spiritual practices interesting and easy. They make the seeker indebted forever to the Guru for initiation from which these 'out of the world' experiences happen. This bestowal of Divine love cannot be compared to any mundane love. Rather, that love makes the seeker experience love everywhere in the universe and all transactions with fellow beings are done with love. This is Shiva-vyapti.

For an intellectual, this kind of regard of a person as Guru or surrendering to a Guru seems like giving up one's own ability to think. In the worldly life of individual freedom, such occurrences of getting a Guru are rare. People are content worshipping a scriptural deity, going to temples, reading saints' works just as a routine without fervor. But one is really fortunate if one meets a Guru and the vague notion of devotion to a statue or impersonal God becomes concrete.

To give a mundane example, if a person has done a Ph.D., the person knows the importance of such one-to-one interaction, and the constant guidance of a Ph.D. guide. That guidance alone, and not mere reading myriads of books, but with only focused reading and lot of one's own independent thinking, helps one to get the Ph.D. There is a difference between just doing one's own spiritual practice without the live company of saints, and following the guidance of a Guru - practicing the mantra given by a Guru. In following a Guru, one never surrenders to a person who is regarded as a Guru. A person calling himself/herself a Guru who demands such surrender from a disciple, asking the seeker to do personal chores, is not a true Guru. A Guru is not interested in the mundane affairs of his disciples. His only goal is the total liberation of the disciple. While doing Ph.D. one follows all directions of a Ph.D. guide, and solves an unsolved problem or throws a new light on an existing situation, showing always individual originality and gets the degree. And one feels great respect for his or her Ph.D. guide throughout one's whole life as someone special. Likewise, a seeker of Truth has a great respect for the Guru as some special saint. The spiritual practice directed by the Guru and contemplation with one-pointedness is similar to the original thinking required for doctoral thesis. Of course, spiritual attainment is far more valuable than doing the Ph.D. thesis. Here, the result is that understanding which leads to knowledge that transcends the duality of knowledge and ignorance. It empowers a person to address all questions of life - spiritual and secular. Following a Guru is never surrendering like a worldly slave. Surrender to the Guru's shakti is giving up one's own limited individual feeling to attain the unlimited 'I AM' state. Following a live Guru is not giving up one's intellect or personality, but on the other hand makes the intellect sharper and personality more attractive. It is acquiring intuitive understanding of our existence. All saints extol Guru's grace. Guru makes the final identification of the disciple with the Self. Ramakrishna used to say to Narendra, Swami Vivekanand, "I have the key to your final experience." Utpaldeva says about initiation or dīkṣā

ददाति ज्ञानसद्भावं क्षपयत्यखिलं मलम् ।
बोधानुवेधाद्-दीक्षोक्ता दान-क्षपण-धर्मिणि ॥

Dadāti jñāna-sadbhāvaṁ kṣapayatyakhilaṁ malam,
Bodhānuvedhād-dīkṣoktā dāna-kṣapaṇa-dharmiṇi.

Diksha is that which gives realization and destroys all impurity. Because it imparts that realization which awakens one from the sleep of ignorance, it is called Dīkṣā. It has the characteristic of both giving (dī) and destroying (kṣa).

BhattaKallata says, "The Guru resides in the heart of the disciple in the form of the Deity of the mantra given at the time of initiation." Unconditional love of the Guru is so powerful that the disciple experiences the Guru in his or her own heart. As the disciple contemplates the love of the Guru, the disciple acquires the state of Guru. Ramana Maharshi says to a devotee, "The extremely visible being of the Guru pushes the mind inward. He is also in the heart of the seeker and so he draws the latter's inward-bent mind to the heart."(*Sri Raman Maharshi*, 38, p.186)

The *Gurugita* extols the Guru and the worship of the Guru. It says at various places, "Salutations to the Guru, by whose remembrance alone, knowledge arises, and who is the ultimate attainment." (*Gurugita* 69) By devotion to the Guru, both indirect and direct knowledge are obtained; there is nothing greater than the Guru. This must be kept in mind by those who follow the Guru's path. (81) On the throne of the center of the heart lotus, the divine form of the Guru is seated; one should meditate on this Guru, luminous like moon, holding in one hand the book of knowledge of the Self and the other hand bestowing blessing. (91) By meditation on the Guru, knowledge arises spontaneously; by Guru's grace; one should feel, "I am free." (98) Know that the nature of the Self, O Parvati, is imperceptible by senses, incomprehensible by mind, without name and form. But the Self is eternal everywhere naturally present, just as fragrance in camphor and flowers is natural, or just as cold and heat are natural. Thus by becoming the Self, one should live wherever on the earth, just as with meditation on the wasp, the larva becomes the wasp. By meditation on the Guru, one will become the Self, and free in the body, state and form. (115-119)

Sage Abhinav Gupta says in his work entitled, *Tantrāloka* (4, 276-277), "The knowledge of the Self alone is the cause of realization of the Shiva Principle. Unlike other philosophies it is not attained by one's efforts alone such as investigation. In this subject not all people are qualified, but only those who have been sanctified by powerful Shaktipat. Just as only a honeybee is interested in the fragrance of a Ketaki flower, and not an ordinary fly, only a rare being blessed by Shiva is interested in the worship of the highest non-dual principle of Shiva. What if such a person has attachments? For a person who is reposing in this sacrifice of Shiva, the proliferation of the world dissolves spontaneously, just as the ice melts away in the hot sun."

In conclusion of this discussion we see how Brahmananda in a poem expresses his concern about a person blessed by Guru but who does not make conscious self-effort to experience Reality described as in Verse 31:

जिसको नहीं है बोध तो, गुरुज्ञान क्या करे
निजरूप को जाना नहीं पुराण क्या करे ।।टेक।।
घटघट में ब्रह्मज्योत का परकाश हो रहा ।
मिटा न द्वैतभाव तो फिर ध्यान क्या करे ।।१।।
रचना प्रभू की देख के ज्ञानी बड़े बड़े ।
पावे न कोई पार तो नादान क्या करे ।।२।।
कर के दया दयाल ने मानुष जनम दिया ।
बन्दा न करे भजन तो भगवान क्या करे ।।३।।
सब जीव जन्तुओं में जिसे है नहीं दया ।
ब्रह्मानंद बरत नेम पुण्य दान क्या करे ।।४।।

Ref. Jisako nahīṁ hai bodha to, Guru-jñāna kyā kare
Nijarūpa ko jānā nahīṁ purāṇa kyā kare.
1. Ghaṭa ghaṭa meṅ Braḥma-jyota kā parakāśa ho rahā
Miṭā na dvaita-bhāva to, phira dhyāna kyā kare.
2. Racanā Prabhū kī dekha ke, jñānī baḍe baḍe
Pāve na koī pāra to nādāna kyā kare.
3. Kara ke dayā dayāla ne mānuṣa janama diyā
Bandā na kare bhajana to, Bhagavān kyā kare.
4. Saba jīva jantuoṅ meṅ jise hai nahīṁ dayā
Braḥmānaṅd barata nema puṇya dāna kyā kare

Of what use is the knowledge from the Guru
For the one who has no right understanding.
If one has not known one's own nature
Of what use are the scriptures?
In every object, the light of the Self is shining
Even then the feeling of duality
does not dissolve
What meditation can he do?
Seeing the creation of God
Even the mighty scholars cannot
cross the ocean of worldliness
Then what can an ignorant person do?
Because of compassion, the compassionate Lord
gave this human birth
If the seeker does not sing his glories incessantly
What can the Lord do?
If one does not have compassion
for all the creatures and critters
What can any amount of merit and charity do
Even though Brahmananda – the bliss of the Self –
is pouring everywhere?

ति श्रीकल्लटाचार्यविरचितायां स्पन्दकरिकावृत्तौ सहजविद्योदयो नाम द्वितीयो निष्यन्दः ।।२।।

2. *Iti ŚrīKallaṭācārya-viracitāyāṁ Spanda-kārikā-vṛttau "Sahaja-vidyodayo" nāma dvitīyo niṣyandaḥ.*

This concludes the second part called 'Sahajavidyodaya'– 'Spontaneous Rise of Knowledge', of the commentary on *SpandaKārikā* written by Shri Kallaṭācārya.

Guru Om.

PART III

विभूति स्पंद - VIBHŪTI SPANDAḤ
POWERS OF SPANDA

The first two parts of *SpandaKarikas* describe the nature of the general Spanda – the Divine Vibration and how a diligent yogi can experience and get established in It. The third part warns about how one's effort and Guru's grace lead to various occult powers and the possible downfall of the seeker who hankers after them. The word 'Vibhuti' has several meanings in Sanskrit: one is a great being, another is ash, what is left over by burning wood. The third meaning is siddhis – occult powers that come to serve a seeker, that arise in a seeker. In order to become a truly great being established forever in the Self one has to regard these siddhis as ashes of no significant value! There are two types of occult powers – one is Māheshwarī - described earlier in the commentary on Verses 26-27 as omniscience, omnipotence, contentment, and so on. These do not bind a seeker. But there are some mundane occult powers such as materializing objects, which if used by a seeker for material gain such as impressing common folk, cause the downfall of a seeker. There is so much attraction for the worldly attachments that it requires an extraordinary ingenuity on the part of the seekers to save themselves from those attachments. Even among those who have experienced the Self only a rare being is so brave that he or she discards the worldly attachments with his or her own power and forges ahead to attain the final goal of experiencing the Lord of all powers and remain in that state.

VERSES 33, 34 AND 35
TYPES OF YOGIS AND FREEDOM

यथेच्छाभ्यर्थितो धाता जाग्रतोऽर्थान् हृदि स्थितान् ।
सोमसूर्योदयं कृत्वा संपादयति देहिनः ।।३३।।
तथा स्वप्नेऽप्यभीष्टार्थान् प्रणयस्यानतिक्रमात् ।

नित्यं स्फुटतरं मध्ये स्थितोऽवश्यं प्रकाशयेत् ॥३४॥
अन्यथा तु स्वतन्त्रा स्यात् सृष्टिस्तद्धर्मकत्वतः ।
सततं लौकिकस्येव जाग्रत्स्वप्नपदद्वये ॥३५॥

33. *Yathecchā-bhyarthito dhātā jāgrato 'rthān hṛdi sthitān*
Soma-sūryodayaṁ kṛtvā saṁpādayati dehinaḥ.
34. *Tathā svapne 'pyabhīṣṭārthān praṇayasyā - natikramāt*
Nityaṁ sphuṭa-taraṁ madhye sthito 'vaśyaṁ prakāśayet.
35. *Anyathā tu svatantrā syāt sṛṣṭis-tad-dharmakatvataḥ*
Satataṁ laukikasyeva jāgrat-svapna-pada-dvaye.

भट्टकल्लटः-यथास्यानभिव्यक्तस्वस्वरूपस्य योगिनो जाग्रदवस्थायां यथा यथा इच्छा भवति, तथैव तस्यानेकार्थ-संनिधानेऽभिमतस्यैव कस्यचिदर्थस्य दर्शनं भवति नटमल्लप्रेक्षादिषु सोमसूर्योदयं कृत्वा चक्षुरादिष्ववधानेन ॥३३॥

तथा स्वप्नेऽपि अभीष्टार्थानेव पश्यति, प्रणयस्यानतिक्रमात् इच्छाभ्यर्थनाया अनतिक्रमात्, यच्च तन्मध्ये हृदयं स्फुटतरम् अभिव्यक्तम् नित्यं तदेतत् स्वप्न-स्वातन्त्र्यम् इत्युच्यते, अयमेव तमोवरणनिर्भेद इत्यर्थः ॥३४॥

अन्यथा तु स्वरूपस्थित्यभावे स्वतन्त्रा स्यात् स्वप्ने आलबिडालदर्शनरूपा सृष्टिः, यस्मात् तत्तत्वं सृष्टिस्वभावं प्रसवधर्मत्वात्; यथा सततं सर्वस्य लोकस्य जाग्रद्वृत्तौ स्वप्नावस्थायां च संबन्धासंबन्धविकल्पाः ॥३५॥

Bhaṭṭa Kallaṭa: 33. Yathasyānabhivyakta-svasvarūpasya yogino jāgrad-avasthāyāṁ yathā yathā icchā bhavati, tathaiva tasyānekārtha-sannidhāne 'bhimatasyaiva kasyacid-arthasya darśanaṁ bhavati naṭa-malla-prekṣādiṣu soma-sūryodayaṁ kṛtvā cakṣurādiṣvava-dhānena.

34. Tathā svapne 'pi abhiṣṭārthān-eva paśyati, praṇayasyānati-kramāt icchā- bhyarthānāyā anati-kramāt, yacca tanmadhye hṛdayaṁ sphuṭataraṁ abhivyaktaṁ nityaṁ tadetat svapna-svātantryam ityucyate, ayameva tamo-varaṇa-nirbheda ityarthaḥ.

35. Anyathā tu svarupa-sthityabhāve svatantrā syāt svapne āla-biḍāla-darśana-rūpā sṛṣṭiḥ, yasmāt tattattvaṁ sṛṣṭi-svabhāvaṁ prasava-dharmatvāt yathā satataṁ sarvasya lokasya jāgrad-vṛttau svapnāvasthāyāṁ ca saṁbandhā-saṁbandha-vikalpāḥ.

Meaning of the verses and BhattaKallata's commentary:

33. The conscious energy within an individual yogi performing regular spiritual practices creates in the yogi's eyes the power of the 'moon and sun' that allows the yogi to discern any object while being aware of the body;

34. In the same way, even in the dream state (of an advanced yogi) the conscious energy brings about contact with the desired object. The reason for all this is the yogi's oneness with the supreme energy which always shines clearly in the central nerve or 'suṣumnā' of the yogi and never violates the trust of the yogi.

35. However, if a yogi even after experiencing the Self does not remain vigilant and become firmly established in the Self, then for that yogi the creation of desires in the waking and dream states keeps going on independently in the same way as it does as for common worldly people (as it is the inexplicable nature of the Spanda to keep creating independently).

BhattaKallata: 33. A yogi in whom a complete expression of the nature of Self has not yet taken place discerns in the waking state any desired object in spite of many other objects being present before him/her. This is because the conscious energy residing within brings about the rise of the 'moon and sun' in the yogi, resulting in a keen power in his/her eyes that enables him or her to focus in on the desired object, much in the same way as people focus on an actor or a wrestler at the center of a stage in spite of so many others being present or so much commotion taking place all around.

34. In the same way, even in the dream state a ripe yogi sees only the objects he/she wants to see, because the conscious energy within never forsakes the yogi's inner strong prayerful desire for oneness. In such a yogi's case, the experience of the conscious energy in the 'suṣumnā' – the central nerve – is ever-present with clarity. This is called the 'independence of dream' state, indicating that the removal of the covering of darkness has taken place in the yogi.

35. On the other hand, if a seeker yogi is not diligent on remaining in the state of knowledge of the Self, then for that seeker the ordinary nature is free to bring about the dreams of owls and cats, as in the case of thoughts of the waking and dream states of ordinary people, because it is the nature of Spanda Shakti to create according to their relevant or irrelevant thoughts.

VERSE 33 DESCRIBES the condition of seekers who are on the path but who have not yet transcended their body identification in spite of their spiritual practices. Such seekers are able to visualize and materialize spontaneously the sensory objects according to their wish in the waking state. Verse 34 describes the condition of those who experience the Self during their waking, dream and sleep states. Their wish is the same as the *icchāśakti* - power of desire of the Self, which is always fulfilled in waking or dream states. They have independence to experience even the dream of their choice. Verse 35 describes the condition of those seekers who are not careful, whether they are still performing their spiritual practices or have experienced the Self, but who are not yet fully established in the Self.

BhattaKallata elaborates on the three types of seekers. The first type is unripened – अपरिपक्व - *aparipakva*, the second type is ripened – परिपक्व - *paripakva*, and the third is inattentive – असावधान - *asāvadhāna*. Their spheres of influence are also described. The first still has body identification, and is in control of the waking state, the second is in control of all three states of waking, dream and deep sleep. The deep sleep state is included with dream, but since it consists of just the impressions and no mental activity it is not specifically mentioned. Third is a yogi who has gained control of the three states but is not diligent enough to be one-pointed on the final goal of getting established in the Self, taking an early exit for material gain such as awards, praise, trying to have followers, and impressing people.

Verse 33 describes how yogis may get whatever they wish in the waking state. The word 'जाग्रतः' '*jāgrataḥ*' has two meanings: It is the one who is literally awake as well as the one who is aware of the conscious energy of the Self. This awareness is due to the power of the 'rise of the sun and moon,' meaning consciousness of the incoming and outgoing breath. Just breathe in and out consciously, concentrate on the object and it manifests. The result is that sudden. It includes not only the objects of seeing but also of the other four powers of perception – smell, taste, touch and sound and of the five powers of action – speech, handling, locomotion, excretion, and sexual action or restfulness. BhattaKallata explains that the yogi experiences these desired objects in spite of other objects being present, just as one concentrates on a play or a boxing or wrestling match in spite of many other persons being present or any commotion that accompanies the event. He also means that in spite of an event such as a play or a match, which might cause noise and distraction, the yogi is focused on experiencing that which he/she desires with the appropriate perceptive faculty.

By this feat of producing anything that the seeker wants for himself or herself or for another person, the seeker can impress common people in the world. There are several stories of people from the past and present, who materialize objects and impress other people to obtain honor and material gain. There was an incident in Swami Parijnanashram's life of Chitrapur Math of Saraswat community to which the author and his wife belong. At that time, Swami Parijnanashram was about seventeen years old. He was initiated as a disciple and successor by Swami Anandashram at the age of twelve. Once he was worshipping his Guru's feet. In the process he materialized flowers in his hands and offered them at his Guru's feet. Swami Anandashram rebuked Parijnanashram and told him not to use this power again, as it was like impressing people offering chocolates to them and a true yogi does not need to do so. Swami Parijnanashram never did this again except for his own puja later in his life, when he produced several alabaster shivalingams or atma lingams which can be seen in his room at his samadhi shrine known as the Karla Math near Pune, India.

During 1975-82 the author and his wife, Chitra, were running a meditation center in New York/New Jersey area for their Guru, Swami Muktanand Paramahansa also called Baba. From 1977 they used to hold Baba's satsang at different devotees' houses once a week on Saturday nights. Sometimes at the request of devotees, after the satsang they would sleep overnight and lead the Gurugita chanting on Sunday morning in the devotees' houses. Once in 1981 after the Saturday satsang was over, a devotee host told the author and Chitra about a great being's visit to their house, who produced a figurine of Lord Dattatreya in his palm out of thin air and gave the devotee as a present who keeps it in his puja altar. That night Chitra had a dream. Baba appeared and said, "Do you want to materialize things? I can easily give that power to you!" Chitra said, "Is it not like taking an exit from sadhana (spiritual practice)?" Baba said, "Yes. It would be a hindrance in the sadhana." Hearing this Chitra said, "Then I don't want it." Baba said, "Okay. You will not have that power."

These powers are spontaneous but can also enmesh the unripe seeker or a non-vigilant advanced yogi back into the world instead of becoming established in the Self.

Verse 34 describes the 'ripened' yogi's state, in terms of obtaining desired objects in the waking and dream states. In the case of a ripened yogi, he or she is aware of the awakened kundalini energy, the energy in the central nerve 'sushumna' acting as the power of desire or icchashakti. That power brings about the 'rise of the sun and moon' which in the yogi's case are the power of knowledge - jnanashakti and the power of action - kriyashakti. The word 'pranaya' used in the verse signifies oneness that guarantees the manifestation, unlike a prayer which is sometimes granted and sometimes not.

In such a yogi's case the *Shiva Sutras* declare 'इच्छाशक्तिरुमाकुमारी (१, १३) 'Icchāśaktir-umākumārī' (I, 13). The word 'ku' means differentiated perception and 'mari' means destroys. This aphorism says that his will, icchashakti, the independent energy of the Supreme Lord, destroys differentiated perception, and directs it to his own nature. Another meaning of kumari is the energy which is playful in creating, maintaining and destroying the universe. The yogi is one with that universal energy. A third meaning: His will is Uma the virgin. As Uma was meditating on the Self and was virgin, meaning fulfilled in the Self and nothing else - no external agency, likewise the yogi is fulfilled in the bliss of his own Self. There is no lack or need of any other object.

In *SpandaKarika 8* also this has been discussed: "Moreover (as a result of obtaining the innate independence of the Self), with just a touch of the Self an individual will become like the Self, then he does not exist as the driving force of the desires." BhattaKallata says in his commentary on this verse: "Moreover an individual does not function according to the driving force of his or her desires; but abiding in one's own nature, whatever Its wish is, following only that, he or she performs inner and outer activities. Then the individual's power is not limited to the objects of the essential internal equipment – antaḥkaraṇa, consisting of mind, intellect, and ego, and ten senses -- but can work anywhere."

Such a yogi does not need to desire anything, having been fulfilled within himself. But if he/she does wish anything in the dream or waking state, the wish is fulfilled immediately by the power of will accompanied by the powers of knowledge and action. In such a case the yogi, being one with the Self, truly becomes an instrument of the all-beneficial Self, and is an instrument of the power of grace toward his or her fellow beings.

Shiva Sutras also claim 'शक्तिसंधाने शरिरोत्पत्तिः । (१,१९) 'Śaktisandhāne śarirotpattiḥ' (1, 19) "With infusion of the energy of Will, the embodiment of the will happens at once." The word sandhāna also means connection. Because of the yogi's connection with or abiding in the Self, Its energy, Spanda – divine pulsation, brings about in the yogi whose mind has been drawn toward the world any object desired in the waking or dream states. One has control over these states. The darkness of ignorance no longer exists. When one keeps completely focused on the Self, one is aware of the intermediate states passing from the waking state to dream state, from dream state to deep sleep state, and so on, including the moment of passing from life into death. Whereas one who is not so focused is not aware of these phases and gets experiences of the cycle of birth and death.

The *Vijnana Bhairava* gives centering practices to develop the focus on the Self alone.

अनागतायां निद्रायां प्रणष्टे बाह्य–गोचरे ।
सावस्था मनसा गम्या परा देवी प्रकाशते ॥ (श्लोक ७५, धारणा ५२)

Anāgatāyāṁ nidrāyāṁ praṇaṣṭe bāhya-gocare,
Sāvasthā manasā gamyā Parā-Devī prakāśate.
(Verse 75, Dhāraṇā 52)

When sleep has not yet come, that is when one is sleepy but not yet asleep, but external awareness has vanished, on that state one's mind should be focused, because in that state ParaDevi – Supreme Goddess – Self's Shakti reveals herself.

पीनां च दुर्बलां शक्तिं ध्यात्वा द्वादशगोचरे ।
प्रविश्य हृदये ध्यायन् मुक्तः स्वातन्त्र्यमाप्नुयात् ॥ (श्लोक ५५, धारणा ३२)

Pīnāṁ ca durbalāṁ śaktim dhyātvā dvādaśa-gocare
Praviśya hṛdaye dhyāyan, muktaḥ svātantrya-māpnuyāt.
(Verse 55, Dhāraṇā 32)

If the breath inhaled and exhaled in a gross way – (pīnām) – is made frail by meditating on the shakti outside the body at a twelve-finger distance from the tip of the nose where one outgoing breath dissolves and the next incoming one begins, and also entering the heart, which is also twelve fingers away from the tip of the nose within the body, where one incoming breath dissolves and the next outgoing breath starts; and if one meditates there on the shakti, one is liberated and gains the independent nature.

The saints also suggest coupling the name - mantra - with breath, or just repeating the name. Then one experiences the Self in spite of all the noise that goes on in the mind and in the outer sensory world. Saint Tukaram says,

आणिक दुसरें मज नाहीं आतां । नेमिलें या चित्तापासूनियां ।।१।।
पांडुरंग ध्यानीं पांडुरंग मनीं । जागृतीं स्वप्नीं पांडुरंग ।।२।।
पडिलें वळण इंद्रियां सकळां । भाव तो निराळा नाहीं दुजा ।।३।।
तुका म्हणे नेत्रीं केली ओळखण । तटस्थ तें ध्यान विटेवरी ।।४।।

1. *Āṇika dusareṅ maja nāhī ātāṅ, nemileṅ yā cittā pāsūniyāṅ*
2. *Pāṅḍuraṅga dhyānīṅ Pāṅḍuraṅga manīṅ,*
   jāgṛtīṅ svapṅī Pāṅḍuraṅga
3. *Paḍileṅ vaḷaṇa iṅdriyāṅ sakaḷāṅ, bhāva to nirāḷā nāhīṅ dujā*
4. *Tukā mhaṇe netrīṅ kelī oḷakhaṇa, taṭastha teṅ dhyāna viṭevarī*

1. *Nothing more is there for me to do now.*
   From the time this mind got focused how!
2. *Pandurang is in meditation, in my mind Pandurang.*
   In waking and dream Pandurang.
3. *It has become a habit to senses all.*
   There is no other disposition at all.
5. *Tukaram says, "My eyes adore with appreciation,*
   that Form standing aloof on the brick[72] *in meditation."*

Saint Jnaneshwar says in his work *Haripath* (Repeat Hari), (Jnaneshwar, 16)

ज्ञानदेवा पाठ हरि हा वैकुंठ । भरला घनदाट हरि दिसे ।

Jñānadevā pāṭha Hari hā vaikuṇṭha, bharalā ghana-dāṭa Hari dise.

For Jñānadev, chanting Hari is heaven itself. You see the world densely pervaded by Hari.

We always have a choice to think. We can use the occult power of controlling the

72 Lord Pandurang's spontaneously emerged statue stands on the brick in the holy place Pandharpur in Maharashtra, India, where pilgrims called 'varakaris' even now gather twice a year. Tukaram is referring to that statue.

waking and dream states as described in Verses 33 and 34 to attain something mundane or use that to experience the Self as the saints use it. The consequence of using the occult powers for material gain is described in Verse 35. Our main problem is not having a one-pointed mind. Our mind flies from one sensory object to another as a butterfly from flower to flower. Even if one tries to make it one-pointed, it is difficult. The *Bhagavad Gita* says:

यततो ह्यपि कौन्तेय पुरुषस्य विपश्चितः ।
इन्द्रियाणि प्रमाथीनि हरन्ति प्रसभं मनः । (२।६०)

Yatato hyapi Kaunteya puruṣasya vipaścitaḥ
Indriyāṇi pramāthīni haranti prasabhaṁ manaḥ.
(B.G. 2/60)

Turbulant by nature, the senses of even a wise discriminating man, who is practicing self-control, forcibly carry away his mind, O Arjuna.

Jnaneshwar Maharaj in his commentary "*Jnāneśvarī*" says: the senses of a yogi or a seeker create new opportunities, such as visions, inner music, new kinds of occult powers – siddhis and prosperity (about which verses 33 and 34 talk about), to tempt him.

The *Bhagavad Gita* further says:

इंद्रियाणां हि चरतां यन्मनोऽनुविधीयते ।
तदस्य हरति प्रज्ञां वायुर्नावमिवाम्भसि ॥ (२।६६)

Iṅdriyāṇāṁ hi caratāṁ yanmano 'nuvidhīyate
Tadasya harati prajñaṁ vāyur-nāvam-ivāmbhasi
(B. G. 2/66)

As the wind carries away a barge upon the waters, likewise the wandering senses, and any (specific) one to which the mind is joined, carry away the discrimination.

From this discussion on Verse 35, it looks as if the senses are going to take the mind away however hard we try to control the mind. We wonder which is stronger – the mind or the senses? But there is a clue right in the words,

यन्मनोऽनुविधीयते ।*yanmano 'nuvidhīyate*, "to whichever sense the mind is joined." This implies that if the mind is not joined to any senses, we won't experience any pain or pleasure, even when the senses are in contact with their objects, our mind will not get carried away. For example, we know that if a child is absorbed in playing, it does not want to eat even if the most delicious food is brought near its mouth. This means the mind is stronger than senses.

Eknath Maharaj says in his *Bhagawat*: "There is no god, man or demon, who can conquer the mind. But I am going to tell you a simple trick that works. So please pay attention." (684)

जेवि हिरेनि हिरा चिरिजे । तेविं मनेंचि मन धरिजे ।
हेंहि तैंचि गा लाहिजे । जैं गुरुकृपा पाविजे संपूर्ण स्वयें ॥
मन गुरुकृपेची आंदणीं दासी । मन सदा भीतसे सद्गुरुसी ।
तें ठेवितां गुरुचरणापाशी । दे साधकांसी संतोष ॥
या मनाची एक उत्तम गतीं । जरी स्वयें लागलें परमार्थी ।
तरी दासी करी चारी मुक्ती । दे बांधोनि हातीं परब्रह्म ॥
सद्गुरुकृपा झालिया संपूर्ण । हें मनाची मनासी दावी खूण ।
तेणें निजसुखें सुखावोन । मनचि प्रसन्न मनासी होय ॥
मन मनासी झालिया प्रसन्न । तेव्हां वृत्ति होय निरभिमान ।
ऐसें साधकां निजसमाधान । मनें आपण साधिजे ॥
(एकनाथी भागवत २३, ६८५–६८८, ६९१–६९२)

Jevī hireni hirā cirije, tevin manenci mana dharije
Henhi tainci gā lāhije, jain Gurukṛpā pāvije sampūrṇa svayen.
Mana Gurukṛpeci āndaṇīn dāsī, mana sadā bhītase Sadgurusī
Ten ṭhevitān Guru-caraṇāpāśī, de sādhakānsī santoṣa.
Yā manācī eka uttama gatī, jarī svayen lāgalen paramārthī
Tarī dasī karī cārī mukti, de bāndhoni hātīn ParaBrahma.
Sadguru-kṛpā jhāliyā sampūrṇa, hen manācī manāsī dāvī khūṇa
Teṇen nija-sukhen sukhāvona, manaci prasanna manāsī hoya.
Mana manāsī jhāliyā prasanna, tevhān vṛtti hoya nirabhimāna
Aisen sādhakān nija-samādhāna, manen āpaṇa sādhije
(Ekanāthī Bhāgavata *23, 685-687, 691-692)*

As a diamond can be cut by a diamond,
mind can be conquered by mind.
When it receives Guru's grace,

mind itself takes control of mind.
This mind is the bonded servant of the guru.
Mind is always afraid of Sadguru.
When it is left at the feet of the Sadguru,
it gives contentment to the seekers.
There is one good habit of the mind.
If it develops a liking for the search
for the highest truth,
It makes the four types of liberation its slaves,
and ties up the Self and delivers It in your hands.
Once there is complete grace of the Sad-Guru,
the mind itself shows the mind the way.
By which it is full of bliss in the ecstasy of the Self.
Mind itself is pleased with the mind.
When the mind is pleased with Itself,
the modification of the mind leaves its pride.
This contentment of the Self seekers can achieve by their mind.

Only saints' company helps us make the mind one-pointed. Jnaneshwar Maharaj says:

ज्ञानदेवा गोडी संगती सज्जनीं । हरि दिसे जनींवनीं आत्मतत्त्वीं ।।

Jñānadevā goḍī saṅgatī sajjanīṅ, Hari dise janīṅ-vanīṅ ātma-tattvīṅ.

Jñānadev experiences the nectar in the company of saints, and sees Hari in people, the forest and Self.

The above remedy is also described by Jnaneshwar in one of the abhangs as follows:

विक्षेपितां नाना उठती कल्पना । पासुनियां जाणा शुद्ध व्हावें ।।१।।
तरीच तें ज्ञान हृदयीं ठसावें । नातरी आघवें व्यर्थ होय ।।२।।
अमृताचें कुंभ सायासें जोडलें । त्यामाजीं घातले विष जैसें ।।३।।
मन हें विटाळ अखंड चंचळ । न राहें चपळ एकें ठायीं ।।४।।
ज्ञानदेव म्हणे गुरुकृपा होतां । लाहिजे तत्वतां ब्रह्मसुख।।५।।

1. Vikṣepitāṅ nānā uṭhatī kalpanā, pāsuniyāṅ jāṇā śuddha whāve.
2. Tarīca teṅ jñāna hṛdayīṅ ṭhasāveṅ, nā tarī āghaveṅ vyartha hoya.

3. Amṛtāceṅ kumbha sāyāseṅ joḍale, tyāmājī ghātale viṣa jaise.
4. Mana heṅ viṭāḷa akhaṇḍa caṅcaḷa, na rāheṅ capaḷa eke ṭhāyī.
5. Jñānadev mhaṇe Guru-kṛpā hotāṅ, lāhije tatvatāṅ Brahma-sukha.

1. All kinds of thoughts arise in the mind.
   Purify yourself from this condition.
2. Then only the knowledge of your true nature
   will be firmly imprinted. Otherwise, everything is futile.
3. It is like putting poison in a jar of elixir
   after obtaining it with great effort.
4. The mind has become filthy,
   restless without a break; it is so fickle that it does
   not stay at one point.
5. Jnanadev says, after Guru's grace is bestowed,
   It brings the bliss of the Self immediately.

VERSES 36 AND 37
OMNISCIENCE DUE TO THE TOUCH OF THE SPANDA

यथा ह्यर्थोऽस्फुटो दृष्टः सावधानेऽपि चेतसि ।
भूयः स्फुटतरो भाति स्वबलोद्योगभावितः ।।३६।।
तथा यत्परमार्थेन यदा यत्र यथा स्थितम् ।
तत्तथा बलमाक्रम्य न चिरात् संप्रवर्तते ।।३७।।

36. *Yathā hyartho 'sphuṭo dṛṣṭaḥ sāvadhāne 'pi cetasi*
Bhūyaḥ sphuṭataro bhāti svabalodyoga-bhāvitaḥ.
37. *Tathā yatparamārthena yadā yatra yathā sthitam*
Tattathā balam-ākramya na cirāt saṁpravartate.

भट्टकल्लटः– यथा किल दूरस्थितः कश्चिदर्थः पुरुषेण पूर्वं सावधानेनापि न लक्ष्यते स एव स्फुटतरो भवति, प्रयत्नविशेषेण निरूप्यमाणस्तत्रैव स्थितस्य ।।३६।।
तथा तेनैव प्रयत्नविशेषेण यत् वस्तु येन रूपेण यदा यस्मिन् काले, यत्र देशे, यथा येनाकारेण संस्थितं, तद् वस्तु तथा स्वबलं स्वस्वरूपमाश्रितस्याचिरेणैव कालेन प्रतिभाति निरावरणस्वरूपत्वात् तेनातीतानागतं ज्ञानं परिमितविषयं न किञ्चिदाश्चर्यम् ।।३७।।

Bhaṭṭakallaṭa: 36. *Yathā kila dūrasthitaḥ kaścid-arthaḥ puruṣeṇa pūrvaṁ sāvadhānenāpi na lakṣyate sa eva sphuṭa-taro bhavati, prayatna-viśeṣeṇa nirūpyamāṇas-tatraiva sthitasya.*
37. *Tathā tenaiva prayatna-viśeṣeṇa yat vastu yena rūpeṇa yadā yasmin kāle, yatra deśe, yathā yenākāreṇa saṁsthitam, tad vastu tathā svabalaṁ svasvarūpam-āśritasyācireṇaiva kālena pratibhāti nirāvaraṇa-svarūpatvāt tenātītānāgataṁ jñānaṁ parimita-viṣayaṁ na kiṅcidāścaryam.*

Meaning of the verses and BhattaKallata's commentary:

Just as a distant object cannot be seen at first by an individual even if the individual is attentive, but appears instantly by utilizing one's own power.

Likewise, whatever exists whenever, wherever, and however, happens to be known in its essential nature without delay after establishing oneself in the power of Spanda.

BhattaKallata: Indeed, just as any object located far away is not seen at first even if one is attentive, yet is discerned more clearly after standing right there and applying special effort,

Likewise, applying special effort alone, whatever object, in whatever form, at whatever time, in whichever location, in whatever shape it exists, that object appears without any obstruction in no loss of time to an individual who has taken refuge in one's own power and in one's own nature. This knowledge of a thing, whether it has already happened or is yet to happen, is nothing significant and not even a little surprise.

THESE TWO VERSES describe that the consequence of being established in Spanda, being vigilant about it leads to being one with the power of knowledge. Verse 36 gives an illustration and Verse 37 gives the description of the power. Suppose you are standing on a sea shore on a clear day and you glimpse at a distance some object out in the sea. You try to look at it more carefully, more attentively but you cannot see at first what it is. Then standing at the same spot, for an instant you close your eyes, turning within, open your eyes and concentrate on the object again. You are able to see the object and find that it is a sailboat. This fact is a common experience. Similarly, a person who is established in the Self and is vigilant has 'omniscience,' in the sense that the person comes to know the past, present and the future of oneself and of anyone else. One also knows any unseen object in all details – place, shape, color, etc., just by a wish. One does not need to learn anything more to possess knowledge. In addition, one does not need to 'do' anything more, because the other consequence is all power, also known as 'omnipotence.' This will be discussed in the next two verses. BhattaKallata also says that the person needs only to be vigilant about the Self, and also that it is not at all surprising. It is just natural.

Saints established in the Self have such omniscience which they use for the benefit of the people. If a person goes to them they know that person's intention, and why the person has come to them. They know why the person is in affliction and what can be done to alleviate it. A lawyer, who worked for our Guru's organization, came to our Guru, Baba Muktanand, as he was deeply worried about a legal problem he was having in his profession. Baba asked him why he was worried, and offered him suggestions which he could try out. Later on the lawyer shared in a talk how Baba helped him solve a complicated legal problem without any formal schooling. Baba has helped this author and his wife in dreams and visions to find out the connection between themselves and Baba in some past lives, and has also guided them as to how to live. Even a seeker also comes to know of the forthcoming events.

In the *Shivasutras* the Sutra 1.20 describes the essence of the sets of verses 33-39:

भूतसन्धान-भूतपृथक्त्वविश्वसंघट्टाः ।

Bhūtasandhāna-bhūtapṛthaktva-viśva-sanghaṭṭāḥ.

The yogi has the power of bringing different elements or objects together, or making them separate, or being free from the limitations of time and space.

In the previous verse, a ripened yogi's will is described as one with the divine power of will. By being one with the power of will, the diligent yogi also attains these different powers. 'Bhuta' means that which exists. Thus bhuta includes the five elements, creatures and objects. Sandhan – means connection or joining. Bhutasandhan is connecting with the object or person or elements. By this power the yogi can easily know what a sick person is suffering from and heal the person. By this power the yogi can help solve another person's problem.

Bhuta-prithaktva – is separating the elements. There is a story in the life of "Sadguru Gñānānanda Giri" (*Guru Gnananand*, 10, p. 126-127). One night Ranganāthan, his attendant, was curious to know why the Guru went out every night. So he stealthily followed the Guru. The Guru went to the Kali temple nearby, and Ranganathan saw a blood-curdling sight. The Guru's head, hands, and legs lay separated from the trunk of his body. Ranganathan was terribly frightened and ran back to the ashram trembling with fear. The next morning the Swami made enquiries of Ranganathan about his nocturnal expedition. Ranganathan still shivering with fright narrated in broken sentences what he had witnessed. The Swami rebuked him and warned him not to indulge in such adventures or he might die out of sheer fright. This type of dismemberment is also known as 'khandayoga.' The Guru had himself told about this yoga of dismemberment to another disciple.

There is an incident in the life of Swami Pandurangashram, the head of Chitrapur Math (1863-1915). Once he was suffering from malaria. While performing his 'sandhya vandan' – a vedic ritual prayer to the Self, he would remove his fever and place it on his yogadanda – the staff some Hindu monks carry – and cover it with a blanket. After the ritual, he would take back in his body the fever from the yogadanda. Someone noticed this and asked the Swami, why he did not leave the fever on the staff only. The Swami replied that malaria was his prarabdha, fruits of past deeds, and no one can escape suffering from the prarabdha, but he did not want it to interrupt his spiritual practices.

The word 'Vishva-sanghatta' literally means 'universe that is fused.' The universe as far as we perceive is full of duality – a conglomoration of distinct objects. To make a logical sense we organize it using space and time. An object is only at a definite place and not anywhere else. It also exists at a particular time. For instance, an airplane is tracked by its GPS (Global Positioning System) or spatial coordinates, (x, y, z) and time, t. For a common person the space and time seem unrelated and absolute. But Einstein has shown that the measurement in time and space is not an absolute grid but is a frame of reference, where we are and when we measure. Such a measurement is a space-time continuum. "The theory of relativity is intimately connected with the theory of space and time." (*Einstein*, 7, p.1) For a common person, matter and energy are unrelated, matter is usually visible and energy is usually invisible. But Einstein showed that light is an electromagnetic force made visible. In special relativity he also shows that $E = mc^2$, where E is energy, m is mass and c is the velocity of light. In short, energy and mass are interconvertible. Matter is nothing but concentrated energy. This led to the atomic fission and later on the atomic bomb, as well as peaceful uses of atomic energy, such as to produce electricity. *Spandakarika* has maintained that the universe or creation is a vibration of energy. The difference between Einstein's relativity and the *SpandaKarika* or Shaiva doctrine is that the energy is regarded as conscious, and this conscious aspect is the focus of study in Shaivism, whereas in Relativity consciousness lies in the person who makes measurements of time and space, and consciousness itself is not studied. In addition, time and space are concepts of the mind. Whereas turning within to experience the Self is transcending the mind. A yogi who is established in the Self has transcended the mind. Hence, he/she has the power to transcend the frame of reference of time and space. In the earlier paragraphs, we have seen examples of this power.

In *Vijnana Bhairava*, there are several dharanas or centering techniques for a seeker to transcend duality and experience the Self.

वायुद्वयस्य संघट्टादन्तर्वा बहिरन्ततः ।
योगी समत्वविज्ञानसमुद्गमनभाजनम् ॥ श्लोक ६४, धारणा ४१॥

Vāyu-dvayasya saṅghaṭṭād-antarvā bahir-antataḥ
Yogī samatva-vijñāna-samudgamana-bhājanam.
(Verse 64, Dhāraṇā 41)

By the fusion of the two breaths, namely exhalation (prāṇa) rising internally in the center and inhalation (apāna) rising externally from the twelve finger distance, the Yogi becomes so competent that there arises spontaneously in the yogi an experience of Equality.

नित्यो विभुर्निराधारो व्यापकश्चाखिलाधिपः ।
शब्दान् प्रतिक्षणं ध्यायन् कृतार्थो ऽर्थानुरूपतः ॥ श्लोक १३२, धारणा १०७॥

Nityo vibhur - nirādhāro vyāpakaścākhilādhipaḥ
Śabdān pratikṣaṇaṁ dhyāyan kṛtārtho 'rthānurūpataḥ.
(Verse 132, Dhāraṇā 107)

"Eternal, omnipresent, without depending on any support, all-pervasive, lord of everything" – the one who meditates every moment on these words in conformity with their sense attains the fulfillment or essence of the words. One has to absorb the meaning of the words 'eternal and omnipresent' which is the nature of one's own Self to transcend 'Time.' One has to contemplate the words 'without depending on any

support, all pervasive' to overcome the limitations of Space. One has to take into consideration the meaning of "Lord of everything" to overcome all limitation.

Saints say that by thinking in limited terms we ourselves condition our experience, by depending on what the senses bring to us. By turning within, by concentrating on the incoming and outgoing breath alone, and by contemplating the words in the above dharana constantly, instead of on the phrases 'I am mortal, I am powerless, I am my body, etc.,' we can experience our true nature. Since limited thinking cannot be undone on one's own, a Guru who is established in the Self is necessary to guide us. The Guru guides us through his teachings and by his own example. It is spiritual practice and earnestness that is required of us. As BhattaKallata says there is no surprise that a person gets omniscience and omnipotence by become established in the Self.

The given verses and the above centering techniques can be used by a seeker to establish her/himself in the Self. At every moment we have a choice of directing our thinking. What the verses declare can be used with the intention of developing powers discussed earlier or with the intention only of experiencing the Self. The Self may appear distant for a seeker because of conditioning to look outside. Hence just as a distant object cannot be seen at first by an individual even if the individual is attentive, but appears instantly by utilizing one's own power – namely, using the centering techniques and thinking only of the Self, which exists forever, everywhere, as the substratum of all manifestation, in the same way it is possible to know the Self in its one's own essential nature without delay after establishing oneself in the power of Spanda! This is summarized by the following abhang ('imperishable song') of Saint Jnaneshwar:

समाधी हरीची समसुखेंवीण । न साधेल जाण द्वैतबुद्धि ॥१॥
बुद्धीचे वैभव अन्य नाहीं दुजें । एका केशवराजें सकळ सिद्धी ॥२॥
ऋद्धि सिद्धि निधि अवघीच उपाधी । जंव त्या परमानंदीं मन नाहीं ॥३॥
ज्ञानदेवीं रम्य रमलें समाधान । हरीचें चिंतन सर्वकाळ ॥४॥

Samādhī Harīcī samasukheṅvīṇa,
na sādhela jāṇa dvaitabuddhi.
Buddhice vaibhava anya nāhī dujeṅ,
ekā Keśava-rajeṅ sakaḷa siddhī.

Ṛddhi siddhī nidhi avaghīca upādhī,
jaṁva tyā paramānaṁdīṁ mana nāhīṁ.
Jñānadevīṁ ramya ramaleṁ samādhāna,
Harīce ciṁtana sarvakāḷa.

Know that the intellect of duality,
will never attain the bliss of equality,
(perfect absorption) Hari's Samādhi,
cannot be attained without the bliss of equality.
There is no other greatness for the intellect
except attaining Viṭhṭhala,
which brings all siddhis
(all powers and achievements).
The wealth of ṛddhis (powers of supremacy)
and siddhis (occult powers) are all hindrances,
as long as the mind is not established
in the supreme bliss.
Contentment joyfully dwells in Jñānadev,
as Hari's contemplation goes on at all times.

VERSES 38 AND 39

OMNIPOTENCE DUE TO THE TOUCH OF THE SPANDA

दुर्बलोऽपि तदाक्रम्य यतः कार्ये प्रवर्तते ।
आच्छादयेद् बुभुक्षां च तथा योऽतिबुभुक्षितः ।।३८।।
अनेनाधिष्ठिते देहे यथा सर्वज्ञतादयः ।
तथा स्वात्मन्यधिष्ठानात् सर्वत्रैवं भविष्यति ।।३९।।

38. Durbalo 'pi tadākramya yataḥ kārye pravartate
Ācchādayed bubhukṣāṁ ca tathā yo 'tibubhukṣitaḥ.
39. Anenādhiṣṭhite dehe yathā sarvajñatādayaḥ
Tathā svātmanyadhiṣṭhānāt sarvatraivaṁ bhaviṣyati.

भट्टकल्लटः- क्षीणधातुरपि तद्बलमुत्साहलक्षणमाक्रम्य यतः कार्ये प्रवर्तते, यथा च कश्चिद् अशक्तोऽपि व्यायामाभ्यासेन महतीं शक्तिं प्राप्नोति उद्योगबलेन, तथानेन स्वभावानुशीलनेन बुभुक्षामपि आच्छादयति योऽतिबुभुक्षितः स्यात्, यतः सर्वत्रैवात्मस्वरूपस्य कार्यकारणसंपादनसामर्थ्यमविलम्बम् ।।३८।।
अनेनात्मस्वभावेन अधिष्ठिते व्याप्ते शरीरे सर्वज्ञतादयो यस्मात्, तत्र स्वल्पयूकाभक्षणमपि क्षिप्रमेव जानाति, तथा स्वात्मन्यवहितस्य सर्वत्र सर्वज्ञता भविष्यति ।।३९।।

Bhaṭṭakallaṭaḥ - 38. Kṣīṇa-dhāturapi tadbalam-utsāha-lakṣaṇam-ākramya yataḥ kārye pravartate, yathā ca kaścid aśakto 'pi vyāyāmābhyāsena mahatīṁ śaktiṁ prāpnoti udyoga-balena, tathānena svabhāvānuśīlanena bubhukṣām-api ācchādayati yo 'tibubhūkṣitaḥ syāt, yataḥ sarvatraivātma-svarūpasya kārya-kāraṇa-saṁpādana-sāmarthyam-avilambam.
39. Anenātma-svabhāvena adhiṣṭhite vyāpte śarīre sarvajñatādayo yasmāt, tatra svalpa-yūkā-bhakṣaṇam-api kṣipram-eva jānāti, tathā svātmanyavahitasya sarvatra sarvajñatā bhaviṣyati.

Meaning of the verses and BhattaKallata's commentary:

38. Just as a feeble person succeeds in doing whatever has to be done when forced to do by drawing his own sheer strength; just as one who is exceedingly hungry under certain situations can overcome his hunger; likewise a ripe yogi though physically weak taking the support of strength of Spanda accomplishes even difficult work easily, and even extremely starved of all bodily needs controls them till a suitable time.

39. Since consciousness pervades the body, an individual experiences all-doership, all-knowledge pertaining to the body. Similarly, when one is established in the Self, one experiences omnipresence, omniscience and omnipotence.

BhattaKallata - 38. Just as even a person whose vitality is depleted based upon his own enthusiasm can carry out work with his own strength, and just as even a weak person by a practice of physical exercises obtains great energy based on his dynamic effort, a starving person by assiduous practice can overcome hunger, because the strength to accomplish all these activities, quickly comes from one's own inner power;

39. With one's own consciousness pervading the body all-knowingness regarding it is experienced, so much so that even the sting of a meager louse is felt immediately, so also for a person who is established in the Self, omnipresence, omniscience and omnipotence certainly happen.

THE EARLIER TWO VERSES referred to 'all-knowingness,' or omniscience and these two verses refer to 'all-doership' or omnipotence. Again the first of the two verses is an illustration and the second is the actual experience.

The first part of Verse 38 describes a weak person utilizing inner strength to do all kinds of work. BhattaKallata elaborates this in two ways: the first is sudden. A person even though weak in vitality, based on the enthusiasm summons the inner strength to carry out work. We see examples of this fact in everyday life. At the time of crisis or where a person is in a situation seemingly impossible to resolve, the person with enthusiasm gets a burst of energy and accomplishes the difficult feat. We call this a 'rush of adrenaline.' The second way is gradual. The person exercises physically or mentally on a regular basis and develops strength over some time and accomplishes the work which he or she could not do earlier.

We see examples of these also in everyday life. The common thing in the two approaches is focusing on the goal. If we are dedicated to attain a goal, we do not care about lack of strength or resources. Others may say 'This is impossible.' and try to dissuade us from the goal. Some other people might come along to encourage and help us out. But if we are steadfast, the power of thought is so great that we develop within ourselves strength suddenly or over a period of time by deliberate study or physical exercise, and all other factors necessary fall in place in time to bring the goal to us. The goal should be a genuine need and not a specific want. With a specific want there might be negative consequences or it may be of limited value. Whereas the genuine need is something general, is far more important and has no negative consequences to anyone. The power many times brings to us our genuine need far more than a specific want. In all such cases, there is one more thing that is common. We are not aware of our individuality. We transcend it and become an instrument of the power of all doership – omnipotence.

But if we are established in Spanda, iccha-shakti - the Divine power of will - is ours and that is accompanied by omniscience and omnipotence. So we are always an instrument of the Spanda and there is no failure in reaching any goal that arises due to iccha-shakti in our mind.

In the second part, Verse 38 talks about 'hunger.' The word 'hunger' also includes the six maladies or perturbations of existence: hunger and thirst of Prāṇa –or body consciousness, sorrow and delusion of mind, and old age and death of body. The verse says that by establishing oneself in Spanda, one can overcome the six maladies of existence. How does that happen? When a person is established in Spanda, all dualities or pairs of opposites have no effect on the person. The person has control over prana, mind and body.

There is a Hindi song which describes the condition of the ecstatic people who have transcended duality.

गहराई में बैठा हो उस को, चंचल लहरें क्या करती हैं,
ना पूरण स्थितिवालों पे असर, बाहर जो कुछ भी गुज़रती है ॥

Gaharāī meṅ baiṭhā ho usa ko, caṅcala lahareṅ kyā karatī haiṅ,
Nā pūraṇa sthitivāloṅ pe asar, bāhar jo kuch bhī gujaratī hai.

To the one who is sitting in the deep,
how can the fickle waves affect?
On the people who are perfect,
whatever happens outside has no effect.

The first part of Verse 39 describes how our body consciousness makes us aware of any part of our body. BhattaKallata gives an example of a louse. If a tiny louse in the hair bites, we suddenly come to know. Similarly, if a little thorn pierces in the foot, we try to take it out right away. Similarly, for a being who is established in the Self the entire world is like a body, so that whatever occurs in it is immediately known; for such a being omniscience is natural.

Shiva Sutra 1.14 says: For a great yogi established in the Self: "दृश्यं शरीरम् । *Dṛśyaṁ śarīram*" *"The entire perceived world is his own self, or His own body is just like an object to him."* Both interpretations apply to such a being. The yogi does not perceive consciousness limited only to his own body. He transcends his waking, dream, and sleep states, and the state of void that is experienced at death. He perceives consciousness everywhere in all sentient and insentient creation. At the same time there is no individual ego that creates an attachment to 'me and mine' – mind and body and other objects – as in other common beings. The yogi considers the whole universe as a witness and regards his body as an object and remains unconcerned. Being one with Sadashiva, he imbibes the 'aham idam' – 'I am all this' principle. Naturally, the yogi has omniscience regarding the entire universe, just as an ordinary person has consciousness all over the body, as illustrated in the first part of Verse 39. The yogi considers all objects as limbs of his/her own all pervasive body. It is just like the yolk of a peacock egg, that contains all the variegated colors of the peacock feathers. The objects remain undistinguished until a specific need arises. Yogis can help the sick, or come into dreams of a seeker and guide the seeker because of omniscience. Thus completely fulfilled in themselves, they remain in the universe only for the benefit of the world.

Vijnana Bhairava has a centering technique 86 for identifying with the Universal Self:

जलस्येवोर्मयो वह्नेर्ज्वालाभङ्ग्यः प्रभा रवेः ।
ममैव भैरवस्यैता विश्वभङ्ग्यो विभेदिताः ।।श्लोक ११०, धारणा ८६।।

Jalasyevormayo vahner-jvālābhaṅgyaḥ prabhā raveḥ,
Mamaiva Bhairavasyaitā viśva-bhaṅgyo vibheditāḥ.
(Verse 110, Dhāraṇā 87)

Just as waves from water, flames from fire, rays from the sun,
So also the variegated nature – waves - of the universe arise from me - Bhairava.

There are two aspects of being established in the Self. "I am one with the Self." The Self has put on me as a garb. "The entire universe is the Self." This leads to the conclusion (by transitivity) that the entire universe is my own manifestation.

Such powers show how truly great a human being can be. What we call miracles or riddhis and siddhis in Sanskrit, sweep the courtyard of such people. Jnaneshwar, Bhagwan Nityananda and many such people are a few of these examples. Namadev, a saint, contemporary of Jnaneshwar, has written an abhang eulogizing Jnaneshwar. (*Namdev*, 25)

काय सांगों देवा ज्ञानोबाची ख्याती । वेद म्हैशामुखीं वदविले ॥१॥
कोठवरी वानूं याची स्वरूप स्थिती । चालविली भिंती मृत्तिकेची ॥२॥
अविद्या मायेचा लागों नेदी वारा । ऐसें जगदोद्धारा बोलविलें ॥३॥
नामा म्हणे यांनीं तारिले पतित। भक्ति केली ख्यात ज्ञानदेवें ॥४॥
(१०४७)

1. Kāya sāṅgoṅ Devā Jñānobācī khyātī, veda mhaiśāmukhīṅ vadavile.
2. Koṭhvarī vānūṅ yācī svarūpa sthitī, cālavilī bhiṅtī mṛttikecī.
3. Avidyā māyecā lagoṅ nedī vārā, aiseṅ jagadodhārā bolavileṅ.
4. Nāmā mhaṇe yāṅīṅ tārile patita, bhakti kelī khyāta Jñānadeveṅ.
(1047)

1. Oh Lord! how can I describe the greatness of Jnaneshwar
He even made a he-buffalo recite the vedas.
2. How far can I praise his state of being
He made the wall of clay move.
3. He did not let the winds of delusion and ignorance touch him.
He was called to uplift the world.
4. Nama says, Jnanadev saved the fallen and sinking.
He made the path of Bhakti available to all.

There are several books[73] on Bhagwan Nityanand describing his miracles. For a seeker though, performing miracles such as these is a wasted effort, taking an exit in a wrong direction instead of focusing on Spanda. At the same time knowing that all-knowingness and all-doership follow after getting established in Spanda is an impetus to do the spiritual practices with a great zeal.

The consequence of being established in the Spanda and having omniscience and omnipotence is a relaxation of total fulfillment. Then there is no anxiety of any kind, no restlessness which even great accomplished people have, a feeling of nothing to do similar to what Saint Tukaram says:

काम नाही काम नाही, जालों पाहीं रिकामा ।।१।।
फावल्या त्या करूं चेष्टा, निश्चळ द्रष्टा बैसोनि ।।२।।
नसत्या छंदें नसत्या छंदें, जग विनोदे विव्हळतसे ।।३।।
एकाएकी एकाएकी, तुका लोकीं निराळा ।।४।।

1. *Kāma nāhī kāma nāhī, jāloṅ pāhī rikāmā.*
2. *Phāvalyā tyā karūṅ ceṣṭā, niścaḷa draṣṭā baisoni.*
3. *Nasatyā chaṅdeṅ nasatyā chaṅdeṅ, jaga vinode vivhaḷatase.*
4. *Ekā-ekī ekā-ekī, Tukā lokīṅ nirāḷā.*

1. *Nothing remains to be done,*
   nothing remains to be done.
   See, I have become free.
2. *I can do whatever arises,*
   by staying steadfast as a witness.
3. *With a strange hobby of unnecessary thinking*
   (about me and mine) and actions
   (about body and related to the body),
   the world is groaning in pain.
4. *All of a sudden, unexptectedly,*
   Tukaram became different among people.

The only way we can experience this state is surrendering to a Guru, receiving grace and by practicing the teaching laid down.

---

[73] For example, *Life of Bhagawan Nityananda* and *Chitdakash Geeta*, English Translation by Deepa Kodikal (Kodikal, 19)

The concluding song summarizes the thoughts of this discussion.

शिवोऽहं वाक्य कहो प्यारे, विचारो हो तन से न्यारे ।।ध्रु ।।
जनम मरण है देह का, दुःख सुख मन का जान
भूख प्यास गुण प्राण के, सांख्य शास्त्र निर्वाण
है तू सत चित आनंद रे, विचारो हो तन से न्यारे ।।१।।
जब तक है अल्पज्ञता, मानता तन निजरूप
ज्ञान भये ते आपको, जाणे शुद्धस्वरूप
न साणी दास भावना रे, विचारो हो तन से न्यारे ।।२।।
एक रूप बहु है दिखै, फूटे दर्पण मांहि
ऐसे अन्तःकरण में, नाना रूप दिखायी
दृश्य ये सत्य नहीं है रे, विचारो हो तन से न्यारे ।।३।।
जैसे कोई स्वप्न में, नाना कष्ट उठाये
तब लग बेचैनी रहें, जब लग जाग न जाये
यह विधि सब व्यवहारा रे, विचारो हो तन से न्यारे ।।४।।
माया मन प्रकृति जगत, चार नाम इक रूप
जब लग ये सांचे रहे, नहीं जाने निजरूप
ब्रह्म परिपूर्ण जगत है रे, विचारो हो तन से न्यारे ।।५।।
शिवोऽहं वाक्य कहो प्यारे, विचारो हो तन से न्यारे ।।

Ref.: Śivo 'haṁ vākya kaho pyāre, vicāro ho tana se nyāre
1. Janama maraṇa hai dehakā, dukha sukha mana kā jāna
Bhūkha pyāsa guṇa prāṇa ke, sāṅkhya śāstra nirvāṇa
Hai tū sata cita ānaṁd re, vicāro ho tana se nyāre.
2. Jaba taka hai alpajñatā, mānatā tana nijarūpa
Jñāna bhaye to āpa ko, jāṇe śuddha svarūpa
Na sāṇī dāsa bhāvanā re, vicāro ho tana se nyāre.
3. Eka rūpa bahu hai dikhe, phūṭe darpaṇa māṅhī
Aise antaḥ-karaṇa meṅ, nānā rūpa dikhāyī
Dṛśya ye satya nahīṅ hai re, vicāro ho tana se nyāre.
4. Jaise koyī svapna meṅ, nānā kaṣṭa uṭhāye
Taba laga becainī rahe, jaba laga jāga na jāye
Yah vidhi saba vyavahārā re, vicāro ho tana se nyāre
5. Māyā mana prakṛti jagata, cāra nāma ika rūpa
Jaba laga ye sāṅce rahe, nahīṅ jāne nijarūpa
Brahma paripūrṇa jagata hai re, vicāro ho tana se nyāre.
Śivo 'haṁ vākya kaho pyāre, vicāro ho tana se nyāre

Ref. O my dear! Say 'Shivoham' – I am Shiva
Contemplate over it and know that you are different from your body.
1. Birth and death belong to the body.
Sorrow and happiness belong to the mind.
Hunger and thirst belong to the Prana.
Nirvana – liberation and bondage belong to the Sankhya.[74]
You are beyond these.
You are existence, consciousness and bliss absolute.
Contemplate this and know that you are not your body or senses.
2. So long as there is a lack of understanding
You regard body as your true nature.
When knowledge arises, you will understand
Your true nature.
Do not forget that you are serving the Guru.
Contemplate this and know that you are different from your body.
3. One object is seen as many, when a mirror is broken.
Similarly, in your inner instrument – antahkarana
Different forms are seen.
These scenes are not real.
Contemplate this and know that you are different from your body.
4. As in a dream, if somebody goes through difficulties
He is depressed and restless
As long as he is not awake
This is also true of all activities of waking state
Think and keep your awareness unattached to the body.
5. Maya, mind, Shakti and the universe
Are four names, but their nature is the same.
These appear as different categories
so long as you have not understood the Self.
But this universe is pervaded to perfection by the supreme Self.
Contemplate this and know that you are different from your body.
O my dear! Say 'Shivoham' – I am Shiva.
Contemplate over it and know that you are different from your body.

[74] An Indian philosophy. See second chapter of the *Bhagavad Gita* or Sage Kapila's works.

VERSES 40 AND 41
DEPRESSION AND ITS ERADICATION

ग्लानिर्विलुम्पिका देहे तस्याश्चाज्ञानतः सृतिः ।
तदुन्मेषविलुप्तं चेत् कुतः सा स्यादहेतुका ।।४०।।
एकचिन्ताप्रसक्तस्य यतः सा स्यादपरोदयः।
उन्मेषः स तु विज्ञेयः स्वयं तमुपलक्षयेत् ।।४१।।

40. *Glānir-vilumpikā dehe tasyāś-cājñānataḥ sṛutiḥ*
Tadunmeṣa-viluptaṁ cet kutaḥ sā syādahetukā.
41. *Ekacintā-prasaktasya yataḥ sā syād-aparodayaḥ*
Unmeṣaḥ sa tu vijñeyaḥ svayaṁ tamupalakṣayet

भट्टकल्लटः– ग्लानिः किल शरीरस्य विनाशिनी । सा च ग्लानिरज्ञानादुत्पद्यते । तदज्ञानम् उन्मेषेणात्मस्वभावेन यदि नित्योज्झितं तदा सा कुतः, कारणरहिता भवेत्? अनेनैव कारणेन वलीपलिताभावः शरीरदार्ढ्यं च योगिनाम् ।।४०।।
एकत्र विषये व्यापृतचित्तस्य यतो यस्मात् स्वभावात् झगित्यन्या चिन्तोत्पद्यते, स चिन्तायाः कारणम् उन्मेषो ज्ञातव्यः । स तु स्वयमेव योगिना लक्षणीयः, चिन्ताद्वयान्तर्व्यापकतयानुभूयमानः ।।४१।।

Bhaṭṭakallaṭaḥ - 40. Glāniḥ kila śarīrasya vināśinī, sā ca glānir-ajñānād-utpadyate. Tadajñānam unmeṣeṇātma-svabhāvena yadi nityojjhitaṁ tadā sā kutaḥ, kāraṇa-rahitā bhavet? Anenaiva kāraṇena valīpalitābhāvaḥ śarīra-dārḍhyaṁ ca yoginām.
41. Ekatra viṣaye vyāpṛta-cittasya yato yasmāt svabhāvāt jhagityanyā cintotpadyate, sa cintāyāḥ kāraṇam unmeṣo jñātavyaḥ. Sa tu svayameva yoginā lakṣaṇīyaḥ, cintā-dvayāntar-vyāpakatayānubhūyamānaḥ.

Meaning of the verses and BhattaKallata's commentary:

40. Mental depression robs the body of its vitality, strength, luster, enthusiasm, health, etc.; it arises due to ignorance. If that ignorance is uprooted by Unmesh – an aspect of Spanda, where can the depression arise from when its cause is gone?
41. When an individual's mind is engrossed in one thought, that which causes another thought to rise is to be recognized as Unmesh – the power of the Self – and must be investigated.

BhattaKallata: 40. Mental depression certainly destroys the body, meaning its vitality, strength, luster, health, enthusiasm, etc. It arises only due to ignorance. If by using the means of expanding Unmesh, the miraculous power of Consciousness – Self, ignorance is uprooted once for all, how can any depression arise? For, depression has no other cause. This is also the reason why yogis' bodies are strong. There is an absence of wrinkles on their bodies or gray hair.
41. If a yogi's mind is totally immersed in some thought, and suddenly some power causes another thought to arise and pervade the mind, that power or principle, should be recognized as Unmesh, and the yogi should contemplate and investigate it. This principle can be experienced in its splendor between the two thoughts – as one is ending and the other arising.

THE SANSKRIT WORD 'vilumpikā' comes from the root 'vilup' which means to rob, steal. Just as a robber carries away the valuables of the house, depression saps away the vitality of the body. In Ayurveda, the Vedic system of medicine, vitality consists of seven bodily constituents – rasa (body fluids), rakta (blood), mānsa (flesh), meda (fat), asthi (bones), majjā (marrow), shukra (seminal fluid). Depression affects all these bodily constituents. This depression proceeds from ignorance. If that ignorance is destroyed by Unmesh, then how can the depression last in the absence of its cause?

The author of the verse has given importance to depression, as depression is the final result of all negative feelings we have. Once the cause is removed all its effects are also removed.

Our essential nature is a compact mass of consciousness and bliss. That bliss disappears when we have the attitude that our body is the self. From childhood we are brought up by parents and society to regard ourselves as limited to our body.

No one in the world, except the people who are established in the Self, teaches us to look within. Consequently we are not experiencing reality to its fullest. We look at the world with a conditioned outlook. Once we had been to Niagara Falls. The view was so breathtaking, that I felt we should have pictures in our album for future enjoyment. Since I am not so good with the camera, I requested my wife, Chitra, repeatedly to take a picture whenever I felt it was an exquisitely beautiful and unique sight. But when the prints came back, many pictures looked repetitious and not so unique at all. I don't think we have opened the album ever since to look at the pictures. The beauty from the camera lens was nothing compared to what our eyes actually saw. In everyday life also, instead of watching the beauty of the present moment unconditionally, we look at it through an attitude conditioned by past memory, planning for future use and losing its freshness. When our nature is Divine Vibration that is the basis of all creation, to regard the body or mind as the self is like observing nature through a camera lens, a very limited view indeed. Another fact is that things that look so important and take so much energy, effort and anxiety at one time seem insignificant after some time. Having the right attitude towards whatever we do would save us so much anxiety.

A natural extension of regarding our body as the Self is that we give too much importance to our position in life. If a person who is in a high position in his job or totally immersed in his work at the expense of any other hobbies retires, he finds it difficult to adjust to the new conditions and gets depressed. A large percentage of people die within a few years of retirement out of boredom. Another consequence is attachment to people and possessions. If drastic changes such as a close person's leaving, which are always unavoidable, take place in life, people get depressed. If one's appearance changes due to aging, a person gets depressed. Even when everything around is good, nothing seems lacking, people get depressed. Even for no apparent reason, people get depressed. Whether it happens due to chemical changes in the brain or whether, as the above verse says, depression causes chemical changes, is a moot point, since suffering is anyway inevitable. That is why the root cause of depression should be investigated. If a person cultivates constructive habits of helping one's fellow beings and contemplating the Self as explained in the verse, changes or losses in life have no effect on the person. Even modern medicine gives importance to meditation, yoga, and living in the company and in harmony with close fellow beings, even pets, for a healthy long life.

Depression, the burglar, steals away the wealth of the highest consciousness and brings about poverty in the form of limitation. This depression arises from ignorance or non-recognition of our essential nature. If that ignorance is removed by Unmesh, which will be discussed later, how can the effect, depression, last when its cause is removed? When depression is removed, its effects on the body, such as illness or sufferings, are also removed. To the extent that they are removed, to that extent our real nature will shine, just as gold shines when tarnish is removed. As the commentator BhattaKallata says because of the absence of the depression yogis' bodies are ever young. There are no wrinkles or gray hair on the body. A constant absence of depression is the goal for all of us.

There is a story of Madālasā, who was a queen, a seer, and who used to bring up her children with the instruction: "Child! You are pure consciousness. You don't have a name. You are now being given this imaginary name. You are not the body. It is made up of five elements. You don't belong to it; nor is it yours. Then why are you crying?

Or you aren't crying! It is the sound that after reaching the prince is manifesting spontaneously! Whatever good and bad qualities seem to exist in the senses, are effects of the five elements. The five elements - earth, water, fire, air and space - making the food, air, and water nourish the body. But they do not nourish or deplete the consciousness that is you. This body is like a covering that keeps decaying. Have no infatuation for the body.

One person is called father, another is called mother, and yet another is called beloved. Some people are regarded as 'mine' and some 'not mine.' Understand that these are mere different manifestations of the five elements. All sense pleasures end in discontent and sorrow. Only the ignorant regards them as means of obtaining happiness."

With this instruction first few of her children became ascetics in childhood, left the kingdom and took off for the forest. The king got really worried. "If all the children become ascetics, who will succeed me?" he thought and asked Madālasā to do something about it. When the next child was born, she started instructing the child: "Child! You are a blessed king. Without any enemies you alone will maintain this earth as your empire of righteousness. All subjects in your empire will be happy that you are their king. Keep in your heart welfare of all. Remember Lord's name and be triumphant over your inner enemies of desire, anger, greed, infatuation, pride and jealousy. Remember, the world is temporary. Overcome the illusion of its reality." Thus great beings and a great king were developed by giving them the right attitude. Modern mothers can take a lesson from Madālasā to bring up their children.

If we watch our thinking carefully, we find that when a thought subsides there is always a pause before the next thought arises. The word "Unmesh" means the energy that creates one thought at a time. It can be experienced in the pause between two thoughts. It is not true that one thought gives rise to another in rapid succession without a break. The thought process looks continuous because we don't take time out to observe it. It is like a movie, which looks continuous, and while watching which we get emotionally involved. Only the film editor knows that the movie is made up of frames and chooses the succession of footage which the audiences watch. Likewise we can choose our thoughts or choose whether or not to act on a thought. By becoming aware of the pause, we can transcend the mind and experience our essential nature and bliss.

We can experience the pause, Unmesh, by focusing the thought only upon one particular object or matter in which the fluctuations of the mind are stilled. The pause arises due to the Spanda - Principle of Divine Pulsation. The entire creation is due to this pulsation, vibration or a throb of absolute reality. Since it is all a pulsation, there is no real difference between subject, object and means of knowledge, or seer, seen and seeing. An experience of Spanda described at the end of the first verse indicates that It is actually a breathing consciousness devoid of the three aspects or emotions with existence alone – "I am." When one concentrates intensely on one particular thought, underlying consciousness swells up; and once the thought of only one object subsides, the entire multitude of thought-constructs are swallowed up in the Divine Pulsation. Unmesh is the efflorescence of the bliss of consciousness. Without any artificial effort we can experience the Unmesh by becoming aware of it. There is really nothing to do, but watch and understand.

We have to know that just as the trees grow on mountains and hair grows on the body, the life force takes care of the functions of the body. The awareness "I am" is the light of the supreme consciousness constantly scintillating within each one of us. That "I am" principle pervades the body to its fullest just as sweetness pervades a drop of honey. That "I am" is the beginning of our thought process - mind - during the time when we are awake or when we are dreaming. With the same certainty as 'I am a woman,' or 'I am a man,' we have to convince ourselves of the fact, "I am consciousness is the beginning of thought. There is nothing special about me. Everything is consciousness. There is absolutely no difference between 'me' and 'them' as consciousness." This is the highest kind of worship of consciousness. It does not require any paraphernalia, rituals or sacrificing anything. It does not require leaving everything and going into a forest to experience It. The 'I am' principle can even be experienced in the hustle bustle of Jersey City, or any other urban area. On the other hand, if we don't have that understanding, no amount of pujas, chanting, sacred reading or sacrifices would keep us in constant bliss. This practice of awareness is not limited to just twenty minutes a day. Twenty minutes of practice might give a temporary sense of peace, but might also generate an ego of being a meditator. Instead, the understanding of transcendent and imminent consciousness, and bringing into practice constantly, makes us experience the pause, Unmesh, definitely keeping us in constant bliss.

Verse 41 clearly analyzes how thinking takes place. There are three important points in the verse. अपरोदयः *aparodayaḥ*, उपलक्षयेत् *upalakṣayet*, यतः स्यात् *yataḥ syāt*. Aparoadayah means the rise of another awareness – or another thought. When a person is engrossed in only one thought, it ends in a completely still mind. That stillness is the Self or rise of 'another' awareness.

A man went to Ramakrishna Paramahansa, one of the well-known saints in India of the nineteenth century and said that he was a simple shepherd, he did not know how to read, how to contemplate God. Ramakrishna asked him what his favorite thing was. The man said, "I have this beautiful goat, which I like the most in this world." Ramakrishna said, "Go and meditate on that." As the man sat in one place and thought one-pointedly about the goat, the goat soon vanished from the thought and his mind became completely still.

In *Vijñāna Bhairava* there is a centering technique:

भावे त्यक्ते निरुद्धा चित् नैव भावान्तरं व्रजेत् ।
तदा तन्मध्यभावेन विकसस्यति-भावना ।।श्लोकः ६२, धारणा ३९ ।।

Bhāve tyakte niruddhā cit naiva bhāvāntaraṁ vrajet,
Tadā tanmadhya-bhāvena vikasasyati-bhāvanā.
(Verse 62, Dhāraṇā 39)

When the mind of the seeker that comes to quit one object is steadfastly restrained and does not move towards other object, it comes to rest in a 'middle position' and through that unfolds intensely the experience of pure consciousness. That is Unmesh.

Similar to the commentary of BhattaKallata on the second verse, there is a centering technique when one has knowledge of two objects or two ideas:

उभयोर्भावयोर्ज्ञाने ध्यात्वा मध्यं समाश्रयेत् ।
युगपच्च द्वयं त्यक्त्वा मध्ये तत्त्वं प्रकाशते ।।श्लोकः ६१, धारणा ३८।।

Ubhayor-bhāvayor-jñāne dhyātvā madhyaṁ samāśryaet,
Yugapacca dvayaṁ tyaktvā madhye tattvaṁ prakāśate.
(Verse 61, Dharaṇā 38)

At the instant when one perceives two objects or ideas, one should take hold of the interval or middle of the two by directed thinking and by abandoning both objects, then in that interval the Principle dazzles.

This is like splitting an atom which appears as one whole entity. A person who has studied modern science knows that enormous nuclear energy is liberated which can be harnessed for destructive purposes such as an atom or nuclear bomb or for constructive purposes such as electricity. Likewise, in the thought process which looks continuous, by becoming aware of two ideas; or in the process of perceiving surrounding objects in a process that looks continuous, by becoming aware of two objects; by abandoning, not by pushing out or destroying but by ignoring, the two objects or ideas and going for the middle, one releases the inherent energy of the Self – consciousness, which one can experience. That is Unmesh.

These are two important dharanas – centering techniques. When our Guru Baba Muktanand was in India somebody asked him, "How can we get contentment?" Baba replied, "By ignoring thought waves."

The second important point in the verse is उपलक्षयेत् - *upalakṣayet* which means "should be experienced." One has to be on one's guard and focused in grasping the Reality. The Reality is not a thing of the senses, one cannot taste It, smell It, see It, hear It, touch or grasp It. Jnaneshwar Maharaj, an expert in this art of contemplation, says in Jnaneshwari, his commentary on the *Bhagavad Gita* as quoted earlier,

आतां आत्मप्रभा नीच नवी । तेचि करूनि ठाणदिवी ॥
जो इंद्रियांतें चोरूनि जेवी । तयासीचि फावे ॥६, २३॥

Ātāṅ ātmaprabhā nīca navī, teci karūni ṭhāṇa-divī,
Jo indriyāṅteṅ coruni jevī, tayāsīci phāve (6, 23)

This feast of the Bliss of the Self is to be enjoyed in the ever new – ever shining fixed light of the Self. However, only the one who hides away from the senses, can make this happen.

Ramana Maharshi, the modern saint, in answer to a question "When can I attain this bliss?" says, "He is daily enjoying that bliss in sleep. There, no sense object is present, and he still enjoys great bliss. We have not got to attain bliss. We are bliss. Bliss is another name for us. It is our nature. All that we have to do is to turn the mind, draw it from the sense objects every time it goes towards them, and fix it in the Self."(*Sri Ramana Maharshi*, 37, p.162)

The third point – यतः स्यात् - *Yataḥ syāt* – indicates a relationship between one thought and its consecutive thought as cause and effect. An effect can never proceed from a cause unless there is some energy that pushes the effect from the cause. That consciousness, which is the source and store of every object pervades both the thoughts – cause and effect. That conscious energy is Unmesh.

Even though this Unmesh always exists in us, as indicated earlier, an active or conscious effort needs to be made. The *Shiva Sutras* 1.5 assures us that success is guaranteed in the conscious effort. उद्यमो भैरवः। *Udyamo Bhairavaḥ* "That effort is Bhairava." When an effort flows out of active consciousness it makes universal consciousness shine within. That active effort itself is Bhairava because it carries us to the state of Bhairava – the Self. The active effort does not occur in stages but it does this all of a sudden, by devouring all other distracting sense energies and ending differentiated conception. In *Mālinī-Vijayottara Tantra* (Mishra, 24), Lord Kartikeya tells the sages:

अकिञ्चिच्चिन्तकस्यैव गुरुणा प्रतिबोधतः ।
जायते यः समावेशः शाम्भवोऽसावुदाहृतः ॥ (२-२३)

Akiñcic-cintakasyaiva Guruṇā pratibodhataḥ
Jāyate yaḥ samāvaeśaḥ Śāmbhavo 'sāvudāhṛtaḥ (2-23)

Even the thinking process ends only by the awakening bestowed by Guru. The state that arises in which one abides is called 'Shāmbhava' *state.*

This bestowal of knowledge on the disciple of the Guru and the subsequent absence of thought makes the disciple's world simply full of light of consciousness and bliss in which ignorance and subsequent depression become history. The disciple remains indebted to the Guru who removes the darkness.

The discussion on the two verses can be summarized in the words of Poet saint Brahmanand as follows:

बलिहारी मैं, बलिहारी मैं
  गुरु चरण कमल पर वारी मैं ।।टेक।।
तिमिर भरे दोऊ नैना मोरे ,चहुं दिश छाये घोर अंधेरे ।
सतगुरु अंजन भर भर मेरे, निर्मल नजर अधारी है ।।१।।
मैं परदेसन राह भुलानी, बन जंगल में फिरूँ हिरानी ।
सतगुरु मिलिया रहबर जानी, सीधे मारग डारी मैं ।।२।।
गहरी नदिया वेग अपारा, डूबत जाय रही मझधारा ।
देकर अपना बांह सहारा, पल में पार उतारी मैं ।।३।।
दुस्तर मायाजाल फंसाई, सतगुरु मेरी बंद छुडाई ।
ब्रह्मानंद स्वरूप समाई, घटघट जोत निहारी मैं ।।४।।

Ref. Balihārī maiṅ, balihārī maiṅ
  Guru caraṇa kamala para vārī maiṅ.
1. *Tīmira bhare dou nainā more, cahuṅ diśa chāye ghora aṅdhere,*
   Sataguru aṅjana bhara bhara mere, nirmala najar adhārī hai.
2. *Maiṅ pardesana rāha bhulānī, bana jaṅgala meṅ phiruṅ hirānī,*
   Sataguru miliyā rahabara jānī sīdhe māraga ḍārī maiṅ.
3. *Gaharī nadiyā vega apārā, ḍūbata jāya rahī majhadhārā*
   Dekara apanā bāṅha sahārā, pala meṅ pāra utārī maiṅ.
4. *Dustara māyājāla phaṅsāī, Sataguru merī baṅda chuḍāī*
   Brahmānaṅd svarūpa samāī, ghaṭa-ghaṭa jota nihārī maiṅ.

Refrain: I surrender, I surrender
To Satguru's lotus feet offer, I myself
1. *Darkness filled both my eyes,*
It was awfully dark on all four sides,
The collyrium Sadguru repeatedly applies,
My vision clears with support he provides.
2. *A stranger was I, forgot my way,*
Lost in the forest woods
After meeting the Sadguru, with tenderness
He brought me to the straight path.
3. *The river was deep with a strong current,*
I was drowning in the current
He offered me His arm as an anchor,
and in no time I went across.
4. *I was caught in the impassable net of Maya,*
Satguru untied me
Brahmanand (the poet) was filled with
Brahmanand – the Bliss of the Self,
In every being I saw Its flame.

Jaya Gurudev!

VERSE 42
EFFECT OF CONTEMPLATION OF UNMESH

अतो बिन्दुरतो नादो रूपमस्मादतो रसः ।
प्रवर्तन्तेऽचिरेणैव क्षोभकत्वेन देहिनः ।।४२।।

42. Ato bindur-ato nādo rūpam-asmād-ato rasaḥ
Pravartante 'cireṇaiva kṣobhakatvena dehinaḥ

भट्टकल्लटः – अतः अस्माद् उन्मेषाद् अनुशील्यमानात् बिन्दुः तेजोरूपः, नादः प्रणवाख्यः शब्दः, रूपम् अन्धकारे दर्शनम्, रसः अमृतास्वादो मुखे, एते क्षोभकत्वेन प्रवर्तन्ते अचिरेण कालेन ।।४२।।

BhaṭṭaKallaṭaḥ - 42. Ataḥ asmād unmeṣād anuśīlyamānāt 'binduḥ' tejorūpaḥ, 'nādaḥ' praṇavākhyaḥ śabdaḥ, 'rūpam' andhakāre darśanam, rasaḥ amṛtāsvādo mukhe, ete kṣobhakatvena pravartante acireṇa kālena.

Having experienced Unmeṣa - the energy that gives rise to thought, occult powers of 'Bindu' – supernatural light, 'Nāda' – supernatural sound, 'Rūpa' – supernormal form, 'Rasaḥ' – supernormal nectar very quickly arise in the seekers, disturbing the seekers, who still give importance to their body, and preventing them from experiencing Spanda.

BhaṭṭaKallaṭa: From this energy Unmeṣa - there arise in a very short time in the seeker 'bindu' – of the form of light, 'Nāda' – unstruck sound called Pranav, 'Rūpa' - power to see objects in darkness, 'Rasa' – taste of celestial nectar in the mouth. These powers disturb the seekers who have not yet transcended the notion of body as the self, and keep them from experiencing Spanda.

THIS VERSE describes the secondary effects of experiencing Unmesh, a collection of occult powers arising within the seeker. These powers are attractive and impress others about the seeker's great individual achievement. But the effect on the seeker is only disturbance in reaching the goal of getting established in the Self. It only establishes the seeker more firmly in the body. At the same time, such experiences can convince vigilant seekers how great they themselves are and all complexes such as superiority or inferiority drop away by themselves, propeling the seekers toward the ultimate goal of being established in the Self, provided they do not mistake the occult powers for their true goal.

The five principles that constitute the body – earth, water, fire/light, air and space -- try to keep the seeker firmly rooted in the manifestation of maya shakti instead of transcending it. In this verse the effect of only the first four principles, excluding air – resulting in the sense of touch, has been described.

In the work titled *SpandaKārikā* Vivritti (4-12) its author describes,

भ्रूमध्यादौ प्रदेशे ध्यानाभ्यास-प्रकर्षप्रवर्धमानोत्तरोत्तरप्रसादस्तेजोविशेषो,
यो बिन्दुभेदाभ्यासाद् धरातत्त्वध्यायिनामभिव्यज्यते ।
वेगवन्नद्योघ-निर्घोषघनोपक्रमः क्रमसूक्ष्मीभावाभिव्यज्यमान-मधुमत्तमधुकर-
ध्वनितानुकारो स्वोच्चरितो ध्वनिविशेषो,
यं व्योमतत्त्वाभ्यासिनः शृण्वन्ति ।
सन्तमसाद्यावरणेऽपि सति तत्तद् दृश्यवस्त्वाकारदर्शनं,
यत् तेजस्तत्त्वन्यक्षनिक्षिप्तमतयो निरीक्षन्ते ।
रसवद्वस्तुविरहेऽपि अमृतास्वादो मुखे लोलाग्रलम्बिकादिधारणा-निरतैर्
अप्तत्वध्यायिभिर्य उपलभ्यते ।

Bhrū-madhyādau pradeśe dhyānābhyāsa-prakarṣapravardhamānottarottara-prasādas-tejo-viśeṣo, yo bindu-bhedābhyāsād dharā-tattva-dhyāyinām-abhivyajyate.

Vegavan-nadyogha-nirghoṣa-ghanopakramaḥ, krama-sūkṣmī-bhāvābhi-vyajya-māna-madhu-matta-madhukara-dhvanitānukāro svoccarito dhvani-viśeṣo, yaṁ vyoma-tattvābhyāsinaḥ śṛṇvanti.

Santamasādyāvaraṇe 'pi sati tattad dṛśya-vastvākāra-darśanam, yat- tejas-

tattvanyakṣa-nikṣipta-matayo nirīkṣante.
Rasavad-vastu-virahe 'pi amṛtāsvādo mukhe lolāgra-lambikādi-dhāraṇā-niratair-aptatva-dhyāyibhir-ya upalabhyate.

As the practice of meditation on the Earth principle at the space between the eyebrows grows by leaps and bounds in intensity, a boon of the dot of the supernatural light is bestowed on the seekers. This practice is known as 'bindubhedābhyās' – or 'practice of breaking the dot.' The meditators on the Space principle hear a special, spontaneous unstruck sound starting with the loud sound of rapids in a river current that gradually becomes subtle to the sound of a bee intoxicated by honey. The meditators on the Fire principle observe objects clearly, even when the objects are enveloped by total darkness. The meditators on the Water principle, even when any juicy substance is absent, taste constantly celestial nectar in their mouth and throat.

The Verse 42 does not discuss the divine touch because it does not cause disturbance as indicated in '*ŚriTantrāloka.*'

अतो बिन्दुरतो नादो रूपमस्मादतो रसः ।
इत्युक्तं क्षोभकत्वेन स्पन्दे स्पर्शस्तु नो तथा ॥११-३२॥

Ato bindur-ato nādo rūpam-asmādato rasaḥ
Ityuktaṁ kṣobhakatvena Spande sparshastu no tathā. (11-32)

In Spanda Bindu, Nada, Rupa and Rasa can cause agitation or disturbance but touch is not of that type.

The nature of 'touch' is like 'an ant crawling over the body' as described in the above text before verse 32. In the current era, in the experience of people whose kundalini is awakened, this experience of touch all over the body is like electricity coursing through the system. In addition, this touch causes delight all the time and is superior to any human touch. The experience of Bindu, Nada, Rupa, and Rasa happens when Kundalini transcends the sixth chakra between the eyebrows – Ājñā chakra.

The current *Spandakarika* verse describes what happens after experiencing Unmesh. But there is no explanation as to why this happens. From the context and contemplation of the earlier verses in *SpandaKarika* the reason can be found out.

'*ŚriTantrāloka* – Ahnik 11' (eleventh chapter) discusses the thirty six principles and explains in verse 24 that the Self or thirty-sixth principle (counted backward from Earth) – as Vedak or the knower shines effortlessly in the heart once all the Vedya – 'knowable' falls away or is transcended. Seeing the elements in their purest form is a natural occurrence. In short, the 'descent' of the Self and Spanda – or Shakti towards the thirty-six principles and Its 'ascent' in the individual to the Self or Spanda naturally gives the experience of the principles in the purest form.

The bindu, nada, rupa, rasa, gandha, and sparsha are in every person and worded in different words by saints of different religious backgrounds. One day a muslim cleric came to our Guru, Baba Muktanand, in Ganeshpuri ashram and said to him, "The blue pearl you have described may be the result of Hindu upbringing." Baba said to the effect, "When I am seeing the blue pearl right now in you, what has religion got to do with it?" In fact, the whole text of *SpandaKarikas* itself is an ancient scientific text which is globally verifiable like any modern science laws and experiments.

The *Shiva Sutra* also discusses this aspect of occult powers:

गर्भे चित्तविकासोऽविशिष्ट-विद्यास्वप्नः ॥ (२.४)

Garbhe citta-vikāso 'viśiṣṭa-vidyā-svapnaḥ. (2.4)

> *In the womb of maya the expansion of the mind is an illusion and is nothing special.*

If a person is satisfied by the limited powers of producing fragrances like ash, or objects, to impress people, his knowledge is also in the sphere of maya – illusion. Then the person gets stuck in the worldly existence of ordinary people.

In *Vijnana Bhairava* there are three dharanas, centering techniques, which show how these occult experiences can be used to go beyond them.

धामान्तः क्षोभसंभूतसूक्ष्माग्नितिलकाकृतिम् ।
बिन्दुं शिखान्ते हृदये लयान्ते ध्यायतो लयः ॥(श्लोक ३७, धारणा १४)

Dhāmāntaḥ kṣobha-saṁbhūta-sūkṣmāgni-tilakākṛtim

Binduṁ śikhānte hṛdaye layānte dhyāyato layaḥ.
(Verse 37, Dhāraṇā 14)

The seeker should meditate on the heart, or at the place/s where the breath ends (a distance of 12 fingers inside or outside the body), or on the bindu, the sparkling bright dot – like a tika, an auspicious mark, applied on a forehead - between the two eyebrows. Then the wandering mind disappears and the seeker is absorbed in the light of supreme consciousness.

अनाहते पात्रकर्णेऽभग्नशब्दे सरिद्द्रुते ।
शब्दब्रह्मणि निष्णातः परं ब्रह्माधिगच्छति ॥ ॥(श्लोक ३८, धारणा १५)

Anāhate pātra-karṇe 'bhagna-śabde sarid-drute
Śabda-braḥmaṇi niṣṇātaḥ param Braḥmādhigacchati.
(Verse 38, Dhāraṇā 15)

The 'unstruck' sound that vibrates uninterruptedly like a rushing rapid river (in any individual but) heard only by a 'competent' person who becomes absorbed or skilled in the sound attains to Supreme Brahman.

This sound is heard first like a handbell, then a flute, then subtle like a stringed instrument – viṇā, then subtler like the buzz of a bee as discussed earlier. When a seeker is absorbed in listening to the inner music, the seeker is absorbed in the space of consciousness.

सर्वस्रोतोनिबन्धेन प्राणशक्त्योर्ध्वया शनैः ।
पिपीलस्पर्शवेलायां प्रथते परमं सुखम् ॥ (श्लोक ६७, धारणा ४४)

Sarva-sroto-nibandhena prāṇa-śaktyordhvayā śanaiḥ
pipīla-sparśa-velāyāṁ prathate paramaṁ sukham.
(Verse 67, Dhārṇā 44)

Cutting off all outgoing senses, by the slow upward movement of the Prāṇa Shakti (through suṣumnā) the sensation like an ant crawling creates supreme delight.

Thus when the mind comes to a stop and the kundalini starts rising, the divine touch experienced by modern seekers as electricity coursing through the system is helpful to the seekers in attaining their true nature.

In other texts such as '*Svaccanda Tantra*' Chapter 6 and in saints' literature all experiences of celestial visions, tastes, smells, touch, music are described in great detail. In Kabir's, Jnaneshwar's, and Tukaram's works one can find the description of these experiences. In *Chitshakti Vilas*, the spiritual autobiography of the present commentator's Guru, Swami Muktanand, he says regarding the visions of brilliant lights and the blue dot – Blue Pearl (*Swami Muktanand Paramhans*, 129-130):

> When I saw the Blue Pearl, the condition of my body and mind, and my way of understanding began to change. I felt more and more delight in myself, and was filled with pure and noble feelings. I started to tire of all forms of external associations and became addicted only to meditation. I did not meditate out of fear, but with enthusiasm and faith and love. I did not meditate to please anyone or to get any benefit from anyone or satisfy a desire, sensual or otherwise. I did not meditate to rid myself of any illness, physical or mental, nor to gain fame through miraculous and supernatural powers I might acquire. No one forced me to meditate. I meditated solely for the love of God, because I was irresistibly drawn to Goddess Chit Shakti, and to explore my own true nature.

When a seeker starts having such experiences it is a personal verification of the facts stated in Vedic and Saints' literature, just as a science student does an experiment in a lab and personally verifies the laws of science. It is no more or no less important. These powers are nothing to be arrogant about or impressing others with. The seeker has to follow the saints' teachings completely to reach the goal of establishing in the Self; visions, etc. are only a passing phase. Then the disturbing effect described in the last part of the Verse will not take place.

With one pointed meditation, the Verse exhorts the seeker to sink his body consciousness and that of the external world, in the real nature, Unmesh, without paying attention to the occult powers.

In his work titled, *Mukteshwari,* where Swami Muktanand (*Sw. Muktanand Paramhans*, 50) advises himself for the benefit of seekers,

जो सिद्धि बहुजनहिताय नहीं, बहुत जनों के प्रयोजन के लिए नहीं,
जो भूखे-गरीबों के काम की नहीं -
मुक्तानन्द! क्या वह सिद्धि दीखने पर भी गन्धर्वनगरी जैसी नहीं है? (७६)

76. *Jo siddhi bahu-jana-hitāya nahīṅ,*
bahuta janoṅ ke prayojana ke liye nahīṅ,
Jo bhūkhe-garīboṅ ke kāma kī nahī -
Muktānand! kyā vah siddhi dīkhane par bhī
gandharva-nagarī jaisī nahīṅ hai?

That 'siddhi' – occult power, which is not for the good of people, which is not of use to anyone, which does not help the poor and hungry, Oh Muktanand! even if this siddhi is concrete and visible, it is surely like a castle in the air.

The following song of Kabir summarizes all the above discussion:

का सिध साधि करौ कुछ नांहीं । राम रसांइन मेरी रसना मांहीं ॥
नहीं कुछ ग्यांन ध्यांन सिधि जोग । ताथैं उपजै नाना रोग ॥
का बन मैं बसि भये उदास । जे मन नहीं छाडैं आसापास ॥
सब कृत काच हरी हित सार । कहै कबीर तजि जग ब्यौहार ॥

Kā sidha sādhi karau kucha nāṅhīṅ,
Rāma rasāina merī rasanā māṅhī.
Nahīṅ kucha gyāna dhyāna sidhi joga,
tāthaiṅ upajai nānā roga.
Kā bana maiṅ basi bhaye udāsa,
je mana nahīṅ chāḍaiṅ āsā-pāsa
Saba kṛta kāca Harī hita sār,
kahai Kabīr taji jaga byouhār.

Why acquire siddhis, when they are nothing?
On my tongue Elixir of Rāma is flowing.
Knowledge, meditation and yoga performed for siddhis
Cause only various diseases like bloated ego and hypocrisy.
What is the use of dwelling in a forest in melancholy
When the mind has not trounced fetters of desires.

"Love for Hari is the beneficial essence of all deeds"
Says Kabir, "Abandon the worldly transactions."

VERSE 43
DISCERNING THE ULTIMATE

दिदृक्षयेव सर्वार्थान् यदा व्याप्यावतिष्ठते ।
तदा किं बहुनोक्तेन स्वयमेवावभोत्स्यते ॥४३॥

43. Didṛkṣayeva sarvārthān yadā vyāpyāva-tiṣṭhate
Tadā kiṁ bahunoktena svayamevāva-bhotsyate.

भट्टकल्लटः- दिदृक्षा द्रष्टुमिच्छा, तदवस्थास्थ इव सर्वान् भावान् यदा व्याप्यावतिष्ठते, तदा किं बहुना उक्तेन, स्वयमेव तत्त्वस्वभावम् अवभोत्स्यते ज्ञास्यति ॥४३॥

BhaṭṭaKallaṭaḥ - 43. Didṛkṣā draṣṭum-iccha, tadavasthāstha iva sarvān bhāvān yadā vyāpyāvatiṣṭhate, tadā kiṁ bahunā uktena, svayameva tattva-svabhāvam avabhotsy-ate jñāsyati.

With the strong desire to discern the Spanda principle, when the seeker remains only in the awareness of the Spanda principle pervading every object, then what more can be said than that the seeker certainly, on one's own, experiences the principle.

BhaṭṭaKallaṭa: 'Didṛkṣā' means a desire to discern the Spanda principle, staying in that desire itself. When the seeker sees all existence enveloped by the Spanda principle, then what more can be said than that the seeker himself/herself will know the principle as experience of as his/her true nature.

THE DESIRE to discern only the Spanda principle, and the conscious practice of seeing It in all existence – the states of waking and dream, and all objects sentient and insentient – brings a seeker to the attainment of the goal. This is not a promise of an experience which will happen sometime in the future; rather it is an outcome of the practice itself. The effect transcends time and space.

In the *Bhagavad Gita*, the Lord says to Arjuna the same thing:

सर्वभूतस्थमात्मानं सर्वभूतानि चात्मनि ।
ईक्षते योगयुक्तात्मा, सर्वत्र समदर्शिनः ॥
यो मां पश्यति सर्वत्र, सर्वं च मयि पश्यति ।
तस्याऽहं न प्रणश्यामि, स च मे न प्रणश्यति ॥
सर्वभूतस्थितं यो मां, भजत्येकत्वमास्थितः।
सर्वथा वर्तमानोऽपि स योगी मयि वर्तते ॥ (६।२९-३१)

Sarva-bhūtastham-ātmānaṁ sarva-bhūtāni cātmani
Īkṣate yoga-yuktātmā, sarvatra sama-darśinaḥ.
Yo māṁ paśyati sarvatra, sarvaṁ ca mayi paśyati
Tasyā 'haṁ na praṇaśyāmi, sa ca me na praṇaśyati.
Sarva-bhūtasthitaṁ yo Māṁ, bhajatyekatvam-āsthitaḥ
Sarvathā vartamāno 'pi sa yogī mayi vartate.(6/ 29-31)

Meaning and commentary by Jnaneshwar: "There is no doubt that I am in all beings and similarly everything abides in Me. This is how the creation is, everything intermingled with each other. The intellect only has to accept this. In spite of the apparent diversity of beings, the individual who worships Me with the conviction that I have pervaded everything without any difference, in whose mind the differences between creatures do not create any duality, but who knows My oneness everywhere, then O Arjuna! It is futile to say that that individual and I are one. Without saying anything, that individual is Me. Just as the lamp and its light are one, that person and I are one. As long as water has its wetness and the sky its emptiness, the person's form embodies Me. Arjuna! Just as there is only the thread in a cloth, the person with the understanding of non-duality discerns only Me; or just as in spite of a variety of shapes of ornaments, gold has no shape, with this type of mountainous firmness in the person's conviction, the person has reached the state of oneness; just as plants exist apart despite the myriad leaves; when the day of non-duality dawns the person has observed the passing of the night of duality. Such a person compares with Me in experience; how can the person in spite of being in a body made up of five elements be trapped in thinking of oneness with the body? With the experience of My vastness, that individual is vast even though not physically so." (*Jñāneśwarī* 6, 391-402)

We observe that the desire of seeing the same consciousness pervade everything leads itself to a firm conviction, and focused practice of oneness with reverence results in our being established in the Spanda.

In Verse 43 the phrase "every object" includes all manifestations sentient and insentient. It includes all worlds – heavens and nether worlds. In *SvacchandaTantra* - Chapter 10 by Abhinav Gupta there is an elaborate discussion of these worlds. The worlds - *bhuḥ, bhuvaḥ, svahaḥ, mahaḥ, janaḥ, tapaḥ, satyaṁ* have been described. *Bhuḥ* is earth, *Svahaḥ* is heaven and *Satyam* is Brahma Loka. There are thousands of nether worlds. Among them 140 are important. People who commit sins reside in these worlds. These heavenly and nether worlds are not fictitious and one can see them in meditation. Under the guidance of her Guru Baba Muktanand, in 1979, Chitra, the co-commentator, had a vision of a nether world. She saw from a distance a woman whose head and hand were visible with the rest of the body submerged in a mudpot, crying 'Take me out.' That lady was in a bubbling mudpot, similar to those seen in Yellowstone National Park, Wyoming, USA. But this mud was all smelly and filthy of urine and faeces. In the vision Baba Muktananda was with Chitra. "It is a nether world," said Baba, and pulled Chitra back, saying, "Leave her alone." Chitra's vision was over. In 2006, while referring to *SvacchandaTantra* regarding the description of other worlds, in Verse 10-41, the commentator came across the description of this nether world which is called अमेध्यक - *Amedhyaka*. The main point of this discussion is that all worlds described in scriptures should not be regarded as someone's fancy but do actually exist and are Shiva's manifestations. One has to practice regarding every object as pervaded by Spanda.

In *Shiva Sutras*, there are three relevant aphorisms. The first one is the aphorism 1.21 'शुद्धविद्योदयाच्चक्रेशत्वसिद्धिः ।' '*Śuddhavidyodayāc-chakreśatva-siddhiḥ.*' The aphorism says that with the rise of shuddha vidya one becomes the master of the universal wheel of power. Shuddha vidya means pure knowledge. This is the knowledge of the Supreme I-consciousness. It is the knowledge of Svātantrya – or universal freedom. In this freedom the yogi is not limited by individuality or his/her body but has an experience of universal expansion as described earlier. This knowledge accompanies the universal powers of knowledge and action.

The yogi does not have any individual desire but has the universal power of will and is capable of creating universal phenomena such as rain, happiness for all, etc. The yogi becomes the master of the shakti-chakra – universal wheel of power. The second aphorism in *Shiva Sutras* is Sutra 2.5 that describes this state in another way. 'विद्यासमुत्थाने स्वाभाविके खेचरी शिवावस्था ।' '*Vidyāsamutthāne svābhāvike khecarī Śivāvasthā.*' After the shuddha vidya (pure knowledge) arises, one naturally flies in the space of consciousness of Shiva. The word 'khechari' means moving in the space of consciousness. It is not a yogic 'khechari' mudra or exercise. It is a state where one regards every object as containing the Self in Its entirety.

The third aphorism in *Shiva Sutras* is Sutra 3.8: 'जाग्रद्द्वितीयकरः।' '*Jāgrad-dvitīyakaraḥ*' 'The waking state is another form of Supreme Consciousness.' The earlier two aphorisms were from parts of the Shiva Sutras called *Śāmbhavopāya* and *Śāktopāya*. *Śāmbhavopāya* is the path or means by which the most highly qualified aspirant attains the Self by means of Guru's grace alone. *Śāktopāya* is the path or means by which an aspirant of medium qualification attains the Self by contemplation. The third aphorism quoted is from *Āṇavopāya*, the path or means where an aspirant needs more physical and mental effort such as contemplation, breathing, and recitation of mantras. All three means emphasize abiding in the Self throughout all the three states of waking, dream, and deep sleep. The first two paths may be spontaneous, but in the third path, one requires conscious effort. That conscious effort is possible only in the waking state. The Verse 43 of *Spandakarika*, which we are discussing, says the power of desire to abide in the Self is so strong that 'this'ness – or perception of objects of the universe – is absorbed into the yogi's expansion into awareness of him/herself as universal consciousness pervading the entire universe.

There are many dharanas – centering techniques – in *Vijnana Bhairava* that help one to abide in the Self.

सर्वं देहं चिन्मयं हि जगद्वा परिभावयेत् ।
युगपन्निर्विकल्पेन मनसा परमोदयः ॥ (श्लोकः ६३, धारणा ४०)

Sarvaṁ dehaṁ cinmayaṁ hi jagadvā pari-bhāvayet
Yugapan-nirvikalpena manasā paramodayaḥ.
(Verse 63, Dhāraṇā 40)

When one without any thought in mind suddenly and with complete conviction regards all bodies and the world as filled with consciousness, there is Supreme awakening, meaning experience of the Supreme Self.

व्योमाकारं स्वमात्मानं ध्यायेद्दिग्भिरनावृतम् ।
निराश्रया चितिः शक्तिः स्वरूपं दर्शयेत्तदा ॥ (श्लोकः ९२, धारणा ६९)

Vyomākāraṁ svam-ātmānaṁ dhyāyed-digbhir-anāvṛtam
Nirāśrayā citiḥ śaktiḥ svarūpaṁ darśayettadā.
(Verse 92, Dhāraṇā 69)

When one meditates on one's Self as vast as space, without any limitation of directions, then the Universal Conscious Energy, transcending all support or thought constructs (ideas), reveals Herself as one's own blissful nature. That is precisely the reason why we like to go to the mountain top and watch the unobstructed scenery; or we like to go to the ocean and see its vastness; or we like to see a view from the top of a tall building; or we like to be surrounded by a vast meadow stretching to the horizon.

स्ववदन्यशरीरेऽपि संवित्तिमनुभावयेत् ।
अपेक्षां स्वशरीरस्य त्यक्त्वा व्यापी दिनैर्भवेत् ॥ (श्लोकः १०७, धारणा ८३)

Svavad-anya-śarīre 'pi saṁvittim-anubhāvayet
Apekṣāṁ sva-śarīrasya tyaktvā vyāpī dinair-bhavet.
(Verse 107, Dhāraṇā 83)

If one becomes aware of the consciousness pervading another body as the same as one's own, then within days one becomes all pervasive, transcending limited body consciousness. Here we must first understand that we actually have four bodies. We have a gross or physical body, made up of the five elements earth, water, fire, air and space, which we experience in our waking state. We have a subtle body which we experience in our dream state that contains our mind, and various chakras experienced in meditation. In transmigration the subtle body and other bodies depart from the physical body of an individual being. We have a causal body which we experience in our deep sleep state. We have a supracausal body which we experience in meditation or the fourth state called Turiya, which acts as the screen for all the three states earlier discussed. What we call our own consciousness is beyond the gross body experienced in the waking state, since we do not experience our gross body in dream or sleep or the turiya states. Similarly, our consciousness is beyond the subtle body experienced in dream, since we do not experience our subtle body in deep sleep; and our consciousness is beyond the causal body in deep sleep and beyond supracausal in turiya, because in the waking state we can narrate those experiences. Our consciousness is the continuing thread that connects all the four states of our existence. This understanding leads to the awareness that the same consciousness exists not only in our body but also in another's body.

यत्र यत्राक्षमार्गेण चैतन्यं व्यज्यते विभोः ।
तस्य तन्मात्रधर्मित्वाच्चिल्लयाद्भरितात्मता ॥ (श्लोकः ११७, धारणा ९२)

Yatra yatrākṣa-mārgeṇa caitanyaṁ vyajyate Vibhoḥ
Tasya tanmātra-dharmitvāc-cillayād-bharitātmatā.
(Verse 117, Dhāraṇā 92)

Whenever through the sensory organs of seeing, hearing, touching, tasting and smelling, we experience any object outside our body or subjectively within, becoming aware that it is the Universal consciousness revealing itself as our own conscious nature, then the mind becomes absorbed, and we are filled with the experience of the Self. Most people living in scriptural times did not know the details of the organs of perception or action; but a student of modern science can observe the intricate fascinating functioning of these various organs. We can study the existence of five elements – earth, water, fire, air and space in our body as follows. Our bones are a clear evidence of the earth element. Our blood and bodily secretions are water. In fact the entire body is about 85% water. The fire is the element evidenced from the normal temperature a body is kept at automatically. It also acts as vision through our eyes. Our stomach acid, mainly Hydrochloric Acid of acidity 3 pH, is a strong acid acting as the digestive fire which makes us digest whatever we put into our stomach through our mouths. The air we breathe in and out through our nostrils, through the pores of the skin, and circulation of the blood providing oxygen to the cells of the body, is the air element. Air also plays a role in our hearing. Air plays a very important role in our speaking. Without air we would not be able to utter words. Also the sound is not conducted in an airless environment. If we did not have space in our body the limbs and organs would collapse in a messy pile. There is also space between any two cells of the body. Electricity and magnetism are inherent qualities of the five elements because of which a radiologist calls our body an electromagnetic field. The five elements – earth, water, fire, air and space – actually work against each other, like water or earth dousing out fire. But it is one's own consciousness that keeps all these elements functioning harmoniously together in a healthy person. This process is called *'Pancikaraṇa'* or 'uniting the five.'

Furthermore, if one has been to an opthalmologist, one can readily admire the various tests the opthalmologist takes. The measurements he/she makes one wonder at the complicated functioning of the eyes. As for touch, see how a minute touch anywhere is felt instantly. How with our fingers we can collect tiny particles from the floor. Likewise the function of any other organ of perception or action is so beautiful, so complicated, and so perfect. The nervous system, endocrinal system, digestive system, etc. work in such a fascinating manner to keep most persons in a tip top condition. In short, if we examine the functioning of our body, we can become aware of the most intelligent consciousness functioning perfectly.

In addition, we also understand that just as when an object is reflected in a mirror, the reflection is of the nature of the mirror, when the sensory perception is registered on the screen of our consciousness, it is of the nature of our own consciousness.

In saints' works also we can find centering exercises to practice having the experience mentioned in the current Verse 43. Jagadish Shastri was a devotee of Ramana Maharshi. He had come to spend a Chaturmasa, the part of rainy season in India conducive to sadhana or spiritual practices, with Ramana. One day the Shastri wanted to write a verse. He wrote on a piece of paper "Hridaya kuhara madhye" meaning "in the cave of the heart," and however much he tried he could not complete the verse. He had to go somewhere. He left the paper under Ramana's seat. By the time he came back, Ramana had completed the verse:

हृदयकुहरमध्ये केवलं ब्रह्ममात्रं, ह्यहमहमिति साक्षात् आत्मरूपेण भाति ।
हृदि विश मनसा स्वं चिन्वता, मज्जता वा, पवनचलनरोधात् आत्मनिष्ठो भव त्वम्॥

Hṛdaya-kuhara-madhye kevalaṁ Brahma-mātraṁ,
hyahamiti sākṣāt ātmarūpeṇa bhāti
hṛdi viśa manasā svaṁ cinvatā, majjatā vā,
pavana-calana-rodhāt ātmaniṣṭho bhava tvaṁ.

In the cave of the heart, only Brahman
Itself is felt directly as the Self only as "I-I"
Enter your own heart mentally;
by inquiry, merging, or breath-control.
and be established in the Self.

This verse forms the essence of Ramana Maharshi's teaching. As soon as we wake up, the pulsation of "I" starts. Consciousness spreads all over our body; and we perceive the world. In the deep sleep state there is no pulsation of "I." The Self, Consciousness, or That which keeps the body alive, just stays as witness. The body goes through its stages of childhood, youth and old age, health and sickness. A woman was meeting her mother after many years; she asked her aged mother how she felt. The mother replied that the body had become old; but she always felt that she was the same person. This sameness is the "I." The continuation of the world we feel is due to the same "I." To become established in the Self, Ramana Maharshi emphasized the practice of shravana (listening to saints' words or scriptural, philosophical writings), manana (contemplation) to get rid of the mind of its outgoing tenedencies, and *nididhyāsana* (absorption).

The bliss we feel is nothing to talk about, it has to express itself as dexterity in our daily transactions.

If a person is not established in the state of bliss, he or she may become confused by a temporary exhilarating experience of the Self obtained by practicing the centering techniques or obtained by saints' grace or by just being in the company of saints. The person may feel that he or she cannot carry out the day-to-day worldly chores. Similarly a person may feel that the spouse may leave the person and become an ascetic if the spouse experiences bliss. Or parents may feel that their son or daughter may leave them or leave a career and may not take care of them in their old age. To allay any such fears, saints' works need to be studied. The saints show by their own example how to live in bliss and do all daily chores efficiently. There is nothing else than Spanda whether we are aware of It or not. People say that while doing some work it is necessary to differentiate between the mind and the Self. Whereas saints say that even while working it is not necessary to differentiate between the two, because for them everything is meditation. There is nothing else. Because of that they can do all the work effortlessly. When it becomes our own experience, we have the correct understanding. After that we continue seeing duality as before. But our understanding is different. In spite of apparent duality we know that in reality it is not so. Therefore we also can easily do all our chores.

It does not matter what work it is. It is going to change. Now there is no attachment regarding that work. Therefore every activity of our life becomes simple. We are at peace while doing work. There is absolutely no conflict while doing any work. Everything is simple. Even though at first we may not have our own strength, just by thinking about the Guru or saints we come across, we can immediately experience their state. In a moment everything in our mind is transformed.

Establishing ourselves in the Self is the most important attainment in the world; then life truly becomes simple. Just as when a student works with a teacher to study a subject, the teacher brings out the hidden mysteries and with the encouragement of the teacher a student soon develops a personal relationship with the subject, in the quest of getting established in the Self a guide or Guru and saints, are also necessary. That process is also known in saints' literature as 'stamping' or 'branding' – in a sense receiving the stamp of approval by the Guru. The Guru knows the capabilities of the disciple and accordingly shows ways to make the quest short. The 'branded' disciple thus does not have to waste time wandering and searching, and encouraged by the Guru focuses on the methods shown by the Guru, and enjoys his/her nature.

This discussion can be summarized by an Abhang 'imperishable song' of Jnaneshwar from his work titled *Haripāṭh* - *'Repeat Hari – Lord's name,'* (*Jnaneshwar*, 16)

साधुबोध झाला तो नुरोनिया ठेला । ठायींच मुराला अनुभव ॥१॥
कापुराची वाती उजळली ज्योती । ठायींच समाप्ती झाली जैशी ॥२॥
मोक्ष रेखे आला भाग्यें विनटला । साधूंचा अंकिला हरिभक्त ॥३॥
ज्ञानदेवा गोडी संगती सज्जनीं । हरि दिसे जनींवनीं आत्मतत्त्वीं ॥४॥

1. *Sādhubodha jhālā to nuroniyā ṭhelā, ṭhāyiṅca murālā anubhava.*
2. *Kāpurāci vātī ujaḷalī jyotī, ṭhāyiṅca samāpti jhālī jaiśī.*
3. *Mokṣa rekhe ālā bhāgyeṅ vinaṭalā, sādhūṅcā ankilā Hari-bhakta.*
4. *Jñānadevā goḍī saṅgatī sajjanīṅ,*
   Hari dise janīṅ-vanīṅ ātma-tattvīṅ.

Whoever attains the understanding of the saints, loses his separateness.
It dissolves in the experience of the Self,

Just as the lighted camphor flames away,
ends then and there, leaving no trace.
One flourishes in fortune in the territory of liberation,
when he becomes God's devotee 'branded' in the company of saints.
Jñānadev experiences the nectar in the company of saints.
He sees Hari in people, forest and Self.

VERSE 44
MEANS TO EXPERIENCE THE SELF

प्रबुद्धः सर्वदा तिष्ठेज्ज्ञानेनालोच्य गोचरम् ।
एकत्रारोपयेत् सर्वं ततोऽन्येन न पीड्यते ।।४४।।

44. Prabuddhaḥ sarvadā tiṣṭhej-jñānenālocya gocaram
Ekatrāropayet sarvaṁ tato 'nyena na pīḍyate.

भट्टकल्लटः- प्रबुद्धोऽसंकुचितशक्तिः सर्वकालं तिष्ठेत्, ज्ञानेनालोच्य गोचरम्-ज्ञेयं परिच्छेद्य । एवमेकत्र तत्त्वसद्भावे विद्यात्मके आरोपयेत् सर्वम् । ततोऽन्येन वक्ष्यमाणेन कलासमूहेन न पीड्यते ।।४४।।

BhaṭṭaKallaṭaḥ - 44. Prabuddho 'saṅkucita-śaktiḥ sarvakālaṁ tiṣṭhet, jñānenālocya gocaram-jñeyaṁ paricchedya. Evamekatra tattva-sadbhāve vidyātmake āropayet sarvam. Tato 'nyena vakṣyamāṇena kalā-samūhena na pīḍyate.

The seeker remaining vigilant in every state of experience should analyze the Spanda inherent in all perceptible objects and dissolve the entire class of objects in the Spanda principle. As a result, the seeker will not be troubled by any other objective phenomenon.

BhaṭṭaKallaṭa: The seeker always – i.e. at the beginning, middle and end of perception --should remain alert regarding the limitless energy, reflecting by knowledge and analyzing the perceptible object. By this means the seeker will not be disturbed by the collection of the 'kalā's to be discussed in the upcoming verses.

IN THIS VERSE Vasugupta, the author of *SpandaKarikas*, asks us to be vigilant toward the Spanda Principle in all states of experience. There are four states of existence – Turiya (also written Turya) or fourth, sleep, dream and waking. Turiya is the state that acts as a screen for all the remaining three states. It is the purest blissful state with awareness and supreme knowledge without limitations of any kind, and it is our natural state.

In *Shiva Sutras*, the aphorism I.6 talks about the seeker, who is a meditating hero: 'जाग्रत्स्वप्नसुषुप्तभेदे तुर्याभोगसंभवः ।' *'Jāgrat-svapna-suṣupta-bhede turyābhoga-sambhavaḥ'* 'In the three differentiated states of waking, dream and deep sleep, the heroic yogi experiences the Turya state.' The meditator is in an active meditation and not passive one. He or she is alert, not yawning or drooping, one pointed and not distracted by extraneous thoughts. A passive meditation ends up in the experience of nothingness which does not have awareness or knowledge of the Self. A passive meditation, as Swami Lakshmanjoo says, is a waste of time. We always have to meditate actively. In that state all knowledge of waking, dream and deep sleep is undifferentiated. We have to be aware of our natural state, as it has been discussed in *SpandaKarika* Verse 3:

"The Spanda principle pervades waking, dream and deep sleep. Even though they are different states, Spanda never undergoes any change in such states. It remains as the sole knower of these states." and BhattaKallata's commentary on this verse is as follows:"Even though an individual experiences mutual differences in waking and other states, the individual's nature itself cannot be hidden since the experiencer is common to all the three states, just as a plant of a poisonous seed has the same poison in all its five parts: root, branches, leaves, flowers and fruit."

The benefits of this awareness of Turya are given in *Shiva Sutras* aphorism 1.11. 'त्रितयभोक्ता वीरेशः।' *'Tritaya-bhoktā Vīreśaḥ'* 'A yogi who experiences the oneness of Turya in all three states of waking, dream and sleep, and who is filled with the bliss of Turya, is a master of all the energies of the senses.' The word 'tritaya' means a group of three. In all the three states there is a triad, a group of three – subject, object and perception. In waking and dream one is aware of it and in sleep the triad is in a seed form. Usually, when we see an object we become aware of the object, but we are not aware of the experiencer, i.e. ourselves, and the process of seeing. When we see an object internally, as in a dream or in a conceptual state or as an impression of the object observed earlier, then also there is the triad but all 'three' are ourselves. Yet we give importance to the perceived object more than the subject and process of perception.

Many people would come to Baba Swami Muktananda and narrate their dreams to him and would ask him the significance of their dream. Baba always facetiously said, "People ask me about the significance of their dreams, but no one asks about the one who sees the dreams.

When we give importance only to the object and not the other two parts of the triad, the world of dualities has an effect upon us. On the other hand a meditating hero is not tainted by dualities or triads of the three states. In *SpandaKarika* Verse 17 we have seen: "That Spanda in Its pure state is incessantly available. The fully enlightened yogi always experiences It in all the three states of waking, dreaming and deep sleep. But It is available to the other, who is not enlightened, only at the beginning and the end of these states." BhattaKallata comments: The enlightened yogi experiences his or her nature as all pervasive consciousness uninterruptedly in all the three states of waking, dreaming and deep sleep, but the one who is a seeker (partially awakened yogi) experiences It only at the beginning and end of the states of dream and deep sleep, and can become aware of It in the waking and the fourth states only with Guru's grace."

That yogi masterfully digests all differences and experiences the bliss of the Self in all perception and action – seeing, hearing and talking, tasting, smelling, touching, etc. and is the master of these energies.

There is a similarity between eating and looking at the world. We eat four different kinds of food: Dry, wet, cooked, and burnt or roasted. Whatever the food, it does not remain food; as soon as we eat it, our digestive system starts breaking it down, and it is converted into blood, nutrients, etc. and the waste is thrown out. This process is automatic in healthy individuals. If the waste accumulates, the person suffers from various sicknesses. Similarly, when we perceive an object through one of our five senses, we have to make it a practice to 'digest' or in other words, understand that the essence of the object is the Self Itself. Then we have health - the correct outlook on the universe. With most people the objects perceived remain as objects only to remain differentiated, and not get 'assimilated' into Self, and the trouble starts. Duality is felt, incompleteness is felt, conflicts start, restlessness starts and one is afflicted by the six inner diseases of desire, anger, greed, infatuation, arrogance and jealousy, and the cycles of sorrow and happiness and ultimately the cycle of births and deaths perpetuate.

In fact, in *Shiva Sutras* there is an aphorism 2.9: 'ज्ञानम् अन्नम् ।' *'Jñānam annam'* meaning 'Differentiated knowledge is his food. Interpreted another way, knowledge of his nature is his food.'

This aphorism is interpreted two ways. The yogi digests the differentiated knowledge of the triads of the three states resulting in the supreme bliss of the fourth state. The other interpretation is 'the knowledge of one's own nature is one's food.' By establishing in the Spanda principle – Self, the yogi is completely satisfied. There is no more desire left in the person to perceiving anything else. In both interpretations, the knower yogi is always aware of the Self. A thief will not steal if he is aware of the police watching him. Similarly if we watch our thoughts, the process of thinking stops. If we are aware of passing from one state into another, that state is not experienced. For instance, if we are aware that we are passing from waking into sleep, we don't sleep; what we experience is Turiya – our own real nature. "This is the greatness of awareness, that if you are always aware in continuation, always one-pointed and residing in the one-pointed state of God consciousness, you won't think anything. If, on the other hand, you are unaware, you will miss the reality of your life." so says great Swami Lakhmanjoo. (*Śiva Sutras*, 2.9)

In order to establish ourselves into this state of awareness, *Shiva Sutras* aphorism 3.20 exhorts us, 'त्रिषु चतुर्थं तैलवदासेच्यम् ।' *'Triṣu caturthaṁ tailavad-āsecyam.'* 'The fourth state should be poured like oil into the three states.' This aphorism is from the third part of *Shiva Sutras* - Āṇavopāya where the seeker has the impurity of feeling insignificant like an atom. The blissful state of Turya is experienced at the beginning and at the end of each of the three states of waking, dream and deep sleep. Normally an individual is not even aware of it, while the seeker is. We noted this earlier in quoting *SpandaKarika* Verse 17. That blissful state has to be deliberately poured or spread like oil in the middle of these states also. Oil when poured is like a continuous stream and not like water that comes in discontinuous drops. Also oil clings to the object unlike any other liquid. We have to hold the awareness that is at the beginning and end of the state to cover the middle of the state. The attempt here is deliberate on the part of the seeker unlike in other aphorisms – Shāmbhava or Shākta upāyas or means quoted earlier where the experience is spontaneous and effortless – like processes of breathing and digesting food.

The seeker, who is not established in Spanda, has a conditioned mind which has a tendency to enjoy the sense pleasures. That is why the attempt is deliberate. That is the reason there is another aphorism in this part of *Shiva Sutras*, aphorism 3.38, 'त्रिपदाद्यनुप्राणनम् ।' *'Tripadādyanuprāṇanam.'* 'Emerging from the fourth state of Turya, insert the bliss, enliven the three states of waking, dream and sleep.' This aphorism gives details as to how to pour the bliss into the three states like oil. 'Enlivening' means becoming aware of the Spanda every moment. In waking and dream, the mind wanders from thought to thought and object to object in an endless chain. First a thought arises about perceiving an object, for a while, while the object is perceived the thought is maintained, then the mind is satiated or even bored with the object, and the perception of the object is dissolved. There is a momentary gap or stillness, and the bliss of the Turya, the background of the scenario, is immediately experienced. A common individual attributes the credit of this bliss to the object just perceived. Then the process of creation to perceive another object begins like a wave emerging. This endless chain of creation, sustanance and dissolution keeps going in the waking and dream states of an individual. To break this chain one must be aware of the link that connects the two triads, the Turya state or Spanda, which is naturally blissful. A Guru breaks the chain for the disciple and by removing the illusion of duality makes the disciple experience the waves of bliss in spite of the absence of objects. Even if the objects are present the waves of bliss of the Self which act as a substratum for all of existence can be experienced by Guru's grace. That is the importance of the Guru.

In *Vijnana Bhairava* the importance of freedom from the thought process is discussed.

दिक्कालकलनोन्मुक्ता देशोद्देशाविशेषिणी ।
व्यपदेष्टुमशक्यासावकथ्या परमार्थतः ॥१४॥
अन्तः स्वानुभवानन्दा विकल्पोन्मुक्तगोचरा ।
यावस्था भरिताकारा भैरवी भैरवात्मनः ।
तद्वपुस्तत्त्वतो ज्ञेयं विमलं विश्वपूरणम् ॥१५॥

14. *Dikkāla-kalanonmuktā deśo-ddeśā-viśeṣiṇī*
    Vyapadeṣṭum-aśakyāsāvakathyā paramārthataḥ.
15. *Antaḥ svānubhavānandā vikalponmukta-gocarā.*
    Yāvasthā bharitākārā Bhairavī Bhairavātmānaḥ.
    Tadvapus-tattvato jñeyaṁ vimalaṁ viśva-pūraṇam.

That supreme state is free from the limitations of directions, time, cause and effect, and cannot be specified by a definite place or designation. It cannot be shown, and is indescribable. That state of Bhairavi, the energy of Bhairava, which is filled with one's own bliss, can however be experienced within by those who are freed from thought constructs. That should be known as the nature of the Self, immaculate and filling the entire universe.

That is the reason why saints recommend to everyone to have a mind free of thoughts. "सोच सोच के दिमाग खराब कर देता है।""*Socha socha ke dimāg kharāb kara detā hai*." "By thinking constantly you are ruining your mind," often said Baba Muktananda. Since the root of all thoughts is the 'I'-thought or ego, this must be investigated. When investigated it disappears leaving the Self – "I"-"I"– the 'Aham Vimarsha' of Spanda uncovered filling the seeker to the brim with bliss. The following dharanas, or centering techniques, relate to common experiences of people and show how one can experience Spanda at these times. They are important as BhattaKallata says in his commentary on the current *Spandakarika* verse: The seeker always – i.e. at the beginning, middle and end of perception - -should remain alert regarding the limitless energy, reflecting by knowledge and analyzing the perceptible object.

शक्तिसङ्गमसंक्षुब्ध–शक्त्यावेशावसानिकम् ।
यत्सुखं ब्रह्मतत्त्वस्य तत्सुखम् स्वाक्यमुच्यते ॥ श्लोकः ६९ धारणा ४६॥
लेहनामन्थनाकोटैः स्त्रीसुखस्य भरात्स्मृतेः ।
शक्त्यभावेऽपि देवेशि भवेदानन्दसंप्लवः ॥ श्लोकः ७० धारणा ४७॥

Śakti - saṅgama - saṁkṣubdha - śaktyāveśāvasānikam.
Yat-sukhaṁ Braḥma-tattvasya tatsukham svākyam-ucyate.
(Verse 69, Dhāraṇā 46)
Lehanā-manthanākoṭaiḥ strī-sukhasya bharāt-smṛteḥ
Śaktyabhāve 'pi Deveśi bhaved-ānanda-saṁplavaḥ.
(Verse 70, Dhāraṇā 47)

69. At the time of sexual intercourse with a woman, an excitement brings about by penetration into her and the orgasm that ensues, where all duality vanishes, is the delight of one's own Self. Shivopādhyāya, a commentator of Vijnana Bhairava says, "If that delight is not recognized as the bliss of the Self then it is only a union of two beasts."
70. O Goddess! Even in the absence of a woman, there is a flood of delight, just by the intensity of the memory of sexual pleasure in the acts

of kissing-licking, embracing-churning, rubbing-scratching-biting. Immersed in this delight, he forgets everything else for a moment. This shows that the bliss is within and not dependent on any external agency. That bliss (not the acts!) one should contemplate.

Even though this flood of delight lasts only moments, common people always look forward to it and make great exertions to experience it, even and making their lives complicated. By contrast, a seeker whose kundalini is awakened with the grace of a Guru experiences this delight every moment without any effort. If the mind gets a superior experience, better than the usual experiences, the mind prefers to dwell on the superior one. These waves of bliss arising from within filling the entire physical being, like an electric current flowing through the body, is the ultimate happiness arising from the touch-perception and make the seeker's mind turn inward and abide in the Self.

The perception of seeing also leads to experience of the Self.

आनन्दे महति प्राप्ते दृष्टे वा बान्धवे चिरात् ।
आनन्दमुद्गतं ध्यात्वा तल्लयस्तन्मना भवेत् ॥ श्लोकः ७१, धारणा ४८॥

Ānande mahati prāpte dṛṣṭe vā bāndhave cirāt.
Ānandam-udgataṁ dhyātvā tallayas-tanmanā bhavet.
(Verse 71, Dhāraṇā 48)

71. At the time when great delight arises after seeing the spouse, a son or daughter, or a parent or Guru, after a long time, or after a poor person suddenly gets a fortune, by meditating on that delight itself, the mind becomes absorbed in the Spanda principle and identified with It.

Likewise, in the perception of taste also one can experience the Self.

जग्धिपानकृतोल्लास-रसानन्दविजृम्भणात् ।
भावयेद्भरितावस्थां महानन्दस्ततो भवेत् ॥ श्लोकः ७२, धारणा ४९॥

Jagdhi - pāna - kṛtollāsa - rasānanda -vijṛmbhaṇāt.
Bhāvayed-bharitāvasthāṁ mahānandas-tato bhavet.
(Verse 72, Dhāraṇā 49)

72. Having eaten some delicious feast or had something exotic to drink, one's mouth opens with delight. Joy also arises after satisfying the physical need of hunger or thirst. The senses of sight, smell, touch and taste are very much together in the eating and drinking processes. That perfect state filled with joy should be contemplated, and then there will be supreme delight of the Self.

Almost everyone loves to hear music.

गीतादिविषयास्वादासमसौख्यैकतात्मनः ।
योगिनस्तन्मयत्वेन मनोरूढेस्तदात्मता ॥ श्लोकः ७३, धारणा ५०॥

Gītādi-viṣayāsvādā-sama-saukhyaikatātmanaḥ
Yoginas-tanmayatvena manorūḍhestadātmatā.
(Verse 76, Dhāraṇā 50)

73. Listening to music or experiencing other sense pleasures of touch, taste, sight, smell, mind gets immersed in the incomparable joy of instrumental or vocal music or the specific sense perception. Yogis being one with joy, with the expanded mind experience identify with the bliss of the Self.

Thus the universe is a place of enjoying one's own blissful nature at every moment in all perceptions or interactions. By being aware of the bliss within, especially when we are not doing anything, we can radiate this joy into all our activities. Since the external activities of life arise first in the mind, whether as a necessity, an objective, or as a reaction to external stimuli, the most appropriate thoughts arise followed by appropriate action. Life becomes worriless, stress free, simple and joyous, and independent of external events.

In order to keep etched in our mind that the joy we get is our own nature and is never from external objects, so that we do not get caught up and carried away in the activities, we must be aware of the temporary nature of this universe. In the fifteenth chapter of the *Bhagavad Gita*, this point has been brought out clearly. In the fifteenth chapter the world is called '*Aśvattha*,' a sacred fig-tree with its roots above and leaves and branches below. The blissful, one-without-second, formless Self is at the top, with the root as Maya. Because of Maya, ignorance of the Self takes place and the world and individual beings with their separate egos are created. Ashvattha (a-shva-ttha) also means 'that which does not remain the same tomorrow.' For common people the tree is attractive and evergreen. Only the knowers understand the momentary nature of the universe. In order to get rid of this tree which arises out of ignorance, the only remedy is knowledge. The knowledge we must have is of our own nature, which transcends the body and notions of 'I' and 'this.' Jnaneshwar Maharaj says in *Jnaneshwari*, his commentary on the *Bhagavad Gita*, that for the knowledge to be permanent, the essential requirement is *vairāgya* – detachment. If a person knows that the food being served has been made with poison, he just walks away from the plate. Similarly, if a person who understands the temporary nature of the world, detachment will run after him.

Those who know their real nature understand their oneness with the Self - Universal Consciousness. It is not that it is something to be obtained anew, but the apparent separateness is like a wave in an ocean; the wave is never different from the ocean. The reader may refer to the end of the first verse in this book regarding the experience bestowed by Guru. Even though bodily they may appear separate, knowers do not identify themselves with the body or with doership or enjoyership. They are established in their own blissful Self. With that knowledge they experience that their Self is all-pervasive, forming the warp and woof of the entire sentient and insentient creation.

Even though the blissful Self is everywhere, because of the experience of duality people who know their nature are happy, experiencing oneness, while those who do not know their nature are unhappy. In order to experience oneness, people have to be in the company of saints and practice their teachings. The knowledge that appears in both the ignorant and the wise is the Self's attributeless knowledge. Only the way they use the knowledge is totally different.

In the world there are two *puruṣa's* - beings - which are two types of consciousness existing simultaneously. One is *kṣara* - perishable and the other is *akṣara* – imperishable. The perishable identifies itself with the entire temporary creation of names and forms from the Creator to grass, resides in and identifies with the body, and regards itself also as perishable. The imperishable identifies itself with nothing – neither with the body nor with the Self – and is full of ignorance with maya and keeps performing all autonomous or mechanical actions of the individual. Then there is a third type of consciousness – called *Puruṣottam*, different from both the perishable and the imperishable. When this third type arises in one, it destroys both the knowledge and ignorance, perishable and imperishable types of consciousness. Even when the universe is destroyed, Purushottam is not destroyed. It supports the universe, Its existence lends existence to the universe, and in Its light the universe appears. It exists eternally everywhere.

Only one who understands that the world is just an illusion, and experiences everything as the Self, is ready to worship the Self, which worship cannot be performed without being one with It. This is the message of Chapter 15 the *Bhagavad Gita*.

Thus at all times the seeker must be alert in experiencing the Spanda principle - Self. The following song of Jnaneshwar's shows how easily this can be done with the help of Lord's name.

सर्व सुख गोडी साही शास्त्रें निवडी । रिकामा अर्धघडी राहूं नको ॥१॥
लटिका व्यवहार सर्व हा संसार । वायां येरझार हरिवीण ॥२॥
नाममंत्र जप कोटी जाईल पाप । रामकृष्णीं संकल्प धरुनि राहे ॥३॥
निजवृत्ति काढीं सर्वमाया तोडीं । इंद्रियां सवडी लपूं नको ॥४॥
तीर्थव्रतीं भाव धरी रे करुणा । शांति दया पाहुणा हरि करी ॥५॥
ज्ञानदेवा प्रमाण निवृत्तिदेवीं ज्ञान । समाधि संजीवन हरिपाठ ॥६॥

Sarva sukha goḍī sāhī śāstreṅ nivaḍī, rikāmā ardhaghaḍī rahūṅ nako.
Laṭikā vyavahāra sarva hā saṁsāra, vāyāṅ yera-jhāra Hari-viṇa.
Nāma-mantra japa koṭī jāīla pāpa, Rāma-Kṛṣṇīṅ saṅkalpa dharuni rāhe.
Nija-vṛtti kāḍhīṅ sarva-māyā toḍīṅ, iṅdriyāṅ savaḍī lapūṅ nako.
Tīrtha-vratīṅ bhāva dharī re karuṇā, śāṅti dayā pāhuṇā Hari karī.
Jñānadevā pramāṇa Nivṛtti-devīṅ Jñāna, samādhi sañjīvana Haripāṭha.

The name of Hari is the sweetness of total bliss. All six scriptures have concluded this. Do not remain idle even for half a moment without repeating the name.
Without Hari, transactions of this entire world are meaningless and lead one through the useless cycle of birth and death.
Repeat the mantra of the Name, so that millions of sins will drop away. Hold on to the thought of Rāma-Kṛṣṇa.
Extricate all your tendencies, cut off all attachments. Don't hide behind senses.

Hold on to the conviction in the holy places - beings and resolutions, tenderness, peace and compassion and make Hari your guest.
Jñānadev has proof - direct knowledge bestowed by Lord Nivritti that Haripāṭh – repetition of Lord's name, brings life-restoring Samādhi.

VERSE 45

MĀTṚKĀ SHAKTI, BONDAGE AND FREEDOM

शब्दराशिसमुत्थस्य शक्तिवर्गस्य भोग्यताम् ।
कलाविलुप्तविभवो गतः सन् स पशुः स्मृतः ।।४५।।

45. Śabda-rāśi-samutthasya śakti-vargasya bhogyatām
Kalā-vilupta-vibhavo gataḥ san sa paśuḥ smṛtaḥ

भट्टकल्लटः- शब्दराशिरकारादिक्षकारान्तः तत्समुद्भूतस्य कादिवर्गात्मकस्य ब्राह्म्यादिशक्तिसमूहस्य; भोग्यतां गतः पुरुषो, ब्राह्म्यादीनां कलाभिः ककाराद्यक्षरैर्विलुप्तविभवः स्वस्वभावात् प्रच्यावितः पशुरुच्यते।।४५।।

BhaṭṭaKallaṭaḥ - 45. Śabda-raśir-akārādikṣakārāntaḥ tatsamudbhūtasya kādivargāt-makasya Brāḥmyādiśakti-samūhasya; bhogyatāṁ gataḥ puruṣo, Brāḥmyādīnāṁ kalābhiḥ kakārādykṣarair-vilupta-vibhavaḥ sva-svabhāvāt pracyāvitaḥ paśur-ucyate.

The genre of Shaktis (energies) that arise from the set of sounds (words) controls the individual and then the individual is called a bound creature. The reason for this is that the collection of kalās (actions associated with groups of sounds) destroys the innate independence of the individual.

BhaṭṭaKallaṭa: The set of sounds or letters (50 in all in Devanāgari – the Sanskrit alphabet discussed later) begins with अ *(A) and ends with* क्ष *(Kṣa) (The first sixteen are vowels and the next thirty-four are consonants. The consonants starting from the letter* क *(K) are divided into five groups of five consonants, followed by two groups of four, and one group of one consonant). From each group arises a power called by different names such as Brāḥmī, and a kalā (movement) associated with it. An individual loses the innate independent nature due to these groups of letters, K and so on, equipped with the powers. Thus the individual dispossessed of his or her independent nature becomes a bound creature.*

THE LAST VERSE incited the seeker to remain vigilant regarding Spanda in all states – waking, dream and deep sleep. Verse 45 shows how one gets trapped by the power and kalās (movements) inherent in words/sounds. No creation is different from Shiva, the Self and His Shakti – Spanda expressing as Its free will (icchā shakti), power of knowledge (jñāna Shakti) and power of action (kriyā shakti). Yet most people through their perceptions and actions get enmeshed in the world due to the powers inherent in words. They become unaware of the innate bliss and freedom and regard themselves as creatures bound by their circumstances and talents.

Yet if we knew the power inherent in letters/words, we would not be trapped in the world and would always be aware of our state of Shiva that transcends our experience of limitations. We would then know that the words really are very transparent and cannot hide the Self. The Self we want to experience is available right now right here, without any effort, without really doing anything. It is all that we are. It is all that we see, smell, hear, taste and touch. There is no time to waste in searching. Swami Lakshmanjoo[75] says, "If you want to perceive the state of Lord Shiva as it ought to be perceived, in its real sense, you must enjoy this universe. You won't find the real state of Lord Shiva in samādhi. In the state of samadhi, you will find His non-vivid formation. You will find the exact state of Lord Shiva in the universe." Realizing all beings as one's own Self, saints teach us through their own life and dedication how to live in this world, see God in one another, be compassionate, work selflessly, and provide help to those who are suffering. A living great saint, *Ammāchi* or *Amritānandamayi Mā*, says, "Today's world needs people who express goodness in their words and deeds. If such noble role models can set an example for their fellow beings, the darkness now prevailing in society will be dispelled."

The word '*Śabdarāśi*' means collection of words or sounds. In everyday life words are so important. They actually rule our life. Thoughts arise within us and take a definite form through our mouth as words. We communicate our thoughts to

---

[75] Swami Lakshman Joo – *Shiva Sutras – The Supreme Awakening*, p.101

another person with spoken words. Angry words of a person make anger or fear arise in us and build in us hatred about the person. Loving words soothe us and generate love in us. Thus words create emotions in our mind. Words residing in our mind as thoughts move our intellect and make our physical body act or react. In Kashmir Shaivism the nature of the Self is '*svātantrya*' or freedom; there is no notion of bondage in the Self. The seeker has to know that bondage felt is due to words, and that bondage can be destroyed by recognizing the power of words, and through words themselves. This is the topic of the present discussion.

We will study several *Shiva Sutras* which explain this bondage and show how to get rid of it. The first explains what the bondage due to *Matṛkā* – power in words – is, in the *Śāmbhavopāya*. - ज्ञानाधिष्ठानम् मातृका । (१-४) *Jñānādhiṣṭhānaṁ Matṛkā* (1-4). The second one in *Śāktopāya* – मातृकाचक्र सम्बोधः (२-७) *Mātṛkācakrasambodhaḥ* (2-7) describes the secret of *Matṛkā cakra* - the cycle of *Matṛkā* - the power in each letter of the alphabet. The third and fourth relevant sutras in *Āṇavopāya* – कलादीनां तत्त्वानां अविवेको माया । शरीरे संहारः कलानाम् । (३-३,४) *Kalādīnāṁ tattvānāṁ aviveko māyā*, and *Śarīre saṁhāraḥ kalānām* (3-3, 4) explain the means along with a few centering techniques, to understand and meditate to get rid of the bondage. Underlying all this, of course, is Shiva – Self and His grace through a human form called Guru.

Bondage:

Shiva Sutra 1.4 says, "ज्ञानाधिष्ठानम् मातृका *Jñānādhiṣṭhānaṁ Mātṛkā*" which means the mother, who is not understood correctly, directs all knowledge. This knowledge has three confining types:

- incompleteness – for example, 'branding' ourselves or feeling 'I am weak, I am no good, I am great, I am famous.' This is also known as 'Āṇava mala – impurity of being small like an atom.'

- differentiated knowledge about objects or creatures – for example, feeling 'No one has this except me; I have the most beautiful house.' This is also known as 'Māyīya mala – impurity due to māyā – the power of illusion.'

- impressions of pain and pleasure – for example, 'Why me? Why did I not get that prize? I received an award. My niece was killed in an accident. My car was stolen.' This is also known as 'Kārma mala – impurity due to actions.'

The last two impurities depend on the first one. If the first one is destroyed, the remaining two are also destroyed. For a detailed discussion of the impurities, see *Pratyabhijñā Kārikā* and Sw. Lakshmanjoo's commentary on *Shiva Sutra* 1.4.

This limiting or limited knowledge is ignorance of our true universal nature, and thinking our individual limited nature is our true nature. The un-understood mother is the power of illusion that Svatantrya - the freedom of the Self - creates to form an individual and his or her world. It is not any actual deficiency but ignorance. An individual while remaining absorbed in the objective or phenomenal world forgets the true energy, mother, which creates the objective world. Bondage manifests in the terms māyā and her five *Kancukas* or confining jackets or coverings, *kalā, rāga, vidyā, niyati, kāla*. They are all inherent in words. Due to our ignorance and objectivity (*māyā*), and our limited knowledge (*vidyā*), we feel incomplete, we experience duality, and we go through the cycles of pain and pleasure. Due to a sense of un-fulfillment, we aspire for an object, which we see or imagine and feel we do not have. The object is known to us as a word. We make use of our limited efforts and talents, which are also called *kalā*, to acquire the object which is confined by *kāla* – meaning time, space and form. Even after acquiring the object (*vācya* or *prameya* in Sanskrit) the only thing that happens in our mind is a relational feeling or cognition (*pramāṇa*) of 'I have that' or 'That is mine.' 'That' is the word for the acquired object (*vācaka* or *pramātā* or possessor in Sanskrit) for which we form an attachment (*rāga*) in general and specifically to the acquired object (*niyati*) - for that word. Thus raga and niyati go together. In this manner, as the work *Tantra-sadbhāva* says, these five principles or coverings make us act in a limited way, know in a limited way, love in a limited way, live in a limited way, and possess in a limited way. Even our spiritual efforts get limited, and if an enlightened being, Guru, tries to guide us, we do not accept the instructions wholeheartedly and remain bound like a beast.

The relational feeling described in the previous paragraph creates bondage. Where no relational feeling is formed, or the triad of listener, word and hearing is not formed, words do not affect us in any manner. For example, if a thought arises in our mind and we don't own it, meaning we don't pay attention or do not act on it, it dies without any consequences, as a cloud that does not produce rain just passes away. If someone for whom we have no attachment dies, that has no effect on us. But if the same person happens to be related to us we feel sad. As long as the 'vachaka' and 'vachya' are separate they are not binding to an individual. Thus in all our limited knowledge the words 'I and mine,' signifying our individual ego, bring out the connection. Our universe is a manifestation of triads of pramātā, pramāṇa and prameya discussed earlier, words taking forms, subtle manifestation as a thought, gross manifestation as an uttered word, and sometimes as the object associated. Basically, the corresponding thought, word and object are not different, even though in the manifested universe they are different. The 17th Century poet Saint Tukaram says in one of his abhangs, "सांडिली त्रिपुटी दीप उजळला घटी ।" "*Sāṇdilī tripuṭī dīpa ujaḷalā ghaṭī* " "The triad abandoned, the Light of the Self started shining in the body."

The word *kalā* is a derivation of the root कल् - *kal* means to move or act. It is also used differently from the confining jacket *kalā* discussed earlier. The universe consists of *kalās* - the movements of Chiti - Shiva. *Pratyabhijñā Hṛdayaṁ* aphorism 2 says 'स्वेच्छया स्वभित्तौ विश्वं उन्मीलयति ।' '*Svecchayā svabhittau viśvaṁ unmīlayati.*' 'Due to Its own free will – iccha shakti, Chiti creates the universe by reflection on Itself as the wall.' The reflection takes place in the opposite order – from the Earth principle to Shakti principle, just as standing in front of a convex mirror one sees one's head and toes upside down. We will see in the following discussion how these movements are described in the Sanskrit alphabet. Each letter/word thus has an inherent power and a corresponding movement or *kalā*. Hence it is important for a seeker to know in detail how and why words bind the seeker. By becoming vigilant regarding the power of words, especially the mantra - few word/s from Guru, the seeker can remain free in Spanda, which is the theme of the last verse.

Śabda-rāshi – Sets of words:

BhattaKallata mentions the vowel A (अ) uttered at the throat, the origin of the mouth, and the last consonant Kṣa (क्ष); and as convention, includes the entire *Devanāgari*, meaning Divine script, or Sanskrit alphabet,[76] containing all vowels and consonants, between the two letters. A specific area of the mouth is used for pronouncing each particular group of sounds. As the groups of consonants progress, the tongue comes forward from the throat into different areas of the mouth, and in the पवर्ग - 'P' group only the lips are used. From the यवर्ग - 'Ya' group onwards each character is a part aspiration or a semivowel. The character ॐ (Auṁ or Oṁ), a compound sound, uses the entire mouth, and consists of the letters A, U, M, which represent Shiva, Shakti and Individual, or three states,

[76] We discuss this later in detail. The reader not familiar with Devanagari can look up the table of vowels and consonants there and can come back to this point.

with the dot representing the fourth state, and many other triads. But we will not discuss it in detail since we can find the discussion in many places such as '*Nectar of Discourses - Pravacana Sudha*' - commentary by Swami Maheshwarananda on the *Bhagavad Gita*, Chapter 7, Verse 8. Thus the Sanskrit alphabet has been constructed very scientifically and has been used in research on developing synthetic speech! Sometimes the letter *Ha* (ह) is regarded as the last letter of the alphabet. In the arrangement in the present verse, the above mentioned last letter '*kṣa*' is already contained as a union of the letters k and s.

Alphabets of all other languages correspond to subsets of the Sanskrit alphabet, because almost every sound that is heard or can be pronounced can be written as just one character, basic or compound, in Sanskrit. The Sanskrit alphabet has fifty basic characters consisting of sixteen vowels and thirty-four consonants, while the Roman alphabet for instance has only twenty-six. Thus, the Roman alphabet requires two characters for almost every sound.

There are sounds – 'shabda' in Sanskrit - which are not in the alphabet. The sound produced by a musical instrument such as a guitar or a drum is not in the alphabet. There are animal and bird sounds which also are not words. For humans these are at 'Madhyama' level and cannot be put into words. Even vocal music from various cultures has sounds which are not in the alphabet. Such sounds produce emotions and feelings of calm or agitation, but do not have in general a binding effect as in sounds of letters, unless a triad of cognition discussed earlier is formed, and hence such sounds are excluded from the Shabdarashi – pile of words. The sound produced by the alphabet in the mouth actually resonates, sending ripples throughout the entire body, if one pays a close attention to it.

Again, in the basic Devanāgari alphabet, A is the first letter and Ha is the last. Hence the word composed of 'a' and 'ha' with the convention of putting a final 'm' in Sanskrit language makes the word 'Aham' meaning 'I am,' that represents the universal 'I Am' enclosing the entire world consisting of 'words' or letters in between. "I am" is also the first word experienced by every individual as soon as he or she wakes up or dreams , and simultaneously the individual's waking or dream state world is also experienced. For an individual, when there is no "I am" as in deep sleep, there is also no world. In other words, 'I Am' is the origin of the world for every individual and causes the bondage discussed earlier. Therefore, the saints, like Ramana Maharshi and Nisargadatta Maharaj, emphasize an investigation into the words, 'I am' that every individual uses. There is another interpretation of 'Aham' based on the power in the individual letters which will be discussed later.

Before going into the individual groups of the Sanskrit alphabet and the powers hidden in them, we consider the power of the word or sound in general. In the sixth chapter entitled '*Śabda-khaṇḍan*' - 'Annihilation of the word' in his work *Amritānubhav – Nectar of Experiences*, Jñāneśwar Mahārāj describes the importance of the sound or word and how the word gets annihilated in the Self. A comprehensive summary follows.

A word is important in reminding. The individual has forgotten his or her original nature. The word is like a mirror that reminds one of one's own face, which one often forgets. Eyes can see an image in a mirror, but a word can make even the blind see. The word given by the Guru can open the eyes of the seeker to his or her own nature.

From the unmanifested Maya principle first the sound or word – Om, and then from Om the five gross elements and consequently all creation have manifested. Even though the creation is not different from the all-pervading Self, creation is given credibility, or temporary factual existence, by the word alone. Even though the word as sound created the first primordial element – space, it is also the quality of space. The word has given a literary form to the formless space. Regarding its own form, the word has none. Before uttering or after it is uttered the word does not have a form and even in the middle of the process of uttering it has no form. It is heard by the ears only and by none of the other four senses – touch, taste, smell or sight. Space would not be recognizable if sound did not exist. The word has spawned the world. It is a torch that shows the correct and wrong paths. 'Bondage and freedom' are word's creations. Investigation into the word indicates that there is nothing else but consciousness. Even though the word is important in bringing into manifestation the world, at the substratum - Self, it has no value.

The Self is pure and has no faults such as impurities, concealment, desire or anger. The word brings individuality to that Self, which imagines impurities and stupidity such as 'I am mortal, I have limited knowledge, I have limited power, I am not free, I am unhappy, I am a sinner.' Thus the word made the pure Self take up impure individuality. But to dispel the individuality and bring one back to Self-hood, again the word which teaches, 'You are not the senses nor prāṇa nor mind nor intellect' is essential. Contemplation and practice of these words brings the individual back to the Self. The word is like a sorcerer who makes the ghost enter and possess an individual and also dispels the ghost. It is the mantra bestowed by Guru -"So ham. Tattvamasi – I am That, Thou art That," due to which the individual gets the knowledge of the Self as the witness of the body and senses.

The sun destroys darkness and then makes the day appear; while the word alone can make appear the contradictory dual tendencies of being interested or being disinterested in the world. An individual feels that to be free of the fetters of worldly unhappiness and sorrow, one has to have the knowledge of the Self; and to attain the Self, the individual seeks the company of saints and studies scriptures and saints' works, which are words. The word exists while showing an object of the world, but the word gets destroyed while turning to the Self, which is Consciousness, self-illuminating, indivisible, and which cannot be illumined by an insentient object such as the word.

The word is useful for reminding, but it has no relation with the Self. A word can remind one of a forgotten object, but what reminder can it give the Self which is eternal knowledge? The Self may remain in the innate knowledge of the pure Self without manifestation, or by contracting and forgetting It may appear as variegated objects. It remains the Self, because there is nothing else to contaminate It. We have also seen in the *SpandaKarika* Verse 29, "... among a word, the meaning or the object it stands for, and a thought, there is no state which is not the Self." But that does not mean that both remembering and forgetting, or words along with their meanings and objects, are characteristics of the Self. The Self which is eternal-knowledge cannot remember or forget what It is, just as the sun does not know what light and darkness are. Even though the word has the powerful quality of reminding, at the level of the Self the word's power is irrelevant, just as a person who is healthy does not need any medicine however powerful the medicine may be.

If one thinks about it, it is foolishness to say that the word destroyed ignorance and gave the knowledge of the Self. What is the meaning of saying that ignorance that existed in the eternal-knower Self was destroyed by the word, and that the word gave the experience of the Self as eternal knowledge? It is foolishness to say regarding the self-illuminating sun that the sun destroys darkness and then rises. How can a person who is asleep get mad at sleep? Or how can the person who is already awake, be said to be awakened? There is no knowledge needed to destroy the ignorance in the Self, since the Self has not moved away from Its state of eternal knowledge.

If we consider ignorance, illusion or the Maya principle, made up of the two letters 'Mā' meaning 'No' and 'Yā' meaning 'Who' – the word maya means 'that which does not exist.' Hence it is ridiculous to say that the word destroys maya or ignorance – which does not exist in the first place. When one is in the dream state, the dream seen is regarded as real. But when one wakes up, one knows that the dream was false. Similarly, when an individual experiences the world, it appears to be real. When one wakes up to one's true nature, that one experiences, "I am existence-consciousness-bliss. I am a detached witness. I am the Self." And one recognizes that one's assumption about the world as a separate entity called the world is an illusion. In the Vedantic philosophy, this is known as 'support' and 'substratum.' There is a subtle difference between the two words 'support' and 'substratum.' If in the twilight, a rope is regarded as a snake, the common nature of 'thisness' of the rope supports both the contradictory notions of the 'rope' and 'snake' at the same time. But when one becomes aware of the special nature of the rope, one becomes aware of the substratum 'rope' and knows that the imposition of a 'snake' on the rope was an illusion. The experience of the Self's special nature - 'thisness' supports both the temporary, duality-ridden world and the eternal, non-dual Self. But the awareness of the common nature of the substratum, Self, gives the experience of the Supreme bliss.

Thus the word can neither destroy ignorance nor show the Self. The concepts of 'knowledge' and 'ignorance' or 'freedom and bondage' do not exist in the Self. They exist only as words. Just as in the deluge the whole creation vanishes, just as the cloudy day vanishes when the clouds disappear, so in the eternal-knowledge Self, the creation of the word vanishes.

In short, Jnaneshwar's discussion, which is according to the Vedantic doctrine, shows that in both Kashmir Shaivism and Vedanta the concepts of individual bondage and freedom exist only as words.

The words we are familiar with consist either of audible sounds as parts of speech or written characters. In this context, it is important to review the origin of speech itself although we have discussed it in detail in Verses 26-27. Both these verses and the current verse can be studied together. Just as all colors in the feathers and body of a peacock are concentrated in the yolk of the peacock egg, all words and creation are concentrated in the *parāvāṇi* – subtle level of speech. In this level there is no duality of *vācya* - meaning or object, and *vācaka* - its verbal representation. Paravani is situated at the gut level. Just as there is an entire tree contained within the tiny fig seed, at the second level of speech, paśyantī, the entire creation exists as a potential but not yet apparent duality. *Pashyanti* is situated at the heart level. Just as there are peas in an unopened pod, at the *madhyamā* level creation exists as apparent but still not manifest duality. Madhyama is situated at the throat level. Just as when a pod is opened the peas spill out, at the fourth level, *vaikharī*, the duality of creation is clearly visible. (*Gurutu*, 12, p.161) It is at the vaikhari level of speech that words are uttered and sentences are formed. The Vaikhari level is situated at the mouth. It is important to keep in mind that Paravani is the substratum of all of these different levels of speech. From the point of view of Paravani, the different levels apparent to an individual do not exist, just as from the point of view of consciousness different objects do not exist, even though an individual perceives them.

The wheel of words or Theory of Alphabet -

Shiva Sutras Aphorism 2.7 states: मातृकाचक्रसम्बोधः। *Mātṛkācakra-sambodhaḥ* - 'The disciple attains the knowledge of the wheel of the hidden mother – matrika chakra - only by Guru's grace.'

The word *Mātṛ* means 'mother', *kā* means 'who,' one who is unknown, and cakra means a wheel or a group. The word *Mātṛkā* originates from the fact that while looking at the world, its creative energy, its mother, remains hidden in the background unnoticed. Swami Lakshmanjoo has described *Mātṛkācakra*, the theory of alphabet, in the commentary on the above aphorism as well as in his work entitled *Kashmir Shaivism –The Secret Supreme*. In the work *Parātriṁśikā* with the commentary by Abhinav Gupta, 800 A.D., this theory has been explained in detail. The grammarian Pāṇinī has also described the fine points of the alphabet, but with some differences from the Kashmir Shaiva theory.

As we shall see, the various letters of the alphabet represent the thirty-six[77] different principles of creation descending from the Shiva principle. They are all regarded as movements of Shiva, the Self.

The 16 vowels presented in Table 1 represent the sixteen movements of Shiva and His energies, representing all internal creation but no external creation. We will examine each of these in turn below.

Table 1

अ A	आ Ā	इ I	ई Ī	उ U	ऊ Ū	ऋ R	ॠ Ṝ
ऌ ḷ	ॡ ḹ	ए E	ऐ AI	ओ O	औ AU	अं ṁ	अः ḥ

His first movement, the letter अ A, is all consciousness. Shiva is *Anuttara* meaning unparalleled, there is nothing comparable to Him. He is also *akula* meaning undifferentiated totality. Abhinav Gupta has given many interpretations of the word Anuttara in his work *Parātriṁśikā*. In one interpretation he says:

वितत इव नभस्यविच्छिदैव, प्रतनु पतन्न विभाव्यते जलौघः ।
उपवनतरुवेश्मनीध्रभागाद्युपधिवशेन तु लक्ष्यते स्फुटं सः ॥
तद्वत् परभैरवोऽतिसौक्ष्म्याद्, अनुभवगोचरमेति नैव जातु ॥
अथ देशाकृतिकालसन्निवेश-स्थितिसंस्पन्दितकरकत्वयोगाः ।
जनयन्त्यनुभाविनीं चितिं ते, झटिति न्यक्कृतभैरवीयबोधाः ॥
तथा च वक्ष्यते उत्तरस्याप्यनुत्तरम्

Vitata iva nabhasya-vicchidaiva, pratanu patanna vibhāvyate jaloughaḥ
Upavana-taru-veśma-nīdhrabhāgā dyupadhivaśena
tu lakṣyate sphuṭaṁ saḥ
Tadvat para-Bhairavo 'ti-saukṣmyād, Anubhava-gocarameti naiva jātu
Atha deśākṛti-kāla-sanniveśa-sthiti-saṁspandita-karakatva-yogāḥ
Janayantyanubhāvinīṁ Citiṁ Te, Jhaṭiti nyakkṛta-bhairavīya-bodhāḥ
tathā ca vakṣyate Uttarasyāpyanuttaram

---

[77]

Five Gross Elements	**Five Subtle Elements**	**Five Organs of Action**	**Five Organs of Cognition**
Earth – Prithvi	Smell – Gandha	Procreation – Upastha	Nose – Grhāṇa
Water – Jala	Taste – Rasa	Excretion – Pāyu	Tongue – Rasanā
Fire – Agni	Form – Rūpa	Feet – Pada	Eyes – Cakṣu
Air – Vāyu	Touch – Sparsha	Hands – Pāṇi	Skin – Tvak
Space – Ākāsh	Sound – Shabda	Speech – Vāk	Ears – Śrotra

Five Internal Organs	**Six Coverings**	**Five Pure Elements**
Mind – Mānas	Limitation of place – Niyati	Pure Knowledge "I" – "this" separate - Śuddha Vidyā
Intellect – Buddhi	Limitation of time – Kāla	"This"ness predominent in "I"ness – Iswara
Ego connected with objectivity – Ahamkār	Limitation of attachment – Rāga	"I"ness in "This"ness – Sadāśiva
Nature – Prakṛti	Limitation of knowledge – Vidyā	"I"ness – Śakti
Ego connected with subjectivity – Purusha	Limitation of creativity – Kalā	Being – Śiva
	Illusion of Individuality – Māyā	

"If there is a heavy cloud cover with incessant rain, if we try to observe the torrents against the background of the sky, they can never be seen due to their subtlety. But if we try to observe them against the background of the wet trees in a garden, or on rooftops, they are easily seen. In the same way, being subtler than subtle, and being beyond the four backgrounds of body, intellect, eightfold[78] *senses and inner organs, as well as the void, Supreme Bhairava can never be experienced against these backgrounds. O Lord! Under these circumstances, the power acting in all places, shapes, time, collections, conditions and efforts makes us experience Your limitless Power of Chiti –consciousness - by taming it to the appropriate acts. Thus You remain "That unfathomable behind each fathomable."*

A mundane example is sufficient to illustrate the point. When we wash a pan, we can become aware of the power with which our fingers move the scrubber around the pot while holding the pot by fingers of the other hand. We notice how intricate the movements of fingers are and become aware of the Chiti that makes this happen.

Shiva's second movement, आ Ā, representing *ānand*, bliss, happens due to His observation of His own nature. When one observes one's own real nature, one is in bliss. The first two vowels thus represent consciousness and bliss. These two energies are inseparable, like fire and its heat. The differentiated reality as the universe is still unmanifest at this stage. The next two movements represent Shiva's intention to express His glory in the external world as the expression of his bliss. These are the two vowels इ (*I*) and ई (*Ī*). I stands for इच्छा (*Icchā*) desire – the subtle state of will and Ī stands for ईशन (*Īśana*) - owning or ruling - the gross state of will. Since there is nothing other than Shiva, the only desire in the subtle state of will is admiration of His own state, the feeling 'I possess this state.' In the gross state of will, by contrast, He wants, in addition to the admiration, to 'own His nature' as if He has moved away from it. The next movement is called *jñāna*, where Shiva discovers that the entire universe exists in His own nature and is full of consciousness and bliss. The letter उ (U) represents उन्मेष - *unmeṣa* – the recognition of the universe or the origin of the universe. The letter ऊ (*Ū*) represents ऊनता - *ūnatā* - lessening, where due to his observation of the differentiated reality of the universe within, the splendor of consciousness and

[78] Five pure senses of perception – smelling, tasting, hearing, seeing, touching and the three inner organs mind, intellect, ego known as the *puryashtaka* - 'city of eight'

bliss moves away. This apprehension about whether the energies of consciousness and bliss would decrease in creation causes a hesitation in moving forward with creation of the universe, and Lord Shiva comes to a standstill.

The next eight vowels, ऋ *Ṛ*, ॠ *Ṝ*, ऌ *ḷ*, ॡ *ḹ*, ए *E*, ऐ *Ai*, ओ *O* and औ *Au*, represent *kriyāśakti* – the Energy of creation. Out of these, the first four vowels, ऋ *Ṛ*, ॠ *Ṝ*, ऌ *ḷ*, ॡ *ḹ*, are called *amṛta bīja* – or Shiva residing in His own bliss. These vowels do not mix with any other letters, which means that they do not modify any consonants as other vowels do. They thus stay separate, representing Shiva remaining in His own nature, without perforing universal creation of any kind. These four vowels are therefore also called eunuch vowels. These four movements respectively represent the intention to return to His nature (the inward movement of iccha shakti), a confirmation of the intention to return, the intention of becoming established in His own nature, and confirmation of the intention of establishment. These letters result in the semivowels र *R* and ल *L* which appear at the end of the alphabet, again representing intention of returning to His own nature after creation of the world. (*Gurutu*, 12, p. 283-286) In fact, according to the Sanskrit rules of sandhi, or letter combination, ऋ = र + इ *R* = *R* + *I* and ॠ = र + ई *Ṝ* = *R* + *Ī* and ऌ = ल + इ *ḷ* = l + I, ॡ = ल + ई *ḹ* = l + Ī. There are no other vowels which are mixed with consonants such as Ṛ and L. These two letters represent the "bliss of resting in the Self."

To utter the ten vowels, the tongue starts at the throat and moves forward to the lips as follows:

Table 2

Vowels		Origin in mouth	Pronounced
अ *A*	आ *Ā*	Gutturals	from throat
इ *I*	ई *Ī*	Palatals	with middle of tongue against palate
ऋ *Ṛ*	ॠ *Ṝ*	Cerebrals	with tip of tongue against roof of mouth – ri, rī
ऌ *ḷ*	ॡ *ḹ*	Dentals	as cerebrals but with tongue against teeth – lri, lrī
उ *U*	ऊ *Ū*	Labials	with rounding lips

Again, the movement to create the universe starts in Shiva. This time the creative energy of Shiva infuses His Consciousness and then it infuses the power of will. The first two of Shiva's five shaktis (energies) – chit (consciousness), anand (bliss), iccha (will), jnana (knowledge) and kriya (action) – are always together. Thus, in the above Table 1 of 16 vowels, the next four vowels (E, AI, O, and AU) are combinations of the first, second and fifth set of vowels of Table 2 (A/Ā, I/Ī, and U/Ū), which correspond to these five shaktis. Iccha is by itself, jnana consists of iccha and jnana, and kriya consists of all three – iccha, jnana and kriya thus forming a triangle with three vertices as the three shaktis.

The Sanskrit letter ए (E) is often drawn like a triangle. It represents kriya shakti, the energy of action, which is subtle or unmanifest creation. The two energies *A* or *Ā* in combination with the two forms of energies of will *I* and *Ī* make up just one form of creation: subtle or unmanifest creation: ए (E). The sandhi rule for this can be expressed as A or $\bar{A} + I = E$ or also as A or $\bar{A} + \bar{I} = E$.

At the letter *E*, a subtle triad of perception is also formed, consisting of perception – *Pramāṇa*, perceiver – *Pramātā* and perceived – *Prameya*.

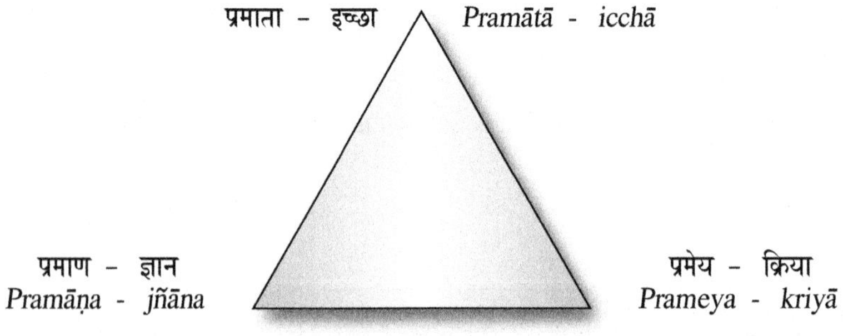

The manifest creation is represented by the next letter, ऐ (*Ai*). This letter is made up of ए (*E*) and the first or the second letter: A or $\bar{A} + E = Ai$.

We can observe even in everyday life that all three energies of bliss, will, and knowledge exist within the energy of action. First, in order to perform an action, the energy of consciousness (bliss) has to be available, otherwise nothing takes place. A dead body cannot perform any action. Then, there has to be a desire to perform the action. Until we have a desire, we would not care to perform any action regardless of how much bliss we have. Then there is knowledge of how to perform the action before we actually perform it. Otherwise the action will not take place.

Energies of consciousness-bliss and knowledge together with the two energies of knowledge create the next two stages of creation, represented by the next two vowels, ओ *O* and औ *Au*, more and most manifest creation respectively: *A* or *Ā* + *U* = *O* and *A* or *Ā* + *O* = *Au*. The letter *O* represents all the subtle triads of Shiva in combination with the corresponding reflected manifest triad of Shakti – the manifest pramata, prameya and pramana – forming a figure called *ṣaṭkoṇa*, a six-pointed star, as follows:

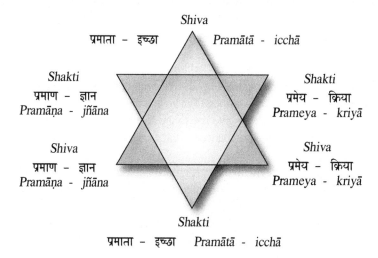

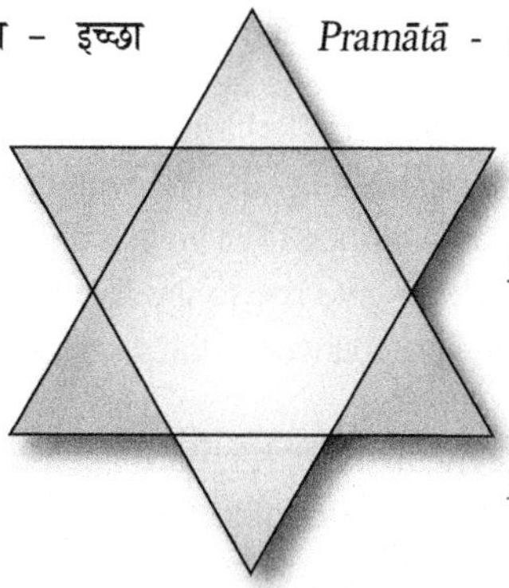

In the letter औ (*Au*) all three energies – iccha, jnana and kriya – merge in one universal point. It represents the most vivid level of creation. The point is also called शूलबीज - *Śūlabīja* – the universe existing most vividly in one point as a sprout exists in a seed. The upward-facing Shiva triangle represents the subtle triad as in the earlier triangle, and the downward-facing Shakti triangle represents the more vivid corresponding individual triad.

If Shiva's form has to be perceived completely, it is necessary to observe the total creation. In samadhi His subtle, unmanifest form is perceived. The creation completely reflects the all-pervasive nature of Shiva in औ (*Au*). The next vowel अं (*ṁ*), called *anuswār*, indicates that even though the creation has taken place in His nature, Shiva has not moved from His own nature. Thus all energies dissolve into this point that represents the dissolution of creation back into Shiva. The last vowel *ḥ* is written ':' as a colon at the end of letters in Sanskrit, is called visarga where the upper dot represents Shiva and the lower represents Shakti, the two together representing two cups where reflection has taken place. The set of vowels representing subjective creation is called 'Bindu' and the set of consonants representing objective creation is called 'Yonī.'

The universe is created by reflection of the Svātantrya – freedom - of Shiva. The five energies *cit, ānand, icchā, jñāna,* and *kriyā* are expansion of this freedom. Each of these five energies are divided and intermingle with each of the five producing twenty-five energies. Thus a matrix of twenty-five consonants is formed. The five shaktis, thirty-six principles and thirty-four consonants[79] related to one another can be described as in the table on the next page.

The table has columns kriya, jnana, iccha, anand and chit in the increasing order of subtlety – each energy containing all five, with chit, the least subtle energy, being predominant in Consciousness. Ten vowels divided into five groups of two as discussed earlier (Table 2) give rise to the five groups of five consonants as rows in the table; they are pronounced in the same area of mouth as the vowels.

Thus अ *A* and आ *Ā* give rise to the क *K* group of consonants. The letter क *K* represents earth, the grossest (36th) principle of Kashmir Shaivism. Other consonants are generated in a similar way until the consonant म Ma. These twenty five consonants describe the making of an individual – Puruṣa. Creation starts with Purusha (subjective Ego) and Prakriti (Nature) and ends with Prithvi (Earth).

Then four semivowels य *Ya*, र *Ra*, ल *La*, व *Va* represent the six coverings of maya. They are generated from the consonants – च *Ca*, ट *Ṭa*, त *Ta*, त–प Ta-Pa. This can be observed from the position of the tongue in pronouncing the letters. Grammarian *Pāṇinī* calls the four semivowels as *antaḥstha* – staying inside an

[79]

1 Gutturals	क *Ka*	ख *Kha*	ग Ga	घ *Gha*	ङ Gṅa
2 Palatals	च Ca	छ Cha	ज *Ja*	झ *Jha*	ञ Yṅa
3 Cerebrals	ट Ṭa	ठ Ṭha	ड Ḍa	ढ Ḍha	ण Ṇa
4 Dentals	त *Ta*	थ *Tha*	द *Da*	ध *Dha*	न Na
5 Labials	प Pa	फ Pha not *Fa*	ब *Ba*	भ *Bha*	म Ma
6 Semi-vowels	य *Ya*	र *Ra*	ल *La*	व Va	
7 Sibilants, Aspirant – *Ha*	श *Śa*	ष *Ṣa*	स *Sa*	ह *Ha*	
8 क - स *K* and *Sa*	क्ष Kṣa				

individual being. Kashmir Shaivism calls them *dhāraṇā* - supporting an individual since they give life to an individual creature. Without these an individual will not be born and creation remains in the Pure elements. Limitation is what gives life to a limited being. There are only four letters but they contain the six principles, because limited creativity कला *Kalā* and Time काल *Kāla* go together in the letter "Ya," Vidya, limited knowledge in "Ra," attachment राग *Rāga* and limitation of place or attachment for a specific object नियति *Niyati* go together in the letter "La" and माया *Māyā* with "Va." (p. 23, *Sw. Lakshman Joo*, 47)

Beyond these, the differentiated perception vanishes as individual self blooms into Unmeṣa – existence. The four letters श *Śa*, ष *Ṣa*, स *Sa*, and ह *Ha* represent internal light, fire and warmth, and are known as ऊष्म *Ūṣma* – or hot letters. Three of these letters are generated from the consonants च Ca, ट Ṭa, त Ta, again seen from the position of the tongue while pronouncing these letters. The letter ह Ha is a 'visarga' or aspiration like अः Aḥ or ḥ. More about the visargas later. The letters of the entire alphabet describe the thirty-six principles ascent through the individual back into Shiva, and given on page 367A.

Each row has its Shakti or energy, manifesting from Chiti. Each shakti performs two functions. First, these shaktis cover the main Chiti – para-shakti or kundalini – situated at Brahmarandhra, which for human beings is at the top of the head. Secondly, these shaktis act on different types of individuals in the following three ways:

1. घोरतरा - अपरा *Ghoratarā* - *Aparā*: Ghoratara work on tamasic or indolent individuals, pushing an individual into bondage of sense objects in the mirage of words by creating various sankalpas and vikalpas – desires and delusions.

2. घोरा – परापरा *Ghorā* - *Parāparā*: Ghora work on rajasic individuals to create good and bad desires, but keep the door to self-inquiry closed, but still open to Self's – Guru's – grace.

3. अघोरा – अपरा *Aghorā* - *aparā*: Aghora are very beneficial to the yogis. They push the seekers up to uncover the secrets and to experience the oneness of the Self.

We have seen the visarga अः *ḥ* written as ":" that represents the starting point of creation, expansion of Being into the Universe. The word visarga is a noun derived from the word – vi – meaning special and the root सृज् *sṛj* which means to create, procreate, release, let go or emit. The upper dot represents the seed of the Universe in Being and the lower its implantation into Shakti. There are three types of visargas: 1. आ *Ā* bliss or Shiva visarga, where the mind is non-existent, or called Chittapralaya. 2. अः *ḥ* is called Shākta visarga – which is considered two ways: Internally, all the three energies dissolve, expanding into bliss; externally, the three energies generate the entire objective universe starting from k to kṣa. The state of this visarga is just one thought - awareness of pure consciousness, and is called Chittasambodha. 3. ह *Ha* - the letter representing Shakti is the third visarga. It is the state where the individual universe dissolves into Shakti, the individual mind becoming one, abandoning all differentiating thoughts. This is also a joyous state where the mind becomes thoughtless or nonexistent. In this world at the end of any satisfying activity we find our mind is thoughtless. The climax experienced in a sex-act of a male and a female is a thoughtless state. All such experiences arise from the Shakti - bliss of the Self. In short, these visargas are the utterances or experiences of "Aha" moments – or blissful moments of the Self.

The creation ends in the fullness of being, in Sadāśiva, and never in inferiority. The corresponding letter is Sa. It represents the experience अहम् इदम् - *Ahaṁ Idaṁ* "I am this whole universe." It is also called the seed of the nectar or अमृतबीज *Amṛta bīja*. The letter Sa indicates satisfaction, happiness, and is uttered automatically when one is very happy. The final experience is प्राणबीज - *Prāṇabīja* – seed of Life force of Shiva, which is Shakti. It is represented by the last letter ह *Ha*. It is also called अनाहत *Anāhata* meaning automatic, without striking, a sound which cannot be recited.

This completes the description of the cycle of words – the theory of alphabet or मातृकाचक्र - *Mātṛkācakra* and associated shaktis, which make a common individual into a bound creature. The *Mātṛkācakra* denotes, as described in the above table, the subjective world, from "Ya to Ha," the cognitive world of the "Ca group"(चवर्ग) representing the subtle senses like smell, and the "Pa group" (पवर्ग) representing the subtle body, ego, etc., or *Puryaṣṭaka* and *Prakriti* and *Purusha*, and the objective world of the "Ka group" (क वर्ग) representing the gross elements – earth, etc. The "Ṭa group" (ट वर्ग) represents the organs of action and the "Ta group" (त वर्ग) represents the organs of perception. We live in the objective world. But how can we reconcile all the three worlds as one and the same? That is the secret of *Mātṛkācakra*. This secret of *Mātṛkācakra* is now being revealed.

Secret of Mātṛkācakra - the wheel of words or Theory of Alphabet -

The letters *Aham* (*A* + *Ha*) and *Kṣa* (*Ka* + *Sa*) are called "*Pratyāhāra*" in Sanskrit, meaning dissolution, or comprehension of totality in one word. The word Aham – includes the entire subjective and objective universe starting from the letter A – Shiva uniting with *Ha* – Shakti into a point '*ṁ*' the *Anusvāra*. It is the perception of the universal I, or '*Ahaṁ Parāmarśa*' in Sanskrit. It is the supreme mantra of Shaivism. The letter *Kṣa* represents another pratyahara - the union of the objective universe starting from the grossest object, *Ka* with the most subtle object, *Sa* – the seed of the nectar – *Amṛta bīja*. The letter *Kṣa* is also called *kuṭabīja* indicating union of two shaktis.

Actually the *Kuṇḍalinī Śakti* or the bliss of 'I am' consciousness of Shiva is the real actor. She generates the three letters from *Ānand Shakti* - letter *Ā*, *Icchā Shakti* – letter *I*, *Jñāna Shakti* – letter *U*, and from them the entire remaining universe - of letters *Ṛ* to *Kṣa* as discussed above. The Guru bestows grace on the seeker, awakening the seeker's Kundalini shakti, the "I Am" consciousness experience inherent in the five fold state of Shiva, viz.: 1. the heart of Shiva - the objective universe, 2. the heart of the body – meaning the all pervasive awareness – or consciousness of each individual body (not the organ called heart), due to which even an ant crawling on a foot is felt, 3. the heart of sound – *Nāda* which naturally occurs as the root of all sounds, 4. the supreme Self – Universal Consciousness and 5. the supreme *Śunya* "Void."

The *Siddhamrita Tantra* says that whatever is said in daily life by one who understands the reality of the *Mātṛkācakra* becomes divine, and such a one is freed from the bondage of life and death. The Guru who bestows this oneness on the disciple is Shiva Himself and not a human being.

Means to experience the secret of the MatrikaChakra

The Guru bestows the secret of the Matrikachakra on the disciple through his/her grace, which comes in the form of awakening the Kundalini by word, touch, look or thought. Often, the word is a mantra, made potent through his/her own experience. Sometimes words are instructions to meditate or perform a specific action, never for the person him/herself but for the benefit of fellow beings. and sometimes through silence alone.

Thirty-six principles	क्रिया Kriyā Action	ज्ञान Jñāna Knowledge
Five Gross Elements	Pṛthvi Earth	Jala Water
चित् Cit आनंद Ānand [1]Vowels अ A आ Ā	क Ka	ख Kha
Five Subtle Elements Energies – इच्छा Icchā Vowels इ I ई Ī	Gandha Smell च Ca	Rasa Taste छ Cha
Five Organs of action	Upastha Procreation	Pāyu Excretion
Vowels ऋ Ṛ, ॠ Ṝ	ट Ṭa	ठ Ṭha
Five Organs of Perception Vowels ऌ ḷ ॡ ḹ	Grhāṇa Nose त Ta	Rasanā Tongue थ Tha
Five Internal Organs	Mānas Mind	Buddhi Intellect
Energy – ज्ञान Jñāna Vowels उ U ऊ Ū	प Pa	फ Pha
Six coverings of Maya consonants – Ca, Ṭa, Ta,Ta-Pa respectively generate these semivowels	Kāla and Kalā - Time and Limited creativity य Ya	Vidyā - Limited knowledge र Ra
Four pure elements - Blooming of the self	Śuddhavidyā - Pur Knowledge "I"- "This" separate	Iśwara Ruler "Thisness" predominant in "I"ness
consonants – Ca, Ṭa, Ta, respectively generate the first three 'sibilants.'	श Śa	ष Ṣa

[1] *Parātriṁśikā* – by Abhinava Gupta – Hindi Tr. by Prof. Nilkaṇṭha Guruṭu, Published by Motilal Banarsidass, New Delhi, India, discusses the formation of these letters, p. 298

इच्छा Icchā Will	आनन्द Ānand Bliss	चित् Cit Consciousness	Shakti
Agni Fire	Vāyu Air	Ākāsh Space	
ग Ga	घ Gha	ङ Gṅa	माहेशी - Māheśī
Rūpa Form ज Ja	Sparsha Touch झ Jha	Shabda Hearing ञ Yṅa	ब्राह्मी - Brāḥmī
Pada Feet	Pāṇī Hands	Vāk Speech	
ड Ḍa	ढ Ḍha	ण Ṇa	कौमारी – Kaumārī
Cakṣu Eyes द Da	Tvak Skin ध Dha	Śrotra Ears न Na	वैष्णवी - Vaiṣṇavī
Ahaṅkār Ego (objective)	Prakṛti Nature	Puruṣa Ego (subjective)	
ब Ba	भ Bha	म Ma	ऐन्द्री - Aindrī
Niyati and Rāga – Place, Attachment ल La	Māyā - llusion of Individuality व Va		याम्या - Yāmyā
Sadaśiva-"I"ness in "Thisness"	Śakti – "I" ness–Vimarṣa		
स Sa	ह Ha		चामुण्डा - Cāmuṇḍā

First we will see the meaning of a few famous mantras. Then we will see various centering techniques or meditations.

The meaning of a few mantras according to the MatrikaChakra:

Here are the meanings of some mantras bestowed by Gurus on their disciples

1. Aum or Om consists of A (अ), U (उ) , M (म). A is Anuttara Shiva, U is Jnana Shakti, M is the individual. There are two more parts of *Bindu, nāda* which are not written. There are many meanings described in *Upanishads* and earlier. Thus literally, AUM is the knowledge of Shiva descending into an individual.

2. 'Aham' is the mantra of the perception of the Universal I, is the supreme mantra as seen earlier.

3. 'Ma-ha-a' is another great mantra that signifies the ascent of individual into Shakti and Anuttara Shiva – Pure Consciousness since Ma stands for subjective individual, Ha – for Shakti and A – for Anuttara Shiva.

4. 'Soham' – the letters sa-ha-ṁ form the mantra 'Soham.' The 'amrit bija' + 'prana bija' + 'anusvar' are the three letters, indicating the perception that Sa - 'I am this Universe,' Ha – or that which goes on automatically - 'Shakti' uniting into one point 'm.' This mantra cannot be uttered by mouth. It goes on automatically as a creature breathes – 'Sa is ingoing breath and Ha outgoing breath.' Sometimes it is described as 'Sa is outbreath and Ha is inbreath.' When a Guru initiates a disciple into this mantra, the disciple experiences the power of the mantra, the heat of the breath and gets hooked into it as described by saints like Jnaneshwar. There is a modern saint known as Mandodari Mata in Maharashtra, who is a cobbler by profession, who does not know how to write, who received the mantra from a Guru, and who has spontaneously dictated a book, "*So 'ham Bhāvāne Brahma-Sakṣātkār*"[80] – "Realizing the Self by feeling or 'being' So 'ham" in Marathi, extolling the transforming effects of this mantra. She says, "There is no other

[80] *So 'ham Bhāvāne Braḥma-Sākṣātkār* – Mandodari Mata, Redkar, Ultra CoOp Hsg. Soc, Lt. Gupte Road, Mahim, Mumbai 400 016, India, 1994.

practice comparable to Soham. It arises out of Kundalini Shakti, which can be awakened only by Guru's grace."

5. The mantra "*Sauḥ*" – made of '*Sa*' '*Au*' and '*ḥ*' represents 'I am this universe,' 'subjective manifestation of the universe' and 'Shakti Visarga.' Again this mantra cannot be recited. When one is aware of the 'Sauh' one understands that the universe is expansion of oneself. It is also known as "Prāsāda" mantra, meaning the mantra that bestows the elevated state which is full of bliss.

6. The mantra, *Oṁ Namaḥ Śivāya*, is called the five syllable mantra *Na* + *Maḥ* + *Śi* + *Va* + *Ya* regarded as the gross form of the five component mantra AUM. The great Vedantic teacher Shankaracharya has written a beautiful hymn consisting of five stanzas. Swami Kashikanand Giriji [1998] has written and published a book containing a commentary on the hymn. He has referred to Vedanta and Kashmir Shaivism for the interpretations. Each of the letters in the mantra represents the light of Consciousness - Shiva. (Sw. Kashikananda, 43)

The letter 'Na' represents consciousness with awareness – Spanda which is like sinusoidal movement of a cobra.

'Ma' represents Purusha – subjective individual ego as per the chart given earlier. 'Ma' is regarded as Jnana Ganga – jnana shakti (as described in the title of the row of the table) - in the individual akin to the river '*Mandākinī*,' slowly meandering river Ganges.

'Śi' stands for Shiva, who bestows liberation by giving pure knowledge (*Śuddha Vidyā*) of Gauri – Shiva's wife Shakti - who is all knowledge without any taint, or pure knowledge like – कर्पूरगौर *Karpūra gaura* - whiteness like camphor - an epithet of Shiva.

'Va' represents the maya creating individuality as per the chart, which is overcome by bringing mind, intellect and all sense organs under control and possessing divine wealth as *Sage Vaśiṣṭha* or *Vasiṣṭha* set an example. The first word *Vaśiṣṭha* means the sage controlled his senses, and the second word *Vasiṣṭha* means he possessed the divine wealth of six types – *tapas* – penance, *śhama* – calmness in the presence of disturbing events, *damana* – steadfast mind without modifications – perturbations, *titikṣā* - forbearance (the sage had forbearance of watching his sons being killed by Vishvamitra.) – *śraddhā* - trust/conviction in the Divinity, *samādhān* – contentedness. *Vasishtha* also possessed the wealth of knowledge. His work *Yogavāsiṣṭha* was instruction to his disciple Lord Rama and inspired Gauḍapādācārya to write *Māṇḍūkya Kārikā*. Sage Vasishtha regarded the universe – maya's work a long lasting dream and delusion of mind. Vasishtha worshipped Shiva.

'Ya' represents Time and limited creativity in the chart on the alphabet. The letter Y in the mantra represents Yaksha which is derived from the root 'yaj' – to worship. The worship of Shiva pleases Shiva who has given to the devotees not just what they wished but infinitely more. He is also beyond time – who is never born and who is eternal. Thus repeating the mantra will overcome the inherent quality of limitation of time and creativity.

Swami Muktanand Paramhansa, our Guru, made the 'Om Namah Shivaya' mantra well known all over the world. He often emphasized that the mind resides on different petals of the heart chakra, anahata, and experiences different emotions. He talked about the *Ājñā* chakra – with the letters *Ham* and *Kṣam* residing on the two petals. People of all creeds and nationalities repeated the mantra with great benefit. Thousands had experience of awakened Kundalini as soon as they received the Om Namah Shivaya mantra card or in meditation sessions in the Ashrams and Centers whether he was physically present or not. The chanting of the mantra which he did in an unusual vilambit (slow) pace in a group chanting has a calming effect on the individuals and surroundings. In any satsangs when it is chanted that way it produces 'pindrop' silence. Everyone goes into meditation, whether they have chanted it or meditated before or not. Baba Muktanand has extolled in his works the benefits of chanting a mantra and this mantra in particular. The authors are beneficiaries of Baba's grace.

7. Guru Om – This is another mantra that Swami Muktananda spoke in devotee's ears and sometimes chanted aloud. This mantra was given to him by his Guru Bhagawan Nityanand in 1947, and awakened Baba's kundalini, as Baba says in his spiritual autobiography. The *Gurugita* has many verses in praise of Guru. In the chart of the alphabet letters '*G* + *u* + *R* + *u* represent limited knowledge, power of knowledge, fire, and power of knowledge

respectively. The individual's universe though has 'fire-power' looks dark due to ignorance and has the pure power of knowledge but only experiences limited knowledge. Thus the word "Guru" replaces individual limited knowledge and perception of ignorance of an individual by the pure unlimited knowledge which has no trace of limitations. "Aum" as seen earlier bestows the fivefold experience of the Universal Consciousness. This interpretation is consistent with the verse of the *Gurugita*, 'गुकारस्त्वन्धकारश्च रुकारस्तेज उच्यते । अज्ञानग्रासकं ब्रह्म गुरुरेव न संशयः ।।' '*Gukāra-stvandhakāraśca rukāras-teja uccyate, ajñāna-grāsakaṁ Brahma Gurureva na saṁśayaḥ.*' - '*Gu*' represents darkness and '*Ru*' represents effulgence and that Guru is the Self that swallows/destroys the disciple's ignorance.

Repeating the guru-given mantra Guru Om, the seeker is established in the state of Shiva. At least two recent sages, Bhagawan Nityanand and Baba Muktanand, lived in that state and assisted seekers to be established in their state.

A few meditations and centering exercises –

Āṇavopāya in *Shivasutras* has two aphorisms: 'कलादीनां तत्त्वानाम् अविवेको माया। शरीरे संहारः कलानाम् । (३-३,४) - *Kalādīnāṁ tattvānām aviveko māyā. Śarīre saṁhāraḥ kalānām. (3-3, 4)*' Ignorance of the undifferentiated knowledge of the 31 principles from *kalā* to the earth is living in the illusive energy of maya. The body can be regarded as five circles one inside another, related by cause and effect. A circle is the cause of its next outer circle and a cause is subtler than its effect. You must make the different *kalās* (circles) in the body enter back into one another, from gross to subtle. Dissolve mentally or by visualization the effect into its cause. (See *Shiva Sutras*, Sw. Lakshmanjoo, p. 137)

Studying the chart of the alphabet reveals that even though the 31 principles are experienced by an individual as different, they arise out of the five Shaktis of Shiva – consciousness, awareness, will, knowledge, action. The objective and cognitive world of 25 principles is covered by the letters Ka to Pa, which is actually held up by the six coverings – maya and her five limiting principles, represented by the four letters Ya to Va. But when we transcend to the letters Sha to Ha we experience pure knowledge. That gives us the knowledge of the Self. This knowledge and the knower, Self, are not different. Attaining the Self is attaining the knowledge. As Saint Jnaneshwar has said in his work Jnaneshwari, it is not necessary to break an earthen jar into pieces and dissolve it back to mud to see that it is made of earth. We only have to know that it is earthen. Similarly it is not necessary to move away from the body and the universe, it is just enough to know that the principles from the earth to kalā are the Self as it is. At the same time to regard the universe of 31-principles as differentiated from the Self and get enmeshed in the actions of the organs of action and perception is delusion.

That is why to get an understanding we must meditate and practice visualization – only visualization – as follows, which is the purport of the aphorism 3.4. "You must make the different kalās (circles) in the body enter from gross to subtle." There are several dhāraṇās of *VijnanaBhairava* to accomplish this.

कालाग्निना कालपदादुत्थितेन स्वकं पुरम् ।
प्लुष्टं विचिन्तयेदन्ते शान्ताभासस्तदा भवेत् ॥ (श्लोक ५२, धारणा २९)

Kālāgninā kāla-padād-utthitena svakaṁ puram,
Pluṣṭaṁ vicintayed-ante śāntābhāsas-tadā bhavet.
(Śloka 52, Dhāraṇā 29)

Sit at a place in a comfortable position. Visualize that the Kālāgni Rudra *– Universal fire arises from the toe of the right foot. Its flames pervade and burn the entire body. You will feel that all impurities are burned away and you are all peace.*

स्वदेहे जगतो वापि सूक्ष्मसूक्ष्मतराणि च ।
तत्त्वानि यानि निलयं ध्यात्वान्ते व्यज्यते परा॥ (श्लोक ५४, धारणा ३१)

Svadehe jagato vāpi sūkṣma-sūkṣmatarāṇi ca,
Tattvāni yāni nilayaṁ dhyātvānte vyajyate parā.
(Śloka 54, Dhāraṇā 31)

Visualize that the gross principles of the body and universe – Earth, Water, Fire, Air, Space, Senses of organ and action have dissolved into the subtle principles of tanmatras – subtle senses and mind, intellect, ego and nature; the subtle principles into maya and the limiting principles; and the limiting principles and maya into the four pure principles – shuddhavidya, Ishwara, Sadashiva and Shakti; and the four pure principles into the Self. This results into the experience of Parāśakti.

This is called '*Ātmavyāpti*' – fusion into the Self or Consciousness.

भुवनाध्वादिरूपेण चिन्तयेत्क्रमशोऽखिलम् ।
स्थूलसूक्ष्मपरस्थित्या यावदन्ते मनोलयः ॥ (श्लोक ५६, धारणा ३३)

Bhuvanādhvādirupeṇa cintayet-kramaśo 'khilam,
Sthūla-sūkṣma-parasthityā yāvadante manolayaḥ.
(Śloka 56, Dhāraṇā 33)

There are three sets of *Vācya* – subjective and *Vācaka* - objective aspects of the universe. Each of them is called adhvā, path or course, and one more subtle than the previous. At the differentiated or *bheda* level there is pada and bhuvana, where the words and their objects are manifest. At the intermediate – madhyama level – or *bhedābheda* level there is mantra and tattva, where the differentiation exists at the thought level but the separation has not actually taken place, and at the non-differentiated *pashyanti* - *abheda* level there is *varṇa* and *kalā*, where subjective and objective exists only as potential. As one contemplates at this level one reaches the state where the mind completely dissolves into the Universal Divine Consciousness.

अस्य सर्वस्य विश्वस्य पर्यन्तेषु समन्ततः ।
अध्वप्रक्रियया तत्त्वं शैवं ध्यात्वा महोदयः ॥ (श्लोक ५७, धारणा ३४)

Asya sarvasya viśvasya paryanteṣu samantataḥ,
Adhva-prakriyayā tattvaṁ śaivaṁ dhyātvā mahodayaḥ.
(Śloka 57, Dhāraṇā 34)

The entire universe on all sides, both objective and subjective aspects, should be contemplated as the Shiva – Supreme Consciousness - principle (instead of step-by-step as in the previous dharana). This is called '*Shivavyāpti.*' Then the universe will appear to the devotee as Shiva Himself and not as a universe. Then the statement made at the beginning of the discussion on the verse will be experienced as true. That statement is now repeated again as follows.

We know that the words really are very transparent and cannot hide the Self. The Self we want to experience is available right now right here, without any effort, without doing really anything. It is all that we are. It is all what we see, smell, hear, taste and touch. There is no time to waste in searching.

To conclude we repeat the song which is credited to Saint Tukaram, and is heard in the movie on him.

आधी बिज एकले. बिज अंकुरले, रुप वाढले.
एका बीजापोटी तरु कोटी कोटी, जन्म घेत सुमनेफळे.
व्यापुनि जगतां तूहि अनंता ! बहुविध रुपे घेसी, परी अंति ब्रह्म एकले.

Ādhī bija ekale. Bija aṅkurale, rupa vāḍhale.
Ekā bījāpoṭī taru koṭī, janma gheta sumane-phaḷe.
Vyāpuni jagatāṅ tūhi Anaṅtā!
Bahuvidha rupe ghesī, parī aṅtī Braḥma ekale.

Before anything there was one seed.
The seed sprouted and form grew.
One seed bore millions of trees that bore flowers and fruits.
Similarly, O fathomless Lord!
Pervading the universe, You also take myriads of forms.
But finally You, the Self, remain the only One.

Sadgurunath Maharaj ki Jay.

VERSES 46, 47 AND 48
SHAKTI AND KRIYASHAKTI

परामृतरसापायस्तस्य यः प्रत्ययोद्भवः ।
तेनास्वतन्त्रतामेति स च तन्मात्रगोचरः ॥४६॥

46. *Parāmṛta-rasāpāyas-tasya yaḥ pratyayodbhavaḥ*
Tenā-svatantratāmeti sa ca tanmātragocaraḥ.

स्वरूपावरणे चास्य शक्तयः सततोत्थिताः ।
यतः शब्दानुवेधेन न विना प्रत्ययोद्भवः ॥४७॥

47. *Svarūpāvaraṇe cāsya śaktayaḥ satatothitāḥ*
Yataḥ śabdānuvedhena na vinā patyayodbhavaḥ.

सेयं क्रियात्मिका शक्तिः शिवस्य पशुवर्तिनी ।
बन्धयित्री स्वमार्गस्था ज्ञाता सिद्ध्युपपादिका ॥४८॥

48. *Seyaṁ kriyātmikā śaktiḥ Śivasya paśuvartinī*
Bandhayitrī svamārgasthā jñātā siddhyupapādikā.

भट्टकल्लटः– परामृतरसात् स्वरूपात् अपायः प्रच्युतिः, तस्य यः प्रत्ययोद्भवो विषयदर्शने स्मरणोदयो यतः, तेन पुरुषोऽस्वतन्त्रताम् असर्वगत्वं च प्राप्नोति, स च प्रत्ययः तन्मात्रगोचरो रूपाद्यभिलाषात्मकः ॥४६॥

स्वरूपस्य स्वभावस्याच्छादने चास्य पुरुषस्य शक्तयो ब्राह्म्याद्याः पूर्वमुक्ता याः, ताः सततम् उद्युक्ताः । यतः शब्दरहितस्य प्रत्ययस्य ज्ञानस्य नास्त्येव कस्यचिदुद्भवः॥ ४७॥

सा चेयं क्रियास्वभावा भगवतः पशुवर्तिनी शक्तिः । यदुक्तम् –
न सा जीवकला काचित् सन्तानद्वयवर्तिनी ।
व्याप्त्री शिवकला यस्यामधिष्ठात्री न विद्यते ॥

इति । सैव च बन्धकारणम् अज्ञाता, ज्ञाता सा च पुनः परापरसिद्धिप्रदा भवति पुंसाम् ।।४८।।

BhaṭṭaKallaṭaḥ - 46. Parāmṛta-rasāt svarūpāt apāyaḥ pracyutiḥ, tasya yaḥ pratyayodbhavo viṣaya-darśane smaraṇodayo yataḥ, tena puruṣo 'svatantratām asarvagatvaṁ ca prāpnoti, sa ca pratyayaḥ tanmātra-gocaro rūpādyabhilaṣātmakaḥ.

47. Svarūpasya svabhāvasyācchādane cāsya puruṣasya śaktayo Brāḥmyādyāḥ pūrvam-uktā yāḥ, tāḥ satatam udyuktāḥ. Yataḥ śabda-rahitasya pratyayasya jñānasya nāstyeva kasyacidudbhavaḥ.

48. Sā ceyaṁ kriyā-svabhāvā Bhagavataḥ paśuvartinī śaktiḥ. Yaduktam -
'Na sā jīvakalā kācit santāna-dvaya-vartinī
Vyāptrī śiva-kalā yasyām-adhiṣṭhātrī na vidyate.'

Iti. Saiva ca bandhakāraṇam ajñātā, jñātā sā ca punaḥ parāpara-siddhi-pradā bhavati puṁsām.

46. If thoughts based on the sensory experiences develop in a person's mind, those thoughts prevent the person from merging with the Supreme Nectar. Then the person experiences bondage and experiences only the subtle senses.

BhattaKallata: 46. The person whose mind dwells on the memories of the perception of worldly objects remains far from merging in the Supreme Nectar of one's own nature. That individual acquires restrictions and limitations. He gets only the experience of the pure senses, whose nature is attraction for the objects of sight, etc., that are only momentary.

47. This person's shaktis are always active in covering one's own nature. Without the fascination for words (related to objects of five senses), the worldly thoughts do not arise.

BhattaKallata: 47. The individual's shaktis, such as Brāhmī which have been mentioned in a previous verse, are always intent on covering the individual's own nature and own being. This is because they cannot arise without the delusive knowledge generated by words (where these shaktis rule) related to the worldly sensory objects.

48. This Matrika Shakti is the Energy of Action (Kriya Shakti) of Shiva, which resides in the creature creating bondage; but when directed towards the Self, and when Its nature is understood, bestows various siddhis (powers).

BhattaKallata: 48. That Matrika Shakti, the Shakti of Shiva, has an active nature, and resides in creatures. As it is said in the following verse –

> *There is no 'jīva kalā' – movement of creatures, which has two children – one of knowledge (three causal instruments - mind, intellect and ego) and the other of action (eleven physical instruments – five senses of perception, five of action and prana – the individual life force, or individual consciousness) - which is not presided by all pervasive 'Śiva kalā' – movement of Shiva.*
>
> *When she is not understood by individuals, she creates bondage, but when understood she becomes the bestower of worldly and divine siddhis (powers).*

VERSE 46 describes how *āṇava mala* develops. This gives rise to the experience of *māyīva mala* as described in Verse 47 and that leads to *kārma mala* as discussed in Verse 48. The three verses together indicate how both bondage and liberation reside in the mental faculty of the individual. BhattaKallata reminds us in his commentary that when we become aware of the real underlying moving energy we experience that energy; but when unaware its manifestations throw us into the fetters of duality.

VERSE 46

A person looking at a movie is so absorbed in the scene that he/she forgets the existence of the underlying screen. An individual being looks at the world of forms perceptible to senses, ruminates over ideas confined to these objects, and is unaware of That which exists as the warp and woof, which is all-knowing, all-pervading, and all-powerful. Ideas, clothed in words, regarding the world, the person's functions, etc., and also the concepts described in various books about the creator, about the Universal Self or religions, as well as the daily limited use of talents and knowledge, bounded in the space-time realm, likewise create more ideas which are limited. Thus a person becomes conditioned and starts experiencing in his/her day-to-day life *āṇavamala* – limitation in creativity, love, and life. This leads to forgetting the unbounded, ever-present bliss that makes a person function in the first place. If the mind is occupied in paying constant attention to ideas and limited knowledge – what it has already known, then the mind experiences what accompanies such attention: emotions of fear, anger, jealousy, desire, diffidence or overconfidence, instead of experiencing constantly arising bliss. It is like paying attention to the waves and foam, rather than to their essential nature, which is water. By the rise of such ideas an individual loses independence. As long as there is a habit of awareness of differences – भिन्नवेद्यप्रथा - *Bhinnavedya-prathā* – one remains bound. In short, Verse 46 says that a person becomes a prisoner of ideas, which are produced out of senses and day-to-day experiences. Oh! What a sacrifice a human being makes by remaining unaware of his own Self!

The aspirant first has to forcibly extricate one's mind from thinking mundane ideas by taking some time out daily, in increasing lengths, from paying constant attention to the world, to contemplate the innate Nature. Then the person has the firm understanding that तस्माच्छब्दार्थचिन्तासु न सावस्था न या शिवः। भोक्तैव भोग्यभावेन सदा सर्वत्र संस्थितः ।।स्पंद २८।। - *Tasmācchabdārtha-cintāsu na sāvasthā na yā Śivaḥ. Bhoktaive bhogya-bhāvena sadā sarvatra saṁsthitā.* (Spanda 28) "Whether it is a word, thought or object there is no state which is not Shiva – Consciousness. The enjoyer alone remains everywhere always as the enjoyment." Then one is freed.

Verse 46 uses the word प्रत्ययोद्भवः '*pratyayodbhavaḥ*' meaning 'born of sensory experience' as a cause of Āṇava Mala or the mental impurity of being 'small.' The independence of Shiva gets conditioned by the power of maya so that Shiva, as the individual, doubts his/her innate perfection and independence. This doubt gives rise to two things. First the individual's awareness of the Self's independence is destroyed, and secondly the individual forgets the Self's independence of action or omnipotence – all power, capability to do anything. With constant attention to sensory perceptions, an individual regards the experience of the world as the reality and doubts the real, Consciousness, regarding it as unreal or unimportant. This is regarding oneself as small.

Due to the conditioning of maya, the 24 objective principles of the world become perceptible. As per Prof. Gurutu, the recent Hindi commentator, in the 46th verse the words *parāmṛta-rasa*, *pratyayodbhava* and *tanmātragochara* indicate all the thirty six principles in a nutshell.

The word परामृत - '*Parāmṛta*' meaning the sublime immortal, refers to the first principle – the light of Consciousness, Shiva the Supreme Self, Prakash. रस - '*Rasa*' – Its nectar refers to the second principle - Its spanda shakti, power of vibration or 'I AM' - awareness – Vimarsh.

Parāmṛta also refers to the next three principles – Sadāshiva – 'I am this universe,' Īśwara – 'This universe is my expression. It is not an illusion, it is my expression' and Śuddhavidyā – 'I am Shiva, this universe is in duality.' These are still pure principles.

The word प्रत्ययोद्भव - '*pratyayodbhava*' includes all the six principles generating the universe – i.e., maya and its five confining jackets: kalā - limited creativity, possessing only certain talents; vidyā - limited knowledge; rāga – attachment or a sense of incompleteness; kāla – limitation of time; niyati – limitation of place. These five principles form a cover over the first five pure independent principles, consequently causing the loss of independence. This is the birth of the individual, starting with the twelfth and thirteenth principles: puruṣa – the subjective individual; and prakṛti – nature consisting of three gunas: sattva, rajas and tamas.

The word तन्मात्रगोचर - '*Tanmātra-gocara*' in the verse indicates the perception of the universe, starting with the 14th through 16th principles: the individual's inner instruments or 'antaḥkaraṇa.' The first principle among them, ahamkār or ego, arises as limited consciousness, and looks at the world as an object. It assumes the doership/ownership of all actions and emotions. As soon as we get up from our sleep we first become aware of this 'I' and then the world of sense objects appears. Then arises the individual's power of selection, buddhi – intellect, which decides and passes the judgment: 'This should be done, that should not be done.' 'This is good, that is bad.' The 'manas' or mind principle comes next, whose function is to create thoughts: 'I have these things to do today.' 'I will do this. I will go there. I have done this and that.' The five senses of perception, 'jñānendriyas' (which are not the actual organs such as nose, tongue, eyes, ears, skin but their respective powers, the functions of smelling, tasting, seeing, hearing, touching) open their shop and start their 'business.' These are the 17th - 21st principles. Then the individual uses the five senses of action, the 'karmendriyas' of speaking (throat, tongue and lips), grasping (hands), moving from place to place (feet), excreting (anus), urinating and having sex (penis or vagina). Again, unless these senses are driven by the directing power of the ego, mind and intellect, the corresponding organs cannot function. These are 22nd – 26th principles. The ten organs described as the 17th through 26th principles carry out their functions in the fivefold subtle sense world of smell, taste, form, touch and sound. These are not actually smell, etc. but are abstractions of these senses. These are the five principles listed as 27th to 31st. While functioning in the subtle sense world, the physical actions take place in the gross world of the 32nd through 36th principles of earth, water, light, air, and space, five universal, primordeal principles. Thus the 46th verse describes the entire set of 36 principles.

Knowing these 36 principles, it is up to the individual at the stage of the twelfth principle of 'Purusha' either to tear down the veil created by maya and the five kanchukas (coverings), and to establish himself or herself in the first five principles of freedom and bliss while looking at the universe; or to look at the remaining 24 principles of the universe from prakriti - nature alone and be baffled. As long as one is aware of one's body as separate from the Self, the universe also exists and appears separate.

There is a centering exercise in the *VijñānaBhairav* to abandon the effect of senses.

इन्द्रियद्वारकं सर्वं सुखदुःखादिसङ्गमम् ।
इतीन्द्रियाणि संत्यज्य स्वस्थः स्वात्मनि वर्तते ॥ (श्लोक १३६, धारणा १११)

Itīndriyāṇi sarvaṁ sukha-duḥkhādi-saṅgamam
itindriyāṇi saṅtyajya svasthaḥ svātmani vartate.
(Verse 136, Dhāraṇā 111)

All perceived through the sense-doors
is confluence of pleasure and pain.
Hence abandoning the senses
established in the Self one must remain.

The activities of the senses lead us to the pleasures of the world. But along with pleasure, sorrow also comes. Instead of getting the mind embroiled in the turmoil of these waves, the mind with the help of intellect should detach itself from the senses. Then one remains calm, resting in the Self. The *Bhagavad Gita* Chapter 2, verse 58 gives an example of a tortoise: "Just as a tortoise brings all its limbs in under its shell at will, the person who brings all the senses and his intellect inward is steady." As per the commentator Jnaneshwar, a tortoise that is happy spreads all its limbs and if it wants it can contract the limbs. Similarly, the person who is a master of senses, has complete control over his senses. Commenting on the next verse of the *Gita* (Verse 59), Jnaneshwar says that even if a person controls all the senses except the sense of taste, the desire for objects surrounds the person in thousands of ways, just as a tree trimmed of foliage but watered at the roots is not destroyed. But one cannot live without taste.[81] Then O Arjuna! When a seeker gets a direct experience of the Self, the seeker can even easily control the sense of taste. After the direct experience of 'I am That,' 'I-am-the-body' feelings are destroyed and the senses forget their objects.

Describing the impending disasters and total destruction from letting the difficult-to-control senses run rampant in the *Bhagavad Gita* verses 60-63, the Lord says in Verse 64, "If a person, whose mind is subdued and senses are under control, moves without attachment and hatred among the objects of sense, that person's mind attains happiness." Jnaneshwar comments on this verse that even if the senses seem to be indulging in their objects, the objects do not harm such a person. Just as the sun in the sky through its rays of light touches all objects on the earth but does not get contaminated by the association, so the one who is detached from sense objects, established in the bliss of the Self, devoid of desire and anger, not seeing anything other than the Self even in the sense objects, for that person what are sense objects and what harm can they cause? Thus the only choice an individual has is to turn the mind within through various methods and meditate on the Self.

Verse 46 describes the mind of the individual. In a similar manner, the first aphorism of Āṇavopāya of *Shiva Sutra* also states the individual's state of mind. "आत्मा

[81] Right here there is a purposeful logical gap, because for the one whose mind is wallowing in sense pleasures, the covering is so dense, that there is not even a desire to look for anything else. But for the seeker, who is making a conscious effort to improve him/herself, Guru's grace pulls the seeker out of the shell of the five kanchukas – confining jackets – and gives the divine taste of the inner treasures. It is up to the seeker to practice the Guru's directions with determination to be established in the sublime experience.

चित्तम् - *Ātmā cittam*" The root cause of Anava mala is that the individual being feels that he or she is the mind saturated with the impressions of sensual pleasures. Here the word Atma does not mean the Self. The word is the derivation of the root 'अत - ata' meaning that which moves constantly. 'अतति इति आत्मा - *atati iti Ātmā*' – "It moves in the cycle of birth and death," by neglecting the knowledge of one's own real nature. Whatever knowledge the individual has is differentiated, causing bondage. Hence the second aphorism says 'ज्ञानम् बन्धः - *Jñānaṁ bandhaḥ*' meaning 'Knowledge is bondage.' Swami Lakshman Joo describes very clearly how this happens. This knowledge is found in the three internal organs (principles 14, 15, 16) – ego, intellect and mind. The mind creates thoughts as to what object is to be enjoyed. The intellect understands the decision and makes efforts for the enjoyment of the object. Finally ego as the enjoyer attaches itself by directing the five senses of cognition and five senses of action toward the object. These three intellectual acts are one with prakriti (nature) through the three qualities – *sukha* - happiness as the *sāttvic* quality of mind, *duḥkha* - sorrow as the *rājasic* quality, and *moha* infatuation – delusion as the *tāmasic* quality. Entangled in the three kinds of differentiated knowledge, the result is what is implied in the first aphorism - constant movement of the individual.

The third aphorism of the *Āṇavopāyaḥ* explains how this happens: कलादीनां तत्त्वानामविवेको माया । *Kalādīnāṁ tattvānām aviveko māyā*. Ignorance of the thirty-one principles starting from *kalā* - limited creativity -- causes one to remain bound in illusion. How does the individual ward off this illusion? The conscious effort towards that goal, which is called *sādhanā*, starts from the fourth aphorism – शरीरे संहारः कलानाम् । - *Sharīre saṁhāraḥ kalānām* meaning "One must make all the kalās dissolve back one into the other starting from gross to subtle." The word kalā here refers to *Nivṛtti kalā* consisting of the Earth principle, *Pratiṣṭhā Kalā* consisting of the 24 principles from water to Prakṛti (nature), *Vidyā kalā* consisting of māyā and her five kancukas – limiting principles, *Śāntā kalā* consisting of the four principles from Shakti to Shuddha vidya, and *Śāntātītā kalā* – Shiva himself; in other words the thirty-six principles discussed earlier. Note that Purusha, the subjective individual which is the principle in the twelfth rank, is not bundled with any of the kalās. It is identical to Shiva. This transcendence from gross to subtle is to be done using the fifth, sixth and seventh aphorisms, by paying attention to the breath at various centers in the body, withdrawing the attention from the sensory world and centering it on the breath, practicing

āsan - posture – holding the awareness at the center of two breaths,

prāṇāyām - control of breath – making the breath subtle and being aware of

the inner vibration, which also gives the experience of divine sounds,
pratyāhār - weaning the mind from the world and inner sounds and directing it toward the Self,
dhyān – meditation, quieting all sounds and going beyond them,
dhāraṇā - holding awareness of consciousness of Shiva constantly and
samādhi - experiencing the universal consciousness of Shiva not only within but also in all activities.

This is described in the *Lakṣmī Kaulārṇava Tantra* 8.11-8.18.

The consequences of remaining established in the Universal Self are described from the eighth aphorism: "His waking state is another form of consciousness." This will be elaborated in the discussion of Verse 48. This is the meaning of the centering exercise in the Dharana 111.

One day a seeker came to Swami Muktanand Paramhans, and said, (Sw. Muktanand Paramhans, 54) "How small we are, and how great the Lord is. Our shakti is so limited and that of the Lord is unlimited. We are a well and the Lord is a sea. What should be done for a well to become a sea? I cannot understand whether the individual soul is only a part or complete." Baba replied:

Baba: As long as the individual self thinks itself to be a part, it remains a part. But when these attributes are gone, it becomes complete. If a well wants to become a sea, it has to merge in the sea, in the sense that the attribute of a well has to be destroyed, just as when a jar breaks its inside space and outside space become one space. The truth is that the space inside a jar and outside is one space. It is already merged with space. Similarly, the individual self is already complete.

Seeker: My intellect cannot go beyond the thought: 'An individual self is only a part of the Self.'

Baba: When your jar breaks then your intellect will understand this matter. Truly speaking, your question is itself unscientific, because you are al ready perfect. The Supreme Self is always available. But because of lack of knowledge It appears to be unattained. This is just like your wearing a necklace of jewels and then searching for it outside. When you learn that the necklace is already around your neck, then would you say, "I found the necklace which was lost" or "The necklace was never lost?"

In the rope-snake illustration of Vedanta a similar thing is said. In that illustration it is 'disappearance of what was not there.' You must decide whether the snake is destroyed, or that which did not exist was destroyed.

It is a surprise that the one who is already free wants to become free. The one who is awake needs to be awakened. Consciousness never changes, then how can you change? You are what you are. Get rid of the idea that you are separate from the Supreme Self. You are, of course, perfect. The wrong understanding that "I am imperfect" which arose due to ignorance regarding the Supreme Self will go away by the knowledge of the Supreme Self. Just as the disease arising from harmful food is cured by wholesome food, what arose due to lack of knowledge will go away by knowledge.

Baba's instruction is also given in various scriptures. In the *Bhagavat*, Chapter 11, the Lord says:

बद्धो मुक्तः इति व्याख्या गुणतो मे न वस्तुतः ।
गुणस्य मायामूलत्वात् न मे मोक्षो न बन्धनम् ।।११,१।।

Baddho muktaḥ iti vyākhā guṇato me na vastutaḥ
Guṇasya māyāmūlatvāt na me mokṣo na bandhanam.
(11, 1)

'I am bound' and 'I am liberated' are only definitions. They happen only because of qualities and are not a fact. The qualities arise from maya. But for me there is neither bondage nor liberation.

Tukaram Maharaj says in one abhang, "सारी जाली मेली लटके वचन । बद्धमुक्त शीण तुका म्हणे ।। - "*Sārī jāli meli laṭake vacana, baddha-mukta śīṇa Tukā mhaṇe.*" "In a game of chess, to say that a pawn died or is alive is only a false statement. Tukaram says bondage or freedom is likewise unnecessary lethargy." In another abhang, he asks, "मुक्त कासया म्हणावे, बंधन ते नाही ठावे ।" "*Mukta kāsayā mhaṇāve, bandhana te nāhī ṭhāve.*" "What should I call liberated, when I don't know what bondage is?"

Jnaneshwar Maharaj describes in the eighth chapter of his work *Amṛtānubhav – Nectar of Experiences* entitled *Jñānakhaṇḍan – Destruction of Knowledge*, how the consequence of knowledge destroying ignorance is that knowledge itself gets destroyed. He says, "My Guru, Nivṛtti, blissfully established me in the Nature of my own Self, that is without knowledge or ignorance, but constant knowledge. That widened my own nature so vastly that it cannot be contained in my own self! I become only 'Itself' – Kaivalya. There are no words to describe our state. That is why the *Upanishads* say 'Not this. Not this.'... Just as there is no darkness in the town of the Sun, how can one even say 'It is light,' since light exists only relative to darkness. When it is dark at night, one needs a light; to take a lamp when it is already daylight is only unnecessary trouble. In the Self which is of the nature of knowledge, both 'unmesh' and 'nimesh' – arising or dissolution – get destroyed."

VERSE 47

Thus all saints and scriptures guarantee that one's own nature is total independence. Yet an individual feels limited for the reasons described in Verse 46. Verse 47 describes how this happens. The feeling of limitation arises due to maya's covering one's own nature so that one becomes aware of differences. Each of the perceptions has words associated with it. Each word has its own associated shakti such as *Brāhmī* described in Verse 45.

There is nothing in the universe which is not associated with a word. Each object is a manifestation of the light of Supreme consciousness, and its associated word is of the nature of awareness – 'I AM.' The key to independence is to grasp the underlying unconditioned consciousness and awareness. The word 'अनुवेध' – *Anuvedha* – meaning 'seeking after' implies that the word seeks after its object.

In the *ShivaSutras*, the third method or '*Āṇavopāyaḥ*' relating to the individual, is given in the 19th aphorism as: 'कवर्गादिषु माहेश्वर्याद्याः पशुमातरः – *Kavargādiṣu Māheṣwaryādyāḥ paṣumātaraḥ*' – "In the world of letters from *Ka* to *Kṣa* the eight presiding goddesses or powers such as Māheśvarī who are the mothers of beasts take control and hold them." The beasts here are ignorant human beings. As per *Mālinī-Vijaya-Tantram* Verses 3.5 through 3.11 it is by Spanda Shakti's power of will, *icchāśakti*, manifesting through the power of knowledge, *jñānaśakti*, and the power of action, *kriyāśakti*, that the universe manifests as the various principles and the Matrika Chakra of 50 letters. The Matrika Chakra consists of 16 vowels and 34 consonants divided into eight groups, presided over by eight goddesses such as *Māheśwarī* and others, as described in the table describing the alphabet in Verse 45. As seen in Verse 45 the power latent in words creates the universe with Consciousness and Bliss as the warp and woof. Words and their objects form the universe. Basically, these goddesses rule over the group of eight: the ego, intellect, mind and the five senses of perception of ignorant bound human beings. The other principles are under the rule of this group of eight. This group of eight in bound beings then rules over the organs of action and sends them after the objects, which are the physical referents of the words.

Words create differentiated knowledge. The message of Verse 47 is brought out also in detail in *Shiva Sutra* 1.4: ज्ञानाधिष्ठानम् मातृका - *Jñānādhiṣṭhānam Mātṛkā* - Matrika Chakra is the Presider over differentiated knowledge. Only the seeker who knows the secret underlying this aphorism, in other words a knower of matrika, the unknown Mother, can understand that as long as the words and objects are separate, such that no organs of action seek after their objects, nothing really happens. The seeker should make every effort not to get into the shackles of worldliness.

In a town there was a young man happily married to a beautiful wife. Once he was introduced to a friend of her wife. The wife's friend's slender body and looks were very attractive. Thoughts (words) about her filled his mind for some time. But he took no action on the thoughts. He did not try to call her, meet her, or delve into the thoughts about her. The result was, as time passed, the thoughts subsided, as clouds in the sky disperse without raining. Thus there was no bondage to the woman friend, no grief for the family, and no complicated life that follows such acts.

To avoid bondage the trick is to watch the thoughts and not indulge in or act on them. Keep the differentiated or worldly knowledge – jnana, and action – kriya (karma) separate by looking at the consequences. This is called 'Viveka' or discrimination in Vedanta. The intellect does this part. Follow the thought into action only if the consequences are beneficial to all, otherwise let the thought disappear without fighting with it. And then again don't get involved with the fruit - success or failure of the action, since there are so many factors that are involved in attaining the goal of action. Practice of discrimination in daily life gives rise to 'Vairāgya' or detachment as called in the Vedanta. Again the intellect plays this part. Discrimination and detachment, called inner treasures by the sages, are necessary qualities required to turn away from the world and its binding sense objects. Adi Shankaracharya in his hymn to the Guru's sandals praises: "विवेक - वैराग्य - निधिप्रदाभ्याम् । *Viveka - vairāgya-nidhi-pradābhyām*." "Guru's sandals bestow the treasures of viveka and vairagya." It is the ego that directs the sense organs of knowledge and action to obtain worldly objects. On one hand the trio of intellect, mind and ego can cause the sense organs to bring together the words and their corresponding objects to limit an individual, and on the other the trio can separate the words and objects, turning the mind inward to be established in the pure bliss, pure free will, pure power of action, and pure knowledge.

Verse 47 – "This person's energies are always active in covering one's own nature. Without the fascination for words (related to objects of five senses), the worldly thoughts do not arise" – contains an inherent antidote to human confinement to limitations! Namely, the logical negation of the conclusion in the verse, thereby refuting the assumptions, which is: "If there are no worldly thoughts, there are no words. And the person's energies do not cover his or her own nature." This indicates that it is the silence of mind, absence of words, that uncovers one's own innate free nature, not the din of thoughts and words.

If we examine the world it is a set of names and forms. If we examine the names then again we are in for a surprise. There is a story which brings out this fact clearly.

There was a saint who lived in a hut outside a town. A seeker liked to be in his company and discuss spirituality. One day he went to the saint's hut, and said, "Maharaj! I want to invite you to my place for dinner. Please come with me in my car. This way I can get some time with you and learn something from you." The saint agreed. The saint was humorous and eloquent. He decided to teach the seeker about the nature of the world, even before starting the trip. He said to the gentleman, "My friend! I don't see your car." The man pointed to his car, and said, "That is my car." The saint insisted that he couldn't see it. The man said, "Is your eyesight all right?" The saint said, "I have a 20/20 vision. I see everything clearly. But I don't see any car." The gentleman walked up to the car, pointed to the windshield, and said, "This is my car." The saint said, "I see some glass; but I don't see any car." The man went to open the door of his car. He said, "Maharaj! This is my car. Please get in." The saint said, "I see a door. But I don't see any car." The man said, "If I cannot prove to you that this is a car, please slap my face." The saint agreed. The seeker showed another part of the car and called it his car, but the saint was equally adamant about teaching him, and kept on identifying it as something else. Finally frustrated, the man said, "Sorry, Maharaj! I couldn't prove the existence of my car. Please slap me." The saint said, "Show me your face." The man pointed to his cheek. The saint said, "This is a cheek! This is not your face." The man pointed to his forehead, and called it his face. The saint said, "This is not your face. This is your forehead." In short, the devotee could not show where his face was and was thoroughly nonplussed. The saint said, "My Friend! Until you prove to me that you have a face, I will not be able to slap you."

He continued, "Just as there is no such thing as a face or a car, so also the so called world which is a conglomeration of names and forms also does not exist. Because of ignorance it seems to exist. Children, spouse, money and everything else appear to exist and make people sometimes happy and sometimes sad, because people do not inquire into the Truth. Only the five elements - earth, water, fire, air and space - are visible as a multitude of colors and designs in the form of these mutable, illusory objects. They are called by various names. Yet, even these five elements are illusory forms of Shiva, Self, Supreme Consciousness. Therefore on the Self, the substratum of all, the creatures and gross world are only superimposed. When one contemplates with a clear and calm mind, only Consciousness the One-without-a-second remains. The so called world independent of the Self vanishes. Therefore to see Consciousness everywhere is true discernment. To see the dual world is not to discern at all." After saying this, the saint and his host got in the car and went for dinner.[82]

There are several dhāraṇās, centering exercises, in the *VijñānaBhairav* that help one to wean oneself away from the world.

अतत्त्वमिन्द्रजालाभमिदं सर्वमवस्थितम् ।
किं तत्त्वमिन्द्रजालस्य इति दार्ढ्याच्छमं व्रजेत् ॥(श्लोकः १३३, धारणा १०८)
आत्मनो निर्विकारस्य क्व ज्ञानं क्व च वा क्रिया ।
ज्ञानायत्ता बहिर्भावा अतः शून्यमिदं जगत् ॥ (श्लोकः १३४, धारणा १०९)

Atattvam-indrajālābham-idaṁ sarvam-avasthitam,

---

[81] Modified from a story by Swami Maheshwaranand Giri – *Pravacan Sudha – Nectar of Discourses* – Verse 17, page 544 Pub: Shanti Mandir, Walden, NY: 2006

Kiṁ tattvam-indrajālasya iti dārḍhyācchamaṁ vrajet.
(Verse 133, Dhāraṇā 108)
Ātmano nirvikārasya kva jñānaṁ kva ca vā kriyā,
Jñānāyattā bahirbhāvā ataḥ śūnyamidaṁ jagat.
(Verse 134, Dhāraṇā 109)

Like a magical spectacle this whole universe is
without any essential reality.
What can be the reality of a magical spectacle?
With this conviction, he attains tranquility.
In the unchangeable Self, how can there be knowledge or activity?
All knowledge is external; therefore this world is a vacuity.

The first of these verses describe the world as a magic show that hence lacks reality. The second says that since the Self has no modifications, there is no knowledge or action in the Self. This is because knowledge and action indicate change. All external objects depend on knowledge and activity. Hence external objects and consequently the world do not exist in the Self. Therefore, the world is void. By contemplating this way, a seeker attains peace.

By knowledge and action in the above, is meant the knowledge and action of the mind, intellect and ego perceived or carried out through senses. They are not the powers of knowledge and action of the Self. These powers are potential energies not dependent on individuality or on ten sense organs or prompted by a sense of difference.

VERSE 48

The 48th verse talks about individual knowledge and action, called *Jīvakalā*, and its relation to Universal knowledge and action, called *Śivakalā*. *Āṇava* mala gives rise to māyiya mala, and both give rise to *kārma* mala. The individual is first created by means of *māyā*, with its nature of three gunas, ego, intellect and mind as explained in Verse 46. Then the individual's knowledge and action are limited or regulated by the five *kancukas* of time, limited knowledge, talent, and attachment arising due to feeling of incompleteness, and of order in time and space, as discussed in Verse 47. We mostly regard maya and her kanchukas as limitations or coverings that deter an individual from experiencing the Self. But we should not have that attitude.

The electrical power generated at a power plant needs to be stepped down using transformers to be of local use for lighting, heating, cooling, ironing, and use in myriad other electrical appliances; likewise, with the four universal pure principles: *Śuddhavidyā, Īṣvara, Sadāśiva*, and its Spanda or *Śakti*, the infinite Universal Self, *Śiva* steps down, descending through maya and its five kanchukas to the individual level, making the individual and a unique 'limited' world and functions appear. The user of electricity never thinks that the power used in the light bulbs and appliances is different from what is generated at the power plant; likewise, it is important for us to regard Maya and the five kanchukas as essential for the Self to express Itself as us and the manifesting universe, but at the same time to recognize that we are in no way different from the Self. But for these essential frills of name and form, the Reality - infinite unchanging universal Self – and the changing world are not different.

The difference between the electric power and the power of Spanda is that the electric power has to be harnessed by humans while the Spanda is independent. It is the only conscious independent creative power, which manifests of its own free will as both kriya-shakti – power of action, and jnana-shakti – power of knowledge. The book *Īśvara-pratyabhijña* describes this Self's power as follows:

> "It is the Creative Power of free will appearing as the dual set knower and known." Due to different forms, place, and order, a variety of actions guided by chronological order, knowers such as the group of eight – mind, ego, intellect, and five senses of perception -- and their corresponding knowns or knowables – as prana, void, colors, jars, happiness-sorrow, etc. – appear by the light of Consciousness. That appearance is the Self's generating power or creative power. It also knows the different created 'knower-known' pairs, and this knowledge of knower-known pairs constantly spontaneously arising is also the Self's creative power."

The creative energy of the Self in the activities "I will expand; I will contract; I will disappear" is the free will nature of the awareness "I Am." All this is only that Principle and there is no order whatsoever.

That independent conscious creative energy has, at the creature level, capabilities of sequencing together various activities of creation, unfolding sequentially. The individual internal desire such as 'I will cook, I have written, I am going to eat' resulting into a corresponding external action is actually the Universal creative power itself. As long as it remains as a mental feeling, there is no chronological order, but as soon as it transforms into external action through the body made of five gross principles it is accompanied by a time-space sequence, and the non-ordered Creative Energy becomes physical and has a certain order. (*Īśvara-pratyabhijñā* and *Vimarṣiṇī* 2.1.8)

Even the modern scientists cannot stop wondering about the spontaneity, order, randomness (free will) and intricacy of nature, when they examine the new galaxies and stars arising from nowhere, observing old stars shrinking into black holes. They agree that the universe is filled with energy, 74% of which they call dark energy, since that is not measurable with their instruments. The only thing they stop short from is calling the energy conscious, the reason being that consciousness is out of the scope of science. Science is in search of truth that is measurable by the senses, thus limiting the scope of research. Consciousness is not measurable and being beyond senses cannot become a theme of science.

Now as we have seen in Verse 45, Matrika Shakti, the power in words, is what is behind the creation of the universe. The 16 vowels *A* to *Aḥ* create the potential universe and the 34 consonants *K* to *Kṣa* create the dynamic virtual manifestation of the universe. It is nothing but a vibration of 'I AM' awareness. The same alphabet, descending from the subtle *Parā* to *Paśyanti* to *Madhyamā* to gross *Vaikharī* level as words and their objects, thereby manifesting the physical universe presided over by the inherent powers as *Brāhmī* and the rest, binds creatures in thoughts of acceptance-rejection and attributes the various sensory actions taking place to the doership of 'I' and 'my body or intellect.' This bondage has been elaborated in earlier verses. Again these words form a logical and tense order.

The last part of Verse 48 describes how when the Matrika Shakti is not known as energy, that energy creates bondage by making the creature experience only the limited sensory world; but when the energy is known, when this true knowledge arises due to some unexpected grace, all activities become only external manifestations of the power of the Self, and 'I' or 'my body or intellect' are not the doers of these manifestations. Thus all the fetters of gross actions fall away on their own. After this experience, Shiva (Self) is experienced in whatever the person does.

Every person experiences painful duality, a play of Lord Shiva who is one-without-another. Swami Prijñānāshram III, [2008] who was the tenth Guru of the Chitrāpur Sāraswat community, accuses Lord Shiva for bringing on this suffering in the following song.

खेळ तुझे जीव घेणे, पाहण्या तू ध्यानमग्न ।
अव्यक्तांशि सख्य तुझे, व्यक्त करी जगी आम्हा ।।ध्रु.।।
प्रतिलेखा आम्ही जाणे, ब्रह्मानन्दी येत विघ्न ।
मायेशि सख्य तुझे, भिन्न माया दावी आम्हा ।।१।।
दुष्ट जग लेणे तुझे रूपे भासि का विच्छिन्न ।
अदृष्टाशि सख्य तुझे कष्टमय दावी आम्हा ।।२।।
कर्ता क्रिया स्वयं होणे, आणीक तू कर्माध्यक्ष ।
कर्त्यापाशि सख्य तुझे सञ्चिताचे ओझे आम्हां ।।३।।
कैंचि देवा ही करणी सांग मी तू का रे भिन्न ।
चक्षुपरी सख्य तुझे मूढ म्हणे गूढ आम्हा ।।४।।

Ref: *Kheḷa tujhe jīva gheṇe, pāhaṇyā tū dhyānamagna*
Avyaktāṅśi sakhya Tujhe, vyakta karī jagī āmhā.
1. *Prati-lekhā āmhī jāṇe, Braḥmānandī yeta vighna*
Māyeśi sakhya Tujhe, bhinna māyā dāvī āmhā
2. *Duṣṭa jaga leṇe Tujhe rūpe bhāsi kā vicchinna*
Adṛṣṭāśi sakhya Tujhe kaṣṭa-maya dāvī āmhā
3. *Kartā kriyā svayaṁ hoṇe, āṇīka tū karmādhyakṣa*
Kartyāpāśi sakhya Tujhe sañcitāce ojhe āmhā
4. *Kaiṅci Devā hī karaṇī sāṅga mī Tū kā re bhinna*
Cakṣuparī sakhya Tujhe mūḍha mhaṇe gūḍha āmhā.

Ref: *Your play is to snatch our life,*
while You seem absorbed in meditation.
Your kinship is with the unmanifest,
while making us in the world manifest.
1. *We know our destiny that becomes*
an obstacle in experiencing the bliss of the Self.
Your friendship is with Maya,
while You show us only an illusion – different maya.
2. *The cruel world adorns You,*
why do you appear to us in distorted forms.
You have kinship with the Invisible,

by which You make arduous to find for us.
3. *You become the doer and the activity,*
and You are in charge of all actions.
Your rapport is with the Doer,
while we carry the burden of accumulated actions.
4. *What kind of doing is this? Tell me why*
You and I are separate.
By keeping Your friendship for namesake,
the dumbfounded says, "You remain a mystery to us."

The *Vijñāna Bhairava* has a centering technique to transcend the duality, to regard the knower and known as one:

ज्ञानप्रकाशकं सर्वं सर्वेणात्मा प्रकाशकः ।
एकमेकस्वभावत्वात् ज्ञानं ज्ञेयं विभाव्यते ॥ (श्लोकः १३७, धारणा ११२)

Jñāna-prakāśakaṁ sarvaṁ sarveṇātmā prakāśakaḥ
Eka-meka-svabhāvatvāt jñānaṁ jñeyaṁ vibhāvyate.
(Verse 137, Dhāraṇā 112)

Knowledge – the light of Self - reveals everything;
Self is revealed by everything.
By this mutually identical nature,
'knowledge and known' should be regarded as 'one thing.'

In the word 'knowledge' is included the knower. Thus the knower (Self) reveals everything, and everything reveals the knower (Self). In the *Śivopādhyāya*, it is said, "What is revealed is not separate from the light of consciousness. That light is not separate from vimarsh - awareness. That vimarsh is none other than 'I AM' awareness. That "I AM" awareness and Consciousness are one and the same." Contemplating that the subject, object and the process of perception are one and the same, one is established in the nature of Bhairava. This is elaborated in Jnaneshwar's work excerpted later on.

Another meaning of the Dharana 112 as per Swami Lakshman Joo is as follows: Knowledge is filled with enlightenment and the knower is also filled with enlightenment. Therefore, you can be enlightened completely by either knowledge or the knower. This is because you will find in knowledge the residence of the knower (Self) and in the knower you will find the residence of knowledge. These are not two different aspects of being, they are only one aspect of being. Knowledge and knower (Self) are, in the real sense, one.

When by the grace of the Lord, we know that knower and known pairs (and the process of knowing) that make up the universe, are one and the same, that "this," meaning the universe of 31 principles and "I," the Self, are one, then there is no bondage. The enlightenment consists of the first five pure principles - *Śuddhavidyā, Īṣvara, Sadāśiva, Śakti* and *Śiva*. Awareness of "this" is always in the mental faculty – mind, intellect and ego. This awareness is a manifestation of 'I AM' awareness – spanda or śakti which is not separate from Shiva.

The *Gurugītā* prescribes daily contemplation at dawn on the Guru's name and form that bestows grace, reassurance, courage, and calm. It reiterates that there is nothing greater than the Guru by the order of Shiva. The three states – waking, dream, deep sleep -- and the fourth that is the substratum - are all Shiva as per His order. By meditating on the Guru in this manner, knowledge arises on its own, and by Guru's grace we experience "I am free." By following the directions of the Guru, we must purify our mind. Whatever temporary pairs of names and forms are perceived by senses, these have to be purged (as separate name-forms). (Verses 95-99) Then it says:

ज्ञेयं सर्वस्वरूपं च ज्ञानं च मन उच्यते ॥
ज्ञानं ज्ञेयसमं कुर्यात् नाऽन्यः पंथा द्वितीयकः ॥ (गुरुगीता १००)

Jñeyaṁ sarva-svarūpaṁ ca, jñānaṁ ca mana uccyate
Jñānaṁ jñeya-samaṁ kuryāt, n'ānyaḥ panthā dvitīyakaḥ.
(Gurugītā 100)

What is to be known is the nature of all,
knowledge is called the mind.
The knowledge and knowable have to be made one.
There is no other path.

In this manner the triad - the knower, the known and the process of obtaining knowledge of the knowable - have to be regarded as the same.The process disappears when the knower and the known become the same, just Being. These statements are not just philosophical statements. Just as chemical formulas or physical laws can be verified in a laboratory, these too can be verified by anyone. These are similar to the thought experiments in Physics by physicists, such as Einstein. These are experiments to experience that transcend thought. The only extra assumption required that is not in Physics or sciences is: "Consciousness is the substratum of the triads." Here the laboratory is the mental faculty, the instrument is the intellect, and the research topic is awareness. The quest should be genuine. There is no extra-ordinary faith required. Just as a science student works in lab with the expert scientist to verify scientific truths, here the aspirant works with a genuine Guru. Then the aspirant can experience that everything is Consciousness.

Again the 8th aphorism of Āṇavopāya of the *Śivasutras* also declares:

जाग्रत् द्वितीयकरः । (शिवसूत्र ३.८)

Jāgrat dvitīya-karaḥ.(ŚhivaSutras 3.8)

The waking state is another form of his real nature of consciousness.

The yogi has the experience of Divine Consciousness everywhere, just as the saint Jnaneshwar says in *Haripāṭh*: "भरला घनदाट हरि दिसे – *Bharalā ghanadāṭa Hari dise*" (abhang 2) – The Lord Hari is seen filling everywhere. Then the waking state is just another opportunity for the yogi to experience his or her real nature. The waking state in the above aphorism includes the dream and sleep states. The only difference is that the waking state is the longest state one experiences, and is experienced as another form of his expansion of self. The yogi already knows that his/her "I"ness - self and the Universal Self, Shiva, are one and the same. But in the waking state the yogi finds this Universal Self manifested in "This"ness or the world. As "This"ness is experienced, it gets digested or recognized as the Supreme Consciousness. This is again elaborated in Jnaneshwar's work excerpted later. This experience is expressed in the following centering technique of the *VijñānaBhairava*.

यत्र यत्राक्षमार्गेण चैतन्यं व्यज्यते विभोः ।
तस्य तन्मात्रधर्मित्वाच्चिल्लयाद्भरितात्मता ॥ (श्लोक ११७, धारणा ९२)

Yatra yatrākṣamārgeṇa caitanyaṁ vyajyate Vibhoḥ
Tasya tanmātra-dharmitvāc-cillayād-bharitātmatā.
(Verse 117, Dhāraṇā 92)

Via hearing, touching, seeing, tasting or smelling,
Wherever is Lord's Consciousness experienced all-pervading
Regard That - form, place, object - filled by the Self alone
with its characteristic only as Consciousness.
The mind then gets dissolved in the Universal Consciousness.

The seeker should practice this technique in order to be established in the Universal Consciousness.

One day Ramana Maharshi (*Sri Ramana Maharshi*, 261-262) was speaking to an elderly visitor, on the two questions the visitor asked him. (1) How am I to search for the 'I' from start to finish? (2) When I meditate I reach a stage where there is a vacuum or void. How should I proceed from there?

"... First one sees the Self as objects, then one sees the Self as void, then one sees the Self as Self, only in this last there is no seeing because seeing is being. What is required is to remain fixed in the Self always. The obstacles to that are distraction by the things of the world (including sense objects, desires and tendencies) on the one hand, and sleep on the other. Sleep is always mentioned in the books as the first obstacle to samadhi and various methods are prescribed for overcoming it according to the stage of evolution of the person concerned. First, one is enjoined to give up all distraction by the world and its objects[83] or by sleep. But then it is said, for instance in the *Gita*, that one need not give up sleep entirely. Too much or too little are alike undesirable. But another method that is prescribed is not to bother about sleep at all. Simply remain fixed in the Self or in meditation every moment of your waking life, and take up the meditation again the moment you awake, and that will be enough. Then even during sleep the same current of thought or meditation will be working. This is evident because if a man goes to sleep with any strong thought working in his mind he finds the same thought there when he wakes."

[83] This has been discussed earlier in the commentary of Verses 46 and 47

Verse 48 says as a result of knowledge one gets siddhis or occult powers. But the bliss and light of the Self is so magnanimous, that as compared to it any other siddhi is trivial, a distraction and a waste of time. If something is needed to carry out a certain activity, it somehow appears through some means inexplicably, when and where required. We should only remain constantly experiencing everything saturated by the Universal Consciousness, following the saints such as Jnaneshwar. The state described in the following is our natural state. We do not need to do anything except to remove our conditioning or confining attitude.

It is so fascinating to know that works of Jnaneshwar Maharaj and verses of *Spanda Karika* have a lot in common as seen from time to time in this work. The last part of Verse 48 has been elaborated by Jnaneshwar in his work *Nectar of Experiences* in Marathi in the ninth chapter titled *Jīvan-Mukta-dashā-kathan – Description of the State of Liberated Life.* The ninth chapter describes that state of knowledge and naturally arising devotion:

> It is as if the fragrance becomes the nose and enjoys itself. The mirror itself becomes the eyes and enjoys looking at itself. The fan and air become one. The head ornament and the head become one. Likewise, in the manifestation of the Supreme Brahman, in the direct firm knowledge of the Self, the triads - the perceptible object of smell, taste, form, touch and sound, the perceiver and the perception or the process, or the triad of seer-seen-seeing vanished and only oneness with Consciousness remained.
>
> Just as a chrysanthemum flower remains as the chrysanthemum flower even if thousands of petals emerge; in the happening of ever-new experiences, there is no knowledge except of the Self, where there is no action of any kind. Thus even if the sense organs experience different new objects, the inner instrument – mind, intellect, ego -- of the knower of Consciousness sees in all of them only one Reality, Consciousness. If an object appears before the knower, his senses run towards the object to experience it. But just as the sight touches the mirror, the eye sees the eye, the perception of the object gives an experience of the Self. If someone goes to lift the wave with one's palm, that person touches only water. If one touches softness of camphor, looks at its whiteness, tastes its pungent taste, or smells its strong smell, still it is just camphor; likewise, different sense organs may experience their respective objects;

but the knower only experiences consciousness in those objects, because in all objects, the knower discerns only consciousness.

Just as the nodes – parts which germinate when slices of sugarcane are replanted - seen near the joints of the sugar cane are not seen in its juice, just as the phases of the moon are not seen in the full moon, it appears only as a light, just as moonlight falling on the moon cannot be distinguished, or just as when the rain falls on the sea, the water is not seen, to the knower the sense objects and the senses appear as the Self. Whatever object appears in front, the mouth talks about it, but the state of silence is not broken, meaning in a word the knower experiences the silent Self. The knower may perform myriad activities, but his established state of non-active, detached Self is not disturbed. Because, the Self transcends all actions and is not a doer, all actions take place externally due to Prakriti - nature according to its qualities of Sattva, Rajas and Tamas (as discussed earlier). When the knower looks at an object, the object seen and the process of seeing are both the Self, so nothing really happens. It is as if the sun went to catch darkness with its rays as its thousands of arms, but remained all alone; or to enjoy the pleasures of the dream, one woke up and found oneself all alone devoid of all dream pleasures.

All yogas such as the eight-fold yoga became useless before the moonlight of the naturally arising devotion. The body-identification tendency got eliminated due to the contemplation of the Self. All outward transactions now take place with the inward tendency of the Self. In the worldly courtyard of duality, it is non-duality that rules. As the transactions of duality increase, non-duality 'multiplies.' The enjoyment of sense objects rides on Kaivalya – Itself alone. In the house of devotion, the goal of devotion merges with the devotee. If a person walks in the house or sits in the house, both the road and destination are the house, since he is already at the destination. Likewise, it is no more necessary to do different practices to attain the Self, as It is forever attained. There is neither remembering nor forgetting. Since the Self is ever-remembrance, there is no remembering the Self relative to forgetting It. Thus, there is no taking or giving up anything in the transactions of this uncommon state. The will becomes the ritual/practice, any behavior within or without ethical rules or regulations is samadhi

– equal vision, a disposition. This state is the goal for which liberation strives. (Just as Saint Tukaram says, "Now we are sitting on the head of liberation.")

The Lord became the devotee, the path and the destination became one, and the Universe became the Ultimate One devoid of differences. Whether somebody became the Lord or somebody became the devotee, where the knower is, it is all the same non-happening. In the knower devotee's temple of intellect, the Deity - Self became so dense, that It swallowed the temple unbounded by the space-time realm. Thus through the desire to serve in the relationship of master and devotee, only the Lord is attained, because both became one. All modes and items of worship – japa, meditation, worship, flowers, sandalwood paste, and so on, the Lord and the devotee became one. Then the devotion and surrender are from the Lord to the Lord. Still, why shouldn't devotion take place? Of course, it can. Aren't the Lord's statue, temple and entourage all carved in the same mountain rock?

All expansion of a tree is tree whether it is a trunk, branch, leaf, flower or fruit and nothing else. Whether a mute person takes a vow of silence or not, it does not matter, likewise whether a knower devotee worships or not, it doesn't matter. Does it matter whether a deity's form made of akṣatās - rice grains[84] - is worshipped with akṣatās or not? Does it matter if a flame of light is asked to wear a cloak of light? If you ask the moon to cover itself with moonbeams, will the moon disappear? What is the point of offering fire-hood to the fire? Likewise, can it happen when the knower devotee worships, he remains a devotee and when he doesn't, he doesn't remain one? Never. He is always Shiva by nature. Now the self of the knower devotee and the Self have become one, and scripture-approved or shunned deeds that are performed by the knower devotee are not different from the Self-hood. Whatever mental, verbal or physical transactions he performs is all service to the Lord.

The words used by the *Upanishads* in praising the Self become ridicule in the sense that the Self transcends all qualifications, but since the Self pervades all the kārya-karaṇa, meaning deeds-instruments, the qualifi-

[84] Rice grains – called akṣatās are integral part of any ritual worship in the Hindu tradition.

cations themselves (described in words) become praises. In the all pervasiveness of the Self, talk of ridicule or praise is all silence – Who is to praise whom? Who is to ridicule whom?

Wherever the footsteps fall, it is the pilgrimage for Shiva. In the world of duality, a ball falls on the ground, bounces back, touches the hand, and falls again to the ground. But if the hand itself were to become the ball, the ball would hit itself, fall on the ground, bounce back, and the process would continue. If one can visualize this, one would understand the play in the oneness of the knower. This worship is natural, untouched by any physical ritual. The tendency of acquiring knowledge is relative only to "This-ness.. [This is described in the *Shivasutras* aphorism *Jāgrat dvitīyakaraḥ* (3.8) quoted earlier.] But the worship that is constant and without attributes transcending "I" and "This" is taking place in the devotee naturally. The worship which is the light of consciousness by nature does not arise or subside; it resonates in the entire body. That natural happiness is indescribable. This is the secret of natural devotion without performing any rituals, where all yoga and knowledge come to an end. As the non-dual being-ness of the Self expanded, the "I-AM" tendency of Shiva and "This" tendency of Shakti both merged in the Self without "I" and "This."

O my Guru, who is the nature of Shiva! On this ground of bliss Your grace has made me Alone, who performs the transactions of give and take in non-duality. You awakened the constantly pulsating waking state of the Self. You removed ignorance that never exists at the Self, and bestowed on me my eternally attained nature. This is such a wonder! We are only Yours (meaning – the individual is the Self by its nature.) That is why when You say repeatedly with love, "You are mine!" it is befitting to You (meaning - You reassure us of our nature). You never accept anything from anyone, nor even give anything to anyone. But how do You get such an honor? By remaining heavy as Guru (literal meaning of Guru) how can You be light like a boat so as to carry the disciple across the ocean of worldliness? If while sharing Your knowledge with the disciple oneness of non-duality got shattered, then why would scriptures sing Your praises? O Benefactor! By bestowing the knowledge of the Self, the universe of "I" and "This" tendencies of the disciple got dissolved and with that delight You became the disciple's relative!

This is the power of knowledge residing in Shiva, manifesting as Guru's grace capable of bestowing on every disciple the state of ultimate freedom, as verified by Jnaneshwar and countless others. The aspirant now does not have anything to seek, but he/she remains a worshipper and remains constantly grateful to the Guru for bestowing this state. Dealing with anything in the world becomes a worship of the Self, and doing nothing also becomes the worship of the Self. Worship means honor, respect, love, devotion for and joy celebrating the meeting with all things mobile or immobile in the nature. That's why Adi Shankaracharya says in his *Mental Worship of Shiva* – "यद्यद् कर्म करोमि तत्तदखिलं शम्भो तवाराधनम् - *yadyad karma karomi tattadakhilaṁ Shambho tavārādhanam*. Whatever work (includes non-work) I do, O Shambho! It is Your worship." We summarize this discussion of the Power with a song which Muktanand Baba was fond of singing.

हरि हा आपणची जग झाला ॥धृ॥
आपणची देव होऊनि भक्त। पूजितो आपणाला ॥१॥
उत्तम अधम योनी जितकी। जिवरूपें भरला ॥२॥
खल्वीदं इति कृष्ण दयार्णव। स्मृती वदती त्याला ॥३॥

Ref. Hari hā āpaṇaci jaga zālā.
1. Āpaṇacī deva hoūni bhakta, pūjito āpaṇālā.
2. Uttama adhama yonī jitakī, jivarūpeṅ bharalā.
3. Khalvīdaṁ iti Kṛṣṇa Dayārṇava, Smṛtī vadatī Tyālā.

Ref. This Hari became Himself this world.
1. By becoming the Deity and devotee, He worships Himself.
2. Highest and lowly species whatsoever, He pervaded them individually.
3. "Indeed This," says Krishna Dayarnav, "the scriptures call Him."

Jai Sadgurunath Maharaj!

VERSES 49 AND 50

PURYAṢṬAKA – THE CITY OF EIGHT GATES

तन्मात्रोदयरूपेण मनोऽहंबुद्धिवर्तिना ।
पुर्यष्टकेन संरुद्धस्तदुत्थं प्रत्ययोद्भवम् ।।४९।।

49. *Tanmātrodayarūpeṇa mano 'haṁ-buddhi-vartinā*
Puryaṣṭakena saṁruddhas-taduttham pratyayodbhavam.

भुङ्क्ते परवशो भोगं तद्भावात् संसरत्यतः ।
संसृतिप्रलयस्यास्य कारणं संप्रचक्ष्महे ।।५०।।

50. *Bhuṅkte paravaśo bhogaṁ tadbhāvāt saṁsaratyataḥ*
Saṁsṛti-pralayasyāsya kāraṇaṁ saṁpracakṣmahe.

भट्टकल्लटः – तन्मात्रोदयः, तन्मात्राणां शब्दादीनाम् अनुभवरूपेण, मनोऽहंकारबुद्धिभिः इति त्रिभिः परामृश्यमानेन पुर्यष्टकेन बद्धः, तदुत्थं तस्मादुद्भूतं सुखदुःखसंवेदनरूपं तदा ।।४९।।

भुङ्क्ते अश्नाति, अस्वतन्त्रो भोगं सुखदुःखसंवेदनरूपं, तस्य पुर्यष्टकस्य भावात् संसरति संसारशरीरे, अतः संसृति–प्रलयस्य जन्म–मरण–प्रवाहरूपस्य संसारस्य विनाशकारणं संप्रचक्ष्महे वक्ष्यामः ।।५०।।

Bhaṭṭa-kallaṭaḥ - 49. *Tanmātrodayaḥ, tanmātrāṇāṁ śabdādīnāṁ anubhava-rūpeṇa, mano 'haṅkāra-buddhibhiḥ iti tribhiḥ parāmṛśya-mānena puryaṣṭakena baddhaḥ, taduttham tasmādudbhūtaṁ sukha-duḥkha-saṁvedana-rūpam tadā.*

50. *Bhuṅkte aśnāti, asvatantro bhogaṁ sukha-duḥkha-saṁvedana-rūpaṁ, tasya*

puryaṣṭakasya bhāvāt saṁsarati saṁsāra-śarīre, ataḥ saṁsṛti-pralayasya janma-maraṇa-pravāha-rūpasya saṁsārasya vināśa-kāraṇam saṁpracakśmahe vakśyāmaḥ.

49. Shiva manifesting as an individual bound creature is bound in the puryashtaka - city of eight gates - consisting of five subtle principles and the mind, ego and intellect. The puryashtaka causes sensory experiences. (These lead to Āṇava, Māyiya and Kārma malas discussed in Verses 46, 47, 48.)

BhattaKallata: The word 'Tanmātrodaya rūpeṇa' has two interpretations – 'Tanmātra' and 'Tanmātrodaya,' meaning 1.) the subtle senses (sound, touch, form, taste and smell) and 2.) effects arising from the functions of the subtle senses (gross senses). Shiva, who as the individual has cognition of the five subtle principles through the mind, intellect and ego, gets bound by this puryashtaka. From the puryshtaka, experiences or feelings of pleasure and pain arise.

50. Consequently, becoming a prisoner of the puryashtaka, Shiva as the individual goes through the current of births and deaths. The means to end this cycle will be discussed in the next verse.

BhattaKallata: The imprisoned individual enjoys the experiences of feelings of pleasure and pain, and because of the existence of puryashtaka revolves through physical bodies in a cycle of births and deaths. Therefore, in the next verse we will discuss how to end the cycle, meaning how to end the worldly current of births and deaths.

THE LAST PART of Verse 48 described the state of a *Jīvanmukta* (one liberated-while-in-the-body) as the result of knowledge of the Matrika Shakti. In these two verses we see the state that results from ignorance of the Matrika Shakti. The basic fact is that by acquiring such knowledge, a seeker transforms into a liberated being experiencing oneness with the Self. Furthermore, the process of acquiring knowledge is through words, spoken or subtle. The power inherent in the alphabet and its consequent manifestations is Matrika Shakti. However, ignorance of the Matrika Shakti arising out of the power of the alphabet causes one to experience duality. Duality is the consequence of Matrika Shakti. The ignorant individual looks only at the sequence of effects or consequences and not to the sole cause. These effects are fed by the five subtle senses of hearing, touching, seeing, tasting and smelling, and the inner instruments - mind, intellect and ego - that make the individual experience pleasure, pain, and attachment to the senses and their objects. This attachment makes the individual go through the round of births and deaths. Thus the ignorant individual becomes enveloped by a shell of sensory experiences, and does not know a way out, even though harboring within all the time the sole cause as existence or Spanda - "I AM"!

We have already discussed the inner instruments and sense organs in Verse 6 of *SpandaKarikas*:

यतः करणवर्गोऽयं विमूढोऽमूढवत् स्वयम् ।
सहान्तरेण चक्रेण प्रवृत्ति-स्थिति-संहृती : ।।६।।

6. *Yataḥ karaṇa-vargo 'yaṁ vimūḍho 'mūḍhavat svayaṁ.*
Sahāntareṇa cakreṇa pravṛtti-sthiti-saṁhṝtīḥ.

That Spanda principle flows as the group of inner causal divinities – shaktis - due to which all sense organs, though inert, acquire activity. By contact with the power of this Spanda principle, the inner causal cycle of powers, such as Khechari (power of knowledge moving in the sky of consciousness), along with the inert sense organs, acquire the power of creation, sustenance, and dissolution.

In Verse 6 we discussed how the *Karaṇa-varga* (the set of inner instruments) – mind, intellect and ego, and the five pure senses -- which make up the puryashtaka, the city of eight gates, though inert, functions as if alive due to Spanda Shakti's 'pancikaraṇa' – quintification. The topic of panchikarana deals with how the five pure elements - sound, touch, form, taste and smell – intermingle to form several other sets of five: 1) the physical five elements – earth, water, fire, air and space; 2) the five senses of cognition – smell (nose), taste (tongue, taste buds), sight (eyes), touch (skin) and hearing (ears); and 3) the five senses of action – sex (procreation), anus (excretion), legs (locomotion), hands (touching, grasping), tongue/larynx (speech) with their respective neural connections and brain functions. The five pure senses and three inner instruments that make up the subtle body of an individual is called the inner soul – 'Jīva' or 'Antarātmā.' 'Jīva' is a vehicle that moves from one physical body to another, causing the individualized Shiva to transmigrate. Thus we see how the puryashtaka is the cause of the individual's cycle of births and deaths. Once we know the cause it is also possible to see how we can direct all our efforts towards ending the cycle.

The five pure senses - smell, taste, sight, touch and hearing – are general capacities, without any specific content. As an example, foul smells, fragrances, etc. are special instances that are all included in the general category of "smell." According to Kashmir Shaivism, the 36th principle, earth, is associated with smell. Similarly, corresponding to the general quality of "taste" are six specific tastes – sweet, bitter, sour, salty, hot, astringent; water is the 35th principle associated with this sense of taste. In the discussion on Verses 6-7 we referred to the work *Pancadaśī* of Vidyāraṇya and its commentary by Swami Kāśikānanda. Here we refer to the work known as पञ्चीकरण-वार्त्तिकम् *Pañcīkaraṇa-vārttikam* – commentary on 'quintification' – of Sureśvarācārya, one of the direct disciples of Adi Shankaracharya. Due to his writing commentaries on this and other scriptures, Sureśvarācārya was called *VārttikaKāra* – writer of *Vārttika*.

According to *Panchikarana-varttikam*, the substratum of the universe is the Self, and the origin of all sounds is the sound Aum or Om. By uttering the sound Aum with concentration, we can experience the Self (Verse 1 of *varttikam*.) While their quintification is described in detail earlier (*SpandaKarikas* 6-7), the first few verses of *Panchikarana* (2-6) emphasize the generation of the pure senses and the five gross elements.

आसीदेकं परं ब्रह्म नित्यमुक्तमविक्रियम् ।
तत्स्वमायासमावेशाद्बीजमव्याकृतात्मकम् ॥२॥
तस्मादाकाशमुत्पन्नं शब्दतन्मात्ररूपकम् ।
स्पर्शात्मकस्ततो वायुस्तेजोरूपात्मकं ततः ॥३॥
आपो रसात्मिकास्तस्मात्ताभ्यो गन्धात्मिका मही ।
शब्दैकगुणमाकाशं शब्दस्पर्शगुणो मरुत् ॥४॥
शब्दस्पर्शरूपगुणैस्त्रिगुणं तेज उच्यते ।
शब्दस्पर्शरूपरसगुणैरापश्चतुर्गुणाः ॥५॥
शब्दस्पर्शरूपरसगन्धैः पञ्चगुणा मही ।
तेभ्यः समभवत्सूत्रं भूतं सर्वात्मकं महत् ॥६॥

2. *Āsīdekaṁ paraṁ Brahma nitya-muktam-avikriyam*
   Tat - svamāyā-samāveśād-bījam-avyākṛtātmakam.
3. *Tasmād-ākāśam-utpannaṁ śabda-tanmātra-rūpakam*
   Sparśātmakas-tato vāyus-tejo-rūpātmakaṁ tataḥ.
4. *Āpo rasātmikās-tasmāt-tābhyo gandhātmikā mahī*
   Śabdaika-guṇam-ākāśaṁ śabda-sparśa-guṇo marut.

5. *Śabda-sparśa-rūpa-guṇais-triguṇaṁ teja ucyate*
Śabda-sparśa-rūpa-rasa-guṇai-rāpaś-caturguṇāḥ.
6. *Śabda-sparśa-rūpa-rasa-gandhaiḥ pañca-guṇā mahī*
Tebhyaḥ samabhavat-sūtraṁ bhūtaṁ sarvātmakaṁ mahat.

The Supreme Brahman, Self, eternally free and immutable, existed alone. Owing to the superimposed identity with Its own Maya, That became the undifferentiated (unformed and unnamed) seed of the universe. From That Self originated Space, which is characterized by sound. From Space, Air, having the characteristic of touch, came into existence. From Air arose Light, characterized by form. From Light arose Water, which is characterized by taste. From Water arose Earth, whose characteristic is smell. (Verse 2 and first part of Verse 3)

The Self has no qualities.[85] Space has only one quality, sound. Each subsequent element acquires the quality/qualities of its predecessor in addition to its own. Air has two qualities, sound and touch. We feel the moving air on the skin and hear a howling sound in a storm or whirlwind. All the elements, such as Hydrogen, Oxygen, Carbon, Nitrogen, etc., are ingredients of air, some of which create fire, and some of which extinguish fire. Light or Fire has three qualities - sound, touch and form. We hear the sound of crackling wood, fire, or thunder associated with lightning; we feel the heat of fire, and see various colors of light that arise. We might see this as blue and yellow flames, or a spectrum of colors as in a rainbow or through a glass prism. Water has four qualities – sound, touch, form and taste. A flowing stream makes a sound, its water is cool to touch, water acquires the form of a drop or flood or shape of any vessel. Water acquires various tastes according to the objects it comes into contact with. It is sweet in sugar cane, hot (pungent) in chilis, salty in seawater or sweat, astringent in Amla or some unripe fruits, sour in lemon juice, bitter in bitter gourds. Aryurveda recommends that the daily diet contain all the six tastes of foods. In garlic all the five tastes except sweetness are included. Earth has five qualities – sound, touch, form, taste and smell. The sediment that is seen when water evaporates shows that Earth is a product of water. In Hawaii, for example, the earth gets formed out of water through flowing lava. This is another example that indicates Earth is a product of water. The metallic elements are ingredients of Earth. Earth is

[85] The following examples from Verses 3-6 demonstrate how the gross manifestation of the five subtle principles – space, air, fire, water, earth –arises from the five pure senses by panchikaran.

regarded as inert or immobile, even though as a planet, it spins on its axis producing days and nights, and also orbits around the sun, producing seasons. When one walks on earth, sound is made. It is sometimes hard to the touch, sometimes slippery, especially when some water comes into contact with it. As a solid it has form and also takes on different forms. It acquires different tastes depending on which minerals are predominant. After rain showers, Earth releases a pleasant smell.

Earth exerts gravitational pull, which is the universal form of *Apāna* (a form of prāṇa – life force), on all objects. Out of the five subtle elements came into being the great, universal, all-pervading principle of prāṇa, vital force, also meaning power of activity, which is inert in nature, and that is called the 'sutra' or 'thread' that passes through all creation. This concludes the explanation of the second part of Verse 3 and verses 4, 5, 6.

Lalita Mauli, the famous modern-day saint of Panavel, Maharashtra, India who left her body in 1997, was a disciple of Bhagawan Nityanand of Ganeshpuri. She advises the seekers as follows in one of her works: (*Lalita Mauli*, 21)

श्री सद्गुरु मुखे पंचिकरण श्रवण । मननाभ्यासें शांतपणें करावे ग्रहण ।
प्रश्नोत्तरें करुनि घ्यावें संशय निरसन ।
झटावे सदा अभ्यासा ॥
खातां पीतां उठतां निजतां सर्व ।
व्यवहारादि क्रियेंत पाहावा एक अपूर्व ।
चैतन्य महाप्रभूचा खेळची सर्वथैव। नित्यानंदमय अद्वितीय स्वरूप ॥ १८-१९॥

Śrī sadguru-mukhe pañcikaraṇa śravaṇa,
mananābhyāseṅ śāṅtapaṇeṅ karāve grahaṇa,
Praśnottareṅ karuni ghyāveṅ saṁśaya nirasana,
jhaṭāve sadā abhyāsā.
Khātāṅ pītāṅ uṭhatāṅ nijatāṅ sarva,
vyavahārādi kriyeṅta pāhāvā eka apūrva,
Caitanya Mahāprabhūcā kheḷacī sarvathaiva,
Nityānaṅda-maya advitīya svarūpa. (18-19)

You should hear about quintification from the Sadguru in his own words; by practice of contemplation you should grasp it peacefully; with questions and answers or inquiry, you should get all doubts cleared; and you should strive to practice. While eating, drinking, waking and sleeping, in carrying out transactions, etc., in all actions, you should see the play and ever blissful unique form of the Greatest Lord Consciousness.

Our Guru Muktanand Baba used to say that it is solely by the five pure senses – sound, touch, form, taste and smell – and their corresponding senses of cognition that the universe exists and creatures get bound. Ears hear sound, no other organ can do that. Skin and no other organ feels touch. Eyes and no other organ see. Tongue and no other organ tastes. Nose and no other organ smells. Nothing else exists that binds a creature. He also quoted from *Jnaneshwari*, Jnaneshwar's commentary upon the *Bhagavad Gita:* "The five elements act as enemies of each other. For instance, Water or Earth douses Fire. Air disappears in Space. Etc. But it is consciousness that brings all these elements together in the body and in their quintification holds them together for a while." "When Kundalini is awakened, three elements dissolve in the body itself, Water dissolves Earth, Fire destroys water, Air (*Prāṇa vāyu*) destroys Fire in the heart and remains as Prana in the form of the body. And after a while it dissolves in the *Murdhni Ākāśa* – the space of the head." (Chapter 6)

Repeating what was quoted earlier in Verse 2, Swami Rama Tirth said in one of his talks in America: "Why does the world appear? Vedanta says, because you see it. Why is the world there? Vedanta simply says, because you see it. If you do not see, there is no world. Close your eyes, a fifth of the world is gone. That part of the world which you perceive through your eyes is no longer there. Close your ears and another fifth is gone; close your nose and another fifth is gone. Do not put any of your senses into activity and there is no world.You see the world and you ought to explain why the world is there. You make it there."[86] In other words, the individual 'I' causes my world to be experienced. Turning the mind, intellect and ego within and investigating the 'I AM' leads one to experience the Self with awareness, and that would annihilate the duality and suffering.

The experience of the individual ego, 'I,' as separate from the Self is the main culprit. The separation gives rise to the worldly experiences through the senses. As a seeker it is necessary for us to understand 'ego's nature' so that it does not remain limited and become a cause of suffering of the cycle of pain and pleasure,

[86] "*The When and Why of the World*," lecture delivered in San Francisco, January 15, 1903, (Swami Ram Tirtha, 57)

birth and death. This has to be done by direct inquiry of 'Who am I' as instructed by Ramana Maharshi and by other means.

Once the author felt that he would like to write an essay on Ramana's teachings. He wrote the article, entitled, *Hridaya Kuhara - The Cave of the Heart* and in the evening read it to his wife. She said that it was too wordy and dry. That night around 2 AM, Ramana Maharshi appeared in the author's vision and sitting next to him told him in thought-form what he should write. Around 2:30 AM the author sat at the computer and revised the article and read to his wife around 5 AM, and she asked what happened overnight, how it was so different. That article is in the appendix of this verse. The article also has been published in August 1999 issue of *Kanara Saraswat* magazine and in Marathi translation in *Sant Kripa* magazine. In short, saints such as Ramana Maharshi keep helping seekers even though they may not be currently in their physical frame.

To continue practicing Ramana Maharshi's teaching of hearing, contemplating, and abiding in the Self – shravana, manana and nididhyasana, we turn to the *Bhagavad Gita*, Chapter 7 Verse 4, where Lord Krishna describes Arjuna that space, air, fire, water and earth along with mind, intellect, ego are regarded as His eightfold material nature. Material nature, which is illusory, is superimposed on the natural state by Maya just as an individual's apparent sorrow overlies the natural state of bliss.

Swami Maheshwarand Giriji says in his commentary on Verse 4, Chapter 7, *Bhagavad Gita:*

> Even though the five elements, like Earth, seem to be inert, visible and divided, in all of them, the power, pulsation and bliss of the one-and-only Brahman (Self) exist in full measure. All these objects are known to exist because of the existence of Brahman; they are perceptible because of Brahman's consciousness; and they become agreeable or disagreeable because of Brahman's bliss. That is why the sages of the Vedas saw Brahman apparent in the five elements.
>
> Having seen the actual Brahman directly in all of them, they sang with the exhilaration of love,"This earth is Aditi - unbreakable - because from the point of view of names and forms it is forever immutable; and since

it is always unchangeable from the point of view of Brahman, it is beyond past, present and future, and is indeed the energy of Consciousness."

They also perceived the blissful Brahman in the water principle. In daily rituals, like oblations with water at dawn and dusk (Sandhyā), they worshipped water as one form of Brahman. They said in the words of the Vedas, "Oh revered water! Being truly of the nature of Brahman, you grant two kinds of pleasures – conditioned or worldly and unconditional or supernatural. Please make us steadfast, peaceful, and focused on experiencing the producer of unbounded contentment, the Bliss of Brahman. We worship You only for the vision of the great Brahman whose perfect nature is bliss, unlike all else. Within You dwells an extremely beneficial essence, that is the pure bliss of Brahman (Brahmānanda). We humbly pray that You allow us to taste that essence."

In the Vedas, the praise and worship of fire is foremost. Worship of fire is "Yajña." Only the praiseworthy is worshipped, so fire, the Deity of Yajna, is placed in front - that is, it exists visibly in front of us. Therefore in the *Śvetāśwatara Upaniṣad*

यो देवोऽग्नौ योऽप्सु यो विश्वं भुवनमाविवेश ।
य ओषधीषु यो वनस्पतिषु तस्मै देवाय नमो नमः ॥ (२।१७)

Yo devo 'gnau yo 'psu yo viśvaṁ Bhuvanam-āviveśa,
Ya oṣadhīṣu Yo vanspatiṣu tasmai Devāya namo namaḥ.'
(2/17)

"*We repeatedly offer our salutations to God, who has entered the Universe as fire, water, plants, vegetation, and trees; who has filled the world of sentient and insentient creation with His existence, consciousness, perfection, and bliss.*" *We regard Fire as the eternal witness in marriage ceremonies.*

In *Taittiriya Upanishad*, Air is revered. 'नमस्ते वायो ! त्वमेव प्रत्यक्षं ब्रह्मासि । (तै. उ. १।१) '*Namaste Vāyo! Tvameva pratykṣaṁ Brahmāsi,*' (*Taittiriya Upaniṣad* 1,1) "Oh Wind! Salutations to you. You are verily Brahman." In *Bṛhad Āraṇyaka Upanishad*, it is said 'खं ब्रह्म (बृ. ५।१।१) 'Khaṁ

Brahma' "Space is Brahman." In this manner our sages used to be immersed in bliss at the thought of Brahman within wind and space. 'यत्साक्षादपरोक्षात् ब्रह्म' (बृ. उ. ३।४।२) '*Yatsākṣād-aparokṣāt Brahma*' (Bṛ. Up. 3,4,2) "This Shruti (revealed scripture) describes Brahman as being as evident as the soul and as directly perceivable as the universe."

The body is also made up of the five elements. They are brought together within the body. In fact, there is no object in the universe not comprised of the five elements. In the body you actually see the hard earth in the form of bones; you see water in the form of fluids such as blood. The principle of fire pervades the body. You can rub both your hands and experience the warmth of fire. The digestive fire burns in the stomach and digests food. Just as the fire principle exists in the body, so does the wind principle. In the body prana - the life force - is everything. Our friendships are with prāṇa, not with people. As long as prāṇa is active, people express their relationships by saying,"This is my husband; this is my wife; this is my brother, son-in-law, father, mother" and so forth. When the deity of prana leaves, the whole game is over. The entire relationship is suddenly broken. No one says,"This lifeless body is my husband, my wife" etc. They say,"He is dead." They are not sorry nor do they beat their breast for the sake of the body, since the body is lying lifeless before them; but they do mourn what is now unmanifest. Relationship can only exist while the life-force remains in the body. We are only in relationships with the life force, not the body.

Moreover, space too exists in the body. If there were no space, there would be no room to breathe, eat or drink, since space creates room. Just as the space creates room inside the body, it also creates room to move and wander about. If it did not, the body would stay in one place impacted and unable to move, seeing as the molecules of the other four elements are packed solid. Because of space, the body can move around.

In this way, the five principles everywhere inside and outside of the body hold the Lord's power, pulsation, and love, and exist everywhere eternally before us in the form of cause and effect, trees, mountains, sun,

---

[86] *Pravachana Sudha – Nectar of Discourses*, Mahamandaleshwar Swami Maheshwaranand Giri, 2006 Pub. Shanti Mandir, Walden, NY Verse 4, pp 77-105

> moon, and so on. Enlightened beings discern the principle of Brahman in both divided and undivided forms, and experience perfect delight.[86]

Native Americans also respect the four elements Air, Fire, Water and Earth, regarding Space as the assumed and obvious element, like "Oxygen." Everyone uses Oxygen, but no one mentions it except in emergencies.

Modern scientists are wonderstruck by the nature of the universe. In the following excerpt from a *New York Times* article of July 11, 2007, Natalie Angiers describes the scientific history of water:

> Some 380 million years ago, a few pioneering vertebrates first made the leap from water to land. We may have lungs rather than gills, and the weaker swimmers among us may be perfectly capable of drowning in anything deeper than a bathtub, yet still we feel the primal tug of the tide. Consciously or otherwise, we know we're really all wet. As fetuses, we gestate in bags of water. As adults, we are bags of water: roughly 60 percent of our body weight comes from water, the fluidic equivalent of 45 quarts. Our cells need water to operate, and because we lose traces of our internal stores with every sweat we break, every breath and excretion we out-take, we must constantly consume more water, or we will die in three days. Thirstiness is a universal hallmark of life. Sure, camels can forgo drinking water for five or six months and desert tortoises for that many years, and some bacterial and plant spores seem able to survive for centuries in a state of dehydrated, suspended animation. Yet sooner or later, if an organism plans to move, eat or multiply, it must find a solution of the aqueous kind.
>
> Life on Earth arose in water, and scientists cannot imagine life arising elsewhere except by water's limpid grace. Behind water's peerless punch, and the reason it rather than alcohol or any other lubricant serves as the elixir of life, is the three-headed character whose chemical name we all know: H_2O. Scientists observe that when two atoms of hydrogen conjoin with one of oxygen, the resulting molecule displays a spectacular range of powers, gaining the mightiness of a molecular giant while retaining the speed and convenience of a molecular mite. "Water behaves very differently from other small molecules," said Jill Granger, a professor of chemistry at Sweet Briar College in Virginia. "If you

want something else with similar properties, you'd end up with something much bigger and more complex, and then you'd lose the advantages that water has in being small."

Because of water's atomic architecture, the tendency of its comparatively forceful oxygen centerpiece to cling greedily to electrons as it consorts with its two meeker hydrogen mates, the entire molecule ends up polarized, with slight electromagnetic charges on its foreside and aft. Those mild charges in turn allow water molecules to engage in mild mass communion, linking up with one another and with other molecules, too, through an essential connection called a hydrogen bond. The hydrogen bond that attracts water to water and to other like-minded players is subtler than the bond that ties each water molecule's atoms together. But subtlety breeds opportunity, and from hydrogen bonds many of water's major and minor properties flow.

With their hydrogen bonds, water molecules become sticky, cohering as a liquid into droplets and rivulets and following each other around like a jiggling conga line. Such stickiness means that water is drawn to the inner plumbing of plants and will crawl up the fibrous conduits to hydrate even the crowns of redwood trees towering hundreds of feet above ground.

Pulled together by hydrogen bonds, water molecules become mature and stable, able to absorb huge amounts of energy before pulling a radical phase shift and changing from ice to liquid or liquid to gas. As a result, water has surprisingly high boiling and freezing points, and a strikingly generous gap between the two. For a substance with only three atoms, and two of them tiny little hydrogens, Dr. Richmond said, you'd expect water to vaporize into a gas at something like minus 90 degrees Fahrenheit, to freeze a mere 40 degrees below its boiling point, and to show scant inclination to linger in a liquid phase. That's what happens to hydrogen sulfide, a similarly sized molecule but with its two hydrogen atoms fastened to sulfur rather than to oxygen; on our temperate world, hydrogen sulfide has long since reached its boiling point and exists as a foul-smelling gas. Same for the tidy troika of carbon dioxide: low freezing point, low boiling point, and, poof, it's up in

> the air. But given its vivid power of hydrogen bonding, water proves less flighty and fickle, with a boiling point at sea level of 212 degrees Fahrenheit, and a full 180 degrees lying between the tempest of a teapot and the tinkling of an ice cube at 32 degrees. A vast temperature span over which water molecules can pool and cling as the liquid assets we love best.
>
> We rely in myriad ways on water's fluid forbearance, its willingness to take the heat without blinking. Earth's oceans and lakes soak up huge quantities of solar radiation and help moderate the climate. As sweat evaporates from our skin, it wicks away large amounts of excess heat. Water also serves as a nearly universal solvent, able to dissolve more substances than any other liquid. It can act as an acid, it can act as a base, with a pinch of salt it is the solution in which the cell's thousands of chemical reactions take place. At the same time, water's gregariousness, its hydrogen-bonded viscosity, helps lend the cell a sense of community. "Water acts as the contact between biological molecules, not just separating them, but imparting information among them," said Martin Chaplin, a professor of applied science who studies the structure of water at London South Bank University. "In an aqueous environment, all the molecules are able to feel the structure of all the other molecules that are present, so they can work as whole rather than as individuals."
>
> There's no end to water's chemical kinkiness, including the way it freezes from the top down and becomes buoyant as it chills. Most substances shrink and get denser and heavier as they cool, and expand and lighten as they melt. Water bucks the norm, and is lighter and airier as ice than when liquid, and so in winter marine life can find liquid haven beneath the floating blanket of ice, and so in summer ice cubes bob and clink in your glass of lemonade.

Likewise, scientists marvel at each of the Elements and have written volumes on their properties. Even the human body is something to marvel about. Its ability to act as an electro-magnetic field, to assimilate food eaten and eliminate waste is a work of perfection of the Spanda Shakti.

Scientists even study the conversation of bacteria with one another! There is a documentary film on a woman biologist from Princeton, who is investigating how bacteria communicate with one another. When the bacteria communicate with each other the whole liquid medium becomes fluorescent in a unique way, just as when we communicate with each other, there is a lot of noise and joy. When she applied for admission to many prestigious graduate schools with her observations, most people regarded this 'bacteria whisperer' scientist as deluded. Only the Chairman of Biology at Princeton who is also a Nobel Prize winner in biology, recognized her talent and admitted her as a doctoral student. She has proven her observations, which could now be used for some bacteria to heal certain diseases. She is currently a professor of Biology at Princeton.

The human body is so complex that there are not only doctors who treat the whole body in terms of its various functions, nervous system, enzymes and magnetic field and so on, but also there are doctors who are specialized to treat only one organ or part starting from hair on the head to the tips of a toe.

In this manner, Spanda Shakti is everywhere if one cares to be aware. Still, some people feel it is hard to see God! As seekers we have to know that from the time we get up until it is time to sleep we must take every opportunity to remind ourselves of the force – 'chiti shakti' – the power of consciousness that actually drives us and the entire universe. We have to make a conscious constant effort to break the thoughts of ignorance lodged in our minds for ages. We have to read daily the stotras such as *Argalā* and *Devi* from *Durgā Saptaśati*, also known as *Caṇḍipāṭh*, to connect ourselves with the Source. Brief meanings of both stotras are given below.

We chant *Argala Stotra* to remove the obstacles we experience in our daily undertakings. We pray to the Divine Shakti to remove our difficulties. These difficulties arise because of our six inner enemies - desire, anger, greed, delusion, pride, and jealousy. These difficulties arise by not knowing who we are. So in almost every stanza we say - Rupam Dehi, Jayam Dehi, Yasho Dehi, Dvisho Jahi: "Grant me the knowledge of who I am, grant me victory, grant me success, trounce over my enemies - the inner enemies." We praise the Goddess Shakti by recognizing that she killed the demons - Madhu and Kaitabh, Mahishāsura, etc. We pray to her to bestow upon us good fortune, good health and greatest happiness. We recognize that Brahma - God of Creation, Vishnu - God of Sustenance, Shiva - God of Dissolution and Indra - King of Gods all bow to her.

Goddess, you gave them Shakti when they needed it. So bless me also. Give me immeasurable bliss, give me a spouse who is compatible, who can help me to go across this ocean of worldliness. This Stotra was written by the sage Mārkaṇḍeya and is sung before *Durga Saptashati* is read.

The second Stotra is *Devi Stotra*. This stotra is for building the correct self-esteem. Modern psychologists say that for successful relationships, for a healthy outlook towards life we have to have good self-image. We must love ourselves. When we think we are the Doer, we become aware of our limitations, due to our separated ego. Reciting this stotra we become aware of who the actual Doer is. We get correct self-image. We recognize that it is the Goddess Shakti who has become everything. We sing to the Goddess: You have become the Maya the veiling power. You are our consciousness. You are our intellect. You are our sleep, dream and waking states. You are hunger in us. You are our reflection in the five elements. You are our physical energy, thirst, all our physical characteristics. You have become our compassion, our personality, our modesty, our faith, compassion, our glow, our talents, our thoughts - or modifications of our mind, our memory, our kindness, our contentment. You have become our mother. The word mother stands for two aspects - one is the physical mother - our mom. The other aspect of mother is Matruka Shakti - The power of words. We become bound if we do not understand the energy that is beyond the power of words. The Word "Aham" means "I am" or it also means ego. The actual meaning is all the letters starting from A to the last letter Ha in Sanskrit alphabet. When we are only aware of letters or words we get trapped in our ego. When we become aware of the Energy, Shakti, which is beyond, we become free. We also say to the Goddess, you have become our delusion also. You are the Presider over all senses. You reside in all beings. As consciousness you have pervaded everything in this universe.

May that Goddess praised by Indra and Gods, fulfill our best wishes, may She do good deeds through us. At present we are troubled by the demons. We are humble with devotion. May she remove all our obstacles. NamashChandikayai – Salutations to Chandi.

There are dharanas, centering exercises in the *Vijnana Bhairav*, which teach a seeker how to experience Spanda, 'I am' divine I-consciousness, in every activity of our life, by addressing the elements in the universe as well as the individual and its functions. The highest state of Bhairava transcends the directions, time, space and designation, and is beyond description in words, but it can be experienced. It can be experienced just by being aware in the stillness of the mind, and in the height of emotion, it can be experienced by taking a plunge into the root of the emotion.

The first dharana is on being aware of the life force, prana, that connects the external five senses to the inner instruments.

ऊर्ध्वे प्राणो ह्यधो जीवो विसर्गात्मा परोच्चरेत् ।
उत्पत्तिद्वितयस्थाने, भरणाद्भरिता स्थितिः ॥ श्लोक २४, धारणा १॥

Ūrdhve prāṇo hyadho jīvo, visargātmā paroccaret
Utpatti-dvitaya-sthāne, bharaṇād-bharitā sthitiḥ.
(Verse 24, Dhāraṇā 1)

The highest Shakti, whose nature is creative, goes downward in the form of exhalation and upward in the form of inhalation. By focusing the mind at the two places of the origin, one experiences the nature of Wholeness.

Continuing in the same vein, but getting subtler, the next dharana directs the seeker to focus at the pause between the inhalation and exhalation. The third dharana takes the seeker still deeper to where the mind's thoughts are dissolved, external breathing process is suspended, and the seeker experiences the state of Bhairava. In all dharanas up to 8 and in dharana 41, prana is used for centering and experiencing Bhairava.

Many dharanas have been considered in the earlier verses, based on awakening of Kundalini, japa – repeating the Guru-given mantra, void, visualization, and postures – āsanas. But the Spanda verses 49-50 are special. They deal with the five subtle senses, the three inner instruments and the quintification of the five elements, and summarize the bondage of individual. It is worth categorizing various dharanas that help the seekers to get out of the trap of the sensory experiences.

Five Senses: The technique is either to observe the five senses and their objects as a witness, or to turn completely inwards, shutting down the senses and their effects. Several dharanas starting with dharana 9 advise the seeker to meditate in his heart by visualizing the five voids, the sources of five senses, or shutting four of them (except touch) off by fingers. The result is absorption in the Absolute Void, the Self. Dharana 76 rejects both the knower or subject and knowledge or object that arises due to sensory perception as without cause or base and advises the seeker to enter the heart to experience the absolute Reality. Dharana 92 directs the seeker to contemplate universal omnipresent consciousness that is revealed through sensory organs, transcending the sensation experienced.

Space - Sound – Hearing - Ears: In dharanas 15 and 18, the seeker is asked to meditate on sound. There is a special unstruck sound which goes on within like a rapid flow of a river. A capable ear can hear it. If that is not possible listening to the sound of a stringed instrument and absorption in the prolonged uninterrupted sound is advised. Dharana 50 directs the seeker mentally to become one with the incomparable joy of song and music. The words of saints, discussions on the spiritual matters, words of the Guru all help turn the mind inward away from senses.

Air – Touch - Skin: To overcome the identification with the body, the seeker should contemplate the skin of the body as an outer shell and visualize that there is nothing substantial within that shell. Then the seeker transcends all. (Dharana 25) At the time of intercourse with a woman - Shakti, an absorption into her is brought about by excitement. The delight of the orgasm is the delight of the Brahman- the Self. (Dharana 46) Even the memory of sexual pleasure obtained in kissing, embracing, pressing etc. floods the body by delight; this shows that the delight is apart from any woman. If one meditates on that delight one experiences the bliss of the divine consciousness. (Dharana 47)

Fire – Form – Seeing - Eyes: Dharanas 36, 37, 43, 48, 53, 56, 57, 64-65 and 69 deal with the sense of seeing.

The technique is to cast the eyes inside a jar, leaving aside the enclosing partitions, meditating on the total void. Casting your gaze on a region which has no trees, on a mountain or a high wall, on the vastness of vacant space, or watching the vast ocean from a beach, all will dissolve the fluctuations of the mind.

The seeker sees a magic performance and meditates on the instant delight that arises.

On the occasion of seeing a friend or relative after a long time, a delight arises meditating on that delight also makes the seeker one with the absolute for that instant. By memory the experience can be prolonged.

In the space surrounding the sun or a lamp rays appear in variegated colors. While observing those, one's own nature of light of consciousness is experienced.

Sitting in a comfortable posture placing the hands overhead in the form of an arch and gazing at the armpits, the mind gets absorbed in that posture of repose, and attains great peace.

In the darkest night of the diminishing phase of the moon, the seeker contemplates the darkness to attain the nature of Bhairava. In the absence of the darkness the seeker first closes his eyes and contemplates darkness, and then in total darkness with eyes wide open, the seeker contemplates the vast dark nature of Bhairava.

Water – Taste – tongue, Earth - Smell – Nose: There are two dharanas, 24 and 49, related to these elements as objectified in a human body. Verse 47, Dharana 24 says, "O deer-eyed one, when one contemplates over the constituents or seven ingredients of one's body – bodily fluids such as saliva and mucous, blood, bones, flesh, fat, marrow and semen – as pervaded with mere vacuity, the contemplation of vacuity will become steady and the light of consciousness will be experienced." We should also consider the contemplation on these elements described earlier by Swami Maheshwaranand Giri. Verse 72, Dharana 49 says, "One should meditate on the condition of pure joy or satisfaction that arises out of eating and drinking (and other bodily functions). There will be supreme delight of the Self." The source of this joy is the Spanda.

Mind, Intellect and ego: Thinking is fundamental to being human. We have to change our mind set. Otherwise, it will be like the following saying:

> If we think the way we've always thought,
> We will always get what we always got.

Shri Shankaracharya writes in his work *Aparokṣānubhūti* – "Direct experience" what a human being should think, since the attitude brings the direct experience. It begins with the inquiry, "Who am I? How did this world originate? Who is its creator? What is its instrumental cause?" and goes into great details in this work. All dharanas involve visualization, discernment, or contemplation, which are functions of the mind. All saints, including our Guru Swami Muktanand Baba, emphasize the importance of keeping the mind focused, one-pointed, on whatever we are doing. Muktanand Baba always quoted the verses on mind, from Upanishads such as, "Mind is the sole cause of bondage or liberation." And "O my mind! Think only auspicious thoughts." His work *Mukteshwari* has couplets 351-368 on the mind. He says, "Kill the mind, You will become Mahadev - Shiva. Let the mind exist, and individuality – 'jeevatva' remains. The Lord is forever attained, look inward in the heart. Due to impurities of the mind, He seems unattainable." (couplets 351-252)

Samarth Swami Ramdas of the seventeenth century has written *Manāce Śloka – Verses for the Mind* totalling 205 verses. He asks the mind to remain in the company of saints, to follow their prescriptions and proscriptions in behavior. He asks the mind to contemplate Rama at dawn and at every waking moment. He says constant contemplation of the sense objects makes one jeeva – limited individual, and ego and ignorance are born. With 'viveka' – discrimination, remain in the Self; 'jeeva' does not originate in the substratum. He asks the seeker to investigate the ego which creates all the sorrow. He says the intellect focused on the body loses what is beneficial and beyond the body. He says the intellect should be focused on the Self in the constant company of saints.

Vijnana Bhairava, Verse 61, Dharana 38 says, "At the moment when one perceives two objects or ideas, one should abandon both and focus on the gap that is between the two. In the gap Reality flashes forth." Verse 92, Dharana 69 says, "When one concentrates on one's self in the form of the sky, unlimited in any direction without support, then the essential nature - Chiti Shakti freed of all props reveals herself. In Verse 94, Dharana 71 we are asked to contemplate, "Within me the inner psychic instrument – mind, intellect and ego does not exist. Because of the absence of thoughts, we will remain thought-free and abide in the pure consciousness which is our essential nature." Verse 96, Dharana 73 asks the seeker to squash a desire the moment it arises; it will be absorbed in the very place from which it arose. It is like squashing a wavelet or foam in the ocean and experiencing the ocean. Verses 97,98, Dharanas 74, 75 also work on withdrawing from desire. Verse 99, Dharana 76 says, "All knowledge is without cause, base and just boggles the mind. From the point of view of absolute Reality, this knowledge does not belong to any person. When one contemplates this alone, one becomes Shiva." Knowledge requires words, words require alphabet a product of matrika shakti. Dharanas 77, 78, 80 and 81 center seekers' mind on contemplating consciousness that is present in all bodies, on immobilizing the mind of all six confining emotions – desire, anger, greed, fear/infatuation, arrogance and envy, not dwell on suffering or pleasure and reject attachment to the body and contemplate "I am everywhere." This makes one enjoy transcendental bliss.

In this world we have come to watch a play. We focus our attention on a multi-stage-multi-act play. But there is only one actor. *Shiva Sutras* say, "नर्तक आत्मा (३.९) - *Nartaka Ātmā* (3.9)" The Self is the actor. The place where the Self takes delight in exhibiting the world drama is the stage called *Antaratma* – 'the inner soul,' or jīva. *Shiva Sutras* say, "रङ्गो अन्तरात्मा (३.१०) – *Raṅgo Antarātmā* (3.10)" The inner soul is the stage. The inner soul consists of the puryashtaka or subtle body experienced in the dream state. Isn't it a Universal Broadway play with its aspects of sound, light or color, costumes, with enhancements of smell, touch and taste and an interesting 'touching' plot keeping the audience completely involved! The audience is the sense organs, as *Shiva Sutras* say, "प्रेक्षकाणि इन्द्रियाणि (३.११) – *Prekṣakāṇi Indriyāṇi* (3.11)" People who are ignorant of their nature think that they are playing the roles themselves. The great critic – Sadguru – knows the mystery plot. He enjoys the play thoroughly. If we approach the Sadguru, he reveals the plot to us. Then we also enjoy the play like him/her.

In order to witness the play, it is necessary to take time out from acting and getting absorbed in our roles and getting to know the real actor. There is a story of two movie actors. One played the Hunchback of Notre Dame in the English movie and the other played the role of Tukaram in the Marathi movie *Saint Tukaram*. They identified with their roles so much, that one became a hunchback for a few months even after the movie was released and the other became like saint Tukaram for the rest of his life. We too have a choice. We can remain attached to our costume of name and form and say the lines of 'I' and 'mine' and remain in misery or we can rise above our costume and identify ourselves with our true nature.

One day Nasruddin was walking by a jewelry store. A necklace in the store was so beautiful and so expensive that the jeweler designed a special glass bubble display for it. Every passerby could see it. It seemed as though anyone could walk away with it very easily, provided one could reach inside the shiny glass bubble. Nasruddin thought that the necklace would be a great gift for his wife, Fatima. He did not have money in his pocket. He reasoned to himself, "Everything in this world belongs to Allah. I belong to Allah. Allah belongs to me. So the necklace is mine anyway. I will just take it from behind the glass." He raised his cane and hit the glass. The glass bubble broke and the necklace disappeared. Nasruddin started crying saying to himself, "I lost my necklace." The store manager came out hearing the noise of falling glass. He apologized to Nasruddin, "Sir, did the glass fall on your head? Did it hurt you?" Nasruddin was surprised and changed the story,"Never mind. You lost your glass jar and your necklace." The jeweler said, "Sir, it was only a 'hologram' image of the necklace. The real necklace is inside. It is just one of a kind. Are you interested in buying it for wife?" "No," said Nasruddin, "Not today! May be tomorrow."

We are also like Nasruddin. We have a convoluted sense of logic and we identify the Truth with Its reflection in all objects seen as the world. We hanker after one attractive reflection after another to obtain happiness and go to all sorts of effort to possess it and once in our possession, we exert to preserve it. Parents think that their children will give them happiness, but the children have their own lives, and walk away as they grow up. What the parents get is disappointment. A person has pride about his or her beauty or that of a spouse, boyfriend or girlfriend, or education or wealth and objects the wealth can bring. That leads to infatuation. Getting to enjoy the objects becomes the person's short lived happiness and losing them becomes sorrow. Some objects that give pleasure for a time no longer are pleasurable. But for getting the unique real 'necklace,' we want to postpone it for tomorrow, and tomorrow never comes. We feel we are the doers and go-getters in the world. This is all a play of 'I' and 'mine,' which is only a reflection of the Self.

But the truth is as stated in *SpandaKarikas* Verse 48:

सेयं क्रियात्मिका शक्तिः शिवस्य पशुवर्तिनी ।
बन्धयित्री स्वमार्गस्था ज्ञाता सिद्ध्युपपादिका ।।४८।।

48. Seyaṁ kriyātmikā śaktiḥ Śivasya paśuvartinī
Bandhayitrī svamārgasthā jñātā siddhyupapādikā.

This Matrika Shakti is the power of Action (Kriya Shakti) of Shiva, which resides in the creature and is a source of bondage; but the same power when realized as the pathway to one's own Reality brings about success – liberation.

In this Verse we see the consequences of ignoring the power of Matrika Shakti. That power is the Spanda principle, the 'I am' awareness of Shiva. Creating the region of eight gates of Puryshtaka, an embodied soul is created and is perpetuated with births and deaths. The soul identifies with ego, mind and intellect and senses or puryashtaka takes the role of a 'doer' and brings upon him/herself the suffering.

A person just keeps worrying. This is due to two reasons: first, due to loss of 'kriya shakti' – capability to perform any action and 'jnana shakti' – knowledge of the Reality; and second, due to acquiring the limited power of knowledge and action reflected in the puryashtaka. The person falls prey to the veiled powers that are inherent in the multitude of words. The person acquires ideas through experiences of senses and objects and education, all of which are not possible without words. When a man dies only the physical body merges with dust. But 'puryshtaka' remains as the subtle vehicle for the soul so that in the next life the bound soul acquires a body suitable to the ideas or impressions stored in the puryashtaka, that once again seek expression. In the present life our ideas are formed according to our interests and desires. The interests and desires are deposited in puryashtaka which determines our future life completely.

Transmigratory existence is stopped by removing impurities from the puryashtaka.

We end the discussion with a song of Purandardas, a 16th Century Kannada poet saint on the human habit of thinking negatively – worrying.

अनुगाल्वु चिंते ई जीवक्के, तन्नमनवु श्रीरंगनोळगॅ मेच्चुवतनका ॥
   सति इद्दरु चिंते सति इल्लदिद्दरु चिंते
   मतिहीन सति आदरू चिंते, पृथिवियोळगे ।
   सति कडु चल्वेयादरे, मितिमेरी इल्लदा मोहद चिंते ॥
मक्कळिल्लदा चिंते मक्कळादरु चिंते, ऑक्काळु होन्नु कोडुव चिंते ॥
   अक्करे इंदली, तुरुगोळु काइदरु,
   कक्कुल्तेय बिट्टु होगद चिंते ॥
बडवनादरु चिंते, बल्लिदनादरु चिंते
हिडिहोन्नु कय्योळादरु चिंते, पोडवियोळगे ।
नम्म पुरंदरविठ्ठलन बिडदे ध्यानिसिदरे
चिंते यागुवदु निश्चिंते ॥

Anugālavu ciṅte ī jīvakke, tanna-manavu Śrīraṅga-noḷage meccu-vatanakā.
Sati iddaru ciṅte sati illa-diddaru ciṅte
matihīna sati ādaru ciṅte, pṛithiviyoḷage.
sati kaḍu calve-yādare
miti-merī illadā mohada ciṅte.
Makkaḷa-illadā ciṅte, makkaḷādaru ciṅte,
aukkāḷu honnu koḍuva ciṅte.
akkare iṅdalī, taru-goḷu kāyadaru
kokkula-teya biṭṭu hogada ciṅte,
Baḍavanādaru ciṅte, ballida-nādarū ciṅte
hiṅḍi-honnu kayyoḷadaru ciṅte,
poḍavi-yoḷage
namma Puraṅdara-Viṭhṭhalana
biḍade dhyāni-sidare
ciṅte-yāguvadu niściṅte

A person worries all the time.
The man is worried if he has a wife
He is also worried if he doesn't have one.
He is worried if the wife is not too bright.
In this world, if the wife is extremely beautiful,
Then he is worried about being hopelessly infatuated with her.
He is worried if he has no children
And he worries even if he has children
If he leases his land to the tiller
He worries about whether he will get enough income.
If he has a herd of healthy milking cows,
The worry doesn't leave him.
He worries if he is poor
He worries even if he is rich.
He is worried even if he has fistful of gold.
Purandardas says, "If one goes into a secluded forest
and contemplates on my Viṭṭhala
Only then does he no longer need to worry about his worries!"

APPENDIX

Hridaya Kuhara - The Cave of the Heart

by

Umesh P. Nagarkatte

Jagadish Shastri, who was a devotee of Ramana Maharshi, had come to spend a Chaturmasa with him. One day the Shastri wanted to write a verse. He wrote on a piece of paper "Hridaya kuhara madhye" meaning "in the cave of the heart." and however much he tried he could not complete the verse. He had to go somewhere. He left the paper under Ramana's seat. By the time he came back, Ramana had completed the verse:

हृदयकुहरमध्ये केवलं ब्रह्ममात्रं, ह्यहमहमिति साक्षात् आत्मरूपेण भाति ।
हृदि विश मनसा स्वं चिन्वता, मज्जता वा, पवनचलनरोधात् आत्मनिष्ठो भव त्वं ॥

In the cave of the heart, only Brahman
Itself is felt directly as the Self doing "I-I"
Enter your own heart mentally;
by inquiry, merging or breath-control.
and be established in the Self.

This verse forms the essence of Ramana Maharshi's teaching. As soon as we wake up, the pulsation of "I" starts. Consciousness spreads all our body. And we perceive the world. In the deep sleep state there is no pulsation of "I." The Self, Consciousness, or That which keeps the body alive, just stays as witness. The body goes through its stages of childhood, youth and old age. A woman was meeting her mother after many years; she asked her aged mother how she felt. The mother replied that the body had become old; but she always felt that she was the same person. This sameness is the "I." The continuation of the world we feel is due to the same "I."

All saints, including Ramana Maharshi, have emphasized that if we want undisturbed peace, and unending bliss, we should inquire into the origin of the "I" or ego. The saints have described their direct experience, after practicing what they taught. This experience is also described in our upanishads. The experience cannot be completely described in words, lest it would become finite and limited. Still, reading their works or listening to them, we immediately feel light-hearted, peaceful and exalted. This is the effect of श्रवण or *listening*. This is not usually a permanent experience. After leaving the saints' physical or literary company, soon the experience subsides.

When we fly with the sun, we never experience darkness, the day seems to go on forever; again in a polar region, when that part of the earth is directed to the sun, there is months and months of daylight, and no darkness at all. Similarly, to experience happiness longer, we have to work on ourselves to keep our mind directed to the source of bliss. This process is called साधना or *spiritual practice*. This can be achieved by practicing the saints' teachings in every activity of the waking state, where we can consciously do something. One of the methods, the saints prescribe, is watching our mind as to what it is thinking, whether it is thinking good thoughts for every fellow being of this earth, whether it is self-degrading or downgrading others. "तन्मे मनः शुभसंकल्पमस्तु." "Oh my mind! Think of only good thoughts" prays an upanishadic seer to his mind. Watching our mind also stops the flow of thoughts, and we experience immediate quietness. The outgoing tendency of our mind acquired from childhood needs to be checked, not by repression but by giving it something sublime.

Since thinking is our mind's nature, we better give it something to think about, like "What is our origin?" Shankaracharya in his book 'अपरोक्षानुभूति' – *Aparakṣonubhuti – Direct Experience* describes how to do the Self-inquiry. It is a small book containing the fundamental wisdom. His famous words are, "कोऽहं कथमिदं जातं, को वै कर्तास्य विद्यते, उपादानं किमस्तीह विचारः सोऽयमीदृशः ।" '*Ko'haṁ kathami-adaṁ jātaṁ, ko vai kartāsya vidyate,Upādānaṁ kimastīha vicāraḥ so 'yamīdṛśaḥ*' "Who am I? How was this world created? Who is its Creator? What is its purpose? The Inquiry should be carried out this way." The same verse can be interpreted as "Who am "I?" How did "this" meaning our mind come into being? Who is its Creator? etc." Thinking about this is called मनन or contemplation. The answer to the question regarding the origin of our mind is also the answer to the questions regarding the world. The answer, which we have to find for ourselves, solves all problems, we feel, we have in the world. This is Self-inquiry.

Along with the Self-inquiry Ramana points to the method of merging ourselves in the Self. The cave of the heart, Ramana mentions, is the place we point to when we say "I did it!" It is not the physical heart which is on the left side, but that place on the right side.

When the mind stops going outside, it merges within the heart. But to merge within our heart, there are so many distractions. We desire so many things to make our life happy. When a desire is fulfilled, the mind is at peace and we feel happy.

There was a prosperous businessman in New York. One day as usual he came home from work in his chauffeur driven Lexus. His servants, which common people rarely have in New York, ran to open the car door. Alighting from the car, he saw his beautiful vehicle, gardens, and house. The sight of his beautiful beloved wife, elegantly dressed and adorned with diamonds, and tender cute dear children dressed in most modern clothing pleased him. He was certain that he was getting joy indeed from his wealth, wife and children. Soon the chef came out, and announced that dinner was served. Platters filled with hot delicious courses were brought out to the dining table. The businessman and his family began their dinner. Conversation was full of laughter, fun and frolic.

Suddenly the phone rang. The businessman lifted his phone, which was next to him on the dining table. Listening to the news from the other end, the businessman seemed stunned as if struck with lightening. His face was pale. The news was that his company stock had crashed. Suddenly the dinner was insipid. The fun and frolic was over. He fell in a nearby easy chair completely disgusted. What was going to happen now? Was he going to lose his house? "Oh Merciful Lord," he said, "Save me. Save my dignity." Now the objects of sight, smell, touch, taste and sound, he had in his world, which he thought gave him happiness, were still surrounding him. But he was so miserable. In an uncontrolled mind there is always a constant commotion.

When the mindwaves get quiet, and one-pointed, the Self reflects through the mind and Its natural bliss comes through. Through the bliss-reflecting mind outer objects seem pleasurable due to delusion. When the mindwaves get scattered, there is no reflection of the Self; and one experiences sorrow.

Our happiness, peace, strength, all we need are in the cave of the heart. Happiness and peace are just other qualified names of the Self. The root of our life is the Self or Consciousness. It bestows upon us peace, bathes us in bliss, and makes us one with the power. This is called निदिध्यासन - *nididhyāsan* or abidance in the Self.

To quieten the mind, Ramana gives the method of breath control. It is not the Hatha yogic exercise. But it is to become aware of the breating. Inhaling, exhaling and duration between the two processes. The mind and breath are related. As we focus our attention on breathing, our thoughts slow down and vanish. What remains is the pure pulsating "I" without attributes, which is Consciousness. The seer, seen, seeing are experienced as Consciousness. Hence the world, a conglomoration of these triads, is experienced as Connsciousness. Within and without it is the same Powerful Consciousness.

The inquiry, merging, and breath-control to enter the cave of the heart and experience the "I" can take place easily in the company of saints. The atmosphere they create makes any one entering it tranquil. "What use is the fan, if a southern breeze is blowing?" asks Ramana. Doing even mundane things, such as drinking tea, cooking, or eating, walking, or just being quiet, in the saints' company, one feels light-hearted, happy and peaceful. They do not need to give specific instructions. We need just be with them. By thinking about them, contemplating about their teachings, or time spent with them, we get the experience of the Self. Then at the opportune time, a special saint, Guru, appears in the life. He/she instructs in silence that to experience the Self constantly is as easy as breathing or as easy as drinking tea. The Self is what we already are. When a Guru comes in the life, s/he guides the disciple in the three ways mentioned by Ramana Maharshi.

Once a disciple had a dream. In the dream, she was standing next to a swimming pool. Her guru was resting on a lounge chair nearby on the deck. He looked at her and said, "People say that there is only one desire that needs to be fulfilled. But once that desire is fulfilled, one more desire follows it. And the cycle goes on. Since this is the situation, how can a person be free from desires?" The disciple felt that the Guru was describing precisely her predicament. She hesitated to answer the question. Suddenly she felt a jolt from inside; and she fell in the pool. As she was drowning in the pool, and swallowing water, she heard the words, "Relax! Relax!" These words were coming out from her Guru; as she opened her eyes and through the water, which was shallow, she could see him sitting in the chair. The words were so soothing, that they made her relax, and she started floating in the water. The Guru came to the pool, gave her a hand, pulled her out and said, "This is what you should do. You should take a leap, a leap into the Self." We too could follow this advice to merge in our heart. This leap is experienced in meditation that happens by Guru's grace.

Sometimes the Guru gives a mantra. Whatever the mantra is, it is actually the

Guru's power instilled in the mantra that removes the cobwebs of the mind, and makes one aware of the meditation that is going in the cave of the heart. Usually the ajapa-japa "So'ham" mantra is given. It is the natural mantra, that keeps going on 21,600 times, during each day and night, in every individual. If we want to experience the Being in the cave of the heart, a start could be made any time.

Breathe in "SO," and breathe out "HUM."
Breathe in "SO," and breathe out "HUM."
When I want peace, I sit some place,
And close my eyes; I become aware of
This Machine that keeps going
Inside my heart, day and night
"Sooo Hummm, Soooo Hummmm."
When I am by myself, sitting, walking, or working,
I wonder from time to time, about this Machine,
This Marvelous Machine, that keeps the beat
"Sooo Hummm, Sooo Hummm."
"So hum" gives me energy; "So hum" gives me insight.
"So hum" gives me strength; And "So hum" keeps me bright.
"So hum" packs in fun, takes "ho hum" out
"So hum" solves the mystery of "What Life is all about."
"So hum" is the mantra, I don't need to repeat,
This Marvelous Machine comes installed with It.

VERSE 51
ATTAINMENT OF MASTERY

यदा त्वेकत्र संरूढस्तदा तस्य लयोदयौ ।
नियच्छन् भोक्तृतामेति ततश्चक्रेश्वरो भवेत् ॥५१॥

51. Yadā tvekatra saṁrūḍhas-tadā tasya layodayau
Niyacchan bhoktṛtāmeti tataś-cakreśvaro bhavet.

भट्टकल्लटः – यदा पुनस्त्वेकत्र स्थूले सूक्ष्मे वा संरूढो लीनचित्तः, तदा तस्य प्रत्ययोद्भवस्य लयोद्भवौ ध्वंसप्रादुर्भावौ नियच्छन् कुर्वन् भोक्तृतां प्राप्नोति । ततः चक्रेश्वरो भवेत् सर्वाधिपतिर्भवति ॥५१॥

Bhaṭṭa-kallaṭaḥ - 51 – Yadā punas-tvekatra sthūle sūkṣme vā saṁrūḍho līnacittaḥ, tadā tasya pratyayodbhavasya layodbhavau dhvaṁsa-prādurbhāvau niyacchan kurvan bhoktṛtāṁ prāpnoti. Tataḥ cakreśvaro bhavet sarvādhipatir-bhavati.

51. When a seeker selecting any one of the gross or subtle puryaṣṭaka, merges his mind with its substratum, the Supreme Spanda principle, the seeker experiences the Spanda principle and its power of Freedom within and without. That seeker controls the puryaṣṭaka, bringing the emergence and dissolution of the puryaṣṭaka at will. The seeker regains the lost position of the enjoyer of the play of consciousness and becomes truly the Lord of all shaktis.

BhattaKallata: 51. When a seeker selecting one of the gross or subtle puryaṣṭaka merges his mind with the Spanda principle, the seeker gains control over the emergence or dissolution of his world of sensory experience and attains his (for-

gotten) position of enjoyer. Then he becomes the Lord of all shaktis or in other words Shiva.

THIS VERSE is a conclusion of the Science of Spanda (Divine Vibration) as well as a summary of all the previous verses.

The words "लयोदयौ (*layodayau*) or dissolution and emergence" in the first part of the verse imply the words "तस्य प्रत्ययोद्भवस्य लयोद्भवौ (*tasya pratyayod-bhavasya layod-bhavau*)," from verse 49, meaning "the emergence or dissolution of his/her world of sensory experience." These words and the forgotten position of enjoyer in BhattaKallatas commentary are best explained by the summary of the verses 1-50 we studied so far.

Before we go on to further explanation, we need to mention the difference between Kṣemarāj's interpretation of this verse, used by Jaidev Singh, another English commentator on the *SpandaKarikas*, and that of BhattaKallata. The word 'ekatra' is explained here in BhattaKallata's version as 'through one of the senses,' whereas Kshemaraj does not deal with the process. He interprets 'ekatra' to mean 'at one place' and starts with establishment in 'one place' meaning the Spanda Principle and its consequences. The process described here by BhattaKallata is useful from the seeker's point of view.

Spanda means vibration; it is power that vibrates, expands and contracts. As given at the end of the commentary on the first verse, we can experience Spanda as that whole mass of conscious blissful breathing presence that dissolves everything. We are It. Once in It as It, there is nothing else – no universe, no individual, nothing but constant steady breathing in and out. That state is natural, beyond effort and effortlessness. In that state actions take place spontaneously and automatically. It is a state that transcends thinking. Once such a blissful state is tasted due to Guru's grace, nothing else in the universe compares with it. To be in that state constantly is the goal of human life. That requires individual effort!

Spanda, also called Vimarsh or Shakti, is the dynamic aspect of Prakash or Shiva. Prakash-Vimarsh or Shiva-Shakti are one and the same: Self and its conscious awareness – "I AM." It is the sole material[88] and instrumental[89] cause for the

[88] Substance – matter like clay used in making pottery
[89] Live agent – potter that makes the pottery

manifestation of the universe. Shiva-Shakti can never be separated. Spanda expands or contracts and dissolves or generates the universe. In that sense, Spanda is the Reality both immanent in and transcendental to the universe. In particular, Shiva manifests as the sentient and insentient universe. Shiva becomes us as us. There are five main principles associated with Shiva – creation, maintenance, dissolution, concealment and grace. The first three are concerned with the sentient and insentient universe. The fourth principle is concealment of the Spanda due to which people's minds are led to confusion in regarding Spanda as false and the universe as the Reality.

Modern science agrees that energy is the cause of the universe. Energy manifests as matter through quantum mechanics and as vibration in string theory. In fact, the first four principles described above (creation to concealment) are the same in quantum mechanics. Investigating Consciousness is beyond the scope of science, since science deals with only the physical universe that can be perceptible to the senses, limited to the waking state of humans. The fifth principle associated with Shiva, grace, makes us understand all the previous four principles. Grace manifests in human form as the Guru and bestows grace on seekers.

The words expansion-contraction (Unmesh-Nimesh) occur in the first verse quoted below and are the cause of the sensory universe - '*pratyayodbhava*,' which is the cause of impurity of being an atom - 'āṇava mala.' From this impurity, the other two impurities arise – *māyiya mala* – impurity due to maya and kārma mala – impurity due to action in an individual.

> Verse 1. "We praise that Śaṅkara, whose nature is the conglomeration of powers that evolve to cause the manifestation of the universe through their junction and disjunction. His expansion (Unmesh) and contraction (Nimesh) causes the universe to dissolve and arise."

This also has another interpretation: The words Unmesh-Nimesh connote the freedom of choice (or Iccha Shakti) of Spanda. The power of concealment inherent in Spanda is called Maya. Concealment hides the nature of reality. It shows duality or separateness where there is none. Because of Maya we experience ourselves as separate individuals who perceive "I am" in relation to the universe. It causes us to feel that there are two types of objects - insentient (jada) and sentient (chetan). Because of maya we make distinctions of high and low.

Unmesh-Nimesh means the expansion and contraction of Spanda. When the awareness of Spanda expands, the universe made up of separate sentient and insentient objects dissolves and Shiva is experienced; and when the awareness of Spanda contracts, the universe as separate objects appears. The last part of the verse describes the means. Vibhava also means experience and Prabhava means manifestation of Shankara. By experiencing the conglomeration of Powers inherent in the universe through intense and fixed awareness, the universe as an entity separate from Shiva dissolves, and we can find the manifestation of Shankara or that grace-bestowing power for ourselves.

Verses 2 through 11 expound the general aspect of Spanda. The entire work of creation, rests on Spanda or Vimarsh – the awareness aspect of Shiva. (v. 2) The states of waking, dream and deep sleep appear quite different from one another to us, but in reality Spanda remains as the unchanging experiencer of these states. (v. 3) The Spanda Principle is the thread on which all experiences of sorrow, happiness, etc. are strung, making them appear in a continuous flow. Actually, it is like a necklace of a cotton string where the beads are also made of cotton. (v. 4) However, from the highest point of view in Spanda there is neither sorrow nor happiness, neither perception nor the perceptor; at the same time there is no inertness in objects such as a rock. (v. 5) Spanda has the freedom, power of Will or Iccha Shakti, out of which the other two powers – Jnana – knowledge and Kriya – action arise, and through which Spanda acts. The seeker must examine with respect this principle, by which the senses of perception and action as well as the inner instrument consisting of mind, intellect and ego become alive and carry out their respective functions. (v. 6-7) An individual is not only an instrument to carry out the Will, but also due to the contact of the strength of the Self experiences the Freedom of will. (v. 8)

Agitation in an individual is caused due to the existence of three malas arising out of the maya principle. The seeker must end the agitation to experience the highest state. (v. 9) Because, when agitation stops it is the Spanda that remains uncovered, just as when the waves subside, the still blue ocean shimmers. Creation cannot cover or hinder Spanda in any way. (v. 10) How can a yogi who is amazed by perceiving his or her Spanda nature's pervasion everywhere in the atoms of the universe enter the cycle of birth and death? (v. 11)

Verses 12-22 describe the Spanda principle as the substratum of everything. Both the experience of the void and the experience of the subjective and objective universe are special manifestations of Spanda. There never is complete Void, the absence of everything. The experience of the yogis who emphasize meditation on the Void is denounced, since there has to be an observer to verify the existence of the void. (v. 12-13) There are two special states of Spanda: the doer or subject and the deed or object, of which the deed is temporary while the doer is imperishable. In the meditation on the Void if the objects disappear then objectivity, of course, also vanishes, but that does not mean that the doer or consciousness also disappears. Only the triad goes away. The foundation of all the triads, the Spanda Principle, remains. (v. 14-15-16) The fully enlightened yogi has an incessant experience of Spanda throughout all the three states of waking, dreaming and deep sleep states, while the partially awakened has the experience only in the transition as one state is subsiding and the other rising. (v. 17) Spanda appears as both knowledge and objects of knowledge in the waking and dream states, and only as consciousness in the deep sleep and turya states. (v. 18) Gunas – Sattva (purity, light, stillness), Rajas (activity) and Tamas (darkness, indolence), which are qualities of the individual nature, cannot cover the general Spanda for those who have experienced their own Spanda nature, since gunas are only special manifestations of Spanda. (v. 19) Although the three gunas cover the experience of Spanda for those people who are not vigilant, the seeker who is alert to discern the Spanda principle attains It without delay. (v. 20-21)

There is a means to experience Spanda in daily life whenever the mind is filled exclusively with a single emotion, by drawing in the mind and directing it to the source of that emotion. The verse also implies that when the mind is fully concentrated, 'in the now' state contemplating only the chore at hand, it is possible to experience Spanda just by becoming aware of the source of this concentration. The only common requirement in all acts is that the mind be filled by only one thought. This easily happens in the extreme emotional state. (v. 22)

Verses 23-32 describe the emergence of सहज विद्या *sahaja vidyā* spontaneous knowledge of the experience of Spanda in the seeker. Vasugupta, the author of the *SpandaKarikas*, encourages the seeker to make the self-effort to attain the state of Spanda. (v. 23). This effort with Guru's grace arouses in the seeker Kuṇḍalini – coiled energy, explained later, through the suṣumnā – the central nerve from the mulādhār (base of the spine) to the sahasrār (top of brain where thousands of nerves come together). Kundalini is usually dormant as three and a half coils (metaphorically)- one coil being I-consciousness attached to objectivity, the second coil being I-consciousness attached to the cognitive cycle, the third coil I-consciousness attached to subjectivity and half-coil is traces of objectivity – Pramiti - reduced in the Pramātā - "Knower" at mūlādhār in creatures. (v. 24) Experience of Spanda occurs in different seekers according to the level of the seekers. (v. 25)

Next the power of mantras endowed with the power of unmasked consciousness, Spanda, Self is described. Saints have extolled the power of live mantras, repeating the Lord's name. (v. 26) The mantras not only uplift the seekers to the Self, like bringing a man drowning in an ocean out to the beach, but also dissolve the seeker's mind into the Self along with the mantras themselves. The all-pervasiveness of the Self flows through that person becoming one with the internal and external objects experienced and participating in their process of creation (creation, sustenance, dissolution, concealment and grace). Every being is all-pervasive; by creating every sense object one experiences it through one's own consciousness alone. Any external object, when experienced, is regarded as a part of one's own body. Thus the body is not limited to what is indicated by the head, hands, and so on. (v. 27) The person loses the identification with the physical body and looks at the whole universe as his/her body. Another consequence is that, among a word, the meaning or the object it stands for, and a thought, there is no state which is not the Self. It alone exists always everywhere as the experiencer as well as the experience. The result is described as a change of outlook towards the universe, now regarding it as the play of consciousness. (v. 28-29-30) The seeker experiences oneness with the Deity merely upon willing to see that Deity or mere will to repeat the mantra. The result of attaining the Self is the acquisition of nectar of immortality. It is indeed an initiation into liberation, which bestows the nature of Shiva on the seeker. The perception is verily the awareness of one's own nature without any covering. (v. 31-32) This is emphasized in the last part of the present verse.

Verse 33 of the *SpandaKarikas* and following describes the 'vibhuti' aspect of the Spanda. The word 'Vibhuti' has several meanings in Sanskrit: one is a great being, another is ash, what is left over by burning wood. The third meaning is siddhis – occult powers that arise in a seeker, coming to serve him or her. In order to become a truly great being established forever in the Self one has to regard these siddhis as ashes of no significant value! The effect of experience of Spanda on the seeker needs to be considered: the conscious energy within an individual yogi performing regular spiritual practices creates in the yogi's eyes the power of the moon and the sun that allows the yogi to discern any object while being aware of the body. (v. 33) Awareness of conscious energy brings about an effect also on the dream state (of an advanced yogi). The reason for all this is the yogi's oneness with the supreme energy which always shines clearly in the central nerve or 'suṣumnā' of the yogi and never violates the trust of the yogi. (v. 34) We are warned that if a yogi even after experiencing the Self does not remain vigilant and become firmly established in the Self, then for that yogi the creation of desires in the waking and dream states keeps going on independently in the same way as it does as for common worldly people. (v. 35) Establishment in the Self is alluded to in the beginning part of the present verse.

But if a seeker is vigilant, then the seeker gets established in the Self. As a result of this, all-knowingness or omniscience is experienced as follows. Just as a distant object cannot be seen at first by an individual even if the individual is attentive, but appears instantly by utilizing one's own power, likewise, applying special effort alone, whatever object, in whatever form, at whatever time, in whichever location, in whatever shape it exists, that object appears without any obstruction in no loss of time to an individual who has taken refuge in one's own power and in one's own nature. This knowledge of a thing, whether it has already happened or is yet to happen, is nothing significant and not even a little surprise. (v. 36-37) Another result is all-doership or omnipotence. Just as a feeble person succeeds in doing whatever has to be done when forced to do, by drawing upon his own sheer inner strength; just as one who is exceedingly hungry under certain situations can overcome his hunger (without physical food); likewise a ripe yogi though physically weak taking the support of strength of Spanda accomplishes even difficult work easily, and even extremely starved of all bodily needs controls them till a suitable time. With one's own consciousness pervading the body all-knowingness regarding it is experienced, so much so that even the sting of a meager louse is felt immediately, so also a person who is established in the Self certainly experiences omnipresence, omniscience and omnipotence. (v. 39)

On the other hand, the effect of ignorance of the Spanda is mental depression that robs the body of its vitality, strength, luster, enthusiasm, health, etc. If that ignorance is uprooted by Unmesh – aspect of Spanda, where can the depression arise from when its cause is gone? (v. 40) The means to experience Unmesh is to focus on just one thought. If a yogi's mind is totally immersed in some thought, and suddenly some power causes another thought to arise and pervade the mind, that power or principle, should be recognized as Unmesh, and the yogi should contemplate and investigate it. This principle can also be experienced in its splendor between the two thoughts – as one is ending and the other arising. (v. 41) The secondary effects of this energy Unmeṣa is that there arises in a very short time in the seeker 'bindu' – of the form of light, '*Nāda*' – unstruck sound called Pranav, '*Rūpa*' - power to see objects in darkness, '*Rasa*' – taste of celestial nectar in the mouth. These powers disturb the seekers who have not yet transcended the notion of body as the self, and keep them from experiencing Spanda. (v. 42) This is the doership – or experiencing power or 'bhoktruta' - in the last part of the present verse referring to losing of Spanda experience.

Instead of dwelling on Nada-Bindu-Rupa-Rasa, the seeker should experience the Spanda: with the strong desire to discern the Spanda principle. When the seeker remains only in the awareness of the Spanda principle pervading every object, then what more can be said than that the seeker certainly, on one's own, experiences the principle. (v. 43) One can experience Spanda in the midst of emotions by remaining vigilant. The seeker always – i.e. at the beginning, middle and end of perception – should remain alert regarding the limitless energy, reflecting by knowledge and analyzing the perceptible object. By this means the seeker will not be disturbed by objective phenomena which is the collection of the 'kalā's (movements) given in the next verse. (v. 44)

Verse 45 describes the vehicle of thought, one of the most important verses of *SpandaKarikas* that explains Mātṛkā śakti, the power inherent in the Sanskrit alphabet. It describes in detail what is mentioned in verse 29 – the word and its object (objective meaning). Every thought has a form – word - consisting of letters (subjective meaning). The set of sounds or letters (50 in all in *Devanāgari* – the Sanskrit alphabet) begins with अ (*A*) and ends with क्ष (*Kṣa*) (The first sixteen are vowels and the next thirty-four are consonants. The consonants starting from the letter क (*K*) are divided into five groups of five consonants, followed by two groups of four, and one group of one consonant. From each group arises a power called by different names such as Brāḥmī, and a kalā (movement) associated with it. An individual loses the innate independent nature due to these groups of letters, *K* and so on, equipped with the powers. Thus the individual dispossessed of his or her independent nature becomes a bound creature. At the same time, the individual who possesses the understanding of the power inherent in a letter of the alphabet, becomes liberated by the live mantra given by a Guru that selects only the beneficial letters!

We learn the effects of thoughts of an individual who is ignorant of Matrika

Shakti. If thoughts based on the sensory experiences develop in a person's mind, those thoughts prevent the person from merging with the Supreme Nectar. Then the person experiences bondage and experiences only the subtle senses. (v. 46) The shaktis such as Brahmi inherent in the classes of consonants are always active in covering one's own nature. Without the fascination for words (related to objects of five senses), the worldly thoughts do not arise. (v. 47)

Matrika Shakti is also the Power of Action (Kriya Shakti) of Shiva, which resides in the creature creating bondage; but when directed towards the Self, and when Its nature is understood, bestows various siddhis (powers). In the commentary on this verse we emphasized the effect of the knowledge of Matrika Shakti by describing the state of liberated beings. (v. 48) The present verse again describes the state of liberated beings.

The effect of the five subtle senses, which is also the origin of the alphabet, as described in Verse 45, is discussed in verses 49-50. Shiva manifesting as an individual bound creature is bound in the puryashtaka - city of eight gates - consisting of five subtle principles and the mind, ego and intellect. The puryashtaka causes sensory experiences, pain and pleasure. (v. 49) These lead to Āṇava, *Māyiya* and *Kārma* malas discussed in Verses 46, 47, 48 and in the *SpandaKarika* 9. The effect of puryashtaka on the cycle of birth and death is described. (v. 50)

Thus we are Spanda with Unmesh-Nimesh which causes our universe to dissolve and arise. The Maya principle creates us as separate purusha (individuals) enmeshed with prakriti (nature) consisting of the puryashtaka – set of eight: शब्द-स्पर्श-रूप-रस-गंध-मन-बुद्धि-अहंकार *śabda-sparśa-rūpa-rasa-gandha-mana-buddhi-ahaṅkār* or subtle sound, touch, form, taste and smell, the mind, intellect and ego; all of which conceals the freedom-of-choice inherent in our Spanda nature. The puryashtaka causes us experience ānava-māyiya-kārma malas making us bound in our three aspects – mind, intellect and ego affected by the remaining five subtle and gross forms of senses. As described in the previous verses 49-50, because of the puryashataka we go through the cycles of happiness and sorrow and birth and death. The current fifty-first verse describes that we can end the cycle by establishing ourselves in Spanda approaching It through one of the subtle or gross puryashtaka components and thus gives details of the means to merge with Shiva alluded to in Verse 1.

There was a sage Abhinav Gupta – who was the Guru of Kshemaraj, a commentator of *SpandaKarikas* in the tenth century.He says,

स्वतन्त्रः स्वच्छात्मा स्फुरति सततं चेतसि शिवः
पराशक्तिश्चेयं करणसरणिप्रान्तमुदिता ।
तदा भोगैकात्मा स्फुरति च समस्तं जगदिदम्
न जाने कुत्रायं ध्वनिरनुपतेत् संसृतिरिति ॥

Svatantraḥ svacchātmā sphurati satataṁ cetasi Sivaḥ
Parāśaktiś-ceyaṁ karaṇa-saraṇi-prānta-muditā,
Tadā bhogaikātmā sphurati ca samastaṁ jagadidam
Na jāne kutrāyaṁ dhvanir-anupatet-saṁsṛtir-iti.

As the pure and independent Consciousness
Shiva is ever pulsating.
And His Parashakti rises in various sense experiences as joy.
Then the entire world appears in Its Self as the wondrous
delight of Pure I Consciousness.
Indeed, I do not know what the sound "World" is supposed to refer to.

Effort for merging with Shiva can happen only in the waking state through body, speech and mind. Any work that is done is with the awareness that it is the Spanda that acts, any word that is uttered is with awareness of the power of Spanda. Any thought that arises is a bubble of Spanda. Regarding the universe, and every object or creature in the universe as a manifestation of Spanda is an attitude or keeping awareness to that effect. For maintaining that awareness, doing ceremonial worship – celebration of holy days also helps. Because the mantras, words, used in the ceremonial worships repeated with understanding are also powerful to focus awareness. But any awareness can only occur in the mind of the seeker. Hence if the mind is merged with Spanda, everything else is just an obvious consequence.

To repeat, the present verse emphasizes that the seekers focus on one of the eight gates – puryashtaka. In the last (10th) chapter of *Amritanubhava*, Jnaneshwar Maharaj describes the effect of focusing on the form – the third puryashtaka. This chapter discusses establishment in Consciousness due to Guru's grace. Jnaneshwar Maharaj says that when one person looks at another, one becomes the seer and the other the seen and vice versa. But that cannot be so, since a 'seen' is something inert like a jar. Then both are seers. But again without a seen there cannot be a seer, since these terms are relative. So related to mutual actions among sentients, the seer is only the light of consciousness. Again the insentient 'seen' appears only due to the light of Consciousness. Thus in the appearance of the universe, it is only the light of consciousness that remains as the Seer. But the light of Consciousness exists before the world appears and after the world disappears. Therefore the only mystery is the light of Consciousness. The light of consciousness is so pervasive that it cannot be a mystery. Even if he (Jnaneshwar) did not say anything, people would notice it. This is the common experience of people who are established in the Self. The differences of liberated, seeker and bound remain as long as one is looking away from the Self, but once one understands one's nature as the Self all those differences drop away.

"So long as seekers do not look at the universe as the play of Consciousness, they are not going to find peace whatever they may do. They may practice yogas, perform yajnas, pujas, they will not find peace. They might earn lots of merits, go through the hard penances, go on to pilgrimages, but they won't find peace. Without the vision of the play of Consciousness which comes by only Guru's grace, a person does not find peace." [page 287, *ChitshaktiVilas*]

Why and how does this happen by Guru's grace? A person, who is unaware of the substratum Spanda, is bound by the four walls, each representing a level of speech – parā, paśyanti, madhyamā, vaikharī - and a chain of 50 links – made up of the fifty sounds – fifty letters of the alphabet, which is attractive and the person would not think of breaking and is also impossible to break by one's own effort. He lives in this jailyard of eight gates with its own vigilant attractive shakti concealing the true nature, by tempting him 'how good the life is,' and making him restless in trying to find lasting happiness through the shaktis – the sensory pleasure of one or more of the five types – sound, touch, form, taste and smell guided or misguided by the mind, intellect and ego. The more he tries to live happily through one of the shaktis this way, the longer is the sentence by lifetimes. Some people start genuinely to search for lasting happiness, tired of temporary pleasures through any of the shaktis ending in painful consequences and yearn to free themselves of the fetters. At the right time Guru arrives and sends a secret message to the disciple as soon as they meet. Guru says, "If you want permanent happiness and get out of this jail of momentary pleasures and pains, there is a cave within you – called the cave of the heart. Steel yourself against the guarding shaktis. Repeat the secret words, "So'ham, So'ham" – "I am the Self, I am the Self," contemplate them in the heart. Find out your real nature. You will find a state where the wonderful bliss reigns. Then not only will you be free from the clutches of your jailors, but you will see that in each of the senses or shaktis there is a liberating experience of the bliss of Self (which is the message of the present verse), and you will be crowned as the ruler over all the shaktis."

While controlling the shaktis and puryashtaka, does he become bound again at any time? No. Only a person who does not know anything beyond the puryashtaka and the matrika shakti is bound. But can a person who transcends them be bound? Just as the sun does not know darkness and fire does not experience cold, such a person will never be bound again.

Focusing on the Guru, Baba Muktanand achieved the Bliss of Freedom – and lived up to his name! He tells us that the secret of achieving this state is love for the Guru and the grace of the Guru. He says in his *Chitshakti Vilas – Play of Consciousness*, "I pursued only my Guru. I was ready to carry out his bidding. I followed the path prescribed by him, never anxious for attainments. I did not even wonder where the path would lead me. My only concern was to ensure that I walked unswervingly on whatever path my Guru pointed out. And as I followed him, I reached where I ought to have. While I was thus traveling, I did not allow my attention to run here and there; nor did I bother about lesser things. I kept the straight path and found what I was to find. What had to happen happened. I did not fall short of my destination, even slightly."

The means to be established in the Self is to merge the mind, another member of Puryashtaka, with Spanda. This is described in *SpandaKarika* as working on the mind 1) by maintaining only one thought; 2) going to the root of one intense emotion; 3) being aware of the gaps in transitions of states of waking and dream, waking and sleep, one thought subsiding and the other arising; concentrating on the pause of outgoing and ingoing breath, being aware of the doer Spanda when one task ends and other begins; 4) using a mantra. The most powerful of all the means is a mantra or the word, which is the first puryashtaka and 'sublime cause' of space or origin of all remaining four fundamental principles of the Universe as discussed in verses 6 and 49, repeating the live mantra given by the Guru with its importance given in verses 26 and 45.

It is not only consciously repeating the mantra, but also feeling the mantra going on in any daily situation. Once Chitra, the co-commentator, had a dream in which she was sitting with our Guru Baba Muktananda. She heard many people shouting at Baba calling him names. Chitra started yelling back at them saying why they were shouting at Baba; that they did not know how great Baba was. Baba was calm and asked Chitra, "Can you hear 'Om Namah Shivaya' in their shouting?" Suddenly, she could hear no more shouts but only Om Namah Shivaya. That ended her dream. As a preparation of writing the commentary on this verse Umesh was reading *Shiva Sutras* on the plane from New York to India. There was a girl on the seat behind who was talking constantly loudly with the fellow passenger. Umesh tried in many subtle ways to stop her loud talking and even using earplugs. Still the noise continued. When Umesh remembered Chitra's dream and he consciously tried to feel the Guru given mantra - Guru Om in the noise, he suddenly felt no more disturbance. The girl also eventually fell silent. He could concentrate easily on what he was reading. Then there was another girl on the seat in front who started talking loudly. Again feeling the same mantra obviated that noise.

Repeating the mantra consciously in a chaotic situation also is very powerful. When two people are exchanging angry words, an observer consciously repeating the mantra mentally to calm down the situation has an effect as quick as a 'bullet.' One has to have a powerful weapon that works instantly in any situation. Guru given mantra is that weapon. Jnaneshwar Maharaj in his work, *Haripath*, also calls Mantra a weapon.

वेदशास्त्रपुराण श्रुतींचें वचन । एक नारायण सार जप ॥ १ ॥
जप तप कर्म हरिवीण धर्म । वाउगाचि श्रम व्यर्थ जाय ॥ २ ॥
हरिपाठीं गेले ते निवांतचि ठेले । भ्रमर गुंतले सुमनकळिके ॥ ३ ॥
ज्ञानदेवा मंत्र हरिनामाचे शस्त्र । यमें कुळगोत्र वर्जियेलें ॥ ४ ॥

Veda-śāstra-purāṇa śrutiṅceṅ vacana, eka Nārāyaṇa sāra japa.
Japa tapa karma Harivīṇa dharma, vāugāci śrama vyartha jāya.
Haripāṭhīṅ gele te nivāṅtaci ṭhele,
bhramara guṅtale sumana-kaḷike.
Jñānadevā mantra Hari-nāmāce śastra,
Yameṅ kuḷagotra varjīyeleṅ.

1. *The Vedas, Shāstras, Purāṇas and Upaniṣads promise that repeating one name Nārāyaṇa is the essence of all spiritual practices.*
2. *Japa, penances, rituals and righteous actions without (the thought of) Hari are unnecessary exertions that go to waste.*

3. *Those who go on repeating Hari remain at peace. They are like the bees absorbed in enjoying honey in the flower-buds.*
4. *For Jñānadev, the mantra of Hari's name is a weapon that makes the Lord of death stay away from one's family and lineage.*

Ekanath Maharaj, a saint of the sixteenth Century in Paithana, Maharashtra, India, who was established in his own nature due to the grace of his Guru Janardan Swami, has described the characteristics of the bound soul and liberated beings. He says, "A bound soul is always attached to "body and mind" and "I and mine." What he says about liberated beings, brings out a full import of the words experiencing the Self through one of the senses and the word 'chakreshwara' in the current verse. He says:

जळीं देखें प्रतिबिंबातें । मी बुडालों म्हणोनि कुंथे ।
कोणी काढा काढा मातें । पुण्य तुमतें लागेल ॥
स्वप्नीं घाय लागले खड्गाचे । तेणें जागृतीं म्हणे मी न वांचे ।
ऐसे निबिड भरिते भ्रमाचें । तें बद्धतेचें लक्षण ॥

Jaḷīṅ dekheṅ prati-biṁbāteṅ, mī buḍāloṅ mhaṇoni kuṅthe
Koṇī kāḍhā kāḍhā māteṅ, puṇya tumateṅ lāgela
Svapnīṅ ghāya lāgale khaḍgāce, teṇeṅ jāgṛtīṅ mhaṅe mī na vāṅce
Aise nibiḍa bharite bhramāceṅ, teṅ baddhateceṅ lakṣaṇa.

He sees his reflection in water and moans, "I am drowning. Help me, Lift me up. You will earn a lot of merit." He receives wounds by a sword in a dream. Waking up he cries, "I am not going to survive." This high tide of delusion indicates symptoms of bondage. Happiness and sorrow of the dream state give him the joy and pain in the waking state, when he is reminded of the dream. Likewise, the sentence "I am my body" makes him suffer. A bound soul forgets that "I am the Self – Shivo 'ham. I am That – Aham Brahmasmi." He is firmly attached to the sense objects, and always absorbed in thinking about them.

But a liberated being even though he has a body does not identify with it. Just as a kingdom or a begging bowl seen in the dream state are equally false in the waking state, likewise, the afflictions of body – diseases and injuries; afflictions of the mind – praise and insult; and those of the prana – hunger or thirst, are equally regarded as false by the liberated one. One who is dead and cremated in a dream does not become ashes in the waking state, similarly the liberated one regards this universe as universe as false, but regards himself as truly one with the Self.

How do the senses of action and perception of a liberated being work? His samadhi of meditation and waking up from meditation are the same. Even when he walks fast on his feet, he does not feel, "I am walking." He might go on a tour of three worlds, but it is as if he has not gone anywhere. It just seems like the moon running through the clouds, where the moon is actually stationary while it is the clouds that run fast covering it. It is like a person sleeping in a carriage and the carriage moves.

When the liberated being looks at different objects the process of seeing brings in the experience of the Self which is beyond seeing. He enjoys what he sees.

When the story consisting of words narrated at one of the four levels of speech reaches his ears, the listener, the story, and the speaker all become his own Self. Thus whatever sound he hears transcends audition and he experiences the bliss of freedom. Then it does not matter whether the words are from the *Upanishads* or are swear words.

When he smells a flower or sandalwood, the source of the smell, the smell, and he become one as the Self. There is no good or bad smell for him.

Now about his taste: The plate, food, the juices and flavors and the tongue become one Swānand – bliss of the Self. The six flavors he knows but he has the same attitude of acceptance for them. He is not hungry. If you feed him a lot, he does not say, "It is enough." What is this strange tongue of the liberated, which goes to taste a flavor but instead tastes the exuding bliss of the Self.

Now listen to his touch. When the cold or heat hits him, cold loses its coldness and heat loses its heat. It is just like the smoke or sandalwood touching the fire becomes the fire. When he touches, the triad of touch – the object and hand merge into his own nature.

Similarly, when the dualities hit the liberated one, the dual nature of dualities vanishes. Since he is in everything to its fullness, there is no wonder that his sense of duality dissolves. If the ornaments of gold are kept in a gold box, then whether you open or close the gold box, you see gold. Likewise, the Self is experienced by the liberated being whether the senses are acting or not.

When he speaks, his silence does not break, because he knows the principle beyond words which is also underlying the words. It does not matter whether the words are chants or abuses. On water there are waves, the nature of waves is water; likewise the nature of sound is silence. It does not occur to him, "I should speak the truth" or it does not happen that on account of greed, he should lie. Whether he chants or quarrels, he does not deviate from the oneness. If he says to someone, "May God save you," God goes and saves that person.

Now about grabbing by hands. If such a being is to hold weapons, he knows how to use them, but there is no doership. If he has to gamble, the sense of winning or losing is not in his experience. If he has to release an arrow, he will hit the target accurately, but he does not seek praise regarding his action.

The feelings of man-woman are not in his mind. He takes on whatever role comes upon him according to his prārabdha, whether it is of a sannyasi – renunciate or a householder. If he has a son – he says, "Oh, Son. You are verily the Self." He experiences that he has become the father, mother and the son. Whatever momentary joy of sex ordinary people experience, far superior joy than that a liberated one has in waves of bliss.

In his three states of waking, dream and deep sleep whatever actions happen are like experience in the waking state of actions performed in the dream state.

Thus no senses can bind him. He knows the secret of life.

The aphorism *ShivaSutra* 1.21 says, "शुद्धविद्योदयात् चक्रेशत्वसिद्धिः ।" "*Śuddhavidyodayāt cakreśatva-siddhiḥ.*" "With the rise of the pure knowledge, comes mastery over the universal wheel." This is what is discussed by Saint Eknath in the earlier paragraphs. The realized being is established in the Spanda which is the source of all creation and experiences. There is no individuality in the background. Along with the experience of Spanda, there is also the experience of 'power of freedom of choice.'

For seekers to establish themselves in the innate Shiva nature there are several centering techniques – dhāraṇās - in the *Vijñāna Bhairava*. Three dharanas in the context of verse 51 are as follows:

अस्य सर्वस्य विश्वस्य पर्यन्तेषु समन्ततः ।
अध्वप्रक्रियया तत्त्वं शैवं ध्यात्वा महोदयः ॥ (श्लोक ५७, धारणा ३४)

Asya sarvasya viśvasya paryanteṣu samantataḥ
Adhva-prakriyayā tattvaṁ śaivaṁ dhyātvā mahodayaḥ
(Śloka 57, Dhāraṇā 34)

Meditating on the Shaiva Principle that manifests this entire universe in respect to all its six levels the seeker experiences the 'great rise.'

The Shaiva principle consists of Prakāśa (Light of Consciousness) and Vimarśa (I-AM awareness). Meditating on this principle, discussed in the beginning of this chapter, seeker's great rise happens – seeker experiences the Light of Consciousness. The dharana preceding to this one explains how the meditation has to be done.

भुवनाध्वादिरूपेण चिन्तयेत्क्रमशोऽखिलम् ।
स्थूलसूक्ष्मपरस्थित्या यावदन्ते मनोलयः ॥ (श्लोकः ५६,धारणा ३३)

Bhuvanādhvādi-rūpeṇa cintayet-kramaśo 'khilam,
Sthūla-sūkṣma-parasthityā yāvadante manolayaḥ.
(Śloka 56, Dhāraṇā 33)

There are three sets of Vācya – subjective and Vācaka - objective aspects of the universe. Each of them is called *adhvā*, path or course, and one more subtle than the previous. At the differentiated or *bheda* level there is *pada* and *bhuvana*, where the words and their objects are manifest. At the intermediate – madhyama level – or *bhedābheda* level there is mantra and tattva, where the differentiation exists at the thought level but the separation has not actually taken place, and at the non-differentiated *pashyanti - abheda* level there is *varṇa* and *kalā*, where subjective and objective exist only as potential. As one contemplates at this level one reaches the state where the mind completely dissolves into the Universal Divine Consciousness.

The entire universe on all sides, both objective and subjective aspects, should be contemplated as the Shiva – Supreme Consciousness - principle (instead of step-by-step as in the previous dharana). This is called 'Shivavyāpti.' Then the universe will appear to the devotee as Shiva Himself and not as a universe. The foregone contemplation on Verse 51 is also a meditation of the prescribed type. The third dharana is

सर्वज्ञः सर्वकर्ता व्यापकः परमेश्वरः ।
स एवाहं शैवधर्मा इति दार्ढ्याच्छिवो भवेत् ॥ (श्लोकः १०७, धारणा ८४)

Sarvajñaḥ sarva-kartā vyāpakaḥ Parameśvaraḥ
Sa evāhaṁ Śaiva-dharmā iti dārḍhyāt-Śivo bhavet.
(Śloka 107, Dhāraṇā 84)

"I am omniscient." "I am omnipotent." "I am all pervasive." "I am the Supreme Lord." This nature of Shiva I am. With this firm conviction one becomes Shiva.

In the company of Guru, such an experience does not require time. Guru has the appropriate means to make the disciple experience the State of Shiva, state of equal vision. In summarizing this verse, we quote an abhang of Jnaneshwar, our favorite saint since his Guru, Nivritti, made his sadhana easy and full of joy, just as our Guru Baba Muktanand did for us.

समाधि साधन संजीवन नाम । शांति दया सम सर्वांभूतीं ॥१॥
शांतीची पैं शांति निवृत्ति उदारु । हरिनाम उच्चारु दिधला तेणें ॥२॥
शम दम कळा विज्ञान सज्ञान । परतोनी अज्ञान नये घरा ॥३॥
ज्ञानदेवा सिद्धि साधन अवीट । भक्तिमार्ग नीट हरिपंथी ॥४॥

1. *Samādhi sādhana saṅjīvana nāma, Śānti dayā sama sarvāṅ-bhūtīṅ.*
2. *Śāntīcī paiṅ śānti Nivṛtti udāru, Hari-nāma uccāru didhalā teṇeṅ*
3. *Śama dama kaḷā vijñāna sajñāna, Paratoni ajñāna naye gharā*
4. *Jñānadevā siddhi sādhana avīṭa, Bhakti-mārga nīṭa Hari-panthi*

1. *The life giving Name is the means*
to experience Samadhi – Equality consciousness.
It is peace and compassion for all creatures.
2. *How generous is (my Guru) Nivrutti.*
He bestowed the Peace of the peace.
He gave me the name of the Lord to repeat.
3. *My mind and senses were subdued by themselves.*
All the indirect and direct knowledge arose from within.
Ignorance will never return to this place again.
4. *Jnanadev attained perfection with a spiritual practice*
that was never dull.
The path of devotion leads straight to God.

Guru Om!

VERSE 52
SALUTATIONS TO GURU AND HIS WORD

अगाधसंशयाम्भोधि-समुत्तरण-तारिणीम् ।
वन्दे विचित्रार्थपदां चित्रां तां गुरुभारतीम् ॥५२॥

52. Agādha - saṁśayāmbhodhi - samuttaraṇa - tāriṇim
Vande vicitrārtha-padāṁ citrāṁ tāṁ Guru-Bhāratīm.

भट्टकल्लटः – अगाधो ह्यप्रतिष्ठोऽनन्तः ॥ ५२॥

Bhaṭṭa-kallaṭaḥ - 52. – Agādho hyapratiṣṭho 'nantaḥ.

I offer my salutations to the speech of my Guru, which has beautiful words with wonderful meaning, which is like a boat that takes me across this unfathomable ocean of doubts.

Bhaṭṭa Kallaṭa: 'Unfathomable' means without base or end.

THERE IS ANOTHER interpretation of this verse. I offer my reverential prayer to Spanda in the form of parashakti, the supreme divine I-consciousness which is full of wonderful transcendental bliss, and which acts like a boat in crossing the fathomless ocean of doubt regarding my essential nature.

This verse is a tribute to the power of the Guru-disciple relationship. The Guru plays the essential role of making the complex world utterly simple for the disciple by reducing everything to Consciousness and Awareness. The disciple has a responsibility to have complete trust in the Guru and accept that the truth could be so simple, that it is almost an anticlimax.

It may be hard to grasp though. That is the reason the *Gurugita* Verse 8 says:

यज्ञो व्रतं तपो दानं जपस्तीर्थं तथैव च ।
गुरुतत्त्वमविज्ञाय मूढास्ते चरते जनाः ॥

Yajño vrataṁ tapo dānaṁ japas-tīrthaṁ tathaiva ca
Gurutattvam-avijñāya mūḍhās-te carate janāḥ

People perform fire sacrifices, ritual worships, penances, charity, do japa – repeat Lord's name, and also go on pilgrimage to a holy place.
But, without understanding the Guru principle, people are wandering about in ignorance.

The reason for all this is the lingering doubt. "Is my Guru real? How can all this that appears so complex, be so simple? He must have some other agenda to say that." Some devotees have various expectations and some set ideas on how an ideal Guru should be. If the Guru as an individual does not live up to their prescribed standards in their observation, or if the newspapers have published certain controversial stories, devotees' doubts grow instead of trust based upon their own experiences. Vasugupta also starts with the words 'अगाध संशयाम्भोधि – *agādha-saṁśayāmbhodhi*' meaning unfathomable ocean of doubt. However great the Guru may be, and however many good things must have happened in the life of a disciple after the disciple has come into contact with the Guru, the ocean of doubt is such that it is endless, as BhattaKallata says. Once a doubt sets in the disciple's mind, Guru's greatness, transcendent attitude to the universe, Guru's unconditional love towards all universal creation, are first doubted. Then issues keep cropping up like tentacles of the doubt, and the mind gets clouded. The mind starts giving justification why depending on Guru, or any one else for that matter, is not good. They give examples of Ramana Maharshi or Krishnamurti who did not have a Guru in a physical form. But they might not have seen Ramana Maharshi's writing: "I thought of You and was caught in Your Grace; And like a spider in Your web You did Keep me captive to swallow me in Your own hour." (*Aksharamanamalai*) Ramana Maharshi indicates that once Guru's grace is obtained, it is just a matter of time to experience oneness with the Self - our

Shiva state of Consciousness and 'I-AM' awareness. The disciple can hasten it by making a conscious effort of thinking of the Guru, coming to Him, regardless of the issues that block at a given time. Since issues are in the mind, when the mind is transformed the issues will be gone. Nisargadatta Maharaj was asked how he realized his Self, within three years of meeting his Guru. He said, "His was the teaching – "That You are," and mine was the trust."

BhattaKallata also says this: The ocean of doubt is baseless. It may be false to begin with! One needs to enquire and search out the origin of the doubt. A doubt is ignorance - mayiya mala, a delusion. Once pure knowledge arises in the mind due to Guru's grace, ignorance cannot exist, just as the sun does not know darkness. There is a dharana or centering technique in *Vijñāna Bhairava* which can help a seeker to make the self-effort to attain the goal of entrance into Shiva.

मानसं चेतना शक्तिरात्मा चेति चतुष्टयम् ।
यथा प्रिये परिक्षीणं तथा तद्भैरवं वपुः ।। (श्लोकः १३५, धारणा ११२)

Mānasaṁ cetanā śaktirātmā ceti catuṣṭayam
Yathā priye parikṣīṇaṁ tathā tad-Bhairavaṁ vapuḥ.
(Śloka 135, Dhāraṇā 112)

When the thought-producing mind, determining consciousness – intellect, prāṇa energy – life force, and the individual self – 'doer' limited by these three, all four merge into Consciousness and I-AM awareness – by regarding them as manifestation of maya, and hence illusory or false, and appear to the seeker as the miracle of Chiti – Consciousness alone, then the seeker is enlightened by Consciousness free from the covering of maya, just as the sun becomes clear after a snow storm. The seeker becomes Consciousness – Bhairava by practicing this dharana.

When a powerful Guru comes in life, and spontaneously transforms the devotee inside-out, without effort on the part of the devotee, the devotee is convinced and accepts the Guru. Our Guru Swami Muktanand Paramahans (Muktanand Baba) (1908-1982) always mentioned caution about choosing a Guru. He always warned people regarding choosing a guru in a hurry, as 99% of gurus are false but 1% are genuine. He always emphasized that before Guru's grace there is disciple's grace. The disciple should approach the Guru with an open mind, full of reverence and faith.

For Chitra and Umesh, the commentators, having an open mind and longing for a Guru was the start. In August 1972, they met Muktanand Baba in Gurudev Ashram, Ganeshpuri, Dist. Thane, Maharashtra, India after a thousand mile tour of ashrams and temples in South India. His was the last Ashram they visited during that trip. Chitra had Baba's picture in her wallet given by a friend, an American, who was an English teacher, in New York. The picture was taken in Baba's preceding world tour in 1970. Baba recognized the person who had given Chitra his picture. Reverence and faith came later, as their lives transformed beyond their own expectations from 1972 to 1974, while they were away from him (as he was in India and they were in New York), before they accepted him as their Guru. Two main things that happened were spontaneous meditation without their making any effort, and the resolution of a long-standing problem with Umesh's getting a Ph.D. Baba was in New York City for the last three months of 1974. In November 1974, he asked them to start a meditation center for him. They waited until Shiv Ratri in 1975 to start the center. The following week they received a harmonium and Chitra started playing the harmonium although she had never played before, by feeling. During the summers, they closed the center. Once the three of them, Chitra, Baba and Umesh were walking around the DeVille ashram, in South Fallsburg, NY, in June 1976, when he stopped and turned around and said, "मी खरा आहे. *I am real*." They said, "We know, Baba." He disliked psychics and miracle mongers who misled people. When Baba was in South Fallsburg many times after that, they rented a cottage away from the Ashram, made his lunch in the cottage, did Guruseva that they received directly from him. The guruseva, was mainly selecting gems from various saints' works on the topics Baba had given them, and writing them in the notebooks. He personally directed their sadhana, removing the individual confining egos, a process sometimes very painful. They ran the meditation center until 1982, after which another couple ran it as they were to join Baba on tour, leaving their jobs, during the summer.

In 1985, when Swami Nityanand started Shanti Mandir in New Jersey, the center merged with Shanti Mandir. Chitra and Umesh's experiences with Baba Muktanand have been published elsewhere in a Shanti Mandir publication, *Mukt-Anand*. Experiences with Baba Muktanand and Mahamandaleshwar Swami Nityanand Saraswati (whom they call 'Nityanand Baba,' instead of a generic 'Gurudev' which many people prefer) have been published in several issues of a Marathi magazine *Sant Kripa*. They have also quoted some experiences in this commentary on the *SpandaKarikas*. Some experiences are very subtle and personal to disclose.

Muktanand Baba always quoted two definitions from the *Kulārṇava Tantra*, 'शक्तिपातक्षमश्च गुरुः, गुरुः पारमेश्वरी अनुग्राहिका शक्तिः *Śaktipāta-kṣamaśca Guruḥ, Guruḥ pārameśvari anugrāhikā śaktiḥ*' which mean "The Guru should be able to transfer the spiritual energy to the disciple and awaken the disciple's kundalini energy. The Guru is not an individual but is the grace-bestowing power of God." Muktanand Baba's was an experiential path. He gave Shaktipat to thousands upon thousands of people around the world, true to Gadge Maharaj's[90] saying of a saint who is like the rain: "पाउस नाही पाहत, हगंधडी आणि शेत। *Pāusa nāhi pāhat, hagandhaḍi āṇi sheta*. The rain does not look whether it showers on a field where people go to relieve themselves or whether the field grows crops."

While in the Yoga scriptures, it is said that to awaken Kundalini one must apply the three physical bandhas (locks) – Jālandhar, Uddiyān and Mula, in most devotees' cases Muktanand Baba's words, touch and look sufficed to spontaneously awaken the Kundalini Shakti in them. The experiences that came match scriptural descriptions and saints' experiences. Most of the experiences happened unexpectedly, some came even in marketplaces. In the center, which Umesh and Chitra ran under the guidance of Baba, children and adults alike received Baba's grace of Kundalini awakening as they chanted and meditated. Each person benefited to make their life a success.

Baba taught his disciples to do sadhana in many ways. All the four yogas, jnana, bhakti, karma and hatha, were combined in his teaching of Siddha yoga, the Yoga of Siddha's grace. He taught people how to sing the name of God ardently and experience the nectar in chanting. In his talks, quotations and stories of modern and ancient saints from all over India appeared. He was a great storyteller. He caused a meditation revolution in his three world tours. He used Vedanta and Kashmir Shaivism to explain his teaching of Love, Honor, and Respect for every creature of this universe. He was strict and loving at the same time. He could appear in dreams and give grace, answer questions in his own beautiful way. Sadhana was never boring with him. He taught Chitra and Umesh how to cook, how to study, how to meditate, how to do their daily chores with full concentration, how to love, honor and respect every one unconditionally, how it is consciousness and awareness everywhere and nothing else. His favorite verse of *SpandaKarika* that applied to himself was:

[90] Gāḍge Mahārāj was a saint favorite of laborers and mill workers. He was contemporary of Baba Muktanand.

इति वा यस्य संवित्तिः क्रीडात्वेनाखिलं जगत् ।
स पश्यन्सततं युक्तो जीवन्मुक्तो न संशयः ॥ ३०॥

30. Iti vā yasya saṁvīttiḥ krīḍātvenākhilaṁ jagat
sa paśyan satataṁ yukto jīvan-mukto na saṅśayaḥ

30. The one who is aware of one's universal nature of consciousness-awareness regards the entire world as one's own play, and watching it, one remains always merged with the Self and is liberated while alive. There is no doubt about this.

Baba Muktananda's Guru was Bhagawan Nityanand. Bhagawan Nityanand met Baba when Baba was a child in a school but initiated him many years later, on 15th August 1947, as described in *ChitShakti Vilas* (*Play of Consciouness*), Baba's famous spiritual autobiography. Bhagawan Nityanand was an avadhut saint. Many people of our saraswat community in South India, in 1920s and 30s, would bring him home, give him a bath, feed him, and let him go. No one knew where he was born, where he did his sadhana, etc. but he was an omniscient and omnipotent being. He liked children. He cured people's illnesses. He gave spiritual guidance to countless people in his own unique cryptic way, and never gave any lectures, but he did quote from the *Upanishads*. One aphorism that fits him perfectly is *Shiva Sutra* 2.5.

विद्या-समुत्थाने स्वाभाविके खेचरी शिवावस्था ।

Vidyā-samutthāne svābhāvike, khecarī Śivāvasthā.

The pure knowledge of God consciousness effortlessly rises and this state of Shiva is realized as one with the state of Khechari.

Bhagawan Nityanand was in such a blissful state. It was the meditation the authors experienced during the visit to his Samadhi shrine that prompted them to visit Muktanand Baba.

Baba Muktanand gave the name Swami Nityanand to his first successor after his own Guru, announcing the succession on the Guru Purnima Day in 1981 in South Fallsburg. Fortunately, Chitra and Umesh happened to be in the audience to greet him soon after the program was over. Swami Nityanand proved his caliber as a saint by going through countless hardships from 1983 to 1985, proving Saint Tukaram's words, "चणे खावे लोखंडाचे, तरीच ब्रह्म पदीं नाचे । *Caṇe khāve lokhaṇḍāce, tarīca Braḥma Padī nāce*" meaning, only when one eats nuts of iron, (one goes through hardships) one dances or is established in the Self. Thanks to late Mahamandaleshwar Brahmanand Giriji Maharaj, Swami Nityanand was protected and reestablished to be of service to humanity. True to his name, Nityanand is in ever-bliss. He has appeared in our dreams and guided us, of course, along with his guidance in the waking state! His loving and informal nature and approachability by anyone has made him a favorite saint of all those who meet him. The best *Shiva Sutra* aphorism that describes him is 1.18: "लोकानन्दः समाधिसुखम् । *Lokānandaḥ samādhi-sukham.*" Meaning: The joy of Samadhi is bliss for the whole universe. For such yogis, the objective and subjective worlds are not separate. They are one and no different from Consciousness. His favorite song of Tukaram applies to him: "आनंदाचे डोही आनंद तरंग - *Ānandāce ḍohī ānand taraṅga*" – In the reservoir of Bliss, there are waves of bliss." Any one can experience that in his company.

It was Nityanand Baba who showered his grace on Umesh, saying six years ago, "You have Baba's grace and Chitra's inspiration. You should write a commentary on the *SpandaKarikas*." The commentary was finished in Nityanand Baba's beautiful Shanti Mandir Ashram, situated in mango groves in Magod, near Valsad, Gujarat, India on the auspicious day of Thursday, 5th June 2008, (Jyeṣṭha Śukla Dvitīyā, Sarvadhāri Samvatsara, Śālivāhana Śaka 1930 as per the Hindu calendar.)

Baba always said, "The Guru is not an individual, but is the grace-bestowing power of God." Soon after coming to Baba and getting closer to him, a conflict arose in Umesh's mind. As per his birth in the Chitrapur Saraswat Community, the community had a 300-year old tradition of Guru Parampara - lineage. Param Pujya (Most Revered) Swami Parijnanashram was the Guru of the Community, and Umesh was very much devoted to and had interacted with P.P. Swami Anandashram (Abode of bliss), his predecessor, who lived true to the name given him by his Guru.

Once as Umesh sat meditating he had a vision, in which he was sweeping the ashram courtyard. From one side of the Ashram building Swami Anandashram appeared, and from the other Baba Muktanand. As he was offering his salutations to both, they merged into Baba. Thus the conflict in Umesh's mind was resolved.

The two gurus showed Umesh that Guru is not an individual, but is the grace bestowing power of God. Now whichever ashrams Umesh and Chitra visit, they experience the same power. There are no conflicts.

Soon after the work of the present commentary started, Umesh and Chitra went to meet P.P. Sadyojāt Śankarāshram Swamiji in Chitrapur Math, Shirali. He was trained by revered Ishwaranand Giri of Mount Abu and had recently been installed to continue the Chitrapur Guruparampara. Thus the Giri order of sannyasis protected Muktanand Baba's lineage and Chitrapur Math lineage. Swamiji is compassionate, loving and strict. Both Nityanand Baba and Sadyojat Shankarashram Swamiji have reinvigorated valuable Hindu tradition among youth, have similar public works projects to help people, and have established a Veda Pāṭhśālā (Sanskrit school for learning Vedic rituals and philosophy) in their ashrams. When Umesh told Sadyojat Shankarashram Swamiji about the *Spandakarika* project, Swamiji said, "Write it from an upāsak's (worshipper's or seeker's) point of view." This has what has taken place in the commentary.

Shri Nānā Kākatkar, the former editor of *Sant Kripa* magazine of Pune, whom Umesh and Chitra had gone to meet, said, "In your commentary of every verse, you must bring in appropriate references from *Shiva Sutras* and *Vijnan Bhairava*. Then it would be worthwhile." That also has happened. Whenever they met him in his old simple Pune office, Shri Kakatkar always encouraged both Umesh and Chitra, saying they should keep writing. Review and reflection are good for seekers.

While writing, Baba's favorite saints, Jnaneshwar, Eknath, Tukaram, Brahmanand, Purandardas, Ramana Maharshi, Lakshman Joo and so on all came to help out. Among them was Jnaneshwar, whose works *Cāngdev Pāsaṣṭi* (65 verses to Changadev), *Jñāneśwari* – a commentary on the *Bhagavad Gita*, *Haripāṭh* and *Amṛtānubhav* (*Nectar of Experience*) Marathi literature of the 12th century fit in appropriately in *SpandaKarikas* of the 8th Century from distant Kashmir, thus making it a rich tapestry of saints' works in the tradition of Baba. The commentary is based on the talks Umesh gave in the meditation center in 1981-82 and Prof. Nīlakaṇṭha Guruṭu's Hindi text based on BhattaKallata's Sanskrit commentary, published by Motilal Banarsidass.

For this verse, the appropriate aphorism from *Shiva Sutras* is 2.6: "गुरुरुपायः - *Gururupāyaḥ*" Guru is the means. The Guru is that person who puts before the disciple the reality of God Consciousness. He can make the disciple realize the 'mantra vīrya' - the power of creative energy and 'mudrā vīrya' – establishment in that creative energy. The great energy of the great Lord is said to be the mouth of the Guru; hence that energy, being the cause of understanding, is the means, as per the *Triśirobhairava Tantra*. (Ref. Commentary of Kshemaraj on *ShivaSutras*.)

We conclude this commentary by Narayana's song on "how can I forget Guru's sandals?"

श्री गुरुपादुकादशक

ज्या संगतीनेच विराग झाला, मनोदरींचा जडभास गेला ।
साक्षात्परात्मा मज भेटवीला, विसरू कसा मी गुरुपादुकाला ॥१॥

सद्योगपंथे घरिं आणियेले, अंगेच माते परब्रह्म केले ।
प्रचंड तो बोधरवी उदेला, विसरू कसा मी गुरुपादुकाला ॥२॥

चराचरीं व्यापकता जयाची, अखंड भेटी मजला तयाची ।
परंपदी संगम पूर्ण झाला, विसरू कसा मी गुरुपादुकाला ॥३॥

जो सर्वदा गुप्त जनांत वागे, प्रसन्न भक्तां निजबोध सांगे।
सद्भक्तिभावाकरितां भुकेला, विसरू कसा मी गुरुपादुकाला ॥४॥

अनंत माझे अपराध कोटी, नाणी मनीं घालुनि सर्व पोटी ।
प्रबोधितां त्यां श्रम फार झाला, विसरू कसा मी गुरुपादुकाला ॥५॥

कांहीं मला सेवनही न झाले, तथापि तेणे मज उद्धरीले ।
आतां तरी अर्पिन प्राण त्याला, विसरू कसा मी गुरुपादुकाला ॥६॥

माझा अहंभाव असे शरीरीं, तथापि तो सद्गुरु अंगिकारी।
नाही मनी अल्पविकार झाला, विसरू कसा मी गुरुपादुकाला ॥७॥

आतां कसा मी उपकार फेडू, हा देह ओवाळुनि दूर सोडूं ।
म्यां एकभावे प्रणिपात केला, विसरू कसा मी गुरुपादुकाला ॥८॥

जया वर्णितां वर्णितां वेदवाणी, म्हणे नेति नेति ति लाजे दुरूनि ।
नव्हे अंत ना पार ज्याच्या रुपाला, विसरू कसा मी गुरुपादुकाला ॥९॥

जो साधुचा अंकित जीव झाला, त्याचा असे भार निरंजनाला ।
नारायणाचा भ्रम दूर केला, विसरू कसा मी गुरुपादुकाला ॥१०॥

Śrī Guru-Pādukā -Daśaka

1. *Jyā saṅgatīne ca virāga jhālā, manodarīñcā jaḍa-bhāsa gelā*
Sākṣāt-parātmā maja bheṭavīlā, visaru kasā mī Guru-pādukālā.

2. *Sadyoga-panthe gharin āṇiyele, aṅgeca māte ParaBrahma kele*
Pracaṇḍa to Bodha ravī udelā, visaru kasā mī Guru-pādukālā.

3. *Carācarin vyāpakatā jayācī, akhaṇḍa bheṭī majalā tayācī*
Paraṁ-padī saṅgama pūrṇa jhālā, visaru kasā mī Guru-pādukālā.

4. *Jo sarvadā gupta-janānta vāge, prasanna bhaktān nijabodha sāṅge*
Sad-bhakti-bhāvākaritān bhukelā, visaru kasā mī Guru-pādukālā.

5. *Ananta mājhe aparādha koṭī, nāṇī manīn ghāluni sarva poṭī*
Prabodhitān tyān śrama phāra jhālā, visaru kasā mī Guru-pādukālā.

6. *Kāhīn malā sevanahī na jhāle, tathāpi teṇe maja uddharile*
Ātān tarī arpina prāṇa tyālā, visaru kasā mī Guru-pādukālā.

7. *Mājhā ahaṁ-bhāva ase śarīrin, tathāpi to Sadguru aṅgikārī*
Nāhī manī alpavikāra jhālā, visaru kasā mī Guru-pādukālā.

8. *Ātān kasā mī upakāra pheḍū, hā deha ovāḷuni dūra soḍū*
Myān ekabhāve praṇipāta kelā, visaru kasā mī Guru-pādukālā.

9. *Jayā varṇitān varṇitā veda-vāṇī, mhaṇe 'neti neti' ti lāje durūni*
Navhe anta nā pāra jyācyā rupālā, visaru kasā mī Guru-pādukālā.

10. *Jo sādhucā aṅkita jīva jhālā, tyācā ase bhāra Nirañjanālā*
Nārāyaṇācā bhrama dūra kelā, visaru kasā mī Guru-pādukālā.

1. In whose company I became detached,
stupidity from the cave of the mind went away.

Verily which caused me meet the Supreme Self,
how can I forget those Guru's sandals?

2. *He brought me home by the true yoga,*
He made me the Supreme Self in the body.
Brilliant sun of knowledge arose,
how can I forget those Guru's sandals?

3. *What pervades the sentient and insentient,*
I keep meeting that incessantly
The union with the highest state is complete,
how can I forget those Guru's sandals?

4. *He Who always communes secretively among people,*
but pleased with devotees reveals the knowledge of the Self.
Is always hungry for true devotion and trust,
how can I forget those Guru's sandals?

5. *Countless millions of my mistakes*
He ignored, digesting all of them
He had to take so much effort to awaken me,
how can I forget those Guru's sandals?

6. *I never served Him even a little,*
yet He redeemed me,
Now at least I offer my prana to him,
how can I forget those Guru's sandals?

7. *My ego is still in the body,*
yet the Sadguru accepts me.
That has not affected my mind even a bit,
how can I forget those Guru's sandals?

8. *How can I now return His favor,*
May I relinquish my body as an offering
I have prostrated with one-pointedness,
how can I forget those Guru's sandals?

9. *Trying to describe the Self repeatedly,*
in embarrassment Vedas only conclude 'Not This, Not This.'
One, whose nature has no end or bounds,
how can I forget those Guru's sandals?

10. *The individual who is acknowledged by a saint,*
the Lord removes his burden.
He destroyed Narayana's delusion,
how can I forget those Guru's sandals?

श्री गुरुचरणकमलार्पणमस्तु ।

Śrī Guru-caraṇa-kamalārpaṇam-astu

Offered at Lotus Feet of the Guru

APPENDIX

SPANDAKĀRIKĀ VERSES AND THEIR MEANINGS

Verse 1 Page 1

यस्योन्मेषनिमेषाभ्यां जगतः प्रलयोदयौ ।
तं शक्तिचक्रविभवप्रभवं शंकरं स्तुमः ॥१॥

1. Yasyonmeṣa-nimeṣābhyāṁ jagataḥ pralayodayau
Taṁ śakti-cakra-vibhava-prabhavaṁ śaṁkaraṁ stumaḥ.

We praise that Śaṅkara, whose nature is the conglomeration of powers that evolve to cause the manifestation of the universe through their junction and disjunction. His expansion and contraction causes the universe to dissolve and arise.
Alternative meaning: Page 19

By experiencing the conglomeration of Powers inherent in the universe through intensive and fixed awareness, the universe dissolves as a separate entity from Shiva, and we can find the manifestation of Shankara or that grace-bestowing power for ourselves.

Verse 2 Page 27

यत्र स्थितमिदं सर्वं कार्यं यस्माच्च निर्गतम् ।
तस्यानावृतरूपत्वान्न निरोधोऽस्ति कुत्रचित् ॥२॥

2. Yatra sthitam-idaṁ sarvaṁ kāryaṁ yasmācca nirgatam
Tasyānāvṛta-rūpatvān-na nirodho 'sti kutracit.

Where this entire creation rests, and from where it has manifested, cannot be concealed by anything. Because of this nature It has absolutely no obstruction anywhere.

Verse 3 Page 41

जाग्रदादि-विभेदेऽपि तदभिन्ने प्रसर्पति ।
निवर्तते निजान्नैव स्वभावादुपलब्धृतः ॥३॥

3. Jāgradādi-vibhede 'pi tadabhinne prasarpati
   Nivartate nijānnaiva svabhāvādu-palabdhṛtaḥ

The Spanda principle pervades waking, dream and deep sleep, even though they are different states, but never undergoes any change in such states. It remains as the sole knower of these states.

Verse 4 Page 53

अहं सुखी च दुःखी च रक्तश्चेत्यादि-संविदः ।
सुखाद्यवस्थानुस्यूते वर्तन्तेऽन्यत्र ताः स्फुटम् ।।४।।

4. *Ahaṁ sukhī ca duḥkhī ca raktaścetyādi-saṁvidaḥ*
   Sukhādyavasthānusyūte vartante 'nyatra tāḥ sphuṭam

It is evident that 'I am happy;' 'I am sad'; 'I am attached,' yet all such feelings exist in a different place, in which happiness and other states are strung together.

Verse 5 Page 63

न दुःखं न सुखं यत्र न ग्राह्यो ग्राहको न च ।
न चास्ति मूढभावोऽपि तदस्ति परमार्थतः ।।५।।

5. *Na duḥkhaṁ na sukhaṁ yatra, na grāhyo grāhako na ca*
   Na cāsti mūḍhabhāvo 'pi tad-asti paramārthataḥ

That is the Spanda principle in the highest sense, in which there is no sorrow, no happiness, no object, no subject, no insentience.

Verses 6 and 7 Page 71

यतः करणवर्गोऽयं विमूढोऽमूढवत् स्वयम् ।
सहान्तरेण चक्रेण प्रवृत्ति-स्थिति-संहृती : ।।६।।

6. *Yataḥ karaṇa-vargo 'yaṁ vimūḍho 'mūḍhavat svayam.*
   Sahāntareṇa cakreṇa pravṛtti-sthiti-saṁhṛtīḥ.

लभते, तत्प्रयत्नेन परीक्ष्यं तत्त्वमादरात् ।

यतः स्वतन्त्रता तस्य सर्वत्रेयमकृत्रिमा ॥७॥

7. *Labhate, tat-prayatnena parīkṣyaṁ tattvam-ādarāt.*
Yataḥ svatantratā tasya sarvatreyam-akṛtrimā

That Spanda principle, flowing as the group of inner causal divinities or Shaktis, due to which all sense organs, though inert, acquire the ability of creation, sustenance, and dissolution, should be examined with great care and effort. By this examination Its innate independence pervading all can be experienced. (As such there is nothing inert per se but it is the degree of consciousness present in an object that makes it inert or insentient like a rock or sentient like a living creature.)

Verse 8 Page 87

न हीच्छानोदनस्यायं प्रेरकत्वेन वर्तते ।
अपि त्वात्मबलस्पर्शात् पुरुषस्तत्समो भवेत् ॥८॥

8. *Na hicchā-nodanasyāyaṁ prerakatvena vartate*
Api tvātma-bala-sparśāt puruṣas-tatsamo bhavet.

Meaning of the verse, as per Kṣemarāj: It is not true that an individual behaves as the driving force of desires. It is due to the touch of Spanda - the power of the Self - that the individual becomes like That.

Another meaning: An individual does not live only as the driving force of the desires. But with just the touch of the power of the Self the individual will become like the Self.

(As continuation of the last verse - benefits of the inquiry:) Then (as a result of obtaining the innate independence of the Self), with just a touch of the Self an individual will become like the Self, then he no longer exists as the driving force of the desires.

Verse 9 Page 101

निजाशुद्ध्यासमर्थस्य कर्तव्येष्वभिलाषिणः ।
यदा क्षोभः प्रलीयेत तदा स्यात्परमम् पदम् ॥९॥

9. *Nijāśuddhyā-asamarthasya kartavyeṣvabhilāṣiṇaḥ*
Yadā kṣobhaḥ pralīyeta tadā syāt-paramaṁ padam.

Due to an individual's own impurity, the individual is incapacitated, unfulfilled, and is therefore desirous of worldly gains to attain fulfillment. When the individual's agitation disappears, the individual experiences the highest state.

Verse 10 Page 113

तदास्याकृत्रिमो धर्मो ज्ञत्वकर्तृत्वलक्षणः ।
यतस्तदीप्सितं सर्वं जानाति च करोति च ॥१०॥

10. *Tadāsyākṛtrimo dharmo jñatva-kartṛtva-lakṣaṇaḥ*
Yatas-tadīpsitaṁ sarvaṁ jānāti ca karoti ca.

Then the natural state of the individual, which has omniscience and omnipotence as its characteristics, flashes forth, due to which, the individual knows and does all that is desired with independence.

Verse 11 Page 121

तमधिष्ठातृभावेन स्वभावमवलोकयन् ।
स्मयमान इवास्ते यस्तस्येयं कुसृतिः कुतः ॥११॥

11. *Tamadhiṣṭhātṛ-bhāvena svabhāvam-avalokayan*
Smayamāna ivāste yas-tasyeyaṁ kusṛtiḥ kutaḥ.

How can the wretched cycle of birth and death exist for an aspirant who observes with amazement one's own nature, that is Spanda, that presides over all activities of life, and that pervades the entire universe?

Verse 12 Page 131

नाभावो भाव्यतामेति न च तत्रास्त्यमूढता ।
यतोऽभियोगसंस्पर्शात्तदासीदिति निश्चयः ॥१२॥

12. *Nābhāvo bhāvyatām-eti na ca tatrāstyamūḍhatā*
Yato 'bhiyogasaṁsparśāt-tadāsīd-iti niścayaḥ

Void cannot be contemplated. Similarly, insentience cannot exist, since the recollection or inference regarding insentience indicates the existence of something. The Principle of Spanda must be present in order to recall or infer something.

Verse 13 Page 139

अतस्तत्कृत्रिमं ज्ञेयं सौषुप्तपदवत्सदा ।
न त्वेवं स्मर्यमाणत्वं तत्तत्वं प्रतिपद्यते ॥१३॥

13. Atastat-kṛtrimaṁ jñeyaṁ souṣupta-padavat sadā,
Na tvevaṁ smaryamāṇatvaṁ tattavaṁ pratipadyate.

Hence that void, like sleep, should always be regarded as artificial. Mere nonexistence or void cannot be contemplated. Spanda Itself cannot be proposed as an object of recollection.

Verse 14, 15 and 16 Page 145

अवस्थायुगलं चात्र कार्यकर्तृत्वशब्दितम् ।
कार्यता क्षयिणी तत्र कर्तृत्वं पुनरक्षयम् ॥१४॥

14. Avasthā-yugalaṁ cātra kārya-kaṛtṛtva-śabditam,
Kāryatā kṣayiṇī tatra kartṛtvaṁ punar-akṣayam.

Our own nature – consciousness (Self) and awareness (Pulsation) – has two states called deed and doer. The deed is temporary and the doer is eternal.

कार्योन्मुखः प्रयत्नो यः केवलं सोऽत्र लुप्यते ।
तस्मिँल्लुप्ते विलुप्तोऽस्मीत्यबुधः प्रतिपद्यते ॥१५॥

15. Kāryonmukhaḥ prayatno yaḥ kevalaṁ so 'tra lupyate,
Tasmiṁllupte vilupto 'smītyabudhaḥ pratipadyate.

When the effort directed towards any deed vanishes, only a fool thinks that he has ceased to exist.

न तु योऽन्तर्मुखो भावः सर्वज्ञत्वगुणास्पदम्
तस्य लोपः कदाचित् स्यादन्यस्यानुपलम्भनात् ॥१६ ॥

16. Na tu yo 'ntarmukho bhāvaḥ sarvajñatva-guṇāspadam,
Tasya lopaḥ kadācit syād-anyasyānupalmbhanāt.

But that inner nature, which has qualities of omniscience, etc., never disappears, as there is no other conscious power that experiences all states.

Verse 17 Page 161

तस्योपलब्धिः सततं त्रिपदाव्यभिचारिणी ।
नित्यं स्यात् सुप्रबुद्धस्य, तदाद्यन्तेऽपरस्य तु ॥१७॥

17. Tasyopalabdhiḥ satataṁ tripadā vyabhicāriṇī,
Nityaṁ syāt suprabuddhasya, tadādyante 'parasya tu.

That Spanda in Its pure state is incessantly available. The fully enlightened yogi always experiences It in all the three states of waking, dreaming and deep sleep. But It is available to others who are not enlightened only at the beginning and the end of these states.

Verse 18 Page 171

ज्ञानज्ञेयस्वरूपिण्या शक्त्या परमया युतः ।
पदद्वये विभुर्भाति तदन्यत्र तु चिन्मयः ॥१८॥

18. Jñāna-jñeya-svarūpiṇyā śaktyā paramayā yutaḥ,
Padadvaye vibhur-bhāti tadanyatra tu cinmayaḥ.

To the enlightened one, Spanda appears with all Its power in the form of the goal of knowledge and as knowledge itself in the waking and dream states respectively, and only as consciousness in the other state/s.

Verse 19 Page 179

गुणादिस्पन्दनिःष्यन्दाः सामान्यस्पन्दसंश्रयात् ।
लब्धात्मलाभाः सततं स्युर्ज्ञस्यापरिपन्थिनः ॥१९॥

19. Guṇādi-spanda-niḥṣyandāḥ sāmānya-spanda-saṅśrayāt,

Labdhātma-lābhāḥ satataṁ syur-jñasyā-pari-panthinaḥ.

Different guṇas which are special emanations of Spanda acquire their individual power from and are always dependent upon the general Spanda. They can never be the enemies of the Knower of the Spanda.

Verse 20 Page 185

अप्रबुद्धधियस्त्वेते स्वस्थितिस्थगनोद्यताः ।
पातयन्ति दुरुत्तारे घोरे संसारवर्त्मनि ।।२०।।

20. *Aprabuddha-dhiya-stvete svasthiti-sthaganodyatāḥ,*
Pātayanti duruttāre ghore saṁsāra-vartmani.

The guṇas and other special currents of the general Spanda are always active in covering the natural state of those who are ignorant of the Spanda. They push them down further in the fearsome path of worldliness so hard to go across.

Verse 21 Page 195

अतः सततमुद्युक्तः स्पन्दतत्त्वविविक्तये ।
जाग्रदेव निजं भावं न चिरेणाधिगच्छति ।।२१।।

21. *Ataḥ satatam-udyuktaḥ spanda-tattva-viviktaye.*
Jāgrad-eva nijaṁ bhāvaṁ na cireṇādhi-gacchati.

Therefore, the one who incessantly strives for discerning the Spanda principle attains one's own nature in the waking state itself without any delay.

Verse 22 Page 207

अतिक्रुद्धः प्रहृष्टो वा किं करोमीति वा मृशन् ।
धावन् वा यत्पदं गच्छेत्तत्र स्पन्दः प्रतिष्ठितः ।।२२।।

22. *Atikruddhaḥ prahṛṣṭo vā kiṁ karomīti vā mṛśan*
Dhāvan vā yatpadaṁ gacchet-tatra Spandaḥ pratiṣṭhitaḥ.

At the height of anger, or in extreme joy, or in a quandary as to 'what am I to do?,' or in a desperate situation such as running for one's life, whatever state is reached, there Spanda is established.

Verses 23, 24 and 25 Page 217

यामवस्थां समालम्ब्य यदयं मम वक्ष्यति ।
तदवश्यं करिष्येऽहमिति संकल्प्य तिष्ठति ।।२३।।

23. Yāmavasthāṁ samālambya yadayaṁ mama vakṣyati
Tadavaśyaṁ kariṣye 'hamiti saṅkalpya tiṣṭati.

This verse is interpreted in two ways: the Seeker's interpretaion and the Knower's interpretation.

Seeker's interpretation: When his mind has nothing else except the only firm resolve, "Whatever this Master of mine will order me to do (easy or difficult to attain), that I will certainly carry out."

Knower's interpretaion: When he remains with no other thought except the resolve, "In whatever way this energy of Spanda makes me experience awareness of my nature I will stay in it."

तामाश्रित्योर्ध्वमार्गेण सोमसूर्यावुभावपि ।
सौषुम्नेऽध्वन्यस्तमितो हित्वा ब्रह्माण्डगोचरम् ।।२४।।

24. Tāmāśrityordhvamārgeṇa soma-sūryā-vubhāvapi
Sauṣumne 'dhvanyastamito hitvā brahmāṇḍa-gocaram

Then in that state both the moon and the sun or Apāna and Prāṇa or mind and Prāṇa, travel fast by the higher path in the Sushumna and abandoning the limitations of body-consciousness merge with the space of Universal consciousness. (Both interpretations of sun and moon happenin devotee's life. See discussion.)

तदा तस्मिन् महाव्योम्नि प्रलीनशशिभास्करे ।
सौषुप्तपदवन्मूढः प्रबुद्धः स्यादनावृतः ।।२५।।

25. Tadā tasmin mahāvyomni pralīna-śaśi-bhāskare
Sauṣupta-padavan-mūḍhaḥ prabuddhaḥ syādanāvṛtaḥ

Then in that sublime space, where the moon and the sun have dissolved, one ignorant remains in a state of deep sleep while the knower-yogi's experience of the Self is not covered by anything.

Verses 26 and 27 Page 237

तदाक्रम्य बलं मन्त्राः सर्वज्ञबलशालिनः ।
प्रवर्तन्ते ऽधिकाराय करणानीव देहिनाम् ॥२६॥

26. *Tad-ākramya balaṁ mantrāḥ sarvajña-bala-śālinaḥ,*
Pravartante 'dhikārāya karaṇānīva dehinām

तत्रैव संप्रलीयन्ते शान्तरूपा निरञ्जनाः ।
सहाराधकचित्तेन तेनैते शिवधर्मिणः ॥२७॥

27. *Tatraiva saṁpralīyante śānta-rūpā nirañjanāḥ,*
Sahārādhaka-cittena tenaite Śiva-dharmiṇaḥ.

Mantras, having arisen from the Supreme I-Consciousness, Spanda, have the power of omniscience, etc. They carry out their assigned functions just as the senses of individual beings function as assigned by the individuals' decisions.

Verses 28, 29 and 30 Page 255

यस्मात् सर्वमयो जीवः सर्वभावसमुद्भवात् ।
तत्संवेदनरूपेण तादात्म्यप्रतिपत्तितः ॥२८॥

28. *Yasmāt sarvamayo jīvaḥ sarva-bhāva-samudbhvāt*
Tat-saṁvedana- rūpeṇa tādātmya- pratipattitaḥ.

A person is all-pervasive because he becomes one with the internal and external objects and participates in their process of creation (creation, sustenance, dissolution, concealment and grace).

तेन शब्दार्थचिन्तासु न सावस्था न यः शिवः ।
भोक्तैव भोग्य-भावेन सदा सर्वत्र संस्थितः ॥२९॥

29. *Tena śabdārtha-cintāsu na sāvasthā na yaḥ Śivaḥ*

Bhoktaiva bhogya-bhāvena sadā sarvatra saṁsthitaḥ.

Therefore, among - a word, the meaning or the object it stands for, and a thought, there is no state which is not the Self. It alone exists always everywhere as the experiencer as well as the experience.

इति वा यस्य संवित्तिः क्रीडात्वेनाखिलं जगत् ।
स पश्यन् सततं युक्तो जीवन्मुक्तो न संशयः ॥३०॥

30. *Iti vā yasya saṁvīttiḥ krīḍātvenākhilaṁ jagat*
Sa paśyan satataṁ yukto jīvan-mukto na saṅśayaḥ.

The one who is aware of one's universal nature of consciousness-awareness regards the entire world as one's own play, and watching it, the one remains always merged with the Self and is liberated while alive. There is no doubt about this.

Verses 31 and 32 Page 267

अयमेवोदयस्तस्य ध्येयस्य ध्यायिचेतसि ।
तदात्मतासमापत्तिरिच्छतः साधकस्य या ॥३१॥

31. *Ayam-evodayas-tasya dhyeyasya dhyāyi-cetasi*
Tadātmatā-samāpattir-icchataḥ sādhakasya yā.

The goal of meditation is attained in the meditating seeker's mind when the seeker experiences oneness with the Deity merely upon willing to see that Deity.

इयमेवामृतप्राप्तिरयमेवात्मनो ग्रहः ।
इयं निर्वाणदीक्षा च शिवसद्भावदायिनी ॥३२॥

32. *Iyam-evāmṛta-prāptir-ayam-evātmano grahaḥ*
Iyaṁ nirvāṇa-dīkṣā ca Śiva-sadbhāva-dāyinī

This is the acquisition of nectar of immortality. It is the attainment of the Self. This is an initiation into liberation, and it is that which bestows the nature of Shiva on the seeker.

Verses 33, 34 and 35 Page 281

यथेच्छाभ्यर्थितो धाता जाग्रतोऽर्थान् हृदि स्थितान् ।
सोमसूर्योदयं कृत्वा संपादयति देहिनः ॥३३॥

33. *Yathecchā-bhyarthito dhātā jāgrato 'rthān hṛdi sthitān*
Soma-sūryodayaṁ kṛtvā saṁpādayati dehinaḥ.

The conscious energy within an individual yogi performing regular spiritual practices creates in the yogi's eyes the power of the 'moon and sun' that allows the yogi to discern any object while being aware of the body;

तथा स्वप्नेऽप्यभीष्टार्थान् प्रणयस्यानतिक्रमात् ।
नित्यं स्फुटतरं मध्ये स्थितोऽवश्यं प्रकाशयेत् ॥३४॥

34. *Tathā svapne 'pyabhīṣṭārthān praṇayasyā - natikramāt*
Nityaṁ sphuṭa-taraṁ madhye sthito 'vaśyaṁ prakāśayet.

in the same way, even in the dream state (of an advanced yogi) the conscious energy brings about contact with the desired object. The reason for all this is the yogi's oneness with the supreme energy which always shines clearly in the central nerve or 'suṣumn;' of the yogi and never violates the trust of the yogi.

अन्यथा तु स्वतन्त्रा स्यात् सृष्टिस्तद्धर्मकत्वतः ।
सततं लौकिकस्येव जाग्रत्स्वप्नपदद्वये ॥३५॥

35. *Anyathā tu svatantrā syāt sṛṣṭis-tad-dharmakatvataḥ*
Satataṁ laukikasyeva jāgrat-svapna-pada-dvaye.

However, if a yogi even after experiencing the Self does not remain vigilant and become firmly established in the Self, then for that yogi the creation of desires in the waking and dream states keeps going on independently in the same way as it does as for common worldly people (as it is the inexplicable nature of the Spanda to keep creating independently).

Verses 36 and 37 Page 293

यथा ह्यर्थोऽस्फुटो दृष्टः सावधानेऽपि चेतसि ।
भूयः स्फुटतरो भाति स्वबलोद्योगभावितः ।।३६।।

36. *Yathā hyartho 'sphuṭo dṛṣṭaḥ sāvadhāne 'pi cetasi*
Bhūyaḥ sphuṭataro bhāti svabalodyoga-bhāvitaḥ.

तथा यत्परमार्थेन यदा यत्र यथा स्थितम् ।
तत्तथा बलमाक्रम्य न चिरात् संप्रवर्तते ।।३७।।

37. *Tathā yatparamārthena yadā yatra yathā sthitam*
Tattathā balam-ākramya na cirāt sampravartate.

Just as a distant object cannot be seen at first by an individual even if the individual is attentive, but appears instantly by utilizing one's own power,

Likewise, whatever exists whenever, wherever, and however, happens to be known in its essential nature without delay after establishing oneself in the power of Spanda.

Verses 38 and 39 Page 301

दुर्बलोऽपि तदाक्रम्य यतः कार्ये प्रवर्तते ।
आच्छादयेद् बुभुक्षां च तथा योऽतिबुभुक्षितः ।।३८।।

38. *Durbalo 'pi tadākramya yataḥ kārye pravartate*
Ācchādayed bubhukṣāṁ ca tathā yo 'tibubhukṣitaḥ.

Just as a feeble person succeeds in doing whatever has to be done when forced to do by drawing his own sheer strength; just as one who is exceedingly hungry under certain situations can overcome his hunger; likewise a ripe yogi though physically weak taking the support of strength of Spanda accomplishes even difficult work easily, and even extremely starved of all bodily needs controls them till a suitable time.

अनेनाधिष्ठिते देहे यथा सर्वज्ञतादयः ।
तथा स्वात्मन्यधिष्ठानात् सर्वत्रैवं भविष्यति ।।३९।।

39. *Anenādhiṣṭhite dehe yathā sarvajñatādayaḥ*
Tathā svātmanyadhiṣṭhānāt sarvatraivaṁ bhaviṣyati.

Since consciousness pervades the body, an individual experiences all-doership, all-knowledge pertaining to the body. Similarly, when one is established in the Self, one experiences omnipresence, omniscience and omnipotence.

Verses 40 and 41 Page 309

ग्लानिर्विलुम्पिका देहे तस्याश्चाज्ञानतः सृतिः ।
तदुन्मेषविलुप्तं चेत् कुतः सा स्यादहेतुका ।।४०।।

40. *Glānir-vilumpikā dehe tasyāś-cājñānataḥ sṛutiḥ*
Tadunmeṣa-viluptaṁ cet kutaḥ syādahetukā.

Mental depression robs the body of its vitality, strength, luster, enthusiasm, health, etc.; it arises due to ignorance. If that ignorance is uprooted by Unmesh – an aspect of Spanda, where can the depression arise from when its cause is gone?

एकचिन्ताप्रसक्तस्य यतः सा स्यादपरोदयः।
उन्मेषः स तु विज्ञेयः स्वयं तमुपलक्षयेत् ।।४१।।

41. *Ekacintā-prasaktasya yataḥ syād-aparodayaḥ*
Unmeṣaḥ sa tu vijñeyaḥ svayaṁ tamupalakṣayet.

When an individual's mind is engrossed in one thought, that which causes another thought to rise is to be recognized as Unmesh – the power of the Self – and must be investigated.

Verse 42 Page 319

अतो बिन्दुरतो नादो रूपमस्मादतो रसः ।
प्रवर्तन्तेऽचिरेणैव क्षोभकत्वेन देहिनः।।४२।।

42. *Ato bindur-ato nādo rūpam-asmād-ato rasaḥ*
Pravartante 'cireṇaiva kṣobhakatvena dehinaḥ

Having experienced Unmeṣa - the energy that gives rise to thought, occult powers of 'Bindu' – supernatural light, 'Nāda' – supernatural sound, 'Rūpa' – supernormal form, 'Rasaḥ' – supernormal nectar very quickly arise in the seekers, disturbing the seekers, who still give importance to their body, and preventing them from experiencing Spanda.

Verse 43 Page 327

दिदृक्षयेव सर्वार्थान् यदा व्याप्यावतिष्ठते ।
तदा किं बहुनोक्तेन स्वयमेवावभोत्स्यते ॥४३॥

43. Didṛkṣayeva sarvārthān yadā vyāpyāva-tiṣṭhate
Tadā kiṁ bahunoktena svayamevāva-bhotsyate.

With the strong desire to discern the Spanda principle, when the seeker remains only in the awareness of the Spanda principle pervading every object, then what more can be said than that the seeker certainly, on one's own, experiences the principle.

Verse 44 Page 337

प्रबुद्धः सर्वदा तिष्ठेज्ज्ञानेनालोच्य गोचरम् ।
एकत्रारोपयेत् सर्वं ततोऽन्येन न पीड्यते ॥४४॥

44. Prabuddhaḥ sarvadā tiṣthej-jñānenālocya gocaram
Ekatrāropayet sarvaṁ tato 'nyena na pīḍyate.

The seeker remaining vigilant in every state of experience should analyze the Spanda inherent in all perceptible objects and dissolve the entire class of objects in the Spanda principle. As a result, the seeker will not be troubled by any other objective phenomenon.

Verse 45 Page 349

शब्दराशिसमुत्थस्य शक्तिवर्गस्य भोग्यताम् ।
कलाविलुप्तविभवो गतः सन् स पशुः स्मृतः ॥४५॥

45. Śabda-rāśi-samutthasya śakti-vargasya bhogyatām

Kalā-vilupta-vibhavo gataḥ san sa paśuḥ smṛtaḥ.

The genre of Shaktis (energies) that arise from the set of sounds (words) controls the individual and then the individual is called a bound creature. The reason for this is that the collection of kalās (actions associated with groups of sounds) destroys the innate independence of the individual.

Verses 46, 47 and 48 Page 375

परामृतरसापायस्तस्य यः प्रत्ययोद्भवः ।
तेनास्वतन्त्रतामेति स च तन्मात्रगोचरः ॥४६॥

46. *Parāmṛta-rasāpāyas-tasya yaḥ pratyayodbhavaḥ*
Tenā-svatantratāmeti sa ca tanmātragocaraḥ.

If thoughts based on the sensory experiences develop in a person's mind, those thoughts prevent the person from merging with the Supreme Nectar. Then the person experiences bondage and experiences only the subtle senses.

स्वरूपावरणे चास्य शक्तयः सततोत्थिताः ।
यतः शब्दानुवेधेन न विना प्रत्ययोद्भवः ॥४७॥

47. *Svarūpāvaraṇe cāsya śaktayaḥ satatothitāḥ*
Yataḥ śabdānuvedhena na vinā patyayodbhavaḥ.

This person's shaktis are always active in covering one's own nature. Without the fascination for words (related to objects of five senses), the worldly thoughts do not arise.

सेयं क्रियात्मिका शक्तिः शिवस्य पशुवर्तिनी ।
बन्धयित्री स्वमार्गस्था ज्ञाता सिद्ध्युपपादिका ॥४८॥

48. *Seyaṁ kriyātmikā śaktiḥ Śivasya paśuvartinī*
Bandhayitrī svamārgasthā jñātā siddhyupapādikā.

This Matrika Shakti is the Energy of Action (Kriya Shakti) of Shiva, which resides in the creature creating bondage; but when directed towards the Self, and when Its nature is understood, bestows various siddhis (powers).

Verses 49 and 50 Page 403

तन्मात्रोदयरूपेण मनोऽहंबुद्धिवर्तिना ।
पुर्यष्टकेन संरुद्धस्तदुत्थं प्रत्ययोद्भवम् ॥४९॥

49. Tanmātrodayarūpeṇa mano 'haṁ-buddhi-vartinā
Puryaṣṭakena saṁruddhas-tadutthaṁ pratyayodbhavam.

Shiva manifesting as an individual bound creature is bound in the puryashtaka - city of eight gates - consisting of five subtle principles and the mind, ego and intellect. The puryashtaka causes sensory experiences. (These lead to Āṇava, Māyiya and Kārma malas discussed in Verses 46, 47, 48.)

भुङ्क्ते परवशो भोगं तद्भावात् संसरत्यतः ।
संसृतिप्रलयस्यास्य कारणं संप्रचक्ष्महे ॥५०॥

50. Bhuṅkte paravaśo bhogaṁ tadbhāvāt saṁsaratyataḥ
Saṁsṛti-pralayasyāsya kāraṇaṁ saṁpracakṣmahe.

Consequently, becoming a prisoner of the puryashtaka, Shiva as the individual goes through the current of births and deaths. The means to end this cycle will be discussed in the next verse.

Verse 51 Page 431

यदा त्वेकत्र संरूढस्तदा तस्य लयोदयौ ।
नियच्छन् भोक्तृतामेति ततश्चक्रेश्वरो भवेत् ॥५१॥

51. Yadā tvekatra saṁrūḍhas-tadā tasya layodayau
Niyacchan bhoktṛtāmeti tataś-cakreśvaro bhavet.

When a seeker selecting any one of the gross or subtle puryaṣṭaka, merges his mind with its substratum, the Supreme Spanda principle, the seeker experiences the Spanda principle and its power of Freedom within and without. That seeker controls the puryaṣṭaka, bringing the emergence and dissolution of the puryaṣṭaka at will. The seeker regains the lost position of the enjoyer of the play of consciousness and becomes truly the Lord of all shaktis.

Verse 52 Page 451

अगाधसंशयाम्भोधि-समुत्तरण-तारिणीम् ।
वन्दे विचित्रार्थपदां चित्रां तां गुरुभारतीम् ॥५२॥

52. Agādha - saṁśayāmbhodhi - samuttaraṇa - tāriṇim
Vande vicitrārtha-padāṁ citrāṁ tāṁ Guru-Bhāratīm.

I offer my salutations to the speech of my Guru, which has beautiful words with wonderful meaning, which is like a boat that takes me across this unfathomable ocean of doubts.

There is another interpretation of this verse. I offer my reverential prayer to Spanda in the form of parashakti, the supreme divine I-consciousness which is full of wonderful transcendental bliss, and which acts like a boat in crossing the fathomless ocean of doubt regarding my essential nature.

BIBLIOGRAPHY

1. Attar, Farid, *Muslim Saints and Mystics*, English translation by many, e.g. Arberry 1966 Penguin Group, London, England
2. Bhartṛuhari (600), *Śatakatrayī - Nīti, Śringār, Vairāgya*, Sanskrit Orig. a n d Marathi Translation by L. G. Vinze, Nirṇayasāgar Prakāśan (1969) Mumbai, India
3. Brahmānand (1800), *Śrī Brahmānand Bhajanmālā* in Hindi, 65th Edition, 1966, published by Hariprasād, Ajmer, India
4. Capra, Fritjof (1991), *The Tao of Physics* An exploration of the parallel between modern physics and Eastern mysticism Flamingo, London ISBN: 0 00 654489 4
5. Dādu (1557-1603) *Dāduvāṇī*, commentary Sw.Nārāyaṇadās, Dādu Mahā-vidyālaya, 1979, Jayapur, India
6. Dennis, Overbye, *Quantum Theory Tugged, All of Physics Unraveled,* The New York Times, December 12, 2000
7. Einstein, Albert, *The Meaning of Relativity* Fifth Edition, MJF Books, 1984 New York, p.1
8. Ekanāth Mahārāj (1590) *Abhang Gāthā* (Collection of Abhangs – devotional songs in Marāṭhi, Sākhare Mahārāj Sampradāya 1977, Kolhāpur, Mahāraṣṭra, India
9. Gondavelekar Mahārāj (1845-1913), *The Saint of Gondavali* by K.V. Belsare, Chaitanyopāsanā, 1988
10. *Guru Gñānānanda,* Bharatiya Vidya Bhavan, 1993, Mumbai 40007, India. p. 126-127
11. Guruṭu, Nīlakaṇṭha (1984) *Spandakārikā* with Sanskrit Commentary by BhaṭṭaKallaṭa – Commentary in Hindī, Motlāl Banārsidass, Delhi, India ISBN (Paperback): 812082332X
12. Guruṭu, Nīlakaṇṭha (1986) *Parātriṁśikā* (original Sanskrit) by Abhinav Gupta – Commentary in Hindī, Motlāl Banārsidass, Delhi, India
13. Jñānadev or Jñāneśwar Mahārāj (1290) *Jñāneśwarī*, (Original Marathi) includes BG – Bhagavad Gita, Mumbai: Government Central Press, 1960, English translation by V.G. Pradhan, State University of New York Press (January 1987) ISBN-13: 978-0887064876
14. Jñānadev or Jñāneśwar Mahārāj (1292) *Amṛtānubhav*, (Original Marathi) –

Commentry by V.G. Jog, Yashwant Prakashan Pune: 1960, English translation (January 1987)

15. Jñānadev or Jñāneśwar Mahārāj (1293) *Chāngdev Pāsaṣṭī*, (Original Marathi) – Commentary by, Yashwant Prakashan Pune: 1960, English translation (January 1987)

16. Jñānadev or Jñāneśwar Mahārāj (1294) *Harīpāṭh*, (Original Marathi) – Commentary by V.G. Jog, Yashwant Prakashan Pune: 1960, English and Hindi translation by Umesh and Chitra Nagarkatte, Shanti Mandir, Walden, NY, USA (2009)

17. Kabīr (1440-1518) – The quotations from unpublished Notebooks of Sw. Muktānand Paramhans

18. Kelkar, Gopal (written in 1896) *Swami Samarth* (1975) Marathi, Anamol Prakāṣana, Pune, India (page 15)

19. Koḍikal, Dīpā, et al., *Life of Bhagawan Nityananda and Chitdakash Geeta*, (English Translation) (2001) Surendra Kalyanpur, Mubai 400 057, India

20. Kṣemarāj (1000), *Īśvarpratybhijñā*, ed. Subrahmanya Iyer, et al 1986, Motilal Banarasidass, Delhi, India ISBN 81-208-0021-4

21. Lalita Mauli (1906-1997) from unpublished work. Nityananda Nilaya Gurukul Trust, Panvel, India

22. Mandodari Mātā, *So 'ham Bhāvāne Brahma-Sākṣātkār* – (Original Marāthī) (1994) Redkar, Ultra CoOp Hsg. Soc, Lt. Gupte Road, Mahim, Mumbai 400 016, India.

23. Mishra, Paramhans (1994), *ŚrīTantrālokaḥ* by AbhinanvGupta, commentary by Jayarath, Varanasi, Sampurṇānand Sanskṛt Vishwa Vidyalaya (Volume 3, 9.152, pages 452-454) ISBN 81-7270-017-2

24. Mishra, Paramhans, *ŚrīMālinīVijayaTantrra* Varanasi, Sampurṇānand Sanskṛt Vishwa Vidyalaya ISBN 81-7270-047-4

25. Nāmadev, *Nāmdev Gāthā* (original Marāṭhī) 1970 edition publisher - Govt. of Mahārāṣṭra, Mumbai , India

26. Nisargadatta Maharaj (1980), *ŚrīSadgurubodha* (Marathi) Keshava Bhikaji Dhawale Publication Mumbai, India (page 65)

27. Panda, N. C., *The Vibrating Universe*, Motilal Banarasidass, 2000, Page 328 ISBN 81-208-1291-8.

28. RamāVallabhDās (1600) He belonged to the lineage of Eknāth Mahārāj. His Śrīkṛṣṇa Jayantī abhangs are popular in Citrāpur Sāraswat Community.The quoted abhang is one of them.

29. Samarth Rāmdās. *Dāsbodh*, edited by Prof. K.V. Belsare, 9th edition, 1995, Samarth Seva Mandal, Sajjangaḍ, Mahārāshṭra, India.

30. Shah, Idries (1971) *The Pleasantries of the Incredible Mulla Nasruddin* E. P. Dutton, New York, ISBN: 0-525-47306-8
31. Śekhāvat, Khiṅv Siṅha, *Gurukṛpā se Merī Bandhanmukti* (Hindi) *Spiritual Diary- My Liberation from Bondage by Guru's Grace* Śrī Rānade Āshram, Nal, Bikaner, Rajasthan, India, 1998, page 6
32. Singh, Jaidev (1968) *Spanda-kārikās* with Sanskrit Commentary by Kśemarāj – Commentary in English, Motlāl Banārasidass, Delhi, India ISBN (Paperback): 978-8120808218
33. Singh, Jaidev (1980) *Pratyabhijñahrdayam, The Secret of Self-Recognition*, Motilāl Banārsidass, Delhi, India ISBN (Paperback): 9788120803237
34. Singh, Jaidev (1979) *Śiva Sutras, The Yoga of Supreme Identity*, Motilāl Banārsidass, Delhi, India ISBN (Paperback): 9788120804074
35. Singh, Jaidev (1979) *Vijñanabhairava or Divine Consciousness, A Treasury of 112 types of Yoga*, Motilāl Banārasidass, Delhi, India ISBN (Paperback): 8120808207
36. Sopāna (1296), Brother and disciple of Jñānadev, abhangas from unpublished Notebooks for Sw. Muktānand Paramhansa 1978
37. Sri Ramana Maharshi - *Day by Day with Bhagawan* - A. Devaraj Mudaliyar (2006) Sri Ramanashramam, Tiruvannamalai, Tamilnadu, India.
38. Sri Ramana Maharshi - *Talks with Bhagawan Ramana Maharshi* - (2006) Sri Ramanashramam, Tiruvannamalai, Tamilnadu, India.
39. Sundardas (1596-1689) *Sundar Vilas* Dadumahasabha, Jaipur, Rajasthan, India.
40. Swami Gambhirānanda (1985) T.U. *Taittirīya Upaniṣad*, Advaita Ashrama, Kolkata, India ISBN – 81-7505-024-1
41. Swami Ishwaranand Giri (2000) *Autumn Leaves* Samvit Sadhanalaya, Mt. Abu, India
42. Swami Kāśikānand Giri Mahāmandaleśwar (1996) *Vidyāraṇyamunīśvar-aviracitā Pañcadaśī* (Hindi) Ānandavana Śodha Samsthān Kāndivli, Mumbai, India
43. Swami Kāśikānand Giri Mahāmandaleśwar (1998) *Oṁ Namaḥ Śivāya* (Hindi) Ānandavana Śodha Samsthān Kāndivli, Mumbai, India
44. Swami Kāśikānand Giri Mahāmandaleśwar (1998) *Pañcīkaraṇa-vārttikam - Sureśvarācārya* (Hindi) Ānandavana Śodha Samsthān Kāndivli, Mumbai, India
45. Swami Lakshman Joo (2002) *Shiva Sutras The Supreme Awakening*, Edited by John Hughes, Universal Shaiva Fellowship, Culver City, CA 90230, U.S.A. ISBN 1-75965-457-3

46. Swami Lakshman Joo (1998) *The Awakening of Supreme Consciousness Lectures of Swami Lakshman Joo*, Edited by Jankinath Kaul 'kamal,' The Ishwar Ashrama Trust, Jammu, page 78.
47. Swami Lakshman Joo (1988) *Kashmir Shaivism The Secret Supreme*, Shri Sadguru Publications, Delhi, India ISBN:81-7030-257-9
48. Swami Lakshman Joo (1996) *Śrī Vātulanāthsūtrāṇi* Ishwar Ashram Trust, Ishber, Srinagar, Kashmir, India
49. Swami Maheshwaranand Giri Mahamandleshwar (1968) *Pravacan Sudha*, 3rd edition – English Translation (2006): *Nectar of Discourses – Nectar of Discourses, Seventh Chapter of the Bhagavat Geeta* by Umesh Nagarkatte, Shanti Mandir, Walden, NY, USA ISBN: 0-9675317-3-X
50. Swami Muktānand Paramhans (1968) *Mukteśwarī* – (Hindi) Siddha Yoga Dham Ashram, Ganeshpuri, India.
51. Swami Muktānand Paramhans (1972) *Paramārth Kathā Prasang* – Hindi, Gurudev Siddhapīṭh, Ganeshpuri, India, p. 138.
52. Swami Muktānand Paramhans (1963) *Play of Consciousness* Gurudev Siddhapīṭh, Ganeshpuri, India, Translation ISBN:0-914602-37-3
53. Swami Muktānand Paramhans (1974-76,78-81) *From the Finite to the Infinite* SYDA Foundation 1989, South Fallsburg, NY, U.S.A. ISBN 0-911307-02-8
54. Swami Muktānand Paramhans (1976) *Gurudev Ashram Patrika* – (Hindi) Ashram Newsletter – Yr. 5, issue 8, August 1976, Siddha Yoga Dham Ashram, Ganeshpuri, India.
55. Swami Narasimha Saraswatī, *Śrī Gurucaritra* (1600). This is a popular Marāṭhī scripture.
56. Swami Nikhilānanda (1995) *Māṇḍukya Upanishad Kārikā with Gauḍa-pādācārya's Kārikā*, Advaita Ashrama, Kolkata, India ISBN:81-7505-022-5
57. Swami Rām Tīrth (1902) *In Woods of God Realization, The Complete Works*, 9th Edition 1978, Rama Tirth Pratisthan, Lucknow, India
58. Tukārām (1598-1656) His thousands of Marāṭhi abhangs published 4th Edition 1982 by K. B. Dhavale, Mumbai, 4000 004, India
59. Ved Vyās (date unknown) *Śrimad Bhagavad Gītā* (BG) Gita Press, Gorakhpur, India.
60. Weeks, J. *How to Visualize Surfaces and Three-dimensional Manifolds*, Marcel Dekker, ISBN 0-8247-7437-X p.269
61. Yājñavalkya ( ) *Bṛhadāraṇyka Upaniṣad*, English Translation – eighth impression 1993 by Swami Madhavananda, Advaita Ashrama Kolkata, India
62. Abhinava Gupta (1200) *Svacchanda Tantra*, 2004 Edited by Vrajavallabh Dvivedi, Parimal Publications, Delhi, India ISBN 81-7110-035-X

INDEX

OTHER BOOKS AND DVD'S AVAILABLE FROM SHANTI MANDIR.

BOOKS

- Nectar of Discourses - on the Seventh Chapter of the Bhagavad Gita 2007
- Mukt Anand (English) 2002
- भक्तांजली Bhaktānjalī (Hindi)
- Lalita-Sahasra-nama (with English transliteration and translation)
- ललितासहस्रनाम (LalitāSahasra Nāma) (Sanskṛt)
- नित्य स्तोत्र Nitya Stotra (Sanskṛt)
- नित्य स्तोत्र Nitya Stotra (Gujarāti)
- Nitya Stotra (English)
- Pearls on the Path – MM Swami Nityanand Saraswati

DVDS (English):

- Swami Nityananda at the University of Delaware 2007
- Mahamandaleshwar – installation ceremony of Swami Nityananda as mahamandaleshwar
- The Mystery of Puja
- Worship of the Goddess
- Honoring Baba
- Navrātra – Nine Nights of The Goddess
- River of Faith – Kumbh Mela 2001
- Tribute Part I – Bhāvānjali
- Tribute Part III – Shraddhānjali

Website: www.shantimandir.com

CPSIA information can be obtained
at www.ICGtesting.com
Printed in the USA
LVOW02s0953090316
478359LV00047B/358/P

9 780988 602519